TEARING
DOWN
THE WALL
OF SOUND

TEARING DOWN THE WALL OF SOUND

The Rise and Fall of Phil Spector

MICK BROWN

ALFRED A. KNOPF   NEW YORK   2007

THIS IS A BORZOI BOOK
PUBLISHED BY ALFRED A. KNOPF

Copyright © 2007 by Mick Brown

All rights reserved. Published in the United States by Alfred A.
Knopf, a division of Random House, Inc., New York, and in Canada
by Random House of Canada Limited, Toronto.
www.aaknopf.com

Originally published in Great Britain by Bloomsbury
Publishing Plc., London.
Knopf, Borzoi Books, and the colophon are registered trademarks of
Random House, Inc.
Grateful acknowledgment is made to Rolling Stone LLC for
permission to reprint an excerpt from "The Phil Spector Interview"
by Jann Wenner, copyright © 1969 by Rolling Stone LLC
(*Rolling Stone*, November 1, 1969). All rights reserved.
Reprinted by permission of Rolling Stone LLC.

Library of Congress Cataloging-in-Publication Data
Brown, Mick, [date].
Tearing down the wall of sound : the rise and fall of Phil Spector / by
Mick Brown.—1st American ed.
p. cm.
Originally published: London : Bloomsbury, 2007.
Includes bibliographical references (p.).
ISBN 978-1-4000-4219-7
1. Spector, Phil, 1940– 2. Sound recording executives and
producers—United States—Biography. I. Title.
ML429.S64B76 2007
781.66092—dc22
[B]
2007004819

Manufactured in the United States of America

First American Edition

The reasonable man adapts himself to the world. The unreasonable man adapts the world to himself. All progress depends on the unreasonable man.

—George Bernard Shaw

Contents

Author's Note

Tearing Down the Wall of Sound is going into production before opening statements in Phil Spector's murder trial. The chapters about the incident of Lana Clarkson's death are based on the information and evidence available at this time and are in no way meant to make any allegations about Phil Spector, or to predict a verdict in the trial.

—March 30, 2007

TEARING DOWN THE WALL OF SOUND

1

"Mr. Spector Likes
People to Walk Up"

On an unseasonably warm day in December 2002 I found myself sitting in a room at the Hyatt Hotel on Sunset Strip in Los Angeles, waiting for Phil Spector to call.

It had been thirty-six hours since I'd arrived in Los Angeles, to find a message telling me that my meeting with Spector, which had taken some three months to arrange, and was scheduled to take place the following day, had been "postponed." It was as if all my worst fears had come to pass.

Between 1961 and 1966, Spector's so-called Wall of Sound made him the most successful pop-record producer in the world, with more than twenty Top 40 hits by such artists as the Crystals, the Ronettes and the Righteous Brothers. In the words of the writer Tom Wolfe, Spector was the "first tycoon of teen"—a mercurial and combustible mixture of genius and hustler, a precocious, brilliant and off-the-wall visionary who would change the face of pop music forever.

In a period when most people, even those who made it, regarded pop as disposable ephemera, Phil Spector alone dared to believe it could be art. Marshaling armies of guitars and keyboards and brass and drums, celestial sleighbells, and voices keening like angels, he made records of a hitherto unconceived-of grandeur and majesty, elevating the themes of teenage love and heartache to the epic proportions of Wagnerian opera—"little symphonies for the kids," as he put it. Spector crammed emotion into a bottle and uncorked it—the clamorous, joyous noise of a small tyrant unleashing his vision, his revenge, on the world. When, in the late '60s, musical fashion overtook his Wall of Sound, Spector moved on to the biggest pop group in the world, the Beatles. He rescued their valedictory album, *Let It Be*. He produced *Imagine* for John

Lennon, and "My Sweet Lord" for George Harrison. Then began the long, slow retreat. In 1979 Spector produced his last album, for the punk rock group the Ramones. And then he was gone. The architect of the Wall of Sound vanished behind another wall—of barbed-wire fences, guard dogs and Keep Out: Armed Response signs, of stories about guns and craziness, rumor, half-truth and legend—much of it, it seemed, of Spector's own creation. The "tycoon of teen" became rock and roll's most enigmatic recluse.

When in the autumn of 2002 I first contacted Spector, he had not given a major interview in some twenty-five years, and to arrange a meeting involved delicate and protracted negotiations. Letters were dispatched back and forth. Michelle Blaine, Spector's personal assistant, and the daughter of Hal Blaine, the drummer who had played on all of Spector's greatest hits through the '60s, happened to be passing through London, and we met for tea at a Mayfair hotel. She was fiercely protective of her employer. What exactly would be the thrust of the interview? Was I familiar with Mr. Spector's records? How familiar? What had I read about Mr. Spector? I would be aware that there had been a great deal of misreporting about Mr. Spector's life and affairs—gossip, scandal; talk of guns, of craziness—all of it exaggeration, myth and lies. Mr. Spector would not countenance any interview that proceeded along those lines.

A week later I was informed that Spector had agreed to talk. My elation was immediately tempered by a deep foreboding that the interview would almost certainly never happen. It was almost to be expected, then, that I should be told on my arrival in Los Angeles that our meeting had been "postponed." I sat in my room, awaiting the call that I was now convinced would never come. And then the telephone rang. A car, I was informed, would be collecting me from my hotel at noon. At the appointed hour, a white 1965 Rolls-Royce Silver Cloud, license plate PHIL 500, drew up outside the hotel. A uniformed chauffeur held open the door. Encased in leather and walnut and hidden behind black curtains—a car that could tell stories—we turned onto the Hollywood Freeway, keeling slightly like some stately ocean liner, and headed east.

After some thirty minutes, we turned off the freeway, following the signs for Alhambra, a nondescript, working-class neighborhood of strip malls and scrubby bungalows. The road wound upwards, and further upwards still, ending at last at a set of high wrought-iron gates, posted with Keep Out signs. The chauffeur stepped out to open them, drove through and pulled to a halt at the bottom of a flight of stone steps, the gates closing behind us. "Mr. Spector," he said, "likes people to walk up." The steps led up through an avenue of lowering pines, the castle visible through the trees.

It was up these same steps that just a few weeks later, in the early hours of Monday, February 3, 2003, Spector would stagger with Lana Clarkson, a sometime actress and model, whom Spector had met just two hours earlier in a Hollywood nightclub. According to the testimony given to the police by Spector's chauffeur Adriano De Souza—the same chauffeur who had driven me from my hotel—Spector was apparently inebriated, and Lana Clarkson was "like grabbing his arm and shoulder and helping him up the stairs." Now, as I climbed, I had the distinct sense that I was being watched, although I might have been imagining this.

Michelle Blaine was waiting for me at the top. She led me through the front door into a cavernous hallway, wood-paneled and red-carpeted. Later, I would try to bring the details of this hall to mind, to match it with the account of the affidavit filed by Detective Mark Lillienfeld of the Los Angeles Sheriff's Department, reporting the scene that he and other officers had found there in the early hours of February 3.

> Your affiant saw the victim slumped in a chair in the foyer of the home. She was wearing a black nylon slip/dress, black nylons, and black shoes. A leopard-print purse with a black strap was slung over her right shoulder, with the purse hanging down on her right side by her right arm. She had what appeared to be a single-entry gunshot wound to the mouth. Broken teeth from the victim were scattered about the foyer and an adjacent stairway. Lying under the victim's left leg was a Colt, 2-inch, blue-steel, .38-caliber, six-shot revolver. This weapon had five live cartridges in the cylinder, and under the hammer, a spent cartridge.

I struggle to remember now exactly where in the hall that chair was placed. The affidavit makes no mention of the two suits of armor that I vividly recall, standing sentinel—stage props for a fantasy of baronial splendor. Spector was nowhere to be seen. Michelle Blaine led me on a tour of the ground-floor rooms. In the music room there was hi-fi equipment, and a guitar that had once belonged to John Lennon, resting on a stand, like a museum exhibit. A narrow room led off it, a bar lined with framed photographs of Spector with various music business luminaries.

In the sitting room a Picasso drawing hung on the wall beside an original John Lennon sketch. A uniformed maid brought iced water and

I settled myself on a sofa beside a coffee table. The affidavit describes the scene that Detective Lillienfeld found in this room.

> In a living room just east of the foyer, your affiant saw that candles had been lit atop a fireplace mantel. The coffee table between two couches had a brandy glass partially filled with alcohol, and atop the table was a Jose Cuervo tequila bottle and a partially empty Canada Dry soft drink.

I waited, suddenly aware that classical music was eddying softly around the room. At length, Michelle Blaine's mobile telephone rang. It was Spector, calling from elsewhere in the house. Phillip, she said, would be with us shortly. He appeared a few minutes later, walking down the staircase, to the strains of Handel. He was wearing a shoulder-length curled toupee, blue-tinted glasses, a black silk pajama suit with the monogram *PS* picked out in silver thread and three-inch Cuban-heel boots. He looked bizarre—like a wizened child in fancy dress—yet at the same time curiously magnificent. I rose from my seat to shake hands, and he peered up at me. "My," he whispered. "You're tall."

He perched on the edge of a sofa, sipping from a tumbler filled with something that might have been cranberry juice, might have been anything. His hands trembled. Close up, his skin was sallow, like parchment, but his expression was puckish, amused. "I don't like to talk," he said. Yet over the next four hours, he talked like a man possessed. About his music, the Ronettes, the Righteous Brothers, the Beatles, about hustling and payola, success and failure.

"I *knew*," he said. "People made fun of me, the little kid who was producing rock and roll records. But I knew. I would try to tell all the groups, we're doing something very important. Trust me. And it was very difficult because these people didn't have that sense of destiny. They didn't know they were producing art that would change the world. I *knew*."

"And you wanted immortality?"

"Yes. Very much. I think when Jefferson wrote the Declaration of Independence he was thinking, people will remember this. When Gershwin wrote, he may have said, 'I don't know about this *American in Paris*,' but I think he said, 'this is something special.' I think Irving Berlin had an ego, that he wanted people to remember this. I think he wanted to be number one. And so did I."

Our conversation was interrupted by a whirring noise, like a cuckoo clock, and a voice chirruping the hour. *"It's two o'clock."* His wristwatch. "Timing," Spector said, "is the key to everything.

"Okay." He jabbed a finger at me across the table. "You ask me, 'What's your name?' And then you ask me, 'What do you do for a living, and what's the most important part of what you do for a living?' Go ahead! Just for the conversation."

"Okay. What's your name?"

"Phil Spector."

"And what do you do for a living?"

"I'm a record producer."

"And what's the most important—"

"Timing . . ." And he broke up in laughter.

I had not expected him to be funny. The scabrous comedian Lenny Bruce had been one of his closest friends—"my Socrates," as Spector described him. And it was as if he was still keeping Bruce's lines warm. "Profanity," he said, "is the last refuge of the inarticulate prick." And: "In a world where carpenters get resurrected, anything is fucking possible." As long as you've got the timing right.

The wristwatch whirred and chirruped. *"It's three o'clock."* Time out. He rose from the sofa and vanished upstairs. I walked in the garden. The sun was shining on the roofs of the houses in the valley below. But among the trees, the unkempt lawn and flower beds, all was shadows and melancholy, and I wondered what could have brought Phil Spector here. Lunch was served in the dining room. I ate alone. When he returned, Spector looked at the food and shook his head. "Let's go in the other room," he said.

For years, he said, he had not been well. "I was crippled inside. Emotionally. Insane is a hard word, but it's manic-depressive, bipolar. I take medication for schizophrenia, but I wouldn't say I'm schizophrenic. But I have a bipolar personality, which is strange. I have devils inside that fight me. And I'm my own worst enemy."

He had first started seeing a psychiatrist in 1960—to get out of the military draft, he said. He never stopped, but therapy was never enough. "There's something I'd either not accepted, or I'm not prepared to accept or live with in my life, that I don't know about perhaps, that I'm facing now." He paused. "To all intents and purposes I would say I'm probably relatively insane, to an extent. To an extent. But I can function in the world."

For years, he said, he couldn't face being with people, and he couldn't face being with himself. He suffered from chronic insomnia, night after night, going crazy. "You don't sleep; your mind starts playing tricks on you. It's a terrible situation."

Finally, he sought help. Always "terrified" of drugs, he began taking medication that would moderate his moods and help him sleep. He had "waged war" with himself. "I just told myself that I would beat it. That I would beat my own brain. And over a slow period of time, and every day getting up and saying, nò, you're not there yet, and months and years going by . . ." He paused. "It's been very slow, very difficult."

Now, he said, he was trying to make his life "reasonable."

"I'm not ever going to be happy. Happiness isn't on. Because happiness is temporary. Unhappiness is temporary. Ecstasy is temporary. Orgasm is temporary. Everything is temporary. But being reasonable is an approach. And being reasonable with yourself. It's very difficult, very difficult to be reasonable." The wristwatch spoke. *"It's six o'clock."*

Six weeks after our meeting, on Saturday, February 1, 2003, my interview with Spector appeared in the *Daily Telegraph* magazine. He was pictured on the magazine's cover in his Louis Quinze wig, grinning lopsidedly into the camera, looking like someone who'd taken too much Prozac. The headline was "Found: Pop's Lost Genius." Two days later, I was sitting in the office of the *Telegraph* magazine when a colleague burst in from the newsroom, telling me to turn on the television. It was 10:00 a.m., California time. Filmed from a helicopter's perspective, the Alhambra castle resembled a Gothic film set, all turrets and dark pines. Cut to camera shots familiar from a hundred crime stories and cop shows: the yellow tape, the police prowl cars slewed in the drive, the stocky detectives in boxy suits moving purposefully around the grounds. An unidentified woman had been found, shot dead in Spector's home. He was under arrest. For a terrible moment, a scene flashed across my mind. Somehow, Spector had read my piece, disliked it intensely, and in a moment of madness—"I have not been well . . ."—taken revenge on his assistant, Michelle Blaine. It was some hours before it would be revealed that the victim was Lana Clarkson. But who Lana Clarkson was, and what she was doing in Phil Spector's castle in the early hours of February 3, it didn't say.

Phil Spector was taken to Alhambra police station, where he was kept for some hours before being released from police custody on $1 million bail. It would be a further eight months before he was charged with murder, a full four years before he was to come to trial. In my interview with Spector, he had spoken with remarkable candor about his fragile mental state and his years on the brink of insanity. And in the wake of the shooting, his comments—"I have devils inside that fight me"—were recycled around the world, an instant template for his psychological condition. I received a telephone call from the Los Angeles Sheriff's Department asking whether there was anything more I could tell them about his behavior on the day we met. There wasn't. I had liked Spector when I met him and found it hard to believe he would kill anybody in cold blood. The coincidence of the article's publication and Lana Clarkson's death left me feeling shocked—in some curious way, implicated. I wrote to Spector to express my sympathy for the predicament he now found himself in, but heard nothing back. Nor did he reply when I wrote to inform him that I intended to write a book about his life and career and to request a further interview.

When the news first broke about the Lana Clarkson killing, one prominent music business figure told me, there was a collective feeling of astonishment among Hollywood circles—"not that a dead body had been found in Phil Spector's home, but that Phil was living out in Alhambra . . . Nobody lives in Alhambra."

Even by his own standards of unfathomable strangeness—even if he was living in a castle—the fact that the most famous record producer in the world should have chosen to seclude himself in a grungy working-class neighborhood of auto repair shops and railway stockyards seemed only to confirm how profoundly estranged he had become from a world where he was once indomitable.

For years, Spector had been a chimera, viewed largely through the distorting lens of his own legend, but seldom seen in public. He was a person whom others traded stories about, each more lurid and fantastic than the last, and in the wake of the killing the stories were exhumed and retold with a vampiric relish; stories of his control-freakery and his drinking jags, his tempestuous marriage to Ronnie Bennett, the lead singer of the Ronettes, the temper tantrums, the bodyguards, and, of course, the guns. There was the story of how he had once pulled a gun on John Lennon, and on Leonard Cohen. Johnny Ramone, of the punk group the Ramones, whom Spector produced in 1979, was quoted in the *Los Angeles Times*, recounting a story of how Spector had once held them captive at gunpoint in his home. Gary and Donte Spector, two of the three sons Spector adopted in the '70s but from whom he had been estranged for years, regaled the tabloid press and celebrity TV programs with lurid tales of the abuse they had allegedly suffered during childhood. "While we don't know if Dad killed this lady," Donte was quoted as saying, "he should be locked up. He's a sick man."

The fact that in the few years before the shooting Spector had actually been leading a quiet and sober life, that his worst problems were seemingly behind him—"I want to be a reasonable man"—and that he had recently returned to the studio for the first time in years, was lost to most people. It was more convenient for all concerned for Phil Spector to be crazy.

There had been record producers before Phil Spector, of course; men with the artistic sensibility and vision to discover and nurture extraordinary talent, like John Hammond at Columbia Records, who discovered Billie Holiday; or with the enterprise, determination and business savvy to build their own record labels, like Ahmet Ertegun at Atlantic, the Chess brothers in Chicago, and Sam Phillips, whose Sun recordings with Elvis Presley, Jerry Lee Lewis, and others laid one of the principal foundation stones for rock and roll in the 1950s. All of these men were talented and smart. But none were to leave quite the indelible mark on popular music that Phil Spector did. Not only did Spector create records in a wholly original style that would influence a succession of artists from Brian Wilson of the Beach Boys to Bruce Springsteen; and not only were they hits. But Spector challenged the very order of the record business at the time, insisting that everything be done on his terms and nobody else's.

He controlled everything himself: finding the artists, co-writing the songs, production, publicity, quality control. Because he made the sound, and the sound was what sold, he became, uniquely for a producer, bigger than his artists—a tiny, strutting tyrant in dandy rags and Cuban heels. "He was the first of the anarchists/pop-music millionaires," the writer Nik Cohn observed. "At last, in him, odium equaled money."

The critic Kenneth Tynan once wrote that, the gift of talent apart, what enables one to exercise that talent is the ability to impose oneself (s'imposer). Roman Polanski, Laurence Olivier, Orson Welles and Marlon Brando were among those whom Tynan named as possessing this gift. "Definition of an imposer," he wrote in his diaries: "one about whom one worries whether his response to one's next remark will be a smile or a snarl."

Spector was an imposer. Physically small and unprepossessing, he was nonetheless a monumentally commanding figure, who by dint of charm, magnetism, genius or sheer force of personality was able to persuade others to follow his vision, inspiring in them a need for his approval and a fear of his disapprobation—the desire, as Tynan would have put it, for a smile rather than a snarl.

When I first started to approach the friends and associates who had known and worked with Spector over the years, I was struck by how forcefully he imprinted himself on people's memories and feelings, and how strongly he divided opinion.

Recalling his first meeting with Spector in the early 1960s, on the threshold of his greatest success, the recording engineer Larry Levine talked vividly of his "kinetic" quality—an abrasive, unsettling aura so palpable that Spector could change the atmosphere in a room simply by walking into it. "It's like the Bermuda Triangle—there's no explanation for what happens in a place, and yet with Phil things happened."

Levine had disliked him on sight, but came to hold a quite different view. He quoted the song that had given Spector his first million-selling record in 1958, when he was just eighteen years of age, its title borrowed from the epitaph on his father's gravestone, TO KNOW HIM WAS TO LOVE HIM. "You need to get to know Phil to love him. I didn't then," Levine told me. "But I grew to love him. And I do now."

Several people quoted this song to me, in tones of affection, reverence, or heavy irony—a recurring punctuation mark to their stories about Spector's brilliance, or his perversity, his kindness, or his duplicity. A successful career woman, sophisticated, beautiful and highly intelligent, whom one suspected had known many fascinating men in her life, described Spector as the most fascinating of all—"completely mesmerizing."

Some refused to believe that Spector could have been responsible for the death of Lana Clarkson. Others saw it as the inevitable fulfillment of a character who had been at best eccentric and at worst dangerously unstable. Don Kirshner, the music publisher who provided many of the songs that Spector alchemized into hits, told me that from the moment he first met Spector in 1961 he had believed he was "a candidate for doing himself or other people harm. You thought he would be someone who would go down in flames to be known, who'd make a statement in a headline." For some, it was as if Spector, in writing the final chapter on his downfall, had himself been the instrument of a revenge that they had been silently wishing on him for years.

Some refused outright to talk to me at all, either out of loyalty to Spector, or, it seemed, out of fear that they would incur his displeasure. Spector not only produced but also co-wrote many of his greatest hits. And while it is more than forty years since his astonishing run of chart success, he continues to control the copyrights of his songs and, by implication, the royalties his co-writers could expect to receive from them.

"You've Lost That Lovin' Feelin'," the song which Spector co-wrote and produced for the Righteous Brothers, holds the distinction of having the most radio plays of any pop single in history. But when I contacted the Righteous Brothers, Bill Medley and Bobby Hatfield, I was told they had no interest in discussing Spector. I persisted and eventually received a letter from Bobby Hatfield. Producing "You've Lost That Lovin' Feelin'," Spector decided to forgo the duo's usual practice of sharing the lead vocals, instead giving almost the whole song to Bill Medley and leaving Hatfield to sing only a minor part. Spector had told me the story of how a peeved Hatfield asked what he was supposed to do while Medley was singing. "You can take the money to the bank," Spector joked back. But Hatfield offered another twist. His letter was capitalized and written in an eerily neat hand, giving the impression of bitterness clenched tightly in an iron fist.

DEAR MICK,
RATHER THAN GOING INTO SEVERAL
REASONS, I THINK THIS ONE BRIEF REASON WILL
SUFFICE. WE NEEDED A "B" SIDE FOR "LOVIN'
FEELING" FAST. BILL AND I WROTE A *TWO CHORD*
PIECE OF SHIT CALLED "THERE'S A WOMAN" IN
ABOUT 20 MINUTES. WE RECORDED IT WITH PIANO,
BASS AND DRUMS. WE *LET* PHIL PUBLISH IT *ALONE*.
WILL *NEVER* FORGET THE FIRST TIME I SAW THE
SINGLE. WRITERS . . . HATFIELD, MEDLEY *AND*
SPECTOR.
RIGHTEOUSLY, BOBBY HATFIELD.

Two months after I received his letter, Bobby Hatfield was found dead in a hotel room in Kalamazoo, Michigan, a few hours before he was due to perform a show. He was sixty-three.

Spector the control freak. That was one side of the story, for sure. But there was more to it than that. Over fifty years, Spector has so compartmentalized his life that it seems that few have truly known him at all. Few people were aware that in the years when he was out of the public eye, Phil Spector was leading an approximation of a normal, domestic life. Ahmet Ertegun, the great elder statesman of the American music business, had known Spector for more than forty years, but expressed surprise when I told him that in the 1980s Spector had been happily married to a woman with whom he had two children. "Phil was married? I had no idea." Spector, Ertegun said, had been a "very good friend to me. But it's hard if you don't communicate. Phil had a lot of acolytes, but I don't think he would really open up to any of them. Maybe he didn't trust anybody enough to do that."

And what about the death of Lana Clarkson? Ertegun sadly shook his head. Sure, Phil was eccentric and things could sometimes get out of hand. But killing somebody? "I can't believe that. Phil doesn't have any meanness in him to kill anybody." He thought for a moment, and then asked, "Was he alone with this girl? He should never have been left alone . . ."

Seated in the living room of his Alhambra castle, Phil Spector told me, "I don't like to talk, and I can't stand to be talked about. I can't stand to be looked at. I can't stand to be photographed. I can't stand the attention. But at the same time I want the recognition." And after four hours' talking he told me that all he wanted was to be "a reasonable man." It was a phrase that came up with everybody I would talk with, and the reaction was always the same. Reasonable! When had Phil Spector ever been reasonable?

2

"It Was Phillip Who
Was Moving Fastest"

Seated in the living room of his Alhambra castle, hand trembling at his glass, Phil Spector looked for some clue to the mental difficulties that had assailed him throughout his life. His parents, Ben and Bertha, had been first cousins, he told me. "I don't know genetically whether or not that had something to do with what I am or who I became. But to all intents and purposes I would say I'm probably relatively insane, to an extent. To an extent . . ."

Both Bertha's and Benjamin's families were from the Ukraine, part of the great diaspora of Russian Jews who arrived in America in the early part of the twentieth century. It was a journey to a new world, a new life and, very often, a new identity. Arriving at Ellis Island, after a voyage that usually entailed extreme discomfort and hardship, new arrivals would mount a staircase to the registration hall, where medical examiners would cast an appraising eye over them, separating the halt and lame from the apparently able-bodied. Long lines would bring them at last to the immigration officials who would check their name against the ship's manifest. There, the new arrivals would often find their European names transformed at a stroke to an Anglicized spelling.

Apparently, such was the fate of Bertha's father, whom American naturalization records would name as both "George Spektar" and "George Spektor," and who was born in the province of Podolia in southwest Ukraine in 1883.

Clara, the woman whom George took as his wife, was also born in Russia, although it is not known when they met or married. But by the time of the birth of their first child, Doraine, in 1906, they were living in France. Bertha was their second daughter, born in Paris on July 15, 1911. She was barely four months old when her father left to make a new home for the family in America. George traveled first to England, and on November 17 set sail from the port of Liverpool on a steamship of the White Star line, the *Adriatic*, docking in New York ten days later. His immigration forms listed his occupation as tailor.

In April the following year he was joined by Clara and their two young daughters, who had sailed on the liner *La Touraine* from Le Havre. George and Clara would go on to have two more children. By 1923, when George signed the last forms of his petition for naturalization—swearing like all new immigrants that he was neither "an anarchist, a polygamist nor a believer in the practice of polygamy"—George Spektor or Spektar had finally settled on the name "Spector."

The family of Phil Spector's father, Benjamin, would replicate this same journey to a new life, and a new identity, a few years later. Immigration records show that "Gedajle Spektus" or "Gedajk Spektres," was born in 1871 in Odessa, Russia—Ukraine's main port city—and arrived in America in June 1913, having sailed, third class, on the steamship *Cleveland* from the port of Hamburg in Germany. He brought with him his wife Bessie, five sons and a daughter, all of whom had been born in Russia. (A second daughter would be born three years after the family's arrival in America.)

Benjamin was the third son, but there is some discrepancy in the official records as to his exact date of birth. The coroner's report on his death in 1949 records his birth date as January 10, 1903. However, the petition for naturalization signed by his father records Benjamin's birth-date as June 4, 1902. This certificate shows that the transformation of Benjamin's father to American citizen was completed with his acquisition of a new name: Gedajle Spektus or Gedajk Spektres now signed himself "George Spector." His occupation was recorded as "dry-goods merchant."

In later years, Spector family legend would have it that Benjamin enlisted in the armed forces when America entered World War I in 1917, and served overseas. But as he would have been at most sixteen years of age at the time of the war's end, this seems unlikely. However, census records show a Benjamin Spector, born in 1903, enlisted in the U.S. Navy at St. Louis in 1920, and was assigned to a destroyer-minesweeper, USS *Eagle*, based in Portsmouth, New Hampshire. Why Benjamin should have enlisted in St. Louis is not known; nor is it known for how long he served in the navy. But it seems that by the late 1920s he had made his way to California, where he found work in the construction industry. By the early 1930s he had returned to New York, and it was there, in 1934, that he married Bertha Spector.

Were Ben and Bertha first cousins? For this to be the case at least one of their respective parents would have needed to be the brother or sister of one of the other set. We can assume that the two Georges were not brothers. This means either that Benjamin's father, George, must have been the brother of Bertha's mother, Clara; Bertha's father, George, the brother of Benjamin's mother, Bessie; or that Bessie and Clara were sisters. Quite which, if any, of these permutations is the correct one is now lost to time. But an intriguing clue to how closely related the two Spector families were lies in the petitions for naturalization filed by both heads of family. The petition for George, father of Bertha, is dated June 2, 1923, and witnessed by one Isidore Spector, a tailor, noted as residing at 102 East 105th Street, New York.

The petition for George, father of Benjamin, is dated four years later—June 1, 1927. This too was witnessed by the same Isidore Spector. There is also the name of a second witness: Clara Spector. Could this have been Bertha's mother, and Bessie's sister?

Benjamin and Bertha settled in the South Bronx, and their first child, a daughter, Shirley, was born in 1935. Then came tragedy. Bertha gave birth to a son who died when he was just two days old. The birth of a second son, then, was a cause of particular joy. According to his birth certificate, Harvey Philip Spector was born in the Prospect Hospital in the borough of the Bronx on December 26, 1939—a birthday he shared with Mao Tse-tung and Henry Miller. But the birth was sufficiently close to midnight of the previous day for Bertha to tell friends that the certificate was wrong, that her son had actually been born on December 25 and, as she would joke, that she had "given birth to the second Jesus."

This confusion over Spector's birthdate would be compounded in later years, when the year of his birth was misreported as 1940—an error that was perpetuated thereafter. For reasons that are unclear, he would also decide to add a second *l* to the name Philip.

Spector's birth certificate lists his father Ben as being "age 36. Birthplace: Russia. Occupation: Ironworker. Place of work: Factory."

Bertha is recorded as being "age 28. Birthplace: Paris, France. Occupation: Housewife. Place of business: Own home."

The family's place of residence was listed as 1029 Elder Avenue, in the Bronx. But shortly after Harvey's birth the Spectors moved a short distance to a new home in the Soundview district. In later life, Spector would romanticize his childhood home, saying that he'd grown up "in a ghetto . . . that's how I came to write 'Spanish Harlem'." But Soundview was hardly that; a respectable working-class residential area, in the early part of the century it had been an Irish neighborhood, although by the time the Spectors arrived, its population was predominantly Jewish.

The family home, at 1027 Manor Avenue, stood in a row of modest, jerry-built, two-storey gray-brick houses, each of which would usually be occupied by two families—one on each floor. The house's crenellated fascia lent it the appearance of a miniature castle; a short flight of steps led up to the front door. In the heat of summer, the steps of the houses along Manor Avenue—the stoops—would become the social thoroughfare as parents pulled their chairs outside in the hope of catching a breeze, and children played on the street.

A hundred yards north of the Spectors' home, an elevated train clattered along the length of the area's main shopping thoroughfare, Westchester Avenue, in those days lined with mom-'n'-pop stores, kosher delis, dress shops, tailors and family restaurants. A movie house, Loew's—or "Lowees," as it was known locally—showed films three or four weeks after they had opened in Manhattan—a few miles but a world away from the teeming streets of the Bronx. At the bottom of Manor Avenue was another broad thoroughfare, Bruckner Boulevard— now widened and fenced off as the Bruckner Expressway—and beyond that a leafy public park and the shoreline of the Long Island Sound.

Ben Spector worked long hours as an ironworker. He would leave the house early each morning, often arriving home after the children were in bed. But he was apparently a reliable provider. The family lived modestly but comfortably and was sufficiently well off to own their own car at a time when private car ownership in the city was comparatively rare, and to sometimes take winter vacations in Florida.

Both Ben and Bertha loved music. Ben played the guitar, and the radio in the small family home always seemed to be on, broadcasting dance music, show tunes and the latest hits of the day—fuel to Shirley's ambitions to be a star of Broadway musicals or Hollywood movies.

The abundance of relatives in the city meant that weekends were invariably given over to visiting or entertaining. The young Harvey grew particularly close to Bertha's sister, his aunt Doraine, who for twenty years shared an apartment with her brother Louis without either talking to the other, although nobody in the family could remember why.

Ben Spector was a short, heavily built man with a cheerful, gregarious manner. Harvey idolized him, and his happiest childhood memories would be of being taken by his father to Coney Island and Radio City, which Harvey thought was "like heaven." Bertha was also short and compact, an intensely house-proud woman, much concerned with appearances, who wore her hair in a tight perm and always made a point of dressing in her best. If Ben—to outward appearances at least—radiated the sense of being at ease in the world, Bertha seemed forever at odds with it. She made high demands of her husband; no matter what Ben did, how much he earned, it was never quite enough.

Harvey, the longed-for son, was doted on by his mother and adored by his elder sister. But he was a sickly child. From an early age, he suffered from bouts of asthma, and his skin was allergic to strong sunlight, which increased Bertha's sense of motherly protectiveness. He was also overweight and often teased at school; he found it hard to make friends—a fact not helped by Bertha's wariness of other children. She discouraged him from inviting his friends into their home, or visiting theirs. Throughout his childhood, Bertha would instill in Harvey the sense that the world was a dangerous, threatening place and that people were, on the whole, not to be trusted.

Many years later, Harvey would tell a story designed to suggest both how "very different" he felt himself to be from other children, and how this difference intimated an authority that would serve him in later life. "I always liked to do different things than everybody else; preferred being in the background. It was always a joke in New York. There was a game called pitcher, batter, catcher, which you'd play with a stick and a ball on the streets. And when I was a kid it was a joke that 'Joe, you'll pitch; Jack, you'll catch; Jim, you'll hit; and Phil, you'll produce the game.' That was how I achieved my success, because I was smarter than most." The story has the ring of fable. Nobody would ever have talked about stickball games being "produced" and nor would any of his friends have had an inkling of what life held in store for Harvey Philip Spector. But the moral is clear. He always believed he was destined for greatness.

There is a photograph of the Spector family, taken when Harvey was around eight years of age. It shows the family seated at a restaurant table, apparently for a celebration—a birthday or an anniversary, perhaps. Ben Spector is smartly dressed in a wide-lapel suit and patterned tie, grinning into the camera, the proud head of the family. Harvey sits to his right, chubby-cheeked, hair neatly spruced and smiling shyly. To Ben's left sits Bertha, as neat as a pin; and beside her, Shirley, lips heavily rouged, eyes devouring the camera with the relish of the movie or singing star she dreamed of becoming.

There is nothing in Ben Spector's expression that hints at despair, but Ben was evidently a deeply troubled man—troubled enough to take his own life. Early on the morning of April 20, 1949, his dead body was found slumped in the front seat of his car, parked outside premises at 1042 Myrtle Avenue, Brooklyn, some five miles from the Spector family home in Soundview. Ben had apparently run a length of tubing from the car's exhaust pipe into the front seat, turned on the ignition, wound up the window and waited to die.

The coroner's report would rule the time of death at 8:05 a.m., and the cause of death as "Carbon Monoxide Poisoning—Asphyxia. Toxicology report notes 0.65 CO in his blood. Death ruled as suicide." No details were recorded as to who had found the body, or at what time.

The body was taken to the Kings County Hospital morgue, and on April 22, Ben Spector was laid to rest in the Beth David Cemetery in Elmont, New York. A year later, an imposing granite headstone was placed on the grave, engraved with a Star of David and the epitaph TO KNOW HIM WAS TO LOVE HIM.

Exactly why Ben Spector should have decided to take his own life is not known. There were stories that he was experiencing chronic financial difficulties, although there is no evidence to support this. There is a suggestion too that Ben had health worries, brought on by increasingly worsening diabetes. But given the mental troubles that would afflict both his son and daughter in years to come, it is not unreasonable to assume that he too suffered from depression, a depression so acute that he was driven to kill himself. Whatever the reasons, it is impossible to imagine the effect of Ben's death on the nine-year-old son who idolized him. Suicide was regarded as a cause for shame, a stigma. Shirley and Harvey were told only that their father had met with an accident. It would be some time before they were to discover that Ben had taken his own life. For the bereaved child the suicide of a parent often gives rise to deep feelings not only of pain and abandonment, but also of guilt and responsibility. In the solipsistic view of a child, the world revolves around their actions; if my father killed himself it can only be because I drove him to it. For Harvey, Ben's suicide would be a cause of pain, confusion and recrimination for years to come, something he would talk about only to his closest intimates, and then only with the greatest difficulty. Fifty-two years later, Phil Spector would sit on the sofa in his Alhambra castle, hand trembling at his glass, reflecting on the "something I'd either not accepted, or I'm not prepared to accept or live with in my life, that I don't know about perhaps, that I'm facing now." That something was surely the suicide of Ben Spector.

The loss of Ben cast an immovable pall over the house on Manor

Avenue. Harvey, the chubby boy who had been teased about his weight, grew sallow and thin, as if the very life was being squeezed out of him. In Bertha it left a legacy compounded of shame, sadness and a deep bitterness that would stay with her for the rest of her life. "Whenever Bertha talked about Ben, she would describe him as 'my lovely husband,' and in the next breath call him a son-of-a-bitch," remembers one friend. "She'd loved him, and he'd abandoned her." Bertha and Shirley argued constantly, and at the age of seventeen, in a bid to escape the growing tensions in the family home, Shirley made a hasty and improvident marriage to a serviceman. But the union quickly faltered in the face of Bertha's disapproval, and Shirley returned home. In 1953 Bertha decided to make a new life for herself and the children away from Manor Avenue and all the memories it held. She had relatives living in Los Angeles, and she decided to join them there. Her father, George, who was by now a widower, moved with them.

California. A new beginning. The cold darkness of the Bronx, and all its bad memories, fading in the cloudless California sky. The family settled in a small apartment at 602½ Spaulding Avenue, a quiet residential side street south of Melrose Avenue in the Fairfax district, the hub of the Jewish population in Los Angeles. Fifty years on, the area remains largely unchanged. The main thoroughfare, Fairfax Avenue, is a broad avenue lined with palm trees, consisting largely of one-storey buildings built in the '30s, lined with dressmakers, grocery stores, small family restaurants, a synagogue. Then as now, its social center was Canter's, a cavernous and noisy delicatessen, perpetually filled with families and students from the nearby Fairfax High School. Bertha took a job as a seamstress, leaving early each morning to take the bus downtown. Shirley took a job as a secretary. Harvey became a latchkey kid. For a year, he attended John Burroughs Junior High School, a twenty-minute walk from his home, on the junction of Wilshire Boulevard and McFadden, in the Miracle Mile district. In 1954, at the age of fourteen, he transferred to Fairfax High School (motto: "Never Say Die, Say Do"), located on the junction of Melrose and Fairfax avenues, just four blocks from the Spector home.

The student body of Fairfax was overwhelmingly Jewish. "On Jewish holidays they'd hold school in a telephone booth. There were about six kids there," remembers one old boy. The school had a high reputation for academic achievement and for producing students who would go on to excel in the law, medicine and business. The standing joke was that Fairfax students had more chance of owning a football team than playing for one. Pupils at neighboring high schools called it "Fairy-fax."

Harvey felt out of place from the first day he stepped through the school gates.

Although he had left the East Coast when he was twelve years old, Spector would always remain, in his own mind, a New Yorker, romanticizing his childhood in the Bronx and intimating an umbilical connection to the urban sensibility of rhythm and blues and street-corner doo-wop that would come to play such an important part in his music.

He had no disposition toward California life. He hated the beach, the big skies, the perpetual sunshine, and anything to do with "outdoors." The heat made him uncomfortable, strong sunlight irritated his skin. As well as suffering from asthma, he had inherited his father's condition and was borderline diabetic. While he would never need insulin pills or injections, he would religiously watch his sugar intake, and in later life become an avid reader of food labels.

California was a land of giants, bronzed, healthy, vitamin-enriched. Spector was small, pale and scrawny, with watery eyes, a receding chin and a whining, adenoidal voice: the outsider, "always different." He disliked everything about himself, even his name. "Harvey" was the sound of his mother whining, the painful memory of his father's voice. By his mid-teens he was insisting that he be called Phillip. Bertha refused, and to Spector's intense chagrin would continue to address him as Harvey throughout his life. In later years, whenever she wrote letters addressed to "Harvey Spector" he would return them unopened.

Phil's physical frailty and the trauma of his father's death had inculcated a suffocatingly protective attitude toward him in Bertha and Shirley. "They were like a tag team," remembers one friend. "Two very driven, bossy Jewish women, fighting for him, driving him and smothering him."

He would seldom invite friends to the small apartment on Spaulding Avenue, and Bertha always seemed to have an excuse for why he shouldn't visit others. "Bertha wouldn't let Phil cross the street on his own. She didn't trust the world. Phil wasn't allowed to do anything without her."

In later life, Spector would tell friends that he always believed his mother favored Shirley, and for Bertha nothing he ever did was good enough. The chiding that had once been directed toward her husband, she now directed toward her son. "Bertha was the kind of woman who's always on your ass," says another family friend. "She was not a nurturing woman. She didn't give love. She just didn't have that in her."

Hanging like a shroud over the family home was the memory of Ben. "There was a lot of shame around the issue. Bertha told him, you will not discuss the specifics of this, ever. Because that's the kind of stuff that spreads on the school yard for months." His father's suicide remained the young Phil's dark secret, too painful for him to bear alone, but impossible to share with anyone else.

Quiet and introverted, he found it hard to make friends. In the jungle hierarchy of Fairfax—as in any other high school—the criteria for popularity were either good looks or sporting prowess, and Spector had neither. While he loved sports—in later life he would own a courtside season ticket for the Los Angeles Lakers—and more than anything would have loved to have been a baseball player, he was too small and weak ever to make the team.

He was a bright child who loved reading. He took a particular interest in American history and developed a fascination with Abraham Lincoln that would last all his life. In later years, one of his favorite conversational jokes was to parrot the line, "Apart from that, how did you enjoy the play, Mrs. Lincoln?" But lacking in either sporting prowess or academic brilliance, to many of his peers he remained almost invisible. "He wasn't a cool guy, he wasn't a smart guy and he wasn't a funny guy," says Burt Prelutsky, who was in the same year as Spector. "Had there been such a thing as 'least likely to succeed,' Phil would have been it."

To earn extra pocket money, for a year he stacked books after hours in the school library alongside a boy named Cary Cooper. New to the neighborhood, Cooper had few friends and felt some affinity with Phil. When Phil told Cary that his father had died (without explaining how) and talked about his unhappy home life, Cary experienced "this overwhelming feeling that he was a sad character. I felt sorry for him. I wanted to support him and didn't want to be one of these other people that rejected him. He felt rejected, I know that. His peer group rejected him."

Most Fairfax students were enrolled in social clubs, not unlike college fraternities. Members would be voted in, the most popular students joining the most elite clubs. Those who were not members of any club were known as "bennies."

"It meant that you were not a popular person, a social isolate," Cooper says. "Phil was in that category. It wasn't just that he wasn't a sports person or good-looking. He didn't seem to have the interpersonal skills to compensate."

For a while Spector served as the school's "town crier"—a role that entailed him standing up in front of the school during assembly in a white letterman sweater, reading out announcements and then leading the assembly in the school song. The town crier also acted as chief cheerleader at the football and baseball games. "It was kind of a prestigious position in some people's eyes," remembers Ron Milstein, who took over as crier from Spector, "but one where most people thought you were a complete and total jerk for wanting to do it."

Spector and Milstein became friends. "Kids who couldn't compete academically would hang out in horticulture, or auto shop, and Phil befriended some of those people. I think he felt compassionate; he felt for those people who were down-and-out or not popular. And there were people who felt for Phil. He was a sensitive person, but he was mixed up. He could be very witty and sharp; he used humor to get through things. It's a good ploy. But I don't think he felt very comfortable in himself."

Milstein believes that Spector also felt "somewhat embarrassed" by his Jewishness, in a time when anti-Semitic feeling often coursed just below the surface of daily life. "We got an invitation to a party out in Burbank, that we knew was going to be predominantly Gentile. Phil decided that because our names were so obviously Jewish we would go under assumed names. He said, 'I'll be Phil Harvey,' and I was going to be Ron Mills. So we get there and we're meeting people and all of a sudden I hear Phil's voice: 'Hey, Milstein, get over here!' He basically blew our cover and we had to talk our way out of the whole thing."

While Spector might have failed to make his mark in any other subject on the Fairfax curriculum, in one, at least, he was outstanding. Growing up in a household where the radio was on constantly, he had developed an early love for dance music, show tunes and the popular hits of the day. He learned to play the accordion and would occasionally perform at weddings and bar mitzvahs for pocket money. Fairfax had a strong reputation for music—alumni would include the songwriter Jerry Leiber, the producer and trumpeter Herb Alpert and, some years later, the singer Natalie Cole. Spector played French horn in the school orchestra, but he could find his way around almost any instrument and had a natural gift for sight-reading and improvisation. In later years, his music teacher, Dr. Homer Hummel, would tell his pupils that he had learned more from Spector in music classes than Spector had learned from him. Phil adored Dr. Hummel, and when he retired some years later, made a point of turning up at his farewell party, to tell his old mentor how important his teachings on harmony had been in crafting the Teddy Bears records.

Bertha encouraged her son's passion, buying him a guitar as a bar mitzvah present on his thirteenth birthday.

The record producer and scene maker Kim Fowley once described pop as "music for lonely people, made by other lonely people." And for Spector, his small bedroom on Spaulding Avenue became his sanctuary. Returning home from school, he would go straight to his room, shut the door behind him, pick up his guitar and turn on the radio.

The music that by the mid-'50s had come to be known as rock and roll had been woven from myriad different strands, but its essence was the appropriation of black musical styles by white performers, and the adopting of what was held to be a black sensibility—visceral, uninhibited, hedonistic—by a teenage audience. Bill Haley's "Shake, Rattle and Roll," which in 1954 became the first rock and roll record to make the Top 10, had earlier been recorded by the rhythm and blues singer Big Joe Turner. Haley's version diluted the lascivious suggestiveness of the original sufficiently to be played widely on the radio, but to its teenage audience its meaning was clear—shake, rattle and roll was sex. In the same year, at the Sun Studios in Memphis, Elvis Presley recorded his first single, "That's Alright, Mama"—a blues song originally recorded by Arthur Crudup, infusing it with a country inflection to create a hybrid that came to be known as rockabilly.

This music came in a variety of regional guises. There was the rolling, piano-driven style of New Orleans, embodied in the recordings of Fats Domino and Little Richard (respectively, relaxed and frenetic—and both of whose songs were traduced in anodyne cover versions by the white ballad singer Pat Boone). There was the Chicago rhythm and blues of Chuck Berry and Bo Diddley; the Memphis rockabilly of Presley, Jerry Lee Lewis and Carl Perkins; and the doo-wop and vocal group sound that flourished primarily in the urban centers of Los Angeles and New York through such groups as the Crows, the Chords, the Platters, and Frankie Lymon and the Teenagers.

But as much as rock and roll, in all its variants, galvanized the teenage audience, its impact on the charts was slow to be felt. The best-selling artists on the *Billboard* charts in 1955 were not Fats Domino and Elvis Presley but crooners, balladeers and close-harmony groups—Frank Sinatra, the Fontane Sisters, Mitch Miller—who already seemed to belong to a passing era.

Turning the dial of his radio in his bedroom, the young Phil Spector would have heard all of these and more. But his favorite station was KGFJ, the home of a disc jockey named Hunter Hancock. Hunter was an anomaly, a white disc jockey who had begun playing what were then still known as "race records" in the late '40s, and who by the early '50s had been voted the most popular disc jockey among black listeners in

Los Angeles. Hancock was to be Spector's introduction to the big-voiced blues shouters, piano pumpers and guitar tyros, like Amos Milburn, Fats Domino and Lowell Fulson, and also to jazz.

The guitar became Spector's entrée to the social world of the school yard, and he would entertain friends during school breaks, vamping on hits of the day. Annette Merar, who would later become his first wife, remembers Spector reminiscing about just one such school yard session. "He was trying to learn a Dean Martin song, so he would just *think* it, bending his fingers around the neck of the guitar, faking it, but with enthusiasm. Everybody else was just singing along, and they never realized he had no idea what he was doing. Phil just thought that was hilarious."

Spector's passion for music was shared by another friend, Marshall Lieb, whom he had first met at John Burroughs. The son of a car dealer, Lieb could not have been more different from Spector. He was tall, dark and handsome, socially accomplished, popular with girls. He took Spector under his wing. The constant feuding with his mother and sister had given Spector a hair-trigger temper and a fast mouth, and on more than one occasion Lieb had to step in to prevent his friend being given a beating. "Phil was rather mischievous in high school—with me alongside him," Lieb would later recall to the writer Rob Finnis. "He'd have a rather big mouth, and he'd get himself in trouble sometimes, and he always knew he could turn to me and I would help him out . . . and I helped him many times." Lieb would be playing much the same role a few years later when the pair toured as the Teddy Bears. "[Phil] wouldn't take any guff, by the same token he wasn't very strong, he didn't have that much power to hurt anyone, yet he felt he had to, so as soon as words came into fighting, that's when I tried to cool it."

Together, the two boys took guitar lessons with a sometime session guitarist named Burdell Mathis, who had a small studio around the corner from Wallich's Music City on Sunset Boulevard. For a while, Spector also took lessons from another session guitarist, Howard Roberts. But he was so shy that he refused even to take his guitar out of its case, simply watching as Roberts demonstrated his moves, before rushing home to practice what he had seen.

On Phil's fifteenth birthday, Bertha and Shirley took him to see Ella Fitzgerald performing a concert in Hollywood. Playing in her backing group was the guitarist Barney Kessel, and Spector watched transfixed as his fingers flew effortlessly over the frets. Born in Oklahoma in 1923, Kessel was a child prodigy who had left home at fourteen to go on the road, playing with big bands, including those of Charlie Barnett and

Benny Goodman. He went on to play with Charlie Parker, Oscar Peterson, and with the paragons of the West Coast "cool school," Chet Baker and Art Pepper, as well as recording a number of acclaimed albums under his own name. He was also one of the most respected session guitarists in Los Angeles. It was Kessel who provided the exquisite guitar accompaniment on Julie London's 1955 hit "Cry Me a River."

Phil had found a new hero. He collected every Kessel recording he could find, and in an act of homage pinned a photograph of the guitarist on his bedroom wall, alongside the pictures of Albert Einstein and Abraham Lincoln. (When Kessel died in 2004, Spector would describe him to one friend as "the Quintessential. The greatest musician I've ever known; the greatest guitarist that ever lived—well ahead of Segovia whom many, wrongfully, think was the greatest.")

So impassioned was Spector about Kessel's playing that when the jazz magazine *Down Beat* ran an interview with Sal Salvador, the guitarist in the Stan Kenton band, in which Salvador singled out his favorite guitarists but omitted to mention Kessel's name, Spector wrote a letter in defense of his hero, saying he was "a little disappointed that when naming his favorite guitarists Salvador left out the name of Barney Kessel, who in my opinion holds the title of the greatest guitarist . . . Sure wish you would ease my pain and have a story about Barney in one of your future issues."

The letter appeared as the lead on the magazine's letters page in the issue dated November 14, 1956, and its publication not only thrilled Spector, but also inspired his sister Shirley to act on his behalf. Tracking down Barney Kessel at the Contemporary recording studios in Hollywood, she explained that it was her younger brother who had written the letter to *Down Beat*, that he worshiped the guitarist and dreamed of following in his footsteps; would Kessel meet him to pass on some advice? Astonished to learn that the correspondent who had championed him so eloquently in *Down Beat* was just fifteen years old, Kessel readily agreed.

A few days later Phil, Bertha and Shirley presented themselves at Du-par's, a coffee shop on Vine Street, close by the Capitol Records building and much favored by musicians on a break from recording sessions, where Kessel was waiting. Spector spent most of the meeting dumbstruck in the presence of his idol, while his mother and sister belabored Kessel with questions about their son's career prospects in the music industry.

Kessel offered some surprising advice. It was one thing to love jazz and to play it, he told them, but he would not recommend a career as a jazz musician. Phillip should look at the big picture. Fashions in music were cyclical, and jazz was on the downswing; it was rock and roll that people wanted to listen to now. If Phillip wanted to make a career in music he should be thinking of becoming a songwriter or a record producer. (Kessel was true to his own advice; as well as working as a guitarist and bandleader, at the time of meeting Spector he was also working as a vice president for Verve Records, where he produced recordings by Fred Astaire and Audrey Hepburn. Shortly after meeting Spector, Kessel would take Ricky Nelson, the sixteen-year-old star of the television program *The Adventures of Ozzie and Harriet*, and produce his first record, a cover version of Fats Domino's "I'm Walkin'," which went on to sell more than one million copies. Kessel would go on to perform on countless pop sessions for artists including Elvis Presley and the Beach Boys, as well as working with Spector himself.)

Kessel was obviously impressed by Spector's determination and ability. As further encouragement, he offered to give his young admirer some guitar lessons and advice on writing songs. According to his son David, Kessel even joined Spector recording a couple of songs at Wallich's Music City, which provided booths where aspirant musicians could record and cut acetates. "My dad was doing all these heavy jazz sessions, winning *Playboy* and *Down Beat* jazz polls, and he takes time out to make a rock and roll record for free for some kid because he believes in him. Barney could see early on that Phil had something special about him."

In the music room at Fairfax, Spector made another friendship, with a classically trained pianist named Michael Spencer, who played piano for the school choir. Spencer was a year older, and his first impression of Spector was of a "birdy guy—a little twerp," who under normal circumstances he would never have paid much attention to. But when he heard Spector play guitar he quickly revised his opinion. "Phillip was very quiet, very sensitive, a little mouse-like creature without a lot of confidence—but when he was playing music, he had a tremendous aggression." Spencer, whose father was an accountant, lived in a large house on Highland Avenue, in a particularly affluent area of West Hollywood. Spector became a regular visitor to the home, and the two boys would sit for hours, improvising together on jazz and pop standards and poring over the family's large collection of albums of jazz, classical music and show tunes. Spector was particularly impressed by his friend's knowledge of classical music and would listen enthralled as Spencer expounded on the symphonies of Wagner and Sibelius.

While Spector never talked about his own home life, Spencer sensed that these sessions were a welcome escape from the stifling attentions of his mother and sister. Bertha would invariably drive him on his visits to Spencer's home. "Then either she would call to say she was coming to collect him, or she'd just show up, because Harvey was quote 'sick with asthma,'" Spencer remembers. "She was hypochondriacal about Harvey and his asthma. But I never saw him have an asthma attack."

On one occasion, Bertha arrived with Shirley, and Spencer invited them inside. It was the first time he had seen the three members of the family together. "And it was like birds in a cage. Shirley, highly strung with this high-pitched voice, squeaking away at Harvey; and Harvey squeaking away at her, both of them walking this way and that. It was so intense. It was fascinating to watch this family unit."

When Spector was sixteen, Shirley left home and moved into an apartment of her own nearby. Phil and Bertha moved to a smaller apartment, on the first floor of a Spanish-style apartment building at 726 North Hayworth Avenue, two blocks west of Fairfax Avenue. Bertha had given up her job as a seamstress and found work as a bookkeeper. The work was less arduous; the pay, better. But her improving circumstances did nothing to alleviate the strained relations between mother and son, and the pair bickered constantly. Whatever the starting point of the arguments—school grades, money, Phil's "unsuitable" friends—they would inevitably progress to the family's festering sore, the death of Ben. "Phil would be berated with that," one friend remembers. "Bertha would say, 'Your father killed himself because you were a bad child.' And then he would say, 'Daddy killed himself because of you.' Your mother tells you this, you attack back with that. They would just attack each other all the time. There's a reason for everything, and with Phil the reason he's the way he is is all to do with his immediate family."

Spector was awkward around girls, but by the age of sixteen he had found a steady girlfriend named Donna Kass. His first attempts to woo her had unfortunate results. When Donna wanted to get out of a class, Phil wrote a note, forged the name of a teacher, and handed it in personally. The teacher looked at the note and asked Phil, "Do you know who I am?" It was his name that Phil had forged.

Kass was a year younger than Spector, timorous and shy. He was her first boyfriend, and she seemed to see in him qualities that others had missed. Phil, she told the writer Mark Ribowsky, was "not a handsome guy, not at all. He was very pale and had no chin. Not real masculine." But behind the unprepossessing appearance and the quirky manner, Kass thought, lay a "great personality" and a "brilliant" mind. "God, he was brilliant," she told Ribowsky. "He was a great historian—he knew *everything* about Lincoln . . . Phil was just so different from anybody else. He was not the run-of-the-mill kid."

When Donna asked about his father, Phil told her the same thing he told most people—that Ben had died of a heart attack, and when she learned from a friend that Ben had actually killed himself, she warmed to Phil even more, understanding his insecurities.

Establishing a pattern that would characterize his relationships with women for the rest of his life, Spector became intensively possessive of Donna, interrogating her on her movements and sometimes tracking her down on the telephone if she went off with other friends without telling him. Donna thought that Phil's behavior was a mirror of Bertha's suffocating possessiveness. Clearly anxious to keep her away from his mother, Phil would seldom invite Donna to his home, and whenever he visited her it would not be long before Bertha would be on the telephone, asking when he was coming home.

To Donna, it was as if Bertha and Shirley saw her as a rival for Phil's affections who was trying to "steal" him away from them. "I always felt they were in love with him or something. They treated him like he was a god. They protected him, and they wanted to protect him from me."

Donna was probably unaware of Bertha's hypochondriacal anxieties over her son's health, and Phil never mentioned it. But the issue would surface from time to time nonetheless. Donna's best friend was Annette Kleinbard, who was still a junior high school student at Louis Pasteur School. One night Donna and Spector were on a double date with Annette and her boyfriend, George, and parked up in a quiet spot in the nearby Hollywood Hills, known among the local teenagers as Pussy Hollow.

"Donna and Phil were in the backseat, and I was in the front with George with his arm around me," Annette remembers. "And all of a sudden I could hear this heavy breathing in the back. Now, I was a virgin, and I assumed that Donna was too. And I was beside myself because the sounds were getting louder and louder and George was trying to get more romantic, and we were both listening to this incredible heavy breathing that was getting more and more passionate. And suddenly I heard Phil's voice from the back: 'I've got to get out of here, I'm having an asthma attack.' It wasn't heavy petting at all. We'd parked up in some weeds."

Money had always been tight in the Spector household, with little available for luxuries. Ron Milstein's parents would sometimes give him the money to buy dinner at Norm's cafeteria on La Cienega. "Phil would come with me with a brown bag and ask the waitress for a glass of water, a toothpick and napkins, all kinds of other things and never buy anything."

For a while he worked after school as a busboy at Canter's, and then as a page at the CBS studios where *I Love Lucy* was filmed, showing the audience to their seats and running errands. (A huge fan of Lucille Ball, in 1966 he wrote the theme song for a television special, *Lucy Goes to London*, which was performed by the Dave Clark Five.) Bertha added to the money he had saved and bought him a secondhand Chevrolet Impala. The car was Spector's pride and joy. On Friday nights he would drive to Dolores, the drive-in restaurant on Wilshire Boulevard, where waitresses delivered the food on roller skates, and which was packed with the scene makers from Fairfax. Spector would park on the edges and lounge against his car, hoping to be noticed, never quite part of the crowd.

Among his schoolmates, opinions of Spector differed wildly; those who were unaware of his musical talent, or indifferent to it, dismissed him as "a doofus," a "nebbish," a runt. Those who had heard him play tended to hold a very different view. As Spector's confidence in his abilities grew, so too did his circle of friends and acquaintances. With Marshall Lieb he was admitted into a Fairfax High social club called the Barons, and would often join a group of friends that included Ron Milstein and a boy named Harvey Goldstein in impromptu music sessions, practicing harmonies on the doo-wop and pop songs of the day. Milstein noticed how Spector increasingly took command of these sessions. "Phil was definitely the leader in that respect. He would sing all the different parts, showing us what he wanted us to do." He had now acquired a hollow-bodied Gibson guitar, similar to the one played by his hero Barney Kessel, and Milstein remembers how he would impress everybody by unleashing a flurry of dazzling guitar licks. "He called it 'doing a Barney.'" Milstein fancied that Spector "had thoughts of being someone special, but in high school there was no way for that specialness to come out." For now, he was just a confused mixture of budding brilliance, frustration and anger.

With Lieb and Michael Spencer he would sometimes play at house parties and weddings. Spencer too admired Spector's growing abilities as a guitarist, but noticed how easily his temper could be triggered: "We'd be playing some party or frat house, and maybe someone was giving him looks, or acting weird, and it would be: 'What are you looking at?' He'd want to take on some of these guys, and you'd have to step in to quiet things down. My guess is there was liquor in the formula, because at frat houses there was always a lot of liquor going on, and Phil could never hold his drink. He was not an easy one to take around." They would often run into another group playing the same circuit, the Sleepwalkers, made up of students from the neighboring University High: the singer Kim Fowley, Dave Shostak, who played sax, Bruce Johnston, who played keyboards, and the drummer Sandy Nelson. Spector would sometimes sit in with the group on guitar.

"We were playing bar mitzvahs at the Brentwood Temple, house parties—the Jewish kids would have their chaperone dances, and the Catholic kids would have theirs—it was all dogshit," Kim Fowley remembers. "In between times we'd be stealing golf clubs. We'd chase ambulances and fire engines, and when some rich guy's house went up in flames we'd go for the golf clubs because we could sell them in the ghetto. Black people wanted to play golf in the '50s. We'd go down to the black neighborhood, and all the other thieves would be there with the toasters and waffle irons.

"The bass players were always wandering in and out, and the guitar players were always the hardest to get. So Phil Spector would come by and play sometimes. But he was just a guy who knew the songs that everybody else knew. He didn't make an impression. Give him ten bucks, or don't give him anything so we can have more."

Bruce Johnston, who would later go on to join the Beach Boys, has a slightly different recollection: "Phil talked a little funny—like a more masculine Pee-wee Herman. And he'd pull faces, like a little grimace now and then, which was kind of strange. But he was light-years ahead of any other teenage guitar player around. Our whole thing was wishing we sounded like the radio, and Phil's guitar playing did that, and it certainly didn't hurt with meeting girls and all that teenage stuff. I remember playing someone's house in Brentwood and Phil, who definitely didn't have movie-idol looks, with all the girls sitting by him as he played, because he had that radio sound. I remember that because they weren't sitting around me."

Occasionally too Spector would play in a scratch group led by a sax player named Steve Douglas, who had been two years ahead of Phil at Fairfax. Douglas's group was managed, after a fashion, by Spector's sister Shirley, who still harbored her own dreams of being a singer, while working full-time as a secretary. Shirley affected a kind of brittle glamour, wearing her peroxide-blond hair in the style of Lana Turner and blowing plumes of cigarette smoke out of the side of her mouth. "She was a real nervous, speedy little chick, who didn't know how to stop talking," Douglas remembered. "Phil would always show up late to rehearsal, or not show up at all, but he was a hell of a guitar player."

Spector was now sucking up influences like a sponge, mastering the rudiments of songwriting and arranging, able to turn his hand to any number of musical styles, and by dint of his abilities and his application, moving toward the center of an extended group of musicians who would play a significant role in the burgeoning Los Angeles music scene. In the spring of 1957, he and Marshall Lieb appeared on a local late-night television talent show, *Rocket to Stardom*, broadcast on KTLA from an Oldsmobile showroom. Singing the Five Satins' doo-wop hit, "In the Still of the Night," the pair won the competition.

"We all were moving, with our own ambitions," Michael Spencer says. "But it was Phillip who was moving the fastest."

But among some of his old friends there was the sense that he had no compunction about leaving them behind. "It was like Phil would go in and out of different social strata and just give up on what had been before," Ron Milstein remembers. "When we finished our friendship it was as if we'd never even known each other. It was the cold shoulder."

In the summer of 1957, Spector left Fairfax High without a backward glance. His feelings about his school years would be best illustrated by a curious vignette at the Class of '57 high school reunion, held ten years later at the Ambassador Hotel. Spector reserved a table at the back of the room and arrived with two bodyguards, who positioned themselves to prevent anybody else approaching him.

"It was pretty strange," Ron Milstein remembers. "Most people went with their dates. Phil went with his bodyguards. But big deal, you know? We were all pretty much the same. But he was richer and stranger."

Burt Prelutsky was by then writing a weekly column for the *Los Angeles Times*. Intrigued by Spector's behavior, he contacted him for an interview, seeking some explanation. "He basically said that he wanted everybody to get as close to him at the reunion as they had in high school," Prelutsky says. "He was still very bitter. It was a question of, he was going to show us . . ." When Prelutsky's article appeared in the paper, he received a gift from Spector: an electric clock, with Spector's picture on its face, and the inscription "Thanks for giving me the time of day."

Revenge would prove an impetus to Spector for years to come; the little guy rubbing the big guy's nose in it, repaying all the slights and taunts, real and imagined, that he'd had to suffer over the years. And damn the consequences. "You count your success by how many enemies you've made" would become one of Phil Spector's favorite maxims.

3

"To Know Him Is to Love Him"

By the time he left Fairfax High, Phil Spector was in no doubt that his future lay in the music business. But Bertha insisted he needed a skill to fall back on. Spector had always taken a keen interest in law, following the progress of big murder trials in the newspapers, and when Marshall Lieb enrolled at Los Angeles City College, studying politics, Phil joined him there, training to be a court stenographer. Michael Spencer observed how attuned Spector was to the training. "Phil was physically sensitive; he had very fine fingers, and his dexterity was incredible. You'd sit with him and he'd be rapping his fingers, as if he was typing out what you were saying on the table, unconsciously practicing. He was always at a high-pitched level. There was very little that was contemplative. But that was Phil. Always buggy."

The work often took him into the local court, transcribing routine criminal cases, and on one occasion he sat in on one of the endless series of appeals for Caryl Chessman, the so-called Red Light Bandit, who in 1948 was convicted on seventeen counts of robbery, rape and kidnapping. One of the kidnapping counts included bodily harm of the victim. Under California's so-called Little Lindbergh Law, in cases involving kidnapping with bodily harm the sentence was either life in prison without possibility of parole or death. The jury did not recommend mercy, and Chessman was sentenced to death in the gas chamber. Chessman became a cause célèbre, and a range of public figures, including Aldous Huxley, Marlon Brando and the evangelist Billy Graham, took up his case. Chessman spent twelve years fighting the sentence, before going to the gas chamber on May 2, 1960.

Growing up in a Jewish household had inculcated in Spector an early awareness of racial and political issues. Bertha was a staunch Democrat, who had organized block parties to support the Democratic Party's nominee Adlai Stevenson when he ran unsuccessfully for president in 1956. Spector became a fervent supporter of Chessman, railing against the injustice of the sentence and the inequities of the justice system with such fervor that some of his friends began to suspect he was a communist. But it wasn't simply a question of Spector sympathizing with the underdog; he saw himself as one.

While he enjoyed his experiences in the courtroom, Spector had no intention of allowing his studies to get in the way of his music. He had come a long way in the last two years, not only building up experience as a musician and a performer, but learning the craft of composition and arrangement, deconstructing the different elements that comprised the records he loved—the crisp slapback technique that the producer Sam Phillips conjured at the Sun Studios on his recordings for Elvis Presley, Chuck Berry's duck-walking guitar licks, the subtle interweaving of voices in doo-wop and the keening harmonies of the Everly Brothers.

It was now time to make his move. With Marshall Lieb and Harvey Goldstein, Spector had been rehearsing a handful of songs written in his bedroom, and in the early spring of 1958, he finally summoned up his nerve and walked into a small Hollywood studio called Gold Star and said he wanted to make a record.

Gold Star was run by two partners, Stan Ross and Dave Gold. Like Spector, Ross had been a student at Fairfax, going on to learn his craft as an engineer in a local studio, Electrovox, where his duties included recording performances off the radio by comics like Jack Benny and Eddie Cantor and then pressing them as shellac discs to give away as gifts and promotional items.

In 1950, Ross and Gold opened their own studio on the corner of Santa Monica Boulevard and Vine Street, in premises that had previously been occupied by a dentist. By the standards of most Los Angeles studios, Gold Star was unprepossessing. The entrance to the studio was down a litter-strewn side alley. The surroundings were cramped and dingy, the carpet tattered. The singer-songwriter Jackie DeShannon would later joke that the bathroom was the best place for crabs in all Los Angeles. The main recording space, Studio A, was tiny—a mere 25 × 35 feet—with a low ceiling that made the room seem smaller. But what the studio lacked in size it more than made up for in atmosphere. The cramped dimensions of the room lent a powerful intimacy to the records made at Gold Star. It also had two echo chambers, built by Dave Gold, that were among the best to be found in any Los Angeles studio. Attempting to replicate the full, resonant sound of recordings made in the Columbia Studios in New York, Gold had made several failed attempts at building the chambers before finally coming up with the right design. Situated behind Studio A, the trapezoid-shaped chambers were lined with two-inch concrete walls. Each was fitted with a speaker, to input the sound of the recording from the control room, and a mike to record and feed it back. The recording engineer Larry Levine, who would work on virtually all of Spector's recordings between 1962 and 1966, recalls that crawling into the dark, tomblike space and simply hearing your own breath resounding in your ears could be a "terrifying" experience.

Gold Star was used primarily as a demo studio—a place where publishers and songwriters would record a rough cut of a song to sell on to interested parties. But the studio occasionally produced a freshly minted hit. "Tequila," a honking instrumental by the Champs, went to number 1 in 1958; and in February of the same year—just a couple of months before Spector walked into the studio—Gold Star had produced a song that would become a classic of the rock and roll era—Eddie Cochran's "Summertime Blues." The song had been recorded as a demo at one of the regular Wednesday afternoon sessions booked by a local music publishing company, and performed by a scratch group including a shipping clerk and a librarian, with Cochran on vocals. "Summertime Blues" would almost certainly have been one of the records that Spector would have heard on the radio that spring as he sat in his bedroom, writing songs and dreaming of making a hit record himself.

When Spector first walked into Gold Star, Stan Ross was unimpressed. "He was just this nervous, shifty little kid," Ross remembers. "He told me he'd just graduated from Fairfax; we're alumni! Then he said he was going to have a hit record." Just like everyone else, thought Ross. Nonetheless, he allowed Spector to visit the studio a couple of time and watch him at work but told him that if he wanted to make a record himself he would have to pay the standard rate—$15 an hour, plus the cost of the tape. For a two-hour session—around $40—Spector could make his record.

Spector turned to his mother for a loan. He could not have chosen a worse time. Just a few weeks earlier Bertha had been involved in a car crash that had left her unable to work, and she was now involved in litigation against the other party. Nevertheless, she was able to provide $10. Marshall Lieb came up with a further $10, and Harvey Goldstein also contributed to the cause. The remainder would come from an unexpected and, it would transpire, particularly serendipitous source— Donna Kass's friend Annette Kleinbard. Kleinbard was just sixteen, two years younger than Spector. He complained to friends that he found her "irritating," but they did have one passion in common: music. It seemed that whenever Spector saw Annette, she would be singing. He liked her voice, but he also saw something else in her—an opportunity to get his record made.

"He came up to me one day," Kleinbard recalls, "and said, 'Do you have ten dollars?' I said, 'I don't have ten cents.' So he said, 'Well, if you can get together ten dollars, you can cut a record with us.'" Kleinbard begged the money from her parents. "I was a belligerent child and very precocious. I kept saying, 'If you give me ten dollars, we're going to have the number-one record in the world, and I am going to buy you a beautiful mansion, and a racehorse'—because my father had once been a jockey."

Over the next few days, Spector rehearsed the group on a song he had written called "Don't You Worry My Little Pet"—an upbeat rock and roll song that was influenced by two of his current favorites, Buddy Holly and the Crickets and the Everly Brothers. And on May 20, 1958, the four teenagers walked into Gold Star, ready for their big moment. Sitting at the controls, Stan Ross watched with amusement as Spector scuttled between the studio and the control booth, adjusting microphones, playing piano and guitar, organizing the four-part harmonies and doing his best to give everybody the impression he knew what he was doing.

"Don't You Worry My Little Pet" evinced a raw and spontaneous youthful energy, but nobody apart from Spector was really convinced the song was any good. Stan Ross would later dismiss it as "a piece of crap," and even Annette Kleinbard thought it was "dreadful." But it was a calling card. Through another friend, Spector effected an introduction to a small, independent label, Era Records, run by Lew Bedell and Herb Newman.

Stooped and balding, in an earlier life Bedell had been a television host and comedian; he was a man, according to Stan Ross, who "only knew pratfalls. His big question, about everything, was: 'Whaddya think?' He could never make up his mind about anything." Newman had worked at Liberty Records, where his cousin, Si Waronker, was president, before joining forces with Bedell in 1955 to found Era. The label enjoyed an early number-one record with Gogi Grant's "The Wayward Wind," followed by a number of middle-of-the-road pop and country hits. But by 1958, Bedell and Newman were making concerted efforts to break into the rock and roll market, setting up a second label, Dore—named after Bedell's son.

Bedell was sufficiently impressed by Spector's first effort to offer the group a "lease of master" agreement, effectively giving Era control of the master recording for a nominal amount. At the same time Bedell agreed to underwrite the recording of three more songs, with the promise that if the songs did well, a more binding agreement would follow.

On July 3, 1958, the four members of the as-yet-unnamed group convened in Bedell's office to sign the agreement. This gave Era "all right, title and interest of whatsoever kind" in, and "exclusive and perpetual ownership" of, each of the four masters.

In return, Era undertook to pay an advance of $40 for each of the masters (recoupable against royalties), with a royalty rate of 3 percent of the net retail cost of each record. In other words, Spector, Lieb, Goldstein and Annette Kleinbard would receive around one and a half cents for each copy sold, to be divided between the four of them. As songwriter, Phil would receive an additional royalty for the license of his copyright.

There was one further hurdle to be overcome. Because all the members of the group were legally minors Era had to obtain a court order approving the signing under the so-called Coogan Law, which protected underage performers.

In the meantime, Bedell and Newman arranged for more studio time at Gold Star. By now, the group had decided on a name, the Teddy Bears, apparently suggested by Harvey Goldstein and inspired by the Elvis Presley hit of the day, "Let Me Be Your Teddy Bear." But ironically Goldstein was not with the group when, in mid-July, they walked into Gold Star to resume recording. A few months earlier, he had volunteered for the U.S. Army Reserve, a term of service that would prevent him from being drafted into the military proper, and he had been summonsed for two weeks' basic training at Fort Ord in northern California.

The song the Teddy Bears were scheduled to record was a ballad called "Wonderful Lovable You," another Spector song that Bedell had chosen as a possible B-side for "Don't You Worry My Little Pet." Bedell and Newman had dropped by the studio to keep an eye on their new investment. But after two hours, most of which Spector spent experimenting with his guitar sound and attempting vocal overdubs on Gold Star's rudimentary two-track equipment, the session was abandoned. A few days later, Bedell and the Teddy Bears reconvened in the studio. Bedell had now decided the song needed a solid backbeat, and Spector had called in his old friend, the drummer Sandy Nelson. But again, things went far from smoothly. Marshall Lieb would later recall that Nelson was so befuddled by the tempo of "Wonderful Lovable You" that Lieb had to instruct him when to hit the downbeat. At length, Bedell left in exasperation, telling Stan Ross that if the song wasn't completed in two hours, he was to terminate the session. With time running short, Spector pleaded with Ross to be given the chance to record another song instead. Ross relented.

For weeks, Spector had been working on a slow, torchy ballad, loosely modeled on the Chantels' hit "Maybe," which had been rising up the charts through the spring of 1958. At first glance, the lyric of the new song appeared to be just another lament of unrequited teenage love and devotion, but for Spector its inspiration cut far deeper than that, to the abiding source of all his pain and unhappiness. Pondering on the epitaph on his father's gravestone—TO KNOW HIM WAS TO LOVE HIM—Spector had only to shift the tense from the past to present—"To Know Him Is to Love Him"—to write a memoriam disguised as a pop song. Annette Kleinbard had no idea of the song's original inspiration. "Phil told me, I love your voice and I want to write a song for it—not for me, because he was going out with Donna, my best friend, and I just wasn't interested in Phil in that way." When he first sang the song to Annette over the telephone, interrupting her in the middle of her school homework, she was unimpressed. "I thought it was really awful, but that was a lot to do with Phil's voice. He was a great producer, but not a great singer." Nor did Stan Ross have any inkling of its potential as Spector hastily set about arranging the song in the studio: "Annette sang it live, then Phil and Marshall did the oo-badda-oo-badda background sounds, and they overdubbed that, with Phil playing guitar. Sammy put the backbeat in. And that was the record. It was Phil's baby completely. I thought it was a good song, but I certainly didn't think that a ballad like that, done the way they'd done it, could be a hit. We cut it in about an hour. All told, it probably cost one hundred dollars to make."

Listened to almost fifty years on, however, it is apparent that notwithstanding Ross's starkly matter-of-fact description something quite magical had happened.

The song seems almost to amble into your presence with a gently strummed guitar, a simple snap on the snare drum and a whisper of softly humming voices, before Annette Kleinbard's voice enters, shaping a melody over the next two verses of almost stately formality, Spector and Lieb's hushed chorus—"and I do, and I, and I do, and I . . ." echoing behind her. In the middle section the song suddenly takes flight, soaring out of the minor register into a refrain of unsurpassable sweetness (Spector told Annette that he had derived the melody from a Wagner opera. "I don't know which one—I hate Wagner—but that's what he told me") before returning to the original theme, to finally fade away in a mist of whispered "And I do's."

The inspiration for "To Know Him" seems to seep into the song like a contagion. Annette Kleinbard might have thought she was singing a simple teenage love ballad, yet her vocal—fragile, innocent, artless—invests it with an unmistakably elegiac quality. Ostensibly a song about yearning it carries a palpable premonition of abandonment and loneliness, as if to confirm the melancholic truth that to gain what one most desires is at the same time to know that one day it will inevitably be lost. It was a song that seemed to resonate with all the pain of Spector's past, and a presentiment of his future.

What nobody seems to have realized at the time, however, was that it was a hit. Lew Bedell certainly didn't seem to think so. Dore 503 had "To Know Him Is to Love Him" as the B-side of "Don't You Worry My Little Pet." Dipping a tentative toe in the marketplace, at the beginning of August, Bedell pressed up five hundred copies of the record and sent them out to his distributors. Two weeks later, on August 14, Bedell, Newman, the four members of the Teddy Bears and their parents convened in a room at the Los Angeles County Superior Court to hear the court's approval of the "master lease agreement" signed a month earlier in Bedell's offices. Under the ruling, Era was instructed to pay all monies arising from the group's recordings into a trust account and told that no payments could be made from the account without the court's approval. The company was also prohibited from passing on the Teddy Bears' contract to any other party that might not have the wherewithal to make good on it, or from changing ownership without the court's approval. Phil Spector was now legally entitled to make his fortune.

Writing off the cost to promotional expenses, Bedell took Lieb and Spector to Mays department store and bought each a pair of white bucks and matching woolen sweaters, which Bertha dutifully monogrammed with the group's name. They were then posed for publicity photographs. "We were very clean-cut," Lieb would later recall. "Remember, we had very short hair, white bucks and weren't rebellious in any way. We had nothing to say about anything that would lead to any kind of trouble."

For a month nothing much happened with "Don't You Worry My Little Pet." Responding to a deluge of requests orchestrated among her friends by Annette Kleinbard, a couple of local disc jockeys flipped the record and played "To Know Him Is to Love Him" instead. The song quickly fell off their playlists, but the flurry of interest was apparently enough to convince Bedell that he should be promoting that song rather than the notional A-side. By early September, "To Know Him" was being played on heavy rotation on a station in Fargo, North Dakota— hardly a hub of the music business. At around the same time, Bedell got word that the programming director of radio station KDWB, in Minneapolis, Lou Riegert, had fallen in love with Annette's voice and was also playing the song to death. In the last week of September, "To Know Him Is to Love Him" finally crept into the *Billboard* charts at number 88.

The *Billboard* Hot 100 had been inaugurated only a month earlier, proclaimed as "the industry's fastest and most complete programming and buying guide" to the popular music of the day. Prior to that, a record's popularity had been measured on three separate charts, showing radio airplay, sales and jukebox plays. The Hot 100, for the first time, combined all these elements to measure a record's popularity.

The new chart reflected both the extraordinary diversity of pop music at the time, and the rapidity with which rock and roll—barely four years old—had begun to assert itself as a significant commercial and cultural force. At number one in the week that "To Know Him Is to Love Him" entered the charts was the Italian ballad "Volare" by Domenico Modugno. At number two was "Bird Dog" by the Everly Brothers. Other artists in the Top 10 included Tommy Edwards, the Elegants, Bobby Day, Jimmy Clanton and Little Anthony and the Imperials.

Number 88 was a respectable enough beginning, but it's possible that the song might have gotten no further had Lew Bedell not been able to call on a powerful ally—Dick Clark, the host of the television show *American Bandstand*, the most important platform for pop music in the country.

Originally known simply as *Bandstand*, the show had been created in 1954 by a Philadelphia disc jockey named Bob Horn who, shrewdly noting the rising storm of rock and roll, devised the simple format of placing performers in front of a camera and having them lip-synch to their current hits, while an audience of teenagers twisted and jived around them—a template that would become the standard for pop shows for decades to come. Broadcast on a local station, WFIL-TV, *Bandstand* offered a profligate display of the new and deliciously dangerous possibilities of rock and roll, each week featuring doo-wop groups like the Flamingos and Frankie Lymon and the Teenagers, and R&B singers such as Fats Domino and Little Richard. A roster of regular girls, always blond and buxom, would give a countdown on the charts and conduct brief, laudatory interviews with the performers. Joe Boyd, who as a teenager was an avid viewer, and who would later become a distinguished record producer himself, recalls the particular *frisson* engendered by the sight of the *Bandstand* babes interviewing "dangerous-looking pompadoured black men in sharkskin suits. It was not lost on us that these were probably the only occasions on American TV in 1955 when white girls and black men could be seen in such close proximity (*Bandstand* dancers being almost entirely white, of course)."

In 1956, Horn's tenure on *Bandstand* came to an abrupt halt when he was arrested on charges of statutory rape and contributing to the delinquency of a minor. The charges, it would later transpire, were a frame-up, seemingly instigated by people who apparently loathed Horn and all his program stood for. He was later acquitted, but by that time *Bandstand* had passed into the hands of Dick Clark—a man whose clean-cut demeanor and twinkling toothpaste smile was guaranteed to offend no one. Clark was in his mid-twenties and was smart enough to observe his audience closely and listen to their opinions. Renamed as *American Bandstand*, and broadcast across the nation each Saturday at noon, the show quickly became mandatory viewing for teenagers anxious not only to hear the new records and see their favorite stars but also to keep abreast of new dance steps and the latest fashion trends. Clark, in keeping with the mood of the times, ensured that these were conservative. Girls that appeared on the show were not allowed to wear slacks or tight sweaters and boys were obliged to wear a jacket and tie. Smoking and chewing gum were not allowed.

Members of the audience quickly developed their own fan following, and on the back of the show's success Philadelphia developed its own music scene of flash-in-the-pan, clean-cut pop idols and forgotten-by-tomorrow dance hits, while Clark himself became arguably the most important man in the record business.

When Clark aired "To Know Him Is to Love Him" on *American Bandstand* in the third week of September, giving the song immediate national exposure, the joy in the Era offices and among the Teddy Bears was unconfined. Clark would become a controversial figure a year later, when a U.S. House of Representatives committee launched its investigation into payola in the music industry.

The investigation was largely instigated by ASCAP (the American Society of Composers, Authors and Publishers), a symptom of the moral panic that swept across America in the wake of the rise of rock and roll. As the longest established performing-rights association, ASCAP held the monopoly on show tunes, Broadway songs and jazz, and had strong ties to the most conservative elements of the music business, not least the handful of major record labels whose dominance had been seriously challenged by the rise of rock and roll. By the late '50s, independent labels had broken the stranglehold of the majors on radio airplay, and songs licensed by ASCAP's rival BMI (Broadway Music Inc.) dominated the charts. ASCAP argued that the only way the pernicious and morally degrading music could possibly be getting frequent airplay was because disc jockeys were receiving payola—cash payments or gifts in kind—to play the records, and duly began lobbying the House of Representatives to investigate. In fact, it was not unusual for a disc jockey to find an envelope stuffed with dollar bills left on his desk with a batch of new releases, or to be treated to dinner, with perhaps a hooker for dessert, by a friendly promo man. Strictly speaking, payola was not illegal, but it was considered unethical, and in 1959 a subcommittee of the House Committee on Interstate and Foreign Commerce, under Judge Oren Harris, launched a far-reaching investigation into record industry practices.

The investigation spread panic through the industry. Disc jockeys all over America resigned or were fired for accepting payola. Among those investigated were Harold Lipsius and Harry Finfer, the owners of Universal Distributors in Philadelphia, one of the principal distributors of "To Know Him Is to Love Him." Also investigated was Dick Clark. Clark, it transpired, had a share in the copyrights in 163 pop songs, 143 of which had been given to him. Furthermore, the investigation suggested, a high proportion of the records broadcast on *American Bandstand* were manufactured by companies in which Clark had a financial interest, or were songs published by companies he owned. "Mr. Clark managed to keep an average of 4.1 records owned by [his] publishing, manufacturing or artist management firms in the charts every week between October 1957 and November 1959," the investigators' report stated. Among the companies in which Clark had an interest was Jamie, the record label owned by Universal Distributors. Clark admitted that he had invested $125 in Jamie, which had returned him a profit of $11,900. It was also revealed that Jamie had paid out $15,000 in payola, although Clark denied receiving any of it. At the request of his employers ABC-TV, Clark quickly gave up all his business interests, and he emerged from the hearings with the commendation from Judge Oren Harris that he was "an attractive and successful young man," albeit one who "took advantage of a unique opportunity to control too many elements in the popular music field." (The disc jockey Alan Freed, generally acknowledged as the man who coined the term "rock and roll," was not so lucky. In December 1962, Freed pleaded guilty to two counts of commercial bribery and was fined $300. But it was effectively the end of his career. He died three years later, bitter, broken and penniless.)

Clark's decision to promote "To Know Him Is to Love Him" on *American Bandstand* was to prove beneficial to all concerned. Two weeks after the song had been broadcast on the program it rose to number 40 in the charts, and by late October it had reached number 4, prompting Clark to invite the Teddy Bears to appear on the program in person. Seizing the opportunity, Lew Bedell booked the group on a whistle-stop promotional tour through New York, Washington and Philadelphia, and in the last week of November, Spector, Annette Kleinbard and Marshall Lieb boarded the plane for New York.

Harvey Goldstein did not make the journey. Even though he had played no part in the recording of "To Know Him Is to Love Him," Goldstein returned from his army reserve training expecting to resume his place in the Teddy Bears. But Spector and Lieb had decided that he was now unneeded. Before the group's departure, Spector informed Goldstein that Dick Clark was paying expenses and didn't want somebody who hadn't sung on the record. Goldstein was out of the group. It was only later that he would discover that Clark did not pay expenses for people to appear on his show. Goldstein would later file suit against the remaining three members, claiming that he owned 25 percent of the Teddy Bears' name. The action was eventually settled out of court; bonds were placed in trust for Goldstein and he continued to be paid royalty checks for a decade to come.

On November 28, the Teddy Bears made their national television debut on *American Bandstand*. The following week, "To Know Him Is to Love Him" rose to number 1, where it was to remain for the next three weeks. (In Britain it went to number 2.) By the time the record finally dropped out of the American charts some four months later it had sold almost 1.4 million copies. As a mark of his gratitude, Lew Bedell reportedly sent Mrs. Dick Clark a mink coat.

For Spector, the success of "To Know Him" was not only a personal triumph, it was a vindication. The small, insignificant, put-upon boy had proved everybody wrong. Success now went to his head like helium.

"Before the song was a hit, Phil used to come in and say, 'Anything doing today, Mr. Bedell?' " Lew Bedell told Mark Ribowsky. "He was so obsequious, I figured he was half Japanese, this guy. Then, after it was a hit, he walks in and it's 'Hey, Lew, baby, we're doin' good.' He starts calling Herb 'Hey, you.' You never saw such a complete change in a little fuckin' Jewish kid."

Nor were relations improved when it came to discussions about what the Teddy Bears should record next. Spector had brought in a ballad called "Oh Why," which played on a similar musical theme to "To Know Him." But Bedell, who as paymaster believed he had the right to decide what the group recorded, disliked the song. In that case, Spector told him, the group would go elsewhere. This was not quite the act of bravado it seemed. Unbeknown to Bedell, Spector had already been approached by Lew Chudd, the head of a rival company, Imperial Records, offering the Teddy Bears a contract at twice the royalty rate they were receiving from Era—three cents a copy. With the group having delivered their four songs for Era, there was little Bedell could do. Cursing Spector and the group for their ingratitude, he washed his hands of them.

Shirley Spector had been watching her brother's burgeoning career with growing interest and, some thought, a degree of envy. "I met her after Phil had his first hit," Bruce Johnston says, "and it was like, all of a sudden the kid has the success that she thought she should have."

While her own ambitions to be a singer had led nowhere, managing Steve Douglas had given Shirley a taste of the music business and a belief that she could prosper in it. She now proposed to Spector that she should manage the Teddy Bears. Bertha too weighed in, insisting that Phil had an obligation to share his success with his sister. Wilting under the two-pronged attack, he reluctantly acquiesced, and in January 1959 Shirley joined the group as they flew to New York for a television appearance on *Perry Como's Kraft Music Hall*—the first stop on a tour of one-nighters and sock hops in cities across the eastern seaboard.

On the flight to New York, Phil kept Annette amused reciting skits from his two favorite comedians, Jonathan Winters and Lenny Bruce, whose first album, *Interviews of Our Times*, had been released a few months earlier. "Phil idolized Lenny and knew every line there was," Annette remembers. "There were things about Phil that were great. He could be great fun, and he was very bright. I was having to take schoolwork with me, and he would correct me on my English grammar. It was Phil who drummed into me that you always have to put that 'ly' on the end of an adjective—so instead of saying 'appropriate,' you say 'appropriately.' I have Phil to thank for that. He and Marshall were very protective of me because I really was so young. They watched out for me. And I remember that they never, never, never ever made a pass at me."

But what should have been a triumph quickly became an ordeal.

Familiar with the fights that had always characterized the Spector household, Annette and Marshall Lieb had swallowed hard when Shirley appointed herself as the group's manager. Now their worst fears were being realized. Shirley and Phil argued constantly, "screaming fights," Annette says. And Shirley quickly turned her temper on Annette herself.

"She could be sweet one minute, and then so mean the next. She always had me off balance because I never knew what she was doing or where she was coming from. I think that Shirley wanted to sing, too; in a sense she wanted to be me, and she resented me, even though it was my voice that had started her brother's career. She made my life pretty terrible, a living hell."

Embarrassed by his sister's behavior, Phil constantly apologized. "I think he was very concerned about her, how irrational she was. But I remember one day saying to myself, 'This just isn't worth it. I am going to lose my sanity over this,' because she was so exhausting as a human being and so neurotic, or that is how I perceived her to be."

It was during this tour that an incident supposedly occurred that was to scar Spector for years afterward. One night, after a performance, some young toughs followed him into the men's room, held him down and urinated on him. In years to come, this story would become a central part of the Spector mythology, to explain his distrust of the world at large, his obsession with personal security and his subsequent use of bodyguards. Curiously, Annette Kleinbard says she has no recollection of the incident. "I don't remember that and I would have known that." But it was a story that Spector himself would recount at various times over the years to friends and intimates.

It is hard to imagine Spector inventing a story that casts him as the butt of such abject humiliation, but his tendency to self-mythologizing was already becoming apparent to those around him. In a hotel in New York, the three Teddy Bears were astonished when Fidel Castro, newly installed as the revolutionary leader of Cuba and on an unofficial visit to the United States, stepped into the elevator behind them, accompanied by a phalanx of bodyguards in combat fatigues. "Phil," Annette remembers, "was making faces at them behind their backs. He was a real prankster." In later years, Spector would inflate this fleeting encounter into a personal meeting with Castro, at which the Cuban leader allegedly offered him a job as a translator.

Back in Los Angeles, apparently keen to exaggerate his growing importance still further, he told Kim Fowley that he had produced the Mystics' doo-wop hit "Hushabye," and "Come On, Let's Go" by Ritchie Valens. When Valens's song "Donna" was a hit, Spector told

Donna Kass that he had written the song for her. What is so mystifying is that Spector could easily be found out. On February 3, 1959, Valens died when the small plane carrying him, Buddy Holly and the Big Bopper crashed in Iowa. Watching the news on television, Donna Kass saw Valens's girlfriend Donna Ludwig, for whom Valens had written the song, weeping, and realized for the first time that Phil had lied to her. But by then, his relationship with Donna was all but over.

Spector now started dating a girl called Lynn Castle, whom he had met through Marshall Lieb. Lynn was seventeen when she met Spector, and like Donna Kass before her fancied she could see in him qualities that most people missed. Lynn had spent her childhood in a Catholic boarding school, and Spector, she thought, was actually as vulnerable and unworldly as she felt herself to be.

"It was like you see in a movie, two lost souls. I felt that. Nobody could see what in the world I ever saw in him. He didn't look like anything that anyone with an eye for glamour would look at. But he was smart, he was sweet and he was funny. I didn't know about his bleakness and blackness, because I had bleakness and blackness too. But I could see his vulnerability. That's what I loved about him. Because he was fragile he was able to see my fragility. And he knew that what would make him feel okay would work for me as well. Water seeks its own level, and that's what happened."

With the proceeds from "To Know Him Is to Love Him," Spector bought his first sports car, a metallic blue Corvette. Late at night, he would drive to Castle's house in the Valley, tap on her bedroom window and climb in and sit on the end of her bed, playing songs for her on his guitar. "Sweet, sweet songs," Lynn says. "I was absolutely crazy about him."

The idyllic mood was somewhat dissipated on the rare occasions when she would visit him at the apartment on Hayworth, to be greeted at the door by Bertha with an arctic glare. Nowadays Bertha was often to be found in Wallich's Music City, demanding to know exactly how many copies of the Teddy Bears record they had sold. And she continued to exercise an iron grip on her son's life. "I was definitely not welcome around Bertha," Lynn says. "The most I can remember is being at the door. I don't even know if I ever got to go in. I don't think anyone was good enough for her son. Bertha ran Phil."

The Teddy Bears' new home, Imperial, was known primarily as an R&B label. Its owner, Lew Chudd, had built Imperial's fortunes by tapping into the rich vein of talent in New Orleans largely overlooked by other companies. His major discovery was the exuberant Fats Domino—one of Spector's heroes—who enjoyed a string of hits in what was known as "the race market" until crossing over into the pop charts in 1955 with "Ain't That a Shame." Chudd's next big success came with Ricky Nelson—whom Spector's mentor Barney Kessel produced for Verve. Nelson enjoyed a huge hit with a cover version of Fats Domino's "I'm Walkin'." But by a strange oversight, Verve had neglected to tie Nelson to a contract, and Chudd quickly signed him to Imperial. Chudd was a pushy, abrasive man who employed a novel approach to keeping abreast of teenage trends. "He'd come down to Hollywood High and take the kids to lunch," Kim Fowley remembers, "have a burger and fries and listen to what they talked about and what they played on the jukebox. He was the old man in the corner; he looked like a guy working in a tailor's shop. He ran his whole business based around his lunch."

With the Teddy Bears hit still lingering in the charts, Chudd hurried the group back into the studio to begin work on an album. Lew Bedell had exacted his revenge, using his influence to make Gold Star unavailable. Instead, Spector found himself in unfamiliar surroundings, at Master Sound Studios. For the first time he also had the benefit of experienced session musicians at his disposal, including the bass player Red Callender and the drummer Earl Palmer.

Spector had written a handful of new songs, and in line with the conventional wisdom of the day Chudd decreed that the remainder of the album should be filled out with a grab bag of standards, including a Jerome Kern and George Gershwin song, "Long Ago and Far Away," and the old chestnut, "Unchained Melody," chosen to demonstrate the group's versatility and broad appeal.

But as the sessions wore on Chudd found himself experiencing much the same frustration that Bedell and Newman had felt watching Spector at work at Gold Star. After two weeks of positioning mikes, moving the group and musicians around the studio to capture the right sound and experimenting with echo, he had recorded only six of the required twelve tracks. Beyond impatience, Chudd called in his house arranger and producer Jimmie Haskell and instructed him to complete the album in one day.

"In those days the musicians' union allowed us to record a maximum of six songs in three hours," Haskell remembers. "Chudd said, 'I've got the session booked for tomorrow; call the musicians and finish up the other six sides.'" Whatever reservations Spector might have felt about being so brusquely pushed aside, he kept to himself. "Chudd was tough," Haskell says. "Regardless of how forceful Phil could be as he got older, Chudd would have overwhelmed him. He loved to be talked back to, but nobody had the guts to do it."

Haskell was given the songs, wrote the arrangements overnight and convened in the studio next day with the group and musicians. The six tracks were dispatched inside the requisite three hours. "But I can tell you this about those sides. They were somewhat on the sterile side. Phil took the time to get a certain sound, and when you do six songs in three hours you get a sterile sound. It can work, and when you have a good vocal on top of it you can have a hit record—but not this time."

Nor was it altogether Haskell's fault. Spector's new songs were largely derivations of a formula established with "To Know Him," but none achieved anywhere near that song's heart-stopping effect. Released as a single, "Oh Why"—the song that had already been rejected by Lew Bedell—reached only number 98. And *The Teddy Bears Sing* would quickly vanish without trace.

The album's most enduring legacy is the cover art—an unintended masterpiece of high kitsch, which shows Lieb and Spector, dressed in their sweaters stitched by Bertha, handing stuffed teddy bears to Kleinbard, who affects an expression of theatrical "Who, me?" coyness. According to the album's liner notes, "Annette, the sixteen-year-old lead voice of the trio is a straight 'A' student and had her mind set on psychology as a profession before 'To Know Him' hit." While "Phil's biggest problem is not to forget the tunes that keep running through his mind. He never steps out of the house without a pencil and notebook. It is not uncommon for him to interrupt a date, dart out of a movie, or wake up in the middle of the night to jot down a new song that pops into his head.

"The Teddy Bears," the notes went on, "are a good example of how today's teenagers have a chance to become famous in the record field . . . In no other field of creative or industrial endeavor can the youngster express himself for so many and reap the lucrative rewards."

For the members of the group, the words must have seemed bitterly ironic. The contract that the Teddy Bears had originally signed with Era Records entitled the four members of the group to one and a half cents for each record sold. With the sales of "To Know Him Is to Love Him" around 1.4 million, they were theoretically entitled to a grand total of $21,000, split four ways. (Annette Kleinbard remembers her remuneration as "disgusting.") As the writer of the song, Spector would have been entitled to considerably more. In later years, he would claim that, in all, he was owed some $20,000 on the record but received just $3,000. It was a lesson he would never forget.

By now the group was in a state of terminal decline. Shirley Spector's behavior was becoming ever more volatile and irrational, what Annette described as her "Jekyll and Hyde" mood swings ever more pronounced, a portent of the mental illness that would soon overwhelm her. When she drew up a contract formalizing her appointment as the group's manager both Marshall and Annette refused to sign it. Tired of apologizing for Shirley's behavior, tired of Annette and frustrated over the failure of their recordings, Spector allowed the Teddy Bears to dwindle away. In September 1959, Annette was driving her new MG sports car along a twisting road in the Hollywood Hills when she lost control, plunging into a ravine. She was critically injured, and spent three months in UCLA hospital, undergoing extensive facial surgery. Spector was not among her visitors.

Even as the Teddy Bears were gliding slowly toward extinction, Spector had been casting around for his next move. As part of his Imperial contract, he recorded a guitar instrumental called "Bumbershoot," and for a brief period led an instrumental group called the Phil Harvey Band, comprised of a loose aggregation of musicians who would gather at Michael Spencer's home. Spencer's parents often traveled to Palm Springs at weekends, and his Sunday afternoon gatherings were famous, bringing together musicians, writers, and what passed as bohemia among the Fairfax alumni of West Hollywood, invariably culminating in frantic jam sessions, led by Spencer on the piano. The circle included Steve Douglas, the sax player who had been briefly managed by Shirley Spector; Mike Bermani, who played drums for Duane Eddy; Don Peake, who would go on to play guitar with Ray Charles; another guitarist, Elliot Ingber, who would later play with Frank Zappa's Mothers of Invention and Captain Beefheart's Magic Band, and the bass player Larry Taylor, later of Canned Heat. The Phil Harvey Band did little else but rehearse, although they did play one gig at a venue called the Rainbow Roller Rink, appearing on the same bill as Ed "Kookie" Byrnes, who had become a teenage cult hero through his appearance on the hit TV show 77 *Sunset Strip*. Bruce Johnston was in the audience. "Phil must have had four guitars up there beside himself," he remembers. "They were tuning their guitars for at least half the set before they played the first song. They played two songs and left the stage." "Kookie" Byrnes, throwing handfuls of his trademark comb into the audience, got a bigger ovation.

But for Spector the project was a mere dalliance. He had now decided that his future lay not in performing, but in producing. Almost fifty years later, he would cast this decision in characteristically romantic terms. "I wanted to be in the background," he told me, "but I wanted to be important in the background. I wanted to be the focal point. I knew about Toscanini. I knew that Mozart was more important than his operas. That Beethoven was more important than his music, or whoever was playing it. I knew that the real folk music of America was George Gershwin, Jerome Kern, and Irving Berlin. Those names were bigger than the music. That's what I wanted to be."

Whether the twenty-year-old Spector was really dreaming of being Beethoven or Toscanini is a moot point. But he realized that if he wanted to progress he needed to cultivate more powerful allies, and it was this that led him to the door of one of the best-connected men in the Los Angeles music business, Lester Sill. Sill was a decorated World War II hero—he had fought at the Battle of the Bulge and the Battle of Sorrento—who after the war moved into the record business, working as the sales manager for Modern Records, the Los Angeles R&B label, before setting up as an independent talent scout and publisher. His greatest discovery was the team of Jerry Leiber and Mike Stoller, whom Sill found as teenagers, and who would go on to write and produce countless hits for such artists as Elvis Presley, the Coasters and the Drifters.

Sill was a short, dapper man, who always dressed in expensive shirts and beautifully cut sports jackets. He had a reputation as a peerless record salesman; one story tells how he would carry sand around in his pocket, ready to throw on the floor and do a sand-dance when a song demanded it. "Lester was one of the funniest people I've ever met," Jerry Leiber remembers. "He was just a happy guy. You saw Lester and it was a good day." "Lester was a gentleman," concurs Stan Ross. "He always looked you in the eye when he spoke to you. He wasn't one of those guys who's looking around the room for someone else . . ."

Sill had been around the Master Sound Studios when Spector was working on the Teddy Bears' album and had taken note of his abilities as a producer, and his precocity. "He looked like he was twelve years old," Sill would recall. In the spring of 1959, with the Teddy Bears' album still warm in the racks, Spector found his way to Sill's office on North Argyle Avenue, where Sill contracted him as a producer and writer.

More than just a mentor, Sill was to become almost a father figure to Spector. Relations with Bertha had by now reached breaking point, and when Spector explained the problem to Lester he invited him to move in to the home in Sherman Oaks where Sill lived with his wife Harriet, his sons Greg and Joel, and his stepson Chuck. Bertha bitterly resented what she construed as Sill's interference and would never forgive him. Relieved to be free of her controlling influence, Phil instructed the Sills to say that he was out whenever she telephoned.

Sill was in partnership with another writer and producer, named Lee Hazlewood. Together they ran a production company called Gregmark (named after Lester's son Greg, and Lee's son Mark). Their biggest act was the guitarist Duane Eddy, whom Hazlewood had discovered while working as a disc jockey in Arizona, and encouraged to play in a deep, twangy style, halfway between country and rock. Eddy's first recording, "Movin' N' Groovin'," was a minor hit early in 1958 and in July of that year he enjoyed his first Top 10 record, "Rebel Rouser." Over the next two years he would go on to rack up a further thirteen Top 40 hits.

Eddy's recordings were released on Jamie Records, the label owned by Universal Distributors in Philadelphia—the same company that had been so instrumental in the success of the Teddy Bears.

Keen for Spector to gain more experience, Sill took him to Phoenix, Arizona, where Hazlewood made all his recordings, in a small, ramshackle studio called Ramco Audio Recorders. Spector sat fascinated, watching as Hazlewood experimented for hours on end with a variety of echoes and tape delay effects to conjure the deep twang that was the trademark of all Eddy's records. But Hazlewood was also highly protective of his techniques and resented Spector's endless questions and remarks. "Lee was a country boy," remembers Stan Ross, "and you have to understand country boys to get along with them. He was the kind of guy who laughs at his own jokes before you do. Lee thought Phil was crazy. They were like fire and ice." After only a short while, Hazlewood told Sill he didn't want Spector around anymore.

Spector had meanwhile come up with another idea—if not a particularly original one. While the Teddy Bears themselves had been unable to follow their success with "To Know Him Is to Love Him," their close-harmony sound had been replicated by a group called the Fleetwoods who enjoyed a Top 10 hit with a song called "Come Softly to Me." Figuring the formula was worth one more go-round, but contractually prohibited from using the Teddy Bears name, Spector went into the studio to record a handful of songs with a makeshift group that he called Spector's Three. He was joined by a session singer named Ricki Page, and Russ Titelman, the younger brother of Marshall Lieb's girlfriend Susan, and one of the group who frequented the jam sessions at Michael Spencer's home. The Spector's Three's first single, "I Really Do"—which bore a strong resemblance to "Come Softly to Me"—was released by Sill and Hazlewood on their own label, Trey, but quickly disappeared.

Titelman was something of a protégé of Spector's. Three years younger, he had been privy to Spector's mercurial rise, watching with fascination when the Teddy Bears sometimes rehearsed in the front room of his family home, and in awe as "To Know Him Is to Love Him" made its inexorable progress up the charts. Titelman's father had died when he was young. "Phil became my role model—him and James Dean."

Spector encouraged Titelman to take guitar lessons from his old teacher Burdell Mathis, and they would often cruise the streets in Spector's Corvette with the radio turned up loud. "Phil would point out, that's one guy playing that part, another guy this part, see how the vocals come in here. That's pretty much how I learned to listen to records."

To Titelman, Spector was a "totally commanding" figure. "He was extremely funny, charming and charismatic. But at the same time he was a manipulator of people. Both of those personalities existed at the same time."

Better than most, Titelman could recognize that Spector's character had been forged in the crucible of a tempestuous and unhappy home life. On one occasion, visiting Spector at the Hayworth apartment, Titelman watched in astonishment as Bertha chased her son around the apartment, brandishing a kitchen knife. "Phil told me to go downstairs and we ran out of the back door and down the steps. He had his Corvette parked in the alley. We get in, and suddenly Bertha is standing there at the end of the alley with a piece of four-by-two, screaming at the top of her lungs at him. Phil starts inching the car toward her—he just kept on going, and she got out of the way. She didn't hit the car. I have no idea what they were fighting about."

Titelman's girlfriend was a petite and strikingly attractive blonde named Annette Merar. When the Spector's Three were invited to perform on a local TV program, *The Wink Martindale Show*, lip-synching to "I Really Do," Spector asked Annette to appear in place of Ricki Page (Spector replaced himself with a friend of Titelman's, Warren Entner). Two years younger than Spector, and a student at Fairfax High, Merar was only dimly aware of who Phil Spector was. "It certainly didn't register that he was on the road to success or was a genius or anything like that." But Spector was immediately taken with Annette, telling her that she was so pretty he wanted her to model for the cover of a forthcoming Spector's Three album. Annette was duly flattered, but the group, such as it was, had run their course. A second single, "Mr. Robin," was released with no more success than the first, and the album was never made. Annette shrugged and assumed that was the last she would see of Phil Spector.

His relationship with Lynn Castle was also coming to an end. Lynn had left her parental home and moved into a small apartment in the Valley. She had dreams of becoming a songwriter herself and had struck up a friendship with Lester Sill and his partner Lee Hazlewood. Spector seemed to resent her growing independence and particularly her relationship with Hazlewood. Annette had met Lynn on a couple of occasions with Spector, and could see his infatuation with her. "I think she was really the love of his life. Phil likes women who live life to the full, and Lynn fell into that category, and he was very comfortable around her because of that. He just loved her, loved her, loved her."

But for Lynn, his jealousy and possessiveness were becoming intolerable.

"His behavior got too frigging crazy, too absolutely crazy. Where are you? What are you doing? What are you thinking? Where are you going? Controlling."

Occasionally, she would be out shopping or in a coffee shop and Spector would suddenly appear from out of the blue. She began to suspect he was following her.

"I couldn't understand that at all; it just made me want to run. And I remember saying to Phil, I can't stand it anymore, because I just felt like I was choking. I mean, who could take anybody *constantly* . . ."

Finally, she could take no more and stopped seeing him. For Spector, the end of the relationship seemed to encapsulate the growing disenchantment he was feeling with his life in Los Angeles. Since the success of "To Know Him Is to Love Him" in the winter of 1958, he had recorded a succession of singles and an album, all of which had been, in commercial terms at least, conspicuous failures. In his conversations with Lester Sill, he began to express a desire to try his luck in New York. Sympathetic to his feelings, and reasoning that it would be in his interests too for Spector to gain more experience elsewhere, Sill contacted his old protégés Jerry Leiber and Mike Stoller and asked whether they could make use of an apprentice. In the spring of 1960 Spector boarded the plane for New York, and a new life.

4

On Broadway

Flying over the great heartland of America, which had embraced him, and forgotten him, in the space of eighteen short months, Phil Spector would have pondered long and hard at the prospect of now being apprenticed to two men at the very summit of the New York music business hierarchy, and how closely he seemed to be following in their footsteps.

Jerry Leiber had first met Lester Sill in 1950, when Sill was working as the sales manager for Modern Records. Leiber was a student at Fairfax High, who after school worked in Norty's, a local record shop specializing in Jewish music—a white boy who revered black music, selling records by rabbinical cantors. According to Leiber, Sill walked in one day, hawking a new record by the blues singer John Lee Hooker. "I told him, I love the record, but the only thing that sells here is songs for synagogues on high holidays. They will not be buying records by John Lee Hooker."

When Leiber told Sill that he wrote blues songs himself, Sill asked him to sing one. Impressed by Leiber's impromptu performance, Sill offered to help circulate his songs and told Leiber to provide him with some lead sheets. "I had no idea what he was talking about. He said, 'Those are the sheets where the notes are written down, and under the notes are the words' . . ."

Leiber was unable to write music, but shortly afterward he made a serendipitous connection when he was introduced to Mike Stoller, another Jewish boy fatally enamored of black music and already an accomplished jazz pianist. Leiber and Stoller quickly formed a partnership, and with Lester Sill's help began to make the rounds of what Leiber describes as "the cottage industry" of publishers and independent labels in Los Angeles.

They were beating a path that Spector would follow just a few years later, working the "music row" around Sunset and Vine peopled with chancers and flimflam men, raw opportunists and rough diamonds. Typical was the music publisher Harry Goodman, brother of the clarinet player Benny—a man, Leiber remembers, who dressed like a Savile Row dandy, spoke "like a Brooklyn butcher" and held court in an office engulfed in the aroma of marijuana fumes.

"The first time we met him, we went over there and asked, 'Can we play you some songs, Mr. Goodman?' And he says, 'What else do you think I'm here for?' So Mike, very tentatively, walks over to the piano and sits down and one, two, three . . . And Harry says, 'These are the lyrics here?' And I said, 'Yes.' And then he says, 'What's your name?' And I said, 'Jerry.' And he says, 'Jerry, I'm going to tell you something. That song you just sang is a piece of shit.' And he's got a wastepaper basket there and he throws the lyrics in the can. 'Let's go on to the next one.' And he does this five or six times and then finally we get to a song, and he says, 'This is a *real* pile of shit—but it's the kind of shit that I need.' "

Gradually, Leiber and Stoller began to place their songs with R&B artists such as Amos Milburn, Jimmy Witherspoon and Charles Brown. Their first significant hit came with "Hound Dog," recorded by Big Mama Thornton, which topped the R&B charts for seven weeks in 1953. It would also provide the writers with a timely lesson in music business practice. The producer on the session was the local bandleader Johnny Otis. When the record was released, Leiber and Stoller were disconcerted to find that Otis had added his name to the writers' credits, and mortified when the record company, Duke, stopped payment on a royalty check. Bruised by the experience, Leiber and Stoller set up their own publishing company, Quintet Music, and their own record label, Spark, in partnership with Lester Sill. Their first signing was a local R&B group named the Robins, for whom Leiber and Stoller wrote a series of songs—"Riot in Cell Block No. 9," "Framed" and "Smokey Joe's Cafe"—which Leiber and Stoller termed "playlets," vivid narrative songs, performed in a humorous, knockabout style that would become one of the songwriters' trademarks.

While only local hits, their work with the Robins brought them to the attention of Atlantic Records in New York. Founded in 1948 by two Turkish-born brothers, Ahmet and Nesuhi Ertegun, Atlantic had established itself as one of the most successful independent R&B labels in America. In 1955 Nesuhi Ertegun approached Leiber and Stoller with a proposition: Atlantic should buy out Spark, and Leiber and Stoller move to New York and make records for Atlantic as independent writer-producers—an unheard-of arrangement in the record business at that time. Under the deal, Atlantic would pay for all the sessions and give the pair a 2 percent royalty on sales. Crucially, Leiber and Stoller also insisted that they should receive a label credit as producers on all their work—another unprecedented move. Atlantic quibbled over the use of the word "producers." "They wanted to call us directors," Leiber remembers. "They said they were the producers because they put up the money." But Leiber and Stoller prevailed.

Their first Atlantic recordings were with established Atlantic artists such as Joe Turner, LaVern Baker and Ruth Brown. For the Coasters—a revamped version of the Robins—the pair crafted a further series of comic "mini operettas," such as "Yakety Yak," "Charlie Brown," "Along Came Jones" and "Little Egypt," honking vaudevillian R&B songs with lyrics that aligned the group firmly on the side of their teenage audience by mocking and ridiculing the adult world, and which Leiber described as "a white kid's take on a black kid's take on white society."

At the same time, the pair landed an unexpected windfall when, in 1956, Elvis Presley recorded their earlier hit "Hound Dog." Presley's version went on to sell 7 million copies, remaining at number 1 on the pop charts for an incredible eleven weeks—still a record for the longest time any record has held the number 1 spot. In addition to their Atlantic work, Leiber and Stoller suddenly found themselves being called upon to provide more songs for Presley as well.

But perhaps their greatest artistic triumph would come with the Drifters, for whom they crafted a glorious succession of hit singles that would take pop music to new heights of sophistication and polish. Their first hit for the group, "There Goes My Baby," which reached number 2 in the charts in 1959, is widely credited as being the first R&B record to employ strings. It was also the first pop record to employ the subtle Latin American rhythm known as the *baion*, which put the emphasis on the first, third and fourth beats of the bar (*one* [two] *three-four, one* [two] *three-four*). Not only did the *baion* become the basis of a succession of Drifters records, from "Save the Last Dance for Me" to "Under the Boardwalk," but Leiber and Stoller's combination of subtle rhythms and arrangements, the "cushion" of sound they constructed in their recordings by using two or three guitarists and three or four percussionists, would serve as one of the most important precursors for what Spector later achieved with his Wall of Sound.

Jerry Leiber was less than enthralled when Lester Sill called him from California to ask whether the pair could find a use for "this talented kid" named Phil Spector who wanted to learn the business. "I said, 'That's an invitation to poach our ideas,'" Leiber remembers. "And Lester said, 'So what?'"

Sill talked up his young protégé, reminding Leiber about Spector's early success with the Teddy Bears. "I told him that we didn't go for that white-bread trash. We wrote for black people—we were race-record makers. But Lester said, 'Hey, come on. He's very talented and he would be so grateful'—which is actually not something that you would ever associate with Phil."

Nor was Leiber any more impressed when Spector walked through the door of his office at 40 West Fifty-seventh Street.

To Leiber, Spector cut an odd-looking figure, small and scrawny, with a "furtive" manner, and a disconcerting tic of widening his eyes and then blinking, "as if he was looking not at you, but through you." Spector gave off what Leiber calls "conflicting signals"; one minute quiet and self-effacing—"he'd had a big, big hit, and that gives people a sense of accomplishment and security, but Phil acted like it had never happened"—the next, pushy, with an eye for the main chance and a self-belief beyond his twenty years. Leiber thought Spector was "a very strange dog."

What did impress him, however, was Spector's talent. Whatever Leiber might have thought of "To Know Him Is to Love Him," it was obvious that Spector was a promising producer, and—of more immediate use to the producers—a gifted guitarist. "He'd studied with Barney Kessel and he carried that strong jazz-guitar discipline. He was very good."

Leiber and Stoller signed him to their company Trio Music on a two-year contract. Lacking funds, for the first few weeks Spector slept on the sofa in their office, his bag and guitar stashed away in the corner, until finding a small apartment of his own.

Spector had now arrived at the epicenter of the American music business and, while sitting in on sessions with Leiber and Stoller, lost no time in exploring the opportunities to hand.

At the age of twenty, Spector had landed, in musical terms at least, at the very heart of the world. The great tornado of rock and roll that swept through America in the mid-1950s had blown up largely from the South. The Sun Records studio in Memphis had been the cradle for Elvis Presley, Jerry Lee Lewis, Carl Perkins, and Johnny Cash—the rough-hewn country and rockabilly roots of rock. Little Richard and Ray Charles were from Georgia; Roy Orbison and Buddy Holly from Texas; Fats Domino from New Orleans. There were thriving music scenes in Chicago, Detroit and, of course, Los Angeles, serviced by small, independent labels. But New York remained the heart of the music industry. Most of the Big Six labels had their headquarters here, as did most of the major music publishers, and the two principal performing rights organizations, ASCAP and BMI.

New York's burgeoning pop music industry was centered around two neighboring office buildings that housed the music publishers and writers who were the engine of the industry. The Brill Building, located at 1619 Broadway, was a ten-storey art deco block, built in 1931, and named after its first owners the Brill brothers, whose clothing store initially occupied the ground floor. In the 1930s, in the face of deepening economic recession, the Brills started renting out space to music publishers, who found the location convenient for the theaters, nightclubs and vaudeville halls that lined the "Great White Way." In the 1940s, the Brill Building was celebrated by *The New Yorker* humorist A. J. Liebling as "The Jollity Building," where sundry Broadway agents, publishers, songwriters and bandleaders camped out in a rabbit warren of cubicle-sized offices, hustling and scuffling for a break. By 1960 the building housed some ninety music publishers, offering what has been held up as the perfect model of "vertical integration"—a writer could sit in one cubicle, penning a song, sell it to a publisher in the next, hastily record a demo in one of the number of small studios scattered through the building, and then make a deal with a producer hanging around in the lobby. The most prestigious company of all was Hill and Range, owned by two brothers, Jean and Julian Aberbach, which among other things managed the publishing catalogue for Elvis Presley, and occupied a location befitting its station at the top of the music publishing tree in the building's penthouse suite.

If the Brill Building was the spiritual heart of Tin Pan Alley, 1650 Broadway, located just a couple of blocks north, was its upstart younger brother, a scruffier block with none of the Brill's art deco grandeur or raffish show business history. A hive of small publishers, independent record labels and songwriters, its most illustrious occupant was Aldon Music, run by Al Nevins and Don Kirshner, where a formidable team of young writers worked day and night in a series of rabbit warren cubicles, fashioning hits for the pop market.

Within days of arriving in New York, Spector had set about forging new alliances. At Leiber and Stoller's office, he met another young aspirant musician and songwriter from Los Angeles named Nino Tempo. A swaggering young Italian-American with Marlon Brando looks, Tempo (born Antonio Lo Tempi) had worked as a child actor and recorded an album of instrumentals (a multi-instrumentalist, his main instrument was the sax), *Nino Tempo's Rock and Roll Beach Party*. He and Spector connected immediately, and the friendship was cemented when Jerry Leiber went off on a summer vacation, and invited Spector and Tempo to housesit his midtown brownstone. Over the next couple of months, until Tempo returned to Los Angeles, he and Spector were inseparable.

"We were as flat broke as you can imagine," Tempo remembers. "We'd sit there in a diner with two bucks between us, saying, 'Well, we can afford one coffee and two donuts, or two coffees and one donut.' Phil was likeable, funny, crazy, wacky, all those things. But you could also tell he was going places. He knew he was good, and it was just a matter of time before everybody else realized it too."

Tempo would come to play a significant role in Spector's career, but Spector forged a more immediately productive friendship over a cup of coffee in a Howard Johnson's diner on Broadway, when he was introduced to a young songwriter named Beverly Ross. Ross was just seventeen when she wrote "Lollipop" for the Chordettes, which reached number 2 in 1958, and she had recently signed to Hill and Range as a staff writer. "Phil's eyes lit up when I told him that," she remembers. "He was very impressed. And I was impressed that he'd written 'To Know Him Is to Love Him.' The two of us were kind of looking at each other thinking, Geez, you're so young and you've had a big hit. We hit it off straightaway."

Spector, Ross recalls, was "very bright, very funny," but she sensed that for all his braggadocio and self-confidence, he was actually lonely and a little homesick. "There's a Yiddish expression my mother used to use—*schmalzgrub*; it's a little warm place. So I brought him in to my *schmalzgrub*."

Ross thought Spector was "a great musician" and "a truly brilliant guitar player," but only a "mediocre" writer. As a team, she believed, they could be greater than the sum of their parts. Together they would sit in Ross's apartment, working on songs, with the television on and the volume turned down. "Phil would sit there with his guitar and these awful commercials would come on, and he would make up these wild riffs, running up and down the scale to match whatever was on the screen; like, for an electronic carving knife he'd hit some dramatic chord, or say it was an ad for a trouser press—he'd do obbligatos on the guitar that were hysterically funny, dramatizing these ridiculous commercials selling products that no one would ever use. He had a great sense of humor, and he liked a very attentive audience."

But her new friend also discerned a deep vein of insecurity. Spector would talk about the early death of his father—he told her that Ben had died of a heart attack—the unhappiness of his childhood, and his insecurities over his size and appearance. Ross quickly came to the conclusion that beneath the veneer of cockiness and wisecracking humor, Spector was actually "filled with self-loathing."

He was particularly self-conscious about his hair, which was already beginning to thin and recede. He bought a special electric comb, fitted with a blue light, which was supposed to thicken hair and prevent hair loss, and he would run it through his hair constantly, examining himself in the mirror to see if it was having the desired effect.

"He would comb his hair and be so nervous and worried, and talk about how attractive this friend was and how handsome that one was, and this friend got on the football team when he was in high school, and he was jealous because he didn't get this girl or that girl. And I remember thinking, Well, he is short, he doesn't have big bulging muscles or anything, but he's witty and funny and he has a lot to offer. But I think he had a terrific rage and anger that he didn't look like Tarzan. You just had this feeling that he wanted to get even with everybody for his father dying so young and for him not growing up as every girl's dream."

Spector, she remembers, would talk for hours, as if to delay for as long as possible the moment when he would have to be alone. "He'd have you there until four in the morning even though you had to get up at eight. It was like a hypnotic spell. I think we had a tremendous chemistry, and one time when I was over at his place he kissed me and we had a powerful boy-girl reaction to each other. I think he was in love with me, and possibly I with him. But I never wanted to get romantically involved. You know when you don't let down your guard because you don't quite trust someone? And I think Phil was bitter about that too."

Ross was not the only connection that Spector was busily cultivating in his first few months in New York. Through Leiber and Stoller he met Ahmet Ertegun and Jerry Wexler at Atlantic Records and Paul Case, the A&R manager at Hill and Range. An avuncular man in his mid-forties, Case was a figure of substance in the Brill Building hierarchy, and he quickly took Spector under his wing, introducing him around the wide number of writers and producers on the Hill and Range roster. Foremost among these was Doc Pomus.

Born in Brooklyn in 1935, Pomus—whose real name was Jerome Felder—had been crippled by polio at the age of six and walked on crutches (he would later be confined to a wheelchair). Like Leiber,

Stoller and Spector, he was a Jewish boy who had started an early love affair with black music. As a teenager he sang in jazz clubs, affecting the pseudonym Doc Pomus to allay the suspicions of his middle-class parents, and working with a number of legendary musicians, including Milt Jackson and Horace Silver. In the early '50s he began writing songs, achieving his first success with "Boogie Woogie Country Girl," recorded by Big Joe Turner. He wrote "Lonely Avenue," an R&B hit for Ray Charles in 1956, and collaborated with Jerry Leiber and Mike Stoller on the Coasters' hit "Young Blood." But it was not until he teamed up with a younger writer, Mort Shuman, and began pitching songs for the teenage market that Pomus really started to enjoy significant commercial success. Together they wrote across a bewildering variety of styles—rock and roll for Elvis Presley, disposable bubblegum pop for Fabian and Bobby Rydell, "Teenager in Love" for Dion and the Belmonts. In 1959, Pomus and Shuman had ten hits on the *Billboard* charts—only two fewer than Leiber and Stoller.

Some of their best songs were for the Drifters, writing in a style that Pomus called "Jewish Latin." Between 1959 and 1961 they provided the Drifters with a string of hits that included "This Magic Moment," "Sweets for My Sweet" and, most memorably, "Save the Last Dance for Me"—a song that Pomus supposedly scribbled on the back of an invitation to his wedding to an actress, Willi Burke. Pomus was a squat, barrel-chested man with twinkling eyes and a goatee beard, who spoke in a scratchy, high-pitched voice that sounded more black than white, punctuating his every utterance with the universal endearment "babe." "Everybody loved Doc," says Jerry Wexler. "If the music business ever had a heart it would be Doc Pomus. He was a very lovable guy, a very cool guy. Super cool. He also was a great songwriter."

Spector adored him and would spend as much time with him as possible, listening to his stories and relaying them to other friends in a perfect imitation of Pomus's rasping hipsterese. He would often tease Pomus about his disability, to the embarrassment and mortification of others who were too polite to mention the obvious, but causing Pomus himself to laugh uproariously. Spector seemed to have a particular dispensation to amuse.

Pomus and his wife had a house on Long Island, but he spent most of his time at the Hotel Forrest, a short walk from the Brill Building, "a dumpy little place" as Ahmet Ertegun remembered it, frequented by a colorful assortment of Broadway show people, quirks and fly-by-nights, and where Pomus would frequently hold court in the hotel's Spindletop restaurant. Spector liked to tell the story of how one dinner-date with

Pomus was enlivened by a contract hit. "[A] guy in a raincoat walks in with a hat and goes up to a guy and boom boom boom, three times in the head, and the guy slumps over dead, just like that." Pomus couldn't understand why Spector was reluctant to eat in the restaurant again. "The place is incredible, right, the salads, I mean how about the service in that restaurant? You have to look on the up side."

For his first few months in New York, Spector doggedly played the role of apprentice to Leiber and Stoller, trailing them to the studio and playing guitar on their sessions for the Coasters, the Drifters and LaVern Baker. But in October he finally got his chance at production when John Bienstock at Hill and Range asked Leiber and Stoller to produce "Corrina, Corrina," a new single for Ray Peterson. An erstwhile country singer who had enjoyed a big hit with the "death song" "Tell Laura I Love Her" the year before, Peterson also had an interest in a label called Dunes, which was a subsidiary of Hill and Range. Busy with other projects, Leiber handed the project on to Spector.

He shared his excitement at the news with Beverly Ross. Together they had been working on a song called "That's the Kind of Love I Wish I Had." Spector told Ross that he would get Peterson to record the song as the B-side, to repay her for all the help she'd given him. But according to Ross, when she suggested that she should accompany Spector to the session, he hedged, giving the excuse that nobody except the artist and musicians were allowed.

"Corrina, Corrina" had been an R&B hit for Big Joe Turner, but Spector's version had none of the bare-fisted rough and tumble of Turner's; instead, he gave the song a light, lilting quality, sweetening it with a pizzicato string arrangement that might have been borrowed from a Drifters record. Peterson's hiccoughing falsetto sounded no different from a dozen other "Bobby" records of the time.

"Corrina, Corrina" charted in November, rising to number 9, and giving Spector his biggest hit since "To Know Him Is to Love Him" two years earlier. Beverly Ross was impressed when she heard the record; less impressed when she turned it over to discover that Spector had dropped the song they had written together, and that he had promised to record as the B-side. In its place was a song called "Be My Girl," credited to Spector and "Cory Sands"—in fact, a pseudonym for his sister, Shirley. Spector was clearly extending a helping hand to his troubled sister. But Ross was "devastated and heartbroken—speechless practically. I couldn't believe he'd done that to me." But what she regarded as a bigger betrayal was to come.

Almost from the moment he arrived in New York, Spector had been badgering Jerry Leiber to write a song with him, telling Ross that if Leiber agreed she would be included too. But Leiber had done his best to put Spector off. "I kept saying it would be very difficult because Mike is my partner and I think that he would feel put out if I wrote a song with somebody else. But Phil kept insisting, 'Come on . . . it's just a song.' So in the end I said, 'I tell you what; if it's agreeable with you, I would like to invite Mike along to write it with the two of us and if that happens then I will be happy to write the song with you.' He said, 'Sure.' I don't know why I was asking him, because he was supposed to be working for me. I didn't owe anyone an explanation. But Phil could put you on the spot like that."

Stoller agreed to the plan and the three men made an appointment to meet at Leiber's apartment at nine in the evening. Spector arrived at 7:30.

"He said, 'Let's get to work,' and I said, 'No, we've got to wait for Mike.' " By 9:30, with no sign of Stoller, Spector's impatience was growing uncontainable, and Leiber agreed to start sketching out some ideas. At 9:45, Stoller called to say he couldn't make the meeting after all.

Over dinner, Leiber had been playing some classical recordings, including Ravel's *Rhapsody Espagnole* and Debussy's *Iberia.* He suggested to Spector they should perhaps write something with a Spanish feel. While Spector sat at the piano, developing a theme, Leiber turned his thoughts to the lyric. Within a couple of hours they had fashioned the rudiments of a masterpiece, "Spanish Harlem," Spector's poignant melody perfectly complementing the lyric's theme of romantic yearning. Later, Mike Stoller would embellish the tune yet further with a naggingly memorable figure of descending triplets, played on marimba in the final recording.

"Phil was an accomplished musician, but we weren't talking about musicianship, we were talking about the music business, which is about the songs," says Leiber. "So I think that he learned a lot by just writing that song with me. By the choices that I made and what I told him to do, shade this and shade that, make this shorter and make that a shade longer, whatever."

On October 20, Spector joined Leiber and Stoller in the studio with Ben E. King, the lead vocalist of the Drifters, who had recently left the group after a dispute with their manager to embark on a solo career. Over the course of three hours, King recorded four new songs: two were collaborations by Spector and Doc Pomus—"First Taste of Love" and "Young Boy Blues." The third was "Spanish Harlem," and the fourth a song hastily improvised at the end of the session by Leiber, Stoller and King himself, called "Stand by Me."

Unsure of the commercial prospects for "Spanish Harlem," King's label Atlantic initially released it as the B-side of "First Taste of Love." It was not until the record was flipped that it registered on the charts, in January 1961, eventually rising to number 10. Three months later "Stand by Me" would surpass it, reaching number 4.

When Spector played Beverly Ross an acetate of "Spanish Harlem" in the offices of Hill and Range, she was less than thrilled. Spector had reneged on his promise, she believed, by not including her in the collaboration with Leiber.

It was the final straw. Spector, Ross was now convinced, was "a user," who had exploited their friendship and then callously pushed her to one side. "It was almost as though he had it planned out. That he was going to eliminate this person and that person and go on and get all the credit for himself."

What Ross perceived as Spector's betrayal was to leave a lasting mark on her. When her contract ran out with Hill and Range, Mike Stoller offered her a job as a staff writer at Trio. "I thought, This is a dream that every writer has, to work for Leiber and Stoller. And then I thought, It's going to mean that every day I'm going to have to see Phil Spector coming in and out of the office or getting charts or being in the studio, and the idea of being in close proximity to him was so hateful to me, so I turned it down."

Ross dropped out of the business for almost two years. "I became a *lemekhal*—something that doesn't move, like an unhatchable egg."

She would eventually pick up the threads of her career, enjoying a Top 40 hit with "Remember Then," a reprise of the doo-wop style by the Earls. "And one day I was walking on the street with a girlfriend and this great big limo with blackened windows starts following me and all of a sudden I hear 'Bev, Bev!' And it's Phil, poking his head out of this big limo. And he said, 'Hey, I hear you got a big smash out there'—like he was watching what I was getting, how come I was daring to have a hit without him. So I said, 'Yeah, it's really doing great.' And he just kept following us, wanting me and my girlfriend to get in his car, but I was so gun-shy of ever becoming vulnerable to someone who'd betrayed me like that, because Phil practically killed me emotionally. I figured I wasn't smart enough to handle the part of his personality I didn't understand. It was like Phil was born without a conscience, and I was his victim. He could be so ruthless. Phil wrote one line in one of the songs we wrote together that kind of tells the story of his life; the song was 'Don't Believe Everything You Hear,' and the line was 'If you hear him lying just walk away.' Don't even turn back. And that really was his whole attitude; if anyone dares to hurt me I'm just going to walk away; I'm not going to look for any explanation, and no matter how much I love them or they love me, I'm just going to walk away. I think he probably had no use for anybody who was good to him; because I think maybe he thought he was shit. Just bad stuff."

5

"A Big Hoot and Howl"

With "Spanish Harlem" under his belt, Spector returned to Los Angeles at the end of 1960 with a distinct spring in his step. He booked into the Player's Motel, next door to the musicians' union offices on Sunset Boulevard, and a popular stop for visiting actors and musicians. Among the old friends waiting to greet him was Michael Spencer. After graduating from Fairfax, Spencer had gone on to study law at Harvard. But he had dropped out after realizing that his true vocation was music. Spencer had not seen Spector in more than a year, and was struck by the change that his time in New York had wrought in him. Spector, thought Spencer, had grown in stature—quite literally; he now wore lifts in his shoes, adding two inches to his height, and his hair curled toward his collar in a length that seemed, by the standards of the day, ostentatiously bohemian. Spector played his friend a demo pressing of "Spanish Harlem," enthusing about how he was now accepted and honored among the high rollers of the New York music business. Spencer was struck by how the "unformed entity" that he knew from high school dates and bar mitzvahs was now "calling the shots and feeling his oats."

Spector's first port of call was his old friend and mentor Lester Sill, who was eager to get Spector to work on a new project. Sill and his partner Lee Hazlewood had hit a rough patch with Duane Eddy, who would shortly abandon them for a new contract with RCA. Casting around for a new act, Sill had picked up the contract of a trio called the Paris Sisters—Albeth, Priscilla, and Sherrell. Managed by their mother, a former opera singer who had modeled the group on the close harmonies of the Andrews Sisters, the girls had been performing in Las Vegas lounges before two of them were even teenagers, disguising their youth with padded bras and lashings of makeup—a subterfuge apparently helped by their father, who worked at the hospital where they were born and was able to alter their birth certificates. Before signing with Sill they had already recorded a couple of singles for Imperial Records, which had gone unnoticed, and earned money singing demos at Gold Star.

The Paris Sisters usually sang in three-part harmony and rarely featured a lead. But meeting the group for the first time, Spector was immediately struck by the similarity between Priscilla's soft, breathy voice and Annette Kleinbard's. The group, he thought, could be his new Teddy Bears. Before long, he and Priscilla were enjoying a brief fling.

"Phillip had such a crush on her," Michael Spencer remembers. "She was so cute. Flat-chested and so shy. Oh my God! When she sang he was just blown away by her. And their mother, like a fairy tale, taking care of all these sisters. Phillip was just blown away by it all."

(Stan Ross offers a contrasting view. "They were nice girls, but they all looked like they needed nose jobs. The mother was a pain in the ass. The mother hen. She used to come by with a lot of makeup and a pushed-up bustier, so she wouldn't look so old. I told her, 'You still look like an agent.' ")

For the group's first single, Spector turned back to the song that he had co-written with his sister Shirley and used as the B-side of Ray Peterson's "Corrina, Corrina," "Be My Girl"—simply retitling it "Be My Boy." Seeking some reassuring faces in the studio, Spector invited Russ Titelman, who had sung with the Spector's Three a year before, to play guitar and Michael Spencer to play piano on the sessions. A moody, romantic ballad, "Be My Boy" strongly recalled the Teddy Bears hit—Spencer remembers "the lights were low, the music slow, and Phil mumbling how it was an aural oral job"—but it lacked the earlier hit's heart-stopping poignancy. When the single was released in April it reached only number 56 on the *Billboard* chart.

Michael Spencer threw a party at his parents' house to welcome his friend home. Spector had brought his guitar and began to vamp on some jazz and blues songs, interspersed with wisecracks and comical dialogue. Among the gathering were Russ Titelman, and his girlfriend Annette Merar, whom Spector had employed lip-synching to the Spector's Three record on television. It had never occurred to Annette before to think of Spector in a romantic light. But success seemed to have given him a new sheen of self-assurance, and watching as he sat with his guitar, entertaining the gathering, her feelings suddenly began to change.

"Watching him play, it didn't make my body shiver, it made my soul just fall in love. It wasn't a physical thing at all. I never noticed what Phil looked like or didn't look like. I never look at that. I just look at soul. I feel it. And he just did it for me the way he played that guitar. He had this charisma and charm and humor, and this wonderful smile—some people's eyes just smile, and Phil was like that. And with all of that together I was just floored."

At the end of the evening, Spector told her that he had to drive out to the Valley to see Lester Sill. "I'll come with you," said Annette.

Russ Titelman thought that Annette was "one of the most beautiful girls on the face of the earth." She was petite, almost elfin in stature, with an aquiline nose, wide green eyes, and a vivacious, palpably sexual intensity about her. She loved literature and poetry, and dreamed of becoming a writer herself. At the time she and Spector started dating, she was just completing her senior year at Fairfax. Over the next few weeks that Spector spent in Los Angeles, the couple saw each other as often as they could, Spector frequently calling at her home. Annette's father was an accountant who was in awe of Spector having achieved so much at such an early age. " 'Isn't he amazing!' That was the theme," Annette remembers. Her mother was a classically trained pianist. "She wasn't a social person, and nor was Phil. So when he came over to the house my mother would disappear and my father would just smile, and Phil would say, 'Let's go . . .' He was definitely the domineering one in the relationship. I was the moth around his flame, and whatever he did was fine. I was so clueless."

The first Russ Titelman learned of the relationship was when he was driving past the Player's Motel and saw Annette's car in the parking lot. Knocking on the door of Spector's room, he discovered them inside. His relationship with Annette was already on the wane, he says. "But it was the secrecy that hurt. That my idol and my girlfriend should be doing that behind my back."

As his friendship with Beverly Ross cooled, Spector wasted no time in forging a new partnership, with another protégé of Leiber and Stoller named Phil Teitelbaum, who had enjoyed fleeting fame as a singer under the name Terry Phillips but was now signed to Trio Music as a writer. Together they wrote some material for Ruth Brown, who was being produced by Leiber and Stoller, and for Johnny Nash, a Houston-born reggae singer whom Spector himself produced for ABC Records. Shortly after his return from Los Angeles, Spector broke some unbelievable news to Phillips. His schmoozing at Hill and Range had apparently paid dividends, he told Phillips; they had been given the opportunity to write some songs for Elvis Presley's forthcoming movie, *Blue Hawaii.** Phillips's incredulity at the news—how had a relatively unknown songwriter like Spector managed to land a deal to write for the biggest name in pop music?—was tempered by a more pragmatic consideration. Both he and Spector were under contract to Leiber and Stoller at Trio Music; how could they write for Hill and Range at the same time? But Spector brushed aside his concerns, assuring him that everything had been taken care of. Phillips moved into Spector's apartment on Eighty-second Street and in a whirlwind of activity set to writing new material.

Spector also had another offer on the table. Since his arrival in New York, he had grown increasingly close to Ahmet Ertegun, the owner of Atlantic Records, where Leiber and Stoller so successfully plied their trade. Even among the colorful array of impresarios, mavericks and hustlers who populated the New York record business, Ertegun cut a distinctive and singularly stylish figure. The son of a Turkish diplomat, he had lived in Switzerland, France, and England before his father was appointed Turkish ambassador to the United States in 1934, when Ahmet was eleven. Through his older brother, Nesuhi, Ahmet acquired a passion for jazz, nurtured by the janitor at the Turkish embassy in Washington, a black man named Cleo Payne, who introduced the young Ertegun to the world of beer joints, boxing, soul food and what Ertegun himself described as the "secret language of the black man." By the age of sixteen, he was absconding from home and traveling to New York to inveigle himself into the joints and jazz clubs of Harlem.

In college, Ertegun studied philosophy, economics and literature, but his heart was in music. In 1947, he became partners with a blues enthusiast named Herb Abramson and his wife Miriam, and with funding from an acquaintance of Ertegun's father, a Turkish dentist named Dr. Vahdi Sabit, founded Atlantic Records. For $95 a month they rented a room in a run-down hotel, the Jefferson, with enough space for their

---

*Hill and Range administered Elvis Presley Music, the company which had been set up by Presley's manager Colonel Tom Parker. Freddy Bienstock, a cousin of Hill and Range's founders Jean and Julian Aberbach, had the sole responsibility for selecting material and presenting it to Elvis personally. "I had a song written by Leiber and Stoller which I thought was very good for Elvis," he remembers. "I went out to Memphis and played it for him. And he listened to the first eight bars and he took it off and said, 'It's not for me.' I was disappointed, and I thought I'll wait. And not the next session, but the session after that, I resubmitted it to him. And he started playing it, and after eight bars he looked at me and said, 'I didn't like it the first time.' I was stunned. He must have heard thousands of songs in between."

desks and for Ahmet to sleep. When they wanted to record, they would push the furniture back against the wall.

The first Atlantic releases were an eclectic grab bag of jazz, blues and gospel recordings. But within a couple of years the label had become synonymous with the raucous, good-time party music epitomized in the recordings of such artists as Ruth Brown and Joe Turner. Within the music industry—if not to its black audience—this music was known as "race music," until a reporter at *Billboard* magazine, Jerry Wexler, devised the more palatable, and evocative, term "rhythm and blues." In 1953, when Herb Abramson departed for the armed forces in Europe, Wexler himself joined Atlantic as a partner. Through the '50s the red and black Atlantic label, stamped with the legend "Leads the Field in Rhythm and Blues," dominated the R&B charts with recordings by such artists as the Clovers, Clyde McPhatter and the Drifters, LaVern Baker and Ray Charles. Wexler and Ertegun were an intriguing partnership. Wexler was rabbinical, erudite, knowledgeable in art and literature— probably the only record producer within a ten-mile radius of the Brill Building who could quote Hegel and the philosopher William James. He was also dogmatic, cantankerous and commercially hard-nosed. It was Wexler who took care of business, arriving early each day to chase orders, hassle contracts with pressing plants and distributors and schmooze disc jockeys, usually only turning his attention to producing at night.

But it was Ertegun who set the tone for the operation, a singular concoction of the hip and the urbane, dapper in horn-rimmed spectacles, expensively tailored suits and a trim goatee beard, equally at home in Southern juke joints or sophisticated Upper East Side restaurants, charming all and sundry with what Wexler would describe as his "semicosmopolite European stutter."

Spector had found a new role model. He was mesmerized by Ahmet's cool vernacular, his sharp dress, his effortless air of hip knowingness and inscrutability. He loved to listen to Ahmet's stories about venturing into the boondocks of Louisiana in search of the great primitive piano genius Professor Longhair ("and when we got there he'd already signed to Mercury!"), recording with Ray Charles and hanging out with the aristocrats of jazz and blues—the Dukes, the Earls and the Counts. Ertegun's savoir faire, his cultured enthusiasm and his encyclopedic knowledge of music set him apart from the run-of-the-mill sharks and hustlers, "the short-armed fatties," as Spector would call them, who populated the music business, and whom he was quickly coming to loathe. The Atlantic label, shaped and informed by good taste and a commitment to musical excellence, was exactly the kind of operation Spector dreamed of one day running himself.

Ertegun, for his part, was a collector and curator of interesting characters, and Spector was a study. He made Ertegun laugh with his practical jokes and corny one-liners, and his uncanny impersonations of other people in the business, including Ertegun himself. "He could do my voice very well," Ertegun remembered.

"I'd never seen anybody like Phil before, and I'm sure I'll never see anybody like him again. You know—you smile and you connect with somebody, and Phil and I connected. He was very funny; a great sense of humor. Very intelligent, and also very hip about the music. He wasn't much into jazz, but he knew everything about R&B and he certainly knew everything about rock and roll."

Like Ertegun, Spector was a student of the Mezz Mezzrow school of hipster slang, and the pair delighted in out-jiving each other. "We developed our own hip way of speaking, our own interpretation of black slang. We'd say 'yayss,' rather than yes. We had our own little things. There was a certain kind of food that we both liked very much— Philadelphia food. Scrapple—kind of leftover bits of meat and grease that you fry; like a fried pâté. Or a Philly cheesesteak sandwich—meat cut paper-thin, which has been broiled, served on something resembling French bread with a gooey cheese melt."

Ertegun was in the throes of divorcing his first wife, Jan, a Scandinavian who seemed to leave so little impression on him that when he subsequently bumped into her some years later at a party she had to remind Ertegun who she was. He was in search of a playmate, and Spector was happy to play the part. They became inseparable, and when Ertegun offered Spector a job as his personal assistant and staff producer Spector, despite his accumulating number of commitments, quickly accepted. "He was already producing records, and he was in demand," Ertegun remembered. "I think he only accepted the offer because we were having a good time together."

Spector shared the news of his new appointment with his old friend Michael Spencer. "He said, 'I've signed one hundred percent exclusive with Hill and Range.' I said, 'Congratulations.' He said, 'I'm also signed one hundred percent with Leiber and Stoller.' I said, 'Double congratulations.' He said, 'Well, that's not it, I just signed one hundred percent exclusive with Ahmet Ertegun. Do you think there's anything wrong with that?' I said, 'It sounds perfectly natural, Phillip. Who am I to say?' Phil's view was that they all adored him and so they would somehow all accommodate him and work it out."

In fact, Spector had grievously overplayed his hand. Contrary to what he had told Terry Phillips, the conflict of interest between Hill and Range and Leiber and Stoller over the offer to write songs for *Blue Hawaii* had not been "taken care of." When Leiber and Stoller got wind of the deal they were furious. Elvis Presley was one of their best clients: Leiber and Stoller demanded half of the publishing rights from Hill and Range on any songs written by Spector and Phillips. Hill and Range refused, and no songs by Spector and Phillips were ever submitted to Elvis. As if that weren't bad enough, Spector was now rubbing salt into the wound by signing on for Atlantic as well. "[Leiber and Stoller] were angry," Lester Sill recalled, "because they groomed him, helped him, honed his craft. They took Phil in, they took care of him, and they were gonna make deals with him, and the minute he got hot, he walked."

But there was little Leiber and Stoller could do—particularly when Spector pointed out that the contract he had signed with them was actually null and void because he had been underage when he signed it.

Shortly after the news of Spector's appointment to Atlantic was published in the trade magazine *Billboard*, Spector and Ertegun both happened to be in Los Angeles.

"Phil was driving this hot Thunderbird, it was souped-up to make a lot of noise, and he had a record player fitted in the front," Ertegun remembered. "So these music publishers were talking, 'Oh my God, Ahmet and Phil Spector are going to be producing a lot of hits; we've got to give them songs.' And most of these were older guys. So Phil said, 'Listen, we'll only listen in our car, because we like to hear how it sounds through car speakers. You want to play the demos, come down and we'll play them in the car.' So we get this poor old guy who's come down with a couple of demos, and we put him in the backseat. And Phil takes off, going through the middle of Hollywood at ninety miles per hour, and the guy's screaming, 'I don't care if you never record any of my songs! Lemme out of the car!' It was just a big hoot and howl."

On the same trip, Ertegun took Spector to a meeting with Atlantic's "great white hope" Bobby Darin, at the home in the Hollywood Hills he shared with his starlet wife Sandra Dee. Darin was eager for Ertegun to hear some new songs he'd written. Darin's musical ideas were often brilliant, but not always. He was also extremely temperamental, and Ertegun had learned to indulge him.

"Good," said Ertegun after Darin had run through the first song. "Good," he repeated after the second. "Fine," he commented after the third. "Interesting," he remarked after the fourth.

"What?!" Spector broke in. "Are you fuckin' crazy or am I? He can't record these songs. These songs are pure shit!"

"Who is this guy?" Darin demanded. "Get him the fuck out of here."

Ertegun's colleagues at Atlantic apparently thought much the same thing. Jerry Wexler would later come to regard Spector as "a one-off genius" and a close friend, but his first impressions were unfavorable. "Phil had come out of California and he was so brash and full of piss and vinegar with his guitar and his one little hit. You would have a meeting with him and he would just lay it down. He didn't care who he was talking to or how much experience he was up against, it was 'Now, this is what I think.' He had one mantra in the studio; if I made a suggestion or wanted to pursue an avenue he didn't agree with, his answer would always be 'Hey, man—I came from California to make hits.' "

Wexler and Spector collaborated on recordings for Billy Storm and, most disastrously, the Top Notes, working on a song called "Twist and Shout," which borrowed heavily from the Cuban wedding song "La Bamba," and which had been brought to Atlantic by its writer Bert Berns. The song had all the makings of a hit, and in the studio, Wexler remembers, he and Spector went at it with "unrestrained ferocity" but succeeded only in "butchering" it, while Berns sat watching in pained silence. Wexler was left to reflect that it would have been better to let Berns produce the song himself, which is exactly what he did the following year with the Isley Brothers, turning it into a major hit.

"Phil and I created negative synergy," Wexler says. "I liked him, but we could not collaborate. But I don't think Phil's a collaborator."

Nor did Spector's idiosyncrasies endear him to others on the Atlantic staff. He would infuriate Miriam Abramson, the label's office manager, by booking rehearsal time, and then turning up late, or not at all. "We'd have artists sitting there in the office, waiting for him. He wouldn't call, and they'd sit there an hour or two and leave, then come back the next day, and finally he'd show up. He was really very autocratic for somebody who was just starting out. You'd think, who does he think *he* is. Phil took advantage of people, because to some extent he was lazy. He knew that Ahmet liked him, that Jerry Wexler would support him. He was absolutely always convinced about his own creativity and talents. He never doubted himself, ever."

The records that Spector produced in the few months he was associated with Atlantic, while all competent productions in the standard R&B mold of the day, hardly bore out his conviction in his own genius, nor did they trouble the charts. But Ertegun did not seem overly bothered by that. He just enjoyed having Spector around. "Jerry in particular got frustrated with Phil. He was waiting for him to deliver as a producer, which never really happened at Atlantic. But Phil understood what people loved. He could play it and sing it and do it, boom boom. I knew it was going to come. In the meantime, he and I were going out to clubs and this and that and having a terrific time."

In March, Michael Spencer left Los Angeles for New York, determined to follow a career in music. In the wake of the debacle over *Blue Hawaii*, Spector's friendship with Terry Phillips had cooled, and when he moved out of Spector's apartment, Spencer moved in. Spector was moving faster than any job description could contain, combining his role at Atlantic with other freelance producing jobs. One of Spencer's first jobs in New York was contracting the musicians and playing piano on another Spector production—"Pretty Little Angel Eyes," sung by a discovery of Ray Peterson's named Curtis Lee. "Pretty Little Angel Eyes" was a mediocre song redeemed only by Spector's use of a black quartet called the Halos providing an infectious doo-wop backing. Like the majority of his recordings at the time, it was a proficient record but hardly a memorable one, and could have been the work of any one of a dozen producers working around Broadway. But for Spector these records were an important step in learning to "play" the studio like an instrument, experimenting with the placement of microphones and the use of echo, learning how one studio differed from the next, and the importance of establishing relationships with engineers and arrangers he could trust.

Jimmy Reed, a blues singer much admired by Spector and Spencer, now deeply in his cups, was performing at Carnegie Hall, and they made a pilgrimage to see him. But it was a saddening experience. "We came in a few minutes late," Spencer remembers. "And Jimmy Reed came out and he faced the rear of the stage and he started singing 'Got me running . . .' and someone walked onstage, and as he was singing turned him around to face the audience. At that point Phillip and I left. It was too desperate."

On another occasion, Spector took Spencer uptown to the Apollo to see Ray Charles. Like Reed, Charles was wrestling with an addiction— in his case, to heroin. "We went backstage, and Ray was walking around with blood dribbling down his arm. And nobody had had the courtesy to clean him up."

Spector regaled Spencer with stories of his accomplishments, and his new network of friends and allies, treating him to his note-perfect impersonations of Ertegun and Doc Pomus. Spencer noticed how he seemed to be making their mannerisms his own, "as if he was re-assembling himself by borrowing this and that. Phil was always looking for the father figure, and Doc played that role to an extent." Spector joked to Spencer how he would tell everybody that he met that he was a genius, "and they all agree with me." Spencer fancied that he could see his friend's burgeoning success "feeding into his ego, and all the forces that were inside of him could manifest because now he had power." But he could also discern more unsettling currents below the cocksure, braggadocio veneer.

Spector had begun to see a Park Avenue psychoanalyst, Dr. Harold Kaplan, on a regular basis. In later years, he would explain that this was a ruse to "avoid the [military] draft." He had a deep anxiety about being drafted, even though he had reached draft-eligible age at a time when the United States was not at war. He told Spencer (who had received his Selective Service card) that he had learned of a scam whereby you could buy your way out for $3,000, although it seemed he never took that option. But while avoiding the draft was a happy consequence of the visits to Dr. Kaplan, it was not the only reason. Spector was plagued by unspecified anxieties and inexplicable feelings of unease. He fretted about his appearance, the impression he made on others and what they might really think of him.

Spencer sensed that he was "emotionally disturbed. Not mentally. Mentally is the processing of data, the processing of factual stuff—reality. It wasn't that. Phil didn't have cognitive problems; he was shrewd and sharp. He could think through things; he was very obser-vant, very astute. It was more the emotional area. There were contradic-tions. It was as if Phil was wired differently, and not all the circuits came into play in the early stages, but as his environment changed these wirings manifested."

Living at close quarters with Spector, Spencer began to notice the personal idiosyncrasies that had not been apparent when they were together in Los Angeles. Sometimes Spector would return from a nearby grocery store and pull out cans of tuna or beans which he had hidden in his pockets, "things he could easily afford to pay for. I don't know why." If Spector was going on a date he would ask Spencer to buy his contraceptives because he was too shy to buy them himself. The smallest thing could rattle him. Spencer had the knack of shaving in a matter of seconds, a few quick strokes with the razor and a rinse. Spec-tor would watch aghast, "terrified" that Spencer would slash his own throat. Spector would spend an age in front of the mirror, carefully scratching away his stubble, endlessly experimenting with new creams and unctions to find the perfect preparation, before finally dousing himself in copious quantities of cologne.

Spector, his friend noticed, was constantly "buggy," constantly on edge. He was uncomfortable in unfamiliar situations, as if he felt physically threatened. Yet at the same time he would provoke confrontations, as if to confirm that his fears were justified, snapping at strangers who stared a moment too long at his hair or his clothes. "There was a chip on his shoulder. It was the chip that would appear sometimes when we played those frat parties. It wouldn't take much to throw Phil over the top."

On one occasion Spencer took Spector on a nocturnal ramble around Forty-second Street between Sixth and Seventh Avenues, at that time a notoriously seedy area lined with peep shows, third-run cinemas and twenty-four-hour automats, frequented by hustlers, junkies and prostitutes. Spencer liked to catch a movie and then sit in Hector's Cafeteria watching the carnival of humanity parade by. But Spector, he says, was "terrified. Phil came from a conservative background and I would say he was basically conservative."

In the apartment they shared Spencer noticed that Spector would stare out of the window or sometimes vanish onto the fire escape. "I never paid it much mind. Then one night I said, 'What's out there?' And he was looking in the window of an adjacent apartment and there were two lesbians in there. And he was just fascinated to watch them. After that, in the park, if he saw two lesbians walking together, or perhaps holding hands, he would just stand and stare. Phillip could get obsessed with things. It was part of his personality."

For a while, his obsession was learning French. "I think Dr. Kaplan told Phil that if he could master something it would help him get a handle on himself," Spencer says. A French tutor would visit the apartment several times a week, and Spector started to use the word "bourgeois" at any and every opportunity. But he quickly tired of the new enthusiasm, and the lessons soon stopped.

Lester Sill was in search of another hit for the Paris Sisters, and as May turned to June he called Spector back to Los Angeles. For his first single with the group, Spector had been able to fall back on one of his own songs, "Be My Boy." But he realized he needed something stronger to follow it. Over the years, one of his principal maxims as a producer would be that "it's all about the right song." A good song could transcend a mediocre performance or a lackluster production and endure forever. But no amount of studio sweat or polish could turn a lackluster song to gold.

Spector revered the great tunesmiths of the '30s and '40s—George and Ira Gershwin, Jerome Kern, and Irving Berlin—had an encyclopedic knowledge of their songs and could sing many by heart. Berlin was a particular favorite, and the felicitous irony of a fellow Jew writing the best-selling Christmas song of all time, "White Christmas," would be a major inspiration behind Spector later recording his own Christmas album.

More than anything, Spector would have loved to be a great songwriter himself, but he had a realistic view of his own limitations. "To Know Him Is to Love Him" had appeared fully formed, almost in the shape of a gift from his father. But he would struggle ever to write a song as memorable again. He had a limited palette for writing melodies— they were sweet but never quite strong enough, and as a lyricist he could never transcend the platitude. Spector knew that if he were to progress as a force in music he needed a reliable source of strong material. And in New York there was no source more reliable than Don Kirshner at Aldon Music—the man whom *Time* magazine would dub "The Man with the Golden Ear."

Born in 1934, Kirshner was the son of a Harlem tailor, who had numbered Billie Holiday and Dinah Washington among his clientele. Tall and powerfully built, Kirshner won a sports scholarship to Upsala University in New Jersey, where he captained the basketball team, and might have made a career in the sport had it not been for a chance encounter at the Long Island resort hotel where he was working one summer as a bellhop. Swimming in the pool one day Kirshner overheard a younger boy playing the piano. Liking the melody, Kirshner offered to put some words to it. Together they sang the song for Frankie Laine, who was performing at the hotel, and who suggested they should make a demo. Borrowing $50 from his father and recruiting the hotel barman to sing, Kirshner recorded the demo and was able to place the song with a publisher.

At around the same time, he was introduced by a girlfriend to another aspirant songwriter named Walden Robert Cassotto. Cassotto not only wrote songs, he also sang, played the piano and acted. He had suffered from rheumatic fever as a child and his fragile health had inspired a burning ambition to become "the most important entertainer in the world" before his time ran out. Fancying he could spot a star in the making, and flushed by his own modest success, Kirshner suggested they should team up. Their first composition together was an advertising jingle for a local department store. Kirshner hefted the tape recorder on his shoulders so that Cassotto wouldn't strain himself. A second jingle for another store followed, this one sung by a girlfriend of Kirshner's named Concetta Franconero. From jingles, the pair progressed to pop songs. When Gene Vincent recorded one of their compositions, "Wear My Ring," as the B-side of his hit "Lotta Lovin'," Kirshner and Cassotto pocketed a royalty check for $2,500. It was a revelation for Kirshner: a B-side earned as much as an A-side. In 1957, the partnership came to an end when Cassotto secured professional management and changed his name to Bobby Darin. (The friendship, however, remained intact: when Kirshner married his wife Sheila two years later, Darin was best man; that same week his record "Mack the Knife" went to number 1.)

Unsure where to turn next, Kirshner played some of his songs to Doc Pomus, who diplomatically suggested that he might try publishing instead. In the spring of 1958, he teamed up with a music-business veteran named Al Nevins; the pair took office space at 1650 Broadway and started trading under the name Aldon Music. Nevins was twenty years older, but it was the perfect partnership. "Al believed in me," Kirshner remembers. "He was like a father. He let me pick the songs and he doled out the money." Kirshner could neither read nor write music, and his own musical taste was more for sing-along standards and show tunes than rock and roll—more Lerner and Loewe than "Good Golly, Miss Molly." But he had an intuitive understanding of what made a hit record, and he quickly recognized that to broach the teenage market he needed songwriters who understood the dreams and anguish of being a teenager themselves. The first people to walk through the door at Aldon were two songwriters, Neil Sedaka and Howard Greenfield, with a mindless confection called "Stupid Cupid." Paul Case at Hill and Range had already turned down the song, but Kirshner sensed it would suit his old friend Concetta Franconero, now better known as Connie Francis, who had already enjoyed two Top 40 hits. "Stupid Cupid" reached number 17. Sedaka and Greenfield's next hit was "Oh! Carol," a love letter to Sedaka's high school classmate Carole Klein, sung by Sedaka himself. Klein also wrote and performed songs, under the name Carole King. And with her husband and co-writer Gerry Goffin she penned a riposte, "Oh! Neil." Amused, Kirshner "schlepped out to Brooklyn" to sign the pair to Aldon, offering Goffin the incentive of $50 a week to give up his full-time job at a chemistry plant. Kirshner's investment was rewarded in 1961 when their song "Will You Love Me Tomorrow?" recorded by the Shirelles, rose to number 1 in the charts.

By then, the Aldon team had been swollen by the arrival of two more writers—Barry Mann, who already had an established track record as a writer before signing with Aldon, and Cynthia Weil, an aspiring actress who had worked at a rival publishing house, Frank Loesser. Mann and Weil quickly became man and wife, and an enduring songwriting partnership.

By 1962, Kirshner had assembled a team of some twenty writers, aged between sixteen and twenty-six, working either singly or in pairs, who between them were responsible for a major percentage of the hits being generated out of New York. He had also started his own label, Dimension, releasing records by such artists as the Cookies, Carole King and Little Eva (who was actually King's babysitter).

"Donny," as he was universally known, was a brash man with a high opinion of himself. His partner Al Nevins was suave, with epicurean tastes—he affected an ascot and collected rare cognacs. Kirshner, according to one producer, "was a bit of a slob. He'd sit around the office with his shoes off and his feet up on the desk. He was the sort of guy who'd invite you out to his mansion in New Jersey for a dinner party and order in pizza. But he had the greatest ears in the business. That man could sit and listen to somebody play eight bars of a song and he could tell you whether it was a hit or not, and he was right so often it was frightening. He was phenomenal."

In his suite of offices at 1650 Broadway Kirshner had fashioned a production line of hits. His writers worked in small cubicles furnished with a piano and a desk, cutting their demos in an office studio, often congregating at the end of the day to compare notes and tunes, while constantly vying against each other for "Donny's approval and largesse." "It was fun servitude," Kirshner says. "You'd come in every day, and I didn't have expensive offices. I couldn't afford it. You'd hear these songs coming through the wall."

While only a few years older than his young protégés, Kirshner had the paternalistic manner of a much older man. "They were like my kids." He was a straight arrow who disapproved of drinking and abhorred drugs of any kind, and who would go home each evening to New Jersey and his new wife Sheila.

There wasn't a writer at Aldon who wasn't Jewish. Just as it had been the Jewish entrepreneurs and moguls of Hollywood who had shaped

America's view of itself through the movies, and the Jewish songwriters of the '30s and '40s—Irving Berlin, Harold Arlen, George and Ira Gershwin—who peddled America's dreams, so Kirshner's writers too were "normal Jewish kids," as he put it, whose songs both shaped and reflected the conservative dreams and aspirations of most American teenagers, with their time-honored themes of infatuation and heart-break, summer romances, the first kiss, dreams of wedding bells and living happily ever after. Two of his songwriting teams—Barry Mann and Cynthia Weil, and Gerry Goffin and Carole King—were married couples, although barely out of their teens, and seemed to be living out the dream themselves.

Almost from the moment he set foot in New York, Spector had targeted Kirshner as a man to be cultivated and made a point of visiting the Aldon offices to pay homage.

Compared to his clean-cut team of writers Kirshner thought "Philly," as he called him, was "an oddball," with his off-center garb, his twitchy mannerisms and his hipster locutions—"he talked like a foreign count or something"—which Kirshner suspected he'd plundered from Ertegun.

"Phil had quirks that nobody liked," Kirshner remembers. "He was a practical joker. He would work at being different and eccentric. I'm sitting with some fairly normal Jewish kids who were going to go home, get married, this and that. And he was walking in with capes, shoes up to your eyeballs or whatever, which stand out in any crowd. Phil had to compensate for his size, his looks, by being different."

But Kirshner was nothing if not a pragmatist. He had heard Spector's work, recognized his potential and quickly took him under his wing.

"I would walk the streets with Phil. There were times we'd stay at the office till two, three in the morning and then I'd take him home. I remember when his grandfather died, he was really depressed because he'd already lost his father, and he came out and stayed at my house in New Jersey. So I would be the father figure, the mentor. But with Philly, it was mostly business. I didn't like to be uncomfortable or eccentric, or if he made a nasty remark or a wisecrack. I thought he was cute, eccentric, charming, all of the above. But I also got to know that Philly was a user and pretty manipulative. To me, Philly was not an overwhelming friend, but a business associate we made a lot of money with."

As one mutual friend put it: "Both of them had their magnificent egos." Relations between the two men were often strained, but the mutual advantage to be gained from the partnership overruled any personal reservations. It was a marriage of convenience that would provide Spector with many of his greatest hits and Kirshner with an unbroken stream of royalty payments for years to come.

Spector was drawn to Kirshner because he had the lock on the teenage market, the best stable of songwriters, and wielded the kind of power that Spector hoped to one day have himself. "Phil needed my writers," Kirshner says. "And he respected me for my knowledge of wedding the right song to the right artist. He knew that if he picked my brains and took my songs he would be a notch above everybody else."

For his part, Kirshner recognized Spector's talent as a producer, and his potential as a hit-making vehicle for his writers' songs. "I wasn't interested in Phil as a writer. My writers were superior to him. But he was a great interpreter of songs. I knew he could capture the essence of a hook in a record and fortify the hook, fortify the drum sound. What he would add to a great song would be a Top 10 record. But what Phil did not like—what he didn't like with anyone—was that I was in a position of power.

"Philly always wanted to be numero uno. And because he had a similar drive to what I had, he resented any authority figures, which I clearly was. If I'd said Phil you're not having my songs, he'd have been finished. So whether he liked it or not, he had to be nice to me. No different if I was pushing to have a song with Wexler and Ahmet, I had to be nice to them. So it was a fact of life. No different than a doctor you use; he may have a lousy bedside manner but you need him. If he's gonna give you the chemo you gotta be nice to him. So it was almost a love-hate thing."

It was on one of his periodic visits to Aldon that Spector first heard "I Love How You Love Me," a composition by Barry Mann and Larry Kolberg—who combined songwriting with his full-time job as a liquor salesman. The song was earmarked for the teenage singer Tony Orlando, who had enjoyed his first hit earlier that year with another Aldon song, "Halfway to Paradise," written by Gerry Goffin and Carole King. But Spector persuaded Kirshner that it was better suited to a female singer and would be perfect for the Paris Sisters.

Mann and Kolberg, who had scribbled the lyrics in five minutes on a restaurant napkin, envisaged the song as upbeat and cheerful. But Spector had other ideas. He flew out to Los Angeles for the sessions, determined to make a record of a richness and majesty that would surpass anything he had achieved before. At Gold Star, he gathered the Paris

Sisters around the piano, working on the vocals over and over again to get precisely the right balance between the voices, slowing down the tune to a tempo more befitting a prayer than a song (when Kolberg first heard the record he likened it to "a funeral dirge"). With the arranger Hank Levine he then spent days crafting a lustrously silken string arrangement.

But it was the mixing that was to prove the most time-consuming process as Spector became obsessed with effecting exactly the right marriage between voices and strings. He was staying at Lester Sill's home, and would take the tapes back each evening, listening to them incessantly in the privacy of his room. "He would wake me up at three or four in the morning, listening to it over and over again at a very low level," Sill remembered. "He must have remixed the strings on that song thirty times; then listened to it for another four or five days before he was sure it was right. Then finally when the record was pressed he listened to the pressing for another two or three days before he gave it an approval. I've never seen anyone more meticulous about mixing, about recording or mastering than Phil, of all the producers I've worked with. And it was really part of him, he became part of what he was doing, I mean, really his whole life was into it."

"I Love How You Love Me" was, in many ways, an echo of "To Know Him Is to Love Him"; sonorous and sweet, but also deeper, warmer and more richly textured—the first true precursor to the Wall of Sound. While Mann and Kolberg had written the song as a simple and affecting celebration of love, Spector's production seemed to carry within it the premonition of heartache, as if this was a love too good to be true. If "To Know Him" had been an elegy disguised as a love song, this was a love song disguised as an elegy. It was almost as if Spector couldn't produce a love song that didn't also carry the fear of loss. "I Love How You Love Me" entered the Top 40 in October 1961, rising to number 5.

When Annette Kleinbard first heard the song she was shocked by its resemblance to the hit she had made with the Teddy Bears three years earlier. "I was driving in my car, and my first thought was 'Is that me?' Before she'd sung more than five words I knew that it was Phil's record. I'd never heard of the Paris Sisters, but I knew it would be a huge record and I wept, because it felt like Phil had taken my voice and passed it on to somebody else. It was just the most beautiful record, but I loved it and I hated it at the same time. Because I had been struggling to make it on my own and never could do it on that level and was so beside myself that

Phil had done it. But Phil knew—he knew what he wanted, and he was a genius. He just had a lock on the heart of the kids of America, of the world."

As Spector labored in the studio producing "I Love How You Love Me" and a handful of other songs for an intended album, Sill's partner Lee Hazlewood grew increasingly frustrated at the amount of time, money and attention that Sill was lavishing on his young protégé. It seemed that whenever Hazlewood wanted to talk to Sill he was busy with Spector. Hazlewood had always resented what he regarded as Spector's cockiness and lack of respect, and pumped up with excitement about the Paris Sisters recordings Spector seemed only to goad Hazlewood even more. "Phil was running around like crazy and giving people a hard time and he was picking fights with Lee," Stan Ross remembered. "Phil wasn't really respectful—he was being Phil Spector, not the easiest guy for anybody to love. Lee said, 'I'm not gonna go in the same room with that little fart.' "

At length, Hazlewood told Sill he had had enough; he was ending their partnership and going back to work with Duane Eddy. "Lee thought I was neglecting our thing," Sill later recalled, "which wasn't true. It was really that Lee saw Phil as a threat, creatively. That's how much Phil had grown."

Sill now put a proposition to Spector. Why didn't they become partners in their own label?

For Spector, the offer was precisely what he had been waiting for. His formative experience with the Teddy Bears, and the fifteen months he had spent working the angles in New York, had provided a salutary lesson in the hierarchy of the music business. Performers—particularly young and gullible ones—came bottom of the pecking order; songwriters, producers and music publishers occupied the next rung; but the real power lay with whoever owned the label and counted the money. Spector had achieved some success as a songwriter and as a staff and freelance producer; but his income was negligible compared to what he could earn if he took complete control of the entire recording process— writing, producing and publishing the songs and releasing them on his own label.

But of even greater importance to Spector was the fact that he would at last have complete freedom to record who he wanted to, how he wanted to and when he wanted to. Spector, it was agreed, would control the artistic direction of the new label from his base in New York, while

Sill took care of sales and promotion in Los Angeles. The label would be called Philles—a blending of its partners' names, Phil and Les. At the same time, Spector set up his own publishing company, dedicating its name to the woman he most loved and hated—Mother Bertha Music.

In search of a distributor for the new label, Sill turned to his old partners Harold Lipsius and Harry Finfer at Universal Distributors in Philadelphia, striking a deal to finance, press and distribute Philles records in exchange for a one-third stake in the profits.

Returning to New York, Spector now began to concentrate his attention on scouting for new talent for the label. His short sojourn with Atlantic, and his carousing with Ahmet Ertegun, was anyway coming to an end. Ertegun was about to marry for the second time, this time to Ioana Maria "Mica" Banu, a former Dior model who had once been married to a member of the Romanian aristocracy, and whom Ertegun had courted by hiding a small orchestra in the bathroom at the Ritz-Carlton in Montreal to surprise her with "Puttin' on the Ritz."

When she and Ertegun married in 1961 the couple bought a house on East Eighty-first for $100,000 which required considerable restoration. Mica undertook the project herself, in the process launching herself into a successful career as an interior designer. Suddenly Ertegun wasn't getting out as much as he used to do. "Phil saw that our every evening was not going to be every evening anymore. And that's when he decided to go on and do something else," Ertegun remembered.

On the day that Mica and Ertegun married, Spector left Atlantic.

Mica and Spector regarded each other warily. On one occasion Spector was invited to dinner at the Erteguns' new home. A fastidious hostess, Mica had carefully arranged placement cards at the table. While she was entertaining guests in another room, Spector mischievously switched the cards around. Mica's suspicions fell on Spector, and for a while he was barred from the Erteguns' table.

Spector meanwhile turned his attention to finding an act good enough to raise the curtain on his new label. He unearthed three possibilities at Hill and Range. The Ducanes and the Creations were both white male vocal groups, singing in a street-corner doo-wop style that was already going out of fashion. Spector cut records with both but passed them on elsewhere—the Ducanes to his friend George Goldner at Goldisc Records, the Creations to his new partners Lipsius and Finfer to release on their Jamie label. The third group, five teenage girls from Brooklyn known as the Crystals, he decided to keep for himself.

6

"They All Thought
He Was a Genius"

Phil Spector might have become the undisputed emperor of what became known as the girl group sound, but he was not its originator. That distinction belonged to a young singer-songwriter named Richard Barrett. Barrett led a group called the Valentines, which had enjoyed a modest string of successes for a small New York label, Rama, run by an erstwhile dance-hall manager and record producer named George Goldner. Barrett also discovered Frankie Lymon and the Teenagers, who, signed to Goldner's label, quickly became one of the most popular acts in rock and roll. But it was his discovery of five black teenage girls, whom he chanced upon singing a cappella backstage at a Lymon concert while waiting to meet their idol, which was to set the girl group ball rolling. The girls were a group of high school classmates from the Bronx who called themselves the Chantels; the song they were singing, a heartfelt harmony called "The Plea," was written by one of the group, fifteen-year-old Arlene Smith.

George Goldner prevaricated when Barrett first brought him the group, arguing that young girl singers were not saleable in the rhythm and blues market, but eventually agreed to record them for his new label, End. The Chantels' first single, "He's Gone," backed with "The Plea," released late in 1957, was a modest hit on the pop and R&B charts. But it was the group's second single, "Maybe," that would establish the earliest template of the girl group sound, pitching Arlene Smith's high, plaintive vocal against a wailing vocal chorus that owed as much to the call-and-response of gospel as it did to pop. "Maybe" reached number 15 on the pop chart, and while the Chantels would never equal its success, their example would prove an inspiration to myriad teenage girls who began forming themselves into groups and practicing harmony singing. Foremost among them were the Shirelles, a quartet from Passaic, New Jersey, who in 1960 rose to the top of the American charts with King and Goffin's "Will You Love Me Tomorrow," which remained in the American Top 40 for almost four months. More significantly, it was the first ever record by a black female group to reach number 1.

Like virtually every other girl group in New York, the five members of the Crystals—Dee Dee Kenniebrew, Mary Thomas, Barbara Alston, Patsy Wright and Merna Girard (who would soon be replaced by Dolores "LaLa" Brooks)—had been inspired by the example of the Chantels, and it was the success of the Chantels and the Shirelles that was no doubt uppermost in Spector's mind when he first encountered the gaggle of shy and ungainly teenagers in the offices of Hill and Range in March 1961. But that was not the only reason he found the Crystals such an attractive proposition. More than most people, Spector understood that the history of American music was largely the story of white imitating or stealing from black. Jazz and rhythm and blues were his own favorite music forms, and in his year in New York Spector had worked with enough black performers to convince him that the emotional rawness and honesty of black voices was his favorite instrument. Black singers, he would later explain, have a way of expressing themselves "because of true suffering, natural suffering. Musically there are a lot of incredible white singers, too. It's just that my soul probably lies somewhere in suffering, and I identify with people who suffer."

Not only did Spector fall in love with the Crystals' warm and soulful harmonies—he also recognized that in all their raw and untutored innocence, the group offered a tabula rasa on which he could stamp his own identity as a producer. They even brought with them a tailor-made song, "There's No Other (Like My Baby)," which had been written by a cousin of one of the group, Leroy Bates. Spector thought he could do something with it. Bates had written the song in a rocking tempo, but Michael Spencer came upon Spector in the Hill and Range offices, working with the group, slowing down the tempo to transform the song into a moody ballad, bringing it a completely different feel, and heightening its resemblance to the Chantels' "Maybe" (Spector added his name to the writer credits in the process).

But the Crystals were under contract to Hill and Range and about to sign to the publishing company's own record label, Big Top. Spector needed to move quickly to make them his first signing to Philles. Waiting for Sill to finalize the arrangements with Universal, Spector turned to another source to fund the Crystals sessions—a music business manager named Helen Noga, whom he had met through Paul Case, his mentor at Hill and Range. In later years, Spector would describe Noga as "the toughest woman I ever met in my life. The toughest *person* I ever met in my life. 'Bout four foot nine, four hundred pounds—huge woman, small, with a mouth like a truck driver. She took a liking to me. All these people loved me; they saw money in me."

Born in 1913, Noga was an extraordinary woman, a pioneer. In the 1940s, with her husband John Noga she founded the San Francisco jazz clubs the Black Hawk and the Downbeat, that routinely hosted performers such as Sarah Vaughan, Duke Ellington, Count Basie and others. In the 1950s she discovered a young Johnny Mathis singing in a college band and became his manager. She signed him to Columbia Records and groomed him as a smooth crooner in the Frank Sinatra mold, quickly turning Mathis into an international star.

Noga rejoiced in her tough reputation. "I'm an Armenian from Fresno," she would joke. "And it takes three Jews to take one Armenian in any business deal."

Perhaps her greatest accomplishment was to break the color bar imposed on black entertainers in Las Vegas. In 1960 she refused to sign a contract for Mathis to perform at the Sands hotel-casino unless he could enter through the front door, gamble in the casino and eat in the restaurant—rights that had been denied to other black entertainers. Nat "King" Cole and Louis Armstrong were among the performers who called Noga, begging her not to make trouble, and warning her that she was putting her own life in danger. "She made a lot of people very angry doing that," her daughter Beverly remembers, "but even the people she made angry or won her point over—like her or not—still had to respect her."

She and Spector hit it off immediately. "Mother recognized that he was a talented young guy, but the talent came second in her mind, strangely enough," says Beverly Noga. "The main reason she adored Phillip was that he made her laugh a lot."

Noga had a home in Beverly Hills, and whenever Spector went out to the West Coast he would make a point of visiting her, often arriving straight from the airport, carrying the suitcase that served as his portable office. "Mother used to say, 'Phillip, if the light's on, you can ring the doorbell.' And he eventually didn't care if the light was on or not. He and my mother would sit there and just laugh and talk about everything—music, people, the industry. It was an insane relationship."

Lester Sill was less enamored of Noga; he thought her "obnoxious";

but money was money. In June 1961, with the first funding from Noga in place, Spector called the Crystals into Mira Sound Studios. It was the night of the girls' prom, and Barbara, Mary and Merna showed up at the studio still in their prom dresses. Spector had assembled just a small ensemble—drums, bass, two guitars and a small string section, led by Michael Spencer on piano.

Leroy Bates had originally modeled "There's No Other (Like My Baby)" on a traditional gospel song, "There's No Other Like My Jesus," and from the opening bars of its spoken introduction, Spector honored the song's antecedents; Spencer's storefront church piano chords, and the chiming truck-stop guitar riffs combined beautifully with a soaring string arrangement to give the song an almost sanctified feel. Watching him work in the dimmed light of the studio, coaching the Crystals in their gospel harmonies, then listening back over and over again to the playback, Spencer reflected that however buggy Phil Spector might have been in the outside world, here he was totally in command, and at peace with himself.

"I would say 'To Know Him Is to Love Him,' 'I Love How You Love Me' and 'There's No Other' were Phillip's three milestone records. They all had the same mood, every song—that yearning feeling.

"I can see his face listening back to 'There's No Other'; he would be repeating the sounds, mouthing the words and listening . . . you could see the emotion running through him. There was that total immersion in the sound, emotionally processing it, and then, when he came out of it, that intuitive feeling of whether he'd got it or not. And he had got it."

Confident that he had got the right song for his first Philles release, but awaiting the pieces of the label to fall into place, Spector continued to work as a freelance producer. For Hill and Range he produced two singles by Arlene Smith, the lead singer of the Chantels—one released on Big Top, the second on a ready-made label called Spectorius (which never produced another record)—both notable mainly for the amount of time and money that Spector lavished on the sessions. "In person Phil could be quiet and agreeable, but when it came to the studio he was very brash," remembers Freddie Bienstock of Hill and Range. "But he was a terrific record producer. He was a perfectionist. He would do so many takes until he thought it was right. And then he would listen and listen. He would take so long, which was very annoying to me because it all cost money, until he finally was satisfied and he considered it to be perfect. Others, including Ahmet and Jerry Wexler, were never such perfectionists."

Spector also produced a second single with Curtis Lee, "Under the Moon of Love," which strongly recalled the 'party in a cardboard box' productions of Frank Guida for Gary "U.S." Bonds. But his most notable recording of this period, and a giant step toward what he would later achieve with the Wall of Sound, was "Every Breath I Take" sung by Gene Pitney, a young singer-songwriter who would come to play a critical part in Spector's career—although not with this record. Pitney was signed with the publisher Aaron Schroeder, who occupied an office at 1650 Broadway. Another aspiring songwriter, Al Kooper, was in Schroeder's office when Pitney walked in to audition "wearing a salt-and-pepper jacket, heavily greased down DA [duck's ass] hairdo, and white bucks. Three dressing schools tied together; very strange. The creature was quickly ushered in, sat down at the piano and proceeded to mesmerize us for two uninterrupted hours with his incredible songs and bizarre voice. He was an original." Schroeder signed Pitney to a contract, according to Kooper, "so thorough it might've included bathroom privileges," and set up a new label, Musicor, as a vehicle for his young prodigy. But Pitney's first two singles for the label vanished without trace. Schroeder then walked down the corridor to the reliable mother lode of Don Kirshner, who provided him with a new song by Carole King and Gerry Goffin, "Every Breath I Take," adding the recommendation that Spector should produce the record.

Pitney would later recall that at their first meeting, at a Chinese restaurant off Broadway, Spector, by way of introduction, informed him that his sister was in a lunatic asylum, "and she's the sane one in the family." "Phil then had long hair, no loot and little success. He was a kind of an angry young man, undirected but not mixed up . . . a very small hunched-up man who didn't want to hurt anybody."

For some reason, everybody of Spector and Pitney's acquaintance—Schroeder, Kirshner, Goffin and King, Leiber and Stoller, and Mann and Weil—decided to turn up for the recording, crowding into the tiny booth at Bell Sound Studios. "It turned out to be the most ridiculous session ever," Pitney told the writer Alan Betrock. "Although Phil wanted to experiment, he didn't have enough control—not to the extent he had later—and there were too many people at the session, making comments. To add to it all, I had a wicked cold and was croaking—I sang the whole thing in falsetto." According to Pitney, at that time the average cost of recording one song, carefully calibrated to the sliding scale of union fees, was around $500.

"For the first three hours, the musicians got regular scale, the next thirty minutes they got time and a half, and after three and a half hours they got double scale. Most people would just do three-hour sessions, and if they weren't finished, would start fresh again next day. It was a lot cheaper that way. But not Phil, he kept on and on. In the end there were only two usable takes for fourteen thousand dollars. It was unbelievable."

But the result was Spector's most startlingly original production to date, a melodramatic concoction that pitched a doo-wop choir, swirling strings and a martial drumbeat behind Pitney's quivering, neurasthenic and adenoidal voice.

According to Pitney, Aaron Schroeder was so impressed that at the end of the session he tried to press a $50 bill into Spector's hand. But Spector, so confident of the record's prospects that he had done the job for nothing, refused. "That was Phil's way of saying 'You can't buy me.' I did my thing. I did you a favor, but that's it. Aaron wanted to grab Phil, put him under contract, but Phil was too smart for that. You could see what was comin' with him. Phil purely had designs on creating his own little empire."

As summer turned to autumn, Spector's relationship with Hill and Range came to an abrupt end, when the company finally woke up to the fact that he had enticed the Crystals away from them. It was Hill and Range that had discovered the group in the first place; Spector had spent weeks rehearsing the girls in their offices, and was himself under contract to make records for Big Top. Spector had spent eighteen months nurturing his relationship with Hill and Range, but had no hesitation in burning it to the ground in a second when the occasion demanded.

"That was one of the things that I loved about Phil," Doc Pomus reflected later. "He knew what the game was, and he played it. Every businessman is your best friend until they've sucked you dry of whatever they want. Phil just got to them before they got to him."

Spector, anyway, had no time to spend on regrets. With the Paris Sisters' "I Love How You Love Me" making its way up the charts, Lester Sill was keen for him to return to Los Angeles and record a new single for the group. Eager to cement his new alliance with the writers at Aldon Music, Spector took with him a new Goffin and King song, "He Knows I Love Him Too Much." A sultry ballad drenched in Hank Levine's strings, the song closely hewed to the formula Spector had established with the group, and rose to number 34 in March. But the trip to the coast was to have an unhappy outcome. Lester Sill had discovered that an assistant had inadvertently wiped the tracks that Spector had recorded a few months earlier for the Paris Sisters album. Spector, and the group themselves, were furious—not least when Sill informed them that the huge royalty payout they were expecting from "I Love How You Love Me" would not now be forthcoming. The expenses in making the album had consumed all the profits from the record. "There was actually a debit," Sill told Mark Ribowsky. "The cost of the album was horrendous. I showed 'em the figures. It must have been $10,000. That was the way Phil recorded. He could be a perfectionist."

Chagrined and suspecting that Sill had not been altogether honest in his accounting, Spector returned to New York. Still awaiting the release of the first Philles single, and eager to get some money in the bank, he now accepted yet another offer, this time as an A&R man for the Los Angeles label Liberty. In his constant to-ing and fro-ing between New York and Los Angeles, Spector had struck up a friendship with Liberty's West Coast A&R man, Tommy "Snuff" Garrett, and when the East Coast equivalent of Garrett's job became vacant, Garrett offered it to Spector.

The deal that Spector struck was remarkably generous. Not only was he given a year's salary of $25,000 in advance to scout and produce artists for the label, but at the same time he was given the leeway to continue producing acts for Philles. His first demand on moving into his new office at Liberty was for a bigger desk. Garrett obliged by installing a huge oak table from the conference room, where Spector sat for the next few weeks, doing nothing much at all. Paul Case was among Spector's first visitors. "He used to fool around with a hockey game, one of those games you can shoot," Case told Richard Williams, "and the only recollections we ever had of going up to the office were of him, the desk, and the game."

Spector's time at Liberty would produce only three singles—for Troy Shondell, Obrey Wilson, and an R&B singer from Los Angeles named Bobby Sheen, who had sung with a revamped version of the Robins and been sent to Spector by Lester Sill. Sheen was tall and handsome with a smooth tenor voice that reminded Spector of one of his favorite singers, Clyde McPhatter. In the early part of 1962, Spector recorded him with a song called "How Many Days." The record was not a success, but within a few months Bobby Sheen would come to play a more significant role in Spector's plans.

· · ·

"There's No Other (Like My Baby)" by the Crystals was finally released in October 1961, with the catalog number Philles 100. It took the record more than a month to enter the *Billboard* charts, where it finally peaked at number 20.

Even before its release, and while notionally committed to Liberty business, Spector had been in search of a follow-up, turning once again to "the Good Housekeeping seal," as Don Kirshner called himself. Barry Mann and Cynthia Weil's "Uptown" was an urban parable about race and class in New York, but which spoke to the frustrations of every young person struggling to be somebody in the stultifying anonymity of city life.

In his magisterial history of the Brill Building era, *Always Magic in the Air*, the writer Ken Emerson recounts that Weil had been inspired to write the song after seeing a young African-American pushing a cartload of clothes through New York's Garment District. Pondering on the scene, she was struck by the idea of a young man who is a nobody in his working life, but who regains his dignity and identity each night when he returns to his home uptown. Weil wrote a lyric from the viewpoint of a girl whose boyfriend may be "a little man" by day, "lost in an angry land," but who is reborn each night in the glow of her love and admiration. Weil would rightly describe it as "one of the first sociological songs."

Don Kirshner was no sociologist—his own taste was for more simple love songs; but he could recognize in "Uptown" "the struggle of the Jews and the blacks, and all the ethnic quality people. I knew it would be a hit." In keeping with the cinematic quality of Weil's lyrics, Barry Mann wrote a melody that he characterized as "very much like *West Side Story* or 'Soliloquy' [from Rodgers and Hammerstein's *Carousel*]."

While the inspiration for Weil's song had been a young Afro-American, Spector's production seemed to recast the protagonist as Puerto Rican, employing a Spanish guitar and flourishes of castanets that gave the song a Latin flavor distinctly reminiscent of Leiber and Stoller's productions with the Drifters. Emerson recounts that Spector also altered a few notes because the Crystals singer Barbara Alston was unable to reach them. When Mann and Weil heard the finished article they were unhappy with Alston's vocal, and prevailed on Spector to rerecord it with another singer, Little Eva Boyd, who subsidized her singing aspirations by working as Carole King's babysitter. But the sessions were a disaster. "He would make her do it over and over again," Weil recalled. "She was totally pissed off, and she would sit there at the mike, cursing, 'He's a bad man. This guy's a motherfucker. I hate him.' "

Eventually Spector abandoned the sessions altogether, and in March released the version he had already recorded with Alston. It would eventually rise to number 13 in the charts.

Spector then tried his hand with another Mann and Weil song that played on the theme of urban dreams and tribulation. Weil had originally conceived "On Broadway" as a story about a small-town girl dreaming of fame and success among the glittering lights of the Great White Way. Spector recorded the song with the Crystals, but was unhappy with the results and decided not to release it as a single. (It would subsequently appear on their first album.) Mann and Weil then took the song to Leiber and Stoller, who immediately recognized its potential for the Drifters, changing the gender of the song's protagonist, from a small-town girl to a musician, down on his luck but determined to make it—"'Cause I can play this here guitar / And I won't quit till I'm a star on Broadway."

On the way to the session, Leiber and Stoller ran into Spector on the street and invited him to join them, and it is Spector's piercing guitar solo that brings the song to its climax, convincing you that for the young player stardom is indeed just a beat away.

It was only some months later that Leiber and Stoller began to hear how Spector had apparently not only played on the record, but had actually produced it. Recalling the incident some forty-five years later, Leiber would still struggle to keep a tone of neutrality in his voice. "It just confirmed the feeling we'd had all along that Phil was a little . . . grandiose."

Spector's relationship with Annette Merar had been growing more serious. In June 1961 Annette graduated from Fairfax High, and the following September she enrolled at the University of California in Berkeley, studying sociology, anthropology, and English. Spector would call her every night from New York, regaling her for hours on end with jokes, stories of his achievements and news of how "There's No Other (Like My Baby)" was rising up the charts. In January 1962, Annette cut short her studies at Berkeley and returned to Los Angeles and enrolled at UCLA in Brentwood. Spector was in town to see Lester Sill, and his relationship with Annette picked up where it had left off a few months earlier. Spector was staying at the Player's Motel, but he would frequently call on Annette at her parents' home. "Duke of Earl" by Gene Chandler was riding high in the charts, a song characterized by an irresistible doo-wop chorus—"Duke, duke, duke, Duke of Earl, duke, duke."

"Phil would sit there playing this on the piano," Annette remembers, "mimicking the song, and he would make it so funny. He would just laugh and laugh."

Annette's dreams of continuing with her studies and becoming a writer began to falter in the face of Spector's ardor, and after a few weeks she made the decision to drop out of college. Spector had been pressing her to come and live with him in New York. "He was there and I was in L.A. and we just wanted to be together." In April she left home and moved to New York, joining Spector in his tiny apartment—a bedroom, a living room, a small kitchen and a bathroom. While there was no financial need for her to work, she took an office job typing and filing.

Spector lost no time in introducing her to the social whirl in New York, dining out in expensive restaurants, kibitzing in nightclubs. "I was in the center of the universe," Annette remembers. "That's how I felt when I was around Phil." On a trip to Coney Island with his friend the arranger Arnold Goland, an amused Spector watched Annette lose money in a boardwalk shell game, before cajoling the con artist into giving the money back.

"People adored Phil," she remembers. "The Brill Building people, Donny Kirshner, Doc Pomus. He was always surrounded by people. They all thought he was a genius."

Throughout the time that they had spent sharing an apartment, Michael Spencer had noticed that Spector would treat the girls he sometimes brought back to the apartment "like trophies." Despite the way that Spector had treated her, Beverly Ross would continue to see him from time to time. "She was a compassionate girl, and very supportive of Phil," Spencer remembers. "But he'd dominated her completely. He *liked* Beverly, but he wasn't nice to her. There was always that contradiction in Phil."

But Spector seemed to be deeply smitten with Annette. While only nineteen, she had a maturity, an intelligence and an independence of mind beyond her years. She knew about music, and Spector valued her opinion—her ears. She would often accompany him to recording sessions, and copy and print his lead sheets. Annette had quickly grown accustomed to the fact that Spector now habitually kept "musicians' hours"—exacerbated by his difficulty in sleeping—and would seldom go to bed until the early hours of the morning. "I was up at his Liberty office real late one night," she remembers, "and I went to sleep on the couch. I remember falling asleep watching him screaming his head off at somebody. I thought: why does he always have to scream like that."

At home they would talk endlessly about music, or watch TV, a classic movie, perhaps, where Spector would perform his old trick of turning down the volume and improvising his own commentary, or making jokes about the commercials, keeping Annette in stitches.

"There was an advertisement for Ivory Soap, and the slogan was '99 and 44/100ths pure.' And Phil would say, 'Whatever happened to the other 56/100ths?' He was so smart and original in his thinking, but he wasn't an intellectual. I respected his creative genius, but I never particularly respected his intellect. He'd skip over things, like he did with the frets when he was playing the guitar. He never heard anything—he never listened."

Spector was proud of his Jewish ancestry, and would observe Jewish holidays, but he had no religious belief, and as he grew older he would become an avowed atheist. Annette thought his Judaism was "political. He was very much a Zionist type." He also showed a deep fascination with Hitler and read *Mein Kampf* to try to understand the roots of Hitler's fanaticism. "Phil's politics were very liberal. But he thought Hitler was an evil genius. I remember, we argued about the difference between a demagogue and a dictator, because he said there's no difference. And I drew a line. I argued that a dictator has formal power; a demagogue has the following, but not the formal power. This argument went on forever, and we could never agree. And I still think I'm right."

Helen Noga's interest in Philles had been short-lived. The seed money she had provided for the first Crystals sessions had been useful, but between Spector and Sill, and Harry Finfer and Harold Lipsius at Universal, there was no room in Philles for another partner. Spector would later maintain that Noga had been paid off, but her daughter Beverly disputes this.

"Mother laughed about that for years. She used to say, 'If a check was mailed I wonder who got it?' She never got paid for leaving the situation. She didn't ask for it. She didn't expect it. She and Phil were so close, and the friendship just kept on going. She was a tremendous supporter of his and was always there to give him advice."

For Spector the fact that he needed partners at all in what he was quickly coming to think of as his company was beginning to rankle. He had not been fully persuaded by Lester Sill's excuses about the vanishing royalties from the Paris Sisters recordings. And while Spector had come to regard himself as the artistic force in Philles, in Los Angeles Sill had been supervising his own sessions for the label. Of the first five Philles releases, only "There's No Other (Like My Baby)" (Philles 100) and "Uptown" (Philles 102) were Spector productions. The remainder had been organized by Sill. Philles 101 was a lightweight pop record, "Here I Stand," by Joel Scott; Philles 103, a piano instrumental, "Malaguena," by another of Sill's protégés, a writer and producer named Al Hazan (who had been the man behind B. Bumble and the Stingers' "Nut Rocker"), released under the name Ali Hassan; and Philles 104, a novelty song, "Lieutenant Colonel Bogey's Parade," by the sax player Steve Douglas. It wasn't that Spector particularly disliked the records—Douglas in particular was a good friend and would come to play an important role in Spector's music in the years to come. It was just that they weren't his. By the early months of 1962, Sill told Mark Ribowsky he could already begin to "smell things falling out a little bit with Phil."

Nor would Spector's next recording with the Crystals help matters. Written by Gerry Goffin and Carole King, as the title suggests, "He Hit Me (and It Felt Like a Kiss)" was a particularly perverse choice as a follow-up to the Crystals' first two hits.

Gerry Goffin would later explain that the song had been inspired by a story told to them by their babysitter, Eva Boyd, after she had turned up for work bearing the scars of a beating by her jealous boyfriend. "But she sort of smiled before she went to her room," Goffin recalled, "and she said, 'He really loves me.'" But the idea of love as a sadomasochistic battle zone—bathing the bruises in tears of reconciliation and regret—appeared to be a recurring theme in the pair's songs at the time. Spector also recorded their song "Please Hurt Me" ("If you gotta hurt somebody, please hurt me") for inclusion on the Crystals' album (Eva Boyd would also record the song as Little Eva), and Goffin and King also wrote "Chains" ("my baby's got me locked up in chains . . .") for the Cookies.

Don Kirshner had his own reservations about "He Hit Me." What he loved about Goffin and King's songwriting was that they wrote "real warm, boy-girl things, songs that got under your skin." "He Hit Me"— a song more likely to make your skin crawl—was, he acknowledged, "different." But Kirshner was prepared to indulge his young protégés.

"Gerry Goffin was becoming an important writer, and I didn't want to stamp on his creativity. Most of my songs had a feeling of romanticism—boy/girl. This was a little more controversial. But I had to give them freedom of expression. It wasn't as much entertainment as it was philosophizing."

" 'He Hit Me' was absolutely, positively the one record that none of us liked," Barbara Alston, the Crystals' lead singer, recalled. "All I really wanted to know was 'Why?' Why would five young girls sing something extraordinary like 'He Hit Me (and It Felt Like a Kiss)'? Yuk, was what I felt."

But Spector had no such qualms, and attacked the song with a manic relish. With its funereal beat, overheated production and melodramatic string arrangement, "He Hit Me" sounds almost comically kitsch by today's standards, if one didn't suspect that Spector was approaching it in deadly earnest.

Lester Sill was the first person to tell Spector that he hated it. And he wasn't alone. The record created a minor outcry, disc jockeys refused to play it, and in June 1962, Philles was obliged to pull it from the shelves.

Preoccupied with the Crystals, Spector had all but forgotten about his arrangement with Liberty—his sole telephone call to Snuff Garrett in Los Angeles in the early months of 1962 had been to complain that the plants in his office had not been watered. But while he might have produced nothing of note, his stay at the label was to provide him with a major opportunity.

On a shopping expedition at 1650 Broadway, Spector visited Aaron Schroeder, who played him a new song called "He's a Rebel," written by his protégé Gene Pitney. The song played on a familiar theme that had inspired the film *Rebel Without a Cause* and any number of other pop songs about the misunderstood teenager. By a pleasing coincidence, Pitney had been inspired to write it after hearing the Crystals' "Uptown."

" 'Uptown' was the first song where I ever heard anyone use funky strings like that," Pitney recalled, "and especially low strings, violas and cellos down that low. I fell in love with it and it hit me. I said, 'I'm gonna write their next single, another song they could do just like that.' "

Listening to the song in Aaron Schroeder's office, Spector knew that he had found a hit. He also knew he had to move fast. Schroeder told him that another producer had designs on the song—Spector's friend Snuff Garrett. Pausing only to tender his resignation at Liberty, Spector took the first plane out to Los Angeles.

In the space of eighteen months, he had burned a trail through the New York music scene, cementing alliances that would stand him in stead for the rest of his career, and destroying others without a moment's thought. He had co-written one rock and roll classic, "Spanish Harlem," and produced a handful more; risen from being a nobody to one of the hottest record producers in the business. Now Phil Spector was about to embark on the most spectacular phase of his career.

7

Building the Wall of Sound

Spector had good reasons for choosing to record "He's a Rebel" in Los Angeles rather than New York. For one thing, union rates were cheaper on the West Coast, but he was also growing increasingly weary of the stranglehold which the New York union, the American Federation of Musicians Local 82, held on his sessions. Although the technique was becoming commonplace, union rules theoretically forbade overdubbing. The union was also increasingly vigilant in policing a closed shop: on one occasion, when Annette had been recruited to rattle a tambourine during a Crystals session, Spector had been anonymously reported for using non-union labor. "He would tell me the union was driving him out of town," Michael Spencer remembers.

More importantly, Spector preferred the musicians in Los Angeles. The New York session players were hardened professionals, who tended to view him with a mixture of bemusement, grudging respect or barely concealed contempt, who would groan audibly at the amount of time he spent on preparing the studio, and the protracted run-throughs before recording began. The musicians in Los Angeles were cooler, more relaxed and more attuned to Spector's iconoclastic approach; nobody thought Spector was crazy, or if they did they certainly didn't say it to his face.

And then there was Gold Star. Spector had worked at three or four studios in New York, but none had proved as congenial as the place where he had made his first records, and none could match the singular acoustics and atmosphere of Studio A. "To Know Him Is to Love Him" and "I Love How You Love Me"—for very different reasons, the records closest to Spector's heart and, not coincidentally perhaps, his biggest hits to date—had both been made at Gold Star. He had come to regard Stan Ross, the studio's co-owner, who had engineered every one of his sessions there, as almost a talismanic presence.

Touching down in Los Angeles, Spector wasted no time in making preparations to record "He's a Rebel." He contacted his old friend, the sax player Steve Douglas, and asked him to contract the best musicians he could find. To arrange the session, Lester Sill suggested Jack Nitzsche, who had once worked for Sill and was now working as an arranger for his former partner Lee Hazlewood.

All Spector needed now was a group to sing the song.

Spector, quite naturally, had earmarked "He's a Rebel" for the Crystals, but the group would never make the session—whether because they refused to fly to Los Angeles or because they were occupied on the road is unclear. Spector didn't miss a beat. It would be a relatively easy matter to find singers in Los Angeles to replace them, he reasoned. All he really needed from the Crystals was their name, and Philles owned that.

It was Jack Nitzsche who suggested that he should audition a group of local session singers called the Blossoms, who were led by a twenty-three-year-old singer named Darlene Wright. The daughter of a Pentecostal minister, Wright had grown up in Texas and Los Angeles, singing in church choirs before joining with four friends—Gloria Jones, Fanita Barrett and sisters Annette and Nanette Williams—to make the Blossoms. The group made a series of singles for local labels, but they became better known as backing singers. Before the Blossoms, much of the session work in L.A. was covered by the Johnny Mann Singers, five white men and three white women, who could sight-read music and be relied upon to provide performances of a saccharine banality. The Blossoms' flawless harmonies, which could pass as either black or white, allowed them to work across a bewildering variety of styles, singing behind artists as diverse as Sam Cooke, Doris Day, Ray Charles, Jan and Dean, and Bobby Darin. They would provide the "sha-dums" on Shelley Fabares's innocuous piece of candy floss "Johnny Angel," and the "shoop shoops" on Betty Everett's "Shoop Shoop Song (It's in His Kiss)." Nitzsche had often worked with the group, and his wife Gracia sometimes sang with them.

When Wright first met Phil Spector, she would later recount in her autobiography, she took note of his "pasty, Lord Fauntleroy face and waiflike frame," and his overpowering aftershave, which "smelled like musk. As dark as it was inside Gold Star, he wore his sunglasses. And when he stood up, in four-inch heels, I was still taller than he was." Spector, she thought, looked like "a little kid in a sandbox."

Seated at a piano, Spector led her through "He's a Rebel." The moment he heard her voice he was sold. But Wright was less convinced. In her autobiography she would recall that compared to the material she'd been recording with Ray Charles and Bobby Darin, "He's a Rebel" sounded "like a trifle—just another tribute to a teen dream, this one from the wrong side of the tracks, or the police blotter." Wright might have been only twenty-three herself, but she had a husband, a child and a mortgage to pay—the transition between her teens and adulthood had "lasted about five minutes." But she could do swooning teenager, if that's what Spector wanted. It wasn't. What he wanted, he told her, was the "low, growling side" of her voice, "the righteous indignation and in-your-face testimony that I usually saved for church."

Spector offered Wright a flat fee of $3,000 to sing lead on the song. Fanita Barrett and Gloria Jones were also booked on the session, for a standard session rate. They were joined by Bobby Sheen, the singer whom Spector had recorded for Liberty the year before.

But there was another problem. Booking Gold Star, Spector had naturally assumed that his old friend Stan Ross would be available to engineer the sessions. But Ross had decided to take a vacation in Hawaii. Ross proposed his cousin, Larry Levine, as a replacement. Spector was furious—he was about to cut the record of a lifetime, and the man he trusted most at the boards had decided to absent himself— but he had no intention of waiting for Ross to return.

At thirty-three, Levine was ten years older than Spector. Tall and quietly spoken, with an easygoing, unflappable manner, he had served in the U.S. Army in Korea as a radio operator and later worked in the aviation industry. When Ross and Dave Gold opened Gold Star in 1950, Levine had taken to dropping by the studio in the evenings, "basically because the people in the music business were more entertaining than the run of the mill," and ended up working there, initially assisting Ross and then engineering sessions on his own, including Eddie Cochran's "Summertime Blues."

Levine had seen Spector around the studio working on the Paris Sisters' sessions, and he was no more enthralled about the prospect of working with Spector than Spector was about working with him. "I thought he was a brat, spoiled or whatever," Levine remembers. "There was something abrasive there. It wasn't anything he said; it was just an aura that he carried with him, and nothing that he can do anything about. But I think that happened with a lot of people with Phil."

Of the musicians that Steve Douglas brought into the studio, only the guitarist Howard Roberts and bass player Ray Pohlman had worked with Spector before. Spector had requested a second bass player, Jimmy Bond. The group was filled out with a second guitarist, Tommy Tedesco; a pianist, Al DeLory; the drummer Hal Blaine, a seasoned session musician who had already played on hits by Connie Francis and Elvis Presley; and two sax players—Douglas, and Spector's old friend Nino Tempo. Used to working with the standard drum/bass/guitar rock and roll combo, Larry Levine was puzzled by the number of musicians trooping into the studio. "I thought, what is this all about?" But whatever reservations he might have had, Levine was diplomatic enough to keep them to himself, patiently following instructions as Spector went through his customarily laborious procedure of organizing mikes and rehearsing the musicians.

Inspired by Spector's use of strings on "Uptown," Gene Pitney had written "He's a Rebel" with the idea that it too should use a string arrangement; but Spector decided to forgo any other adornment, instead cutting it as a tough, swaggering rock and roll song. Al DeLory cast an eye over the musical charts, which Jack Nitzsche had written, and with his right hand began to improvise a naggingly insistent five-note gospel figure that was to become the song's introduction and central motif. Steve Douglas added a booting sax solo in the middle section. Recording the vocal, Darlene Wright did exactly as Spector had requested, tearing into the song with a gospel fervor. As the song went into the fade, Wright got so carried away testifying—"No, no, no"— that she lost the rhythm and sang off beat. "I'll sing it again," she told Spector, but he said that wasn't necessary. "I like the mistake." Wright was aghast. What kind of man, she thought, lets mistakes into his records?

It was only when Spector was mastering the recording that he discovered that Snuff Garrett had recorded his own version of "He's a Rebel" with a virginal young singer named Vikki Carr. It would have been hard to imagine a less appropriate marriage of singer and song. Carr's release, in the last week of August 1962, was heralded by a full-page ad in *Billboard* trumpeting "The Original!! The Hit!!" Three weeks later, Spector's version stood at number 66 on the charts, while Carr's lodged at number 120.

In the first week of November, "He's a Rebel" reached number 1, supplanting the novelty hit "Monster Mash" by Bobby "Boris" Pickett and the Crypt-Kickers (ironically, another song on which the Blossoms sang backing vocals). The first that the Crystals knew of "their" new recording was when they heard "He's a Rebel" on the radio as they were traveling through Ohio on a tour. It was only by chance that they happened to be sharing a bill with Gene Pitney, who was able to coach them in the song so they could perform it onstage. Cursing Spector silently under their collective breath, the Crystals stepped out each night to bask in the applause for a record they'd had absolutely nothing to do with.

At the end of August 1962, Spector returned to Gold Star. The song that he brought with him was, superficially at least, a bizarre choice. A favorite from his childhood, "Zip-a-Dee Doo-Dah" was from the 1946 Walt Disney film *Song of the South*, a slice of happy-go-lucky, not to say mindless, optimism, written by two Tin Pan Alley songwriters, Allie Wrubel and Ray Gilbert.

In search of an even fatter sound, Spector assembled a group consisting of three guitarists (two acoustic, and Billy Strange playing a fuzz-tone electric), three bass players, two sax players, a drummer and a percussionist. Al DeLory was again on piano, but he was now joined by Spector's old friend Nino Tempo—on the same instrument—DeLory playing the upper register, Tempo the lower. A third pianist, Leon Russell, also played on the song. It was a weekend session, and Stan Ross was again unavailable, so Larry Levine was back at the controls. To perform the song, Spector had once again called on Darlene Wright, Fanita Barrett and Bobby Sheen.

Recording the instrumental track, Spector and Levine, who had no idea of the title of the song, worked for three hours moving the mikes around the studio and setting the sound levels. Jack Nitzsche's arrangement was so clotted that Spector decided there wasn't even room in the mix for a full drum kit; he instructed Hal Blaine to play only his bass drum. Spector kept asking Levine to turn up the faders on the instruments for more volume. Levine did as he was instructed until the meters on his dials were pinging into the red zone. Realizing that if he tried to record at that level, the sound would distort, Levine turned off the faders and brought the meters back to zero.

"Phil looked at me for a moment like I was crazy, and then he started screaming at me: 'I just about had it! I had it! You can't do that!' I said, 'I had no choice, I couldn't record it.' "

Levine started the process all over again, bringing up the microphones one at a time, balancing the sound of each instrument against the other. He had reached the point where all the microphones were turned up except for the lead guitarist's, Billy Strange, when Spector stopped him again. "That's it! That's the sound!" Leaking through the other microphones into the control-room speakers, Strange's guitar sounded like an angry wasp.

"But I don't have Billy's mike on yet," Levine protested.

"Tape it!" said Spector.

The track was done in one take. At its conclusion, Levine turned to Spector and asked, "What's the title of this song again?"

"Phil said, ' "Zip-a-Dee Doo-Dah," ' " Levine remembers. "And I said, 'Yeah, sure—that's a big put-on. What's it really called?' And he said, 'No, really, it's "Zip-a-Dee Doo-Dah." ' And when I realized that's what I was hearing, I literally fell out of the chair. Because this was just the greatest thing."

Spector had taken the jaunty refrain and turned it completely on its head. The rhythm section clunked and rolled like a slow train rumbling through a tunnel, carrying a deranged, wailing gospel choir as freight. It was dark, incantatory and disturbingly sexual; Larry Levine says he had never heard a record like it.

"Later on Phil told me that when he took the demo back to New York, he played it for a publisher, and after four bars—that clunk, clunk, clunk that starts the song—the publisher walked over, lifted up the needle and said, 'I'll give you ten thousand dollars up front now, without even hearing what the rest of it sounds like.'

"People would come into Gold Star and I'd say, 'I'm going to play a tape for you, and if you tell me there's a chance this is not a Top 10 record I'll eat the tape right in front of you.' And they'd look at me like I was crazy. But nobody ever suggested I eat the tape. I was playing that record for everybody. When Phil came back to town he said, 'Jesus, I've got to put this record out now; everybody in Hollywood's heard it.' But I couldn't resist it."

Casting around for a name for his ad-hoc group, Spector settled on a pun on the teenage sartorial craze of the time. Credited to Bob B. Soxx and the Blue Jeans, "Zip-a-Dee Doo-Dah" entered the charts in December 1962. Larry Levine had no need to eat the tape—the song peaked at number 8—and he would work on virtually every Phil Spector session for the next four years.

Even as the Philles label was gathering momentum, Spector's relations with Lester Sill were going from bad to worse. Spector was still disgruntled at his partner for wasting money on inferior recordings that he regarded as a blemish on the Philles label. And the debacle over the lost Paris Sisters album continued to rankle. Furthermore Spector now began to suspect that Sill was holding out on him on Philles royalties. Sill could hardly fail to be aware that he was being frozen out when Spector stopped returning his phone calls and became unusually elusive.

In late summer of 1962, Spector approached Lipsius and Finfer, offering to buy out their one-third share in Philles. Lipsius agreed, and Finfer—a minority shareholder to Lipsius in the one-third Philles interest—had little choice but to go along with it. Spector now controlled two-thirds of Philles to Sill's one-third. With Finfer out of the way, Lipsius, who was an attorney, now began to represent Spector, pressuring Sill to sell his share. Visiting Sill one day at his office, Al Hazan found him sitting on the floor, desperately riffling through the papers strewn all around him. "He was saying, 'Phil's told me he's going to ruin me.' He was more concerned about that than sad that the partnership had broken up. Lester was a very hard-nosed business guy. He wasn't the type of guy to get sad about things."

At length, Sill relented, demanding a figure based on a year's worth of Philles's recordings royalties. He eventually settled for far less—around $60,000. Sill told friends that he knew the price was a steal, but he was just happy to be free of the heartache.

In September 1962, as "He's a Rebel" was making its way up the *Billboard* charts, Spector circulated a letter to his distributors advising them that he had acquired "complete and absolute control of Philles Records, Inc." More than just his partner, Sill had been Spector's mentor, the man who had given him back his career when it seemed to be all but over, but Spector showed no hesitation, or sentiment, in cutting him off. "Lester wasn't cheating on Phil," Annette Merar says. "Although there might have been a little bit of suspicion on Phil's part because Lester was a good businessman, too. I just think Phil didn't need Lester anymore, and his personal value system allowed him to think, I can do this alone, so fuck Lester Sill. That's what it amounts to. Phil didn't want to share it anymore, and Lester had outlived his usefulness."

Michael Spencer saw it another way. "Lester was a father figure, and Phil always turned on the father."

In the autumn of 1962, Phil and Annette moved out of their small apartment and into a penthouse on Sixty-second Street, close to the East River. Downstairs Spector took a suite of offices for Philles. Standing on the huge balcony of the penthouse apartment and looking down over the Fifty-ninth Street Bridge to the lights of Queens shimmering on the far side of the river, it seemed to Phil Spector as if he had arrived on top of the world.

But there was to be one final parting shot at his old partner. According to one story, as part of his settlement with Sill and Finfer, Spector was required to give them the royalties from the next Philles single. Begrudging the thought of sharing anything more with his former partners, Spector devised a plan that would fulfill his obligations while costing him next to nothing. At the end of January 1963, he called the Crystals and three musicians—Michael Spencer on piano, bass player Leonard Gaskin and drummer Herbert Lovelle—into Mirar Sound Studios and recorded a mindless five-minute bump-and-grind dance song he had written himself called "(Let's Dance) The Screw." Spencer remembers the session as being "as boring as beans." A handful of copies of the record were pressed with the catalogue number Philles 111, and copies sent to both Sill and Finfer. Whether the record was actually made to fulfill contractual obligations is debatable. Under those terms, it would have needed to be properly pressed and distributed—which it wasn't; and the same catalogue number was subsequently used for the next Philles production, "He's Sure the Boy I Love." But whatever the reasons behind the record, the implied meaning of the title—screw you—was not lost on Lester Sill.

"Lester didn't speak too kindly of Phil after that," says Russ Titelman. "He felt he'd been betrayed. But then everybody Phil touched felt that in the end."

Yet despite whatever bitterness he might have felt, Sill behaved remarkably charitably toward his estranged partner, urging his stepson Chuck Kaye, who had helped him handle affairs in the Los Angeles office, to continue working for Philles. Sill himself continued to work in the music business, first for Screen Gems and then Jobete Music, right up until his death in 1995. As the years passed, he would often talk fondly of Spector to friends and associates. "Lester didn't harbor a grudge against Phil," remembers one acquaintance of both men. "If anything it was the other way round. I could never figure out why." Spector, for his part, seemed seldom to miss an opportunity to disparage Sill in public, sometimes joking that his old partner was "the less" in Philles; yet privately he seemed to retain a deep affection for him. The pair would often talk on the phone, gossiping about the music business and hashing over the past. But when I interviewed Spector in December 2002 he was curt about his former partner.

"Lester was like Mr. Nice Guy. He turned out to be a little deceitful, but he was a nice guy who knew everybody in the business. He introduced me to people, gave me references. I would say, 'Introduce me to this person, get me to that person,' and he did that."

And that was all he said.

Riding on the success of "Zip-a-Dee Doo-Dah," Darlene Wright, Fanita Barrett and Bobby Sheen had been touring the eastern states as Bob B. Soxx and the Blue Jeans, as part of a package tour with Marvin Gaye, the Orlons and Little Eva. It was a miserable experience. The weather back east was atrocious, and the group was earning only $900 a week between the three of them. Now at the end of 1962, Spector called them back into Gold Star, eager to capitalize on their success both as "The Crystals" and Bob B. Soxx and the Blue Jeans.

But first he had to placate Darlene Wright.

Chafing at the lack of recognition she had received for her performance on "He's a Rebel"—a number 1 record, and no one ever knew her name!—and the fact that she had received only a flat fee—albeit one that was three times the standard union rate—Wright confronted Spector. If he wanted her to record again it would be under her own name, and with a proper contract, or she wouldn't do it at all. Spector assured her he would get the deal done, but it was only when she threatened to quit altogether that he finally got his lawyers to draw up artist contracts for both Wright and Fanita Barrett.

With Wright once again taking the lead, Spector recorded the group singing the thundering rock and roll song "He's Sure the Boy I Love," written by Barry Mann and Cynthia Weil. But when the song was released, it was once again under the name of the Crystals. The first Wright knew of it was when she heard the song on the radio. Furious, she confronted Spector in the studio, and in the heat of the moment he made a slighting remark about "you people." Spector had an almost religious devotion to black people, and it was unlikely he meant the remark as a racial slight. But Wright took it that way, and stormed out of the studio.

"It was like Phil was God, and we were all his little angels," Gloria Jones remembers wryly. " 'You just stand there and sing the song and I'll decide whose it's going to be.' Then we'd hear on the radio, that's Bob B. Soxx and the Blue Jeans or that's the Crystals. We never knew when we were recording whose song it was going to be."

"The singers were nothing to Phil," Darlene Wright would note many years later. "He used to say it was all about 'his music.' So I'd say, 'If it's all about your music, why aren't you making instrumentals?' "

In search of fresh material, Spector meanwhile had turned to another songwriting team, Ellie Greenwich and Tony Powers. Born in Brooklyn in 1940, Greenwich had worked briefly as a high school teacher and failed as a singer before turning to songwriting. A brief collaboration with Doc Pomus led her to Leiber and Stoller's publishing company, Trio Music, where she forged a partnership with Powers. Her first meeting with Spector in the Trio offices in August 1962 was not auspicious. Greenwich was sitting at a piano playing a song called "It Was Me Yesterday" when Spector walked in. "Phil was walking around the room, fixing his clothes, looking in the mirror and adjusting his hair—all the time making noises while I was playing my song," Greenwich recalled. "Finally I said, 'Either you want to hear my songs or you don't.' Phil exploded and stormed out of the room, and everyone in the office felt that Spector was gone for good." A short while later, however, Spector heard a demo of another Greenwich-Powers song called "(Today I Met) The Boy I'm Gonna Marry" and arranged another meeting with the writers at his office on Sixty-second Street. The pair turned up at 2:00 p.m. as arranged. Spector arrived at 6:00.

"When he came I was really mad. 'Hey, Phil, if you make an appointment and can't keep it, you should let us know. You were very rude!' And I think he just liked the idea that I stood up to him, because we hit it off right away."

Spector took two Greenwich and Powers songs back to Los Angeles to record (adding a few embellishments, and his name to the writers' credits, in the process). The first was a vamped-up variation on the doo-wop idiom, called "Why Do Lovers Break Each Other's Heart?" which was ascribed to Bob B. Soxx and the Blue Jeans, and reached number 38 in the charts in March 1963.

The second was "(Today I Met) The Boy I'm Gonna Marry"—a delightfully melodic celebration of what was held—in the early '60s, at least—to be every young girl's dream. Once again, Darlene Wright took the lead, cushioned in an appropriately opulent and romantic arrangement with a celestial choir and percussion that pealed like church bells. This time, Spector promised her, the record would be released under her name—or at least a name that he had decided to give her. Darlene Wright, he had decided, did not have the necessary sass and distinction.

Instead, Spector decreed, she would be named Darlene Love, after one of his favorite gospel singers, Dorothy Love Coates. Wright simply shrugged and took the change in her stride. "I figured Phil would just decide to call me something else again two or three records down the road." But it was Darlene Love she would remain for the rest of her career.

By the end of 1962, Phil Spector had begun to gather around him a team of some twenty-five musicians who would form the bedrock of what would come to be known as the Wall of Sound. Not all would play on every Spector record, but the majority would play on most of them. They included the guitarists Billy Strange, Glen Campbell, Irv Rubin, Bill Pitman, Dennis Budimir, Al Casey, Tommy Tedesco and Spector's idol and mentor, Barney Kessel. On drums were Earl Palmer, Richie Frost and the legendary Hal Blaine, who would go on to become probably the most celebrated rock drummer in history, playing on more than 120 Top 10 hits between 1961 and 1971 alone. On keyboards were Don Randi, Leon Russell, Larry Knechtel, Mike Rubini and Al DeLory. Steve Douglas, Jay Migliori, Ollie Mitchell, Dave Wells, Lou Blackburn, Nino Tempo and Roy Caton played horns. On bass were Jimmy Bond, Ray Pohlman, Carol Kaye and Wallick Dean. Anyone and everyone played percussion, including Frank Kapp, Julius Wechter, Gene Estes, Victor Feldman and Sonny Bono.

These musicians, who became the core group for countless Los Angeles sessions throughout the '60s, would later become famous as "The Wrecking Crew," a name given to them by Hal Blaine, although they more usually referred to themselves as "the clique." They were far from being rock and roll punks. Most were older than Spector; seasoned professionals who'd cut their teeth on the road with jazz combos, or working sessions with MOR singers at Capitol and Columbia. They wore sports jackets and ties, kept up their mortgage repayments, had drinks cabinets at home and relaxed by going bowling. Along with Jack Nitzsche, several of them played on a bowling team called Spins and Needles—a play on a song that Nitzsche and Sonny Bono had written for Jackie DeShannon, "Needles and Pins."

Gold Star was far from being the most sophisticated studio in Los Angeles—most regarded it as a dump. But for Spector it provided an environment where he was totally at ease, totally in command. He became the studio's most ubiquitous client and would wrangle with Stan Ross to have it available whenever he required.

"I remember Phil doing an interview one time, where he para-phrased the great Swedish film director Bergman," Larry Levine says. "Bergman had been asked why he wouldn't direct movies in America, where the facilities were so much better. And he said, well, he knew there were great facilities and great technicians, but there's a time, maybe two or three minutes during filming where you can be totally creative, and he needed to totally trust the people he was working with so he could be free to create within that period. And Phil said that was the way he felt about me and the people he worked with at Gold Star. He could be cre-ative because he trusted us."

In his earlier recording sessions in New York and Los Angeles, Spec-tor had usually worked with the standard-size group—bass, drums, piano, a couple of guitarists, sometimes three. He had begun to use strings. But the sound he achieved was never quite as big as the sound he was hearing in his imagination. Listening to a symphony orchestra play "The Ride of the Valkyries" or the *1812 Overture* it was as if you could hear great armies on the march. Why couldn't a rock and roll record sound as big, as powerful, as thrilling as that?

In 1962 this would have been a wildly fanciful ambition. Most people—even most people who made it—regarded pop music as instantly disposable ephemera. Records were shaped and made in the heat of the moment, a flash of sheet lightning, forged from passion, excitement or rank opportunism, which might or might not illuminate the charts, and would be forgotten as quickly as they were conceived. Nobody consid-ered pop music an art form. But Spector approached each record as if he were creating a masterpiece, lavishing an unprecedented amount of time, care and attention on the song, the preparation and the recording.

Theoretically, there were two ways to achieve the sound that Spector wanted. One was through overdubs—an option that the available tech-nology of the day hardly allowed. The other was through using multi-ples of instruments in unison. Why stop at one or two guitars when you could have three, or even four? Why one piano when you could have two or three? Instead of a trio or quartet of backing singers, why not a choir? Instead of a rock and roll band, why not a rock and roll orchestra?

"I was looking for a sound that could produce fifteen hit records and more," Spector once explained. "I imagined a sound so strong that if the material was not the greatest, the sound would carry the record. It was a case of augmenting, augmenting. It all fitted like a jigsaw." Thus were laid the foundations for what would become the Wall of Sound.

This was an evolutionary process rather than an overnight decision. But in the six or so months that elapsed between "He's a Rebel" and

"(Today I Met) The Boy I'm Gonna Marry" you can hear how the Wall of Sound was beginning to take shape, and to grow.

Spector preferred to work at night, usually beginning his sessions around eight p.m. The musicians he used were frequently in demand elsewhere, and he liked to have them available at the end of the day, so he could run into overtime if he felt like it. It was in these long sessions, often stretching into the early hours of the morning, the studio crowded to bursting point with musicians, littered with coffee cups, soda cans and cigarette butts, that the Wall of Sound was incubated and born.

The standard approach to producing was to begin with the nucleus of the rhythm section—drum and bass—establishing a firm rhythmic foundation around which the other instruments would be built. But for Spector the first building block was always the guitars—three, four or sometimes more, playing the same eighth chords over and over again to create an insistent wash of sound. In the long warmup sessions before recording actually began, as Larry Levine positioned microphones and checked recording levels, Spector would walk along the ranks of guitarists, whispering into their ears "Keep it dumb. Keep it dumb."

Virtuosi musicians playing eighths interminably! It was like calling in Picasso to paint a door! But Spector didn't want displays of virtuosity, nor was he interested in the individual sound of the instrument, only its integral value to the sound as a whole.

Nino Tempo, whose first instrument was sax and who readily admitted that he was a distinctly average guitarist, sometimes found himself enlisted to join the "chorus" of guitarists four or five strong. "I could be sitting next to Barney Kessel and you couldn't tell which one of us was Barney Kessel and which one of us was the bad guitar player. But this was what Phil did. And he did that because, of course, he wanted the prestige of Barney, but he also knew that if he needed someone to stand up and do something great, then Barney would do it. So he always got the best guys because he respected the musicians." Some couldn't take it. Howard Roberts, Spector's old guitar teacher, played on "He's a Rebel" and never came back, complaining that the regime made his fingers bleed and the music was too stupid for words.

"Start with the guitars, then blend everything into the guitars; that was the basis of the whole rhythm section, the guitars. Phil was unique in that," says Levine.

"He'd have them play and play and play—those poor guys. And then he'd hear something and he'd have them try something else and they'd play and play, and when it became a viable sound he'd bring in the pianos—which made it unviable again. And so then you knock out the piano and try again with the guitars, and then pianos again. And then, when they're in, you bring in the basses, the horns. Phil never wanted to hear horns as horns, which I thought was so great because all it would do was modulate the chords; you'd hear the chords changing, but there weren't any instruments to say 'I'm changing,' so it would be in the mind of the listener that these moving parts were moving."

Nailing the whole edifice to the ground like metal tent spikes in a storm were the drums. A clean, hard backbeat was the cement in the Wall of Sound, and Spector was obsessive in his search for the perfect drum sound. Sometimes he would arrive at the studio before anyone else, and experiment on modifying the sound by stuffing blankets, pieces of wood or stones into the bass drum, stomping on the pedal until he had it the way he wanted it. It was a ritual that he would repeat incessantly over the years, as if searching for some perfect timbre that would remain forever just out of reach.

"One of the first things that impressed me about Phil was hearing how he just walked in and lifted all the cymbals away from Hal Blaine," remembers the producer Denny Bruce. "Because without even thinking about it drummers will throw in a cymbal clash. It's cliché. And Phil didn't want cliché. He just wanted this strong, throbbing, pulsating backbeat."

To this would be added the defining characteristic of the Spector sound, the final garnish of percussive effects—maracas, tambourines, chimes, bells and castanets. Jack Nitzsche would provide a pithy summary of the whole process: "Four guitars play eighth notes; four pianos hit it when he says roll; the drum is on two and four on tom-toms, no snare, two sticks—heavy sticks—at least five percussionists . . ."

"A Phil Spector session was a party session," the drummer Hal Blaine remembers. "Phil would have a notice on the door of the studio, 'Closed Session,' and anyone who stuck their head in, he'd grab them and give them a tambourine or a cowbell. There'd sometimes be more percussionists than orchestra. I used to call it the Phil-harmonic. It was an absolute ball."

Assembling these different elements, striking the right balance between them and capturing the precise sound that Spector wanted was a long and arduous process. In a union-mandated standard session of three hours, most of the time would be spent on preparation and rehearsal—adjusting microphones, moving the musicians around the studio to get the balance right, the endless process of repetition and modulation.

"We almost never rolled tape on a session until we were two, two and a half hours into it," Levine says. "And sessions always ran overtime; he'd always work at least three and a half to four hours on the one side doing the rhythm and horns.

"Most producers spoke in generalities. They didn't have the sense of what they wanted to hear until after it was presented to them. But Phil really knew, and he was always very specific about what he wanted. He had the sound in his head and that's what he wanted to capture. The musicians he hired were all great musicians, but in a funny way maybe their greatness was a detriment to what he wanted to achieve. It was as if he was going three hours to tire them out enough so they weren't being individualistic, and they were fitting into this mold that he wanted. But once we finally got round to making a take it was very rare that we needed to do it more than once or twice.

"Every time we'd get something he'd have to listen and then he'd listen again until he heard something that said to him, 'This is what I want to do and this is the way I want to go.' He had to listen always. I remember it was very tiring working with Phil because I had to mix it as if it were a final record so he could hear the perspective of what was happening and it always meant being alert and I got very tired."

No other producers worked this way—it seemed that none could work this way. On one occasion, Larry Levine was approached by another producer, wanting him to engineer a session and reproduce the Spector sound. Levine initially turned the offer down.

"I thought it would be disloyal to Phil to take what I knew and give it to somebody else. But then when I thought about it, it always comes down to the song. And the songs that Phil wrote with these other people, and Phil's creativity, made for something that nobody else could match.

"So this guy hired all the musicians, the Wrecking Crew; and I started doing it the way Phil would do it—start with the guitars then adding in the other instruments. Then the producer starts in with, 'What's that guitar playing? I don't hear him. I'm paying him. I want to hear him.' So we ended up making something totally different. No one could achieve what Phil achieved anyway."

By the standards of most recording studios Gold Star's Studio A was extremely small—just twenty-five feet by thirty-five feet—and its ceilings unusually low. But its peculiar dimensions, and its primitive equipment, became a crucial ingredient in Spector's sound. In a sense, the studio was his most important instrument. Because the room was so small and invariably crowded with up to twenty musicians at a time, it was impossible to achieve any kind of meaningful separation between the sounds of the different instruments.

The only baffles were around the drums. And while every instrument was miked separately, the sound of each would inevitably bleed into the next, creating a dense impasto, like a Rothko painting.

The vocals would usually be recorded at a separate session, and seldom "live" with the band. Gold Star had only a one-track monaural recorder, and a two-track recorder. The instrumental track would be recorded on the monaural recorder, and then transferred onto one track of the two-track machine. The vocals would be recorded on the second, free track. The two tracks would then be mixed together, striking the right balance between music and voices, and bounced back onto the monaural recorder—"back to mono," as Spector's slogan would later have it.

Spector liked to record and to mix at a deafening volume. Most producers, says Levine, preferred to capture the sound of music as it was heard in the studio. At Gold Star, the huge speakers in the control room, and the lashings of echo applied to each song, would transform the music into something that seemed to have a life of its own. "The control room at Gold Star was the greatest listening environment imaginable. It just consumed you, enveloped you—all of the sound coming out of these three speakers. It was more than being in the record. See, it was not truthful at all. What everybody strives for in studio speakers is truth; this didn't in any way duplicate what you heard in the studio; it was just exciting and thrilling and full-bodied. The musicians would come into the control room for the playback and just be blown away," he remembers. "They simply couldn't believe that what they were hearing was what they'd been playing, and it made them excited."

As the coup de grâce, Spector would then play the finished track through a speaker the size of a car or transistor radio—the way the kids would hear it. Only if the song passed this most crude and rudimentary test would he allow the recording to be mastered and pressed.

From "Zip-a-Dee Doo-Dah" onward, Spector followed the practice of releasing his singles with deliberately redundant B-sides, usually an instrumental track that had been hastily improvised at the end of a session. There was little point, he reasoned, in wasting a good song, and putting a piece of disposable junk on the B-side ensured that disc jockeys would not turn the record over and dissipate airplay. The titles were in-jokes: "Brother Julius" was the man who ran the shoeshine stall out-side Gold Star, "Bebe and Susu" were the names of the mothers of the Ronettes, "Tedesco & Pitman," two members of the Wrecking Crew.

Sometimes Spector would not even bother to supervise the sessions himself, assigning the task of composing and producing them to musicians such as Don Randi. "Phil would call me up and say I want you to go in and do a B-side," Randi says. "And if it starts sounding good, stop. It's a little sore point with me, because I feel I wrote some of those songs, and I never got credit for that. I'd go in and do it and Phil would figure them out at the end. And then put his name on them."

While the musicians in New York had tended to view Spector with a mixture of superior disdain and grudging respect, the team he built at Gold Star came to regard him with unbridled affection.

"Musicians respected him because he could play himself and under-stood the trials and tribulations of making music," says Don Randi. "All the guitar players in particular loved to work for him because he under-stood the guitar better than any other producer, and he could play it so well. If Phil had decided not to be a record producer and become a jazz guitarist, he could have done that, no question."

"Phil would push the musicians to the limit, but you never saw them get upset," remembers the Crystals singer LaLa Brooks. "Some musicians in New York, they'd say, 'Listen, man, I've had enough, I'm going home, stick it up your ass . . .' I've seen them do that. Fifteen takes! They wouldn't even go to five takes! They'd be collecting their instruments and 'We're outta here! Because he's a nut!' But at Gold Star it was a family. They had positive and they had negative, but everybody chipped in, and they would stay there hours to produce that sound. If Phil said he wanted a kettle drum, then somebody would go and find a kettle drum, and everybody else would just sit there and wait."

Spector could be imperious, dogmatic, demanding, but he knew how to create an atmosphere in the studio that would encourage the musicians to give of their best. Gifts would be sprinkled like confetti. When Leon Russell played a piano part that Spector particularly loved, he stopped the session and wrote out a $50 check on the spot.

He would frequently leaven the sessions with bouts of joking and horseplay. "The bane of my recording career is that I didn't have a tape recorder running during those sessions," Levine says. "When things were going well—and that was most of the time—Phil would do stand-up comedy. He'd get on the talkback microphone into the studio and he'd do twenty-five minutes of one-liners, just throwing them out there. And then the guys would come back at him; Barney Kessel in particular had a really wry sense of humor. It was Phil's stage. And he loved it, and we all loved it. Even I loved it, and I was the brunt of the jokes that Phil would crack, which was okay with me because it was never meant other than in humor, and I knew that."

The musicians would respond in kind. When Spector turned up at the studio wearing a T-shirt bearing a picture of Beethoven, Ray Pohlman organized for everybody to turn up at the next session wearing T-shirts bearing a picture of Spector. He loved it. Don Randi recalls another night when Hal Blaine arrived with a movie-prop phone that he set ringing in between takes. "Phil's going, 'What the fuck is that?' Hal picks it up and says, 'Phil, it's for you.' It totally destroyed the mood but it was great."

"Phil didn't mind spending studio time that way," says Levine. "As long as the work got done. He always paid the Gold Star bill and the musicians. He never stinted on that. I remember one time he said, 'This is where I live, and you've got to pay the rent on where you live.' "

Spector's brushes with the musicians' union in New York had made him more cautious working in Los Angeles. "The greatest thing Phil did for musicians was observing union contracts," says Don Randi. "Everything was put on a contract; he insisted upon it. And he made all the other producers go along with the program, so we benefited enormously. Where that comes back is that fifteen, twenty years later, I will go to my mailbox and there'll be a residual check for three hundred dollars or seven hundred dollars where they've reused the track. We would do anything for him."

But if Spector treated the musicians like kings, he showed less consideration for the singers. "The musicians were all pros," says Levine. "The singers, for the most part, were just kids." But Spector regarded them simply as components in the machine, useful only for as long as he needed them and eminently disposable if he didn't. There was only room for one ego at Gold Star.

He would often keep them waiting for hours while he listened back to the tracks, thundering around the studio at deafening volume, indifferent to their boredom or needs. They would often curl up on sofas and try to sleep, until roused by Spector to provide another take. And he thought nothing of summoning them from their homes at a moment's notice if their services were required. Spector seemed to particularly relish the power he had over them to make or break their careers. "Phil would say, 'They're all mine,' " remembers Annette Merar. " 'Without me, they're nothing. They will do what I want.' Again, it was full power, full control."

"He rode the singers hard," Don Randi says. "Sometimes to get a performance he would go to such lengths that I would have to leave the studio. He had an ear, and if somebody was off-pitch—look out. Things were said, hurtful things. He could be brutal to get that performance out of them. This was out of the singers, but never the musicians."

"Oh, he was so critical!" remembers Gloria Jones. " 'The clapping's not right . . .' So we'd do that for ten or twelve takes. 'That note didn't make it.' The sessions would just go on and on and on and on. He was a genius-maniac—that's what I call Phil. He threw his little weight around, and he would kind of frighten people because of the way he acted. He was like God to a lot of people."

But not to Darlene Wright. As much as Spector loved her voice, and Wright would come to respect his talents, the two would argue constantly. "Darlene would say just what was on her mind to Phil, and he would back up like a little kid," Jones remembers. "Sometimes Phil would have it so cold in the studio, and Darlene would say, 'Turn that air-conditioning off,' and he'd turn it off. She had the balls to stand up to him, and he listened. I think he knew what he had in Darlene."

Jones, for her part, found Spector "scary"; the aloof, faintly menacing air, the dark glasses. But she fancied she could see vulnerability behind the façade. "I remember I had to come into the studio one time to get my money, and my husband came with me, not for any particular reason. And you could tell Phil was scared to death—like I was bringing my husband to beat up on him or something. Phil might have been a genius, but he was just a little punk, throwing his little weight around. I respected him because of his talent, but I didn't like him at all."

Jones's close friend and fellow singer Fanita Barrett saw things differently. "Nobody has a nice thing to say about Phil, but to me he was a nice man. He tried to make people laugh, but none of his jokes were ever funny. But he fascinated me, and I loved the way he worked. He made those sessions feel like family. I was just in awe—he was such a genius. I remember one time I was pregnant, and he told me, name the baby Philles and you'll never have to worry about her again. He offered to pay for her college education and everything. And you know what? I didn't do it. I called her Crystal—and I didn't know he was feuding with the Crystals at the time. Stupid idiot that I was, my poor baby never got a dime."

8

"He Wanted to Be
Thought Of as Interesting"

Shy and painfully self-conscious, Bernard "Jack" Nitzsche was the antithesis of hip when he first came into Phil Spector's orbit. Medium height and slight of build, he wore his hair in a short brush cut, dressed conservatively in short-sleeve sports shirts and a tie, and blinked from behind thick horn-rimmed spectacles—"sweet and a little nerdy-looking," according to Fanita Barrett. Everybody knew him as "Specs."

Nitzsche and Spector had much in common. Nitzsche had grown up on a farm in Michigan, under the shadow of a protective and overbearing mother—like Spector, a lonely child who had found consolation in music.

"Jack had music running in his veins," one friend remembers. "He could listen to windshield wipers and tell you what time signature they were in, and what songs would go along with it. I remember being with him in a car when 'Summertime Blues' came on, and he turned on the wipers to prove his point. They matched exactly."

Like Spector, Nitzsche had a particular reverence for black music, holding a lifelong belief that rock and roll—including whatever he would create himself—had been stolen from the black man. His son Jack Jr. would describe Nitzsche as "prejudiced in reverse. He hates white people."

He and Spector shared a passion for Motown and a fascination with the sound that Berry Gordy Jr. was conjuring from his small storefront studio in Detroit, which Gordy, with characteristic bravura, had christened "Hitsville USA." Nitzsche enjoyed telling the story of how one day he and Spector were driving down Sunset Boulevard when Marvin

Gaye's "Stubborn Kind of Fellow" came on the radio. Spector immedi-ately turned the volume to full blast—a sure sign a record had his atten-tion. When the drums kicked in, Spector and Nitzsche looked at each other in amazement and said in unison, "Who the fuck is playing the drums?" (It was Marvin Gaye himself.) Spector was so excited he lost control of the wheel, the car spinning on its axis to face the oncoming traffic. As cars weaved past them, the drivers sounding their horns and giving them the finger, Spector brought the car to a halt, he and Nitzsche clutching each other in laughter.

To Annette Kleinbard, Spector and Nitzsche were "the perfect match. Jack was somehow able to totally get into Phil's mind, and he knew exactly what Phil wanted. Nitzsche," she says, was "a modern-day Stravinsky. He never got the recognition he deserved."

"If Phil was the visionary, Jack was the architect," says Denny Bruce, who was a close friend of Nitzsche and managed him in later years. "He could draw the blueprint that you handed to the guys who were doing the building, so at least they'd know what the ground floor was sup-posed to look like. You're getting the feel, the tempo, the important things before you build any more. So the Wall of Sound was structured the way an architect will build a house; yeah, the closet doors do close. Jack was really meticulous about writing and copying charts, and he had such a good ear. There might be three or four acoustic rhythm guitars playing the same thing and it would be, 'Hold on, Glen—I think it's your high E string.' Jack would hear everything, but what he really excelled in was tempo and groove."

Nitzsche shared Spector's love for classical music, and his growing symphonic ambitions. As big as Spector wanted the Wall of Sound to be, Nitzsche was happy to encourage him to make it bigger still.

"Jack was musically educated," remembers one friend. "If Phil said, 'I want some Strauss here,' he'd know what he meant. They just bounced off each other. Phil was ready to go out on a limb and Jack was ready to go out there with him. Phil would say, 'It needs a saxophone,' and Jack would say, 'Let's double it,' and Phil would say, 'Let's triple it.' Jack was having the time of his life, and liberties were taken all the way around, which was the beauty of it all. They were like two scientists in a laboratory, experimenting, and they got tremendously lucky. They became very close friends."

Nitzsche was one of the few people around Spector in the studio who would answer him back and dare to contradict him. Spector would defer to Larry Levine on matters of technical expertise and frequently ask for his opinion on a particular performance or instrumental phrase. After a while, he even trusted Levine to do edits in the studio. But Levine was always aware that he was first and foremost an employee. Nitzsche felt confident enough in his abilities to be able to challenge Spector when he disagreed with something. "They had terrible fights," says Denny Bruce. "Jack was always walking out on Phil. But he would always come back."

Nitzsche idolized Spector to the point of brushing his hair forward in the same way and affecting the same dark glasses, rain or shine. On one occasion, Spector took him to New York and introduced him around the Brill Building, radio stations and trade papers as "my partner." Nitzsche was thrilled; Spector had finally given him the acknowledgment he felt he deserved. But Spector never used the word again.

Nor was Nitzsche generously rewarded for his efforts—he was paid just the standard $50 a session. But he took a pragmatic view. Not only was working with Spector a unique experience, he would later explain, but "the credits helped secure employment for years." Even while working for Spector, he was busy elsewhere as an arranger. With Sonny Bono he wrote the song "Needles and Pins," which became a hit for Jackie DeShannon and, later, the British group the Searchers. And in 1963 Nitzsche enjoyed a minor hit himself with the instrumental "The Lonely Surfer," written by his friend Al Hazan.

Finally, he felt emboldened enough to go to Spector and ask for a raise. Spector turned him down. "He told Jack, 'Look, the body of work you're making here is going to keep you going for the rest of your career,'" Denny Bruce remembers. "But Jack had a wife and a child to support. And there wouldn't be a session for a month or two, so he would work with other producers who wanted a Phil Spector sound. He was with Phil in Martoni's restaurant and one of the guys Jack was going to work with was there, and Jack was talking to the guy. And when he went back to the table, Phil said, 'I don't want you talking to him anymore.' Jack said, 'Well, I'm going to do some work with him.' And Phil said, 'I don't like him and he doesn't like me, and you are in my camp.'"

Nitzsche dropped the session. Whatever he could get working for others was nothing compared to the joy he derived from working with Spector. "Maybe other producers liked their records," Nitzsche would later recall. "Phil *loved* his records. Phil really was the artist, and it wasn't just out of ego. Phil understood the teenage market, he could relate to their feelings and buying impulses. He was a kid. He'd call me at four a.m. and want to go out for ice cream.'"

Sonny Bono was one of Jack Nitzsche's closest friends. Born in Detroit, the son of Italian immigrants, Bono had grown up in Los Angeles, an aspiring songwriter who worked bagging groceries and driving a tug at Douglas Aircraft before landing a job at Specialty Records as an A&R man. Bono had given Nitzsche his first break when he arrived in Los Angeles, writing out lead sheets for arrangements for three dollars a piece. When Bono lost his job at Specialty and was down on his luck, he slept for a few weeks on the couch in Jack and Gracia's apartment. When Nitzsche started working as Spector's arranger, Bono was desperate to join him. Like Nitzsche, Bono was in awe of Spector's talent, and his hit rate. Spector, he thought, was someone he could learn from. He was also anxious to promote the career of his new girlfriend, a seventeen-year-old runaway called Cherilyn Sarkasian LaPierre. Known as Cher, she had briefly dated Nino Tempo before meeting Bono. Bono was convinced that with the proper production and coaching Cher could be a star.

In late 1962, at Nitzsche's urging, Bono called Spector, asking for work.

"And what do you wanna do for me?" Spector asked.

"Anything," Bono replied. "Anything."

"I don't know if there's an opening under that job description," Spector said. "I'm in the record business, you know?"

After leaving Specialty, Bono had worked as a promotions man for a distribution company, Record Merchandising, peddling new releases to radio stations on behalf of a number of small, local labels. He knew from experience that promo men would push hardest on the records they figured would be hits, that DJs often expected "incentives" in cash or kind to get behind a song, and that the vast majority of new releases ended up in the garbage. Philles, he told Spector, was too important a label to entrust its releases to someone who was also handling product from other, rival labels. What Spector needed was his own West Coast promotions man.

Spector took Bono on, but quickly found other uses for him as an all-purpose sidekick and gofer, sometimes joining the choir of backing singers or playing percussion, other times being sent out to collect hamburgers or deli as the sessions stretched interminably into the night. Before long, Bono started to bring his girlfriend Cher to the sessions. Cher had a honking voice, so powerful that whenever she sang Larry

Levine would move her to the back of the group, away from the microphone, so she wouldn't drown out the other voices. She was also worldly beyond her years. When Spector, teasingly, asked in French if she wanted to go to bed with him, Cher snapped back at him—also in French—"Yeah, okay. For money."

Bono was an obliging foil, happy to play the part of Spector's flunky, always ready to laugh at his jokes and indulge his whims. "Phil only had to look like he wanted something and Sonny would be jumping—whatever," Gloria Jones recalls. Lester Sill would put it more bluntly. "Sonny had his nose up Phil's ass a mile." On one occasion Bono was awoken in the middle of the night by a call from Spector asking whether he wanted to meet for a bite to eat. Groggy and befuddled, Bono dutifully climbed out of bed and drove to collect Spector from his hotel and on to Denny's, a twenty-four-hour diner on Sunset Strip. For the next hour they sat in total silence as Spector ate his meal. Spector, it seemed, simply didn't feel like talking.

In his autobiography Bono writes that Spector "wanted to be thought of as interesting." He was obsessed by his appearance and how other people would see him. Spector, Bono and Nitzsche would sometimes take photos of each other, practicing the coolest way of sitting in a car or striking a pose—sunglasses on, sunglasses off . . . "He would put one arm on the window, try steering with one finger, all sorts of different poses," remembered Bono. "Then he would have me stand outside the car and ask how he looked."

For a while, Spector harbored an infatuation with the singer Jackie DeShannon. One day he asked Bono, "If she saw me driving, do you think she'd like me better with my glasses on or off?"

Bono replied that he had no idea.

With a handful of surreptitious phone calls, Bono was able to find out DeShannon's schedule and calculate that she would be driving down Sunset Strip at a certain time. Spector and Bono stationed themselves on the street and, when DeShannon drove past, set off in pursuit. At length they pulled alongside her car. "Phil positioned himself so that he was sitting almost completely sideways," Bono remembered. "Most of his back was toward the window. He was, he thought, looking as cool as possible. From Jackie's point of view though, he was barely visible."

For a mile Spector drove parallel to DeShannon, holding the pose, until at last DeShannon turned off the Strip, apparently oblivious to the fact that it was Spector in the car beside hers. Spector, Bono remembered, was "crestfallen. 'Damn,' he said, 'the sunglasses probably scared her.' "

Spector's fastidiousness about his wardrobe and appearance could be comical, but it seemed to hint less at vanity than at some more troubling, underlying insecurity. Preparing for a recording session or a meeting, he would spend hours posturing in front of the mirror, matching different shirts and jackets, testing colognes and experimenting with different ways of combing his fast-thinning hair, which only Annette Merar was allowed to cut.

"And every single strand would have to be perfect . . . 'Okay, so fix it at the back to make it compensate for the bit at the front that's long.' But to me he was adorable, and a very sexy guy. I remember one occasion when we were living on Fifty-eighth Street, and he was going off to work dressed in a Beau Brummel kind of velvet vest and a jacket; his hair was perfect; he was just mesmerizing, and I just loved him so hard, but I never said anything. He walked out and closed the door and it was . . . 'Oh my God.' He was my type of guy."

Spector's obsession with his appearance would never leave him. For years afterward, whenever he was in company he would leave the room at frequent intervals to preen and primp in front of a mirror. "It wasn't arrogance or egotism," Annette says. "It was like the opposite that drove him to be perfect."

Joel Adelberg was a tall, cadaverous man with a sense of humor not so much dry as parched—Beverly Ross would describe him as "the funniest man I've ever met." Born in Brooklyn in 1938, Adelberg had developed a childhood fascination with cowboy legend and lore that never left him (Mike Stoller would describe him as dressing "like the Marlboro Man"). As a teenager he sang in doo-wop groups and made a couple of singles, changing his name to the more memorable (and Gentile) Jeff Barry, before deciding to concentrate on songwriting. He collaborated with Beverly Ross—shortly before Ross met Spector—and in 1960 had a Top 10 hit co-writing the "death song" "Tell Laura I Love Her" for Ray Peterson. In that same year he met Ellie Greenwich and they began writing and recording the occasional song together. When they married in 1962, Greenwich brought her songwriting partnership with Tony Powers to an end.

Spector would regard the partnership that he forged with Greenwich and Barry as the most productive of his career, and the happiest he had with any of his teams of writers. "Jeff and Ellie really understood me, really knew what I wanted, and were able to deliver. The others understood, but not as much as Jeff and Ellie did."

In *Always Magic in the Air*, Ken Emerson would provide an astute analysis of how Greenwich and Barry differed from Spector's other songwriting partnerships, and the particular sensibility they brought to their songs.

> They had little interest in Broadway musicals or the Great American Songbook, and even less in classical music or jazz. Unburdened by the past and by the ambitions and doubts that the past can inspire, they took themselves and their music less seriously. This freed them to write entirely and unself-consciously in the present tense of teenage rock 'n' roll.

Unlike most other songwriting teams that generally followed a division of labor between lyricist and composer, Greenwich and Barry both moved easily between each discipline. This open-ended creative fluidity made it easier to accommodate a third collaborator in Spector.

"In the beginning Spector was sort of like an ideas man, bouncing off things and we were really doing the majority of the work," Greenwich told the writer Rob Finnis. "He would more or less say, 'Oh, I think we should write a song about the most important thing in the world—love,' and Jeff and I would start dribbling and Phil would be eating a sandwich and then suddenly go, 'Ooh! Go back a little bit. The third line you played. Start from there.'

"Really it was a hotchpotch way of writing, because the three of us were spewing out ideas simultaneously. I'd be pounding on a piano, Jeff would be playing a tambourine or banging something and Phil would be strumming his guitar and the three of us are singing away like maniacs at the top of our lungs . . . we'd find some melodic thing, or lyrical thing, that hit all of us at once more or less, because our minds were on the same wavelength, you could say. There was just something about the three of us together that sparked off one another."

The first collaboration between the three, in the early part of 1963, would exemplify all the winning charm and innocence of the team's "silly little things," as Jeff Barry described the songs. "Da Doo Ron Ron (When He Walked Me Home)" was composed over the space of two days in Spector's office on Sixty-second Street. The title—which serves as a punctuation for each stanza, as well as the chorus—was a piece of gobbledygook made up on the spot until a proper lyric could be written, but Spector liked it so much that he decided to keep it—its infectious, nursery-rhyme charm a perfect illustration of Jeff Barry's songwriting dictum of keeping things "simple, happy and repetitive."

A friend of Spector's, Bill Walsh, an independent promotions man from Boston, happened to drop by as Spector, Greenwich and Barry worked on the song, inadvertently inspiring the rhyme for the song's opening line about meeting a boy on a Monday, "and my heart stood still / Some boy told me that his name was Bill." Once again, Spector decided to use the Crystals' name, although the group themselves had become largely superfluous to requirements. Darlene Love had effectively become the voice of the group. But when Spector recorded her singing "Da Doo Ron Ron" he had a change of heart. The song was designed to be infused with all the giddy, adolescent joy of falling in love for the first time. Love's voice, he decided, was "too old," too knowing, to put the song's lyric across effectively. Instead, he turned back to the group whose name he intended to put on the record.

Barbara Alston was nominally the Crystals' lead singer and had taken the lead on the group's first three singles for Philles. Alston's voice was light and seductive, but it lacked projection, and when "He's a Rebel" became a hit, it was the youngest member of the group, LaLa Brooks, who took the lead on the song onstage. Brooks was only fifteen, but she sang with a full-throated power that bore a closer resemblance to Darlene Love, and she diligently applied herself to imitating Love's Southern-inflected diction.

Spector had a particular soft spot for LaLa. While she thought he was "sweet" on Barbara Alston, he treated LaLa herself like a younger sister, sometimes singling her out for special favors. At Christmas he gave all the other Crystals identical sets of luggage, but LaLa was treated to a special set, printed with red and black roses, "classier and more expensive," she remembers. On another occasion she was riding with Spector in a limousine when he suddenly stopped the car and stepped out, instructing her to wait. Returning a few minutes later, he presented her with a gift-wrapped box. Inside was a black toy poodle. "I was so happy. But then I was afraid to take it in the studio because Dee Dee and Barbara and all the others would see it and I didn't know how they'd feel."

Recognizing the strength of LaLa's voice, when recording the Crystals in New York Spector would move her away from the microphone, to prevent her overpowering the rest of the group. Now, he decided, her combination of gutsy projection and teenage innocence was just what he needed for "Da Doo Ron Ron."

Spector flew LaLa out to Los Angeles, leaving the rest of the group to continue on a tour with Sam Cooke. It was the first time LaLa had ever been on a plane, the first time she had ever been separated from the protective circle of group or family. Sonny Bono was waiting at the airport with another gofer, Tom, to meet her. "I'll never forget, they were teasing me about how Tom had had an eye transplant, to help me loosen up. I'm a black girl from Brooklyn in a car with two white guys and it was a little bit scary—not that they would do anything, but the company wasn't of black people."

In the studio, Brooks was mystified when Spector talked her through the song for the first time. "I said, 'Phil—da doo ron ron—what does it mean?' He said it doesn't matter what it means, just sing it. It sounded so funny on my tongue. But me being a kid it sounded kind of cute, it fit right into my age and character. And I think that was why it came out so good."

Good hardly describes it. A cloudburst of handclaps, Don Randi's driving piano triplets and honking saxes, Hal Blaine's drum fills rattling like gunfire, "Da Doo Ron Ron" is probably the most irrepressibly exhilarating song that Spector ever recorded, LaLa Brooks's vocal a gust of sheer, heart-lifting, lovestruck joy. You can almost see the smiles spreading from ear to ear around Gold Star as the song fades into the distance.

"The minute I heard the title was 'Da Doo Ron Ron' I knew this was gonna go Top 10 so fuckin' fast your hair'll fall out," Don Randi remembers. "It was so silly, but so great. That record had every hook in the book to make it a hit."

For LaLa Brooks it was "the most exciting moment of my life"; for the rest of the Crystals, it was further evidence of their increasing obsolescence; for Darlene Love, a reminder that to Spector nobody was indispensable. "But that was Phil," remembers LaLa. "He was a perfectionist all the way, and he didn't care if people's feelings got hurt. It wasn't about feelings, it was about Phil. And whoever could pull it off, that's who he would use. He didn't give a damn."

"Da Doo Ron Ron" entered the Top 40 in the second week of May 1963, eventually rising to number 3.

Its follow-up, "Then He Kissed Me," would capture even more perfectly the essence of the Barry, Greenwich and Spector collaborations—the juxtaposition of a lovely melody and a sweet and heartfelt sentiment with a production of painstakingly crafted towering grandeur, "this great wall of enormous sound," as Doc Pomus once described it, "and somehow through it all there was this lovely . . . romantic, sentimental innocence."

The song opens with a simple chiming guitar figure, before a flourish of castanets establishes a shuffling variation on the *baion* rhythm;

Jack Nitzsche's string arrangement soars above the dense impasto of massed guitars, keyboards and brass; a choir echoes LaLa Brooks's lead lines, and then peels off to swathe the song in a chorus of ethereal sighs—the sonic equivalent of the dream of satin, tulle and eternal love conjured in the lyric: "I felt so happy I almost cried / And then he kissed me." It was the closest thing to perfection pop music had ever produced.

But for LaLa Brooks, the song's lyrics had a particular poignancy. "I was fifteen years old, and I'd never kissed a boy! That's the honest truth. So to sing those lyrics, 'Well, he walked up to me and he asked me if I wanted to dance . . .' I was wondering, 'Well, who is going to kiss me— and where the hell is he?' "

9

Little Symphonies for the Kids

At the age of twenty-three, Phil Spector was the most successful rock and roll producer in America. In the eighteen months since founding Philles he had produced ten Top 40 hits, four of them Top 10, and one—"He's a Rebel"—a number 1 smash. With his "little symphonies for the kids," he had shaped a palette of teenage yearning, desire and heartache; the ecstasy of a good-night kiss, the agony of being too young to be married; innocent and knowing, neon-bright and dungeon-dark all at the same time. He had alchemized the base metal of his own pain, alienation and resentment into something fabulous, mythical and beautiful. The school yard loser, the nerd, the loner, was now a figure of power and substance. He dressed in bespoke suits from Sy Devore—the Hollywood tailor who styled himself as "the man who dressed the Rat Pack"—silk waistcoats, ruffle-front shirts, bootlace ties, pointy-toe stack-heel boots. He had taken to sporting a neat little jazzbo goatee beard, of the kind favored by Ahmet Ertegun and Mike Stoller, and dousing himself in expensive Caesar cologne. He walked with a bantam-cock strut. To the outside world Spector might have been small, strange, a disturbing presence; in the studio he was a god, shaping his own universe.

Watching Spector's endless flow of hits from the East Coast, Ahmet Ertegun was deeply admiring of his friend and former apprentice—if ruing the fact that the promise he had always detected in Spector was now coming to fruition elsewhere.

"What Phil was doing was unbelievable," Ertegun told me. "If he'd stayed at Atlantic and made those records it would have been our greatest period. But I don't think he could have done that so easily in New York. Part of that was being able to use Gold Star studio like his own place. I had recorded at Gold Star too, but he somehow built that sound, and with those musicians, into something that was uniquely his. They were mostly the same musicians that I used, but he got his thing going to such an extent that in a sense he's the *only* producer who could produce a hit record without having a hit artist. He could just get a session singer—any session singer—and have a hit. The production was everything.

"What Phil had was a vision. All good producers have that, but he had it more than most. You have to go in there with an idea of what you want, otherwise what the hell are you doing in there? It's like I've told some of my groups, 'What would you do if you didn't have a producer? You'd have to get somebody else to roll the joints.' "

Ertegun's partner, Jerry Wexler, brought a more analytical eye to how Spector's approach was revolutionizing the role of the producer in pop music. Before Spector, Wexler argued, there had been two kinds of record producer. The first was what Wexler called "the documentarian," like Leonard Chess, the founder of Chess Records in Chicago, who in the late '50s took the raw urban blues of performers like Muddy Waters and transplanted them from the bar to the studio, simply recording them as Muddy played them.

The second category, into which Wexler put himself, was what he described as "the servant of the project," whose job was to enhance; to find the right song, the right arrangement, the right band and the right studio; in short, to do whatever was necessary to bring out the best in the artist.

Spector had created a third category: "the producer as star, as artist, as unifying force." To Wexler, every Spector record was "an intaglio," an intricate design carved by a single hand into the surface of a stone. The rhythm track, the *sound*, the background vocal, the lead vocal—every aspect of the design was of Spector's making.

But Wexler was no great enthusiast of the essential element of Spector's Wall of Sound. The way in which the individual ingredients were melted together into what Wexler described as "a fascinating treacle," to a point where it was impossible to tell which instrument was which, offended Wexler's purist principles. "That gargantuan leakage, everything leaking out of everyone else's mike, was something we guarded against fanatically at Atlantic. To me it was like a muted roar. I didn't like it, and I still don't like it. But I recognized its incredible, incredible value. Phil was making hits."

Wexler also recognized some essential, deeper truth in the way Spector made records. "Rather than develop his artists' careers, Phil developed himself; rather than serve the artist, the artist served Phil."

. . .

Among the Los Angeles music business cognoscenti, Spector's sessions became the place to be. He enjoyed an audience, and the tiny booth at Gold Star would often be crowded with visitors—record executives, musicians, friends and hangers-on—all eager to witness his Midas touch at firsthand. Annette's sister, Renee, was going steady with a lawyer named Mitchell Geffen (they would marry in September 1963), whose younger brother David had ambitions to be in the music business. David Geffen had dropped out of his course at the University of Texas after less than a year and come to Los Angeles to stay with his brother, taking a menial clerical job in a bank. When Annette was in town, she would often invite Renee, Mitchell and David to tag along with her to the studio. Soon, David began turning up by himself, sitting quietly at the back of the control room and watching wide-eyed as Spector went through his paces. Geffen came from a poor, working-class Jewish family, just like Spector, and he was in awe of what the producer had achieved. "David saw Phil as a model," says Annette. "He was kind of like a puppy around Phil." Geffen was so obsequious around Spector that the actor Dennis Hopper, who would sometimes drop in on sessions, assumed he was on the payroll, "like a roadie or something. Phil would send him out for hot dogs and stuff." Spector, for his part, regarded the young Geffen as an irritant and an ingrate. At the end of one session, he invited Geffen to join him and a group of friends at a restaurant. Geffen was thrilled, but when they arrived Spector told Geffen to go and sit with his chauffeur instead. "David never forgot that," says his brother Mitchell. "It was such a slight. He felt like a schmuck."

But for all his braggadocio posturing, it seemed that no amount of success could assuage Spector's constant, nagging feelings of insecurity. Spector would sometimes confide his doubts to his old friend Nino Tempo, who had become a regular at the Gold Star sessions. A versatile musician, Tempo could play sax, drums, piano or guitar; he was a good pair of ears. Long after the sessions had ended and the musicians had gone home, Spector and Tempo would often still be at the control desk, playing back and critiquing the tracks.

"I remember when he'd had four or five hits in a row—something that hadn't been done too often in those days—and he said to me, 'How long can I go on without making a flop?' I said, 'What difference does it make? You're talented enough; you'll always make hits. So you only have three out of five, or two out of five. What's so terrible about that?' But Phil needed five out of five. The thought of anything he made not being a hit was painful to him. There was always this thought in his mind, How much longer can I keep doing this? And he was pushing and pushing himself. He couldn't bear it."

Spector might have crowed that he was "a genius." But Tempo sensed something else. "Phil's problem wasn't that he thought he was too good. It was that he never thought he was good enough."

For Spector, success was always provisional, his good fortune something that might be snatched from him at any moment. To be cast back into anonymity and poverty was a thing of terror. Jack Nitzsche would recall an occasion, visiting New York, when Spector acted as his Virgil, guiding him through the bacchanalian sleaze and squalor of Times Square (much as Michael Spencer had acted as Spector's guide a few years before).

"Very strange big-city scenes were being played out all around us," Nitzsche remembered. "Guys with handkerchiefs around their heads—that kind of tough guy—were walking down the street. I saw someone pull off a pickpocket routine right in front of me. It was the first time in my life I'd ever seen drag queens in two-piece bathing suits. These black prostitutes were threatening to beat up Phil because they said he was staring at them strangely. I said, 'Phil, let's get out of here.' He told me, 'No, we have to stay here and soak it all in, man—we have to see how it would be like if it had gone the other way.' Very serious."

No matter how great his achievements, Spector always seemed to need people to believe he'd done more, and could never resist an opportunity to self-mythologize. Bruce Johnston remembers driving down Sunset Boulevard one day with Spector and Terry Melcher—the son of Doris Day, and a singer who would himself become a highly successful producer—when Elvis Presley's "Can't Help Falling in Love" came on the radio.

"Phil was saying, 'I should have had more guitar on there . . .' I said, 'Excuse me?' 'Oh, I don't know, maybe it's the voice is too loud . . .' 'So you produced that?' 'Uh-huh . . .' " As far as Johnston knew, Spector had been nowhere near the session. "With all the success he was having on his own label, and he was claiming he'd produced Elvis . . ." It was as Doc Pomus once said: "Phil always told a lot of stories, but here's the reality: what actually happened, what Phil wished could have happened, and what he *says* happened."

Johnston, who had played with Spector at bar mitzvahs and house parties, could see the change that had come over his old friend, how the small, nervy, unprepossessing teenager with the Pee-wee Herman voice was now wreathed in an air of grandiosity and self-importance. Spector produced a single by Melcher, "Be a Soldier," notionally for Philles but that was eventually released under the name of Terry Day on Columbia. "Terry said Phil spent most of the session on the phone. And that's when Terry thought, Okay, bye, Phil . . ."

In the studio, Spector's mood could swing wildly between elation—the palling-around and backslapping, the endless stream of jokes—and periods of dark, moody depression.

"People would say that Phil was a tyrant, or Phil was a horrible person, but I wanted to make him happy, because he was so hard to make happy," LaLa Brooks remembers.

"I'd be singing these things—'da doo ron ron, da doo ron ron . . .'—and it used to weigh on me that he would be so stressed-looking if I didn't get it right. You'd be doing a song, and it would be like Sonny doesn't like my phrasing or Jack likes the phrasing. And Phil would be sitting there—you wouldn't know whether he liked it or he didn't. He would sit there and squirm in a chair and put his legs up, and sometimes you'd think, Where is he? His head would be down, or he'd have this deadpan expression on his face, and he would always have things like raisins and nuts there on the desk, and he'd take from the raisins and nuts and stoop down into a chair and you could never feel where he was, where his emotions were. Phil would never say to you, 'This is great.' Never. Sonny would say it as his mouthpiece. And Sonny would tell him, 'It's great, it's great, leave it.' But that wouldn't work, and Phil would have you do it over and over and over because he was never satisfied. And even then, when it was perfect, and he did get hits out of it, even then you never knew. Even with 'Da Doo Ron Ron,' which was one of the biggest, even with that, Phil never came up to me and said, 'Thank you, LaLa.' Never, never, never."

"Phillip was always a very strange person," Sonny Bono would tell the writer Justine Picardie. "He always had a tough time staying rational, a real tough time. I don't think it was any reason you or I would know—you'd have to go back into his family history and trace it. It was more than just his success that was the crux of the problem . . . His sister, his whole family was a turbulent family. His mom would come to every session and drive us all nuts. He hated his mom and [we] hated it when she came to the sessions. His sister was committed [to an institution]—and sometimes I'd have to go and give his sister money from him, and I'd have to slip it under the door. It was a strange family."

Bono would recall how sometimes, when things in the studio got particularly difficult, Spector would call a halt and vanish into another room to telephone Dr. Kaplan back in New York, the musicians and singers killing time for an hour or two until Kaplan had managed to talk him down. The psychiatrist's long-distance contribution would be acknowledged in one of Spector's throwaway instrumentals, "Dr. Kaplan's Office," which appeared on the B-side of "Why Do Lovers Break Each Other's Heart?" The studio, Bono said, "was like a road-show Dr. Kaplan's office."

The conversations with Dr. Kaplan would often revolve around Spector's greatest fear. From the moment he had first set foot in an aircraft, at the age of eighteen, traveling with the Teddy Bears from Los Angeles to New York, Spector had had a mortal terror of flying. And the constant shuttling back and forth between the East and West coasts in the years since then had done nothing to assuage his fears. For Spector, every flight was an agony. Being 30,000 feet in the air, with only a thin skin of aluminum between you and certain death; the sudden bucking and swaying in turbulence; the sheer lunacy of entrusting your life to the total stranger in the pilot's seat—it was all fuel being poured on to the flame of the one thing that Spector feared most—losing control. Sometimes he would plead with Jack Nitzsche to fly with him. "He told me he didn't want to die alone," Nitzsche remembered.

One of the most frequently told stories about Spector concerned the occasion when he suffered a panic attack on an aircraft shortly before takeoff from Los Angeles, obliging the captain to turn back to the gate so that Spector could get off the plane. The story first appeared in a profile written by Tom Wolfe, and published in the *New York Herald Tribune*'s Sunday magazine in 1965, under the title "The First Tycoon of Teen." Wolfe's account began in a dazzling burst of high-octane prose. "All these raindrops are high or something. They don't roll down the window, they come straight back, toward the tail, wobbling, like all those Mr. Cool snow heads walking on mattresses. The plane is taxiing out toward the runway to take off, and this stupid infarcted water wobbles, sideways, across the window. Phil Spector, twenty-three years old, the rock and roll magnate, producer of Philles Records, America's first teenage tycoon, watches . . . this watery pathology . . . It is sick, *fatal.* He tightens his seat belt over his bowels . . ."

Jeff Barry, who along with his wife Ellie Greenwich was on the flight with Spector, recounted the story to the writer Richard Williams a few years later. "We were on the plane waiting, boarded . . . plane's loaded. I was sitting across the aisle from Phil, and he leans over to me and says, 'Hey, man, I don't think I can make it.' Does his Ahmet Ertegun imitation. And says, 'Hey . . . it's filling up . . . I don't know. Look there, Jeffrey, all the way in the back, it's filling up . . . people . . . losers.' So I said, 'Yeah, that's it,' and he says, 'I gotta get off. Miss, I gotta get off this plane.' And he's flying . . . he's always on pills when he's flying and he's flying before he's flying. So the stewardess went up front and evidently the pilot gave permission to let this guy off . . .

"Phil gets off, and Ellie and I sit there, and I think, Phil Spector's too bright. I don't wanna bet against Phil Spector. *Let's get off the plane.* So we raised our hands also, and asked to be excused. All these fairly straight people were sitting there, and I had a two-day growth of beard because we'd been in the studio, and Phil looks weird as shit anyway, and they were all saying, 'Who are these weird people? This blonde, and this other tall, skinny jerk and this little twerp, what IS GOING ON?' Anyway, like fifty people wanted to get off the plane.

"The plane was held up, the captain was grounded on the spot for opening the doors again in the first place . . . So we got off and Phil got off and I understand that a lot of other people got off. The flight was delayed, and they had to get another captain to take over. They took our luggage off, we waited for it, and when it came we ran right over to get on the next flight . . . And then Phil comes staggering down, and the word went from one airline to the next, not to let this guy on. He could not get out of Los Angeles—he had to go to another airport someplace else, where the word hadn't gotten out yet."

This picture of Spector, the frightened flier, would become part of music business legend. Joe Smith, who worked as chairman of Warner Bros. and Capitol Records and was a long-standing acquaintance of Spector, enjoyed telling the story of another occasion when Spector was flying, this time with Ahmet Ertegun.

"Phil really didn't want to fly. Ahmet was saying, 'I'm with you, I fly all the time, I'll hold your hand,' blah, blah. Now, Ahmet is a man who if he's flying to Indonesia, as soon as he fastens the seat belt—click—he's asleep. And he doesn't wake up until they're telling you not to stand up until the doors are open. So they get on the plane. And Phil is immediately imagining the engine's on fire, and they haven't even left the ground. Ahmet's trying to go to sleep, and Phil's prodding him, he's terrified. So Ahmet says to him, 'Listen—this plane is either going to make it, or it's going to crash. And you know what'll happen if we crash? We'll all die. And you know what'll happen then? Atlantic Records will take out an ad in all the trade papers, rimmed in black, and it'll say, "Ahmet Ertegun, born when-ever/died whenever. Phillip Spector, born whenever/died whenever." And at the bottom it'll say, "and don't forget the great new Solomon Burke hit," because Jerry Wexler wouldn't waste a dime . . .' "

10

Going to the Chapel

On February 18, 1963, in the rabbi's chambers in an Upper West Side synagogue, Phil Spector enacted the traditional Jewish wedding ritual of crushing a wineglass under his foot—a symbolic representation of the sacking of the Temple in Jerusalem—a reminder in the midst of joy that bad things may happen. Standing beside him, Annette Merar thought "it was the happiest day of my life."

Getting married, she says, "was one of the few mutual decisions Phil and I ever made. I remember he was in the bedroom and I was lying on a couch in the living room. And I was like, should we go back to L.A. and have a wedding? And Phil said, 'What's the point? We're here, why not just do it?' Okay . . ."

In the time that they had been living together, Spector had continued to see Dr. Kaplan on a regular basis. He never disclosed what was discussed in these sessions. But then, even with Annette, he would seldom talk about his anxieties, the difficulties of his childhood, and never about the trauma of his father's death. "Other people sometimes talked about it, with regard to the way he was or to explain some of his behavior, but Phil never talked about it. It was as if he just shut down so hard with that. I picture the image of a deadbolt just slamming shut. I think he just couldn't deal with the pain and the loss. And blaming himself. But with Phil, I could never determine what were his genuine internal dynamics, and what might be the result of traumatic events like the suicide."

Annette had never set eyes on Dr. Kaplan, but with the wedding looming, Spector now insisted they should meet. "He said, 'My doctor wants to meet you, and you have to come and talk with him.' I think he wanted to check me out, like a test."

Annette was not impressed. "Phil was very dependent on him. But

Dr. Kaplan became very dependent on Phil too. Phil was like the boy genius, and Dr. Kaplan was into power, success and money."

Nevertheless, if it was a test, she passed.

The marriage was planned for Valentine's Day, but February 14 fell on Shabbat, a Friday night. Instead, they married on the following Tuesday. Annette's parents and friends had been unable to make the journey. Of Spector's friends, only the arranger Arnold Goland attended the ceremony, as best man. Helen Noga loaned the newlyweds her Manhattan town house for the reception, where some forty people, mostly Phil's friends from the music business, toasted their health. As the couple cut the cake, Michael Spencer caught Spector's eye. "He looked at me askance," Spencer remembers, "like 'Is this for real? Do you believe this?' It was as if he wasn't taking it seriously."

There was no honeymoon. On the day after the wedding, Spector flew to Los Angeles for a recording session. It was a portent of things to come.

Now that they were married, Annette wanted to pursue her own dreams as a writer; she abandoned her secretarial job and enrolled at Hunter College, studying English literature and creative writing. With Lester Sill out of the way, Spector had drawn up papers making Annette vice president of Philles. He continued to commute furiously between the two coasts, recording in Los Angeles, and running his business out of the downstairs office on Sixty-second Street. He took on a secretary, Joan Berg, and Chuck Kaye, Lester Sill's stepson, now joined him in New York, spending his days yammering on the telephone to distributors, disc jockeys and the trade papers.

From his earliest days with the Teddy Bears, Spector knew how quickly and easily money could be taken from you in the music business, and how hard it could be to extract what you were owed. But with Lester Sill out of the picture he had finally achieved the total independence, and the total control, he had always craved. Spector no longer needed to go cap in hand to a distributor or major label to finance his recordings. He paid for everything—the musicians, the studio costs, the pressing, the promotion—and he owned everything. Most important, he retained control of the masters. The masters were his fortune and Spector would never let them out of his grasp. For the rest of his life, whenever he was recording, at the end of every session the tapes would be carefully boxed and carried home with him for the night—the gold bars under the mattress—to be brought back to the studio next day.

Philles was now so hot that he no longer needed to plead with distributors to handle his records or pay their bills. Now, if they didn't bow to his terms and pay promptly he could threaten to withhold product, depriving them of any share of future revenue from the seemingly endless flow of hits. "As well as being a musical genius, Phil was also a very good businessman," Annette says. "He had a natural talent for that. He knows how to cover his ass. He liked musicians, he liked creative people. But he really didn't like the people in the industry, the distributors and so on. He'd talk about the cigar-smoking fatties. He always felt he was butting heads with the industry rather than complementary with it. And he just assumed the posture with everybody that they were an antagonist before they were a friend. He'd come on to people in a very aggressive way."

Almost from the moment he left school, Spector had kept musicians' hours, often not going to bed before three in the morning, seldom rising before ten. He had a small music room in the office downstairs, with a piano, guitars and tape equipment, where he would usually work until the early hours of the morning, to Annette's growing frustration.

"He never came home for dinner, whether it was cooked or not. Many, many nights I'd phone down. 'Hello, Phil—where are you?' 'I'll be right up,' blah, blah, blah. And he never was. He was married to music. And that's okay, but I just didn't know . . . and it's very difficult when you wait and wait and wait, and then go to the studio and wait and wait."

Annette had always accepted her husband's traveling, his long absences, but as Philles grew more successful, and his schedule more hectic, so Spector's absences grew more frequent and longer. In the early stages of their relationship, music had been one of the things that bound them together; Spector respected Annette's taste and judgment and would frequently call on her for advice or an opinion about a song. On occasion, she had been enlisted in the studio as a backing singer, or banging a tambourine. But that was no longer the case. Music began to keep them apart. It was as if now that Spector had captured Annette he felt he no longer needed to pay her the attention required to keep her.

As their marriage began to unravel, Dr. Kaplan suggested that the couple should see him together for counseling, but after a handful of sessions Spector gave up on the idea. Instead, he and Annette continued to see Kaplan separately—and drifted further apart.

"Phil was just not available as a husband, partner or friend," Annette says. "And I made the mistake of believing that whatever he did was right, and I did was wrong, so I never took much initiative or challenged him, even though he may have been wrong in lots of ways about lots of things. For me, our love affair was the courtship: as soon as we were married everything started going to hell."

. . .

Even as Phil Spector was reciting his marriage vows to Annette, he had another girl on his mind. Veronica Bennett was the lead singer of the Ronettes, three spectacularly beautiful girls from Spanish Harlem, who embodied the racial melting pot that was New York. The mother of nineteen-year-old Veronica and her twenty-year-old sister Estelle was half black and half Cherokee, and their father was white. Their eighteen-year-old cousin Nedra Talley was half Spanish.

Of the three girls, Veronica—or Ronnie, as she was known—was the most extrovert; the precocious child who would push herself forward at family gatherings to sing and dance, the attention seeker, the best singer and the natural focal point for the group.

Inspired, like every girl group of the period, by the Chantels' "Maybe"—Nedra Talley remembers sitting in her bedroom and listening to the song "over and over and over again"—the group started singing in local sock hops and talent contests. They landed a job dancing at the Peppermint Lounge, and performed at the disc jockey Murray the K's "caravan of stars" nights at the Brooklyn Fox Theater. The standard demeanor of girl groups of the day was one of demure innocence. Publicity photographs would usually show the groups modestly attired in formals, like high-school prom queens, or in their Sunday best. But the Ronettes looked as if it was Saturday night and they were cruising for trouble—figure-hugging dresses, hair piled into improbable beehives, and lashings of mascara, which transformed the youthful high school girls into vamps. In 1961, the group signed for Colpix, the recording arm of Columbia Pictures, and was put together with the house producer Stu Phillips, who had enjoyed a number 1 hit earlier that same year with the Marcels' "Blue Moon."

"This wasn't an amateur-looking bunch of little girls who were shy and retiring," remembers Phillips. "They were nice-looking, trim and danced like crazy, and they had the big hair, which was important in those days. They put on a show. They looked like they could *taste* being stars."

But try as he might, Phillips couldn't find the right musical formula for the group. They released a handful of singles on Colpix, and the label's R&B subsidiary May, under the names Ronnie and the Relatives, and the Ronettes, but without success. They were on the verge of quitting the business altogether when, in the first months of 1963, they met Phil Spector.

Accounts vary as to how this happened. Writing in her autobiography, *Be My Baby*, Ronnie Spector tells the story of how the girls, frustrated with their lack of success, decided to track down Spector themselves, dialing information and asking for the number of Philles Records. When Estelle called, she was put straight through to Spector, who immediately invited the group to audition. Nedra Talley offers a less fanciful account, recalling that Spector was told about the group by his friend Arnold Goland, and went to see them perform at one of Murray the K's shows at the Brooklyn Fox. After the show, he went backstage to introduce himself and invited the group to audition for him. A few days later, the Ronettes duly presented themselves at Mira Sound Studios, where Spector put them through their paces. "He sat there hunched over his piano, attacking it, playing different songs for us," Nedra Talley says, "and I remember looking at him and thinking, Boy, he's really not much to look at; but he had this reputation for being a boy genius. I was impressed with him in that sense. So it was okay, but what could he bring to us?"

Spector himself was apparently no more impressed with the group as they launched into a rendition of the song on which they had traditionally practiced their three-part harmonies, the old chestnut "When the Red, Red Robin Comes Bob Bob Bobbin' Along." But when Ronnie took the lead on the Frankie Lymon hit "Why Do Fools Fall in Love" he was galvanized. "Stop!" Ronnie would describe him saying. "That's it. That is it! *That* is the voice I've been looking for."

The problem was that the Ronettes were still under contract to Colpix. Knowing full well that Colpix would balk at any attempt by him to buy out the group's contract, Spector instead suggested the girls tell the label that they were giving up singing to follow other plans.

"They came into Colpix," Stu Phillips remembers. "And one of them claimed she had nodes on her vocal cords and couldn't sing anymore; another one said she was sick of the business and was going to be a nurse. I said to my boss, Paul Wexler, 'Don't believe them; I think they're full of shit.' But Paul said, 'We're not having any success, let them go.' The next thing I hear is that they're on Philles. I put my head in my boss's office and said, 'I don't want to say I told you so . . . but I told you so.' "

In March 1963, the Ronettes signed with Philles. Spector quickly moved the group to the top of his list of priorities, and for the next few weeks devoted most of his time to rehearsing them in New York. LaLa Brooks was given an early portent of the Ronettes' growing importance when the Crystals were gathered in Spector's office one day, and the

Ronettes walked in, giving every sign of being very much at home. It was the first time the two groups had met. "That was the end of our rehearsal. All of a sudden he wanted to rehearse them." LaLa also noted a certain chemistry between Spector and the Ronettes' lead singer. "Ronnie was paying a lot of attention to Phil, and he was married to a very nice girl."

In May 1963, after a few weeks of rehearsal in New York, Spector was ready to take the Ronettes out to California to record. Spector and Ronnie had begun stealing kisses between rehearsals, and it was now clear that, in his mind, Nedra and Estelle were already beginning to fade into the background. Telling them he could not afford to pay the airfares for all three members of the group, Spector flew to Los Angeles with Ronnie—with her mother Beatrice in attendance as chaperone—leaving Nedra and Estelle to make the 3,000-mile journey by car with Bobby Sheen.

One musician remembers Spector walking into Gold Star with the Ronettes for the first time, looking like the cat that'd got the cream. "He whispered to me, 'Can you imagine just piling the three of them on top of each other and just . . . licking . . . ?' I said, 'Well, yeah, there's an idea . . .' "

Later, Spector and Jack Nitzsche gave the girls a lift back to their hotel. At a stoplight, a car filled with young black men drew up next to them, and the men started shouting and wolf-whistling. Staring fixedly ahead, Spector jokingly barked at Nitzsche, "Jack, if they open the car door, give 'em the girls . . ."

At Gold Star, Spector recorded the group singing a new Ellie Greenwich and Jeff Barry composition, "Why Don't They Let Us Fall in Love?" The group was thrilled with the result, but received an early tutorial in Spector's working methods when he told them that he had decided not to release the song, instead sending them out on the road to polish their stagecraft.

It was to be another few weeks before he would summon them back into the studio to record the song that would launch them to the top of the American charts.

Whether or not Spector intended "Be My Baby" as an explicit declaration of his growing feelings for Ronnie, the song he composed with Jeff Barry and Ellie Greenwich in his Sixty-second Street office seemed a portent of the part each would soon come to play in the other's lives—a heartfelt declaration of a need that was flowering into full-blown love.

In Los Angeles, Spector visited Nino Tempo at his parents' house and played him the finished song on the piano. Tempo told his friend he didn't think much of it. "Phil said, 'You will by the time I finish with it . . .'"

On July 29, Spector marshaled the full complement of his troops in Gold Star—battalions of pianos and guitars, brass, strings, the full regiment of backing singers—determined to make his most towering production yet. Jack Nitzsche suggested a thunderously nagging drum figure to Hal Blaine that would kick the song into orbit from the second the needle dropped on the groove—*Boom, boom-boom, bang! Boom, boomboom, bang!* Spector took the soaring melody and brought to it all the classic ingredients of the Wall of Sound; a sinuous rhythm that hinted at the *baion*, dramatic castanet flourishes, a cushion of ecstatic harmonies, an achingly romantic string section, Hal Blaine's magisterial drum fills. Michael Spencer was one of the four keyboard players on the session. "On my right was Al DeLory. On my left was this fellow in a three-piece suit with a DA hairstyle. That was Leon Russell before he took acid. We each had a different kind of piano. That session took three and a half hours. There's this pause toward the end of the song where the drums go boom-ba-boom-boom before the song picks up again. I remember that by the fortieth or forty-first take I was so punchy, I played right through it, and we had to do it again. And that subsequent take was the one Phil used."

In her autobiography, Ronnie recounts that she was so nervous about recording that she would spend hours in the ladies' room at Gold Star, endlessly fixing her makeup and teasing her hair while developing the heart-clutching whoah-ohs that would become her signature vocal mannerism. It took three days to record her vocal, but her performance struck a perfect balance between teenage innocence and sexual precocity—sweet, seductive and totally irresistible. Jack Nitzsche would later declare himself "amazed" at the vibrato in Ronnie's voice. "That was her strong point. When that tune was finished, the speakers were turned up so high in the booth that people had to leave the room."

In August 1963, "Be My Baby" entered the American charts, eventually rising to number 2. Ronnie would later recall that the group was on tour when Spector presented them with their first royalty check for $14,000, taking them to celebrate at an all-night diner with coffee and pie. At the end of the meal, Spector proffered a $100 bill. When the waitress told him she wouldn't be able to provide change at that late hour, he asked the girls if they would mind picking up the check. "For a millionaire," Ronnie writes, "he sure could be cheap."

• • •

Even as he was recording "Be My Baby," Spector was planning his next, and most ambitious, project yet. Notwithstanding the fact that he was Jewish, Christmas was Spector's favorite time of year. He enjoyed the seasonal bonhomie, the ritual of cards and presents, all the trappings and frills, the cornier the better. (When, a couple of years later, he bought his own mansion, he would regularly deck it out with twinkling fairy lights, illuminated reindeer and snowflakes—"it looked like Disneyland," remembers one friend.)

He also loved Christmas songs, the schmaltzier the better—"The Bells of St. Mary," "Rudolph the Red-Nosed Reindeer" and, of course, "White Christmas": the fact that the Jewish Irving Berlin would reap a harvest of ASCAP royalties for the song that defined the most important date in the Christian calendar was a source of particular amusement. What could be better, Spector reasoned, than giving his favorite Christmas songs the Wall of Sound treatment? Little symphonies for the kids to wake up to on Christmas morning: yesterday's Christmas sound today.

The idea was hardly original. Elvis Presley had recorded a Christmas album in 1957. In 1961 Cameo Parkway Records, one of Philles's principal rivals, had released an album of Christmas songs set "to the beat of today's popular music" by two of its best-selling artists, Chubby Checker and Bobby Rydell. Brenda Lee's "Rockin' Around the Christmas Tree" had been a hit in the same year, and in 1962 the Four Seasons recorded their own album of Christmas songs. But Spector was to take the genre to a completely different level, and one that has never been surpassed.

In August, Spector called all his performers into Gold Star, and over the next six weeks, in the sweltering heat of high summer, cajoled, bullied and charmed them into capturing the spirit of Christmas. "Recording the Christmas album was just the best time of all, because it was all the artists together," Nedra Talley remembers. "You could sense that there was this side of who was gonna get what songs, and the fact that Ronnie and Phil were becoming an item, the others might have felt that there might be some favoritism to the Ronettes. But the other side was that it was so much fun being together and supporting each other and all singing on each other's songs."

Sparing no expense, Spector kept the studio booked for almost twenty-four hours a day, sometimes working through the night until dawn. "You'd get so tired you'd get hysterical," Nedra says. "I remember one night we were all sitting around waiting for the music track to come back—Darlene, Bobby and Fanita Barrett—and by this time we're all delirious—and Darlene throwing back her head, laughing at something, and her wig flying off. That was it. There was no more recording after that, nobody could get their composure."

For Larry Levine, the project became a nightmare. "It got to the point where Phil and I were at each other's throats because night after night we were in for six weeks doing that album," he remembers. "He had to have it out and then he wanted the tracks done as *singles*, not as album tracks. I never wanted to work with Phil again after that. My nerves were shattered, and everyone was exhausted."

Spector poured everything into the record—sleigh bells, chimes galore, the sound of music boxes and neighing horses. Darlene Love singing "White Christmas," the Ronettes performing "I Saw Mommy Kissing Santa Claus," and LaLa Brooks singing "Parade of the Wooden Soldiers"—the result should have been kitsch of the highest order. But Jack Nitzsche's gorgeous arrangements, and the sheer, unadulterated joy evident in all the performances, elevated the music to something quite magical—innocent and knowing at the same time: a vision of all the happy Christmases Spector had dreamed of and never known.

The title of the album, *A Christmas Gift for You from Phil Spector*, was a measure of just how much Spector now saw himself as the main attraction. But his most vainglorious gesture was to be found on the final track. While violins played "Silent Night" and an ethereal choir crooned behind him, Spector delivered a soliloquy of wincingly contrived sincerity, thanking all those who had worked on the album, and his audience "for giving me the opportunity to relate my feelings of Christmas through the music that I love." Larry Levine would recall that the soliloquy originally lasted more than five minutes, Spector "extolling his virtue, how great he was, while trying to sound humble," until he was persuaded to trim it back to two minutes.

Afterward, according to Denny Bruce, Spector and Jack Nitzsche amused themselves by recording alternative versions: "Hello, this is Phil Spector. It's Christmas—why don't you go fuck yourselves."

As well as playing on Spector sessions, Nino Tempo was also pursuing a career as a singer. Along with his sister April Stevens, he recorded singles for United Artists and Capitol, before signing for Ahmet Ertegun's Atlantic subsidiary, Atco. Their first release in 1962, "Sweet and

Lovely," charted at number 77, but the follow-up, "Paradise," failed even to make the Top 100.

Spector felt he could do better with the duo and, one night over dinner, told Tempo that if he could extricate himself from his Atlantic contract, he, Spector, would sign Nino and April to Philles "and make us stars." Tempo asked Ahmet Ertegun to be released from his contract, but Ertegun told him that Atlantic wanted one last try; if the next record flopped, then Nino and April were free to go. The record Ertegun decided to release was a version of the 1934 standard "Deep Purple." Recorded at the same sessions as "Paradise," the song had already been dismissed by Ertegun as "embarrassing" and "unreleasable."

Tempo couldn't have been happier. "I played Phil a DJ copy on this little broken-down Victrola at my parents' house, and he said, 'This could be a smash.' I said, 'It could be, but it won't—it'll be one of the best-kept secrets in the world.' So after about three weeks and bad reviews, Phil says, 'How's it doing?' I said, 'It died.' He said, 'Okay, good. Start looking for material.'

"Then one day I'm gazing at the sun in the backyard and the phone rings: 'This is Jerry Wexler at Atlantic. Do you realize that you've got a smash? It's breaking all over the place.' And all I could think was: Oh shit!"

In the autumn of 1963, "Deep Purple" went to number 1 in the charts. Tempo never signed with Philles. But his friendship with Spector stayed strong. Whenever he was in Los Angeles, Spector would make a point of dropping by the family home, where Tempo still lived with his parents, for the ritual spaghetti dinners. Spector adored Tempo's father, and had his own pet name for him, Daddy Sam (it was the name that Tempo gave to his music publishing company, aping Spector naming his company Mother Bertha). Some years later, when Tempo's mother died, Spector would confess to his friend that he had always envied Tempo the warm family life that he had never experienced himself: "Phil told me it was almost like his own mother had passed away."

By comparison, Spector's relationship with his own family was as fraught as ever. Shirley had once been devoted to her younger brother, but his burgeoning success had put an increasing distance between them. At the same time, the incipient symptoms of mental neurosis that had been apparent to Annette Kleinbard and Marshall Lieb on the Teddy Bears' tours—the mood swings, the irrational temper tantrums and screaming fits—were now flowering into mental illness. Don Randi would remember her as "never quite all there." Spector had attempted to help Shirley, writing out checks and sometimes adding her name to his compositions so that she would receive some income from royalties.

He would often answer the phone to find her on the other end of the line, rambling incoherently. On one occasion, when Spector was at home in New York with Annette, Shirley called in a highly distressed state, claiming that her doctor wanted to hospitalize her, but that she didn't have the proper pajamas. A bemused Spector immediately contacted the doctor to see whether the hospitalization was necessary. When the doctor started talking about the cost of the hospitalization, Spector, suspicious he was being taken advantage of, started haggling over the price. "That was very characteristic of the way Phil did things," says Annette. "Very aggressive, and just nail them . . ." He eventually agreed to pay up—the first of many such payments he would make for Shirley's treatment.

His relationship with Bertha was no less fraught. Bertha was often to be found in Wallich's Music City, counting the number of Philles records that they stocked and sold, just as she had in the early days of the Teddy Bears. In her canasta and mah-jongg games with her friends, she would boast proudly about "my son the record producer." But in private she would reproach him constantly for his shortcomings, real or imagined. "They always argued," says Annette. "Bertha was very verbal, as is Phil. And that was odd to me because my family were very low key; there was never a cross word. But they would just scream at each other, about everything, whatever they were talking about, whether the color was brown or black. It really wasn't the issue; they were just arguing. It was always confrontational."

More disconcerting still for Spector was the way that Bertha would frequently arrive unannounced at Gold Star during sessions. "She was a funny woman," Stan Ross recalls. "She used to walk into the studio and touch the walls, like she was going to fall down, like a security thing. And she wasn't that old."

LaLa Brooks would find her sitting in the studio's small lounge, sometimes for hours on end—"a short lady with a perm and a pleasant smile; a typical Jewish mom"—clutching a sandwich or a carton of soup, waiting patiently to see her son.

"And it would be: 'LaLa, would you please tell Harvey that I am still out here waiting . . . Would you please tell Harvey I have a sandwich out here if he wants it . . .' And he would never let her in. I could never figure that out—because your mother is your mother, right? She would say, 'LaLa, would you please go in there one more time and ask Harvey if I can come in.' And Phil would say, 'Leave her out there. Leave her.'"

Sometimes I would bring the sandwich through, but he wouldn't eat it. He'd just push it to one side. And he'd scratch his head or pull his ear . . . one of those little tics he had. And I would think, Oh dear, both of them are crazy."

LaLa fancied that she could sense "a softness in Phil that could not get out. You could see it in his eyes, his body language. I always thought that if his childhood had been better as far as nurturing went, he could have been the softest, the most kindest person that anyone could have imagined. But there was this coldness there whenever his mother was around. I never once saw him open the door for her to the studio welcomingly, unless she pushed herself in when I wasn't there."

Jack Nitzsche enjoyed telling the story of the day Bertha did exactly that, walking into the control room unannounced, in the middle of a session. Hearing his mother's voice—"Hello, Harvey"—Spector exploded, "Get the fuck out of here!" Bertha simply crossed her arms and turned to Hal Blaine, who was also standing there. "Hal," she said, shaking her head, "do you talk to your mother like this?"

In the grip of his deepening obsession with Ronnie, Spector began to push the other artists on Philles to the back of his mind. Darlene Love was arguably the greatest female singer that Spector had ever worked with. Full of grit, passion and fervor, hers was one of the great soul voices of the era, and she should have been a much bigger star than she was. Love's second solo single, "Wait 'til My Bobby Gets Home" reached number 26 in September 1963, thirteen places higher than "(Today I Met) The Boy I'm Gonna Marry." Her third single, "A Fine, Fine Boy," written by Spector, Greenwich and Barry, was her best performance yet, a thunderous gospel-style song, which combined the galloping beat of "Da Doo Ron Ron" with a soaring get-happy chorus. But according to Love, Spector seemed to lose interest in the song as soon as he'd recorded it, and it stalled at number 53. Bob B. Soxx and the Blue Jeans had also been forgotten—"Not Too Young to Get Married" would be their last single. Affable and easygoing, Sheen was a particular favorite of Spector's. They would sometimes socialize together, which Spector rarely did with his other performers, and Spector would occasionally give the singer money for his traveling and hotel expenses. Sheen had worked uncomplainingly as Bob B. Soxx and singing backup on virtually every Philles recording, but whenever he broached the possibility of being given a shot as a solo performer, Spector would change the subject.

"Bobby felt that Phil never made the most of the acts he had," remembers Sheen's widow, Frances. "He said there were certain songs and things he wanted to do, but Phil would never let him do it. He didn't want Bobby to be a star. Bobby figured it was because he was a man, and Phil didn't want to have any male stars, only females. I think Bobby always felt that Phil really wanted to be the star, but Phil couldn't sing. He was living his life through the singers, but he kept them under his thumb. But I don't think Bobby felt hard done by. I think he was grateful to be out there singing—that was enough for him."

LaLa Brooks too felt that Spector "lived through his artists. Phil didn't have what it took to be a singer, but he wanted so bad to be that star, and he certainly didn't want anybody around him to be bigger than him. With Phil it was: 'I made you and I can break you.' He would rather kick your ass, destroy you and put you out on the street because that way he has the control. Because when you're ditched and gone, he's still Phil Spector, the genius. He was never going to let you out of the cage."

From the moment she first met Ronnie Bennett, LaLa Brooks had noted her sexual precocity, her seductive, come-hither manner.

"I can see her now with her minidress, her hair up and a drink in her hand . . . woo! She look *grown*! Ronnie was just down-to-earth, sleazy—but on a nice level. She would say, 'Girl, how the fuck are you?' Ha, ha, ha. 'Girl, you are so fucking pretty . . .' That was how she spoke. She was always open and she was always a goodhearted person from the day that I met her.

"We'd be in the studio, and she'd have these nice, sexy little outfits on—I think all the musicians would be thinking, Voom, voom, voom! She carried herself sexy with everyone in the studio, so you wouldn't necessarily think of her as just Phil's—even though she was. She'd have that body language of getting up close to him, but Phil would be trying to play it cool. He'd say, 'Go back on the mike and do that note over again.' You wouldn't see that feeling on him as much as you would see it on her. But you knew it was there."

In the autumn of 1963, the Ronettes were invited on tour with Dick Clark's Cavalcade of Stars. But Spector told Ronnie he needed her in the studio to record a follow-up to "Be My Baby," a new song he had written with Greenwich and Barry. Nedra and Estelle were superfluous; anybody could provide the backing vocals. Ronnie's cousin Elaine took her place on tour.

If writing "Be My Baby" had been Spector's love call to Ronnie, her performance on "Baby, I Love You" was her answer. The whoa-ohs that open the record sounded not only like a heart-clutching sigh, but also a premonition of something dangerous—a love affair that was gathering in intensity as inexorably as Spector's production, carried along on a titanic choir and a drift of strings, the sound both spacious and dense.

From the earliest days of Philles, each new release would be stamped with a small, barely perceptible testament to Spector's love for his wife—the words "Phil + Annette" inscribed on the run-out grooves. With "Baby, I Love You," the practice ceased. By now Spector and Ronnie had started an affair, meeting surreptitiously in hotels and, under the guise of "rehearsals," at his office on Sixty-second Street. For Nedra Talley, the growing intimacy between Ronnie and Spector was evidence not only of how intent he now was on separating Ronnie from the rest of the group, but also of her cousin's growing ambition.

"We'd started out as a trio, and that's what it was supposed to be. So there was a side where I could see where Phil's motives were to control Ronnie—promise her that she would be a star on her own. And when Ronnie began showing an interest in Phil, I knew. This was not the romantic thing with the wind blowing in the hair. There was no wind blowing. Ronnie and I had grown up so close, our lives were completely intertwined, that I knew her personal taste in men. And I said this to Ronnie—'Oh, here's Phil Spector and he's this gorgeous guy that you just can't stop looking at? That is not Phil Spector.' Phil was this little guy that was weak of chin and drooled a little bit, so let's get real. My cousin knew what she wanted. She wanted to be a star."

In her autobiography, Ronnie Bennett claims that when she began her affair with Spector she had no idea that he was married. The women's clothes that she once saw in his apartment, Spector explained away as belonging to his sister Shirley. It was not until Darlene Love took her to one side in Gold Star that she learned the truth. She evidently took it with a commendable mixture of sangfroid and pragmatism. "I felt terrible for a few days, like somebody had died," she writes, but "for a girl singer in the sixties, your producer was your lifeline . . . The way I saw it, my choice was simple. I could keep my mouth shut and hold on to my career, my relationship, and my family. Or I could confront Phil now and throw it all away."

She kept her mouth shut.

The first Annette knew of the affair was when a friend told her. Spector had told Annette that he was going to the studio for a rehearsal, and she paid a visit to a friend, Lindy Foreman, who had recently moved to New York and who was well connected in the music business. As they talked, Lindy mentioned the rumors that Phil was getting rather close to Ronnie. "I had had complete trust and faith in him up to that point," Annette remembers. "My heart kind of clutched." Through the window, she and Lindy could see into a neighboring apartment; a man had pulled up his shade and was masturbating in full view of them. "The two of us sat there, thinking men are dogs, and you know that's true."

Annette hurried home and telephoned the studio. Spector wasn't there.

"It was about midnight now. Then I thought, Oh God, he's downstairs in the office and he's not alone. We had an intercom between our apartment and the office. I thought, okay, he's busted. So I buzzed. He picked up the phone, and I said, 'Okay, what's happening?' And he fumbled out, 'I'm here rehearsing.' And I got very upset. I didn't say anything. I just went downstairs and started banging on the door. And he wouldn't answer.

"I went back up to the apartment in tears, and he called me back on the intercom, and I said something about 'your whore.' I'm not saying I handled it well, but it was difficult. I was pretty hysterical.

"Then he came up and proceeded to start yelling at me—the argument side of him. He said, 'Look, I'm with Ronnie and it's not what you think. Come downstairs and we'll be standing there and you can see; don't come out of the elevator.' So I went downstairs, the door was open and I could see them face-to-face. And I literally thought I was going to puke."

That same night, Annette moved out of the apartment into a hotel. Within a couple of weeks, however, Spector had taken a new apartment around the corner on York Avenue and Annette moved back into their old home.

She was, she says, in a state of total shock. "I had never expected anything like that would happen with Phil. I had the idealism of youth. I had no perspective, no clue. And he never admitted it. He never said he was sorry. That night we argued and he was just screaming. I'd seen him screaming before, but not at me. But Phil's like a boxer on the ropes. He would just come back flailing and swinging. When he's faced with an adversary, he's a fighter to the end."

Looking back, Annette began to wonder whether Spector had ever really loved her at all.

"I think I represented a challenge, someone with a mind. I think he saw me as a combination of somebody he looked up to, and like a trophy—a pretty woman. But his actions did not show he loved me, ever.

"I don't think Phil knows how to love. I don't think he has equal relationships. He doesn't see the value in another person. It's: 'Where do you fit into my puzzle, what piece can I put you in?'

"He was funny, charming, charismatic and talented. He had a great personality and a wonderful sense of humor. But he was totally unconnectable. He needed his yes men and his bodyguards and people around him, but he would never let anybody get close to him emotionally. He said to me once, 'I don't need love, I don't like love. I don't want love.' But to me that was a defense mechanism of a man who needed and wanted love desperately. It was deeper than being afraid of love. It was *cannot.* I even thought at times, God this guy is stunted.

"It was as if all his emotional life went into his music. That became his modus operandi and his survival mechanism. And it was such a huge gift that he could make his entire identity from that. He identified only as the music maker, the genius, the manipulator, the Svengali. All those things that drove him and drove him. It was his way of saying, 'This is me. I'm the greatest. Number One.' I think if Phil hadn't had that and was just a regular guy, he would have killed himself."

In the first week of November, "Baby, I Love You" entered the American Top 40, eventually rising to number 24. At the same time, copies of *A Christmas Gift to You* were being shipped out to distributors, ready to deluge the Christmas market. On November 22, President John F. Kennedy was assassinated in Dallas, Texas.

The Ronettes were on tour and happened to be in the city on the day that Kennedy died. "We heard the president was coming, so we stayed up all night to see him," Nedra remembers. "We were looking out of the window, waiting, and the TV was on in the room and all of a sudden he was shot. We were completely blown out of the water. Of course, we didn't perform. And then we were checking out of the hotel, just sitting there in the bar, waiting for the bus, and it came on TV when Ruby shot Oswald. Everybody was devastated."

In the mood of national shock and mourning, Spector immediately withdrew the Christmas album from release. "A president died and the public changed," he would later explain. "How would you like to put out a fifty-five-thousand-dollar album the same week as something like the president being assassinated took place?"

Spector too went into mourning, for Kennedy and the record.

11

"The Wall of Sound, It Kinda Sounds Tired"

In January 1964, Phil Spector traveled to Britain for the first time. He had negotiated a deal to release Philles records in Britain on the London-American label, a subsidiary of Decca, one of the three major companies (the others were EMI and Pye) that effectively controlled the British music industry. The Crystals, Bob B. Soxx, and the Ronettes had all enjoyed massive hits, and Spector was now being trumpeted as American pop's new wunderkind.

The Ronettes had arrived in England shortly before him, topping the bill on a tour of provincial cinemas and theaters. Their support act was a coming English rhythm and blues band called the Rolling Stones. In their slinky, figure-hugging dresses and teased hair, the Ronettes were catnip, and Ronnie was puzzled why the Stones seemed singularly immune to the girls' charms, merely nodding to them before and after shows. It was only when she asked the group's manager Andrew Loog Oldham why "the boys" were being so unfriendly that the reason became clear. Spector had telegrammed Oldham with a terse instruction: "Keep the Stones away from my girls."

Oldham and Spector had history. In the early '60s, Oldham was the nearest equivalent to Phil Spector the British music scene had to offer— a cocky, precocious brat, who combined nerve and style in equal measure, who threw tantrums and made demands. Before Oldham, the English record business was run largely by hangovers from Tin Pan Alley, cautious men in bad suits who tended to view pop music as an aberrant and short-lived branch of the light-entertainment industry, and liked to play things by the book. Oldham, who saw pop music as a higher calling, tore the book up.

A war baby, the illegitimate son of an American airman, he demon-

strated an early infatuation with glamour. As a student at Wellingbor-
ough he affected a hearing aid in honor of the "Prince of Wails," Johnnie Ray, and did a piano act à la Liberace. Leaving school at sixteen, he
quickly moved on to the Chelsea scene, working as a window-dresser
for the fashion designer Mary Quant by day, and by night waiting on
tables at Ronnie Scott's jazz club. His true gift was for insinuating himself into the affections of movers and shakers. By the age of nineteen he
had sidestepped into the pop business, working for the Beatles' press
agent Tony Barrow, until a tip from a music journalist led him to a dingy
pub in south London where he discovered his Holy Grail—an unknown
group called the Rolling Stones. Oldham was transfixed, less by the
Stones' rough-and-ready versions of black rhythm and blues songs, than
by the palpable wave of sexual energy coursing through the young girls
hugging the front of the narrow stage as the group performed. Oldham
could recognize his destiny when it was staring him in the face.

Within a matter of days, he had proposed himself as the group's
manager, and quickly set about shaping them in his preferred image by
a series of adroit maneuvers. He fired the hapless pianist Ian Stewart,
because he was "ugly." ("Stars," Oldham would later write in his autobiography, *Stoned*, "must be killers, always striking first and last." Stewart
obligingly stayed on as the group's road manager.) He finessed their first
single, a reworking of Chuck Berry's "Come On," into the charts by rig-
ging sales at chart-return shops. And he shrewdly encouraged Mick Jagger and Keith Richards to start writing their own songs, by locking
them in a bedroom and refusing to feed them until they had produced
the goods. More tellingly, he fostered a dishabille "bad boy" image that
would guarantee newspaper column inches. Ironically, it was the popularity of the Stones' rivals the Beatles that made this ploy possible. The
Beatles were working-class boys whose rough edges had been blunted
by their more conservatively minded manager Brian Epstein. The triumph of the neatly suited, parent-friendly mop-tops left a yawning gap
for a group that would appeal to more rebellious teenage spirits. In
1963, when Oldham engineered the newspaper headline "Would You
Let Your Daughter Marry a Rolling Stone?" the shudders of revulsion
across middle England were palpable.

With his partner, Tony Calder, Oldham set up his own management
and music publishing company. He went on to discover Marianne
Faithfull ("in another century you'd set sail for her, in 1964 you'd record
her") and to found one of Britain's first independent labels, Immediate
Records.

Spector was Oldham's model, his hero, his inspiration. Like Spector,

Oldham affected the dandified clothes, the twenty-four-hour shades, the air of cocky, sardonic languor. He rode around town in a Cadillac; his driver carried a gun, not only illegal in Britain but virtually unheard of. As Spector had taken on "the short-armed fatties" of the American music business, so Oldham determined to wage a similar war of attrition against the plutocrats and Denmark Street spivs who ran the British industry.

In 1963 when Oldham and Calder traveled to America, to make connections, Oldham's first priority was to pay homage to Spector. "Andrew was in awe," remembers Calder. "First of all, Phil was American! We hadn't seen Americans before. Americans were exotic! And it was all there: the hair, the arrogance—he was very arrogant, and rightfully so because he was so successful—the high-pitched Ahmet Ertegun voice. Ahmet was Phil's hero. You'd say, 'We saw Ahmet last week.' And it would be: 'That cocksucking douche bag.' If you didn't know Phil you'd think he was being insulting. But it was actually total respect. And that was the only way he knew how to express it."

Recognizing something of himself in Oldham, and flattered by his attention, Spector obligingly played the role of mentor. "He gave us the rundown on everything," says Calder. "Distribution, how you get records on the radio, how you put them in the right places, where you put the stock. It was a master class. For Andrew, it was a case of being wrapped up in the game. Idolizing, respecting—and getting some fucking great ideas off him, because we always worked on the basis that whatever we nicked and adapted we always took the best. And at that time Phil Spector was the best. He'd shown the bravado, the bullshit. These are the enemy—all the straights—we'll beat them. And it was like a Panzer division coming toward you. He blew open doors just by walking up to them. 'Hi Phil, how are you?' 'Fuck off.' And that bullshit works. It really works."

At the end of their stay, to cement the friendship, Spector presented Oldham and Calder with a gold watch apiece from Sy Devore. Calder wore his for years, "until my wrist went green . . ."

When Spector landed at London's Heathrow airport, Oldham was waiting to greet him. He was accompanied by Maureen Cleave, a journalist for the London *Evening Standard*. A clever girl of impeccable breeding, with a Mary Quant bob and a cut-glass accent, Cleave was one of the first journalists in Britain to write seriously about pop music, and her columns were hugely influential. It was to Cleave, two years later, that

John Lennon would confide his belief that the Beatles were "more popular than Jesus."

Spector, Cleave noted, had traveled from New York dressed in "a dark suit, lined in scarlet, a black brocade waistcoat with the pattern standing a quarter-of-an-inch off the surface, a pin-tucked mustard shirt, and mustard silk handkerchief. At the end of the tight trousers were long, pointed, brown shoes with spats to match. In his tie was a pearl stickpin; looped across his stomach a gold watch chain. And he carried a small briefcase with the word 'Phillip' tooled in gold in one corner." He walked "a little like Charlie Chaplin, i.e., for every three steps forwards he takes one backwards or to the side. He is a man you can't take your eyes off."

"I've been told I'm a genius," Spector informed Cleave, en route from the airport. "What do you think?" Cleave took note of his prodigious accomplishments—"fifteen hits in a row," the musical breakthrough of the Wall of Sound. His records, he told her, were "built up like a Wagner opera. They start simply and they end with dynamic force, meaning and purpose. It's in the mind. I dreamed it up. It's like art movies. I aimed to get the record industry forward a little bit, make a sound that was universal."

"He has a Cadillac limousine," Cleave wrote, "and a tendency suddenly to give everybody presents. He originally meant to be a lawyer and can stenotype 300 words a minute. He admires Abraham Lincoln and Lenny Bruce." "I am the least quoted man in the industry," Spector told her. "I stick to my little bourgeois haunts and I don't bother with the masses."

Arriving at their destination, Spector stepped out of the car. There was a stiff wind, Cleave now remembers, and she noticed that he involuntarily put his hand up to clutch at his head. After years of fussing and fretting over his thinning hair, Spector, it seemed, had finally surrendered to the inevitable and was now wearing a toupee.

Decca had arranged for Spector to be installed in an efficiency in Dolphin Square, close by the Thames Embankment, and a young assistant from the promotions department named Tony King was assigned to look after him. On his first day in town, Spector announced that he wanted to go shopping. King took him to a West End department store, where Spector embarked on a hurricane spending spree. When it came to settling the bill, King was dismayed when Spector announced that he had no money, and that he expected Decca to pay for his purchases out of his royalties. An anxious King was obliged to telephone his office for authorization. "I was shocked, but Phillip was deeply satisfied at the outcome. I think he was trying it on. He was very funny—tiny, tiny with that strange high-pitched voice—and kind of sweet-natured really. But a bit like a naughty schoolboy, not helped by the fact that Andrew was tagging along with him most of the time. Andrew was obsessed with Phil and obviously modeled himself on him. They were getting into all sorts of mischief."

The satisfactory outcome of this small demonstration of his power appeared to reassure Spector that he was in good hands.

Over the following week, Spector made all the mandatory stops on his Grand Tour of the English pop scene, feted as if he were a greater star than any of the artists he produced (he was), and luxuriating in the attention and acclaim. He dined with George Harrison of the Beatles, enjoying Harrison's tale of how the group had included their version of "To Know Him Is to Love Him" on their demo recording for Decca— and been turned down. He appeared as a guest on *Juke Box Jury*, a television show in which a panel of celebrities would adjudicate on the new releases, voting them a hit or a miss, and put in the obligatory appearance at the studios of Britain's most influential pop music television program, *Ready Steady Go!* The Ronettes were in London, having concluded their tour, and one night in their room at the Strand Palace Hotel Spector rehearsed them on a new song, "(The Best Part of) Breakin' Up." "Sitting there listening to them, my scalp tingled," Tony King remembers. "But the funny thing was, we got a phone call from the front desk complaining about the noise. I thought Phil would flip, but he just laughed it off and we all went off for dinner. It was pretty obvious there was this thing between Phil and Ronnie; you could just feel the connection."

On another occasion, during a dinner at Mirabelle, apparently beside himself with excitement, Spector dashed out of the restaurant, commandeered the Rolls and drove off alone into the night, returning with the news that he'd almost crashed the car driving on the wrong side of the road.

At Oldham's instigation, Spector tried to arrange a meeting with the eccentric English producer Joe Meek, who worked out of a home recording studio above a leather-goods shop in a run-down area of north London. Meek was one of the first producers to experiment with reverb and electronic effects, and his instrumental "Telstar," by the Tornadoes, had been a number 1 hit on both sides of the Atlantic. But when Spector got through to him on the telephone, Meek railed against him, accusing him of stealing his ideas, and slammed the phone down with such venom that he broke the receiver.

Spector loved the Stones and wanted to release the group's records in America on Philles. Oldham was thrilled at the offer and together they went to meet the chairman of Decca, Sir Edward Lewis—a man who wore the chalk-stripe suits and mannered air of a merchant banker. But Lewis refused to release the Stones from their contract. "He was the first person to say no to Phil Spector," Tony Calder says. "Phil was extremely pissed off."

That same evening, Spector attended a Stones recording session on Denmark Street. As the evening wore on, they were joined by Graham Nash and Allan Clarke from the Hollies, and by Gene Pitney, who had arrived straight from the airport, carrying a cache of duty-free brandy. The session quickly degenerated into a drunken jam session, culminating in an improvised tribute to Oldham, "Andrew's Blues," sung by Spector and Mick Jagger in a parody of Sir Edward Lewis's pukka English accent.

> *Yes, now Andrew Oldham sittin' on a hill with Jack and Jill*
> *Fucked all night and sucked all night and taste that pussy till it taste*
> *just right . . .*
> *Come and get it, little Andrew, before Sir Edward takes it away*
> *from you.*

Tony Hall, Decca's head of promotions, was a ubiquitous and popular figure on the London music scene, and his gatherings were legendary. Hall lived on Green Street in Mayfair, directly opposite an apartment where George Harrison and Ringo Starr were staying at the time. "Any time they wanted to come over, because there were always kids hanging around outside their door, they'd have to order a taxi, leap into it, drive round the block and come back on my side of the road, where I'd be waiting with my door open."

The Beatles were preparing to leave for their first visit to America, and Hall threw a farewell party for them and the Ronettes.

"It was a very sweet evening," remembers Tony King, "because the Beatles, as big as they were at that time, had no idea what was about to hit them when they went to America, so they were very apprehensive. And Estelle and George had started to be interested in each other. Everybody was drinking Scotch and Coke and getting a bit pissed. We were all dancing along to Martha and the Vandellas' "Heat Wave," and Ronnie suddenly let rip, joining in with that great vibrato of hers. And I can remember John Lennon's face, looking at her and registering 'oh, you're the real article.' "

"Ronnie," Tony Calder remembers, "was the bird that everyone wanted to shag. Everybody was salivating over this incredible little thing sitting in this chair. Then Andrew came in, flapping around all over Phil, and Phil was being 'This is my party'—even though it wasn't. He was getting very wound up about the attention everybody was paying to Ronnie. You could feel the sexual tension, every guy in the place looking at her. Because she was exotic. And she was American!"

Two days later, on Friday, February 7, the Beatles boarded Pan Am flight 101 from Heathrow airport, with Phil Spector in tow. He had originally planned to take an earlier flight but, paranoid as ever, had changed his arrangements to travel with the group, trusting to the fates that no plane carrying the biggest pop group in the world could possibly crash.

Dressed in a short overcoat and a corduroy Beatle cap, Spector followed the Beatles down the gangway of the plane at John F. Kennedy International Airport into a furnace of adulation. The only problem was, it wasn't for him. Spector's visit to London had consolidated his position at the top of the music business tree. He had cemented friendships with the two biggest groups on the British music scene, the Beatles and the Rolling Stones, who would soon follow their British rivals to America.

Spector was thrilled at the music, the breath of fresh air it carried. But he could little have imagined that the impending British Invasion was to prove the harbinger of his decline.

A week before their arrival in America, the Beatles' "I Want to Hold Your Hand" went to number 1 on the *Billboard* charts. On February 15, their first American album, *Meet the Beatles*, also went to number 1, where it would stay for the next eleven weeks. In the last week of February, to meet the burgeoning demand of Beatlemania, half a ton of Beatles wigs were shipped to America, quickly followed by 24,000 rolls of Beatles wallpaper. The torrent had become unstoppable.

Spector's initial response to the phenomenon was to attempt to capitalize on it. Sonny Bono had been pestering him to give his girlfriend Cher a chance to record. Spector now hurried her into the studio to record a "tribute" to the Beatles' drummer, "Ringo I Love You," hastily scratched together by Spector and two New York songwriters he had recently begun working with, Vinnie Poncia and Pete Andreoli. Rather than using Cher's name, Spector released it under the pseudonym Bonnie Jo Mason. Nor did he wish to sully the name of Philles. The record was released on a subsidiary label, named in honor of his wife Annette— a gesture, according to Vinnie Poncia, that was intended to "anesthetize the situation between them," but which, given the abysmal quality of the record, must have seemed more like an insult. It was a relief to all parties when the record sank without trace.

In the months following his return from London, Spector made several attempts at reconciliation with Annette. His triumphant visit to Britain had reinvigorated his self-confidence, temporarily banishing his worries and self-doubts. "He was very happy about his reception there," Annette remembers. "You could see his attitude changing with all the recognition and success."

On his journey to London, Spector had been shadowed by a powerful and imposing presence that went by the name of Red—or "Big Red," as Spector called him. Red would be the first in a succession of bodyguards that Spector would hire over the years, partly for protection, but mostly it seemed as a demonstration of his rising status and power. "Phil wanted to be Elvis and Frank Sinatra combined," one friend remembers. "Those were his heroes. And he wanted that kind of persona, the cool, aloof thing, the entourage—all that protected crap."

Spector's flamboyant appearance—the hair, the elevator shoes, the ruffled shirts—had always drawn stares, and sometimes insults, but now with bodyguards at his side, he seemed almost to relish the prospect of confrontation, safe in the knowledge that if anybody caused trouble he had muscle on hand to deal with it.

"In 1965, you walk into a Hollywood restaurant looking like Phil Spector, there would be silence," Denny Bruce says. "Like, what the hell is that?! Which is why he'd have bodyguards. He would stand there with shades on, a P. J. Proby billowing shirt, a vest, two guys behind him. He'd walk over to somebody who'd laughed out loud, and it would be: 'What's so funny?' He antagonized people. And he enjoyed that attention."

"Phil thrived on being different," Nedra Talley says. "He didn't want to just be a little Jewish boy. So he developed a look, but with that look he got a lot of harassment. People would be calling him faggot and all kinds of things, and he'd just have to swallow it. But when he had his bodyguards with him, it got to be that he would pick fights. We'd be in a restaurant and he'd walk out first, and it would be just like a magnet where people would be drawn to say something to him. Then Phil would say something back to them, and just when it was getting ugly he would step back and his two guys would step out from behind and handle the situation. It was like a trap."

Like LaLa Brooks, Nedra sensed that Spector's braggadocio was actually compensation for a much deeper underlying insecurity. Spector, she thought, was "a tortured soul." He had told the Ronettes the story of how when touring with the Teddy Bears he had been set upon in a lavatory and pissed on.

"When he told us that, something inside of me went out to him. I loved that song, 'To Know Him,' and the thought of this little guy who was too small to defend himself getting pissed on for just trying to do his thing, it broke my heart. So I always thought that, with the bodyguards, Phil was just getting his own back."

But, to others, it seemed that Spector never quite knew when to stop. On one occasion, he even instructed his bodyguards to beat up Larry Levine, after an argument at Gold Star. "I walked out of the studio," Levine remembers, "and he sent these guys out to hit me—a couple of young gorillas. They didn't know what to do; they obviously weren't going to hit me. It was just another way of exhibiting power."

After the run of successes they had provided for the Crystals and the Ronettes, Ellie Greenwich and Jeff Barry had fallen out with Spector. The cause was a song called "Chapel of Love," which the three partners had written together in the autumn of 1963. It was a song that returned to one of Barry and Greenwich's perennial themes—marriage and happy-ever-after—with an infectious, sing-along melody that seemed to lodge in the brain and wouldn't let go. Spector recorded the song with both the Ronettes and LaLa Brooks, but apparently unconvinced, decided not to release either version.

Barry and Greenwich, meanwhile, had been in discussions with Jerry Leiber and Mike Stoller about joining forces in a new label that Leiber and Stoller had set up called Red Bird. Their first signing was a trio of girls from New Orleans called the Dixie Cups—the perfect vehicle, Greenwich and Barry reasoned, for "Chapel of Love." "We always believed in that song," Ellie Greenwich would later tell Alan Betrock, "and we called Phil and asked him, 'Are you putting it out?' He said, 'I don't know . . . I don't think so . . . no, no, never coming out . . .' So we said, 'We're thinking of doing it,' and he said, 'No, no, you can't do that.' He always wanted to have total control over everything he had to do with. I don't know how happy he was that Jeff and I were going to do something on our own on the production level without him. He wasn't totally thrilled, but he didn't stop it."

Released in April 1964, "Chapel of Love" quickly went to the top of the American charts, replacing the Beatles' "Love Me Do" and remaining there for six weeks.

With Barry and Greenwich out of the picture, Spector started casting his net for other songwriters. He contacted his old friend Paul Case at Hill at Range, who introduced him to Vinnie Poncia and Peter Andreoli. At a meeting at Spector's office, Poncia and Andreoli ran through a number of song ideas. When they mentioned a title they were working on "(The Best Part of) Breakin' Up," Spector stopped them and told them they had a deal.

The song became the next Ronettes single. But while Barry and Greenwich's compositions flowed, this one stuttered, reaching only number 39 in the charts. (The throwaway instrumental on the B-side, "Big Red"—named in honor of Spector's bodyguard—seemed to be part of Spector's ongoing attempts at conciliation with Annette: she was credited as writer and therefore entitled to royalties.) In short order, Spector released two more singles sung by Ronnie under the name of Veronica, "So Young" and "Why Don't They Let Us Fall in Love?"— the first song the Ronettes had recorded at Gold Star a year earlier—but neither troubled the charts.

Spector seemed to have one obsession, and one obsession only. During the recording sessions he now insisted that Ronnie should sit with him in the control room, rather than fraternizing with the other singers and musicians. When they lunched with the producer Herb Alpert, Ronnie noticed that Spector put himself between her and Alpert, leaning in front of her whenever she spoke, apparently to prevent Alpert looking at her. In *Be My Baby* she recounts that when one evening during recording she and Nedra ducked out from the studio with Sonny Bono to pick up some hamburgers without telling Spector where she was going, he threw a fit, knocking over mike stands and strewing spools of tape over the studio. On another occasion, when she and Cher went dancing at the Purple Onion on the Strip, Spector tracked her down to the club and dragged her off the dance floor.

In his constant progress back and forth between New York and Los Angeles, Spector had neglected his business affairs. In the autumn of 1964, Chuck Kaye resigned, complaining that his salary wasn't enough to afford even a square meal. To replace him, Spector turned to a man named Danny Davis. Short, stocky and a spieler, Davis had once worked the Borscht Belt as a comedian before going into the record business as a promotions man. He worked for Big Top Records, where Spector first met him, promoting the Ray Peterson records that Spector produced for Dunes.

In 1963, Davis went to work for Don Kirshner, as vice president of Kirshner's Dimension Records. He had been there only a few months when Kirshner and his partner Al Nevins made a deal to sell Aldon Music to Screen Gems, the recording and publishing subsidiary of Columbia Pictures. Kirshner and Nevins were reported to have received some $2 million for the company. Nevins became a consultant to Columbia Pictures, while Kirshner was named executive vice president, responsible for all Columbia Pictures–Screen Gems publishing and recording activities. His team of Aldon writers dutifully followed him out of 1650 Broadway to new offices on Fifth Avenue, next door to Tiffany. Kirshner promptly folded Dimension Records, and Danny Davis found himself out of a job.

The situation Davis inherited at Philles was growing increasingly parlous. Not only had Spector's constant absences made his day-to-day business dealings more difficult; more significantly it was clear that he was losing his grip on the marketplace. The Ronettes' first single, "Be My Baby," had been an enormous hit, but successive releases had proved disappointing. While "Baby, I Love You" reached number 24, both "(The Best Part of) Breakin' Up" and "Do I Love You?" had barely scraped into the Top 40. Both singles by Veronica had vanished without trace, as had a single by Darlene Love, "Stumble and Fall." It was to be her last for Philles.

In desperate need of inspiration, Spector turned back to the reliable mother lode of Don Kirshner. It had been almost two years since he had worked with Barry Mann and Cynthia Weil, and like other writers of the Aldon (now Screen Gems) family, the pair had struggled to find a place in the new musical order being shaped by the British Invasion, despite contributing "We Gotta Get Out of This Place" to the Animals. They jumped at the chance to work again with Spector, and over two weeks in the autumn of 1964 the three writers convened in Spector's New York office, bent on fashioning a song that would restore the Ronettes to the charts.

In October, Spector called Ronnie and his musicians into Gold Star to record "Walking in the Rain." Barry Mann would later try to distance himself from the song, dismissing it merely as an imitation of the girl group style that came so easily to Jeff Barry and Ellie Greenwich—"I was just trying to sound adolescent." But he was wrong. "Walking in the Rain" was the most gorgeous Ronettes song yet.

Beginning with a thunderclap (from a sound-effects tape unearthed by Larry Levine), the song struck a perfect note of wistful longing. Spector's production—the gently resounding chimes, a discreet horn figure, the celestial choir, and the way the sound effects of distant thunder joined seamlessly with the percussion—seemed to create a vast, echoing backdrop for Ronnie's yearning vocal. She had never sung better, and would never sing better again.

Spector was exultant and convinced it would be an enormous hit. He was crushed when it reached only number 23. Nor was Larry Levine consoled when he found himself nominated at that year's Grammy Awards for Best Sound Effect for "Walking in the Rain." "It was just a sound-effects tape! Can you imagine the dearth of nominees they had in order to make that a nomination? It was great to be nominated, but I felt so stupid."

For Spector, the failure of the record seemed only to vindicate his growing sense that the industry was turning against him. In January 1964 he gave an interview to the British music paper *Melody Maker* in which he prophesied that his sound would "die because of the natural animosity in the record industry on the part of DJs. I guess they get a bit resentful of a guy all on his own doing so well. But more than anything, I feel they're jealous because I'm so young to have made so much money in a business they thought they knew everything about. They never seemed to believe what I always thought—that every record can be a hit if you concentrate on it enough."

As Philles' West Coast promotions man, Sonny Bono was in a better position than most to realize that the Wall of Sound was beginning to crumble. Making his customary round of the local radio stations to promote "Walking in the Rain," Bono had received the same ominous message. When he played the song to a usually reliable DJ at the L.A. radio station KFWB, the response was distinctly lukewarm. "He gave me a less than enthusiastic look—actually a grimace," Bono would later recall. " 'You know, the thunder and the tricks and the Wall of Sound . . . it kinda sounds tired.' "

Steeling himself, Bono telephoned Spector to recount the conversation. It was, he later recalled, "my fatal mistake." There was an agonizingly long pause at the other end of the line that Bono recognized as his death sentence.

Bono's gaffe fueled the growing resentment that Spector had been feeling toward his gofer. After spending almost two years in Spector's shadow, quietly watching and learning, Bono had begun making efforts to further his own and Cher's careers. In the spring of 1964 he wrote a song called "Baby Don't Go" and produced a demo of himself performing it with Cher. Bono played it to Spector in the hope that he would produce the song for release. Spector passed, but he did offer Bono $500 for half the publishing rights. Encouraged, Bono began producing records on the side for the Vault and Reprise labels. To Spector, it all smelled dangerously of disloyalty. The telephone call was the final straw. Spector now decided to dispense with Bono's services. Rather than tell him personally, Spector instructed Danny Davis to deliver the coup de grâce by telephone from New York. Bono left without so much as a good-bye.

12

"The Last Word in Tomorrow's Sound Today"

At first glance, the Righteous Brothers presented a picture of Mutt-'n'-Jeff incongruity. Bill Medley was tall, dark and cadaverous with an undertaker's pallor; Bobby Hatfield, short, fair, fresh-faced and button-nosed. But improbable as they might have looked, they were the blackest white singers Phil Spector had ever heard. Medley sang in a dark and throaty baritone; Hatfield, in a keening tenor, which reminded Spector of one of his favorite singers, Clyde McPhatter. Together, their sound was pure, impassioned storefront gospel—"righteous," in the opinion of the black servicemen at the El Toro Marine base in San Diego where they often performed: hence the name. In 1962, they signed for a small Los Angeles label, Moonglow. Their first single, the exuberant "Little Latin Lupe Lu," went to number 39 in 1963. "Koko Joe"—a cover of an R&B hit for Don and Dewey that had been written by Sonny Bono in his days as an A&R man at Specialty—and a third single, "My Babe," written by Medley and Hatfield, both failed. All these records were made at Gold Star, and it was his old friend Stan Ross who first alerted Spector to the group. The Righteous Brothers had also performed on a bill at the Cow Palace in San Francisco with the Ronettes, where Spector himself appeared as "guest" leader of the band, quietly standing at the back of the stage, playing guitar.

Spector was galvanized—not only by the Brothers' singing, but also by the prospect they offered of a way out of his impasse. Shooting the messenger had not altered the harsh truth that Sonny Bono had delivered to Spector. The Wall of Sound—more specifically, the girl group sound—*was* getting kind of tired. And even Spector was beginning to recognize it. Jack Nitzsche would later recall how recording the

Ronettes' follow-up to "Walking in the Rain," "Born to Be Together," Spector had taken him to one side and told him, "It's all over. It's over. It's not here anymore." "The enthusiasm was gone," Nitzsche said. "We had done it so many times. The musicians were changing. They didn't want to work overtime for a deal. Everybody. It just wasn't the same spirit anymore. The spirit of cooperation started to change. And for Phil as well. It was a combination of things, and it just stopped being so much fun. The Beatles were coming . . ."

The Righteous Brothers provided a vision of redemption. Not only did they have precisely the kind of soulful voices Spector loved, but the fact that they were white men, he reasoned, would make them easier to sell to radio, television and a pop audience increasingly enamored of British pop groups. However, there was a downside to all this: Spector had grown used to working with artists he could easily manipulate and control; the Righteous Brothers had opinions of their own. Furthermore, they were already contracted to Moonglow—the best Spector could do was arrange a deal leasing them to Philles, rather than signing them directly, as he would have wished. But these, he believed, were just minor obstacles. Only later would they become major ones.

The deal that Spector signed with Moonglow's boss, R. J. van Hoogten, gave him the rights to record and release the Righteous Brothers on Philles in the United States, Canada and the United Kingdom, while Moonglow retained the rights for all other territories.

In search of material for his new signing, Spector turned back to Barry Mann and Cynthia Weil, sending them copies of the Righteous Brothers' Moonglow recordings. A new hit from the Motown group, the Four Tops, was rising up the charts at the time, the deliciously romantic "Baby I Need Your Loving." "[The Righteous Brothers] were singing Sam and Dave kind of stuff," Barry Mann later recalled. "We thought, Well, it would be great to do a ballad. We loved 'Baby I Need Your Loving' and it was kind of an inspiration . . ."

Sketching out a preliminary verse and chorus, the two songwriters flew out to Los Angeles, where Spector joined them in their suite at the Chateau Marmont to develop the song. The tune that Mann and Weil had written was in the same medium tempo, and with all the heart-clutching, anthemic quality of the Four Tops' song—and more. Cynthia Weil's lyric took the Four Tops' theme of yearning and transmuted it into loss, starkly declaring in its opening lines the evidence of a dying love—"You never close your eyes anymore when I kiss your lips . . ."

Even the title was a respectful nod to the song's original inspiration: "You've Lost That Lovin' Feelin'." Spector loved it but suggested that the tempo should be slower still, and added a masterstroke—a dramatic middle section, measured by a bass riff modeled on "La Bamba." With the change in tempo and the addition of the new section the finished song was almost twice as long as Mann and Weil's original demo— almost twice as long as any pop song of the time. But Spector refused to change a note. As autumn turned to winter, he prepared to make the biggest record of his life.

Despite his deepening involvement with Ronnie, and the acrimonious way in which their marriage had ended, Spector had been unable to let go of Annette. He had never admitted his infidelity, and he pleaded with her for them to get back together again, telling her that he would even drop the Ronettes from their contract if she would return to him. But for Annette it was impossible. "I just said, 'No way.' It devastated me."

By early 1964 she had moved out of the apartment on Sixty-second Street, but Spector would occasionally drop by to see her in her new home—"If I'd had a shred of self-respect at that point I would never have let him in the door"—and they spoke frequently on the phone. With his professional associates, he would wear his customary face of cocksure bravado and self-confidence. There were few people to whom he would dare to confide his fears, but Annette was one of them. Sometimes she would answer the telephone at three or four in the morning to find him on the other end of the line in California, anxiously seeking reassurance that he had not lost his gift, or his position, at the summit of the pop music hierarchy.

"It would be: 'Okay, the Beatles are number one, and the Stones are number two, but am I before Bob Dylan or after Bob Dylan?' And I'd say, 'No, you're definitely number three and Dylan's number four'— even though I didn't really think so. He never talked about Dylan's lyrics or his music. But always these conversations about where Phil fit in."

Now, as Spector worked with Mann and Weil at the Chateau Marmont on the new song for the Righteous Brothers, Annette flew out from New York to see him, staying with him at Brynmar, the modest, Spanish-style house that Spector rented in the Hollywood Hills. One night he played her a tape of the song-in-progress. Annette thought it was wonderful. "And then Phil told me that he'd come up with the phrase 'You've lost that lovin' feeling' and that it was written for me. It wasn't nice when he said that. Because he was totally another woman's man. I just remember at five in the morning I bolted up and said, 'I'm out of here.' I grabbed my stuff, and I went back to New York on the train that day."

Apparently unperturbed, Spector pressed on with his preparations for the sessions. For the first time since "He's a Rebel," two and a half years earlier, Jack Nitzsche had told Spector that he was unavailable. Nitzsche had begun to see a world beyond Phil Spector. When the Rolling Stones recorded some sessions at the RCA Studios in November, he was invited to sit in on keyboards, beginning a relationship with the group that would flourish over the next few years. Working with the Stones was a liberating experience for Nitzsche. He told Bill Wyman that they were "the first rock and roll band he'd met that were intelligent," and he relished the freedom to experiment and the way the Stones followed their own instincts in the studio. "The great new thing about them was, they'd record a song the way they had written it," Nitzsche said. "If it didn't work, nobody thought twice about making it a tango! They tried every way possible. Nobody had the big ego thing about keeping a song a certain way. That changed me. That was the first really free feeling I had in the studio." Over the next two years, Nitzsche would become something of a "sixth Stone" in the recording studio, playing piano and harpsichord on songs including "(I Can't Get No) Satisfaction," "Play with Fire" and "Let's Spend the Night Together."

Nitzsche had also accepted an offer to work as the arranger on *The TAMI Show*—TAMI stood for Teenage Awards Music International—a television special that brought together the cream of American and British Invasion performers, including the Stones, the Beach Boys, the Supremes and James Brown. When Nitzsche told Spector he was unable to arrange the Righteous Brothers session, a disgruntled Spector accused him of "a lack of loyalty" (notwithstanding the fact that he agreed to make a cameo appearance on *The TAMI Show* himself). Instead, he was obliged to take on another arranger, Gene Page.

When Spector first played "You've Lost That Lovin' Feelin' " to the Righteous Brothers on the piano in Gold Star, they were unimpressed. They were used to singing frenetic, gospel-tinged rhythm and blues; this sounded like a dirge. Furthermore, they were used to singing in unison: Spector wanted Medley to take the first two verses solo, with Hatfield only joining him when the song was more than halfway through.

"Bill really didn't want to do it," Larry Levine remembers. "He was the vocal one. He said, 'This is not right, because we're an act; we sing everything together, but Bobby sings almost nothing in this; it's all me.'

They really weren't impressed. And I remember saying to Bill, 'How could you not be excited by this? This could be a number-one record, a smash, and you're not excited!' "

But not even Spector could have guessed that what he was to conjure over the next two weeks in Gold Star's Studio A would be his greatest record ever, a work of epic grandeur that would become the most played pop single of all time.

From the first magisterial incantation of Bill Medley's deep, rich baritone—sounding as if it were echoing across a storm-tossed sea, to the measured beat of distant chiming bells—"You've Lost That Lovin' Feelin' " is a record that stops the heart. For the first two verses Medley beseeches and coaxes, laying bare the depths of his desolation. From the far distance, a choir, strings and the rattle of tambourines bear witness to his suffering, the verse punctuated by a bass note of almost funereal sorrow. Now the song builds teasingly to the second, glorious chorus, a storm no sooner conjured than it subsides into the middle section, as hushed and heartfelt as a prayer. A momentary respite, for now—fully two minutes, three seconds into the song—Bobby Hatfield's voice enters, as if from the wings, to engage in a furious call-and-response with his partner, each, it seems, urging the other to further extremes of despair. Now the fatalistic anguish of loss becomes a desperate plea for reconciliation and redemption—*Bring back that lovin' feelin'* —a plea that finally drifts into a far-distant silence, leaving you stunned in its wake. A masterpiece of chiaroscuro, of searing emotional light and darkness, of pain and catharsis, "You've Lost That Lovin' Feelin' " is the very summit of the producer's art.

Larry Levine for one was convinced that he had been present at a moment of greatness. "Absolutely, there was not a shadow of doubt in my mind about that. Particularly when it got to the ending, and it went to the congas—that was so amazing. But I remember Phil pacing up and down. His big concern that he voiced to me was: 'I don't know . . . it's the only song I've ever done without a backbeat; it doesn't have a back-beat, something you can tie on to, and I don't know if it's going to work.'

"There was an A&R guy doing something else at Gold Star, a friend of Phil's, and I remember Phil brought him into the control room. Phil wanted this guy to hear the song, because he really felt his input was meaningful. He was the first person to hear it, and so I played it back, and this guy said, 'Play it again.' So I did, and he said, 'Play it again. This is the greatest thing I ever heard.' So that's what Phil had even before he took the record back to New York."

Spector's own reservations about the record were compounded by its duration. At a time when most singles ran no longer than two minutes, thirty seconds, "You've Lost That Lovin' Feelin' " clocked in at an unprecedented 3:46. But Spector refused to cut a second of it and, in a hapless attempt to dupe radio programmers, printed a timing of 3:05 on the label.

The response from programmers and disc jockeys to the song was one of bemused incredulity. Bill Walsh, an independent promotions man in Boston, had long been one of Spector's most ardent champions and reliable sounding boards—the first person to whom Spector would send test pressings of each new release, soliciting an opinion. Walsh was "blown away" when he heard "Lovin' Feelin'." "But people just didn't get it," he remembers. "A common complaint was: 'It's too fucking long. Why don't you edit it, cut out a verse? We'd be able to play it then.' Secondly: 'It sounds like it's the wrong speed. He keeps yelling!' The Bill Gavin 'sheet,' which was the bible of the radio industry, actually said 'blue-eyed soul has gone too far'! My view was: Are you people insane? I remember I had to lock the door and pin this program director in Providence, Rhode Island, up against the wall, just to prove my point. I said, 'Do nothing else for the next five minutes but listen to this record, and bring up the volume while you're about it.' I got that record played under force and duress. But Phil's music required undivided attention, and not everybody could understand that."

But whatever the initial reservations of the radio industry, the song was unstoppable. By mid-December, five weeks after its release, "You've Lost That Lovin' Feelin' " had entered the Top 10. By Christmas it was number 1.

In Britain, an unlikely rival challenged the record's progress. Cilla Black had been spotted by Brian Epstein while working as the hat-check girl at the Cavern Club, and added to his roster of Liverpool artists. Earlier in 1964 she had enjoyed a number 1 record in Britain with a cover version of Dionne Warwick's "Anyone Who Had a Heart." Even before the Righteous Brothers' song had been released in Britain, Epstein had Black's own, distinctly insipid, version on the market.

Fearing that the Righteous Brothers' version would vanish without trace, Tony Hall, the promotions director of Decca, hastily contacted Spector and begged him to put Medley and Hatfield on a plane to London for a round of promotional appearances. At the same time, Spector's greatest champion, Andrew Loog Oldham, took up the challenge on his behalf, buying up advertising space at his own expense in the British music weeklies to issue an indignant clarion call.

YOU'VE LOST THAT LOVIN' FEELIN'
THE RIGHTEOUS BROTHERS

This advertisement is not for commercial gain, it is taken as something that must be said about the great new PHIL SPECTOR record, THE RIGHTEOUS BROTHERS singing YOU'VE LOST THAT LOVIN' FEELIN'. Already in the American Top Ten, this is Spector's greatest production, the Last Word in Tomorrow's Sound Today, exposing the overall mediocrity of the Music Industry.
Signed
Andrew Oldham
P.S. See them on this week's *Ready Steady Go!*

"We had a mad week of promotion," Tony Hall remembers, "and eventually through all the TV I managed to force the airplay. Cilla was at number three and the Righteous Brothers got to number eight. I had a party at my flat in Green Street, and Cilla was there with Eppy. He said, 'We'll be number one next week. You haven't a hope in hell.' I said, 'Give me a week, and I'll prove you wrong.' And the next week, the Righteous Brothers leapfrogged to number one."

Cilla Black, it was reported, graciously cabled her congratulations to the Righteous Brothers.

Many years later, Spector would reflect that "Lovin' Feelin' " was the summit of his achievements with Philles.

"You know, you don't make anything in the record business that lasts very long," he told the writer Richard Williams, "and when a record like that lasts a long time, it's really startling, because you don't have any Academy Awards for it. It's just nice to know that some people think that out of all the records ever made, it might be the very best. We wrote a very good song at that time."

13

"A Giant Stands 5'7""

By 1964 Phil Spector was beginning to gain recognition far beyond the confines of the music industry and to become a figure of national curiosity. Despite Beatlemania, pop music was still regarded largely as cultural detritus, seldom dignified with coverage in the mainstream American media, its language and customs apparently still a mystery, and an outrage, to the arbiters of culture and taste. But with his prodigious success, his wiggy outfits and his outspoken opinions, Spector was a story, and he increasingly found himself in demand from newspapers and television shows, to talk about the "teenage" movement, how it expressed a new kind of freedom—and how he, more than anyone, had his finger on the pulse of the times.

Invited to appear on a special edition of David Susskind's *Open End* show, dedicated to exploring "Rock 'n' Roll: The New Loud Sound from Tin Pan Alley," Spector found himself facing a combined assault from Susskind and the disc jockey William B. Williams, whose program *Make-Believe Ballroom* on the New York radio station WNEW was a redoubt of the swing jazz and crooners that rock and roll was rudely elbowing aside. (Williams, who gave Frank Sinatra his moniker "the Chairman of the Board," had a legendary loathing of the new music. WNEW once ran a newspaper advertisement with the caption "We asked William B. Williams what he thought of rock 'n' roll" over a large photo of the disc jockey holding his nose.) When Susskind started reciting the lyrics of "A Fine, Fine Boy" in a bored monotone, intended to demonstrate their banality, Spector responded by banging on the table in time to Susskind's voice—"What you're missing is the beat"—then rounded on Williams, asking how many times he played Monteverdi and Scarlatti on his radio show—"That's good music, why don't you play that? I don't hear you play that"—before delivering his parting shot: "I didn't come on this show to listen to somebody telling me I'm corrupting the youth of America. I could be home making money."

To Larry Levine, Spector's posturing on television was all part of a calculated attempt to build a public persona, and a measure of how much he was coming to believe it himself. "He really began believing in his own image, and I think it really affected him because whenever he had contact with the press or TV people, he'd live out the whole image with the dark glasses and the garbled manner. All the time he knew what was going on and he knew what to say and what not to say to sustain the image, and he was really always very together but he liked to give the opposite impression."

In January 1965, the *New York Herald Tribune* published Tom Wolfe's profile, lionizing Spector as the "first tycoon of teen." Beginning with the story of Spector turning round the airplane at Los Angeles, Wolfe went on to paint a portrait of the inexorable rise of the young, imperious, Cuban-heel-booted impresario, from what Spector described as "average lower middle class" origins, to become the most powerful man in American pop music.

Reading Wolfe's account one can detect evidence of Spector's gift for storytelling, and laying the foundations for myths that would endure for years to come. Wolfe describes how following the success of "To Know Him Is to Love Him" Spector had "decided to come to New York and get a job as an interpreter at the UN" but the "night before the interview he fell in with some musicians and never got there" (no mention of Lester Sill's call to Leiber and Stoller); how Phil had written "Spanish Harlem" (no mention of Jerry Leiber); how he had worked with Elvis Presley; how Phil "does the whole thing. He writes the words and the music" (no mention of his other writers or collaborators). Here was Phil, "a millionaire, a business genius," living in his penthouse twenty-two storeys up, with a limousine and a chauffeur and a bodyguard and staff. Here was Phil, "a twenty-three-year-old man [*sic*], with a Shelley visage, with a kind of page-boy bob and winkle picker boots," sitting in his beige office, taking a call from Andrew Oldham—"It's the Rolling Stones. They just got in!"—tearing into the short-arm fatties of the record industry, the "animals" who point and stare and abuse him when he's on the street or in a discotheque, the uncomprehending numbskulls who put down his music. "I feel it's very American. It's very today. It's what people respond to today. It's not just the kids. I hear cab drivers, everybody listening to it."

"Every baroque period has a flowering genius who rises up as the most glorified expression of its style of life," wrote Wolfe, switching gear into hyperbolic overdrive. "In latter-day Rome, the Emperor Commodus; in Renaissance Italy, Benvenuto Cellini; in late Augustan England, the Earl of Chesterfield; in the sal volatile Victorian age, Dante Gabriel Rossetti; in late-fancy neo-Greek Federal America, Thomas Jefferson; and in Teen America, Phil Spector is the bona fide genius of teen."

Spector, needless to say, was thrilled by the piece and gave copies to all his friends.

A month after the publication of Wolfe's article, a more sober appraisal of Spector's accomplishments appeared in *Time* magazine. Describing Spector as "personifying the bizarre, make-believe world he dominates," the piece shrewdly pointed out how his policy of releasing only a handful of records that he was convinced would be surefire hits differed from the approach employed by most in the record business, and analyzed the different components of the Wall of Sound and Spector's preference for using singers that expressed what he described as "a soulful yearning that every teenager understands."

Taking note of his "$600 a month" psychoanalyst, Spector, the piece declared, appeared to be suffering a "maladjustment stemming from a feeling of non-acceptance by the adult world."

"We're the only ones communicating with the teenagers," he said. "They are so prone to anxiety and destruction, and they can't intellectualize their wounds. . . . Our music helps them to understand."

His next project, the piece continued, would be a documentary, starring himself, to be called *A Giant Stands 5 ft. 7 in.* For some reason, it was never made.

The irony was that Spector was being fêted at precisely the time when his supremacy was most under threat. The music business that he had once dominated so assuredly was changing at a phenomenal pace, driven by the two great avatars of the age, the Beatles and Bob Dylan. The arrival of the Beatles had not only heralded the British Invasion of the American charts; they had inspired a legion of American imitators— young musicians who wrote their own songs and were less reliant on the producers and songwriters who had traditionally governed the pop music machine. The Brill Building writers who had furnished Spector with his string of hits were among the first to feel the wind of change;

with performers expressing themselves, who needed tunesmiths in cubicles?

The Righteous Brothers might have recently given Spector the biggest hit of his career. But, one by one, other acts on Philles had been allowed to fade away. Only two singles were released under the name of the Crystals in 1964—"Little Boy" and "All Grown Up," which even Larry Levine thought were "messy," and neither of which troubled the Top 40. Cast aside, the group eventually bought out their contract from Philles and signed with United Artists. Bob B. Soxx and the Blue Jeans, a studio construct in the first place, had long since ceased to exist. Tired of being neglected, Darlene Love went back to session work and with Fanita Barrett took a weekly gig as a backing singer on the TV show *Shindig!* In 1965, only five singles would appear under the Philles imprint, two by the Ronettes and three by the Righteous Brothers (compared to ten Philles singles in 1963, and seven in 1964). And the Ronettes, the jewel in Philles's crown, were beginning to look distinctly tarnished. A song written by Spector, Gerry Goffin and Carole King, "Is This What I Get for Loving You?" reached only number 75 in May 1965.

While Spector seemed to have exhausted all the possibilities of the girl group sound that he had pioneered, others had picked up the baton. Following "Chapel of Love," Red Bird went on to have other hits by the Dixie Cups and the Jelly Beans, produced by Greenwich and Barry. Even more successful were the Shangri-Las, whose trashed-out "bad-girl" looks and theatrically melodramatic songs about death and heartache, written and produced by the enigmatic George "Shadow" Morton, brought a whole new, mordant aesthetic to the girl group genre.

More aggravating still to Spector was the way in which Berry Gordy, his old adversary at Motown Records, was going from strength to strength. Spector habitually affected an attitude of Olympian disdain to his rivals, dismissing them as also-rans, amateurs and schlock merchants. But he held Gordy in singularly high regard. He would scan the *Billboard* charts, anxiously following the progress of Motown Records, and often call on his circle of DJ and radio-programmer friends to give him advance intelligence on Motown releases.

Nineteen sixty-three had been Spector's annus mirabilis, when he had enjoyed an unparalleled run of Top 40 hits, and could rightfully claim to be the most successful record man in America. But by 1964 Gordy had usurped him with female performers such as Mary Wells, the

Marvelettes, the Supremes, and Martha and the Vandellas, and their male counterparts Marvin Gaye, the Temptations, the Four Tops, and Smokey Robinson and the Miracles.

Working out of a converted house on West Grand Boulevard in Detroit, which he dubbed Hitsville USA, Gordy had assembled around him a supremely talented team of writers, producers and artists, fashioning a distinctive signature sound that combined the driving backbeat and testifying vocals of gospel and R&B with the whipped-cream melodicism of pop. More than any other American record man, Gordy had managed to withstand the inroads of the British Invasion, creating a sound that, uniquely, appealed to both black and white audiences, and which Gordy felt emboldened enough to declare "The Sound of Young America."

"Phil was very competitive with Berry Gordy," Annette Merar remembers. " 'He's got the Supremes, but I've got the Ronettes. He's made x amount of dollars with this, but I made y dollars with that.' Very competitive. But at the same time he never considered Berry Gordy to really be in his category, because he was not a producer and musician to the degree that Phil was. But then Phil thought he was superior to everybody in the entire universe, including God."

Notwithstanding the obvious difference, that Spector was white and Gordy black, the two men shared many similarities. Both were small men with Napoleonic egos, self-centered, highly driven and ruthlessly competitive.

Both had built their fortunes from nothing—Gordy had been a professional boxer and worked on the production line at General Motors before breaking into the music business as a songwriter. Both recognized that a good song was the most important factor in the business of making hits—and both could smell one at a hundred yards.

But as similar as they might have been in all these respects, they could hardly have been more different in others. While Spector was generous in his praise of Motown, and obsessively monitored their new releases, Gordy seemed hardly even to acknowledge Spector's existence. "Berry never mentioned the Ronettes or the Crystals or Phil Spector," Diana Ross remembers. "He never talked about the opposition at all. He was so individual in his approach to his groups, his people and how he ran things."

Realizing the limitations of his own production and writing talents, Gordy had quickly learned the value of delegation, building a team of in-house producers, writers and musicians, on call virtually twenty-four hours a day, who would fashion an endless stream of hits, like newly polished cars rolling off the production line. Spector was too stubbornly independent to delegate, and would never have considered spending the money to hire a full-time team. Instead, he recruited musicians as and when he needed them, and continued to draw on the well of New York writers, even at a time when the old Brill Building formula was beginning to pall.

Both men were highly selective in what they released, disdainful of the "shit on the wall" approach of so many companies, which would throw any number of records on the market in the hope that something might stick. For both men, flops were anathema. Yet their methods were radically different. Gordy would evaluate Motown's recordings at weekly "quality control" meetings, where his team of producers were encouraged to be unsparingly critical of each other's work before Gordy himself made the final ruling on which songs were the strongest and therefore worthy of release.

Spector tended to keep things closer to his chest, only occasionally soliciting the opinions of those around him. "You might say something ten times and then two months down the line Phil would act on it," remembers one friend, "but he would never give you the benefit of thinking it was your opinion he was following." And he was always racked with uncertainty, agonizing over whether to release a record or not and shelving huge amounts of material, often songs that others were convinced were surefire hits.

"These could be the greatest records in the world," Larry Levine says, "and Phil wouldn't put them out. He would just have a feeling about it. But I always thought that had a lot to do with Phil's fear of failure. You have one hit after the other, and it puts a fear in you whether you can top that."

But perhaps the major difference between Spector and Gordy was that Gordy thought in the long term. He was concerned to build his artists' careers, to the point of setting up his own Motown "charm school," where his young charges would be tutored not only in singing and choreography but also in matters of style and deportment—how to dress, hold a cigarette or decant elegantly from a limousine—with a view to taking their place in the more refined echelons of show business.

Spector, on the other hand, worked in sudden and intense spurts of enthusiasm that would be quickly exhausted before he was on to the next thing. While he respected talent, he often acted as if his artists were disposable. Today's hot act was tomorrow's has-been. Only the sound was constant, and the only career he was really interested in building was his own. While Gordy had sublimated his energies and his ego into developing Motown as a corporate brand (most record buyers didn't even know, much less care, who Berry Gordy was), for Spector, his name was the brand. In his mind, they weren't Philles records, or even Crystals, Ronettes or Righteous Brothers records; they were Phil Spector records.

"The thing about Phil with all his artists is that he'd get them to a place of greatness and then get tired of them, and go on to the next one," Don Randi says. "And there were a lot of good producers around he could have passed them on to. I would have loved to have a chance; Jack, Sonny . . . But it just wasn't in Phil's nature to do that. As big as Philles was, it could have been one hundred times bigger. But with Phil there was always this attitude of this is mine and this is what I choose to do, and if I can't do it, nobody else can."

Spector did attempt to tear one leaf from Gordy's playbook. As Motown grew, realizing that DJs would be unlikely to include more than one or two new records from one label on their weekly playlists, Gordy set up a series of subsidiary labels to spread his new releases.

In 1965, Spector set up his own subsidiary label, Phi-Dan—partly to give an increasingly restless and underemployed Danny Davis something to do. Phi-Dan released a handful of records by artists including Betty Willis, the Lovelites, and Spector's regular pianist Al DeLory performing a version of the Beatles' "Yesterday," none produced by Spector himself, and all of which quickly vanished without trace.

This changing order in music was manifest in another way—the rise of the 33 rpm long-playing record, or album, as the foremost creative medium—and the dominant commercial currency in pop music.

Like everybody else in the pop music business in the late '50s and early '60s, Spector had always regarded albums as little more than an excuse to milk the success of a single, padding out one or two hits with the addition of highly disposable filler—throwaway B-sides, cover versions of current hits, or songs hastily composed with a mind to the publishing royalties rather than quality control: "two hits and ten pieces of junk," as Spector himself once put it. Albums were largely the domain of jazz, classical music and show tunes.

But now artists began to explore their potential as an extended vehicle for self-expression. The Beatles' *Rubber Soul*, released in June 1965, was to prove a significant bellwether; rather than a disparate grab bag of hits and misses, here was a coherent suite of songs, each as carefully crafted, and as brilliant, as the last. The decision by the group's American label Capitol not to release a single or two as calling cards before releasing the album itself reinforced the perception that *Rubber Soul* should be regarded as a complete and indivisible entity.

But it would be Spector's most devoted disciple and apprentice who would bring the medium to its most glorious fruition.

Brian Wilson, the leader of the Beach Boys, had idolized Phil Spector since the moment in 1962 when he first heard Darlene Love singing "He's Sure the Boy I Love." Years later, Wilson would explain how that record "opened up a door of creativity for me like you wouldn't believe. Some people say drugs can open that door. But Phil Spector opened it for me."

The early songs that Wilson wrote for the Beach Boys—blissfully innocent celebrations of the teenage California holy trinity of sun, sea and surfing—had been bolted together from two basic elements; the guitar riffs of Chuck Berry and the keening harmonies of the Lettermen. But Spector's magisterial productions were to imbue Wilson with a grander sense of vision. "I was unable to really think as a producer until the time I really got familiar with Phil Spector's work," Wilson would later explain. "That was when I started to design the experience to be a record rather than just a song." To Wilson, Spector represented the summit of the producer's art; not only was his music epic, moving, "so large and emotional," as Wilson put it; it was also hugely successful—a fact that Wilson, who always hungered for commercial success, regarded as a critical measure of a record's true worth.

Wilson would occasionally visit Gold Star to watch Spector at work. While recording the Christmas album, Spector invited him to sit in on piano, but a flustered and nervous Wilson was unable to read the lead sheets and backed down. As much as he was in awe of Spector, he was also intimidated by him. "I studied Spector at work in the studio, noticing that like me he was one hundred percent hung up on creating a perfect song," Wilson would later be quoted as saying in his autobiography, *Wouldn't It Be Nice*. "The other similarity, which I failed to notice and didn't recognize until many years later, was that his aberrant personality was perhaps his best tool in making records, allowing him to manipulate people into doing exactly what he wanted. He didn't bend to the world; it bent for him."

Spector, for his part, treated Wilson with a paternalistic indulgence, happy to have him around in the studio, accepting Wilson's hero worship as his due, acknowledging his talent, but not for a moment considering him as a serious rival. It was not in Phil Spector's makeup to consider anyone as a serious rival.

Wilson was particularly smitten with "Be My Baby," which he regarded as the greatest pop record ever made. "Brian must have played 'Be My Baby' ten million times," says Bruce Johnston, who joined the Beach Boys in 1964. "He never seemed to get tired of it." Inspired by the song, Wilson wrote "Don't Worry Baby," intending to offer it to Spector for the Ronettes to record. But, fearing rejection, he changed his mind and recorded the song with the Beach Boys instead. It reached number 24 in June 1964.

As fragile as he was gifted, in the same year Wilson suffered his first nervous breakdown. While the Beach Boys continued touring, he retreated into the studio. Eager to replicate the magic of Spector's recordings, he began to use musicians from the Wrecking Crew on Beach Boys records. The songs about surfing and hot rods gave way to more subtle reflections on love and self-identity. But it was hearing the Beatles' *Rubber Soul* that would provide his Damascene moment. "When I first heard it, I flipped," he would later recall. "*Rubber Soul* was a collection of songs . . . that somehow went together like no album ever made before, and I was very impressed. I said, I want to make an album like that . . . a whole album with all good stuff."

In the summer of 1965 Wilson started writing songs in collaboration with a lyricist named Tony Asher, and at the beginning of 1966, he went into the studio to begin work on the album that would become *Pet Sounds*. A cycle of songs about adolescent yearning and lost innocence, the elegiac melodies framed in arrangements of a startling sophistication, *Pet Sounds* would raise pop music to a new gold standard. Wilson would explain that "it wasn't really a song concept album, or lyrically a concept album . . . It was really a production concept album." The Beatles might have set the yardstick in terms of songcraft, but it was Spector's genius in the studio that Wilson was trying to emulate. He would later claim that even the album's title was an act of homage, bearing the same initials as his hero (although, given the fact that the title was supposedly dreamed up by fellow Beach Boy Mike Love, this seems unlikely).

But *Pet Sounds* was to be Wilson's Waterloo. Driven to surpass his own masterwork, and increasingly enmeshed in drugs, Wilson slowly became unhinged. His obsession with Spector had always had a darker side. As much as he idolized Spector, he also feared him. Now he began to believe that Spector was "a mind-gangster" who was monitoring his brain. Watching the Rock Hudson movie *Seconds*, he "heard" Spector talking to him from the cinema screen. "Just thinking about Spector activated a switch in my head," he would write later. "I felt intimidated, fearful. I kept thinking about the perfection and greatness I was striving for and the likelihood that I might never reach it."

Over the next twenty years, Wilson would spiral downwards through drug abuse, psychosis and chronic obesity, until finally recovering his footing in the 1990s. Yet he would continue to regard Spector with a mixture of awe and fear. When I met Wilson in November 2001 he would describe Spector as "a very scary person. He was egotistical and self-centered. A very scary kind of talking style. A very scary person."

"Brian was just mesmerized by Phil and his work," Bruce Johnston says. "I remember going with him to a session for the Righteous Brothers; Phil was totally in command, and Brian just sat there, having a fan-adulation meltdown. He thought Phil was a genius. But to me, while the brilliance belongs to Phil, the genius belongs to Brian.

"The big thing Brian did was hire the band. By hiring the Wrecking Crew—this rhythm section, horn section and string section—it gave Brian more tools as his music was growing, he was able to grow the tracks—but from bar one he leapt past Phil. You could say the Beach Boys' 'Surfin'' was on the same plane as 'To Know Him.' 'California Girls' compares to 'Be My Baby.' But Phil never got past that into the stratosphere that Brian went into with *Pet Sounds.* There was a limitation for Phil on how far he could go with his Wall of Sound. He was like a little boy who does something really cute and gets applauded for that, and so he starts figuring out how to get the applause back, but then it's not quite as cute again. I think Phil started believing his own legend and press. I don't think Brian ever did that, and to this day Brian never knew how good he was. He was like Cary Grant growing up without a mirror."

By 1965 Spector could hardly have failed to be aware of how dramatically the music scene had changed. It was there every time he turned on the radio; and every time he landed in Los Angeles after the grueling, nerve-jangling flight from New York. The major power brokers in the record business may still have been located on the East Coast, but the energy and the creativity had moved west.

Los Angeles was now spawning its own vibrant music scene, centered around the string of clubs blossoming along the Sunset Strip—the Trip, the Whisky a Go Go, and Ciro's, where Los Angeles's "own Beatles," the Byrds, reigned supreme. On Friday and Saturday nights the scene on the Strip resembled a circus parade, thronged with longhairs and freaks in shaggy Beatle haircuts, girls in miniskirts and go-go boots. The Byrds' dreamy, jingle-jangle version of Bob Dylan's "Mr. Tambourine Man," the harbinger of the fashionable new genre of folk rock, was one of the songs dominating the airwaves in the summer of 1965. Dylan's own "Like a Rolling Stone"—the gunshot, according to myth, that would change rock music forever—was another. A third, Sonny and Cher's "I Got You Babe," must have been particularly galling for Spector. Being fired by Spector had turned out to be the best thing that could have happened to Sonny Bono, or "Sonny Bozo," as Spector had taken to calling him. After releasing singles with Cher under the name Caesar and Cleo, Bono had finally struck the mother lode, producing a song that managed to combine the folk rock sound of the Byrds, Dylan's nasal drawl and the shimmering, spacious sound of a Spector production. The obliging gofer and the honking backing singer now affected matching furry vests and bellbottom pants and were installed in the number 1 position on the charts as America's favorite hippie sweethearts. As if to rub salt into Spector's wounds, the follow-up to "I Got You Babe" was "Baby Don't Go"—the song that Bono had offered Spector, and that he had turned down, a year earlier. It reached number 8.

Spector had spent the past four years commuting between the coasts, retaining his apartment and office in New York, and latterly leasing a modest, Spanish-style house—Brynmar—in the Hollywood Hills. But now he made the decision to relocate permanently to Los Angeles. For all that he had grown up there, Spector never felt comfortable in Los Angeles; he hated the heat—California didn't have weather, he complained, it had climate—and the absence of street life. But Los Angeles was where Gold Star, and the action, was. And the constant flying was killing him. Dr. Kaplan advised against the move. But Spector reasoned he could maintain his equilibrium by calling long-distance whenever he needed instant therapy—just as he had when things got too much in the studio.

In the summer of 1965 he took possession of a new property that he felt more properly befitted his Olympian status in the music business— a rambling, twenty-one-room Spanish-style mansion at 1200 La Collina Drive, a gated private road a short walk from the Sunset Strip. Built in 1910, the property had once been the main residence of a substantial estate, with a series of cottages and carriage houses scattered throughout the grounds. But over the years, most of the land had been parceled off and sold for new developments. Spector's new home sat in two acres. At the front of the house was a paved courtyard set with an ornamental fountain; at the rear, gardens and the inevitable swimming pool. The singer Eartha Kitt was a near neighbor. She and Spector would never get on.

The Spector family: Harvey, Benjamin, Bertha and Shirley.
A celebratory dinner, circa 1947.

The Teddy Bears, 1958.
(Left to right) Phil Spector,
Annette Kleinbard and
Marshall Lieb.

ABOVE: With Jack Nitzsche *(left)* and Darlene Love, Gold Star Studios, 1963.

RIGHT: With Larry Levine and Annette Spector, Gold Star Studios, 1963.

With the Ronettes, Gold Star Studios, 1963.

With Tina and Ike Turner, Gold Star Studios, 1966.

ABOVE: Phil Spector and George Brand guarding the La Collina mansion, 1975.

OPPOSITE, TOP: The Pyrenees Castle, Alhambra, photographed on the morning of Spector's arrest.

OPPOSITE, BOTTOM: Phil Spector after his arrest on the morning of February 3, 2003.

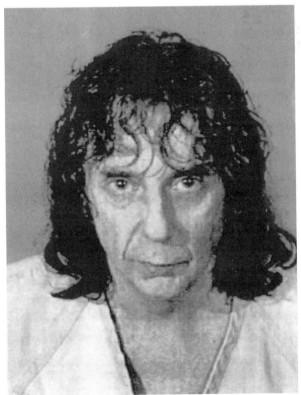

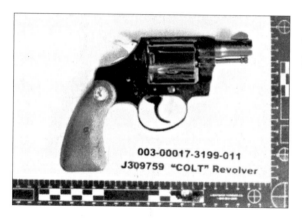

The Colt revolver that killed Lana Clarkson.

003-00017-3199-011
J309759 "COLT" Revolver

Police diagram showing where Clarkson's body was found.

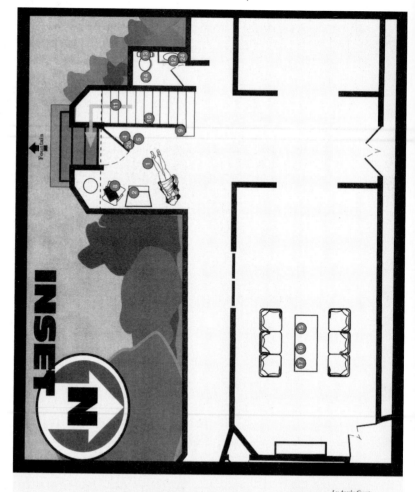

INSET

Fountain

N

1" = 4'- enlarged to
fit board,
use this scale

4'   8'   12' 16' 20'

Los Angeles County
Sheriff's Department
FILE NO.: 003-00017-3199-011
LOCATION: 1700 Grandview, Alhambra, CA
DET. HANDLING : M. Lillefeld
DIAGRAM BY: S. ENSLOW, G.A. UNIT, SHB

Lana Clarkson.

Rachelle Spector.

Phil Spector appears in court, May 2005.

The billionaire tobacco heiress Doris Duke had once lived there, but the house now belonged to Lance Revilot, a racing driver, pilot and playboy, and the son of the Woolworth heiress Barbara Hutton. Spector led friends to believe that he had bought the property; in fact, he had been given the option to buy it for $300,000, but chose to lease it instead. It would prove an expensive decision. At frequent intervals over the following years, when the lease came up for renewal, he would be offered the option to buy, but always refused. "I think," one friend says, "it was a symptom of Phil's general reluctance to commit." By the time he finally gave up the house twenty-one years later, in 1986, Spector had paid the original asking price many times over.

Along with the house, he acquired all of the furnishings, the French Empire furniture, the marble-topped consoles and the nineteenth-century oil paintings. Life-sized blackamoors, dressed in gold leaf, lined the hallway; a Steinway grand piano stood in the living room. In the library, Spector installed a mammoth sound system, with industrial-sized speakers from Gold Star, and a pool table. Just as he did in the studio, he kept the air-conditioning set to almost arctic temperature, the drapes closed to shroud the house in a perpetual twilight. In the sitting room a large fish tank provided the main source of illumination. "It was dark, dark, dark—like a dungeon," one visitor remembers. The entrance hall became his gallery, where over the years Spector would hang photographs of himself with sundry music celebrities, actors and sports stars—some simply taped over the nineteenth-century oils. For Spector, any association with fame, no matter how tenuous, was an affirmation of his own status. The photographs were his trophies.

There was an oil painting of Muhammad Ali; signed photographs of the basketball player Wilt Chamberlain, Elvis Presley and Fred Astaire. Spector adored Astaire, once entertained him at the La Collina house and continued to correspond with him for years afterward. Spector could never resist kitsch ephemera or a joke-shop novelty, and scattered around the house were whoopee cushions and chattering teeth, Batman paraphernalia, and satin cushions from the tourist shops on Hollywood Boulevard embroidered with the names of his heroes Stan Laurel and Bela Lugosi.

Over the years the house would become like a menagerie. Shortly after he'd moved in, a friend gave Spector a live chicken as a joke. Taking the joke one step further, he kept it upstairs in its own room, feeding and looking after it until the novelty waned. He kept a mynah bird in the kitchen, and an ostrich in a pen in the backyard, as well as a succession of dogs of varying sizes and degrees of ferocity.

Visitors to the house thought it looked "like a stage set," with Spector, as one described him, "like Little Lord Fauntleroy."

"It was Phil's idea of being classy," Michael Spencer says. Spector employed a cook, George Johnson, who had worked for Humphrey Bogart and Lauren Bacall, and now served dinner on white linen tablecloths with silver service.

When Spector told Annette he was moving into a big Hollywood mansion, her response was scathing. "I thought, How foolish is that. I asked him, 'Why? What do you need that for?' And the answer was because it made him feel that he was worth something."

After almost two years of living in limbo, Annette had finally asked for a divorce. Spector prevaricated, saying that she would have to arrange it herself. But eventually he relented, and late in 1965 he flew to Tijuana to obtain a Mexican divorce. Annette was granted $100,000 alimony, spread across five years of weekly payments—half of Spector's income for the one year that they had been married. As a condition of the settlement, she was also obliged to sign papers relinquishing her position as vice president of Philles, forsaking any further income from the company. She kept her pear-shaped diamond engagement ring, which she still wears today.

Casting around for acts that could connect him to a new audience, in the summer of 1965 Spector turned his attention to a New York group called the Young Rascals, a white rock band who played in a black soul music style; precisely the recipe that had made the Righteous Brothers so successful. The leader of the Rascals was a gifted singer and writer named Felix Cavaliere, who had occasionally performed at the Peppermint Lounge when the Ronettes were dancers there, and it was Ronnie who first alerted Spector to the group.

Spector was not the only person with his eye on the Rascals. The group was managed by the New York promoter Sid Bernstein—the man who brought the Beatles to Shea Stadium. Bernstein's stunt of broadcasting a message on the electronic scoreboard at Shea—The Rascals Are Coming!—during their performance angered the Beatles but created a palpable buzz of excitement around his young protégés. Bernstein had also been courting a number of industry figures, Jerry Wexler at Atlantic among them.

Wexler traveled out to Long Island, where the Rascals had a residency at the Barge, a floating club moored off Westhampton Beach. "Everyone from the music business was there; Jerry Leiber and Mike

Stoller, about three different lawyers, the Aberbachs," Wexler remembers. "And somehow Jerry and Mike seemed to have some sort of clutch on the guys from the band. Every time I tried to talk to them, Jerry and Mike would whisk them away to the toilet."

Wexler wanted to sign the group to Atlantic, and when Bernstein told him that Phil Spector was in town on a shopping expedition and would be meeting with the Rascals that night, Wexler immediately called Ahmet Ertegun, who had a house on Long Island, and asked him to get out to the Barge and clinch the deal. That night, after the show, Ertegun and Spector each took turns with the group for what Wexler describes as "a riffing contest." It was the old master versus the cocky apprentice, "strangely Oedipal," Wexler says. "But Ahmet wiped Phil out. As they say in the blues, don't mess with the messer. And Ahmet was the messer."

The Young Rascals' first single for Atlantic, "I Ain't Gonna Eat Out My Heart Anymore," reached number 52 in the charts later that year, presaging a run of hits for the band over the next four years.

Having failed to secure a white R&B group, Spector now turned his attention to the coming genre of folk rock. He had been sent a demo of a song called "Do You Believe in Magic," by a New York group called the Lovin' Spoonful. Led by a young folksinger named John Sebastian, the Spoonful played a ragged, slap-happy variant of jugband music. Spector thought he could make something of it and, with Jack Nitzsche in tow, he went to see the group perform at the Night Owl Cafe in Greenwich Village and offered them a deal. But Sebastian shrewdly reckoned that the Spoonful's singular charm and personality would be swept away in the Wall of Sound and turned down Spector's offer. "Do You Believe in Magic" entered the charts in September of that year, rising to number 9.

Spector finally found what he was looking for on the Sunset Strip. The Modern Folk Quartet had started life as a traditional folk outfit modeled on the Weavers and the Kingston Trio—all acoustic guitars and close harmonies. But following the example of other erstwhile folkies like the Byrds, and the Mamas and the Papas, they had gone electric, securing a residency at the new cradle of folk rock, the Trip. Spector met with the group's manager Herb Cohen, and made a deal, and over the last weeks of summer set about rehearsing the group at the house on La Collina.

"We'd go over there just about every day," remembers Henry Diltz, who sang and played banjo in the group. "Phil would be upstairs somewhere. If we were supposed to get there at one he would show up at four. We'd go in and play pool, have a few tokes in the garden, and eventually he'd come down the stairs—'Oh, you guys are here!' He'd sit at the piano, we'd stand around him and sing harmonies—old '50s songs, different things. It was like a musical boot camp."

To polish their musicianship, Spector added Diltz and his fellow member Jerry Yester to his army of musicians on sessions for the Righteous Brothers and the Ronettes.

"I remember sitting next to Barney Kessel, thinking how in the world am I next to this giant?" Diltz says. "I couldn't even read the lead sheet. Jack Nitzsche would walk through the room and plonk it in front of you. It would say five-string banjo—F sharp 7 . . . sus 4. I could play chords, but I couldn't for the life of me understand this. And Jerry would lean over and whisper 'Put your little finger here . . .'—talking me through it. They were beautiful chords, like big band chords, and I was just an amateur."

One night, Spector even joined the MFQ onstage at the Trip, playing twelve-string guitar as they sang "Spanish Harlem." After several weeks, Spector finally took the group into Gold Star to make their first recording, a song called "This Could Be the Night," which had been brought to Spector by a young Los Angeles songwriter named Harry Nilsson. Nilsson had written the song as a tribute to Brian Wilson. Spector's production sounded as if it had been recorded in a school gymnasium—a vibrantly echoing mélange of chiming guitars, bells and exuberant, sunny harmonies. It could—oh, the irony!—almost have been a Beach Boys record. Brian Wilson happened to visit Gold Star as the song was being completed.

"We could see him in the recording booth, in his robe and slippers," Diltz remembers, "sitting there in silence, playing our song over and over, for what seemed like hours. He was our god, and he was there because Spector was a god to him."

"This Could Be the Night" was a breath of fresh air, the most contemporary-sounding record Spector had made in a year. But his nerve failed him. Once again racked by uncertainty, Spector prevaricated and put the recording on the shelf.

"We thought we'd made it," Diltz remembers. "Phil Spector's produced our song; Brian Wilson is in love with it. We sat around for weeks waiting, and nothing happened. We'd call the office and nobody would know anything. I've since come to understand that this was a period when Phil had become paranoid about putting out a song that wouldn't be number one. He didn't want to put out something that would only make it to ten or seven. And we were an experiment. He wasn't sure enough that it was going to be the smash hit that he needed it to be, because of who he was."

He bought a Rolls-Royce and opened an office on the Strip, in the Sunset Building, a five-minute walk from the house on La Collina, although, of course, he would always be driven.

Danny Davis moved from New York to handle the business, but Spector would visit each day, holding court behind a desk like the flight deck of an aircraft carrier, set on a raised dais, "like a throne," as one friend remembers. Pictures of Ronnie covered the walls—"like some kind of bizarre shrine," she would reflect later—along with a Picasso drawing, *The Matador*, which Spector had bought from Richard Burton and Elizabeth Taylor.

He had developed a new enthusiasm: karate. Watching television one night Spector was enthralled to see a martial arts expert named Santi Josol demonstrating how to smash a brick in half with the blade of his hand. Josol and his partner, Victor Lipton, ran a martial arts school called the Tokyo Karate Federation, which had walk-up premises above a store on Santa Monica Boulevard, close to Gold Star Studios. Spector hired Josol and Lipton as sometime bodyguards and to teach him karate. At the same time, Jack Nitzsche took up fencing, and for a while both men would walk around in their respective uniforms, Spector in his karate gi, Nitzsche in his fencing bags, as if they were the latest fashion statement.

Spector became so enamored of karate that he invested in the Tokyo Karate Federation, financing a second studio in Culver City. Too busy to take care of Spector's bodyguard duties, Josol introduced him to another martial arts expert, Emil Farkas. The son of Holocaust survivors, Farkas was born in Hungary and migrated to Canada with his family in 1956, after a popular uprising was quashed by Soviet troops. To defend himself against anti-Semitic slights, Farkas took up martial arts. By the age of eighteen he held black belts in both judo and karate. He was just twenty-two when he took the job as Spector's bodyguard, along with another karate expert named Lazlo.

To Farkas it seemed that having bodyguards was more of a status symbol for his new employer than a necessity. "My feeling was that it was the old story of when you reach a certain level of money, what's the first thing you do? Buy a limousine. And then you need a chauffeur. Then you need a big house. And what else makes you a bit bigger than the other guy? Bodyguards—whether you actually need them or not."

Unless he was doing a session, Spector would seldom leave the mansion before ten at night; the primped-up crown prince of pop, clad in his Doc Holliday suits and waistcoats, his Ben Franklin shades, his Beau Gentry ruffled shirts and his Beatle boots from Lennie's Boot Parlour, enclosed in the walnut and leather sanctuary of the Rolls, descending to the clubs along the Strip to receive the homage of his subjects.

"Say we go to the Whisky or the Trip," Farkas remembers. "Everybody would be standing in line and Phil would just walk to the front and somebody would object to this and Phil would say 'Fuck you,' because he knew we were behind him. In that sense it empowered him to be able to push people around. And for Phil it always had to be the front table, so anybody who was performing would come up and 'Hey, Phil . . .' And for them it would be like 'I know Phil Spector . . .' He liked to be recognized, he liked people running up to him. And he'd be like the king of the mountain. He *was* the king of the mountain. He was the guy that had the touch."

Another friend from this period remembers him as "the lurking little boy. Always intrigued, yet intimidated by his surroundings. Phil was a stargazer himself, so he loved to be gazed at, especially by stars. He would sit at a table with someone but never allow himself to engage in any real conversation—he was too busy absorbing everything that was happening around him, and he liked to sit with people who would draw attention, thereby drawing attention to himself. Oh, there's Billy Wyman, he's one of the Rolling Stones. Who's he with? Oh, that's Phil Spector the famous record producer . . ."

But once back in the mansion, Spector was a man who for all his success and recognition seemed to Farkas curiously dislocated, empty. A man who had climbed to the top of the mountain only to find there was nothing there after all. "Phil was like a guy who had everything but didn't know what to do with himself. He'd sit there and say, 'What shall we do now?' He was like a little kid in that way. It was sad. Here was a guy who had everything, but most of the time he didn't know where he was going from one step to the next. In many ways, he was a lonely guy. He needed people around him. Half the time we'd just hang out, watch television and chitchat.

"You'd come home and sometimes there'd be people on the doorstep, just hoping to meet him, and he'd take them in and give them a drink or whatever. He had that side, especially with women—not to get involved, but just looking after people.

"If he liked you, he could be very nice, no question. He would let his guard down if he felt comfortable. With Phil it was always when he was out there and felt he had to prove himself that this other side, this ugly side, would come out. It was almost like two people. But I don't think he ever enjoyed the position he was in. He was always worried about what other people thought of him, what their attitude to him was. And worried about losing it. And that's a tough way to live."

Karate, says Farkas, was "a whim," and when his enthusiasm began to pall, Spector found a new obsession—shooting pool. He took to spending time in pool halls and private clubs around Hollywood. Determined to become the best, he sought out Willie Mosconi, a professional pool player who had won the world championship fourteen times, and paid him to become his personal tutor. Spector had never quite got the hang of karate; he might have worn a black belt tied around his gi, and he might have boasted to journalists that "in case of real trouble I could literally kill a guy," but according to Emil Farkas "he just play-acted. He'd do a lot of chopping his hands in the air, but he was nowhere near a black belt." But when it came to pool, he was a hot shot.

"Phil was paying Willie Mosconi $175,000 a year or something and had him staying in the house," Ahmet Ertegun remembered. "Phil was pretty good, but Willie was unbelievable. They'd go to pool halls and take bets from people who didn't know who Willie was and then he'd make shots like you couldn't believe. Phil loved that.

"I remember I went with them once. I never played pool; the best I could do was not rip up the cloth. People in the hall could see I had no idea what I was doing. But Phil made a bet on me that I could make all the balls go in the pockets with just one shot. It was a dumb bet. I could have even missed the cue ball. So this guy set up the balls and Phil said to me, 'Just hit it straight ahead'—and it happened! All the balls went in the pockets! I still don't know how. And he and Willie picked up ten thousand dollars. They wanted to give me a couple of thousand. I said, 'Keep me out of it.' "

He told Ronnie he had bought the mansion for them both, but Ronnie came and went. She continued to live at home in New York, keeping her affair with Spector a secret from her mother Beatrice. Whenever she flew out to Los Angeles for recordings or rehearsals, Emil Farkas would be dispatched to the airport in the Rolls-Royce to collect her, a single rose carefully placed on the backseat.

When she left town, Spector would cruise the nightclubs of the Strip in search of approbation and company. Emil noticed what others had observed before, how ill at ease Spector seemed to be in his own skin, how he would do almost anything to avoid being alone. There were often parties at the mansion—scene makers, hangers-on, waifs and strays collected from the Strip. Spector would sometimes vanish for hours on end—a stranger at his own gathering—then reappear, anxious to stave off the moment when the night would end. He did not like to be left, particularly by women.

"Phil would get very upset if women walked out on him," Farkas says. "He would rant and rave—you'll never work again, I'll get you fired, whatever. But then again, you'd have this thing at parties where you might have twenty girls and each one would try to outlast the other to see who was going to stay the night with him. But the feeling I got was that Phil sort of realized that most of these people were around for the external rather than the internal, and he would have preferred that he wasn't liked for the limousines and the money and all that. Phil would have really liked to be loved for himself. And there were girls who liked him for that. I think the problem was that Phil could never believe that these people could love him for who he was."

Ahmet Ertegun came to Los Angeles and happened to run into Spector in a club on the Strip. "He said, 'Come on back to my house,' " Ertegun recalled. "So we go out on Sunset Boulevard. It was across the street from Ben Frank's. It was a Saturday night. The place was jammed with motorcycles, kids. Phil had this big limousine. He said, 'We'll stop at the Gaiety and get some sandwiches, and let's take some girls.' He said, 'Which one of those girls do you like?' I said, 'I don't give a shit.' He had four or five guys with him, so he sends one of his bodyguards—'Go and get that one, that one and that one.' And these girls were all with guys. But his bodyguards go over and say, 'Mr. Spector would like to invite you to come up and have a drink at his house.' 'Oh, we'd love to!' 'No, not you—just her.' The guys were put aside, and the girls came! And I said, 'Phil, these girls are just teenagers.' So he says, 'Oh, let's get a couple of older ones for Ahmet.' So he sends the guys over and they get a couple of girls. So we all get in these limousines. And we stop at the Gaiety, and he orders a whole bunch of sandwiches, but in two groups; one is pastrami on rye . . . good deli sandwiches; and then he ordered like cheese on white bread, peanut butter and jelly—'That's for the schmucks that are working for us,' meaning the bodyguards, 'cos all these guys are from the karate school, regular American idiots. So we have two huge bags. And we go back to Phil's. And he gives these guys a bag and says, 'Go eat your sandwiches and come back in three hours to take everyone home.' Off they go. And we open up our bag and it was all the white-bread sandwiches! And the car's gone. So we were stuck with this junk—except the girls liked those sandwiches. Now that's the kind of fun evening that Phil didn't want to end. And I heard that sometimes he made people stay in spite of their wishes. But with me there, no problem. We all had a good time. We all left. Good night. Everybody safe and sound."

Linda Lawrence had been the girlfriend of Brian Jones of the Rolling Stones, and she was the mother of Jones's son, Julian. When they broke up in 1965 Jones gave Linda some money to buy a car. When they were together, whenever he was on tour with the group, Jones would send postcards, telling Linda about the excitements of life on the road. He made California sound like the Promised Land, and Linda wanted to see it for herself. She sold the car and bought an airplane ticket to Los Angeles. "I wanted to go there because the Stones had been there, and I felt that's where Brian had left me." She was seventeen.

In Los Angeles, Linda stayed with a friend named Catherine (now Catherine Sebastian), who worked as a model in TV commercials. Linda had met Phil Spector in London, on the night when he dropped into the Rolling Stones' recording session, and at a party in Hollywood she introduced herself and they became friends. He invited Linda and Catherine to recording sessions, and they would sometimes visit the house on La Collina. Catherine was astonished at his musical ability and knowledge. "He'd sit down at the piano and he'd take a set of changes— C–G–F, whatever—and he'd just play song after song with those changes, hundreds of them, segueing from one to another. It was absolutely fascinating."

It was a platonic relationship, as if Spector had adopted the two young girls, taken them under his wing. "People would tell me how evil, crazy and uptight Phil was," Linda says. "But I never had that feeling at all. To me he was only kind and caring."

One night, Linda and Catherine dropped acid and went to the Trip nightclub on the Strip.

"We started getting very freaked out by it. We had to leave the club, and I said, 'Let's go up to Phil's.' We walked up there and got to the gates. It was all locked up. I've no idea how we got in, but somehow we did. We rang on the doorbell, but there was no answer; so we walked around the back, stroked the dogs—that everybody said would eat you alive, but we knew them—and walked into the kitchen. We started play-ing around, being silly, sliding up and down the banisters, waiting for Phil to come home. Which he did. He was a bit shocked to find us in the house and told us off. 'You naughty girls, I could have killed you coming in.' But I knew he wouldn't. But he let us hang out there until we'd come down and we were able to go home. So he had that generosity of spirit. Obviously when you're feeling like that, you won't go somewhere you don't think you'll be welcome."

On another occasion Catherine was taken ill, and Spector invited both girls to stay, his staff taking care of her until she recovered.

Catherine, who came from a privileged Philadelphia family, was struck by the incongruity of the surroundings, the nineteenth-century oil paintings and French provincial bedrooms. "It didn't feel owned. It seemed like Phil was just passing through. The music room was his room. Everything else seemed like a stage set. When my mother came up one day, she said it reminded her of walking into one of her friends' houses on the Main Line in Philadelphia."

Sometimes Linda would be woken up by Spector calling in the middle of the night, asking if she would come over. His biggest problem, she thought, was loneliness. "But I felt that way myself. I recognized in him a lot of myself. We'd both been wounded by life."

Just as he had with Beverly Ross in their long, rambling, nocturnal conversations, Spector would confide his feelings of unhappiness and insecurity to Linda. "His father's death had obviously been the big thing in his life, which deep down he'd never dealt with, and which nobody had ever really helped him with. And he was this tiny little guy who'd been bullied at school. He felt insecure and inferior to the other guys who would always get the girl. So these were all the things that would pour out of him. And he'd say, 'But look at me now!' Like he'd got back at those people in some way. It was revenge in a way, a kind of satisfaction he felt. Phil definitely had a thing about that—this need to prove to everyone that he was cool and that he'd achieved something."

Sometimes, when restlessness came upon him, they would drive to another of Spector's favorite hangouts, Canter's on Fairfax Avenue. By dint of being one of the few places in Hollywood to remain open twenty-four hours a day, the family restaurant where Spector had whiled away his time after school, and where he'd worked as a busboy, had now become the early-hours gathering place of choice for music business scene makers and night owls. Spector liked to arrive around 2:00 a.m., holding court at a corner table, Emil and the nameless suits stationed in an adjacent booth. Spector, Catherine sensed, was never properly at ease in fancier restaurants where people sniggered and stared, but here, among "the dem and dose guys"—the schmoozers, hustlers and wiseacres—he felt comfortable. "He was a success in that restaurant."

One of his most frequent companions at Canter's was the comedian Lenny Bruce. Spector had idolized Bruce since his years as a teenager, riffing on the comedian's monologues while traveling with the Teddy Bears, and he had finally been introduced to him by Helen Noga— "Lenny," says Noga's daughter Beverly, "was another of my mother's little babies."

Bruce's irreverent shtick about religion, sex, politics—what newspapers called his "sick comedy routines"—had made him the most controversial comedian in America. His unapologetically confrontational style is illustrated in a story told by his former publicist Grover Sales, about an appearance at the San Francisco nightclub, Off Broadway, when the black comedian Dick Gregory happened to be in the audience.

"Spotting Greg, Lenny peered at the audience for an unnerving interval: 'Are there any niggers here tonight?' Gregory stiffened like a retriever, with the rest of the audience. In 1962, nobody had ever heard that word onstage, not in a white nightclub. Lenny began a mock soliloquy: 'Ohmygod, did you hear what he said? "Are there any *niggers* here tonight?" Is that rank! Is that cruel! Is that a cheap way to get laughs? Well, I think I see a nigger at the bar talking to two guinea owners, and next to them are a couple of wops, one kike, two greaseballs, a squarehead, three gooks, one frog, two limeys, a couple of sheenies, two jigaboos, one hunkey, fonky boogie—bid 'em up! Bid 'em up! Six more niggers! I pass with two dykes, four kikes, and eight niggers!' "

The once-frozen audience now gave way to hysteria, the sweet laughter of liberation only Lenny could unloose: "Now, why have I done this? Is this only for shock value? Well, if all the niggers started calling each other 'nigger,' not only among themselves, which they do anyway, but among the ofays. If President Kennedy got on television and said: 'I'm considering appointing two or three of the top niggers in the country into my cabinet'—if it was nothing but nigger, nigger, nigger—in six months 'nigger' wouldn't mean any more than 'good night,' 'God bless you,' or 'I promise to tell the truth the whole truth and nothing but the truth, so help me God'—when that beautiful day comes, you'll never see another nigger kid come home from school crying because some ofay motherfucker called him a nigger."

"Gregory turned to me: 'This man is the eighth wonder of the world. You have to go back to Mark Twain to find anything remotely like him. And if they don't kill him, or throw him in jail, he's liable to shake up this whole fuckin' country.' "

A year later, Gregory published his book *Nigger*, dedicated to "Dear Momma—Wherever you are, if you ever hear the word 'nigger' again, remember they are advertising my book."

Gregory's remark about death or jail was to prove prophetic. Between 1961 and 1964 Bruce was arrested half a dozen times on obscenity and drug charges. He was banned from entering Australia and the U.K., and blacklisted by any number of nightclubs in America that refused to run the risk of prosecution by having him perform. By the time he came into Spector's life, he was bankrupt, terminally depleted by his struggles against the law and a heroin addict—a man who was giving a passable impersonation of someone fighting for his life, and losing.

The record producer Denny Bruce (no relation), who was then playing drums for Frank Zappa's Mothers of Invention, remembers accompanying Zappa to a meeting with Spector and Bruce in Canter's in the autumn of 1965. (Like Spector, Zappa idolized Bruce, thought he was "a saint." Zappa's manager, Herb Cohen, had once run a nightclub, Cosmo Alley, which was busted for obscenity when Bruce performed there in 1959, and Cohen and Zappa later released a double album by the comedian, *The Berkeley Concert*, on their Bizarre label.)

Expecting to meet the sharp-suited, wisecracking legend, Denny Bruce was shocked to be confronted by a bloated, ashen-faced figure in a stained sweatshirt and jeans. "It was like he was in jail. And his whole conversation was: 'You know, the Fourth Amendment . . .' Not one joke. Nothing."

In many ways, Bruce was the embodiment of the hipster Spector himself had always yearned to be; the towering, uncompromising iconoclast who had taken on the system. While Spector had fought against the short-armed fatties of the record industry, the legion of uncomprehending straights, and earned only their opprobrium, Bruce had taken on the establishment in a more profound and dangerous way—and paid a far higher price. He was a true martyr to his genius, just as Spector fancied he was a martyr to his.

Bruce became a frequent visitor to the La Collina house. Politics, history, society—these were the stuff of Lenny's shtick, and his travails had made him unusually well versed in law—all subjects that fascinated Spector and on which he was also well informed. "They'd sit there and chitchat for hours," Emil Farkas remembers, "intellectualizing about how America was going down the drain because there was no freedom and you couldn't get up and say what you liked, et cetera, et cetera. Phil felt that both of them were on the same page—Phil was anti-establishment, anti-cop. It was the whole era. And he loved the fact that

Lenny had the balls to stand up to anything and anybody, to tell people they were full of shit. Phil loved that, because that's the way Phil wanted to be himself. The difference was that Phil didn't have the balls to get up on the podium and speak his mind, so he could live that vicariously through Lenny."

But now that Spector was a man of substance he could do more than just idolize Lenny. He could help him. He took up Bruce's cause, writing a stream of letters to the government, law enforcement agencies and lawyers, pleading on his friend's behalf. He made his offices and staff on Sunset Strip available for Bruce whenever he wanted to use them, and would write out checks when he needed money—which was often. He would drive miles out into the boondocks to support his friend whenever Bruce could find a club willing to book him. He produced an album, *Lenny Bruce Is Out Again*, which was released in October 1965, and financed a fifteen-day residency at the Music Box Theatre on Hollywood Boulevard, where Bruce played to largely empty houses. Some regarded Bruce as "an expert leech," but Spector helped his friend generously and uncomplainingly, and Bruce's appreciation was genuine enough.

One night Spector took his young friends Catherine and Linda to meet Bruce at his house in the Hollywood Hills, prepping his young friends en route. "He was saying, 'Don't mention the FBI, don't mention the police; Lenny's got some problems and we don't want to make him all sad,' " Catherine remembers. "It was obvious that Phil idolized him, and that this was a special thing we were doing. It felt like he was giving us a special gift."

At the house, Bruce answered the door and ushered them inside. Catherine was shocked. "I come from a nice middle-class home where my mother always had things looking nice. But this place . . . there were dishes in the sink, mattresses on the floor, everything filthy. I couldn't understand it. He was living there with his daughter. She was about the same age as me, close enough that I identified and felt so sorry she had to live like this. But Lenny had such a gentle heart and was blazingly intelligent. And he and Phil behaved very lovingly to each other. They were clearly good friends."

For two hours they sat around talking, Bruce disappearing from time to time—presumably, Catherine thought, to fix. When finally he began to nod out, Spector told them it was time to go. As they left, he embraced Bruce and kissed him tenderly on the cheek.

14

River Deep, Mountain Low

Number 1 for three weeks, seven weeks in the Top 3, "You've Lost That Lovin' Feelin' " had brought Phil Spector the biggest hit of his career, at a time when he needed it most, and for a while the momentum it generated seemed unstoppable.

As a reward for their efforts, Barry Mann and Cynthia Weil might have expected Spector to gift them with the follow-up. Instead, he turned back to another favored songwriting partnership, Goffin and King. Their collaboration, "Just Once in My Life," closely modeled on "Lovin' Feelin' " with its lavish orchestration and opening section sung by Bill Medley, reached number 9 in May 1965. A third single, "Hung on You," stalled, until disc jockeys flipped the record and began playing the B-side—an impassioned version of the standard "Unchained Melody" sung entirely by Bobby Hatfield. The record reached number 4 in September.

But all was not well between Spector and the Righteous Brothers. Spector's ploy of appending his name to "There's a Woman"—the "piece of shit" composed by Medley and Hatfield that had appeared on the B-side of "Lovin' Feelin' "—thus entitling himself to a third of the songwriting royalties, still rankled. And Medley was proving to be a far more independent-minded figure than Spector was used to dealing with.

From the moment "Lovin' Feelin' " had begun its rise up the charts, Medley had been agitating with Spector to release an album to capitalize on the single's success. But Spector balked at producing one without another couple of hits to include. When Larry Levine weighed in on Medley's behalf, Spector relented, agreeing to let Medley, who fancied himself a producer (he had overseen a handful of songs by the pair at Moonglow), bring the project to fruition.

The result was distinctly mediocre but successful enough to persuade Spector to relent once more when Medley began demanding to produce more tracks for a second album. *Just Once in My Life...*, released in May 1965, contained only two productions by Spector, the single of the same name and "Unchained Melody."

To make matters worse, relations between the Brothers themselves were also deteriorating. Medley's growing self-importance was a cause of concern not only to Spector but also to his partner Bobby Hatfield. Hatfield had never quite got over being relegated to the secondary role on the pair's greatest hit, "You've Lost That Lovin' Feelin'," and as Medley flexed his muscles in his studio, Hatfield began to feel even more the junior partner. Emboldened by his own starring role in "Unchained Melody," Hatfield now threatened to sever the partnership altogether and go solo.

Spector, suddenly alarmed at the prospect of seeing his greatest asset evaporate before his eyes, suggested a compromise—an album for the Christmas market, entitled *Back to Back*, that would give both singers equal solo prominence and that would also include their own compositions. Medley would produce his own songs; Spector would produce Hatfield's.

It was during the recording of the album that matters became ever more vexatious. Suspicious of R. J. van Hoogten's accounting, the Brothers had ordered an audit of Moonglow's books, which revealed that van Hoogten had allegedly shortchanged them by some $28,000 on royalties owed for their earlier recordings. Meanwhile, van Hoogten was pursuing his own argument with Spector. Under the original contract between Philles and Moonglow, Spector had the rights to release Righteous Brothers recordings only in America, Canada and the U.K. Van Hoogten planned to capitalize on the Brothers' success by releasing their recordings in other territories, but now alleged that Spector had failed to turn over a number of masters.

Van Hoogten dispatched a letter to Spector, alleging breach of contract and terminating his agreement with Philles, at the same time instructing the Righteous Brothers to cease all recording with Spector forthwith. Convinced that they could make it without Phil Spector, and seeing an opportunity to escape their obligations to both their paymasters, Medley and Hatfield filed lawsuits against both van Hoogten and Spector, claiming that because van Hoogten had breached their Moonglow contract, his contract with Spector was no longer enforceable.

Desperate to bring the proposed Christmas album to completion, Spector attempted to persuade the Brothers to return to the studio, but they declined, letting it be known that they were being courted by a rival company, MGM. Spector promptly riffled through the tapes of unreleased material produced by Medley and came up with six songs that he slapped on the album, *Back to Back*, which was released in December.

Medley and Hatfield were furious. In January 1966, an item in *Billboard* announced that the pair had signed for MGM. Spector immediately filed suit against MGM. In late January, the Righteous Brothers went into the studio to cut their first single for MGM, "(You're My) Soul and Inspiration." The song's writers were Barry Mann and Cynthia Weil. Forgetting how he had overlooked the writers after "Lovin' Feelin' " and stung by what he perceived as a massive betrayal, Spector pleaded with Mann and Weil to withdraw the song—but to no avail. In May, "(You're My) Soul and Inspiration" went to number 1. The Brothers enjoyed only two more Top 40 hits for MGM before fading away. It would be a further eight years of struggle, breakup and reconciliation before they were back in the Top 10.

For Spector, not even the $600,000 he extracted in settlement from MGM could assuage his fury at his prize assets deserting him. He would never forgive them. Three years later, in 1969, talking to Jann Wenner of *Rolling Stone*, he would dismiss the Brothers as "a strange group in that they really were non-intellectual and unable to comprehend success. They couldn't understand it and couldn't live with it and accept it for what it really was. They thought it was something that could be obtained very easily and once it was attained, it could be consistently obtained . . .

"I just think it was a great loss, because the two of them weren't exceptional talents, but they did have a musical contribution to make. I loved them: I thought they were a tremendous expression for myself. I think they resented being an expression. I think now if they had it to do again, they never would have left."

Even those closest to Spector felt the depth of his hurt. Don Randi was not only one of the mainstays of the Wrecking Crew; he regarded himself as Spector's friend. Like all of the Crew, Randi played on a variety of sessions around town. When he was called in by MGM to play a Righteous Brothers session, Randi was happy to be reunited with Hatfield and Medley, and with the paycheck.

"And about a week later I got a call from Phil. 'Why did you work for them?' 'Why did I work for who?' 'You know who I'm talking about . . . Bill and Bobby.' He said, 'How could you do that? They were my artists!' I said, 'Phil, I work for who I want. If you want me to work exclusive to you, I've got a price and I'd be glad to do it.'

"He said, 'You should have walked out.' 'I can't walk out!' I think he felt really bad because he could have gone on and on with Bill and Bobby. But that was it with Phil and me. Not only that. After that, Jack Nitzsche does a date for Lester Sill. So I was helping him out. He asked me to bring something down to Lester; I was working next door. So I dropped the music off. And Lester Sill goes, 'Get out of here! And don't you ever come down to my sessions.' I didn't understand what the fuck was going on. But Lester hated Phil at that point, and because he knew I was close to Phil . . ."

It would be more than twenty years before Randi worked with Spector again.

The farrago over the Righteous Brothers was not the only thing preoccupying Spector in the autumn of 1965. He had been asked to work as associate producer and musical director on *The Big TNT Show*, a televised concert modeled on *The TAMI Show*, which had aired the previous year and been so instrumental in breaking the Rolling Stones and introducing James Brown to a rock and roll audience.

Recorded on two days at the end of November at the Moulin Rouge Theatre, *The Big TNT Show* presented a curiously mixed bag of performers, reflecting the diversity of the pop charts at that time. Among them were the current heartthrobs of Sunset Strip, the Byrds; the English singer Petula Clark; the folksinger Donovan; country singer Roger Miller and R&B acts Bo Diddley and Ray Charles. (Robert Marchese, the stage manager of the show, would enjoy telling the story of how Charles approached Spector during the recording. "Are you Mr. Phil Spector?" Charles asked. "Yes." "Are you the Boy Genius?" "Yes." "Are you the inventor of the Wall of Sound?" "Yes." "Are you the guy who had over twenty hit singles in a row?" "Yes." "Then, Mr. Spector, how come there's no toilet paper in the bathroom?") There was the odd spectacle of the folksinger Joan Baez singing "You've Lost That Lovin' Feelin'," accompanied by Spector himself on piano. But the undisputed stars of the show were its closing act, Ike and Tina Turner.

Ike Turner was one of the unsung giants of R&B. Guitarist, pianist, producer and bandleader, Turner's career had started when he was eleven years old, playing piano behind the blues singers Sonny Boy Williamson and Robert Nighthawk. He had worked as a disc jockey, arranged and played piano on what is widely regarded as the first proper rock and roll record, "Rocket 88," a number 1 R&B hit for Jackie Brenston in 1951; worked as a talent scout for Sun and Modern records, and produced and played on dozens of sessions for blues performers like Elmore James, B.B. King and Howlin' Wolf.

In 1959, in St. Louis, he discovered an eighteen-year-old singer named Annie Mae Bullock and recruited her as the vocalist for his group, the Rhythm Kings. He changed her name to Tina, and they married in a wedding parlor in Tijuana. Ike made his new bride the centerpiece of a live revue, featuring a full band and a trio of shimmying backing singers, the Ikettes, with Tina herself a vision of lust incarnate, prowling the stage like a lioness in heat, wig flying, legs pumping like pistons in heart-attack miniskirts. By the mid-'60s the Ike and Tina Turner Revue rivaled James Brown as the most thrilling act in rhythm and blues, and had enjoyed a string of hits on the R&B charts with songs like "It's Gonna Work Out Fine" and "Fool in Love." What they had not done, however, was break out of the "chitlin' circuit" of black clubs and theaters into the mainstream.

Spector had seen the Ike and Tina Turner Revue more than once, and he loved them with a passion. "That word—revue . . ." he would recall later. "It means something symbolic; it has class. And the show was just mesmerizing; I said, God, if I could make a number-one record with her she could go on *Ed Sullivan*, she could go to Las Vegas; she could break the color barrier. I was just devastated by her."

Most of all, he loved Tina's voice. Barbara Alston, Darlene Love, LaLa Brooks and Ronnie Bennett—all had offered different expressions of the soulful voice that Spector so admired and loved to work with. But Tina was something else again—raw carnality, hurt, passion, power— she was "The Voice" incarnate.

For months, as he surveyed his crumbling empire, a single question had been gnawing at Spector: what next? Watching Tina Turner bring the house down on *The TNT Show*, he knew he had his answer.

What Spector did not need, however, was her husband. Ike Turner's years on the road had earned him a reputation for being suspicious, truculent and volatile. He was particularly possessive of Tina. With Danny Davis in tow, Spector visited Turner at home and spelled out his plan. He would record Tina, and he would give her a number 1 record that would transform her and Ike's career, break them out of the R&B circuit into the mainstream and make their fortune. His only stipulation was that Ike himself would have nothing whatsoever to do with it.

"Ike was a doll," Spector remembers. "Because he was interested in Tina, other women. He was not interested in drugs at the time. He'd never had a drug in his life. He was a gun-carrying black man who grew up in the South; who had to make it on his own; who pistol-whipped his band; who had them on time . . . *like. that*. Whose revue was spot-on. Whose Ikettes moved. Who had to compete with Bobby 'Blue' Bland, B.B. King, Bo Diddley, James Brown and all those people. He had to grow up, top-book himself . . . You ever think why the black artists of the '40s called themselves what they did: the jazz artists? They couldn't get booked. They called themselves Count Basie; Duke Ellington, Nat 'King' Cole. To shove it up the white promoters, y'know? You call me King Cole. You call me Count Basie. They had to sleep, of course, in the barn; but they always kept that Count, King . . . They started it all.

"But Ike was easy to deal with. I had no problem with him. See, when you're going straight ahead, you have blinders on. Everybody dealt with Ike like *Ike Turner*! I didn't deal with Ike like Ike Turner."

Danny Davis would remember it differently. Spector, he would later recall, was "scared to death of Ike."

But Turner accepted Spector's request unhesitatingly. "Phil said he wanted to produce a record on Tina and would I agree to let him do it," he recalls. "He said he didn't want me to interfere. Well, why would I interfere? My attitude was, if you think that you can do it, then take a shot . . ."

Ike made only one stipulation. While he agreed that he would have nothing to do with the record, his name must appear on it.

Ike and Tina were contracted to Loma Records, the R&B subsidiary of Warner Bros. Spector paid $20,000 to lease their contract to Philles, and in the first weeks of 1966 set about planning the record that would decide his future.

One by one, Spector's options had closed down. The Righteous Brothers had gone. The Ronettes had ground to a halt. The glory days of Philles were a fast-receding memory. Spector knew this was his last throw of the dice. For the last three years, his success had been built on a kind of incremental gigantism—from "He's a Rebel" to "Be My Baby" to "You've Lost That Lovin' Feelin' "—each bigger, bolder, more ambitious and grandiloquent than the last. Spector didn't do small. Now, like a beleaguered general, he marshaled all his forces for the last stand.

In search of a song that would do justice to his ambitions he turned back to the writers with whom he had enjoyed his greatest run of success, Jeff Barry and Ellie Greenwich. In the two years since they'd last worked with Spector, Barry and Greenwich had enjoyed a string of hits at Red Bird. But now Red Bird had folded, and their marriage with it; they divorced in December 1965, just a few weeks before Spector approached them. But despite the emotional upheaval in their own lives, despite the lingering ill feeling over "Chapel of Love," Greenwich and Barry agreed to Spector's request. As a gesture of conciliation—and in a demonstration of his own pressing need—rather than insist they come to Los Angeles, Spector flew to New York and together they began to work on new material. "It was like vomiting it out," Greenwich told the writer Ken Emerson. In less than a week they had produced three new songs.

Was "River Deep—Mountain High" the best? Certainly it was the most idiosyncratic. In the heyday of their collaboration, all three writers would sit around the piano, swapping ideas and themes. But now friendship had given way to estrangement. According to Greenwich, each arrived at the writing sessions with a different part: Greenwich provided the melody of the verse; Spector provided the melody of the chorus; and Barry most of the words. Even before it was recorded, the effect was an awkward fit; two quite separate songs that seemed to have been plucked from opposite corners of the room and forced to dance together— although the stop-start tempo made dancing almost an impossibility. And what the hell was the song about anyway? In a self-conscious attempt to get away from the "silly little songs" he had written for the Ronettes and Crystals, Barry had contrived a tortuous lyric using the childish devotion to ragdolls and puppies as metaphors for adult love. "Lyrically, we just all jumbled, jumbled on the chorus," Greenwich recalled. "When you think about 'River Deep—Mountain High' that lyrically says a lot about where we were coming from at that time. It was also a big sound, almost a desperate sound—but exciting! It breaks out: freedom!"

Back in Los Angeles, Spector began rehearsing Tina at the mansion. "I remember her coming home and saying, 'Well, this guy is really different,'" Ike Turner says. "I said, 'What do you mean?' She said, 'You can't vary his lines . . . he doesn't want you to vary his lines.' Phil didn't tolerate any improvisation at all. I mean, Tina was real trained before he met her—anyone who has been around me a lot can sing. But he really put her through it."

In February, Spector gathered his troops at Gold Star and the assault began. It would require five sessions and more than $22,000 to complete. The first two sessions were spent merely preparing the musicians and establishing the shape of the backing track. Word quickly spread through Hollywood that Spector was working on something truly special, the ne plus ultra of the Wall of Sound, and the control room filled with onlookers. Rodney Bingenheimer, the teenage "scene maker" of the Sunset Strip, arrived with Brian Wilson. Jack Nitzsche, who was also recording with the Rolling Stones, brought Mick Jagger. Dennis Hopper moved around the room, taking photographs.

For the third session, on March 7, Tina Turner arrived at Gold Star to find herself confronted by twenty-one musicians, an equivalent number of backing singers and a gallery of gaping onlookers. She was so intimidated by the crowd and the atmosphere of feverish expectation that she was unable to sing, and the session was abandoned.

A week later, she returned to the studio, this time with Ike. As she went through take after take, Spector pushing her remorselessly toward his vision of perfection, the temperature rose and the sweat flew. "We were a little more naïve about things then than we are now," Larry Levine says. "After a couple of hours of this, Tina said, 'Do you mind if I take my blouse off when I sing?' Well, Phil looked at me and I looked at Phil, and we didn't mind. I don't know how Ike felt about it. We just had one light lit on the wall so she could see her music. But to watch her was fantastic. What a great body. I don't think Ike was too happy, but I don't recall ever seeing Ike happy. I seem to recall he and Phil had some words about something or other—probably money."

Over two more sessions Spector added strings and mixed the record. When all was finally done, spent but exhilarated he turned and embraced Jack Nitzsche. "Jack said that he and Phil looked at each other and they both smiled because they knew this was as good as it was ever going to get," Denny Bruce remembers. "I think they both knew that things had now run their course; they'd had an incredible run, but it had come to an end." But, finally, it was all too much. In trying to surpass himself, Spector had actually outreached himself. The sound was titanic, huge and echoing, an unstoppable hurricane, but like a hurricane it left destruction in its wake. Turner's vocal, monumental itself, was buffeted and bruised in the tumult of the arrangement. The wildly colored threads of melody were twisted and bent until their shape and color were all but lost. It was the simulacrum of all Spector's grandiosity, his overarching ambition; it was all his passion, his thirst for revenge and his madness. It was a record that swept you up into its peculiar psychosis and left you stunned and exhausted in its wake. You could be enthralled by it, moved by it, but you could never love it.

"River Deep—Mountain High" was released on May 14, 1966. *Billboard* featured it among its top 60 picks, describing it in the curious demotic of the trade: "Exciting dance beat production backs a wailin' Tina vocal on a solid rock tune penned by Barry and Greenwich." On May 29, the record entered the *Billboard* charts at number 98. The following week it crawled to 94. A week later, to 93. By June 18 it moved up to 88. The following week it dropped out of the charts altogether. Spector's biggest production had become his biggest failure.

After the death, the inquest. For Ike Turner, the failure of the record was a simple case of the institutionalized racism of America in general, and the music business in particular. "If Phil had released that record and put anybody else's name on it, it would have been a huge hit. But because Tina Turner's name was on it, the white stations classified it as an R&B record and wouldn't play it. The white stations say it was too black, and the black stations say it was too white, so that record didn't have a home. That's what happened to 'River Deep—Mountain High.' "

For Jeff Barry it was hubris, the inevitable consequence of Spector pushing himself further and further forward, at the expense of the artist and the song. Spector, Barry told Richard Williams, "has a self-destructive thing going for him, which is part of the reason that the mix on 'River Deep' is terrible. He buried the lead and he knows he buried the lead and he cannot stop himself from doing that. If you listen to his records in sequence, the lead goes further and further in, and to me what he is saying is: 'It is not the song I wrote with Jeff and Ellie, it is not the song—just listen to those strings. I want more musicians, it's me, listen to that bass sound . . .' That, to me, is what hurts in the long run."

For others, the record's failure was a matter of revenge. The "Tycoon of Teen" had become too arrogant, too overbearing, too complacent for his own good. There were stories that Spector now considered himself too important to glad-hand with the foot soldiers in the radio stations and trade magazines, that he was "too busy" to give interviews; rumors that he had been informally blacklisted by DJs, because he refused to deliver the usual blandishments in cash or kind to have his records played. The industry had turned on him.

"Phil antagonized some people," Jack Nitzsche would later reflect to the writer Harvey Kubernik. "Phil had a way to always bring up the idea that he had more money and that was power, which it probably was. He had thirteen hits in a row without a miss. Around 'River Deep—Mountain High,' people started to want him to fail. That's how it is with sports and everything. You get too good and people don't like it, too successful and people don't like it. There was no competition for Phil in those days."

"Phil was an abrasive character," Larry Levine says. "And to a large degree he grew into the character that he was portrayed as by the media. He started to enjoy being that. A lot of people envied him, and a lot of people were waiting for him to fail—hoping for him to fail. So it didn't take much to push it over that edge, to the degree that *Cash Box* and *Billboard* both came out with only a B-plus for the record, which was effectively the kiss of death. But I always felt, and I still feel, that Phil tried to take that record to a place where the available technology couldn't go. It just wasn't enough for what he wanted to do. But that had a lot to do with Phil's personality too. He wasn't content to do what he'd done before. Phil was always looking to move on to the next plateau, until there just wasn't a plateau there to move on to."

In later years, Spector would attempt to make light of the failure of "River Deep." Talking to *Rolling Stone*, he would explain that the record "was just like my farewell. I was just sayin' good-bye and I wanted to go crazy, you know, for a few minutes, that's all it was. I loved it and I really enjoyed making it, but I didn't really think there was anything there for the public." Talking to *New Musical Express* a decade later he would go further still, arguing that had he been egotistical the failure of the record might have affected him. "But I'm not egotistical. I am an ego-maniac. My ego is so high you just can't beat me down."

But in truth, he was devastated. When Catherine and Linda visited him at the house, he cried as he told them how sure he had felt that "River Deep" would be a big hit. "It was the only time I ever saw him really depressed," Catherine recalls. "He said, 'I was sure people would love it; I just don't understand it.' More than upset, he felt betrayed by the American public."

In Britain, the story could hardly have been more different. The record quickly climbed the charts, and by the middle of July it had peaked at number 2. But its success seemed only to inflame the hurt and anger Spector felt at the American industry and public. In a fit of self-righteous pique he took out ads in *Billboard* and *Cash Box*, invoking the name of the American general who during the War of Independence had plotted to surrender the fort at West Point to the British: "Benedict Arnold Was Right." And they hated him even more.

Then Phil Spector closed the door of his mansion, and disappeared from view.

15

Marriage in Purgatory

The brave face that Spector put on the failure of "River Deep—Mountain High" was just that—a face. The failure of the record left him spent and exhausted. The manic energy and drive that had propelled him for the past three years now drained out of him.

"With Phil, it was as if they'd given him the ball, and one day he woke up and the ball had gone," Tony Calder reflected. "The minute he went cold, the business buried him, they killed him. He'd had the success and he'd crapped on everybody. He's just fucking died . . . push him down in his own shit. It's human nature . . ."

He was too depressed even to go near the studio. The writing sessions with Barry and Greenwich had produced another song, "I Can Hear Music," which Spector allotted to the Ronettes. But he was so uninterested that he passed the production over to Jeff Barry (the record went nowhere, although the Beach Boys would have a Top 30 hit with the song three years later). Another producer, Bob Crewe, was invited to record a handful of sessions with Ike and Tina Turner.

Jack Nitzsche had quickly put the disappointment of "River Deep" behind him and was in demand as a producer and arranger for artists like Lou Christie, Bobby Darin and Bob Lind, whose single "Elusive Butterfly" went to number 5 in December 1966. The musicians of the Wrecking Crew were now occupied on sessions for virtually every record of note that was coming out of Los Angeles.

For six years Spector had focused all his energies and dreams on one thing—the desire to transmute rock and roll, and the base metal of his anger, genius and monumental ambition, into art. He had taken on the music business on his own terms, and won. His vision had changed rock and roll forever, but in changing, it had left Phil Spector behind.

Throughout the making of "River Deep—Mountain High," Dennis

Hopper had been holding out to Spector a vision of a new future—film production.

Hopper had a reputation for being volatile, hard-drinking, temperamental and brilliant; a man who saw himself in the tradition of the great Hollywood hell-raisers such as John Barrymore and Errol Flynn. He had been a close friend with James Dean, acting alongside him in two films, the seminal "misunderstood teenager" movie, *Rebel Without a Cause*, and *Giant*. Hopper idolized Dean, and Dean's death in a car crash in 1955 seemed to throw him off balance. Shortly afterward, working on the set of *From Hell to Texas*, Hopper got into a fight with the director Henry Hathaway after Hopper's insistence on improvising his lines required upward of one hundred retakes. He was fired from the film and effectively blacklisted by Hollywood for several years. He moved to New York, studied acting with Lee Strasberg and made a career in television shows, mostly Westerns, usually playing the part of brooding and misunderstood desperadoes, for which he seemed to be typecast. He also developed a serious reputation as a photographer, moving in New York art circles, photographing every contemporary artist of note, including Warhol, Lichtenstein and Jasper Johns, while at the same time assembling a modest collection of their works.

Hopper and Spector had been acquainted for two or three years. "We hit it off really well right from the beginning," Hopper remembers. "Hanging out in Canter's, chasing girls. Phil had been through some really bad trips—his father committing suicide; you don't get rid of those things. And he'd been attacked, physically. You see all these rap guys running around with bodyguards nowadays—well, Phil Spector really needed bodyguards. There really were people after him. And when he put out 'River Deep' and they refused to play it, that was a disaster for Phil. They shot him down and Phil was really hurting after that."

Hopper had been around Gold Star, chronicling the epic progress of the "River Deep—Mountain High" sessions (which he would remember with a haiku-like concision: "Long hours. A lot of big orchestras. Phil being a perfectionist. Ike doing nothing. It was fabulous"), and he would go on to shoot the cover photograph for the Ike and Tina Turner album of the same name. His primary ambition, however, was to direct films. With his friend Stewart Stern, the screenwriter for *Rebel Without a Cause*, he had come up with the idea for a film called *The Last Movie*, about a Hollywood film crew shooting a Western in a tiny Mexican village, and the chaos and confusion they leave in their wake. A parable of corrupted innocence, the film had been inspired by Hopper's own experiences making the John Wayne film *The Sons of Katie Elder* in the Mexican town of Durango. Hopper had paid Stern to prepare a preliminary treatment by selling some of his paintings (Hopper had no cash). Jennifer Jones and Jason Robards expressed interest in starring. Enthused at the prospect of breaking into movies, Spector offered to produce the film and made an agreement with Stern to write the screenplay. He gave Hopper office space at Philles to work from, and began talking up his new career.

In June 1966—at the moment that "River Deep" was disappearing from the American charts—he gave an interview to Peter Bart of the *New York Times*, declaring that he had now "lost interest" in the record business, and was in need of "a new creative outlet.

"Art," he mused, "is a game. If you win that game too regularly it tends to lessen your motivation," adding that to carry on making records "would just be playing for public approval, not for what suits me."

The Last Movie, he declared, would be in the tradition of the directors he most admired, Truffaut, Kubrick and Fellini.

Asked whether his lack of experience in film would be a hindrance, Spector declared that if anything it would be an advantage. "It's helpful to come to something fresh. That's why I want to make my next career in movies. I'm not fresh to records anymore." Filming on *The Last Movie*, he said, would begin in September. He confidently predicted it would win first prize at the Cannes Film Festival.

While Hopper and Stern set to work on the project, flying down to Durango to scout locations, Spector moped in his mansion, unsure where to turn next. As a film producer, he was finding out, there wasn't really that much to do. He invited Tony Hall, the Decca promotions man in London who had been so instrumental in the success of "Lovin' Feelin'" and "River Deep," to come and stay. Hall and his wife had never been to Los Angeles before. They were met at the airport by a Cadillac and driver and taken to Spector's mansion. "It was extremely weird. Phil eventually appeared, greeted us and promptly disappeared again, saying he'd see us later. We waited, and eventually, at about three a.m., he came back and said, 'I'll show you the town.' He insisted on driving—this tiny little figure in this huge Cadillac. He took us to some really sleazy hamburger joint—all very odd—then drove us back at around five a.m. We didn't see him again for days. We hadn't got a rental car, we were unable to go anywhere. It was like being in prison.

Periodically he would poke his nose around the door and say hi, and on one occasion he drove us down to see Gold Star, because I'd asked to see it. But half the time—and I later discovered this from other people—he was hiding in one of the other rooms in the house." After five days, thoroughly bemused, Hall and his wife cut short their visit and left.

Lynn Castle was another visitor. Castle had always harbored her own ambitions to be a singer and songwriter, but in the years since she and Spector had dated she had made her living as a hairdresser, the "hot scissors" for half of the Los Angeles rock fraternity, including Sonny and Cher and the Byrds. She was a close friend of Jack Nitzsche and Lee Hazlewood. In 1966, she recorded her own composition, "Rose Colored Corner," along with a song called "The Lady Barber," which Hazlewood produced and released on his LHI label. Castle was striking-looking, with luxuriant brunette hair that she wore in a twist, adorned with a rose; she wore miniskirts and knee-high boots. It was a look that Nancy Sinatra would adopt when she released her single "These Boots Are Made for Walkin'," which Hazlewood wrote and produced.

Castle had not spoken to Spector in some five years, and was astonished one night to receive a telephone call completely out of the blue—"I was so happy to hear from him," she remembers—in which Spector launched a tirade of abuse at her. Castle was deeply shocked, but rationalized the outburst as an extreme symptom of Spector's old jealousies. "I think his feelings were hurt because I was such close friends with Jack and Lee. I said to him, 'Why are you saying all this?' It was so mean, and so sad. And I just hung up on him."

A few months later Castle was out carousing with Jack Nitzsche. "Jack was drunk and it was: 'Okay, what are we going to do tonight? Let's go see Phil!' So we were out there, howling behind that iron gate: 'Phillip!' And he opened up for us."

It was the first time Castle had been inside the mansion. "And my God, talk about the Little Prince . . . All that stone, all that huge emptiness, and this endless dining room table. And there was little Phillip—my God, he looked so lost. And I thought, Who would want this? What are you doing here? What is this big lonesome? I mean, do you like this? Because I would never want to be here. It's too big, too cold, too lonesome. Is this just a thing about you're strong and you're powerful and you can live in a big frigging castle? Like, who gives a shit? Does that actually make you feel big about yourself? It was like somebody who feels so insecure and frightened inside. It made me so very sad."

For a while after that, Castle and Spector would sometimes talk on the phone. "And I'd hear him on the other end of the line, he'd be hollering out, 'Yeah, go and get that, bring that here.' As if there was somebody else with him. But you'd never hear a voice answering him. Like, who are you talking to, Phillip? Who's there . . . ? And it felt like there was nobody there." And then she stopped hearing from him altogether.

Spector's devotion to his old friend Lenny Bruce was so intense that, according to Ronnie, he hung a blow-up poster of the comedian in the master bedroom. Spector, she would later complain, often fell asleep before she did, and she would lie awake with the image of the haggard, puffy-eyed Bruce staring down at her from the wall.

Spector regarded Bruce as his closest friend, "like a teacher or a philosopher . . . like a living Socrates." But for all his good intentions, Spector's attempts to resurrect his friend's flagging career and spirits had come to nothing. Bruce had become increasingly lost to the world in a stupor of heroin and depression. In Spector's words: "Lenny had a nail tied to his foot and was going around in circles." He now passed his days poring over law books, fighting adversaries real and imagined. Occasionally he would turn up at Spector's offices on Sunset Strip, bearing an armful of documents to be typed and photocopied by Spector's obliging staff, and Spector continued uncomplainingly to put his hand in his pocket whenever Bruce needed anything. Dennis Hopper had known Bruce when the comedian was first starting out, long before he had attained national notoriety, when Hopper himself was working as a contract player at Warner Bros. "I went into this strip club. The regular comic had been taken sick. Lenny's mother had been a stripper, and handled strippers, so Lenny got up and performed, and they yanked him off the stage—in a burlesque house—because he was just too dirty." Hopper would often spend time with Bruce and Spector, in Canter's or in the mansion. "Phil was wonderful with Lenny," Hopper remembers. "He got very involved with helping him. But this was a side that people didn't see. There was this idea that Phil was a monster, but the truth is he was the most generous, the kindest guy."

In April 1966, Bruce was fined $260 and given a one-year suspended sentence and two years' probation for a narcotics violation—possession of heroin—which had been hanging over him for more than three years. The sentence was a mere slap on the wrist—anybody else might have expected a jail term—but it did little to ease his paranoia and anxiety.

At the end of July, Spector telephoned Michael Spencer asking whether he would like to meet Bruce.

"I said I'd love to. Phillip said, 'Well, Lenny's strange: I'm going to have to call him,' then he calls me back to verify it's me and not the police who are harassing him. So about five minutes later Phil calls me back and says it's okay." Spector drove Spencer and a couple of friends to Bruce's house in the Hollywood Hills. "So Lenny leads us into this little study, and there was yellow paper from legal pads strewn all over the floor. I picked up a piece of paper to see what it was. And it was one word in the middle. Pick up another piece of paper. One word. He was so disassociative at that time, so out of it, he would just write one word and throw it on the floor. That's what he was doing at that time. He had a tape he wanted to play Phil of some routines he said he'd been working on. And he was spewing out venom so fast it was impossible to understand what he was saying on this tape. Phil stood there listening, and after about five minutes it became too oppressive. So we excused ourselves. As we were leaving, Phillip said, 'I'm sorry, Lenny can be weird.' "

Four days later, on the evening of August 3, John Judnich, a friend of Bruce's who was staying at his house, walked into the bathroom— Bruce's favorite sanctuary—to find Bruce lying on the floor dead, his trousers around his ankles, a hypodermic syringe in his arm. Bruce had evidently been fixing while seated on the toilet and toppled forward. He had died of a morphine overdose. He was forty years old.

The moment Spector heard the news on the radio, he summoned Danny Davis and drove as fast as he could to Bruce's house. The scene was crawling with police, reporters and television crews. Spector was horrified. His friend's death had become a media circus. Pushing his way through the crowd he somehow managed to get into the house, where he began shouting at police "You killed him!"

Outside, Spector went from one photographer to the next, offering to buy up any pictures they might have taken of Bruce's body, to spare his friend the final indignity of public exposure.

According to Davis, the next morning a police lieutenant arrived at Spector's offices and presented Davis with a manila envelope. Inside was a sheaf of glossy 8 × 10 pictures—the official police shots of Bruce lying dead on the bathroom floor. "They could make one helluva album cover," the policeman told Davis. "The price is five thousand dollars." Davis immediately phoned Spector, who instructed him to buy them.

Bruce was buried two days later. Spector paid for his funeral, and delivered the eulogy at a memorial service held on August 21 at the Eden Memorial Park Cemetery in Mission Hills, where cemetery officials had tried to block the service after advertisements appeared urging mourners to bring box lunches and noisemakers.

Already depressed by the failure of "River Deep," Spector went into a state of almost theatrical mourning for his friend, locking himself away in his study and playing Bruce's recordings over and over again.

The Ronettes had been invited to tour with the Beatles. (The group would play their last ever concert on August 29 at Candlestick Park, San Francisco.) Ronnie was beside herself with excitement at the prospect of renewing her acquaintance with the group that had now become the most successful in the world. But Spector forbade her to join the tour, giving the excuse that he wanted her in Los Angeles to concentrate on more recording. Her cousin Elaine took her place. Spector made no move to take Ronnie into the studio, but in the autumn she rejoined the Ronettes for a tour of U.S. Army bases in Germany. By Ronnie's account, whenever they booked into a hotel, a message would be waiting for her to call Spector, and they would talk deep into the night, Ronnie often falling asleep with the phone line open, awaking in the morning to his voice on the other end of the line. Ronnie thought it was impossibly romantic. Her sister Estelle told her it was Phil's way of making sure she didn't spend the night with anyone else.

The tour was to prove the Ronettes' swan song. As a recording act they were clearly a spent force. Nedra had been seeing an English disc jockey named Scott Ross, and they now made plans to marry and have a family. Both would shortly become born-again Christians, and Ross would train for the ministry. Estelle was also in a relationship, with the Ronettes' tour manager, Joe Dong. And Spector, it was clear, had no interest in attempting to revive the group's fortunes as a recording act. By Christmas 1966 the Ronettes were no more. Only Ronnie remained, freed from the encumbrance of her sister and cousin, confident that Spector would now concentrate his attentions on making her what she had always dreamed of being—a solo star.

In January 1967, apparently at a loss to know what to do next, Spector stirred himself to go into the studio once more to record Tina Turner, calling on his old allies Jack Nitzsche and Larry Levine. "I'll Never Need More Than This" was one of the songs left over from his writing sessions with Jeff Barry and Ellie Greenwich a year earlier. Where the melody of "River Deep" had been as complicated as algebra, this had a hook that recalled the glorious simplicity of Barry and Greenwich at their best. But the production was overblown, gusty with echo (Turner sounded as if she were singing from the far end of the Grand Canyon), almost a parody of the titanic excesses of "River Deep." "We were trying to copy a sound, which turned me off a little bit because we weren't going on to something new," Larry Levine would recall. "We were coming back to what we'd done."

The record was never released.

Within a year, the music business had changed beyond all recognition. The Wall of Sound was obsolete; girl groups, a thing of distant history. There was no place for Phil Spector. His muse—anger, frustrated genius, revenge, the need to prove himself—had fled. Spector would make no more records in 1967; the closest he came to Gold Star was a large picture that he acquired from the Beat artist Wallace Berman, to whom Spector had been introduced by Dennis Hopper—a collage of Spector himself standing behind the control board of Studio A, with his arms outstretched, like an Old Testament prophet. The picture took pride of place in the living room of the mansion.

With no product to work, Danny Davis grew bored and distracted. "I was getting $800 a week, but I'd go into the office every morning and there'd be nothing to promote, no records," Davis later recalled. "Instead there'd be a list on my desk, from Phil, of maybe fifteen things to do that morning.

1) Call the garage to have my mother's car serviced.
2) Call Minnesota Fats and see if he wants to shoot pool at my home this weekend.
3) Call Shelby and see if they can get four new tires for my car, etc., etc.

"Never anything to do with records."

Nobody's gofer, and anxious to make a career elsewhere, Davis eventually walked out, with four months still left on his contract. Spector threatened to sue him for a quarter of a million dollars, but then dropped the case. He closed down Philles Records and the office on the Sunset Strip. It was taken over by the coming record producer Richard Perry, who in turn would pass it to another mogul-on-the-make, named David Geffen.

Emil Farkas had gone. As his driver and principal bodyguard Spector took on a bearish Armenian named Mac Mashourian, whose fearsome appearance disguised a surprisingly refined and delicate temperament. Unmarried, Mashourian lived with his sister and her family, and his favorite topic of conversation was his mother, of whom he spoke with a rhapsodic sentimentality. "I can't imagine that she was still living," one friend remembers, "although Mac was not that old—he just seemed old." To Spector he became as much a friend as an employee.

Sometimes Spector would set forth in his Rolls-Royce with Mac at the wheel, immaculate in black suit and tie, to cruise his old watering holes. But the thrill had gone. Not only a new generation but a new species seemed to have descended on the Sunset Strip, decked out in Day-Glo and love beads. Spector was only twenty-seven, but already he seemed to belong to another age. Drugs seemed to have wrought some peculiar metabolic change in the record business. Marijuana was the new martini; LSD, the holy sacrament. Spector hated dope, the sense of time standing still, the woozy introspection, the touchy-feeliness of it all. LSD simply terrified him. He had taken the drug only once, under the supervision of Dr. Kaplan for psychotherapeutic purposes and, according to Danny Davis, it had triggered his most deep-rooted trauma: he had imagined himself watching his father commit suicide.

"Phil always said he hated his father for what he did, taking the easy way out," Davis would recall. "The acid went right to the heart of that hatred, to the pain, and it horrified him."

He could not bear the thought of losing control.

In his interview with Jann Wenner of *Rolling Stone*, Spector would talk of how much he distrusted the growing influence of drugs in music. "A lot of people said they've listened to 'River Deep' stoned, and they had their earphones on, and they just freaked out, you know, with the sound. Well, you know nobody was stoned when they made the record, I can tell you that . . . Drugs tend to frighten me a little in an audience because it doesn't make for good hearing and concentration. Now, I'd hate like hell to have an incoherent jury listening to me when I'm tryin' to plead a case . . . just spaced out. I'd get frightened. Just like I hate to bet on a fighter or horse that's drugged. That's scary. I don't give a fuck what they do in their own time, but if a disc jockey is going to review my record, and he's stoned, well, you know, he can go either way. It depends on how good the stuff he took was, and he's either gonna love my record or hate my record. But, I mean, you shouldn't be judged that way. In fact—art can't and shouldn't be judged at all! Because it's all a matter of taste."

The Monterey International Pop Festival, held over three days in June 1967 in the small northern California town of that name, was the harbinger of the new cultural order, a gathering of the new aristocracy of rock: Jimi Hendrix, the Who, Jefferson Airplane, the Grateful Dead.

Also appearing on the bill was the soul singer Otis Redding. Already a success on the chitlin' circuit and the R&B charts, Redding was an unknown quantity to most of the hippie audience at Monterey, but his high-octane "gotta, gotta, gotta" performance made him a surprise hit of the festival. Redding recorded for the Stax label, an affiliate of Ahmet Ertegun's Atlantic Records, and after the concert he traveled down to Los Angeles for a meeting with Ertegun.

Ertegun took Redding to Spector's house, where Spector sat at the piano and paid tribute to his old friend and mentor, playing Redding a medley of songs that Ertegun had composed. "Otis was blown away. He knew some of the songs, but he had no idea I'd written them." Then Ertegun suggested an excursion, to a club in Watts where Esther Phillips was performing. "Otis and Esther sang duets together for hours," Ertegun remembered. "Phil was playing the piano, and he'd remind them of different songs and play the introduction and sing behind them. We were there until five in the morning. Two of my all-time favorite singers, Otis and Esther, and Phil on the piano. It was one of the greatest evenings of my life."

Six months later, on December 10, 1967, Otis Redding died when the small plane he was traveling in crashed into Lake Monona, in Madison, Wisconsin.

The Last Movie was grinding slowly to a halt. September had come and gone, and by spring 1967 the film was no nearer to beginning production. Spector pulled out. According to Hopper, he encouraged Spector's withdrawal from the project. "We went around to all the studios and got turned down by all of them. And Phil finally said that he was going to put up the money himself. I said, 'How much money do you have, Phil?' He said, 'I have a million and a half dollars.' Even though it was something I wanted more than anything else in the world, I told him I wasn't going to let him do that. So that's something that he thanked me for for his entire life."

Stewart Stern, who had been busy working on the screenplay, remembers it differently. "[Spector] didn't understand what the situation was, that you have to do research, that you have to spend time alone, that you have to write—all that stuff. He had the itch. But it turned into a terrible business."

According to Stern, Spector refused to pay his fee—"not one dollar"—and Stern took legal action. "I hated to do it, but I had no alternative. As I remember it, my lawyer was doing everything in every way to serve him, and Spector was doing anything he could to outfox him and refuse to accept the subpoena." In the end, the case was settled out of court.

Hopper himself would eventually complete *The Last Movie* in 1970. It did not win Cannes, but it did win the Critics Prize at the Venice Film Festival. But American critics hated it, and two weeks after its release in New York the film closed. Dennis Hopper would not direct another film for a decade.

The collapse of *The Last Movie* did nothing to impair Spector and Hopper's friendship. They continued to spend time together at Canter's or at the La Collina mansion, often in the company of Hopper's friend, the actor Peter Fonda, with whom Hopper was now busily developing another film project, *Easy Rider.* The son of Henry Fonda, Peter seemed to be in a state of permanent rebellion against the conservative strictures of his upbringing. After a series of clean-cut film roles, he had become a cult figure acting in two Roger Corman films, *The Wild Angels* (a biker flick which earned Corman the singular distinction of being sued by the Hells Angels for what they perceived as a negative portrayal of their image), and *The Trip*, in which Dennis Hopper also appeared. Fonda had given up alcohol for pot and acid, and lived on raw eggs, bananas, milk and vitamin compound, mixed in a blender. He rode around Hollywood on his Harley motorcycle, dressed in a tuxedo and an assortment of military headgear. He wrote terrible poetry. He was close friends with the Byrds and their producer Terry Melcher.

Spector may have been "bizarre," Fonda remembers, but he "wasn't weird yet. There was something wonderful about Phil. He was a gentle person, and somewhat afraid. But I was impressed. There was this diminutive fellow who obviously had all sorts of personal conflicts, but had still been able to make this wonderful music. Most record producers in those days were slightly slimy, slightly shady; you'd get the feeling they'd cook the books on you if they could. But Phil didn't give that impression at all."

Fonda felt a particular kinship with Spector, founded on mutual tragedy. When Fonda was ten, his mother, the socialite Frances Seymour Brokaw Fonda, suffered a nervous breakdown and was committed to a sanatorium. It was there, on her forty-second birthday, that she committed suicide, cutting her throat from ear to ear with a razor blade that she had supposedly secreted in a framed photograph of Peter and his sister Jane.

Incredibly, Peter Fonda was never told the truth of his mother's death. It was not until 1960, when he was twenty-one years of age and working in a summer stock theater in upstate New York, that a man in a diner pulled out a yellowing news clipping from the *New York Times* reporting the suicide. Fonda was completely traumatized and would later tell the story of how he took to wearing a T-shirt with the words of the Beatles' song "Day Tripper" printed on the front describing how it had taken him so long to find out . . . and on the back, "but I found out."

Spector never discussed his father's suicide with Fonda, but after Fonda learned of it from a mutual friend he began to understand Spector's air of vulnerability. "I felt such empathy for him over that; it was a point of acknowledgment of what that abandonment felt like."

In February 1968, Hopper and Fonda began work on *Easy Rider*. The film is an elegy to the counterculture, which tells the story of two bikers who on the proceeds from a cocaine deal set out on a voyage of discovery across America.

Spector was invited to play the part of the drug dealer. "We wanted Phil because we knew we'd get his Rolls-Royce and Mac for free," Fonda jokes. "But he also had a great look for the part."

The brief scene required Spector to meet with the two biker heroes, Captain America and Billy (played by Fonda and Hopper respectively), test the cocaine with a single snort and complete the transaction. Hopper had scouted a suitably desolate location, a slip road at the end of a runway at Los Angeles International Airport, and the shoot was conducted to the deafening roar of jets coming in to land. "I didn't realize that Phil didn't like loud noises, even though he was the Wall of Sound," Fonda remembers, "and with his fear of flying as well . . . You see him cowering when a plane comes over; that wasn't acting. He was scared shitless."

With the Ronettes no more, Ronnie had now more or less moved into the mansion on La Collina Drive. Knowing that her mother would not tolerate her "living in sin," Ronnie told Beatrice that she was staying in hotels, busy with rehearsals and recordings. As Beatrice's suspicions mounted, Spector proposed a radical solution. According to Ronnie, he telephoned her mother in New York, wildly improvising a story that he and Ronnie had just been married by "two practicing rabbis" in "an obscure Hebraic ceremony." When Beatrice threatened to come out and see for herself, Spector, apparently convinced that she would accept the situation once she realized the luxury in which her daughter was living, offered to pay the fare himself. Beatrice arrived a couple of days later. Furious to discover that there was no wedding ring on her daughter's finger and that she had been misled, she ordered Ronnie to pack her clothes and told her she was taking her back to New York. According to Ronnie, as the taxi pulled out of the drive to take them to the airport, Spector pulled a wad of $500 bills from his pocket and threw them on the ground, pleading, "It's all yours. Just leave my wife here!"

Back in New York, Beatrice moved her daughter from one relative to the next, in an attempt to avoid Spector's increasingly desperate phone calls. To kill the boredom of watching television soap operas all day long—and in ominous portent of things to come—Ronnie had discovered a new distraction, drinking. "After two glasses I actually started to enjoy watching *As the World Turns*," she would write in *Be My Baby*. At the same time, according to Ronnie, the financial implications of her affair with Spector were beginning to sink in among her family. "Not once did anyone ever talk about Phil without mentioning money in the same breath."

At length Spector himself arrived in New York, tracking down Ronnie to an aunt's house in Spanish Harlem. The following day they left for California.

In March 1968, Spector finally proposed that they should marry. Ronnie was giddy with the vista of unbroken happiness spreading before her. "First off, I'd be a star again," she wrote in her autobiography. "Phil would be so inspired by married life that he'd climb right out of his rut and write half a dozen new songs for me. . . . We'd be the king and queen of rock and roll, and our life would be one never-ending party. Elvis and the Beatles and all the stars from *The Late Late Show* would drop by the mansion just to be around us."

The wedding day was set for April 14. On April 4 Martin Luther King Jr. was assassinated in Memphis. King was one of Spector's heroes, and just as he had been by the death of Lenny Bruce eighteen months earlier, he seemed to be thrown completely off balance. According to Ronnie, he retreated to his room and locked the door behind him, playing recordings of King's speeches over and over again, only emerging three days before the wedding.

The ceremony in the Beverly Hills City Hall was as subdued as Spector's first wedding had been four years earlier. Beatrice had flown out from New York. She, Mac Mashourian, his brother Serge, who acted as best man, and Serge's wife were the only guests. To celebrate,

Spector took the wedding party to a Mahalia Jackson concert. Spector adored Jackson. Ronnie could not have cared less. After the concert, he told Mac to take his new wife back to the mansion, and instructed Serge to drive him to his mother's house. He had yet to tell Bertha that he was getting married. The encounter with his mother was evidently fraught; Bertha did not approve. (She would later lament to friends that her son had married "a schwarze," and complain bitterly that the marriage was "like a thorn in my butt.")

According to Ronnie, when Spector returned to the house two hours later, there was a furious fight during which he accused his new bride of only marrying him for his money. She spent her wedding night with her mother, locked in the bathroom with Spector pounding on the door. It was an unhappy omen.

"Phil and Ronnie getting married was an ego merger," one friend says. "Phil loved the fact that other men were attracted to her but he was the one who had her. He loved her voice. She was his passion. 'She's mine.' But he didn't really want to spend time with her. And Ronnie wanted him so he would produce her and only her, so she would be the star, and also to be lavished with his money. They married for all the right reasons in the Gospel of Rock and Roll, and all the wrong ones in terms of having a reasonable relationship, or any kind of relationship at all."

Marrying Spector, Ronnie had boasted to friends that she was "the only girl who ever married the boss in the music business. Not even Diana Ross married Berry Gordy." But whatever dreams of happiness— and self-advancement—she had entertained about being Mrs. Phil Spector quickly began to evaporate.

Spector now spent most of his time brooding in his study. He seldom left the house, and when he did, it was never with Ronnie. Elvis and the Beatles didn't come to call. Whatever independence she had once enjoyed quickly faded away. She had no bank account of her own, no cash; if she wanted money, she had to ask Phil. According to Ronnie, he installed intercoms to monitor her movements throughout the house. It was his way of showing he cared.

He filled the house with symbols of togetherness that mocked the emptiness of the marriage, and the fast-receding memory of her career: napkins, towels and notepaper monogrammed with "The Spectors"; photographs of them in the studio together. But Ronnie had not been near a studio in more than two years. Spector appeared to have forgotten that she had once had a career. With no distractions, and no friends, there was nothing for her to do all day but mope around the mansion.

As one friend observed, there was "no sign of 'the little woman' in a bone of her body. Ronnie was incapable of boiling an egg." Not that Spector would have allowed her to. He insisted that staff take care of all the household duties. She read movie magazines, watched television soap operas and took up painting-by-numbers.

At night Spector would sit in darkness, endlessly playing old Hollywood movies. Edward G. Robinson, James Cagney, the slapstick heroes Laurel and Hardy and Harold Lloyd. But his favorite film was *Citizen Kane*. How could he fail to identify with Orson Welles's parable of ambition, hubris and spiritual desolation? And how could he fail to identify with its creator? Like Spector, Welles was a prodigy—he had made *Citizen Kane* when he was just twenty-six—a genius who refused to compromise and bent the world to his vision. And as much as *Citizen Kane* was a study of power and the isolation it brings—the plutocrat locked in his mansion of Xanadu, surrounded with everything money can buy but unable to find the one thing that would bring him happiness—so it was also a prophecy of Welles's own future, the inexorable decline of early promise and brilliance. According to Ronnie, Spector would play the film endlessly, weeping at the final scene, in which Rosebud—the sled—the symbol of childhood joy and innocence, is incinerated.

What on earth did they talk about? Spector with his feelings of betrayal and martyrdom, his collection of vintage Hollywood films, his Lenny Bruce recordings and Martin Luther King speeches; Ronnie with her thwarted ambition, her collection of nail polishes and hair preparations, her painting-by-number sets. In Spector's own Xanadu, time passed as if in purgatory.

For Ronnie's twenty-fifth birthday on August 10, 1968, he presented her with a Camaro sports car, gift-wrapped in white silk ribbon. According to Ronnie, however, her delight was short-lived, when he then presented her with an inflatable life-sized mannequin, dressed in a shirt and pants, to keep on the passenger seat beside her. "Don't you get it?" he told her. "Now nobody will fuck with you when you're driving alone."

The gift seemed to do little to pour oil on the troubled waters of the marriage. Shortly afterward—and barely four months after their wedding—Ronnie hired a Los Angeles attorney, P. F. Caruso, to begin divorce proceedings. Caruso's petition claimed that Ronnie and Phil had separated on August 20—just ten days after Spector had presented her with the Camaro and the mannequin.

Listing Ronnie's net worth as "nothing" and estimating Spector's fortune at "5 million," the petition asserted that everything Spector owned was community property and requested the court to authorize the hiring of a certified public accountant to provide an inventory of all his business records so that Ronnie could see exactly what she was entitled to.

"Since the marriage of the plaintiff and defendant," the complaint read, "the defendant has treated plaintiff in an extremely cruel manner and has inflicted upon her great and grievous mental and physical suffering, and said conduct on the part of the defendant has defeated the object of matrimony.

"The defendant has a mean and ungovernable temper and has grabbed plaintiff violently and has threatened to stick his fingers in her eyes and he has stated to her that he could not permit her to get a divorce from him."

Ronnie, the complaint went on, was "currently under a doctor's care for nerves," and it requested that Spector be enjoined from "annoying, molesting, or harming [her] in any way whatsoever."

Spector responded to his wife's petition by promptly filing one of his own. In answer to Caruso's claim that all of Spector's assets were community property, Spector's lawyer Jay Cooper asserted that "there exists no community property of the parties herein." Cooper's complaint also charged Ronnie with "extreme cruelty" against her husband, but without specifying its exact nature.

Evidently, the dispute was quickly put to rest, however. Ronnie continued to live at the mansion, and by April 1969 both suits had been dismissed by the lawyers who filed them.

Bored and frustrated, Ronnie now started to drink more heavily, smuggling the booze into the house on her occasional expeditions to the outside world. In desperate need of a life for herself, her thoughts began to turn toward motherhood. "I knew I'd make a great mom," she wrote in *Be My Baby*. "All I needed was a kid." It seems appropriate that the solution should have been suggested to her by her most constant companion: the television. Watching a program about unwanted babies, she was immediately struck by the idea that she should adopt a child. That same afternoon, she drove to an adoption agency and selected a mixed-race baby boy, named Donte. Within four weeks, Donte was hers. As odd as this spontaneous gesture may have been, Spector's response was odder still. Apparently delighted at the prospect of fatherhood, he immediately set about preparing cards announcing the happy event—"Presenting the smash-hit production of Donte Phillip Spector"—that cast Donte's arrival as a three-act play, in which Ronnie appeared to be playing the part of the child's natural mother.

When Ronnie expressed her doubts about the implication that she'd given birth to Donte herself, Spector replied, "If I say you were pregnant, who's going to say any different?" Ronnie, he suggested, should stick a pillow under her shirt when anybody visited the house. She apparently went along with the plan without demur.

Nedra Talley had recently given birth to her first child, a daughter Christina, and when she learned that Ronnie too had "given birth," her first reaction was one of incredulity. "It was so confusing. I'd only been with her like a couple of months before, and suddenly—'We just had a baby!' I was trying to figure it out. She said it was premature; I said, 'Well, maybe you were two or three months pregnant and you didn't know it.' " When Nedra discovered that Donte was actually adopted she began to think it was just another, albeit extreme, example of Ronnie's old competitive instincts. "Ronnie had always had this thing that if I did something, she had to do it, too; if I was getting married, she had to be married; if I had a baby, she had to have a baby. It just couldn't be that I was beating her."

When Donte first arrived in the house, Spector played the role of doting parent, suspending his customary nocturnal hours to help to feed and bathe him. But the novelty quickly palled. Not quite trusting Ronnie to do the job herself, he appointed a nurse to look after Donte and turned his thoughts back to his career.

16

"Out There, but in a Beautiful Way"

The two years he had been away from the music business had left
Phil Spector feeling estranged, bitter and afraid. The possibility
that his career was over, that the world had already written him
off as a spent force, exercised him endlessly. Just twenty-nine, he was
terrified that his best years were already behind him.

In his 1969 interview with Jann Wenner, Spector would admit how
he felt he could no longer communicate with anybody in the record
business. "I can't really bullshit with them; I don't have friends in the
record industry. I don't talk with them. We don't jell; we don't communicate; because I'm too bitter I think. I'm still involved with why 'River
Deep' wasn't a hit and what the fuck was . . . and am I that hated? Am I
too paranoid? You know, you can antagonize people if they think you're
not human, if you say, 'Aw fuck, I ain't afraid.' A lot of people will get
very angry at that, disc jockeys in particular . . ."

Talking with Wenner, Spector sounded as sour and reactionary as
the "straights" who had mocked his music four or five years earlier—in
his own words, "an old-timer wishin' for the groovy young days."
Nothing was as good as it used to be. Black music had gone, the "group
on the corner" turned into "a white psychedelic or a guitar group."
The charts were full of acts that are "going to bore everybody to
death." Artists of today, he lamented, "just sing. They don't really
interpret anything." Even the Stones were "just makin' hit records
now. There was a time when the Stones were really writing *contributions*. See, that's a big word to me—'contributions!' " He talked of how
he felt he could bring something to Mick Jagger, Janis Joplin and
Dylan. "I'd do a Dylan opera with him . . . You see, he's never been
produced. He's always gone into the studio on the strength of his lyrics,
and they have sold enough records to cover up everything—all the

honesty of his records. But he's never really made a production. He doesn't really have to."

Then there were the Beatles. "I would like to record them a certain way because, again, other than what they do themselves—there's nobody. I don't know how influential their producer is, and I am sure they have a great deal of respect for him and he's the fifth Beatle and all that, but I don't think he thinks the way I would think . . ."

But then nobody, in Spector's opinion, thought the way he did, no producer could hold a candle to what he'd done. "I'm not interested in knocking everybody's brain 'cause I'll *always* make a good record, and it'll be better than all that shit out there today. 'Cause *they* really don't know how to record. They don't know anything about depth, about sound, about technique, about slowing down."

But Jagger, Dylan, the Beatles . . . none of them had called.

Retirement bored him. The studio was Spector's home, his world, the milieu where he was most in command of everything, including himself. Adrift in the echoing rooms of the La Collina mansion, he was nothing but a ghost. Philles was dead, and Spector did not have the appetite either to revive it or to start afresh. But in the summer of 1968 an opportunity presented itself through a flourishing independent Los Angeles label, A&M. The initials stood for the labels' owners, the trumpet player Herb Alpert and Jerry Moss. Alpert was a former student at Fairfax High, who had gone on to work as an A&R man at Dore Records, around the time when the Teddy Bears recorded "To Know Him Is to Love Him" for the label. Moss was an independent promotions man who had prowled the corridors of the Brill Building before moving to Los Angeles in 1960. In 1962, Alpert and Moss formed their own label, releasing "The Lonely Bull"—a mournful trumpet instrumental by Alpert and the Tijuana Brass, inspired by a visit to a bullfight in Tijuana, and recorded in the studio he had built in his garage. The record became a Top 10 hit. This early success was consolidated with middle-of-the-road acts like Sergio Mendes, the Sandpipers and Chris Montez. But by 1968 the label had broadened its roster, licensing releases by British acts such as Procol Harum, Joe Cocker and Free.

Spector was acquainted with both Alpert and Moss, but it was Larry Levine who was most instrumental in bringing him to A&M. Levine had left Gold Star in 1967, when Alpert (whose records Levine had engineered at Gold Star) offered him the job of chief engineer at A&M's new recording studios in the old Charlie Chaplin film studio on La Brea Avenue. In the five years they had spent together working shoulder-to-shoulder at Gold Star, Levine had come to develop an almost filial affection for Spector, regarding himself as something of an elder brother figure. But even Levine had never quite come to terms with the contradictions in Spector's behavior.

"I had a strange experience with Phil that kind of illustrates that. The first year I was at A&M, I got a really nice Christmas bonus. I was already getting a good salary, plus profit-sharing. And when I got the bonus I said to my engineers and the people working for me, 'The drinks are on me—I just realized that if things stay like this until I'm eighty, I'm going to be worth eighty million dollars!' And Phil happened to be there, and he really wasn't happy about that. It was a ridiculous thing. I got the sense that he didn't want me to be independent of him, or be on a par with him money-wise or any other way. It was as if it was threatening to him. It wasn't a question of me being happy. He saw this eighty million dollars as a realistic attainment. I'd meant it as a joke. Everybody laughed except Phil. But Phil needs to be in charge.

"But at the same time there could be this enormous generosity, too. I remember another time at A&M when something went awry somewhere and I got a note from someone berating me. Phil read the note, and he ended up writing three pages to this guy, giving him hell for having the effrontery to do that to me. I mean, three pages! And it was beautifully phrased. Phil would do that kind of thing."

For Jerry Moss, the fact that Spector had not been in a studio in more than a year, and had not had a hit record in more than three years, was an irrelevance. "Our view was that Herb and I just wanted to work with great people," Moss remembers. "It didn't matter to us if somebody was in fashion or out of fashion—as far as we were concerned, this guy was the tops and he made great records. He was intriguing and wouldn't it be fun." Learning of the new partnership, Spector's old partner Lester Sill could not disguise his skepticism. Phil, he told friends, was "roaming and using," just as he always had.

Given carte blanche by A&M to record anyone he liked, Spector returned to first principles, choosing a relatively unknown act that embodied the medium he understood best and loved most—the black voice. He had found a group that were neither "a white psychedelic or a guitar group." Checkmates Ltd. were a mixed-race soul group featuring two strong black singers, Bobby Stevens and Sonny Charles, who alternated on lead vocals in a manner reminiscent of David Ruffin and Eddie Kendricks of the Temptations. "Discovered" by Nancy Wilson, they had been working the circuit of nightclubs and Las Vegas lounges for a number of years; signed to Capitol, they had released a series of singles and an album, *Live at Caesar's Palace*, which included a showstopping version of "You've Lost That Lovin' Feelin,' " with Stevens and Charles trading the Bill Medley and Bobby Hatfield lines. Spector could hardly have failed to notice the similarity when he saw the group perform, and he was excited with the prospect of working with a soul vocal group that he could fashion in his preferred image.

In search of material, in the last months of 1968 he traveled to New York. The old contacts he had relied on in earlier days had scattered to the winds. Don Kirshner had gone on to enjoy great success as executive producer for the Monkees and was now occupied with the TV cartoon group the Archies; the songwriting teams of Goffin and King and Green-wich and Barry were no more (Barry was working for Kirshner on the Archies). But in a Chinese restaurant on Broadway Spector happened to run into Toni Wine, an acquaintance from the Brill Building days. Wine had signed to Kirshner's Aldon Music when she was just fifteen, writing songs and sometimes recording demos for Goffin and King and Mann and Weil. From time to time Kirshner had even suggested that she and Spector should write together. "But at that time," Wine says, "I wasn't even allowed out at night." She had gone on to pursue a career that com-bined singing and writing, recording a handful of singles for Kirshner's Colpix label, enjoying a huge hit in 1966 with her composition "Groovy Kind of Love," recorded by the British group Wayne Fontana and the Mindbenders, and composing advertising jingles. At the time she met Spector she was working with a songwriting partner, Irwin Levine.

Within a few days of their meeting, Spector joined the pair at Wine's apartment on Eighth Avenue to begin writing together. Their first col-laboration was a song called "Black Pearl," a sweet, plaintive soul ballad inspired by the Sidney Poitier film, *For Love of Ivy*, about a black maid who decides to leave the white family she has served for many years to return to school. The lyric contained a deliciously double-edged trope—the black pearl, it ran, might never have been pretty enough to win a beauty show, "But you're my Miss America, and I love you."

"The original lyric was 'you're my Miss America, from Lenox Avenue'—Lenox Avenue being *the* street in Harlem," Wine recalls. "We all thought, That's so real, so perfect, so wonderful. But then Phillip made the 'executive decision' to change it, because how many people are going to know where Lenox Avenue is? But even to this day, when I sing it, I sing it with the original line."

Satisfied with the outcome, at the beginning of 1969 Spector invited Wine and Levine out to California to work on more songs. Enthused at the fact of working again, Spector was at his most charming and endearing, in "a wonderful frame of mind," Wine remembers, a solicitous and generous host, who plied his guests with deli brought in from Greenblatt's and kept them amused with a stream of practical jokes. The two enormous wolfhounds that roamed the grounds, he warned them, were trained to "kill on command" ("lick you to death, maybe," says Wine). On one occasion he called Doc Pomus in New York, spoofing Pomus by conducting the entire conversation in an uncanny impersonation of Pomus's own rasping hipster-speak—"What's up, babe?" On another, he casually handed Wine a packet of chewing gum, then watched in mounting amusement as she worked through the pack, discovering that Spector had removed every stick of gum and carefully rewrapped the empty package.

"We'd sit at the piano, walk around the room, sing, write, talk about our mothers . . ." Wine remembers. "Phil has incredible pitch, and I do too, and sometimes he and I would sit at the piano and sing purposely off-key. It drove Irwin nuts. And Phil would just burst out laughing and say, 'What's wrong, Irwin?' People would say, 'Oh, Phil's crazy, he's nuts,' but I saw no side of that other than he was just hilarious. He was eccentric and pixilated. He was out there, but in a beautiful way, not in a scary way."

In the two weeks they worked at Spector's house they saw nobody other than Spector and his bodyguard. If Ronnie was there, they never saw her. "Years later, when all this came out, Irwin and I would say, 'Jesus, maybe she was locked in a room upstairs . . .' "

With "Black Pearl" in his pocket for the Checkmates, Spector now decided to hold fire with the group. Instead, to raise the curtain on the A&M deal, he turned back to a long-running project, one that had already brought him success, failure and no little heartache—his wife. Was it a residual belief in the talismanic properties of the group's name? A gesture of love and appeasement to Ronnie? Or did he genuinely believe it was an inspired idea? Whatever his reasoning, in February 1969 Spector took Ronnie back into the studio for the first time in almost three years, recording another of the songs from his collaboration with Wine and Irwin—"You Came, You Saw, You Conquered"— and releasing it a month later under the name of "The Ronettes, Featuring the Voice of Veronica." Ronnie was exultant at the prospect of being back in the studio and resurrecting her career. But her hopes were quickly dashed. Uncomfortable in A&M's spanking new studios, Spector struggled to replicate faithfully the old Gold Star Wall of Sound with massed strings and choirs, but the effect fell curiously flat, and the record sounded merely dated. Whatever cachet the Ronettes name once had had long since evaporated, and "You Came, You Saw, You Conquered" vanished without trace.

Spector now turned his attention to the Checkmates, recording their first single, "Love Is All I Have to Give," a melodramatic throwback to the mid-'60s testifying soul ballad, written by Spector and Bobby Stevens, and showcasing Stevens's gruff, rasping, preachy style. But not even Spector appeared confident about the record's prospects; within a matter of weeks he was rushing out a second single, the first song he had written with Wine and Levine in New York, "Black Pearl." Beautifully sung by Sonny Charles, wrapped in a lavish and irresistibly warm production, and with a string arrangement that might have been borrowed from a Temptations record (even Irwin Levine would describe it as "a Detroit record"), it was Spector's most affecting piece of work since "Walking in the Rain."

Released under the name of Sonny Charles and the Checkmates, the record gave Spector his first Top 40 hit in more than three years. He now turned his thoughts to an album. But he quickly seemed to grow bored with the project. Irwin Levine would remember him whiling away the time in the studio on the pinball machine. Nor were matters helped by the growing rivalry between Bobby Stevens and Sonny Charles over the solo billing that Charles had received on "Black Pearl." Envisaging a reprise of the problems that had undermined the Righteous Brothers, Spector withdrew from the project, leaving the arranger Perry Botkin Jr. to complete the album, which would eventually be released under the title *Love Is All We Have to Give*.

Even more distressing to Spector was the sudden death of Mac Mashourian during the recording of the album. Spector marked the passing of his old friend with a dedication in the album's liner notes— ". . . to the memory of a very dear friend of mine, Mac Mashourian. Though he has left his mortal coil, he will live forever. For as my friend, he showed me that love is really mental attraction in the presence of emotional security and for that reason I will love him forever—for after all—'Love is all we have to give.' "

Spector now took on a new bodyguard and factotum, a retired sheriff's marshal named George Brand. Spector would usually call on his bodyguards as and when he needed them. But Brand actually took up residence in the mansion, in a basement apartment. A man of quiet, avuncular authority, Brand was of a different order to the martial arts experts that Spector usually liked to surround himself with, and he had one qualification that Spector particularly liked—Brand was licensed to carry a gun. Spector already kept a gun around the house as a security measure, but having a bodyguard who packed heat in the holster under his jacket seemed to add a certain frisson to the whole business of being Phil Spector.

17

The Lonely Bird in the Gilded Cage

Nik Cohn had much in common with Spector. The son of an academic, Cohn had been born in London but grew up in Ireland—an outsider, Jewish in a country of Catholics—the smallest and youngest boy in class, like Spector, disdained and put upon. As soon as he could, Cohn packed his bags for London and started writing. In 1965, at the age of eighteen, he published his first book, *Market*, a series of studies of street-market characters. The *Daily Telegraph* wrote that it begged comparison with Zola. Cohn went on to write a novel, *I Am Still the Greatest Says Johnny Angelo*, about a pop's star meteoric rise and fall, and in 1968 he published *Awopbopaloobop Alopbamboom*—the first serious literary appraisal of rock and roll's short history. Written in an exhilarating and effusive firecracker prose, it was both paean of praise and epitaph to a golden age that Cohn considered was already at an end.

Phil Spector was the only figure in popular music who continued to exercise a fascination for Cohn—the music's last authentic genius, he believed, a man who "superseded rock and roll." Cohn duly approached him, expressing his desire to write his biography. Spector suggested he fly to Los Angeles to talk about it. Arriving at the Chateau Marmont, Cohn contacted Spector's office and was told he would be collected from his hotel. A week later, George Brand turned up in Spector's Rolls-Royce to ferry him to La Collina Drive.

In what was now an established ritual for any visitor to the mansion, Cohn was ushered into the sitting room and asked to wait—"a very long time." Placed on a coffee table were three copies of an anthology of Tom Wolfe's writing, *The Kandy-Kolored Tangerine-Flake Streamline Baby*, each with a marker at Wolfe's 1965 essay on Spector. The long wait, the carefully placed reference material—Cohn felt it was all designed to tell him something. "It was letting me know that I was not important. The placing of the Tom Wolfe piece was showing me that a better-known and greater man had trodden this path before me and I was bloody lucky to be there. Tom Wolfe had waited for an hour and a half. I could wait for two and a half . . ."

At length, Spector appeared, "a tiny, wispy figure, impenetrable shades . . . The whole idea was obviously intimidation, but what I felt from him was a terrified little boy. But I was something of an expert on terrified little boys, because I'd grown up as one myself."

Over the course of the next four weeks, Cohn would make regular pilgrimage to La Collina Drive, to sit in the arctic semidarkness and talk. The mansion appeared all but deserted. Once he heard a woman singing in another room, a few bars of "Black Pearl." He assumed it was Ronnie. Arriving on another day he glanced up to see a face looking down from an upstairs window, "like the first Mrs. Rochester."

Spector regaled Cohn with stories of his childhood, his school days and how he had revolutionized and conquered the record industry. He sang old songs, showed Cohn trick shots at pool, and almost beat him at pinball (at which Cohn was expert). One day, "like a Jewish mother rampant," Spector prepared a feast of lox and cream cheese on rye. But behind the effusive manner, Cohn sensed a man fearful that his time had passed.

"He would go into long, long monologues, about Lenny Bruce, and *Easy Rider*, which he seemed to think was the greatest film ever made," Cohn remembers. But what he really liked was martyrdom—osmotic martyrdom, as it were; in other words, people being crucified in a way that he saw himself as having been crucified by the industry. As far as he was concerned, people had turned their backs on him and he was in Siberia. Philles was gone. The Checkmates didn't seem to greatly excite him.

"At that time, Los Angeles was awash in kaftans; a whole generation with a new explanation, and your head is in a beautiful bag, man—which somebody actually said to me. As well as beautiful young people, there were a lot of the older school of Jewish record industry people—fat, fifty and over the hill—suddenly reinventing themselves in kaftans and beads. On one level Phil Spector was on their side—*Easy Rider* and so on; Lenny Bruce, civil rights—the whole counterculture thing. But on the other hand, peace and love didn't temperamentally sit well with him.

"He could see what was going on around him, that the music and the attitude behind it was changing; that he needed to adjust, but seeing that and actually acting on it was not something he could really do.

"I don't think it was lack of nous that undermined him. I think it was temperament, because he was an exceptionally angry person. I think there was a terrific war going on within Phil Spector between the conscious side that said, this is what's going on—love is all we need—and the real spring of his creativity, which was anger—or even more specifically, revenge."

One day, when Spector grew tired of talking, he suggested they take a drive. They drove along Sunset Boulevard and past the Aquarius Theatre, where the organizers of the hippy musical *Hair* were throwing a party in the parking lot. Spector told George to slow down, and rolled down his window to appraise the scene. Somebody in the crowd recognized him, called his name and the car was immediately engulfed in a crowd of capering and cavorting freaks, banging on the roof and blowing him kisses. When a hand came snaking through the window, attempting to touch him, Cohn remembers, Spector recoiled in fear and disgust, and shouted to George, "Get me out of here!"

Shaking, he turned to Cohn. "Who were they?" he asked, as the car headed back to the safety of the mansion. "I mean, who were those *animals*? My God . . . sweet Lord, what have I done?"

At length, Cohn decided he could stand no more. His appetite for writing a book had deserted him. He had come to write a life; but now he realized that whatever he wrote "would have been an obituary," he says. The heat and fury and vision that had driven Phil Spector had all but gone. All that was left, Cohn concluded, were the "motions of mystique"—the mansion, the bodyguards, the gold-rimmed shades, none of it able to disguise a terrible "blankness."

"It seemed that he had no more great pleasures, no passions, not even all-consuming hatreds," Cohn would later write. "Sometimes he would say he was happy, and he smiled. At other times he shook his head and looked tragic. But mostly he simply sat, and survived, and let time pass."

One evening, Cohn asked the question that had been exercising him from the first moment he had walked through the doors of the mansion. Was Spector entirely exhausted? Could anything important lie ahead? Or was his life, in essence, already over? Spector, Cohn wrote, "looked surprised, a mite baffled. Playing for time, he removed his shades and peered past my ear, off into infinity, to signal profound thought. He pondered, reconsidered, delayed. In the end, however, the question must have defeated him, outstripped his range, for he only shrugged his shoulders and put his shades back on. 'I guess it is,' he said offhand, and we talked about pool instead."

Cohn left Los Angeles shortly afterward. He did not write the book.

However, he did write an article about his encounter with Spector, which appeared in an English rock magazine *Cream*. It dwelt on Spector's troubled childhood, lauded his early accomplishments and lamented the death of early promise. A portrait of a man lost to the world, estranged even from himself, it was precisely the obituary Cohn feared that his book would have become.

In 1976, Cohn's piece was reproduced in *The Rolling Stone Illustrated History of Rock & Roll*. By then Cohn's own career had taken another, yet more improbable, twist. An article that he had written for *New York* magazine in the early '70s about the disco craze had been turned into the film *Saturday Night Fever*. Cohn was living in New York, enjoying his unexpected windfall, his meeting with Phil Spector long since pushed to the back of his mind. He was astonished then to one day receive a telephone call from a woman announcing herself as Phil Spector's sister, Shirley. She had read the article, she told Cohn; how, she demanded to know, could he have written those terrible things about her mother? Cohn was taken aback. Whatever he had written, he said, was based on what Spector had told him; indeed, if he remembered correctly, Spector had actually told him a great deal more than he'd actually used in the piece. He had erred on the side of kindness.

Brushing his explanations aside, Shirley went on: she wanted Cohn to know that her mother had also read the article and been so shocked that she had suffered a heart attack and was now in the hospital in critical condition.

A shaken Cohn barely had time to stammer his apologies and sympathies before Shirley hung up.

Cohn left his apartment for a meeting, asking a friend who was staying to take any messages. A couple of hours later Cohn telephoned his apartment. There had been a message. Shirley Spector, Cohn's friend told him, had called again. She wanted Cohn to know that her mother had died of the heart attack, and she hoped that Cohn would "rot in hell."

It would be almost thirty years before Cohn would discover that Bertha Spector had not suffered a heart attack at all, and that, in fact, she did not die until 1995.

Motherhood had not proved the panacea that Ronnie Spector had hoped. Depressed over the failure of "You Came, You Saw, You Conquered" and resigned to the fact that her career was now all but over, she began drinking more heavily. On August 10, her twenty-sixth birthday, she and Spector flew to Las Vegas to see Elvis Presley perform. After the show, they went backstage. According to Ronnie, Spector left her stranded while he pushed his way through to meet Elvis on his own. It was only when Elvis's young wife Priscilla—"the only girl there wearing even more mascara than I was"—took her hand, that Ronnie was able to enter the inner sanctum. Spector stayed on, and sent Ronnie back to the hotel, returning a few hours later to find her passed out, drunk, in front of the TV.

The next day, Spector and Ronnie returned to a Los Angeles enshrouded in fear. In the early hours of August 9 a group of misfits and runaways acting under the orders of a habitual criminal and self-styled cult leader named Charles Manson broke into a house on Cielo Drive in Beverly Hills, murdering five people, including the actress Sharon Tate, the wife of Roman Polanski, and the celebrity hairdresser Jay Sebring. The following day, a wealthy supermarket executive Leno LaBianca and his wife Rosemary were found murdered in their home in Los Feliz. Scrawled on the walls in the victims' blood were the words "Death to Pigs," "Rise" and "Healter Skealter"—a misspelling of the Beatles' song "Helter Skelter."

The Manson murders struck a mortal terror into the heart of the Los Angeles music community. Manson had designs on being a singer and a songwriter. He had become acquainted with Dennis Wilson of the Beach Boys after Wilson picked up two of the Manson "family" hitch-hiking; Wilson had allowed Manson and his followers to stay at his house before becoming rattled by their behavior and throwing them out. (The Beach Boys actually recorded one of Manson's songs, "Cease to Exist," retitled as "Never Learn Not to Love.") Wilson introduced Manson to the record producer Terry Melcher, who at the time was living in the house on Cielo Drive where Sharon Tate would be murdered, and where Manson was a frequent visitor. At one point, Melcher actually considered offering Manson a recording contract but then thought better of it. Melcher was convinced that he had been Manson's intended target.

In the wealthy enclaves of Bel Air and Beverly Hills, the shutters came down. Infected with the paranoia, Spector now took steps to turn his mansion into a fortified redoubt. The house was already secluded behind a high wall and an electric gate, but he now had a new chain-link fence erected inside the grounds, and within a few feet of the house itself. Barbed wire was strung around the courtyard with warning signs indicating that the wire was electrified and high-voltage. He acquired two attack dogs, which he named Duke and King, who roamed the property, terrifying visitors and snapping and barking at passersby from behind the wall. (He was eventually obliged to get rid of them after complaints from the neighbors.)

"Phil was paranoid to begin with," Peter Fonda remembers. "And the Manson killings were the proof of the pudding. After that he just shut down. You had the fence, and the fence within the fence. Even as he was withdrawing and withdrawing, he was never a freak. But after that it seemed like he became really freaky and really scared."

Watching through the bottom of a glass, Ronnie was apparently convinced that the new precautions were simply another step to make her a prisoner in her own home. Spector's desire to keep her from the world had now become a pathological obsession. By Ronnie's account, the doors to the house were always locked. If she wanted to go out, she would have to ask George Brand or George Johnson to unlock them, and they would only do so with permission from Spector. Whenever visitors came, she would be sent upstairs to her room. Occasionally, Spector would bring her down, as if to show her off to his guests—his prize possession—before banishing her upstairs again.

Ronnie's tales of her imprisonment—the lonely, broken bird in the gilded cage—would come to assume the dimensions of myth. In later years she would claim that she would only be allowed to leave the house on her wedding anniversary. In fact, she would return periodically to New York to be with her mother, and Beatrice would often come to Los Angeles, staying in her own quarters in the guest room above the garage. Nedra Talley found herself being drawn into the marriage as a confidante and counselor.

"Phil would call and say, 'Ronnie's doing this, Ronnie's doing that.' Then Ronnie would get on the phone and say, 'No, Phil is doing all these things to me.' She was going crazy in that house. If she wanted to go out, he would send George with her to watch her, always to watch her. Or his mother would be there—like, babysitting; if you want to go out, then let my mother go with you. And it was driving Ronnie insane."

One day, Don Kirshner came to call. Despite the millions each had made for the other, Kirshner and Spector had maintained a deeply equivocal relationship over the years. But their shared publishing interests required a show of at least cordiality between the two men.

"We had a mutual respect," Kirshner says, "but we never really liked each other. With Phil it was always about Phil Spector winning and being number one. It was never Darlene Love had a great voice, or

Mann and Weil wrote a great song, or it's Donny Kirshner did that. You'd think nobody else ever contributed. There's a word Phil lacked, and the word is gracious."

According to Kirshner, he and Spector were shooting pool when Kirshner became aware of a persistent "thumping noise" upstairs. "I said, 'Phil, what's that?' " Kirshner remembers. "And he said, 'I locked Ronnie in the closet.' I said, '*You what?* Are you nuts?' I went upstairs, opened the door to the closet and there she was, cowering inside. He said they'd had a falling-out, this and that. I was furious. I got her out of the house right away."

It would be some years before Kirshner would see Spector again.

"I'll never forget it. I was in my office in New York and Phil just walked in. Phil was always walking around with bodyguards. I never knew why. And he had a guy with him now. I was sitting behind my desk, and for some reason which I still don't understand, I walked around and leaned back on the edge of the desk. Phil was sitting maybe three or four yards away; the guy was maybe five yards away. And Philly turned to the guy and said, 'Do it!' And the guy does a Chuck Norris/Bruce Lee triple-kick thing. You remember the boots with the pointed toe, like a cowboy boot? He winds himself up and lunges at me with his foot and the toe ends up about a quarter of an inch from my nose. I could feel the breeze, the vibration. I can tell you this: if I'd sneezed or moved my head, I'd have been permanently disfigured. Forget terrifying—if I'd coughed, he would have killed me. I shouldn't say this, but the guy was brilliant. And thank God he was, otherwise I'd be dead.

"I can take pretty good care of myself, but not with this guy. I must have turned white. And when I composed myself I said, 'What did you do that for?' And Phil said, 'Oh, Donny, I'm just kidding around.' I said, 'You get your ass out of here,' and I kicked them out of the place. He'd obviously planned this as a practical joke. I felt it was a case of I'm going to show that big shot, that authority figure, that I can shake him up a little. But that was way above what Phil had ever done before."

Kirshner never saw Spector again.

Toward the end of 1969 Ronnie was involved in a car accident, drunk at the wheel of the Camaro. Spector now insisted she see a psychiatrist to try and get her drinking under control. The psychiatrist suggested that Spector should join in her group therapy, but according to Ronnie, he refused. In an attempt to stop her drinking, Spector put a padlock on the liquor cabinet. Ronnie forced it open with a screwdriver. "When he found the lock broken, he'd replace it with a bigger one. Then I'd find a bigger screwdriver." After Ronnie had been drunk for three days straight, Beatrice was summoned from New York to intervene. Nedra Talley and her husband Scott had moved to a small Christian community in upstate New York, and in an attempt to save Ronnie from her marriage and herself, they invited her to stay. "She came up and I was telling her, you need something to happen in your own heart so that you can stand on your own two feet; you need something that is bigger than you to make this work. I knew what Ronnie had grown up with, because when Ronnie stood up to be baptized as a child, I stood up to be baptized with her. So I really tried to pull her back to some of our foundation and truths that I thought would help her. And she prayed with me for the Lord really to come into her life and help her. But my personal feeling is she couldn't lay Ronnie Spector down in order to come to that place."

After eighteen months, the A&M deal stuttered to a close. Spector had delivered just two albums, by the Checkmates, and Ike and Tina Turner—and that a grab bag of material dating from the recording sessions in 1966—and a handful of singles. In a trade paper story, a spokesman for A&M described the parting as "not amiable." Spector, it was reported, was now going to Europe, "to discuss new projects." It did not specify what they were. There was no mention of the fact that Spector's prayers had been answered, and he had been thrown a lifeline by the biggest group in the world.

18

With the Beatles

The son of a kosher butcher from Budapest, Allen Klein had an unhappy childhood. Klein's mother died just a few months after his birth, in 1931 in New Jersey, and his father put Klein and his two sisters into an orphanage. When his father remarried, Klein was sent to live with an aunt.

As a young man, he worked two or three jobs at the same time in order to put himself through accountancy school. He took a job with a firm that looked after the books for several show business figures, among them the singer Bobby Darin. One day he happened to run into Darin at the wedding of a mutual friend. Klein asked the singer if he'd like to make $100,000. "What do I have to do?" Darin said. "Nothing," Klein replied. A few months later, Darin received a check for outstanding royalties and fees that Klein had managed to unearth from his record company. Word of Klein's skill in hunting out the discrepancies in record companies' bookkeeping, and his tenacity in recovering the money, quickly spread. In 1962 he became Sam Cooke's business manager, securing an unprecedented agreement for Cooke in which the singer received all his master tapes, site fees, gate revenues for concerts and 10 percent of all records sold and back royalties.

In 1965 Klein was hired as business adviser by the Rolling Stones' manager Andrew Oldham—but that relationship quickly turned sour. Klein went on to represent other British groups, such as Herman's Hermits and the Dave Clark Five. But it was the biggest pop group of them all, the Beatles, on whom he had his sights trained; and in January 1969, Klein arrived in London, ready to make his move.

Their five-year reign as the most popular group in the world had exacted its toll on the Beatles. The friendship between John Lennon and Paul McCartney had disintegrated into a state of mutual acrimony about musical direction and money, and a combination of poor business decisions and cavalier profligacy had brought the group close to bankruptcy. John Lennon had broken the news to the English music press that, if their company Apple were to go on losing money at the current rate, "we'll all be broke in six months." Lennon himself was "down to my last fifty thousand pounds."

When Klein sent word that he was in London, Lennon was the first to take him up on his invitation, arriving at Klein's Dorchester Hotel suite with his wife Yoko Ono in tow.

Thorough as ever, Klein had carefully prepared his pitch, as Lennon would later remember.

"Not many people knew which was my song and which was Paul's, but he'd say, 'Well, McCartney didn't write that line, did he?' And I'd say, 'Right,' you know, and that's what really got me interested, because he knew what our contributions were to the group."

To Lennon, the fact that Klein had once been a "penniless orphan" also weighed in his favor. "How insecure can you get," Lennon reasoned with dubious logic, "with nothing to hang on to?"

Lennon listened attentively as Klein quickly summarized the cause of the Beatles' problems and his proposals for remedying them. By the end of the meeting Lennon had made his decision. Borrowing Klein's pen, Lennon scribbled out a note to Sir Joseph Lockwood, the chairman of the Beatles' record company EMI. "Dear Sir Jo—from now on Allen Klein handles all my stuff."

Not everybody shared Lennon's enthusiasm for Klein. Paul McCartney wanted the Beatles' affairs to be put in the hands of his new representative—and father-in-law—the New York attorney Lee Eastman. Lennon's championing of Klein also sent shivers of apprehension through the Savile Row offices of Apple—which were in no sense eased when Mick Jagger telephoned Peter Brown, who was in charge of administration at Apple, to warn him of the potential problems ahead if Klein took over. "I said, 'Why don't you come in and tell the Beatles that?' " Brown remembers. "And Mick, to his great credit, was willing to come to the Apple office and say to the four of them, 'This will be a disaster.' So I got them to come in to the office; and John, in his perversity, got Klein to come to the meeting. Poor Mick walked in the door to be confronted with Klein as well. And of course he couldn't say anything."

In May 1969, with the sanction of Lennon, George Harrison and Ringo Starr, Allen Klein moved into his new office at Apple and began his task of reorganization with an executioner's zeal. His first act was to dispense with Apple's managing director Ron Kass and A&R man Peter Asher. The Beatles insisted that Peter Brown and Neil Aspinall, the director in charge of artistic affairs, should stay on. Intent on generating income for his new clients, Klein then cast a calculating eye over Apple's available assets. Foremost among these was an uncompleted Beatles' album, provisionally entitled *Get Back*, which had been recorded in a mood of lassitude and finality earlier that same year. *Get Back* had been conceived by McCartney as an "honest" album to restore the Beatles' compact with their audience, a record that would convey all the spontaneity and raw energy of the group's earliest performances, and at the same time appease John's disgruntlement with "overproduced" albums like *Sgt. Pepper.* To make the idea go further, it was decided that the making of the album would be turned into a film.

In January 1969, the group convened at Twickenham film studios, where in happier times they had filmed *A Hard Day's Night* and *Help!* But after ten ill-tempered days, that location was abandoned and they instead adjourned to the studios in the basement of the Apple offices in Savile Row. All the intended spontaneity and "honesty" quickly evaporated as the sessions became bogged down in a quagmire of recrimination and indecision. By the end the group had recorded dozens of different tracks, consisting of new compositions and songs from their Hamburg and Cavern days.

Thoroughly sick of the project and each other, neither the Beatles nor George Martin could face the task of editing and remixing the tracks. For months they sat on the shelf untouched. The engineer Glyn Johns took a stab at assembling them into an album, but his efforts failed to win the unanimous approval of the group.

It was at that point that Klein suggested that his old friend Phil Spector should be given the opportunity of salvaging the project.

"I think it was Klein trying to prove to John that he knew about music," Peter Brown says. " 'I'll help get this out, I know how to get it finished.' Because Klein always needed to prove himself. And I think he was rather proud of himself that he'd found somebody of such . . . eminence to bring in. So Phil was asked. John at that time would have done anything to fuck anyone, he was so disenchanted with everything, he just wanted out. So Phil was a puppet in a way."

In the first week of January 1970, Spector flew to London with George Brand in attendance, and put up at the Inn on the Park on Park Lane. Ronnie had returned to New York with Donté, to be close to

Beatrice, moving in to Spector's apartment at the Hotel Navarro on Central Park South. "Donte was just starting to walk," she recalled in *Be My Baby*, "and I loved being able to take him to Central Park just like any other mom. That time I spent in New York was the happiest period in my marriage."

Spector did not travel well. Apart from his previous visit to Britain in 1964, and a brief excursion to Tijuana to secure a Mexican divorce from Annette, he had never left America. He had little curiosity about the unknown, was never the type to jump on a plane to India to meet the Maharishi, or to travel to Florence to see the Uffizi. "Phil wouldn't even go to Hawaii," says his friend David Kessel. "He liked to sit in his mansion. It was his little niche."

Not only was the lengthy transatlantic flight an instrument of torture, but Spector did not even have the consolation of his familiar creature comforts waiting for him at the end of it. He complained to friends about the food—Can you believe it? The English put cheese and mayonnaise on white bread and think it's a delicacy?—the fact that shops closed at 5:30 p.m. and pubs at eleven, and that there was nothing on TV.

But the Beatles were worth any inconvenience or discomfort. "At that point in his life Phil was like Sherlock Holmes without a case," David Kessel says. "He'd had people offering tapes, acts, none of which he was interested in. But when the call comes to save the Beatles, yeah, okay, that's exciting."

Spector's appointment had served only to deepen the divisions in the Beatles. While Lennon and George Harrison—both great fans—were enthusiastic, and Ringo was prepared to accept anybody who would finish the record, McCartney would prove less welcoming. Peter Brown remembers Spector arriving at the Apple office, "this little bundle of nerves and enthusiasm. He had the biggest act in the world; he'd been asked to get involved. But he was in a very difficult position, because there was one member of the group who didn't want him under any circumstances. Paul didn't want to have anything to do with John or Klein. But my view was that this was a man of great talent, who respected the group enormously and wanted genuinely to help."

Spector had been in England barely a week before he was in the studio—but not with the *Get Back* tapes. The first of the Beatles to strike out on his own, John Lennon, had already recorded two singles, "Give Peace a Chance" and "Cold Turkey," with Yoko and a loose aggregate of musicians he called the Plastic Ono Band. At the end of January, struck by sudden inspiration, he hastily organized a session at Abbey Road Studios, to record a new composition, "Instant Karma (We All Shine On)," calling on the services of George Harrison, the drummer Alan White, bass player Klaus Voormann—and Spector. Voormann recalls that Lennon was in such a hurry that he hadn't even bothered to inform the other musicians that Spector was producing the session.

"It was very strange. John came running in the studio, went to the piano, played the song; we thought, Oh yeah, great. Went to our instruments, started running through, and then suddenly we heard a different voice in the control room. We had no idea who it was. 'Can you put the cymbals a little higher; or take them off?' Then after a while this guy came into the studio, and he had PS monogrammed on his shirt. It still didn't dawn on me. He went back in the control room; we did a couple more takes and then went into the control room. Everywhere there were tape recorders, equipment—it was just ridiculous; stuff Spector had brought in from all the other studios. He turned up the volume all the way, and we heard the count in . . . even that sounded incredible. And what followed just blew us away. It was not only the volume; it just sounded incredibly good. That was the moment when I knew it was Spector."

Intent on beefing up Lennon's sound, Spector had Lennon playing on one grand piano, while Alan White and George Harrison hammered at either end of another and Voormann played electric piano. Voormann was bemused when Spector reprised his old trick from the Gold Star days, telling the drummer Alan White to remove all his cymbals. "It looked crazy. Normally you can never see the drummer because he's hidden behind all these cymbals. But I think Phil told Alan to take them off to resist temptation. And he also ordered Alan to lay a towel over his tom-tom. All these tricks. You really got the sense this was a guy who knew what he was doing." Spector pushed White's drum to the front of the mix, adding handclaps and percussion, to create a sound as stark and propulsive as a jackhammer, while Lennon's voice, laced with echo, acquired a harsh urgency never heard in Beatles records. In search of more voices to emphasize the chorus, someone was dispatched to the Speakeasy, a favorite music-business watering hole, to recruit volunteers.

Spector wanted to overdub strings, but Lennon, thrilled with the results, was adamant the record should be released just as it was. It was only later, when he heard the American release of the single, that he realized Spector had remixed the song without his approval, producing a somewhat cleaner and smoother version. Lennon complained that

"It's the only time anyone has done *that*," but Spector was let off the hook. As far as Lennon was concerned, he'd passed the audition.

Doing his best to ignore the divisions around him, Spector now set about salvaging the *Get Back* tapes, installing himself first in the basement studios at Apple and then in Abbey Road.

He would later complain to his friend the musician Dan Kessel. "It was a near impossible job, the tapes were that bad," Kessel says. Phil had to do lots of edits, listen to take after take, and find the one good verse from one take and the one good chorus from another, and then make copies to piece it together. He was doing extensive surgery, just to get the skeleton of the song, even before it came to overdubbing strings or whatever else he was putting on there."

Faced with bare bones, Spector chose to do a radical overhaul on everything. He added strings to George Harrison's "I Me Mine"; on the song "Let It Be" he added a brass section, and rummaged through a host of outtakes to find the sharp and lyrical guitar solo from George that punctuated the song. But the most radical makeover was reserved for Paul McCartney's ballad, "The Long and Winding Road" a pretty song that had sounded feeble in its original version. Spector decided to embellish it with strings, choir and a celestial harp that added a sugary coating of chocolate-box sentimentality to the song's theme of romantic longing.

McCartney was not consulted on Spector's revisions and when he heard "The Long and Winding Road" he was furious. He immediately dispatched a letter to Allen Klein, demanding that the added instrumentation be reduced, the harp part eliminated, and that he should "never do it again." But Klein ignored his demands and released the song as a single. According to the Beatles' publicist Derek Taylor, McCartney thought it was "the shittiest thing anyone had ever done to him, and that was saying something."

A month before the release of the album, now entitled *Let It Be*, in May 1970 McCartney released his own solo album and formally announced his departure from the Beatles. When, in January of the following year, he began court proceedings against his fellow Beatles he would cite Spector's remodeling of "The Long and Winding Road" as an example of Klein's "intolerable interference" and one of his reasons for seeking the dissolution of the group.

The critics would prove no kinder to Spector's revision than McCartney had been. "They just panned the shit out of me," Spector later told the writer Richard Williams. "It was fun to see people getting into it ... 'how Spector ruined the Beatles' ... There was also the fact that most of the reviews were written by English people, picked up by the American press, and the English were: an American, I don't care who it was, an American coming in, taking over."

While it may not have pleased the critics, the mood of plangent sentimentality that Spector invested in the song captured the imagination of the public as the perfect epitaph to the Beatles' career. Released in America as the group's last single in May 1970, it sold 1.2 million copies in the first two days, and on June 13 it became the Beatles' twentieth and final number 1 single in America. When, later that year, *Let It Be* won a Grammy, Paul McCartney had no hesitation in going to collect the award.

Much as he had come to loathe everything about the Beatles, and much as he wished to cut himself free of all that being a Beatle entailed, the bitter and rancorous disintegration of the group drove a final nail into the fragile psyche of John Lennon. For years, the group had been the instrument of transformation and catharsis for all of Lennon's frustration, anger and pain; the childhood wounds inflicted by the desertion of his father Fred when Lennon was just nine years old, his abandonment by his mother Julia, and her early death; his conviction in his own genius; his deep, underlying insecurities. Drugs, sex, Transcendental Meditation, fame, money—even Yoko and evangelizing for world peace—all had failed to exorcize Lennon's demons. By March 1970 he had taken to his bed in his Georgian manor house, Tittenhurst Park, apparently in the grip of a minor nervous breakdown. It was then that salvation arrived, in the form of a bulky package from America, containing a book *The Primal Scream*, written by a Los Angeles psychologist named Arthur Janov.

Janov had devised a process, which he called Primal Therapy, that involved regressing a patient back to the moment of his birth, and replicating the "primal scream" of infant anguish, when all wants and needs demanded to be fulfilled. In the re-creation of this moment, the theory went, all of the neurotic defense mechanisms that the patient had built up through his life would be demolished, and the patient would be reborn in a condition of prelapsarian purity and innocence. Janov claimed his treatment was a panacea that could cure not only neurosis but also "homosexuality, drug addiction, alcoholism, psychosis, as well as endocrine disorders, headaches, stomach ulcers and asthma."

Lennon, who had been silently screaming all his life, was galvanized. At Yoko's instigation, Janov traveled to England to lead the couple through their first sessions at Tittenhurst Park. Janov would later recount that Lennon "had the kind of pain that would knock a patient off the floor it was so catastrophic." For his part, Lennon would greet Primal Therapy as "the most important thing that happened to me besides meeting Yoko and being born." Duly converted, at the end of April the Lennons returned to Los Angeles with Janov, where they would spend the next four months in therapy. Spector, who remained in London, magnanimously put his home, his staff and his refrigerator at their disposal. Lennon was bemused some months later to find that Spector had billed Apple for food and accommodation costs.

With the Lennons in America, Spector now turned his attention to another Beatle. George Harrison had been so delighted with Spector's work on *Let It Be* that he had no hesitation in inviting him to produce his first post-Beatles solo album. Nor did Harrison have any shortage of songs to bring to the project. Having long been frustrated by being fobbed off with the inclusion of only one or two of his compositions on Beatles albums, Harrison had accumulated a formidable catalogue of work—the ensuing album, *All Things Must Pass*, would comprise twenty-three of his songs.

The number of musicians that Spector assembled for the sessions, which took place between May and August at Abbey Road, almost equaled the size of the team that had once filled Gold Star. There were the drummers Ringo Starr, Jim Gordon and Alan White; Klaus Voormann and Carl Radle on bass; the keyboard players Gary Wright, Gary Brooker and Billy Preston; the horn players Bobby Keys and Jim Price; guitarists Dave Mason, Eric Clapton, Pete Drake and Harrison himself, along with members of the Apple group Badfinger. Voormann, who had played on the "Instant Karma" session, was fascinated and impressed to see Spector now working with a much larger ensemble of musicians, reassembling his old Wall of Sound on the foundations of a massed battalion of guitarists and keyboard players.

"When you analyze what Phil did, it was just amazing," Voormann remembers. "He took away all the baffles between the instruments, because he wanted the sound of each to meld into the other. And he was very particular about where he positioned the acoustic guitars, sitting them right in front of the drums so he got this live drum sound from the room sound. He somehow managed to get the sound so it sounded like glass on top. And then he would have a completely 'dry' bass drum, and a completely 'dry' bass and a completely 'dry' voice, against this whole thing. It sounded just incredible."

The sessions quickly fell into an established pattern. Spector would arrive at Abbey Road each afternoon, habitually dressed in neatly pressed jeans and wearing outsized aviator shades that were forever sliding down his nose. He would complain noisily about the antiquated air-conditioning and lighting, setting the temperature as close to "arctic" as possible, and plunging the studio into a state of near darkness. Saffron-robed Hare Krishna followers drifted in and out delivering vegetarian food. At the end of each session, Spector would depart with George Brand to be chauffeured back to his hotel, leaving the musicians to unwind in a series of prolonged jam sessions that would be boiled down to the "fourth side" of the eventual album.

For the first few weeks things went well, then Spector began to grow impatient. Harrison—as much a perfectionist as Spector, and now particularly anxious that his first solo project should be as perfect as possible—constantly fretted over his vocals and his guitar playing. Usually, it was Spector who kept people waiting. Now the boot was on the other foot.

The more Harrison belabored his performance, the more irritated Spector became—at Harrison, and everything around him. He couldn't sleep in his hotel. England was dank and drafty. He hated the food. He felt perpetually homesick. He hated television: he phoned a friend in California and complained that he'd been "watching someone painting a wall for six hours." His growing boredom and unhappiness now began to manifest in another way. He started drinking.

Spector had always been abstemious in his habits. Drugs exaggerated his perpetual fear of being out of control. He would occasionally smoke a cigarette, or more likely a cigarillo, but it was not a habit. When he drank, it was sparingly. If musicians turned up at his sessions drunk or stoned he would become apoplectic. It offended his perfectionism.

But now he started drinking in earnest himself, gulping down Courvoisier in the long hours as the sessions ground on. He would later explain to the *Los Angeles Times* journalist Robert Hilburn that he was "letting his hair down" after all the hard work of the '60s.

"I ran a company all that time. I didn't even think about drugs and I never had any alcohol, to any extent, until 1972 [*sic*] when I went to England to work with George Harrison and I started getting bored."

But that was only part of the problem. As much as anything else, Spector was drinking to ease his nerves. More than anyone, he respected the Beatles' place at the pinnacle of the musical hierarchy, revered them. For all his outward displays of arrogance and bravado, Spector was thrilled to have been acknowledged and, finally, accepted by them; at the same time he was terrified of the possibility of failure and rejection. He particularly idolized Lennon, who by this time had begun to drink heavily. Anxious and insecure, Spector followed suit. Spector would quickly go from being a garrulous drunk to an unpleasant one. Alcohol, according to one friend, was "poison to his system. Phil would have two drinks and he'd become Mr. Hyde. It was like he'd taken some kind of potion. He would turn on people and be horrible."

The longer the sessions wore on, and the more he drank, the more his mood began to sour. "Phil started getting pretty obnoxious," Voormann remembers. Now it was Spector who began wasting time, performing in the control room with a stream of ad libbing and teasing. He took particular delight in making fun of the tape operator, Eddie Klein, who was endowed with a prominent nose. "Phil was on him all the time," Voormann says. "If Eddie did anything wrong, there'd be half an hour of jokes and laughing at his expense. Cruel for Eddie perhaps, but great fun for everybody else. You could have a great time with Phil making you laugh and all that. But then it got to the point where you realized, My God, he's fucking up the whole session, so can he please go home so we can get some work done."

On one occasion, Spector was so drunk he fell off his chair, injuring his arm badly enough that he was obliged to absent himself from the studio for a few days.

In August, with the basic tracks completed, and his patience and enthusiasm apparently exhausted, Spector flew back to America, leaving Harrison to handle a number of guitar and vocal overdubs himself. On August 19 he dispatched Harrison a five-page memo outlining the work he felt was still required to bring the album up to scratch, written in the temper of a weary schoolmaster marking the homework of a particularly recalcitrant pupil.

"Awaiting on You All": The mixes I heard had the voice too buried, in my opinion, I'm sure we could do better . . . "All Things Must Pass": I'm not sure if the performance is good or not. Even the first mix you did which had the "original" voice, I'm sure is not the best you can do . . . "My Sweet Lord": An acoustic guitar, perhaps playing some frills, should be overdubbed or a solo put in . . . "Behind That Locked Door": The voice seems a little down . . . I think you should spend whatever time you are going to on performances so that they are the very best you can do and that will make the remixing of the album that much easier. I really feel that your voice has got to be heard throughout the album so that the greatness of the songs can really come through . . . Much love. Regards to everyone. Hare Krishna, Phil Spector.

Harrison would later protest that Spector had paid insufficient attention to the project. But Spector was unmoved by what he described to friends as Harrison's "complaining. There's a real problem if I have to be there to tell a Beatle how to sing."

"I know George said that he would have liked Phil to be present more," Dan Kessel says. "But Phil's view was: Hey, I did what I needed to do and I was there as much as I needed to be. I'm sure it wasn't necessary for Phil to hold George's hand while he was doing the twelfth over-dub track of the third harmony part on the slide guitar for the last cut on side Z. In the film business, they have second units and second-unit directors for that kind of thing. And George received producer's credit for his second-unit work."

Released in November 1970, *All Things Must Pass* was universally greeted as a masterpiece. Rather than engulfing Harrison, Spector's densely textured production served to brilliantly illuminate and complement the strength of his songs and performances. The album went to number 4 in Britain, but spent seven weeks at number 1 in America, while the exultant "My Sweet Lord" reached number 1 in both countries—the first single by an ex-Beatle to top the charts. Thirty years later, Harrison would reissue a remixed version of the album on a CD box set, explaining in his sleeve notes his feeling that some songs required "liberating" from a production that "seemed appropriate at the time but now seems a bit over the top with the reverb in the wall of the sound." Harrison also paid credit to Spector. "In his company I came to realize the true value of the Hare Krishna mantra." Whether as an expression of universal love or personal forbearance in the face of trying circumstance, he did not specify.

John Lennon returned from America galvanized by his sessions with Arthur Janov and inspired to write a series of songs, bitter and cathartic, spewing out all his venom, anger and frustration—against life, the Beatles and everything. In September 1970, Lennon, Yoko and Spector assembled at Abbey Road, to begin work on what would become *John*

Lennon/Plastic Ono Band. Klaus Voormann, who again played bass, remembers that the album was recorded in an adrenaline rush, with little time expended on discussion or rehearsal. "John had written down the lyrics and underneath he wrote C, F, G or whatever the chords were—that was our guide. And the words were written bigger than normal. He wanted us to really listen, to understand them and play something that fitted the lyrics."

Lennon would later describe Primal Therapy and the album that resulted from it as like being given a mirror to look into his soul—"and I wasn't looking in it from a sort of mystical perspective which tended to color things, or a psychedelic perspective or being-the-famous Beatle perspective or making-a-Beatle-record perspective, all those things gave a color to what I did."

Lennon had never written songs more revelatory, nor more corrosively powerful—and nor would he ever again—about personal abandonment, the hypocrisies of the British class system, the opiates of religion, wealth and fame: "God is a concept by which we measure our pain . . ." he sang in the magnificent "God," offering a renunciation of all the things he did not believe in—Jesus, Elvis, Beatles. "I just believe in me."

Spector listened carefully. Putting aside whatever thoughts he might have had of rebuilding the Wall of Sound, as he had for George Harrison, he instead fashioned a stark and spare production that perfectly matched the tenor of Lennon's songs, from the brittle, snapping anguish of "Mother" (heralded by the tolling of a funereal bell) to the gossamer delicacy of "Love," employing only a piano (played by Spector himself), bass and a gently strummed acoustic guitar.

"I think Phil himself had strong ideas about how the record should sound, and he and John talked about it," Klaus Voormann remembers. "It certainly wasn't just a case of Phil saying 'I do what John wants me to do'; it was more that Phil knew what was the best approach for this particular album. But that's where he's so brilliant. He didn't have to do his big sound; he could do something very fine, delicate and sensitive, whatever was appropriate for the song and the moment.

"He was very calm, very concentrated, very reliable; a really, really good producer. And he was incredible when he was just sitting at the piano, playing songs, whether it was one of John's he was working on before recording, or one of his own. I remember one day he did a version of 'River Deep—Mountain High' as a ballad, just him on the piano, with his funny, squeaky voice, and it was so beautiful. You knew then, this man is a genius. But he wouldn't let it be captured on tape. He was always hyper-aware of what was going on around him. You sensed he would know if a tape machine was running three rooms down the corridor. He's a tough cookie from New York; nobody can cheat him . . . that sort of attitude."

Recording the *John Lennon/Plastic Ono Band* album had the effect of forging the bonds between Spector and Lennon. They had much in common. Musically speaking, both shared a love of early rock and roll—the Sun recordings and Chuck Berry—and each had enormous respect for the other's work. But the ties went to a deeper, more symbiotic level than that. For both men, the wellspring of their creativity was an anger at the world, born of a deep unhappiness. Both had been nine years old when they lost their fathers—Lennon's deserting him, Spector's taking his own life (one can only imagine Spector's feelings listening in the studio as Lennon performed the song "Mother," addressing his absent father with undisguised fury—"Father, you left me, but I never left you . . ."). Spector could identify with Lennon's view that "talented people must always be in great pain—their sensitivity is what makes them great artists." Spector had always found it hard to forge deep and abiding friendships. He did not readily give of himself to other people. His guard was always up. But in John Lennon, he believed he had found a kindred spirit, someone who had suffered as he had, and who was just as vulnerable. He would come to describe Lennon as "like the brother I'd never had."

Spector had never before deferred to anybody in the studio, but he had no hesitation in subordinating himself to Lennon as "co-producer." "John knew how to shut Phil up," one friend remembers. "He was one of the few people who'd let Phil know if he was out of line. Other people didn't have the courage."

Nor did Spector raise any objection when it became apparent that Yoko had equal say in all matters. Spector's attitude toward women could be haughtily dismissive, but he indulged Yoko, listening attentively to her suggestions (even if he seldom acted on them), all too aware that, without Yoko on his side, Lennon would be lost to him. "Actually, it wasn't difficult to work that out," Peter Brown says. "John deferred to Yoko in everything and put her on this pedestal. But it was perfect for Phil and for Yoko. It gave him something to work on, and she was desperate to make music that would be recognized. She was a very single-minded person. She saw Phil as a tool; somebody who was very powerful in the business, who clearly could be used because he wasn't a Beatle person. Their agendas coincided."

"Everybody talks about Phil as this crazy man, out of control," Klaus Voormann says. "But behind all that he was actually this very quiet, intelligent man who had a great sense of humor. And he got on with Yoko particularly well. He could talk to her, make jokes with her—and it must have been hard for him, because she said lots of things to him that, for a professional, were unbelievable. She wouldn't know technically what was going on, and she would say something that didn't hit the spot at all, that was completely wrong, but he would find a way to explain it to her, or overlook it. He was very diplomatic."

Spector himself would talk later of Yoko being "quiet and helpful, and good to have around. And I gave her credit on the label. I had no choice. John was a brother and he loved her, so I had to figure out a way to use Yoko for my benefit. And the way I used Yoko was that I worked with John twenty-four hours a day, or sixteen hours a day, and when it became sleep time and crazy time for us, I sent him off to Yoko. She could see the value of me, like Ike Turner could see the value of me. Ike was dominating Tina until I came along, and he said, 'Go to it.' He let me rehearse with her, take her along, do anything I wanted, because it was in Ike's best interest. And for Yoko, it was in her best interest, because she was along for the ride. And she was getting more famous. But my ego is so in control and I'm so confident in my ego and talent and ability that I didn't mind giving her a credit on the label."

With Spector preoccupied with his work with Lennon and Harrison, Ronnie had been languishing in New York, convinced that her career was now all but over. But in February 1971 Spector gave her news that lifted her spirits. George Harrison, always a fan, had written a song especially for her—a stately ballad called "Try Some, Buy Some." Ronnie, astonished and delighted at the prospect of recording a Harrison composition, flew to London in high optimism and gave interviews to the British music press, talking enthusiastically of resurrecting her career. But when it came to the recording at Abbey Road, she was completely baffled by the song. "Try Some, Buy Some" was a long way from "Be My Baby." Harrison had written a hymn about rejecting materialism and embracing Krishna that Ronnie could not even understand, let alone invest with any meaning.

Spector dressed the song in a richly textured arrangement of strings and mandolins, which seemed more the point of focus than Ronnie's voice. Ronnie herself would describe it as "like a movie where the star only appears now and then" and would candidly admit she thought the record "stunk." The record flopped. Her comeback over before it had begun, Ronnie packed her bags and returned to New York.

Spector, by comparison, was working at a rate to rival his furious energy of the early '60s. In June, he joined the Lennons at their home recording studio at Tittenhurst Park, to begin work on yet another album, *Imagine*.

The anguished catharsis of *John Lennon/Plastic Ono Band* had proved strong meat for Beatles fans, and the album had been only an equivocal success, reaching number 6 in America and number 8 in the U.K., its sales a drop in the ocean compared to those of Harrison's *All Things Must Pass*. Stung perhaps by the success of the man he had always regarded as very much a junior partner, Lennon had now come up with a collection of songs rich in hooks and melodies that equaled, in some cases surpassed, anything he had written for the Beatles.

Throughout the three-week sessions, Spector once again subordinated his role, attending principally to faithfully rendering all the nuances of Lennon's songs, infusing them with a rare warmth and intimacy, and encouraging him to sing more movingly than at any time in his career.

During the recording of the title track, Lennon's hymn to utopian peace and brotherhood, proceedings were enlivened by the arrival of Spector's friend Dennis Hopper, who had flown over from Cannes. In the years since *Easy Rider*, Hopper had been vigorously pursuing a regime of mind-altering drugs and alcohol and he presented a querulous and quixotic figure. "At one point," Hopper recalls, "Phil came up to me and said, 'John just took me aside and told me "your friend Hopper has a gun hanging out of his pocket. Maybe he should do something about that."' So guess I had a pistol in my pocket. Well, I *did* have a pistol in my pocket. But the truth is, I didn't know too much about anything at that point."

In July, Spector took the completed tracks to New York, to add string arrangements. Lennon would later point out that while many of the songs shared similar themes to those explored on the *John Lennon/ Plastic Ono Band* album, *Imagine* had "chocolate on it for public consumption." But Spector did much more than simply sweeten. Rather, he crafted a series of perfect settings and caught a mood that would make *Imagine* the most perfectly realized and most commercially successful album that Lennon would ever record, and in the title track provide a song that would endure as a globally acknowledged anthem for peace. If a work is to be measured by its enduring impact, the hearts it touches, the hope it inspires, then, in a sense, *Imagine* was Spector's finest accomplishment as a producer. Even if his name was only in small type.

In search of new stimulation, and in a bid to escape the constant sniping at Yoko by the British media, the Lennons had now decamped to New York, taking up residence in a suite at the St. Regis Hotel. Exalting that New York was "the modern Rome," Lennon threw himself into a new life—indulging every avant-garde and radical diversion the city had to offer. He posed for the obligatory portrait by Andy Warhol, jammed with Frank Zappa at the Fillmore East, and found himself being courted by the self-proclaimed revolutionaries Jerry Rubin and Abbie Hoffman, eager to recruit Lennon to their sundry causes. Putting his own career to one side, Lennon threw his energies into supporting and promoting Yoko in her calling as avant-garde filmmaker and artist, bankrolling her films *Up Your Legs Forever* and *Fly*. In October 1971, an extensive exhibition of Yoko's work, *This Is Not Here*, opened at Everson Museum of Art in Syracuse, upstate New York. Spector, now an inseparable part of the Lennon circus, flew up from New York with a group of friends including Klaus Voormann. Drinking to anesthetize his fear of flying, Spector passed the flight in a state of inebriated agitation, shouting across the crowded seats to Voormann, who was sitting at the rear of the plane, "Klaus Voormann! We know you're the son of Martin Bormann"—"so that was nice," Voormann notes wryly. At the press conference that opened the exhibition, Spector—still somewhat worse for wear— spotted a journalist who had written an article about Lenny Bruce that Spector had taken exception to, and harangued him from the stage. "The journalist just wanted to die," Voormann remembers.

The opening of the exhibition coincided with Lennon's thirty-first birthday, and a group of friends, including Ringo Starr and Allen Ginsberg, celebrated in the Lennons' hotel room. As Ginsberg sang William Blake's "Nurse's Song," Spector insisted on holding his hand, while Ringo beat out percussion on an upturned wastepaper basket. Then a raucous Spector drowned out everybody else on sing-alongs of "Yellow Submarine," "Twist and Shout" and "My Sweet Lord."

The caravan moved back to New York, where at the end of October Spector produced Lennon's peace anthem "Happy Xmas (War Is Over)." As a gesture of proletarian solidarity, the Lennons now quit the St. Regis and moved into a dank basement flat in Bank Street in Greenwich Village that had previously been occupied by Joe Butler of the Lovin' Spoonful, and took up every passing revolutionary cause, appearing at a benefit for John Sinclair, the Yippie leader who had been imprisoned for possession of a single joint of marijuana, speaking out on behalf of the Attica Prison rioters and against the jailing of the black radical Angela Davis. By January 1972, the FBI had opened a file on Lennon with the expressed intention of finding grounds to deport him.

Lennon recruited a local band, Elephant's Memory, and with Spector as co-producer began work on another album, *Some Time in New York City*—a collection of agitprop songs including "Woman Is the Nigger of the World," "Sunday Bloody Sunday" and "Attica State." Spector's role was purely as a facilitator. Sympathetic as he was to the Lennons' plight, writing letters to the media and congressmen on their behalf, he was less animated by the fate of John Sinclair or the cause of the IRA. The album was a perfunctory favor. Nor did it capture the imagination of Lennon's audience when it was released in June 1972, rising only as far as number 48 in the charts before sinking from view. Devastated by its commercial failure, Lennon would not record any music for almost a year. Phil Spector's Beatle sojourn was over.

19

"These Are Pretty Wild Sessions, They Get Pretty Out There"

Late in 1971 Spector returned to Los Angeles. He had spent most of the previous two years away in London and New York, at a safe remove from Ronnie and the unhappiness of his marriage. But any expectations that matters might have improved were to be quickly dashed.

Only an incurable romantic could have conjured the records that Spector had made with Ronnie—idealized fables of a love that was too perfect to be true. And his possessiveness too was a sort of love, a symptom not so much of how little he trusted her, but of how little he trusted himself to be able to keep her. Control was Spector's way of guarding against the thing he feared most—being abandoned. But instead of security, marriage had brought only disillusionment, bitterness and recrimination. "The whole bottom line of Phil's life was pain," one friend says. "He had spent his whole life trying to understand that, and deal with that, and never getting it right. But Ronnie was just not sensitive enough to see that. For her the marriage was just some kind of fantasy of the big-shot producer making her a star. She didn't understand Phil at all."

The couple quickly fell into the familiar ritual of arguments, most of them to do with Phil's possessiveness and Ronnie's continued drinking. When, after one particularly horrendous drinking binge, she had a seizure and collapsed, Spector, at his wits' end, had her admitted to a sanatorium. She was apparently so taken with the facilities—the agreeable company of fellow patients, the volleyball games—that she came to regard it as "a vacation playground." Visiting the sanatorium "became my habit," she wrote in *Be My Baby*. "When things got bad at home, I'd get raging drunk, pass out, and then spend ten days in rehab."

Nedra Talley, who had come to regard Spector with a mixture of distrust and disdain, saw his eagerness to push Ronnie for treatment less as a mark of his concern than just another way of controlling her. "The way Ronnie was approaching it was like the clinic was the in-place to go," Nedra remembers. "But I was telling her, Phil is going to use this against you; when he decides to put it to you, there's going to be a list which he'll hold against you. And it's not going to be 'the clinic was a cool place to be'; it's going to be 'you were sick and you can't have your child.'

"Ronnie thought she was smart marrying Phil, but she had someone smarter than her, playing her. He played her in separating her from her sister and her cousin; he played her in cutting her off so that she didn't have any friends; he played her by putting her in hospital. She had a drinking issue of her own; but it was like, if you're with a crazy person for long enough and you have your own crazy side, then you'll go *really* crazy."

Driven to distraction by her drinking, and in a desperate attempt to salvage the wreckage of their marriage, in December 1971 Spector turned to precisely the course of action that Ronnie had employed two years earlier—adoption. By Ronnie's account, the first she heard of the idea was when Spector collected her from the sanatorium after one of her drying-out bouts and drove her to a playground, where he pointed to a pair of fair-haired little boys playing on the swings and told her he was considering adopting them. By the time they had returned to the mansion, the boys and officials from the adoption agency were apparently waiting to greet them.

The adoption of six-year-old twins Gary and Louis was a measure not only of Spector's desperation, but of just how divorced he had become from the reality of his marriage. Adopting Donté two years earlier had done nothing to bring him and Ronnie closer together; the arrival of two more children could only make matters worse. To Ronnie it was merely another example of what she perceived as Spector's desire to curtail her freedom. Within just three years of marriage, she'd acquired "three kids, five dogs and twenty-three rooms," she wrote.

While acknowledging that they were "adorable," she wanted little to do with the twins, although at Spector's instigation she did begin to attend AA meetings in an attempt to bring her drinking under control. Spector was seemingly in no better a state to assume the duties of parenthood, and it quickly fell to the ever-obliging George Brand to assume the role of surrogate father to the children.

Spector had now begun behaving with conspicuous carelessness. At the end of January, Spector was arrested in the Daisy club in Beverly Hills, after police received an anonymous call from a woman claiming that a man wearing a "maroon jacket with a karate emblem" had pointed a gun at her. Officers arriving at the club located Spector, noticed a bulge under his jacket, searched him and found a loaded handgun in his waistband. He was charged with the misdemeanors of carrying a concealed weapon and carrying a loaded firearm in a public place, ordered to pay a $200 fine and placed on one-year summary probation, with the condition that he not possess any dangerous or deadly weapons.

In May, he wrote to Jerry Wexler. During Spector's brief sojourn at Atlantic in the early '60s, the two men had regarded each other with mutual suspicion, but both shared an enormous affection for Lenny Bruce, and the death of the comedian had served to bring them closer together, mourning his loss. Albert Goldman's biography of Lenny Bruce, *Ladies and Gentlemen—Lenny Bruce!*, had just been published. Goldman had approached Spector to talk about his friendship with Bruce, but when it came to Lenny, Spector explained to Wexler, he claimed the right to remain silent. Lenny, he wrote, had told his own story brilliantly and eloquently in his autobiography and his recordings, and Spector would not read or see a single book, movie or play about his old friend, much less contribute to one. As for himself, he wrote, he was "up to my pippin" in the fight against John and Yoko being deported and the primary campaign for Democratic candidate George McGovern. "Roughly translated, that means I'm living in frenzied despair, which is a little hamlet on the outskirts of Desolation Row." He urged Wexler to come visit sometime. "We can pick up some sandwiches and tiptoe through the tar pits together."

On June 16, 1972, at approximately 11:00 a.m., William Valantine, an employee of the Speedy Attorney Service, arrived at the house on La Collina to serve divorce papers on Phil Spector. According to an affidavit filed to the Superior Court, County of Los Angeles, Valantine approached the front-gate entrance of the property, where he was confronted with "numerous signs warning all persons not to enter the property, that there were guard dogs and armed guards on duty. There was approximately a three to four-paragraph sign posted adjacent to the front gate warning any person entering beyond that point would be in violation of certain sections of California Penal Code (I did not write down the sections), and that there were sentry dogs and armed guards on duty and that if I entered I would be risking my life and I should leave immediately."

Undaunted, the intrepid Mr. Valantine drove through the open gate. In the courtyard he noted "several chain-link fences blocking all entrance way to the front door or access. Also, barbed wire was strung loosely around the courtyard with warning signs indicating that the wire was electrified and high voltage, I also noticed several more signs warning against the sentry dogs, no trespassing et cetera. I also observed large floodlights mounted in several upstairs windows of the residence aimed into the courtyard area which, obviously, would be turned on at night if anyone entered. I saw absolutely no sign of life on the property."

After sounding his car horn for five to ten minutes and receiving no response, Valantine left the property. When he telephoned the house a few minutes later, a "female voice" answered, asking him to state his name and business and telling him to call back in five minutes. When he did so the same female answered the telephone, this time identifying herself as Veronica Spector.

According to Valantine, "Mrs. Spector stated that she did not want her husband served today." It would be another couple of days before the papers were actually served.

The four-year marriage between Spector and Ronnie had finally reached a climactic end four days before Valantine's visit, on June 12. In her autobiography, Ronnie offered a graphically lurid account of the events of that evening, recounting how she had returned from an AA meeting to find the door of the mansion locked. Eventually, Beatrice, who was staying at the house, let Ronnie in through the servants' entrance. According to Ronnie, a drunken Spector confronted her in the hall, accusing her of having a boyfriend at the AA group. He then wrestled her to the floor, snatching her shoes, and shouted, "Don't even dream about divorcing me." After a further scuffle, Ronnie spent the night in her mother's room, and they both left the next morning. Ronnie's book suggests that she never returned to the mansion again. However, affidavits sworn for the ensuing court proceedings tell a slightly different story.

In an affidavit sworn on June 23 Ronnie stated that on the night of June 12 Spector "came to my mother's room, told me I should get a lawyer to get a divorce, and he hit me in the face while I was sitting down, my cigarette falling to the floor"—an account that appears to contradict her later claim that he had warned her "Don't even dream about divorcing me."

According to her affidavit, Ronnie ran downstairs, pursued by Spector, who "then pushed me out of the house through the kitchen door. When I left the house, I had no funds or assets of any kind."

After spending the night of June 12 in a hotel, Ronnie returned to the mansion, where she spent the next three nights in her mother's room. On June 16—the day Mr. Valentine called—Ronnie's Beverly Hills lawyers, Jay Stein and Daniel Jaffe, informed Spector that an action for dissolution of the marriage had been filed. Ronnie apparently left the mansion that same day. "Thereafter," she stated, "I was afraid to return to my home for fear my husband would harm me, and my mother and I have since been living in a hotel. In a telephone conversation with me Friday evening, June 16, 1972, my husband told me that he had thrown all my clothes in a garbage can on La Cienega Boulevard."

Ronnie and Beatrice were to continue living in the Beverly Crest Hotel for the remainder of the summer, as the affidavits and the insults flew back and forth. Donte and the twins Gary and Louis continued to live with Spector in the mansion. On July 6 Ronnie filed a motion to obtain sole custody of Donte (she appeared to have no interest in the twins), designed to demonstrate Spector's unsuitability as a parent. Stating that "my husband has a very suspicious nature," she elaborated on the security arrangements that had been described by Mr. Valentine, adding that there were "on the premises, more or less continuously, five dogs, including two German shepherd dogs, which are trained to attack on command, and one Irish wolfhound . . . One George Brand is employed by my husband (or one of his companies); he resides on the premises and acts as a bodyguard." (In a later motion she would add that "moreover, respondent [Spector] keeps and displays a number of weapons.") Ronnie requested that Spector should be ordered to pay sufficient support for her to rent a house or apartment in Beverly Hills, "comparable in furnishings, decor and comfort to the family residence," and adequate for the children (together with their governess) to be able to stay. She also suggested that she was willing to have a court-ordered psychiatric examination of all concerned to press her case.

In late July, Spector's lawyer Godfrey Isaac retaliated by filing an opposition to the proposed psychiatric examination, arguing that everyone involved, including Gary and Louis, had already been seen by psychiatrists before the divorce proceedings began. Moreover, Isaac maintained, he had evidence that Ronnie had had "repeated commitments to psychiatric wards," and that while Spector had been commuting between New York and London, she had "sustained an emotional breakdown." Spector, Isaac added, was willing to pay for Ronnie's lawyers to go to New York to interview the psychiatrists who had treated her if the court needed any more evidence. Ronnie's lawyers fired back, alleging that Spector had been swamping the switchboard at the Beverly Crest Hotel with calls, and "verbally abusing, threatening, harassing and intimidating staff," when Ronnie instructed them not to put the calls through.

At the end of July, the court ordered Spector to start paying Ronnie's hotel bills, and to allow her visitation rights to see Donte. Before long, Ronnie was filing another deposition accusing Spector of refusing to pay in full the bill for her stay, refusing to absent himself from the house when she exercised visitation rights to see the children and of refusing to return her "full-length mink coat, wallet and driver's license."

In August both sides began taking depositions from each other at the Santa Monica courthouse. When Spector's lawyers belabored Ronnie for her drinking, she responded that she had "partaken of alcohol" only since her marriage, "usually only with her husband," and that she drank to "shut out the continuous stream of shrieking by the respondent." At his own deposition, on August 21, Spector arrived with a stenographer's machine, which sat unused on the desk beside him as the deposition progressed. When Ronnie's lawyer Stein asked him why he was not taking anything down, Spector supposedly replied, "I'm waiting for you to say something important."

Stein and Jaffe would later attest that, leaving the courtroom, they were "made the objects of a ten-minute string of vehemence, obscene epithets and screaming" by Spector, "who was literally foaming at the mouth."

When the court ordered Spector to pay his wife interim support payments, he wrote out a check for the first $1,250 in court. A month later, three employees of Brink's—"two being armed guards and one holding a shotgun"—arrived at Jay Stein's offices to deliver the second payment of $1,250—in nickels.

In the meantime, in search of "community property," Ronnie's lawyers had ordered a certified public accountant, Arthur Linsk, to make an examination of the books of accounts of Spector and his company Phil Spector Enterprises.

In his affidavit, Linsk noted that the financial picture relating to Spector was "a diverse and complicated one." Spector, he noted, "does business under the fictitious name of Phil-Spector Productions," and had created at least three trusts in 1970: "Phil Spector Family Trust";

"Phil Spector 1970 Short-Term Trust" and "Phil Spector 1970 Insurance Trust." The Family Trust was funded with securities; the Short-Term Trust funded with copyrights of any interests in "musical compositions."

Spector's income, Linsk noted, was derived from numerous sources. Payments by "Phil Spector Enterprises Inc." included a personal salary as well as "substantial personal expenses," which Linsk noted "appear to be improperly charged as expenses of such corporation."

Itemizing Spector's income for the year of 1971, Linsk stated that Spector had paid himself a salary of $56,000 (approximately $266,000 in today's money). The Family Trust had rendered him $15,818, and the Short-Term Trust $40,897. Factoring in interest and other miscellaneous income, Spector had received a total of $120,223. To that was added personal expenses paid by Phil Spector Enterprises of approximately $75,000. Spector's gross income therefore was approximately $195,000.

Against that figure, Linsk calculated the living expenses of Spector and Ronnie at $44,000, plus the $75,000 personal expenses "improperly charged" to Phil Spector Enterprises—a total of $119,000 for the year.

Among the assets available for liquidation and use by Spector was $15,000 in savings accounts in the Chase Manhattan and Chemical Bank; securities of $372,000 in the Family Trust; and a salary of $3,000 per month for the months of June, July and August due from Phil Spector Enterprises, that Spector had not yet paid himself.

Further investigation revealed that in the period from 1970 to March 1972 Spector had earned producer royalties from Apple Records (for his work with Lennon, the Beatles and Harrison) of $375,366.88, of which $354,015.01 had been advanced or paid—leaving a balance due of $21,351.87. According to Linsk, it was with money from these royalties that Spector had purchased securities worth around $200,000 that had been paid into the Family Trust, and this money should be regarded as "community property," which Ronnie's lawyers calculated at no less than $225,000. Spector and his counsel insisted there was no community property.

At the beginning of August, after recommendations by Dr. Henry Luster, a psychiatrist hired by her counsel, and in an apparent bid to shape up for the custody battle, Ronnie checked into a psychiatric ward of the St. Francis Hospital, where she remained on and off for six weeks, before returning to the Beverly Crest Hotel. On September 14 her lawyers were called to the hotel by the manager, where they found her in "an intoxicated condition." A few days later, her lawyers were called again, this time to be informed that Ronnie had "accidentally set herself afire in bed." (By Ronnie's own account she had drunk a fifth of vodka and "drifted off faster than expected" leaving a cigarette burning. She was rushed to the UCLA Emergency Clinic, where she was found to be unharmed.)

Beatrice had left for New York, apparently telling Ronnie that she had to help Ronnie's sister Estelle with her new baby. And on September 21 Ronnie followed her there. Four days later, in a bizarre twist of events, she wrote to Stein and Jaffe, firing them as her lawyers, and canceling any fee agreements with them. Convinced that Spector had somehow got to Ronnie, Stein replied, expressing his concern that in light of her mental and emotional problems Ronnie "might be acting under the influence and dominance of others who do not have your best interests at heart." Warning her that a delay in going to court might jeopardize her claim to half of all the community funds that Linsk had unearthed (the approximately $225,000), Stein told her that until he and Jaffe had met with her personally, "to determine if you are acting on your own," they would continue to regard themselves as her lawyers.

Ronnie responded with a lengthy sworn affidavit sent directly to the court. In this she alleged that Stein and Jaffe had taken unfair advantage of her "emotional and mental" problems, had hospitalized her against her wishes, and kept her "through doctors and hospitals, incoherent so much of the time with medication and drugs [that] I was in no emotional condition to cope with that type of situation." Stein and Jaffe's motives, she claimed, had been solely to obtain "a large sum of money for themselves, and for their friends and associates, from Mr. Phillip Spector and myself, which was certainly not my intention at all.

"I definitely feel and have always felt that I can settle the divorce matter between Mr. Spector and myself very amicably and I in no way want to fight. In fact I really do not want nor did I ever want anything at all from Mr. Spector."

In November, Stein responded to Ronnie's affidavit, with one of his own, making clear his belief that Spector had "put the words" of the discharge letter and the affidavit in Ronnie's mouth. Declarations signed by Ronnie in the past, Stein maintained, reflected her "complete domination" by her husband. She had stated that Spector had a "violent temper and is domineering," and that in the past he had "physically abused and injured" her, and "imposed his will" on her "by the use of force, threats and violence."

Stein went on: "We believe the fact that we have ascertained . . . substantial community property constitutes a threat to the respondent [Spector], causing him to renew his effort to reach [Ronnie] and by reason of his domination and control over her, to get her . . . to discharge us."

Responding to her allegations that they had acted on her behalf without authorization, Stein stated that the fact that Ronnie "was and is a disturbed human being and is in need of psychiatric help is without question." It was in light of her past history of psychiatric treatment, he went on, that he and Jaffe had felt it necessary to call in Dr. Henry Luster, who had stated that Ronnie "reminded him of a recently orphaned child, whose mental state fluctuated from suicide and withdrawal to desperate clutching and clinging to anyone who offered her some assistance."

Everything they had done for Ronnie, Stein maintained, had been done with her full agreement, and at no time prior to her departure for New York had she expressed any dissatisfaction with their services. According to Stein, Ronnie had been repeatedly advised in the past that she was free to effect reconciliation with her husband, and on one occasion Dr. Luster had arranged a meeting with all parties in his office. Spector had failed to turn up, calling to explain that he was "unable to attend because of the children's purported illness and that he could talk for only a few minutes, whereupon he proceeded to harangue Dr. Luster for a considerable period of time."

Stein's riposte seems to have thrown cold water on Ronnie's application. By the end of November she had changed her mind yet again and decided to press on with the divorce case, with Stein and Jaffe continuing to represent her. It would be a further eighteen months before the case was finally settled. Spector was in London when he learned of Ronnie's decision. He dispatched her a note, neatly typed on Apple notepaper—his version of the last two verses of Bob Dylan's song "Positively 4th Street": ending that if she could look from in his eyes "then you'd know what a drag it is / To see you."

One day toward the end of November 1972 Joe Boyd, who was then working as the executive in charge of music for Warner Bros. films, received a phone call from Phil Spector's personal assistant. Spector had seen the film *Deliverance* and wanted to book "Lonny," the inbred and mentally retarded Appalachian boy who played the theme "Dueling

Banjos" in the film, to perform at his birthday party. Boyd explained that the boy in question—a sixteen-year-old named Billy Redden—did not actually play the banjo, and that the tune had been performed by Eric Weissberg. (In fact, Redden—who was neither inbred nor mentally retarded—was unable even to mime playing the banjo; director John Boorman had another child, wearing Redden's shirt, finger the chord changes.) "I tried to explain this to the assistant," Boyd recalls. "I could hear her talking to Spector with her hand over the phone. Then she said, 'Phil says he saw the movie, and the kid does play the banjo.' I said, 'Eric Weissberg plays the banjo. I was there, I recorded the track.' 'Phil says he doesn't believe you.' He was determined to book the weird, demented kid who played the banjo and he wouldn't get off the phone."

Another woman was beginning to play an increasingly important role in Spector's life. He had first met Janis Zavala in the mid-'60s when she was a high-school student working part-time in the Hollywood clothes shop Beau Gentry, where Spector was a regular customer.

Janis was petite and strikingly attractive; she wore her brunette hair to her waist and dressed in a bohemian style. She and Spector developed a platonic relationship; they would often talk on the telephone and in time he became something of a mentor to her, taking an active interest in helping with her studies. "Phil was very proper with Janis, like a Victorian gentleman, very respectful," says Dan Kessel, who attended L.A. City College at the same time as Janis. "Even though she was ensconced in the midst of the hip, Hollywood milieu, he discerned that she was a special young lady of quality and didn't regard her as a typical Hollywood chick. But they were just friends back then."

After working in publishing, Janis gravitated toward the music business, taking a job, quite by chance, with Spector's old partner Lester Sill at Screen Gems. As Spector's marriage drew to an agonizing and acrimonious end, he turned more and more to Janis for comfort. When Ronnie finally departed, Spector and Janis began dating. Their relationship would prove to be the closest and most enduring of Spector's life.

In June 1973 Tim Blackmore, a BBC radio producer, visited the La Collina mansion to interview Spector for a documentary series, *The Story of Pop*. Spector was in an expansive mood, treating Blackmore and his assistant Jane Lucas to bad impersonations of a Liverpudlian accent, regaling them with stories about his triumphs and accomplishments, spinning yarns, claiming to have played guitar on Big Mama Thornton records, to have produced the Drifters' "Save the Last Dance for Me," to have made hit records before "To Know Him Is to Love Him," "but it's not important to talk about them . . ."

His entire career, he said, he had "just tried to do artistically what was best. Artistically you can do better than anybody else, if you really believe in it. And I really believed in what was going on. And I did try to change the music. It was a painful experience; it was hard, basically because there were not many people to do it with. There was not much help. It really rested upon my ability to do things with my music and sounds." Was there any music, Blackmore asked, that owed a direct allegiance to Spector and what he had done?

"Everything. Including the Beatles. I don't know whether it pays to be a humble moron or a belligerent wiseguy. I don't know what's the difference . . ."

And then the declarative statement of intent. "I can make great records today. I made great records a year ago. Nothing can stop me."

Blackmore was alarmed when, at one stage, Spector suddenly asked, "Are you guys scared of guns . . . ?" He left the room, reappearing a few minutes later, dressed in a blue serge uniform with security-guard epaulettes, wearing a yellow straw hat, and brandishing a pistol. Why the outfit? asked Blackmore. Spector explained that paparazzi sometimes stood outside the gate; he liked to go out in disguise and shoo them away. He presented Blackmore with a shirt, handed the yellow straw hat to Lucas as a souvenir, and then led them on a tour of the house. Pausing at a closet, he opened the door; inside was a box full of yellow straw hats, identical to the one he had just given Lucas. According to Blackmore he took the hat off Lucas's head and put it back into the box, saying "Phil Spector needs all the hats he can get." He then led the bemused couple upstairs to the bedroom of the twins, Gary and Louis, waking the boys to "say hello to my visitors from England." Back downstairs, he entertained his visitors by playing a succession of acetates of unreleased Philles recordings by Darlene Love and the Ronettes. It was growing late, and Blackmore and Lucas were anxious to leave, but Spector showed no sign of wanting the evening to end. "You could be in here for twenty-six days," he told them, "and nobody would even know you were here." They passed the next two hours uneasily, as Spector continued to play music and regale them with stories. It was past two in the morning before they were finally able to make good their escape.

With the Beatles sojourn at an end, Spector was impatient to get back to work, and in the summer of 1973 his business manager Marty Machat negotiated a deal with Warner Bros., giving Spector his own boutique label Warner-Spector under the umbrella of the company.

Machat was a short, stocky man—"he could look Phil right in the eye," remembers one acquaintance—who favored custom-made suits, expensive colognes and large cigars. In earlier days he had dabbled in artist management, representing among others the Four Seasons and the boxer Sugar Ray Robinson. He had a reputation as a tough negotiator—"a very smart, fun fella who fought for his artists and double-checked the fine print," remembers Joe Smith, who was chairman of Warner Bros. Records at the time. "You'd check your jewelry when you shook hands with Marty. He knew how to play the angles."

Smith enjoyed telling the story about Jac Holzman, the founder of Elektra Records, who retired and moved to Hawaii. On a visit to Los Angeles, Holzman had dinner with Smith and Mo Ostin, the president of Warner Records. "And we said, 'Do you miss the music business?' And Jac said, 'I do. Sometimes I even think of getting back into it—and then I remember Marty Machat . . .' "

Spector's new relationship with Warner got off to a shaky start. Early in the negotiations, he invited Smith, Ostin and Warner's head of A&R, Lenny Waronker, to the mansion, and as Smith remembers, "pulled one of his numbers. He was drinking. He locked the doors. And he had what he claimed were his guard dogs outside and he wasn't going to let us go. I later learned they weren't guard dogs, but the three of us couldn't get out. It was just his practical joke. But we didn't think it was very funny. We sat there for another hour or two. Maybe he wanted to exert some power; show us what we were dealing with."

(Stan Ross was another who would experience Spector's compulsive need for control—or fear of abandonment. He recalls an occasion when Spector called "out of the blue" saying he had something he wanted to discuss. Spector sent George Brand to collect Ross and the songwriter Tommy Boyce. "We get to the house, and Tommy says, 'You guys talk,' and he just slides under the grand piano and closes his eyes. I say, 'This won't take too long, right, Phil?' He said, 'No, I just want to ask you a couple of questions about a project I want to do.' So blah, blah, blah, this goes on. And finally I say, 'It's time to go.' So Phil says, 'A few more minutes.' So we give him a few minutes, and I say, 'Phil, we really got to go back to work.' He says, 'Don't go out the door! You gotta wait until I press a button, because if I don't press a button the guys outside will shoot. They have instructions to shoot first and ask questions later.' I said, 'You push all the buttons you want, we're leaving.' Then I realize we don't have a car. I say, 'Phil, we need your chauffeur.' He said, 'I think he's sleeping.' He was just playing his game. But don't play with me. So eventually we get out. Nobody knows why he does these things. He's got to be different.")

Joe Smith was disconcerted still further when, as a gesture to mark the new partnership, he invited Spector to join a party to watch Muhammad Ali fight Ken Norton at the L.A. Forum. Smith had laid on a luxury bus to ferry his guests, who included some of the cream of the music aristocracy, among them Bob Dylan, Neil Diamond and James Taylor. Spector was the only one to turn up with his own bodyguard, George faithfully dogging his footsteps. "We had to park in the lot across the street where the buses park," Smith remembers. "These people never parked anywhere except under the stage; they didn't even know how to get across the street! I said, it's going to be like summer-camp buddies—everybody hold on to somebody so we know where we're going. I had to hold hands, literally, with Bob Dylan and James Taylor. I was leading, and Mo Ostin and somebody else from the record company were at the back, in case we lost anybody. And then I noticed that Phil had a gun, strapped around his leg. I said, 'What's that for?' and he said, 'Oh, it's security.' I said, 'Who cares about you here? We're going to the fight! Nobody's going to shoot you!' But Phil was strange like that . . ."

After the fight, Smith took the party to Trader Vic's for dinner. Sitting in the restaurant, three tables away, was Frank Sinatra, who had an interest in Warner Bros. through his Reprise label. "He sent a message to me, saying, 'What are you doing with those creeps?' " remembers Smith. "I went over and said, 'These creeps have each sold more with their last release than you have with your last two.' He said, 'I think I'd better come over and say hello.' He came over and just blew them all away—Hi, guys, bang, bang, bang . . ." Spector, in the presence of one of his idols, was for once speechless.

Whatever Spector's eccentricities, Smith and Ostin were confident that he would deliver the goods. "Phil had a fantastic reputation as a producer," Smith says. "We didn't need the cachet. I felt he still had a shot. It's not like he'd been living in a cave—well, he had been living in a cave, but he'd been aware of what was happening in music. We felt if he was willing to put his name on the line, we'd just as soon bet on him than on two new acts, which is what the cost would be. No sure thing, but we'd rather lose with Phil Spector than somebody else."

But Spector was apparently in no hurry to deliver on his end of the deal. Another, more enticing, proposition had come his way.

In the eighteen months since he and Spector had last worked together, things had gone from bad to worse for John Lennon. He had been engaged on two legal fronts, fighting for the right to remain in America, and crisscrossing America with Yoko in her attempts to gain custody of her daughter Kyoko. Demoralized by the bad reviews and sales of *Some Time in New York City*, he recorded a more overtly commercial album, *Mind Games* (that would be released in November 1973), then took to his bed once more, drinking heavily to anesthetize his unhappiness. In March 1973 the Lennons severed their relationship with Allen Klein as their business manager, apparently feeling that Klein had been neglecting them (it would take a flurry of lawsuits and a payoff of $4.2 million to make the divorce absolute).

To look after their affairs, they turned to Klein's former right-hand man, a lawyer named Harold Seider, who had resigned as chief counsel of Klein's company ABKCO in 1971 and moved to California. Seider flew to New York and met the Lennons at the Bank Street apartment. Seider was shocked at the Lennons' living conditions. "Talk about an embarrassment; it was in a cellar, two or three rooms, and in the back room no windows, nothing." Lennon had shaved his head, and looked, Seider remembers, "like something that had come out of a German concentration camp." Seider immediately found the Lennons new lodgings, in the Dakota apartment building on Central Park West.

May Pang, a twenty-three-year-old Chinese-American, had once worked for Allen Klein, before becoming the personal assistant to Lennon and Ono. Her duties included assisting Ono on her art films *Fly* and *Up Your Legs*—"The idea was 365 legs for peace, like her bottoms thing. I'd be calling up people like Andy Warhol and Jacqueline Onassis, saying, 'Hi, I'm from John and Yoko; we'd like to shoot you from your toes to your thighs.' "

By the summer of 1973, according to Pang, Lennon's indolence had reached a stage of virtual paralysis—"He really felt he couldn't do it anymore"—and relations with Yoko were now at the breaking point. "It was awful. The two of them . . . it was hammer and tongs, chalk and cheese, whatever you want. It was just not there. I would be in the office; John would come in, talk to me; a minute later Yoko would walk in and say, 'Where's John?' I'd say, 'Didn't you just see him?' That's how estranged they'd become."

In August 1973 Yoko approached May with an unusual request. She and John were not getting along, Yoko told her young assistant, and it was likely that before too long he would start seeing other women. Better, in that case, Yoko suggested, that John should have an affair with May. "I know you'd treat him right, so go out with him." May was taken aback. Her relationship with Lennon was strictly professional; she liked him, but it had never occurred to her that she would like to have an affair with him. Lennon was apparently equally taken aback by Yoko's scheme. "He told me he was shaving when Yoko said, 'I've fixed it for you to go out with May,' " she remembers. "He said, 'I almost slit my throat.' He didn't ask for it, and he didn't expect it. But Yoko was pushing for it, and he finally said, 'I'm tired of being miserable. If she says go for it, I'm going to go for it.' "

Duly authorized, May and Lennon began a tentative affair. In the first week of September, Yoko left town for a feminist conference. Harold Seider was leaving for Los Angeles; without telling Yoko, Lennon and May left with him. They moved into Harold Seider's apartment, until the producer Lou Adler offered to lend them his Bel Air home. (Adler and his girlfriend, the actress Britt Ekland, moved out to his beach house in Malibu.) Lennon, paranoid about his separation from Yoko becoming public, introduced May to everybody as "my nurse."

In the meantime, Harold Seider had been poring over the former Beatle's accounts, and now delivered some bad news: Lennon's earnings from the Beatles had been frozen in the ongoing court case over the dissolution of the group. He had been living on a £5,000-a-month stipend from the receiver, plus money borrowed from Allen Klein. And now, Seider informed him, Yoko had demanded $300,000 "security" money in his absence. The former Beatle was effectively broke. He was also facing another problem—a lawsuit from the music publisher and boss of Roulette Records, Morris Levy, alleging that Lennon had plagiarized his song "Come Together" from Chuck Berry's "You Can't Catch Me." Looking for a quick solution, Seider persuaded Lennon's label, Capitol, to trump up an advance of $10,000 for Lennon to record an album of rock and roll standards, and as a way of settling the action with Levy negotiated a deal whereby Lennon would include a number of songs controlled by Levy on the album, theoretically guaranteeing him a royalty windfall.

Lennon now contacted Spector to see if he would produce the album.

"John told him, 'I want to do an album of the songs I love,' " Pang says. "He said, 'I just want to be the singer in a band; I don't even want to produce.' And Phil was like, 'You're giving me the whole thing?' Because that had never been. It had always been co-productions before. John said, 'Yup, I just want to be a singer in the band.' And we were all thinking, this is trouble."

Spector would arrive each night at the Adler house for rehearsals. He had developed a fleeting enthusiasm for amyl nitrate "poppers," which gave a short and euphoric rush, but left his clothes, May remembers, smelling of "old socks." He would often be wearing a holster, "sometimes one on either side, under his arm. He'd be waving these guns around, and John and I would look at each other thinking, Can this be? Surely George, his bodyguard, wouldn't let him have real bullets in them."

Working on Lennon's albums in Britain, Spector had been on foreign soil. Now he was on his turf, doing things his way, and he started to put the call out for musicians to play on the sessions. Lennon had requested that they use the drummer Jim Keltner and the session guitarist Jesse Ed Davis; in keeping with the "back to the roots" nature of the project, he expected to be working with a small group of musicians. When he and May Pang arrived for the first session at A&M Studios, they were astonished to find a seemingly endless procession of illustrious session players filing into the studio, among them Hal Blaine, the guitarists Steve Cropper and Larry Carlton, and keyboardists Leon Russell and Barry Mann. "So many," Pang remembers, "they were trying to figure out where they could all sit."

Spector arrived customarily late, accompanied by George Brand, and proceeded to spend the next four hours painstakingly testing sound levels and mike placement and laying down the backing track. Finally, at three in the morning, Spector declared he was ready to do the vocal. With May sitting beside him, Lennon completed his takes within half an hour.

Among the troupe of musicians Spector had invited to the sessions were Dan and David Kessel, the sons of the guitarist Barney Kessel. Both in their early twenties, Spector had known them since infancy, from the times when Barney would bring them along to Gold Star sessions (Dan had played percussion on a Crystals session when he was eleven), and had always held a special fondness for the two brothers. They were like family. When Spector was in London, working with Lennon and Harrison, he had sent the boys postcards and souvenirs that he knew they'd get a thrill out of—Apple wristwatches, notes written on the Beatles' stationery. Both played guitar, and Dan also played drums. On the first night of the Lennon session, Jim Keltner was late arriving. "Phil was running the song down, getting an initial balance, so I volunteered to play the drums," Dan Kessel remembers. "He said, 'Okay, let Hal play the fills; you just keep the time.' So I go out there, sticks up. The other musicians were wondering who I was and what was going on. And Phil said, 'Wait a minute; this is Barney Kessel's son; and if Barney Kessel's son says he can play the drums, he can play the drums.' " After a while Keltner turned up and took his place behind the drums. But at the end of the session Spector invited the brothers back the following evening. "He said, 'And bring your instruments,' " Dave remembers. "We said, 'Okay.' And then he said, 'You do play, don't you?' "

On the second night, Spector arrived at the studio dressed as a surgeon, in a white lab coat, with a stethoscope hanging around his neck—his pun on Lennon's nom de plume of Dr. Winston O'Boogie. As he followed his customarily painstaking preparations, Lennon grew increasingly restive.

Spector had developed a fondness for a new tipple, Manischewitz, a sickly sweet wine used in Jewish rituals such as Seder (the high sugar content made it potentially disastrous for Spector, a borderline diabetic). He was now drinking Manischewitz "slowly, but steadily," Dan Kessel remembers, while Lennon was swigging vodka straight out of the bottle. "Anybody, at a certain point, you've had too much, but Phil was holding it better. The production was like this huge behemoth moving very, very slowly—John was waiting and waiting—and finally he cracked. He said, 'When are you going to get to me, Phil?' And Phil said, 'I'll get to you, John . . .' And John was like, 'You'll get to me! You'll get to me!' taking it as an insult, as if to say, 'You may be the great Phil Spector, but I'm the great John Lennon, don't talk to me like that.' And really there was no insult intended. It was just two people who'd been drinking a lot. So it all got a little testy."

The argument was a portent of things to come. Over the next few weeks, the booze flowed and the mood grew increasingly sour.

Tony King, who as a young promo man working for Decca had been responsible for looking after Spector on his first visit to London in 1964, was now working for Apple, and arrived in Los Angeles with the unenviable job of keeping an eye on Lennon. King was shocked at the change that had come over Spector in the years since he had last seen him. The charming, funny and thoughtful man who'd led the Ronettes singing in the Strand Palace Hotel, who'd sent King sweaters as a gift of thanks, had vanished. "He'd lost that boyish, mischievous personality that I first encountered. There was this slightly wild side to him, that made you feel you had to be careful."

King sensed that Spector was "suffering from having been big, and no longer being as big as he was, but still wanting everybody to think he was. So there was all this grandiose posturing going on—very L.A. Very Phil-insecure—a lot of challenging remarks, putdowns, which I found very uncomfortable to be around."

King was staying with an old friend, the English songwriter and musician Mike Hazelwood, whom Lennon had invited to play guitar on some of the sessions. King made a point of keeping away from the studio, but he began to suspect something was amiss one evening when he noticed Hazelwood packing a bottle of vodka into his guitar case, like a gunman packing his piece before a showdown. "I said, 'What's that for, Mike?' And he said, 'These are pretty wild sessions; they get pretty out there.'"

Elton John came to town, and one night King took him to visit the studio. "We went in and Phil was running around, spieling like a madman. John was trying to keep the situation under control, because by this stage Phil was the mad one and John didn't want Elton to think there were two madmen there. Elton was looking at me, kind of 'Is this okay?' We stayed for a respectable amount of time, and when we left Elton looked at me and said, 'Is it always like that?' We were both glad to get out."

In an attempt to lighten the mood, Spector took to turning up at the sessions in an assortment of fancy dress. The doctor's outfit was followed by a priest's cassock and then the dark glasses and white cane of a blind man. One evening he surprised everyone by walking into the crowded studio with an accordion strapped over his shoulders, playing a wistful and note-perfect version of Al Jolson's "The Anniversary Song"—a staple of Jewish weddings—concluding to a thunderous burst of applause.

Paulette Brandt, Spector's personal assistant, had a friend who happened to be dating Chuck Berry, one of Lennon's heroes. As a surprise treat, Paulette arranged for Berry to come to Spector's home to meet Lennon. But Spector insisted on playing his music so loudly that nobody could talk, and after a cursory exchange of pleasantries, Berry left.

The interlude did nothing to ease the mounting tension between Spector and Lennon. "Phil wanted control," May Pang says. "That's basically what it came down to. And he kept holding John at bay—like, It's my show, not yours. It was an ego trip. Fucking with John's head. It was unbearable, because I could see the pain in John from this." One night, Spector arranged to meet at Gold Star to do some vocal overdubs. Lennon arrived, only to pass the evening with Gold Star's boss Stan Ross, waiting in vain for Spector to turn up. "We kept phoning saying, 'Where are you?' " Ross remembers. "And Phil'd say, 'I'll be there in ten minutes.' And an hour later it'd be the same thing—'I'll be there in ten minutes.' At the end of the evening I said to John, 'It's been a pleasure and I'm sorry we couldn't do anything.' He said, 'He's a prick.' Next day I called Phil and asked him, 'What happened?' He said, 'Oh, I had problems and couldn't leave.' So tell us! But that would be too simple for Phil."

At one stage in the evening, Lennon had a heated telephone exchange with Yoko back in New York and smashed the receiver against the mixing board, causing some minor damage. Spector later offered to pay Ross for the repair, but Ross decided to keep the desk in its damaged state, "as a souvenir."

On another night, Lennon became so drunk that Spector was obliged to abandon the session altogether. With George Brand's help, he bundled Lennon into a car to take him back to Lou Adler's house.

"They got John upstairs into the bedroom," May remembers. "John was going, 'Come on, Phil, I love you'—in a drunken, melancholy way. And George was sitting on top of him. In John's mind, I think he thought he was getting into some kind of three-way sex situation. He couldn't tell what was happening. So he freaked out. They brought me upstairs and I was in shock to see that they'd tied John up. He was screaming at me. 'This is it!' I said. 'What did you guys do?' They said, 'Don't worry, he'll be okay, just let him sleep it off.'

"Phil and George left, with John upstairs screaming every awful thing you could imagine. Everything he wanted to say about Yoko was just coming out. It was just anger at everybody, Phil, Yoko, everybody."

In desperation, May summoned Tony King to help. By the time King arrived, Lennon had broken free of his ties and was standing at the front door, bellowing, King remembers, "like a mad bull. I got him in the house and he was a mess, sobbing, saying, 'Why did they do it, how could they do that?' Then all of a sudden he started fighting me. We were rolling around on the floor. Finally I got him where I was laying on top of him with his arms pushed out to the side, my face six inches away from his, and he was in some kind of blackout. He looked up and saw my face, and he said, 'I didn't know you were that strong, dear . . .' We both ended up laughing. And that broke it. The house was just a wreck; windows broken, Carole King's gold records were all over the floor, bent out of shape; Lou's collection of silver-handled walking sticks were scattered everywhere. The next day we went off to breakfast, and John just kind of laughed it off. He said, 'Well, that was a funny night, wasn't it.' I thought, All right for you to say—I've got to repair the bloody house."

That night, Spector arrived at the studio wearing makeup, to cover the black eye Lennon had given him in the struggle.

In November, the sessions were evicted from A&M after Jerry Moss, the head of the company, received reports that Spector had been waving a pistol around. The circus moved to another studio, the Record Plant.

It was there that Spector discharged a gun into the ceiling. "We were doing 'You Can't Catch Me,' " May Pang remembers. "Mal Evans [the Beatles' former roadie] was around, and I remember Phil's mother was in the control room. A very nice, well-dressed lady. And suddenly there was this pop! Everybody went, 'What's that?' and crouched down—including his mother. I went for the door, and in the anteroom outside, Phil was holding a gun and Mal was reaching over saying 'Give me that.' John was cowering with his hands over his ears. He was saying, 'Phil, if you're going to shoot me, shoot me; but don't fuck with me ears, I need them to listen with.' They'd been playing around and Phil kept hitting Mal with his hand, and he'd hurt his nose. Mal had complained, and Phil being Phil—'Oh yeah? I'm going to show you'—had pulled out the gun, and as he pulled it out, it went off. My thought was, Did he always have the safety off? The next day John and I were having dinner and Mal came by and said, 'Here's the bullet from last night.' What bullet? Because all this time John and I thought they were blanks . . ."

In December, Ronnie returned from New York for a court appearance as part of her ongoing divorce proceedings from Spector. In a display of solidarity, Lennon and May accompanied Spector to court, along with Spector's old friend and bodyguard Emil Farkas. Farkas had not seen Spector in more than four years. "He called me out of the blue," Farkas remembers. "He was frantic. He had to go to court and he wanted someone to be with him, so I went. I felt sorry for him. He ranted and raved. He was so crazy, the judge said, 'Mr. Spector, if you don't shut up, you're going to jail.' Phil had this big-time lawyer with him. He went up to the judge and said, 'You have to understand Mr. Spector is a genius in his own way, and you sometimes have to overlook things because of that.' The judge said, 'Well, tell your genius to cool it.' " Embarrassed, Lennon and May walked out. It was the death knell for the rock and roll album.

A few days later, Lennon reportedly received a call from Spector saying the sessions for the album would have to be canceled; the studio had burned down. Alarmed, Lennon phoned the studio, to be told that nothing had happened at all. A week later, Spector allegedly called again, telling Lennon, "I got the John Dean tapes!" When Lennon asked what he was talking about, Spector replied that the "house was surrounded by helicopters. They're trying to get them!" The penny dropped: what Spector was telling him, Lennon surmised, was that he had the tapes of the rock and roll sessions, and would not be handing them over.

Lennon and May Pang left for New York, leaving Harold Seider to settle the matter of the tapes.

When Seider contacted Marty Machat, Machat told him that it was Spector, not Capitol, who had paid for the recording sessions, and therefore owned the tapes. Seider suspected that Machat was attempting to broker the recordings to Warner Bros. as a sweetener for Spector's new deal with the company. "Marty told me 'We'll be able to make a deal with EMI and Capitol,' or words to that effect," Seider remembers. "Because that was basically how Marty operated. He didn't push the envelope—he split the envelope, he opened it up, he burst it open. He was calculating that to avoid problems most companies will do whatever the artist wants, and that if you faced them down they'd capitulate. But I said, 'Marty, you're wasting your time, because as long as I am in the picture, I am going to tell John Lennon, and the answer is no, he is not going to allow this thing to take place.' "

In the end, it was left to Bob Mercer, the managing director of EMI in London, to recover the tapes some months later. Mercer had not been party to the original negotiations over the record, and the first he learned of a problem was when his accounts department told him they had received a bill from Warner Bros. for £90,000 for recordings with John Lennon. Spector, it seemed, had been charging the recording costs to Warner under his new contract with the company.

Mercer now took charge of retrieving the tapes, and eventually managed to track down Spector and make an arrangement for them to be collected from an office on Sunset Boulevard. Mercer contacted a colleague, Chan Daniels at the A&R department at Capitol, EMI's sister label. Daniels had once been in a group called the Highwaymen, who enjoyed a hit with "Michael, Row the Boat Ashore." "Chan went down to the office on Sunset," Mercer recalls, "and about ninety minutes later I got a call from him, quite definitely hyperventilating. He had gone over and presented himself at reception. The receptionist said he was expected and Phil would be out in a minute. She buzzed Phil, and Phil came out with an axe. Chan ran down twelve flights of stairs. In the end I had to send in a U.S. marshal to get the tapes."

The John Lennon album *Rock 'n' Roll* was eventually released in 1975, comprising five of the tracks produced by Spector and a further eight recorded by Lennon in New York. It was quickly forgotten.

At around the same time, the chapter of Spector's marriage to Ronnie was closed with a final settlement. Ronnie was awarded $50,000 in community property and $2,500 monthly spousal support for three years. In return she was obliged to disclaim any interest in any of Spector's business interests, as well as any interest in the three trusts. Spector was awarded custody of Donte, Gary and Louis.

On the back of each alimony check Spector would stamp a short expression of his enduring feelings for her, that Ronnie would be obliged to sign over or under when presenting the check to a cashier. The message was just two words: "Fuck off."

20

"Let's Take Five"

The chaotic tribulations of the John Lennon sessions had the effect of bringing the Kessel brothers, Dan and David, even more into Spector's life. Before long, "Barney's kids" had become his favorite hangout buddies, the sorcerer's apprentices and protégés—the sons that Spector's own adopted children would never be.

The Kessels were chalk and cheese: Dan was quiet, measured, pensive; David, three years younger, was a fiery extrovert and a martial arts enthusiast. The brothers had enjoyed the benefit of an eventful Hollywood upbringing. Barney Kessel and the boys' artist mother Gail had divorced when the boys were young, and for a while Gail went out with the Hollywood actor Lawrence Tierney, "a two-fisted, macho kind of guy," Dan remembers, who would occasionally take the boys on his lunchtime drinking excursions around Irish bars, often culminating in a brawl in which Tierney would see off all-comers. Barney's second wife, B. J. Baker, was one of Los Angeles's premier session singers (Hal Blaine called her "Diamond Lil"), and the brothers would often sit in on her sessions for the likes of Elvis Presley, Frank Sinatra, Ray Charles, and Spector.

The first time Spector invited the brothers up to his house he greeted them wearing a .38-caliber pistol in a shoulder holster. "He asked David and I if we wanted to wear guns, too," Dan remembers. "I said, 'Well, I can wear a gun or not, it doesn't matter.' So then he asked if we wanted to do some target practice. We said 'Sure,' so we went into the backyard, and he had some old 45s that he'd set up on a tree off in the distance—they were records he didn't like—and we shot them to smithereens. He was as impressed with our marksmanship as we were with his."

Spector was a huge fan of *The Godfather* (Al Pacino was one of his favorite actors: "Don't you think he's handsome?" he'd ask friends), and that night he entertained the Kessels for dinner, ordering in Italian food and, shoulder holster in place, putting on his Marlon Brando routine— "Come . . . eat at my table." The evening passed trading scenes from the film—the fish wrapped in newspaper, the horse's head in the bed . . .

The Kessels were unfazed by Spector's enthusiasm for guns. For Dan Kessel it was "completely understandable" why Spector would wear a gun. "It's for protection. It's an insurance policy. But I never saw Phil do anything unsafe with a gun."

But for Spector, wearing a gun seemed to be more than just "an insurance policy." A gun gave him swagger, authority, machismo. It assuaged his insecurities, and made him feel he was somebody. Sometimes he would put in a call to Mo Ostin or Joe Smith at Warner, and turn on the speakerphone so the Kessels could listen in. To Dan Kessel it was "exhilarating to see him packing heat and talking to these top record executives, like he was Jimmy Cagney or Humphrey Bogart. He was tough with these guys and they were being nice to him. I was impressed."

To David, Spector was "the epitome of the American pop-music hero; the epitome of achievement in the United States; the epitome of coming from humble beginnings, delivering the goods and becoming great." Phil, David thought, "is a self-made man of the highest order."

The Kessels were trying to make their own way as artists and producers, and they regarded Spector as a model and a mentor. David had studied law with a view to being a music business attorney, "but plugging back in with Phil on this level it was like, Forget all that stuff; this is what I want to do." Spector would tell them, "I'm all the industry you need." And for the two brothers just being around him was like a master class in music history and the record business.

Spector had a jukebox loaded with vintage rock and roll and R&B— "My True Love" by Jack Scott; the Fireflies' "You Were Mine"; the Drifters, Little Richard, Fats Domino, Jessie Hill, the Olympics—and he would sit for hours with the Kessels, pointing out the finer parts of the songs, telling stories about where and how they were made.

"We'd discuss things like, what's your favorite Johnny Cash song," David remembers, "or the difference between Roy Orbison's recordings on Sun and Monument. You talk about rock and roll, R and B, classical or jazz—all of it—and Phil was totally there. We'd try to out-encyclopedia each other: who was conducting the Leipzig Gewandhaus Orchestra in 1932? Is there such a word as 'irregardless' in the English language? We only went home to sleep five hours a day."

Dan Kessel remembers an occasion when the brothers tagged along with Spector to visit a woman friend at the Hotel Bel-Air. "David, Phil and I started getting into 'Is You Is or Is You Ain't My Baby?' When Phil was in a good mood, he loved to do Ahmet Ertegun and Wolfman Jack imitations. He was spoofing on Wolfman Jack, '*And that was Buster Brown . . . We havin' us a good time; ain't we havin' us a good time?*' And the girl said, 'Yeah, we're having a good time!' And Phil spun round, and gestured to David and me and said, 'No, *we're* havin' a good time.' He wasn't being cruel, but it was funny."

The Kessels, remembers one friend, "were like Phil's kids." He called them "Danny" and "Davey." He liked them to dress uniformly in dark suits and black shirts. When they went out they flanked him "like bookends." Along with George Brand, he would take them to restaurants, parties and boxing matches. Spector was a big fight fan, and would often attend live bouts at the Forum and big-screen live broadcasts. Dan Kessel remembers he and his brother joining Spector to watch the "Rumble in the Jungle" fight in 1974 between Muhammad Ali and George Foreman, which was shown at a theater in Beverly Hills. Spector had placed a substantial bet on Ali with a bookmaker in Nevada. Shortly after the fight, he took receipt of two suitcases loaded with $2 million in cash. When Kessel remarked, "That's a nice chunk of change," Spector replied, "Now I can afford everything on my chili dog at Pink's." Sometimes Spector would boost his entourage with his friend and sometime bodyguard Mike Stone, a martial arts expert who had been a pupil of Bruce Lee, and who himself worked as instructor to many Hollywood celebrities. Stone's most famous client was Elvis Presley, and he would later become the karate instructor to Presley's wife, Priscilla. Their affair would be one of the factors in the Presleys' divorce. Spector took the Kessels to Las Vegas to see Elvis Presley performing at the Hilton International, calling on him in his dressing room after the show. (Stone wisely declined to join them on the trip.) "There was just Dave, me, George and Phil," Dan remembers. "Elvis had the full Memphis mafia. It was very intense—the full Phil trip, and the full Elvis trip. They knew who each other were. They were like two panthers checking each other out. You could tell—mutual respect. It was definitely one of those moments."

To Dan Kessel, Spector was "fundamentally just too rock and roll for some people, including most so-called rock and rollers. Some people just don't get Phil. They don't know when he's being funny, or being playful. They can't keep up with his energy, his mind, his personality. So they say, 'Oh, this guy's crazy.' I never once thought that."

Behavior that others might have regarded as crazy, reckless, irresponsible, the Kessels simply regarded as "Phil pushing the envelope." "He liked that we were pretty fearless," says Dan. "Whether it involved the possibility of violence with armed gangs in different ethnic neighborhoods, or being able to drive over one hundred miles an hour around the Hollywood Ranch Market and on through the narrow alley behind Gold Star at four a.m. We never lost our cool, regardless of what was happening. To David and me it was all a giggle." Over the next seven years they would play on all of Spector's sessions, help him with preproduction, be privy to his business deals and be his most constant companions. Spector dubbed them "the Three Musketeers."

On April 11, 1974, *Rolling Stone* magazine ran a story headlined "Phil Spector in Mystery Mishap," stating that Spector had been involved in a serious car accident "on or about February 10, somewhere between Los Angeles and Phoenix." Spector, it was reported, had suffered multiple head and body injuries and burns and had undergone surgery. No other details were available. "The complete shroud of mystery—rare in the music business but common with Spector—has prompted some cynical speculation that there may not have been an accident after all, that Spector merely wanted to get away from it all, or that he's having cosmetic surgery, possibly a hair transplant." A "friend" of Spector, Pauline Elliot [actually his former personal assistant], was quoted as rejecting that suggestion as "silly. He has plenty of hair, all his own."

The report was an intriguing compound of fact and myth. Spector had not been involved in a car crash driving between Los Angeles and Phoenix. Nor was he having cosmetic surgery or a hair transplant.

Speculation raged that Spector, seemingly apprehensive about his new deal with Warner Bros., and the farrago over the John Lennon tapes, had spread the story of the accident to buy himself some time.

In fact, Spector had been involved in a car crash, which almost killed him. Driving his Rolls-Royce along Melrose Avenue in Hollywood late one night, he was involved in a head-on collision with another vehicle. Spector was catapulted through the windshield. He was rushed to the hospital and required extensive plastic surgery for facial injuries. He would be picking tiny shards of glass out of his face for years to come.

When finally he re-emerged in public he was sporting a collar-length shock of gray frizzy hair. "I said, 'What's with the gray hair?'" David Kessel remembers. "And he said, 'I want people to think I aged ten years in the accident.' A few days later, he dyed it gold. He had the gold hair and he'd started wearing a cape. Then he started wearing a cross. He said, 'I need it to protect myself.' I guess he felt bad after the accident. But he was just doing it to be ridiculous.

"He also told people he'd lost his hearing in one ear—which he hadn't. He said, 'If you really want to have fun, get on this side of me which everybody thinks is deaf now and listen to what they say about me. And if you hear anything interesting, let me know.' "

By the spring, Spector was finally ready to begin fulfilling his contractual obligations to Warner Bros. It was indicative of his state of mind, and his uncertainty, that for his first production he should turn to the past. Cher had come a long way since the days when Larry Levine would move her to the back of the crowd of session singers gathered around the mikes at Gold Star to prevent her voice drowning out everybody else. After "I Got You Babe," she had enjoyed hit records under her own name, and she and Sonny Bono had gone on to become America's favorite television couple with their own variety show *The Sonny and Cher Comedy Hour.* But now the couple was mired in an acrimonious divorce, and Cher had signed a solo contract with Warner Bros.

The first song to come from her sessions with Spector was "A Woman's Story," a song written by Spector with his friend Nino Tempo and Tempo's sister April Stevens; a dark lamentation in which a prostitute looks back over a life in which she's "seen every room with a bed inside it." Spector filled Gold Star with a cast of musicians that exceeded even the heydays of the '60s—no fewer than nine guitarists and four keyboard players, along with brass and half a dozen percussionists, marshalling them to produce a funereal backbeat over which Cher intoned with a lugubrious fatalism.

The next song, a reworking of the Ronettes' "Baby, I Love You," was an even more telling indication of Spector's mood. That he should have chosen to revisit one of his greatest hits was a sure sign of how much he was now looking over his shoulder; that he should have stripped the song of all its original joyfulness and exuberance, rendering it as a plodding dirge, seemed almost willfully perverse.

But to David Kessel, that seemed to be precisely the point. "Phil loves the fact that he'd achieved, but what he always hated was everyone's waiting for him to slip on a record. It was as if he'd trapped himself by being so brilliant. He wasn't allowed to just go in the studio and make a record. He'd say, 'Why can't I just make a record like anybody else, and you either like it or you don't?' And I think at the Cher point he'd kind of given that up and decided he was just going to make the records he wanted to make."

Toward the end of the sessions, proceedings were enlivened by the arrival in the studio of David Geffen. The callow teenager who had once loitered around Gold Star, watching Spector in awe and amazement and dreaming of one day following in his footsteps, was now a major player in his own right. Geffen had swiftly progressed up the ladder from being an agent at William Morris, to managing artists—Crosby, Stills and Nash and Joni Mitchell among them—to founding his own record label, Asylum, in the process shaping the "soft-rock," singer-songwriter genre that now dominated the American charts. In the course of Cher's traumatic breakup with Sonny Bono, Geffen had become her lover, confidant and de facto manager. Spector had always regarded him as an irritant, believing that Geffen's early hero worship was just a way of getting close, to see what he could learn. Geffen, for his part, had never forgotten the slight of being told to "sit with the chauffeur" all those years ago. His first client as a manager was the rarefied Laura Nyro, whose music combined a deep affection for '60s girl group R&B with performances of operatic intensity. Spector was much taken by Nyro and approached Geffen, wanting to produce her, but Geffen turned him down. When Geffen moved into the old Philles offices on the Sunset Strip it reaffirmed Spector's feeling that Geffen was trying to walk in his shoes. And as Geffen's power and standing in the record industry grew, and Spector's waned, so the old animosity grew more intense.

"Phil hated the fact that David was so powerful, because David had no musical talent whatsoever," says Geffen's brother Mitchell. "David can't even sing in key; his genius was to take the most heavyweight creative people in the whole world and convince them that he was important to them. And that must have galled Phil to the very end, that David was the king in a business where Phil was the real genius on the music side. Here's this little *pischer* come along and he's the richest man in Hollywood. It's gotta hurt."

Now, as the Cher session wore on, Geffen committed the cardinal sin of making comments and suggestions about what Spector should be doing in the studio. Without warning, Spector suddenly turned from the recording console and punched Geffen, knocking him to the ground, and screaming "Get out of here, you fucking faggot." "Everybody was astonished," David Kessel remembers. "And Cher just said, 'Oh Phillip, behave yourself.' And he went back to work. But that's Phil's thing. 'Don't tell me what to do; don't tell me how to make a record. Just don't.' "

Spector had intended to produce a complete album with Cher, but the sessions would provide only one more song, a duet with Harry Nilsson on another familiar song, "A Love Like Yours." In the years since writing the ill-fated Modern Folk Quartet song "This Could Be the Night," Nilsson had gone on to enjoy phenomenal success both as a writer and performer with a series of highly regarded albums, providing hits such as "Everybody's Talking" and "Without You." He was now busy squandering his talents on drink and drugs. He arrived at Gold Star carrying his own case of wine, prompting David Kessel to tease, "You're gonna stay for fifteen minutes?" and spent the session methodically working his way through his supply and snorting coke. "Even Phil told him he was drinking too much," Kessel remembers.

Spector seemed to be drifting. Attempting to capitalize on the current fad for disco (well, everybody else was), he made two new signings: a group called Calhoon and a New York singer named Jerri Bo Keno. He was so uninterested in Calhoon that he passed the production duties to the engineer Walt Kahn, who produced two singles that quickly vanished. Spector produced Jerri Bo Keno himself on a song prophetically entitled "Here It Comes (and Here I Go)," which he had co-written with Jeff Barry, but had no more luck.

When he decided once more to conjure some of his former glory by recording Darlene Love, nobody was more surprised than Love herself. Love had never quite got over her bitterness toward Spector and the feeling that she had been hung out to dry. After leaving Philles she had worked as a backing singer with numerous artists, including Elvis Presley and Tom Jones, all the time dreaming of being able to resurrect her own solo career. Her break finally arrived in 1973, when she signed with Philadelphia International, which had supplanted Motown as the most energetic force in black music in America with acts like the O'Jays, Billy Paul, and Harold Melvin and the Blue Notes. Eager to get into the studio, Love was shocked when the label's owners Kenny Gamble and Leon Huff one day announced that they had decided to invoke a clause enabling them to sell her contract to whomever they chose. It had been bought by Phil Spector. (Love would subsequently learn that the "agent provocateur" in the deal was Marty Machat, who was also Gamble and Huff's lawyer.)

At the end of 1974, a disgruntled Love presented herself in Los Angeles, where Spector played her the demo of a new song written by Barry Mann and Cynthia Weil—a paean to feminism entitled "Lord, If You're a Woman." Love thought it was "tripe." In the studio, all the old resentments bubbled to the surface. No matter how acute their differences, Spector, she believed, had always respected her talent; but now, she would later write, he treated her "like a slave," ordering endless retakes, seemingly just for the fun of it. Yet the tension seemed to inspire her performance. Out of her frustration and resentment, Love conjured a vocal of coruscating power, to match Spector's driving, tumultuous production. The record was a glorious reminder that of all the singers Spector ever worked with, none had better served his vision than Darlene Love. But the relationship was too combustible to last. Love walked out on Spector at the end of the session, and would never work with him again, and it would be another three years before "Lord, If You're a Woman" even saw a release.

After almost twenty years living in the Hayworth Street home where Spector grew up, Bertha moved to a larger apartment a few blocks away on Sweetzer Avenue. She kept one bedroom for her son, reproducing it almost exactly as it had been when he had last lived at home, including the collection of old records that he had left behind, and that Phil insisted were filed in exactly the same order.

To David Kessel, the more time he spent with Spector, the more apparent it became just how much his life had been shaped by his tempestuous family relationships, and how much his music had been born from paradox. Only an incurable romantic could have made the records that Spector did in the early '60s with the Ronettes, the Crystals and the Righteous Brothers—shards of passion, brilliance and light, idealized visions of a happiness all the more poignant because it seemed that Spector could never attain it himself. He was the small child looking through the railings at a garden where the blossoms seem all the brighter and more sweetly scented because he was unable to pick them himself. The chaos and misery of his childhood had left a deep legacy, not of scars but of open wounds. If Spector's records were perfect expressions of love, as David Kessel observed, their driving force was actually closer to pain and hostility. "With Phil, it was like, I'm going to shove this love up your ass. It was: What you're hearing, isn't that brilliant? He was getting back at all the people and things he had hostility for. The industry. Anybody that got in his way. His dad for dying. His mother. His sister. Everybody. With Phil, it was just like: Get out of here; I'm fucking taking over.

"He grew up being the young guy having to fight two tough old broads. His mum used to say to him, 'You just got lucky.' Just totally belittle him. And then go out to her canasta club and say, 'You know my son just had another number one record; my son's the greatest this and the greatest that.' A twisted relationship, in that way, and yet they had great love for one another, and he helped support her financially.

"At La Collina there was a circular driveway around the fountain. On one occasion she spent two days just driving around and around the driveway, pestering him for no real reason, honking her horn to try and get Phil to come out; and he wouldn't come out. She finally did it long enough that she had to get a new set of tires—and she had the bill sent to him. Phil was furious: He said, 'That's my mum . . .'"

Spector's difficult upbringing had hardly prepared him for a family of his own—particularly one that had been assembled on a series of whims in a desperate attempt to salvage a marriage that was now behind him. While he cared for the children, according to one friend, "Phil was at a total loss as to how to be a father."

His nocturnal hours meant he was seldom around to interact with them in a normal way. Maids took care of the children's domestic needs. But for the most part the faithful George Brand acted as their surrogate father. Brand's role in Spector's life went far beyond that of bodyguard; he was friend, companion, minder—at times almost a paternal figure. When Spector ventured out in company, Brand would usually sit quietly at another table, like a watchdog, ready to step in if things got out of hand, to protect Spector from others or—more usually—from himself. When Spector drank too much, as nowadays he increasingly did, George would come over and whisper quietly in his ear—"It's time to go home now, Phil" and Spector would usually accede.

Dan Kessel remembers an evening in 1974 when Brand's presence was sufficient to prevent what might have otherwise been serious trouble. "We were in La Trattoria on La Cienega Boulevard. There was a couple sitting next to us at an adjacent table. They'd obviously just seen the film *Lenny* and were discussing it, very passionately. And this was kind of like tearing the scab off an emotional wound for Phil. Phil asked if we could move, but there were no other tables available. Eventually he said something to the guy like 'Excuse me, sir, would you mind please not discussing the *Lenny* film? You're going on and on about him and everything you're saying about him is wrong and you really don't know what you're talking about and it's breaking my heart.' And the guy said, 'Who the hell are you to tell me what to talk about?' Things got really heated up, really tense and then some tough-looking Italian guys materialized out of the woodwork and there were a lot of threats about fighting on both sides. George was packing and I know those Italian guys were packing, but just when I thought there was going to be a blood-bath, the other guy said to Phil, 'You're crazy, you know that? I could have you all killed in a heartbeat.' So George helped diffuse the situation and got the restaurant manager to give us a private table in another room, which is what we had requested in the first place."

Brand had little time for the celebrities and hangers-on that Spector liked to have around. He treated the La Collina home as if it were his own. If Spector was entertaining, George would often curl up to sleep on the French embroidered love seat in the main hallway, or even on the floor, sometimes dressed only in his shorts. "People would walk by, give a shocked glance, then just keep going on to the powder room at the end of the hallway," one visitor remembers. "No one ever mentioned it."

George didn't ask questions, or raise objections or make a fuss about anything that wasn't his business, which was most things. If Spector got lonely and didn't want his guests to leave, which was sometimes the case, then that was Spector's business, not George's. Sometimes the drink would be flowing, and the stories going on and on, and the guest would be yawning, wondering if the evening was ever going to end; and they might say, "It's really time I was going now, Phil, and could you please unlock the door . . ." and Spector might get agitated and jumpy and start issuing threats—you know the guard dogs are trained to kill, the fence is wired?—and if anybody raised an objection, George would be the soul of polite obduracy—"I'm sorry, but it's Mr. Spector's instructions . . ." And the night would go on until even Spector grew exhausted and at last everybody could go home . . .

A petite and vivacious brunette, Devra Robitaille was in her early twenties when she came to work for Phil Spector in June 1975. Robitaille had been born and grown up in London. Her father, Martin Slavin, was a respected composer and arranger, who had written numerous film scores as well as working with pop singers like Frank Ifield and Helen Shapiro. Her mother was a lyricist. Devra herself had trained at the Royal Academy of Music and played classical piano to concert standard.

When Devra was twenty, her family moved to Los Angeles, and Devra started work in the music business. Ironically, her first job was working for Spector's old partner Lester Sill at Screen Gems. She worked at Jobete Music, Motown's publishing arm, where she met and married a Motown engineer, Robert Robitaille, before moving on to Warner Bros., where she worked in the recording-royalties department. One day she picked up a phone call from Spector—a query about recording budgets. He teased her about her English accent, they got talking, and before long she became his main liaison person in the company. He invited her to Gold Star to watch the Cher sessions, where Devra joined the chorus of backing singers. In June 1975, a report in *Cash Box* magazine announced that she had been appointed as "Administrative Director" of Warner-Spector. "A glorified title," she says, "for personal assistant."

For Devra, working for Spector was "like Alice stepping through the looking glass. There was something compelling and charismatic and utterly amazing about him. And there was something almost frightening about the man, too. It was almost a thrill; you were never quite sure what you'd get. But I liked him so much because he was so *interesting*."

Spector would summon her to the house to talk about business and the minutes would stretch into hours as he held forth on everything— the rock business, politics, human nature, "how come the sky is blue . . . Just sitting there in the dining room at La Collina, they were some of the most amazing times in my life. It was an education. And then all of a sudden he'd start screaming, ranting and raving and he'd storm out of the room and slam the door, and I'd be left sitting there, not knowing what to do. Should I go or should I stay? Sometimes he'd leave me sitting there for hours."

To Devra, Spector's life was as unfathomable as his character, a series of Chinese boxes. When he stepped out of the room, she had no idea where he went, or what he did. He could have been leading an entirely separate life in a different part of the house—perhaps two lives—and Devra wouldn't have known. The mansion and its occupants were a riddle. There was George—"a sweet man," Devra remembers—who would materialize at Spector's shoulder as if summoned by telepathy. Sometimes Devra would glimpse a dark-haired woman whom she later discovered to be Janis Zavala, but Devra was never sure whether Janis was a secretary, a lover or a friend. Spector never explained. There were the children, Donte and the twins, who clearly lived there, but who, to Devra, seemed almost to belong somewhere else.

"It was not like the world I came from. In my world everybody talked to each other and knew what each other did and understood each other. Here everything seemed vague. I'd arrive and Phil would put me in the dining room; and I'd sit there waiting to take dictation or whatever. And then he'd go off, and I'd hear voices in the kitchen and he'd come back and shut the door. And he wouldn't say anything to me, like 'Oh, I was just talking to Janis in the kitchen,' or 'The kids are eating,' or anything. He'd just sit down. And then he and I would talk and laugh and interact. Then sometimes he'd disappear and I would be dismissed. And other times, he'd disappear and I hadn't been dismissed, and I'd sit there for hours, wondering what was going to happen and what I was supposed to do. Nothing was ever explained. It was always a games condition."

People were drawn into Spector's circle—the singer Ronee Blakely, the basketball player Magic Johnson, the actor Harry Dean Stanton—and just as suddenly vanished. "And you were never sure whether it was because Phil had grown tired of them or because they'd got tired of him—because he was nuts and it was all a big game that was fun for a while, but then, Jeez, I don't want to be around this anymore . . ."

Sometimes Devra would be summoned when Spector had gatherings at the house, "trotted out like a little ballerina," and he would ask her to perform. " 'Ooh, you should hear how good Devra is . . . ,' and he'd sit me at the piano, and I'd find myself playing Bach and Beethoven for all these luminaries. And after I'd played my little thing, he'd smile and say, 'Isn't she great?' and put me away again, stick me back in the corner and I'd have to be quiet."

Devra's first major job as Spector's "administrative director" was organizing the sessions for a new project—an album with the rock and roll singer Dion DiMucci. Spector felt a particular affinity with Dion. They were of the same generation, and had grown up within just a few miles of each other in the South Bronx. In the late '50s, while Spector was enjoying his first success with the Teddy Bears, Dion and his group the Belmonts were on the charts with the doo-wop hits "I Wonder Why" and "Teenager in Love." As a solo artist, Dion had gone on to make tough rock and roll records like "Ruby Baby" before losing his way with drugs. In 1968 he enjoyed a comeback hit with "Abraham, Martin and John." Reinventing himself as a folksy singer-songwriter, he began performing in concert halls and coffeehouses, recording the memorable "Your Own Backyard," about his struggle with heroin addiction. Signed to Warner Bros., he had made four albums, which moved Bruce Springsteen to describe him as "the real link between Frank Sinatra and rock and roll," but his career was in the doldrums when Spector told Mo Ostin that he wanted to produce him. "Mo was astonished," Dion's manager Zach Glickman remembers. "Warner were about to write Dion off."

Mindful of Spector's reputation, Dion was bemused when Spector instructed him to come to the mansion alone for their first meeting, specifying that the singer should wait at the corner of Sunset and

Doheny, where a car would collect him. "Dion thought it was because Phil didn't want him to know where he lived," says Glickman. "I think it was just Phil being considerate. He didn't want Dion to get lost."

Over the course of a couple of weeks, Spector did his customary prepping at La Collina Drive, choosing and rehearsing songs. And at the end of August 1975 he assembled his troops in Gold Star.

Spector would arrive at the studio each night armed with his supplies—a caseload of Manischewitz, a sixteen-ounce plastic tumbler with a bendy straw—and drink methodically through the session. People talked of there being "two Phils": the "private Phil" who could be sweet and intelligent, considerate and thoughtful, and the "public Phil," who could be arrogant, mean and confrontational. And the difference between them was usually drink. Being drunk gave Spector the license to act out the role of the rock and roll eccentric people expected him to be—or, at least, that he thought they expected him to be.

He would drink in jags. Long periods would pass without him drinking at all; followed by intense bursts, usually when he was recording, when it seemed he was seldom sober. Dan Kessel thought that for Spector drinking served as "an insular cushion during grueling hours of hard work"—a way to cope with the pressures and responsibilities of creativity, of being Phil Spector; a way of keeping things "groovy and under control," as Kessel puts it. "Being in perpetual Alexander the Great mode can be very taxing, physically, emotionally and otherwise, and drinking can help you to stay the course. And making records you can get away with it up to a point where you couldn't if you're a surgeon or an airline pilot."

In the old days, Spector would never tolerate drinking or drugs in the studio; drug-taking among his musicians was still something he abhorred. Dan Kessel would remember him calling time on a session and sending everyone home when he discovered a couple of musicians trading cocaine in the studio. But drinking was another matter, at least for Spector himself. There had barely been a recording session in the past five years when he hadn't ended up loaded, even if he didn't start that way.

Drinking brought out the best and worst in him. One or two drinks and he would be dazzling, the riffs, skits and wisecracks crackling like lightning, the ideas and enthusiasm flying like sparks off a generator. Three or four and he could be foul. "Phil could be a lovable drunk," remembers Devra Robitaille, "but he was more often an ugly and hateful one."

He would sometimes drink to a point of insensibility, and awake feeling so full of shame and remorse that he would be unable to face anybody for days.

Gold Star's co-owner, Stan Ross, who had known Spector longer than anyone and who was engineering the Dion sessions, was alarmed at his old friend's escalating rate of consumption and the effect it had on him. "Drinking changed Phil, and I didn't like that. I can't handle anybody with alcohol, and he'd get stinko. Not only would Phil drink a lot, but he wasn't sociable. He'd sit there with his Manischewitz, the worst wine you could drink, drinking it by the bottle. You'd say, 'Don't you offer anybody else anything?' But no. It was his own thing. And his skin would stink from the smell of it—that smell people get when they drink a lot and perspire. One night, I said to him, 'Phil, you stink.' He said, 'Nobody told me that before.' Maybe nobody had dared to tell him, but it was the truth."

Dion had trouble accustoming himself to Spector's mercurial mood changes, his imperious manner and his way of ordering people around in the studio. Dion considered himself an artist, and felt that Spector was not showing him the proper respect. When he confided his worries to his manager Zach Glickman, Glickman suggested he should talk to Spector's friend Nino Tempo, who was working as arranger on the sessions. "Nino told him, 'Just tell Phil how you feel. Say you're here to make a record, you're a respected artist and you want to be treated as such,'" Glickman remembers. "So Phil listened to what Dion had to say, and after that it would be 'Okay, you cocksucking motherfuckers . . . and Mr. DiMucci.'"

One night, Roy Carr, a journalist from the *New Musical Express* who had traveled from Britain to meet Spector, arrived at the studio with Bruce Springsteen, who was in Los Angeles promoting his new album *Born to Run*—a bravura work whose panoramic, wide-screen production paid explicit homage to the Wall of Sound, and which had seen Springsteen hailed as the new messiah of rock.

Spector was working on the track "Baby, Let's Stick Together," and Springsteen, Carr remembers, "was in awe. It was the full Phil Spector experience, with the bells and chimes and Dion! Phil turned round jokingly at one point and said, 'Hey, doesn't that make *Born to Run* suck?' And Bruce just laughed and put his arms round him. He was in heaven."

But to Carr "most of the session seemed to be Phil just pissing around—being Phil Spector. 'Hey guys . . . Gene, Gene give me more attention—oh great, he's just taken his cock out . . .' That kind of thing. He was just entertaining everybody. Then he did a couple of run-throughs. And five minutes before the scheduled end of the session, just when all the musicians were thinking, Great, we're going into overtime, he did two takes, and said, 'That's it.' "

To Nino Tempo, it seemed that Spector wasn't taking the sessions, or the arrangements he was providing, seriously at all. "He didn't seem to have the concentration, and he didn't want to spend the time necessary to go through each part. He'd say 'Oh we'll get it in the session' or 'You write something; I'm sure it'll be fine.' He didn't seem to have the patience that he used to have. And the frivolity, the party-animal kind of mentality—that had never happened in the old days; there'd be no partying around—it was work. But now it was almost like he cared more about entertaining everybody in the booth than about what he was recording. Always talking and laughing, telling jokes. And this is time that musicians were getting paid.

"Things were going into golden time—that's double, double time. In one overnight session I must have made a couple of thousand dollars on two short arrangements and a couple of thousand dollars just being the bandleader. You would think that I didn't care what happened. But I had a certain sense of pride in my work. We started on a midnight session and by four in the morning we hadn't recorded anything. Finally I got pissed off, I told every musician to shut the fuck up. And I said to Phil, 'What are we going to do? Are we finally going to record something?' And do you know what he said? 'Let's take five . . .' I was so pissed that I just packed up and went home. And then the next day I got a telegram, apologizing and asking me to come back tomorrow night, there's another session. He said, 'Just make the money,' and then it was a party all over again."

Spector had always been a perfectionist in the studio, always worked to his own coordinates, indifferent to the opinion or needs of others. In the past that perfectionism had been directed toward a specific end, which Spector could see, even if nobody else could. But increasingly it seemed that his coordinates were shot.

Recording the title track, "Born to Be with You," Spector asked Dion to perform a "guide" vocal for the backing track, and then declared it was the only take he needed. Dion knew he could do better, but Spector didn't seem to care.

Yet seemingly good performances would be passed over, with Spector calling for endless retakes. "Whatever he did, it never seemed to be good enough," Devra remembers. "Something would be great, but he would want to redo it, remix and remix, over and over again. It drove everybody mad."

The finished album contained just seven tracks produced by Spector (with two earlier songs, including "Your Own Backyard"), and the results were as distracted as the mood in which it was created. It wasn't that Spector was short of ideas: the album brimmed with sonic wonders—chiming guitars, zithers, bells. The extraordinary "He's Got the Whole World in His Hands" in particular, which had an echoing Dion battling against a titanic string arrangement and what sounded like the Mormon Tabernacle Choir, attained a weird, transcendent beauty. But if anything, there were too many ideas; what was lacking was coherence and fire. Much as he had with the Cher sessions, Spector had elected to render one song after another as a monolithic plod. Where once the Wall of Sound had conjured an irrepressible optimism and joy, it now sounded burdened with the worries of the world. Where once there had been blue skies, now there were dark, brooding clouds.

So ponderous were the final mixes that when Zach Glickman heard them he was convinced that Spector had slowed the tapes down even more, so that what should have been playing at 33 rpm now sounded as if it were playing at 25. Dion, appalled at the results, fulminated to Glickman that it sounded like "funeral music" and effectively disowned the project. He would later offer a more considered, and astute, appraisal, reflecting that working with Spector could be "exciting, frustrating, even a little sad at times. He's a real artist and one who liked to surround himself with spectacle, but it seemed to me that he was afraid of failure. He's got the image of a genius and that puts a lot of pressure on himself, always trying to outdo his last masterpiece."

The executives at Warner Bros. were no more enthusiastic about the album. Where was the energy? Where was the life? David Kessel remembers that Spector was furious with the response. "It was: What's wrong with these fucking people? But Phil Spector does not make records for record executives; he *is* the record executive. You have to be the biggest idiot in the world to make a deal with Phil Spector and not expect to get a Phil Spector record."

For Devra, Spector's insistence that the record was a work of genius, that the record company were the fools, not him, could barely conceal the pain he felt at its rejection. "You know how people somehow manifest defensiveness in a bullying way? When they feel picked on, their dukes come up? That's how Phil was. But I think it must have really messed with him to have that kind of criticism. It's one thing to be a mad genius, but when people start saying you're finished musically, that must have really done his head in. I'm sure that was why there was all the *angst* and the drinking and the craziness. He was like a drowning man, desperately floundering for some sort of retrieval."

Chagrined at the response, Spector withdrew the record altogether. It would be another twelve months before *Born to Be with You* was eventually released, and then only in Britain, under a new deal that Spector and Machat had negotiated with Polydor to release Spector material under the banner of Phil Spector International Records. It would be a further twenty years before a new generation of critics and musicians would start hailing *Born to Be with You* as Spector's "forgotten masterpiece."

Marty Machat had invited Roy Carr to Los Angeles with a view to writing a treatment for a film about Spector's life. The working title was *To Know Him Is to Love Him: The Phil Spector Story*. It should be a celebration of his life, his struggles and his triumphant accomplishments, Spector explained. He had already decided that Al Pacino would play the leading role.

But the more time Carr spent with Spector, the more it seemed that what he was seeking was not only approbation but reassurance. "He liked to impress you, with his music, his accomplishments, whatever. There was a bit of a Napoleonic complex there. But I think at the back of his mind was the fear that he was yesterday's man. People would pay lip service to him—Brian Wilson, John Lennon, whoever—but it wasn't being translated into record sales. And there was Bruce Springsteen with *Born to Run*, Roy Wood, Meat Loaf, all these people paying homage to his style, and having massive success. And Phil wasn't making records—or if he was, he was not releasing them, or he was screwing them up. He'd been a great American success story, an icon. And then it was all taken away from him. And that was very hard for him to accept. All the time his catchphrase was, nobody makes better records than I do—all the time. And he wanted you to reply, 'That's right, Phil, that's right.' I think deep down inside he just wanted to be loved by everybody."

Carr put up in the Sunset Marquis hotel, and every few days would make his way to the mansion for meetings. Sometimes his phone would ring at two in the morning, and it would be Spector, telling him a limousine was on its way to collect him.

In the half-darkness and arctic cold, Spector would hold forth long into the night. "It was never what you'd call a conversation," Carr says.

Stories and more stories. He told Carr that he had been in Paris during the student unrest of 1968, working "with an armed undercover unit" in a capacity that was never specified; he would talk about the evenings in the '60s when he would entertain Lenny Bruce, Stan Laurel and Bela Lugosi in the mansion. When Carr mentioned that he was planning a book on the martial arts expert and movie star Bruce Lee, Spector started to cry. Lee, he said, had once worked as his personal bodyguard and lived in the house, and Spector himself had invested money in *Enter the Dragon*, the film that Lee had completed shortly before dying in mysterious circumstances in 1973. Spector told Carr that Lee had been murdered by a martial arts *dim mak* (death touch) and implored him not to write the book, "Because if they can kill Bruce Lee, they can kill you and your family."

Carr was forthright with an acerbic sense of humor, a man whose long experience as a journalist had inured him to the self-regarding fantasies of pop stars. "I remember talking to John Lennon; he really liked Phil, but he told me 'Phil's full of bullshit, but you don't have to put up with it. If you stand up to him he respects that.' So I kept that in mind."

The more Spector talked, the more outrageous his claims became, the harder it became for Carr to tell what was fact and what was fiction. "It got to the point where if he'd told me he was smuggling guns for the contras, I wouldn't have been surprised."

One night, in mid-conversation, Spector stood up and announced he needed to use the bathroom. Carr sat in the semidarkness, awaiting his return. Ten minutes passed. Thirty. An hour. The house was as silent as a tomb. "And suddenly the doors sprung open, and there he was, stripped to the waist, a revolver in his waistband, playing the accordion. I said to him, 'You always did go in for wonderful entrances.' He was pissing himself with laughter."

Carr quickly came to the conclusion that Spector was "a very lonely man. It would get to three o'clock in the morning and I'd say, 'Phil, I'm really bushed; I've got to go.' And he'd look panic-stricken. 'No, stick around.' I remember once I left there and walked down to Ben Frank's on the Strip—I hadn't eaten anything—and I looked out of the window and there was Phil's limo. It was almost like he was following me. I walked back to my hotel and the car followed behind. Whether he was just seeing I got back safely or not I don't know, but it was very strange."

Devra had been assigned to look after Carr, and on another occasion she was summoned to give him a lift back to his hotel. Driving along the Sunset Strip she noticed a Cadillac suddenly looming in her rearview mirror. It was Spector and the Kessel brothers. "They had shotguns poking out of the window," she remembers. "They chased us all the way down Sunset Boulevard, with Roy holding on and me driving like a maniac to get away from them. We ended up driving all the way up into the Hollywood Hills to shake them off." The incident was never explained.

Carr recalls another night at the mansion when Spector organized an outing to his favorite Chinese restaurant, Ah Fong's. "Two cars drew up, and they proceeded to fill the boot with pump-guns and shotguns, like a private army. There was me, the Kessels, a couple of mysterious people. We went to Ah Fong's, and half of it was roped off for us. When we came back afterward, Phil just pulled out his revolver and started shooting at the tree—this is in the front courtyard."

When Carr commented that Spector's security arrangements were "like Fort Knox," Spector explained that he was taking precautions against his children being kidnapped. "He said if anybody kidnapped them they would know that people like him would pay anything—'but they also know that if they harmed them, I would hunt them down like dogs and kill them.' There was a side to Phil where he seemed to see himself as some kind of mercenary."

Spector offered Carr a job and asked what he wanted to do. Philles, Carr told him, was a rich part of rock music's heritage; he suggested going through the entire back catalog and repackaging and presenting it in a historical context, maybe reassembling all of Spector's old artists—the Crystals, Bob B. Soxx, Darlene Love—and producing a Philles show for the stage. But Spector was unenthusiastic. "He was worried he'd be looked on as a nostalgia act." When Carr also suggested he should produce the Beach Boys, Spector looked appalled. "But I think what he had was a fear of failure. He'd already experienced that with A&M. There was this sense of, What happened if there was a big campaign to reestablish Phil Spector as a major player and the public didn't go for it?"

Carr concluded that what Spector really wanted was not an employee but "a playmate. He wanted someone around who knew his history, who loved his music, who would listen to his stories and tell him 'Phil, you're wonderful.' But there's only so many times you could say that."

At length, it was time for Carr to return to England. At a small gathering at the mansion Spector announced he wished to make a presentation. "He pulled out this lovely wooden box. I opened it and it was a Magnum, sitting on a velvet cushion. He said, 'It's for you, Roy.' I said, 'Phil, I usually use a credit card, and I can't take this through customs.' I told him to keep it in the safe."

21

"Leonard, I Love You . . ."

A Los Angeleno through and through, Harvey Kubernik had grown up steeped in Los Angeles musical history, and Phil Spector's illustrious part in it.

"He's a Rebel," "Be My Baby" and "You've Lost That Lovin' Feelin' " had provided the soundtrack for Kubernik's youth. As a child, he would be taken to Canter's by his parents and occasionally see Spector at his corner table, noshing deli. Kubernik began writing for local music papers and then became *Melody Maker*'s Los Angeles correspondent, and he would occasionally see Spector around town: at A&M Studios, where Spector was producing the "Bangla-Desh" sessions; at a Bobby Bland show at the Whisky a Go Go, when having shouted and screamed throughout the opening act, the Dixie Hummingbirds, an inebriated Spector was escorted out before Bland even appeared onstage. Before long, Kubernik had been admitted to the charmed circle that was allowed to watch Spector at work in the studio. Personable and obliging, Kubernik became "the food runner." Spector would spring a $100 bill for deli for everyone from Canter's—"and don't forget the receipt . . ." "The first time, I didn't bring anything back for myself," Kubernik remembers. "Phil said, 'What's your mother's name?' I told him and he said, 'She's doing a good job.' " But when Kubernik asked if he might bring some musician friends to a session, Spector upbraided him with a curt warning: "Nobody does any business off me."

Kubernik's encyclopedic knowledge of music particularly endeared him to Spector, and made him a natural ally of the Kessels. When Spector invited him to play percussion on the Dion sessions, Kubernik was the only person in the room, including Dion, who could not only name all of the singer's early recordings for Laurie Records, including the B-sides, but also who had published them. Spector was usually suspicious of journalists, but Kubernik was careful not to abuse the friendship, and Spector took an almost paternalistic interest in his career. When Kubernik sent Spector a birthday greeting, typed on his rickety old typewriter, Spector telephoned to say that he had a number of electric typewriters at the house and that Harvey was welcome to use one. The grateful journalist drove over to collect it.

Kubernik used the typewriter for months, always careful to thank Spector for the gift whenever he saw him. One day, he received a call: Spector and the Kessels were having dinner at the Cock 'n Bull, a restaurant on the Sunset Strip. Would he like to join them? Kubernik offered his apologies. For weeks, he had been dating a young actress, and tonight he was on a promise. "I made the mistake of bragging 'she's coming over to my apartment, and she's never really gone all the way with a guy . . .' I told him my game plan. We were going to wait till midnight, when she was turning twenty-one. Phil said, 'What's next, spin the bottle?' "

That evening, at 11:45, with Kubernik and his girlfriend having worked their way through half a bottle of Southern Comfort, clothes scattered over the floor, there was a sharp rap at the door. A furious Kubernik opened it to find George Brand standing there. "You are in possession of Mr. Spector's typewriter," Brand announced. "He would like it back." Gun bulging ostentatiously in its holster, Brand walked through the living room into the kitchen, picked up the typewriter, and walked out without saying a word. Kubernik's girlfriend promptly burst into tears. "It was as if the Mob had come over. She wouldn't even let me walk her to her car. It was the end of the relationship."

For days, Kubernik stewed over the incident. Did Spector really need the typewriter that badly? Couldn't it have been collected during the day? Perhaps, Kubernik thought, he had not been profuse enough in his gratitude: He had written a thank-you note, but perhaps one note wasn't enough—he should have written more. Perhaps it was a mistake to have told Spector that part of his seduction plan was to play the *Motown Christmas* album—a favorite of Kubernik's: he should have told him he would be playing the Philles Christmas album instead. Kubernik finally concluded that Spector was "teaching me something. Phil does these Gurdjieff-type exercises on people. I think he wanted me to learn about ownership, and not being reliant or co-dependent on anything or anybody. Especially a tool that was going to be my future."

It was some weeks before he got a call from Spector's office, inviting him to meet at the studio. "I went in and Phil said, 'No notes in the mail from you recently . . .' The Kessels were there, and David said, 'We had a real good time at the Cock 'n Bull. Phil wanted to get you big-time . . .' "

The erratic hours that Devra kept, working for Spector, had exacted a toll on her marriage to Robert Robitaille. They argued more frequently. "I was beginning to think there must be more to life than this." Late one night at Gold Star, toward the end of the Dion sessions, Spector walked Devra to her car, and took her in his arms and kissed her. "I know I should have been thinking, 'This is not right; it's not an ethical thing to be thinking of doing to my husband.' But I wasn't thinking that. I was twenty-four years old, and I'd been transported."

The next day, when Devra arrived at the house with some papers to sign, Spector led her upstairs.

The transition from being Spector's employee to being his lover seemed only to exaggerate the extremes of their existing relationship. It was unlike any love affair she had ever had. Where once he had been kind, Spector now became loving; where once cold, he now became cruel.

"I really, really loved him. But I still don't know if I was in love with him, or just incredibly enamored of him as a fascinating and amazing person. There would be times when I'd go up there, and we'd talk for hours about everything under the sun. That seemed to fulfill a need he had at the time. Other times I would arrive and he would literally launch himself at me and pull me upstairs and then afterward we'd come down and have tea, and he'd give me some notes and things to be done; and then all of a sudden he'd lose his temper and start screaming at me and order me out. And then next time I'd come up he wouldn't be there, or he'd shove a package through the door and not let me in at all. I'd go back to my car and open the envelope and it was handwritten instructions. Call this person, check the liner notes, whatever. I couldn't understand why he was being so horrible to me. And then the following day he'd be all sweetness and light, ushering me in and there'd be a little gift—a wallet, flowers . . . I always felt he was toying with me. Cat and mouse. It's not something one would like to admit, that you would allow yourself to be mesmerized by someone's strong will, but that's what it felt like. Often I found myself doing things that I never would stand for from another human being. But at the same time, I went along with it, because for me, nobody was ever as fascinating as Phil."

His paradoxes were constantly bemusing. She had never met anybody more arrogant, more convinced of his own genius, nor more insecure—constantly stealing glances at himself in the mirror and primping his hair, thrown into rage or apoplexy by any criticism or slight, real or imagined. He could be intelligent, sensitive, unerring in his capacity to spot bullshit in other people, yet at the same time would swagger around with a gun under his shoulder or tucked into his boot— an affectation that Devra thought was simply "silly. I wanted to sit him down and just say, 'Stop this nonsense; it doesn't make you a big man, it just makes you a big idiot.' "

To Devra it sometimes seemed the one thing Spector could stand least of all was an even keel. The eccentricities, the insults, the arguments, and the quixotic flights of temper—all were simply a way of provoking a reaction, *any* reaction. "He was like one of those beings that lands on planet Earth from another world, and was flicking the little earthlings to see what they would do. He couldn't stand for things to be boring. So he'd pull the rug out to shake things up."

His temper could be volcanic. He would shout and scream until the veins on his forehead bulged and it seemed as if his eyes would pop out of his head, but he never once struck or slapped her.

One night, in Ah Fong's after a squabble over the bill, he reached for a bowl of noodles and upturned it over her head. "I got up and stalked out and had to take a taxi home. I quit. And then two or three days later tons of roses turned up. But that was a pattern—me quitting, followed by roses."

His fear of abandonment could be almost pathological. "There were times when he would drag me around Beverly Hills, to restaurants or whatever, and I'd be so exhausted I could hardly keep my eyes open and I'd be pleading, 'Please just let me go home, I want to go to sleep,' and never be allowed to."

But Spector, she says, was "indefatigable. He'd get really drunk, and the more drunk he got, the more he needed someone to talk to. And at that point it almost didn't matter who you were. It was like a plug in the wall; he needed someone to get the electricity from. And as the night wore on, you'd get more and more tired of it all. And eventually it would be four a.m. and you'd have to put your foot down."

One night at the mansion she was desperate to leave and voices were raised. "And he locked the door, and then he got out a shotgun and he put it to my temple and he said, 'If you try to leave I'll pull the trigger.' I remember being quite calm. I wasn't frightened. I just wanted to go home. I said to him, 'Phillip, just stop being silly, put it down and open the door.' And eventually he did. I remember stumbling out and getting in the car and driving away like a bat out of hell. I don't think I ever thought he'd kill me, but I was terrified he could have by accident. But the really extraordinary thing was the next day I came back to work . . ."

Not all such confrontations were resolved so privately. In November 1975 Spector was involved in an incident at the Beverly Hills Hotel with a parking valet named Kevin Brown. According to evidence submitted in September 2004 for the grand jury hearings in the Lana Clarkson case, Brown was at work outside the hotel when he heard a woman scream "Get away from me" and looked over to see Spector and Marty Machat arguing with a woman near the front door. When Brown approached and asked what was happening, Spector allegedly pointed a revolver in his face and told the valet to "Get the fuck away from me," before climbing into a silver Cadillac with Machat and driving away. Spector subsequently pleaded guilty to one count of misdemeanor brandishing of a firearm. He was placed on two years' formal probation, with the condition that he not use or possess any dangerous or deadly weapons.

By the end of 1976 the deal with Warner Bros. had petered to a close, leaving Joe Smith with a feeling of lingering disappointment. "We were never looking to Phillip to sign Elton John or whatever, but we were looking to him to sign somebody and make a signature record, and that never really worked out. It wasn't a good deal. The biggest thing I got out of it was going to the studios and watching Phil work. But the problem with Phil was that he was carrying a big monkey on his back. He's Phil Spector and people expect whatever he does to be a Phil Spector record. And he couldn't do the same record, because people will just say he's repeating himself, but he couldn't come up with anything else either."

But Smith was philosophical. "With rock and roll artists you have to assume the human brain is like a computer with chips that govern its behavior. Well, these people can take blank sheets of paper, put markings on it and take that into the studio, make music out of it that pleases millions of people. They can do things we can't do. They've got chips we don't have. But to make room for those chips, out falls sanity, reason, logic, gratitude . . ."

Spector had not been in the studio in almost a year, and in an attempt to keep some momentum going in his career, Marty Machat now proposed that he should produce another of his clients—Leonard Cohen. On paper, it seemed the most unlikely of partnerships. Cohen was a Canadian poet and author who had become a singer almost as an after-thought—he was thirty-three when he released his debut album, *Songs of Leonard Cohen*, in 1967. His reputation rested on a body of thoughtful, introspective and highly literary songs—bleak and melancholic medita-tions on love, sex and mortality, leavened with a dry, fatalistic humor. He sang in a flat, nasal monotone, framed either by his own acoustic guitar or discreet chamber arrangements. Nobody seemed more sur-prised by his success than Cohen himself.

But Cohen's life and career were now in need of restoration. It had been almost three years since his last album, *New Skin for the Old Cere-mony*, and his record company, Columbia, had taken the step of issuing a *Best of* album—a sure sign that their patience was wearing thin. His family was breaking up and he was drinking heavily; in an attempt to find some equilibrium in his life he had been cultivating an interest in Zen Buddhism and spending time at a Zen retreat, Mount Baldy, in Cal-ifornia.

One night Machat brought Cohen to a small gathering at the man-sion. Cohen would later recall that he found the occasion "tedious," the mansion "dark, cold and dreary." When the other guests departed, and Spector locked the door and refused to let Cohen leave, Cohen was nonplussed. "To salvage the evening, I said, 'Rather than watch you shout at your servants, let's do something more interesting,' " he later recalled. "And so we sat down at the piano and started writing songs."

Over the next three weeks, they composed fifteen numbers, the writ-ing sessions fueled by copious amounts of wine and liquor. Doc Pomus, who was visiting from New York, would remember them as "like two drunks staggerin' around." Alarmed, Cohen's friends tried to warn him off the project. Joni Mitchell was particularly insistent; she had been recording her album *Court and Spark* at A&M studios at the time Spec-tor had been recording the rock and roll album with Lennon and was aware of the turbulence around those sessions. Spector, she warned Cohen, was past his prime and "difficult." Her words were to prove prophetic in a way no one could imagine.

In June 1977 recording began at the Whitney Studios in Glendale. Larry Levine was now back in the fold, engineering the sessions. The studio had a pipe organ that Spector wanted to use on a couple of songs, but on the playbacks Spector had the volume so loud that he blew out the studio's speakers. The recording moved to Gold Star.

After eighteen months, Spector's sporadic love affair with Devra Robitaille had finally come to an end in an abrupt fashion, but she con-tinued to work as his personal assistant. "There was never a discussion.

We just were lovers, and then we weren't. But I think he still trusted me, still relied on me, and we still had a rapport. And I was still very loyal, always did what I was supposed to do with his best interests at heart."

But the Cohen sessions were trying even Devra's patience and loyalty. Going into the studio with Spector was "like a crapshoot. He could be in a great mood, or he could be a raving lunatic. He could go and make magic, or he'd be throwing things around and it would just be this debacle. A lot of it was the drinking. Someone would say something, or he'd just get in a mood and stalk off. Everybody would be hanging around, and then tempers would start to build, and I'd be the pivot point; people would be coming up saying, 'What's going on with Phil? Jesus Christ, when are we going to get out of here, when are we going to get a take?' And Phil would be joking around, getting drunk, walking up and down in the hall, disappearing into the bathroom for hours at a time, fixing his hair. Just prevarication. And it's five o'clock in the morning and everyone's exhausted and our prospective wives and husbands are furious with us, and he hasn't gotten a take yet. And you'd just want to shake him. 'Get on with it!' There were a couple of times when he'd pass out drunk, and Larry and I would have to haul him back into his chair and revive him. And sometimes he'd somehow rally and that would be the brilliant take, the moment of genius."

The boozy camaraderie between Spector and Cohen had quickly degenerated into fractious arguments—about song tempos, structures, arrangements, everything. "They didn't see eye-to-eye at all," Devra says, "and there were a lot of creative differences. It was always very tense, very uncomfortable."

Effectively relegated to the role of sideman, Cohen was doing his best to keep an even temper in the midst of the growing chaos. "Phil was pretty wacky on those sessions—animated," David Kessel remembers. "But what I dug about that was that you had Phil with all of his stuff going on, and then Leonard being like Dean Martin—just cool. It gave Leonard a chance to perfect his Shaolin priesthood stuff and become one with the universe."

Cohen recognized what Spector himself, and few around him, were prepared to acknowledge or admit—that Spector was not simply *eccentric* but seriously disturbed. "In the state that he found himself, which was post-Wagnerian, I would say Hitlerian, the atmosphere was one of guns," Cohen would later reflect. "I mean, that's what was really going on, guns. The music was subsidiary, an enterprise. People were armed to the teeth, [and] everybody was drunk, or intoxicated on other items, so you were slipping over bullets, and you were biting into revolvers in your hamburger. There were guns everywhere."

Cohen would later recall how on one occasion in the studio Spector approached him with a bottle of Manischewitz in one hand and a pistol in the other, placed his arm around Cohen's shoulder, shoved the gun in his neck and said, "Leonard, I love you." Cohen, with admirable aplomb, simply moved the barrel away, saying, "I hope you do, Phil."

On another evening Spector pulled a gun on the violin player Bobby Bruce and held it to his head, after Bruce had made some remarks to which Spector took exception. Larry Levine quickly stepped in to quiet things down. "Phil wasn't angry at Bobby; he was just showing off. But Bobby's gotta be scared shitless. And I said, 'Phil, I know you don't mean anything, but accidents happen. Put it down.' And he wasn't willing to do that. It was like 'Hey, I can handle my life.' So finally I said, 'I'm turning off the equipment and going home unless you put that down right now.' And that's when he finally realized I was serious and put the gun away. I loved Phil, and when you love somebody, you do what you can do to bring it back to the rational. I'd seen him both ways, so I knew that wasn't the real Phil."

The sessions finally ground to a conclusion in a bitter mood, with Spector refusing to allow Cohen to be present for the mixes, or to hear the finished album. Cohen would later claim Spector did not even properly complete his vocals, instead using 'guide vocals' which Cohen had intended to redo later.

Spector was equivocal about the result, scribbling a note to Larry Levine on the master tapes: "I'll tell you something, Larry—we've done worse with better, and better with worse!" For Devra Robitaille, the album was to prove the last straw. Spector would thank her on the album's liner notes for her "grave concern in the face of overwhelming odds." But her sympathies had been exhausted. "I came to the conclusion that I had no business putting myself in a position where I was behaving like a groupie. I disrespected myself. I was an accomplished musician; I was bright and able, and I let myself get trashed." She resigned from her job, and went back to working for Warner Bros.

On its release in 1978, the critics savaged *Death of a Ladies' Man*. Spector was accused of assassinating Cohen's poetic sensitivity with grotesquely inappropriate arrangements and an overwrought production. But the critics were wrong. Out of the fog of alcohol and recrimination, Spector had somehow fashioned a series of almost vaudevillian settings that were perfectly pitched to Cohen's unsparing depiction of himself as a weary boulevardier, desperately seeking spiritual consolation in the pleasures of the flesh, in the face of advancing years and diminishing opportunities. A melancholy waltz for "True Love Leaves No Traces"; bump-and-grind burlesque for "Iodine." "Paper Thin Hotel," a minor-key, bittersweet rumination on infidelity, was dressed with choirs, pedal steel guitars and pianos, with a melody that recalled the work of Jimmy Webb at his most wistfully romantic. In this context even the hokey country hoedown arrangement of "Fingerprints" made a bizarre kind of sense.

Death of a Ladies' Man may not have been Phil Spector's greatest production, but it was certainly the oddest, and in many ways the most compelling.

Cohen attempted to distance himself from the record, describing it to *Rolling Stone* as "an experiment that failed," while acknowledging it had "real energizing capacities." In the final moment, he said, Spector "couldn't resist annihilating me. I don't think he can tolerate any other shadows in his own darkness. I say these things not to hurt him. Incidentally, beyond all this, I liked him. Just man to man he's delightful, and with children he's very kind."

The album would be the worst-selling of Cohen's career. Spector laconically told a friend that he had "got hate mail from all eight of Leonard's fans" and would never miss an opportunity thereafter to make a joke at the poet's expense. In 1993 he was approached by an academic seeking a contribution for a proposed volume of tributes to mark Cohen's sixtieth birthday.

Spector replied by sending a copy of a letter he had recently written to another correspondent, who had seemingly written to Spector seeking his opinion of—of all things—the Partridge Family. While Spector made clear that he regarded the Partridge Family as "an obscene joke," there was one distinguished artist of his acquaintance, he wrote, who had confessed to being "extremely influenced" by them. "And that artist is Leonard Cohen. Underneath that brooding, moody, depressed soul which Leonard possesses lies an out-and-out Partridge Family freak." Spector suggested that his correspondent might even wish to contact Cohen to discuss the Partridge Family further.

Signing the letter, "Cordially, Phil Spector," he helpfully appended Cohen's telephone and fax numbers, just in case his correspondent wanted to get in touch.

22

"Thank You, Folks—
Have a Good Life"

Life had not been easy for Ronnie Spector in the years since leaving Phil Spector. She continued to receive her alimony payments ("Fuck off"), and four times a year she would fly to California to see Donte under the terms of her visitation rights. Ronnie would check into a hotel where Donte would be delivered to her in the back of Spector's Rolls-Royce, stepping out, Ronnie would recall, "like some midget prince."

With Nedra and Estelle having retired from the business, Ronnie recruited two other singers to work as the Ronettes, but the project was short-lived, and she had no more luck as a solo artist until an introduction to Steve Van Zandt, the guitarist for Bruce Springsteen, led to her recording a Billy Joel song, "Say Goodbye to Hollywood," with Springsteen's E Street Band. In the summer of 1977, a promotional tour brought her to Los Angeles, where Harvey Kubernik met her in her hotel on the Sunset Strip. Afterwards he paid a visit to Spector. "I told him I'd just interviewed Ronnie. He said, 'You interviewed Ronnie Spector. I was married to her. That's the end of this conversation.'"

The Dion and Leonard Cohen albums had both been commercial failures—interesting failures, perhaps, but failures nonetheless. Spector had no interest in the music that now dominated the American charts: the solipsistic, Californian singer-songwriter musings of the Eagles and Jackson Browne; the numbing stadium rock of groups like Journey and Kansas; the increasingly bland and mechanical repetitions of disco.

At the age of thirty-eight, Spector might have been expected to feel even more estranged from the rude arrival of punk rock, but the opposite was to prove to be the case.

The Kessel brothers had made an early connection to the Los Angeles punk rock scene that was incubating at a Hollywood club called the Masque, with bands like the Bags, the Weirdos and the Germs. When a New York punk rock group called the Ramones made their Los Angeles debut at the Roxy Club in August 1976, the Kessels were in the audience, and they quickly became friends.

In fact, the Ramones were less a "punk" group than a cartoon of one. They dressed in a uniform of black leather jackets, ripped Levi's and shaggy Beatle-esque haircuts, and each member affected the group's name as a surname. They displayed none of the self-conscious "art" posturing of other New York bands of the period such as Television or Talking Heads, nor the working-class agitprop of British punk groups like the Sex Pistols and the Clash. The Ramones' medium was dumb garage-band pop; a lineage that went back to ? and the Mysterians and the Count Five, the Kingsmen and greasy-haired, street-corner doo-wop. Signed to Sire Records, a New York label run by an old acquaintance of Spector's from the Brill Building days named Seymour Stein, the group released their debut album in 1976—a collection of comical three-chord teenage mantras like "Chain Saw" and "Now I Wanna Sniff Some Glue," all played at breakneck speed and none lasting longer than two minutes. The album was over almost as soon as it had begun.

When the Ramones performed at the Whisky a Go Go early in 1977, the Kessels took Spector to see them. But it was Blondie, the group they were sharing the bill with—or more specifically the group's Monroe-esque singer Deborah Harry—that caught his eye. After the show, he invited Blondie back to the mansion and expressed an interest in producing them, but nervous of Spector's reputation, they turned down his offer.

Later that same year the Ramones returned once more to Los Angeles, where the Kessels produced two songs with the group at Gold Star for the brothers' own label. At the end of the session, Dan Kessel played the songs over the telephone to Spector, and he invited them up to the house.

The journalist Roy Carr happened to be visiting, still in discussions about the film that was never going to be made, and Spector was at his most expansively entertaining, playing his old records, regaling the assembled company with stories and showing off his firearms. "They were just a bunch of kids from Queens," Carr remembers. "Dee Dee was particularly dumb. He said something quite innocently which Phil took exception to. And Phil pulled this pistol out and pointed it at him. Dee Dee was shouting, 'Okay, if you want to shoot me, shoot me. Phil Spector wants to kill me!' "

Spector seemed to "get" the Ramones immediately; their irreverence, their vitality, and the way they connected to an earlier, less self-conscious, era of rock and roll. "Phil just loved their music," David Kessel says. "It was like, God, you mean there's a rock and roll band around? The simplicity of the chords; the lack of improvisation. He understood that it was back to Buddy Holly. He thought they were the best rock and roll band in America."

He was particularly taken with the group's lead singer. Tall and gangling, Joey Ramone (born Jeffrey Hyman) was Ichabod Crane in shades and tennis shoes. "Phil and Joey clicked immediately," David Kessel says. "Joey had his rock and roll history shit together. And they had all that New York street-corner stuff in common. In L.A. you don't care where the street corner is because even if it's half a block away you're still going to get in the car. Phil and Joey talked street corners, they talked doo-wop. The rest of the group were in shock." As the evening wore on, Spector's enthusiasm for working with the group seemed to grow.

"I remember he asked them how many records they'd sold," Roy Carr says. "They didn't know shit from Shinola, so Phil disappeared for about ten minutes and came back with this big computer printout and told them their sales figures. Obviously he was tapped into the Warner mainframe. And their sales were going down."

Spector offered to sign the group on the spot. "He said, 'I'll give you $150,000 and you can have it tonight. I'll get Marty to come over and sort it out.' And he said, 'Roy's going to be your manager.' I said, 'This is news to me, Phil, thank you very much.' Then the group turned to me and said, 'What shall we do?' I said, 'Don't ask me.' "

The Ramones turned Spector down. Instead, at Seymour Stein's suggestion, he turned his attention to another Sire act, a power pop duo from Boston called the Paley Brothers—Andy and Jonathan. The brothers had recorded one, eponymous, album for Sire, and had already discussed the possibility of being produced by two of Spector's former associates, Steve Douglas and Jack Nitzsche (whom Andy Paley remembers as being "totally obsessed with Phil").

Paley was staggered to be awoken at 3:00 a.m. one morning in Boston by a telephone call from Spector himself, asking whether the brothers would be interested in working with him. It took Spector some minutes to convince a disbelieving Paley that he wasn't a friend playing a prank. The brothers were on a plane to Los Angeles three days later. Paley passed the flight reading *Elvis: What Happened?*, a book by three of Presley's former henchmen. Paley's attention was particularly taken by a passage where Presley allegedly ordered one, Red West, to kill his karate instructor Mike Stone, suspecting that Stone had been having an affair with his wife Priscilla: "Mike Stone must die. He must die."

After checking into their hotel the brothers were ferried up to Spector's house. Sitting in the lounge waiting for Spector to appear, Andy Paley was staggered when a handsome, well-built man walked into the room and introduced himself as . . . Mike Stone.

Spector spent most of the next month rehearsing the brothers at his home, breaking off for the occasional excursion to clubs and restaurants. He had acquired a beaten-up VW van with darkened windows, which he loved to drive, he told them, "because nobody would realize anybody famous was inside."

"He'd separate us off," Andy Paley says. " 'Andrew, you go back to the hotel I need to work with Jonathan.' Then a few hours later Jonathan would come back and say, 'Phil took me to this movie; he didn't think you'd like it.' And then a few days later he'd say, 'Andrew, I want you to stay behind'—and he'd take me off to a party, and say, 'I didn't think your brother would be into this . . .' I could never really figure that out."

At length, Spector rounded up some of his old musicians from the Wrecking Crew and took the Paleys into Gold Star. After all the preparation, the sessions lasted less than a week, and produced only a couple of tracks. "We'd get phone calls, Christmas cards," Paley recalls, "but the record never came out." Eventually, the Paley Brothers split up, and Andy Paley embarked on a new career as a producer.

An unexpected financial windfall arrived in the form of the teenage actor, Shaun Cassidy. The half brother of the pop idol David Cassidy, Shaun was the star of a television program *The Hardy Boys*, and had recently signed with Warner Curb Records, a label owned by an entrepreneur named Mike Curb, who had started in the business hiring out musical instruments. Larry Levine would remember Curb as "a little nebbish," who was occasionally seen hauling a keyboard into Gold Star for a Spector session. It was a period that Curb evidently remembered with some fondness. Looking for a song for Shaun Cassidy's first single, Curb steered the young singer toward "Da Doo Ron Ron."

To promote the song, someone at the label came up with the idea of featuring Spector in the video. The scene called for him to be shown seated in the backseat of a limo, pulling away from the sidewalk, pursued by a knot of screaming girls, as Cassidy turns to the camera and asks, "Who was that guy?" It was a reasonable question. "Frankly, I didn't think any of Shaun's fans would have a clue," remembers Nola Leone, who was managing Cassidy's affairs at the time. "But I thought it was kind of hip. And Shaun thought so, too."

Spector, apparently happy to participate in any legend-building exercise, agreed to take part.

On the day of the shoot, Cassidy, Leone and the film crew presented themselves at the mansion to collect Spector before proceeding on to the location. Spector emerged holding a goblet filled with wine in his hand—"it looked like a chalice," Nola remembers—executed a series of theatrical karate kicks, and then invited Cassidy and Leone inside the house to talk. Leone was alarmed when he steered them into the ground-floor powder room and locked the door behind them. For the next hour, he regaled his captive audience with a list of his accomplishments. "The gist of it," Nola remembers, "was that he was the greatest producer in the world, that he should have produced Shaun's record, and anyone could have had a hit with it because it was such a great song—just on and on and on. Every once in a while I'd say, 'There's a lot of people waiting—we should probably go.' And he'd just ignore me. He said, 'You be quiet; you're lucky to even be here.' It wasn't that we were afraid; it was just very strange. And finally, after what seemed like an eternity, he opened the door and we went out."

Spector was persuaded into his limo, and the party drove to the location. At the end of the shoot, Spector offered Cassidy a ride back to the mansion. What Nola Leone remembers as "a look of panic" registered in the young singer's eyes, and he politely made his excuses and refused. Cassidy's version of "Da Doo Ron Ron" would subsequently go to number 1.

People came and went, with vague plans of work, projects that would never come to fruition. Spector's eccentricities had become a thing of legend, and any encounter could be relied upon to provide a suitably vivid anecdote. The '60s English model Twiggy, who had enjoyed an improbable renaissance as a singer with an album called *Please Get My Name Right*, would recall in her autobiography visiting Spector with her husband, the actor Michael Whitney, for discussions about Spector producing her. Unsettled by the guard dogs, the looming presence of George Brand and being made to wait for almost two hours in the darkened mansion before Spector eventually appeared, Twiggy was finally undone when he began brandishing a gun. She fled, never to return. Annette Kleinbard, the voice of "To Know Him Is to Love Him," had an even more disturbing encounter.

Kleinbard had long since lost contact with Spector. After the breakup of the Teddy Bears, she had changed her name, first to Annette Bard and then to Carol Connors, recording a number of singles before turning to songwriting, enjoying early success with "Hey Little Cobra," which was a hit for the Rip Chords. In 1977 she co-wrote the theme for the film *Rocky*, "Gonna Fly Now," which was nominated for an Academy Award. Connors was acquainted with Marty Machat, who suggested that she and Spector might possibly work together. Machat organized a meeting at the Polo Lounge of the Beverly Hills Hotel, where Spector had had his altercation in 1975 with a parking valet. Walking out after the meeting, Connors remembers, they passed a woman who took one look at Spector's bristling hairpiece and let out a gasp of amused disbelief.

"She obviously came from Iowa or somewhere and she had never seen anything like it. But Phil just went off the deep end. 'How dare she?'—ranting and raving. She was with some guy, who walked up to make something of it, and Marty was coming between them, trying to get Phil away from there. And the next thing I knew Phil had a gun in his hand. I don't know if it came from his jacket, his shoe, his belt. I just remember that it was there, and it hadn't been there before. I don't know if Phil was going to fire the gun, but there was just this *anger* there, and then Marty was getting him into the car and away from the hotel. And I remember vowing to myself, 'I will never be in Phil Spector's company again as long as I live—ever.'"

For the past four years, Janis Zavala had been the one constant, stable presence in Spector's life—although to most who knew Spector, she hardly seemed present at all. Self-contained and independent-minded, she continued to work at Screen Gems, with Spector's old partner Lester Sill. She seldom visited the studio when Spector was working and seems to have largely absented herself when visitors came to the La Collina mansion. To some, it seemed as if she was Spector's special secret. One day when Harvey Kubernik was visiting he walked upstairs and happened to bump into Janis on the landing. Kubernik fancied that he had come to know Spector well over the previous two years and had visited the house on several occasions, but he'd never even heard of Janis before, much less met her. Kubernik concluded that Spector deliberately kept her out of sight. "I think Phil was afraid that people would hit on her. It was his idea of being charming."

Spector's domestic life was a secret to everyone, which seemed to throw his public one into even sharper relief. If the private Spector was "a sweet, humble man," as one friend maintains, when he stepped out of the mansion, and on to the public stage, it was as if his personality would change. The "Phil Spector Show" would take over—the big limousines, the bodyguards and hangers-on, the tantrums, the insults, the drunken scenes. It was as if Spector felt he needed to put on a mask to impress people and to hide the truth about the vulnerable, insecure— and frightened—man he really was. It was a paradox that Janis Zavala evidently found harder and harder to reconcile.

Gradually, she seemed to play a less important part in his life. She was seen at the mansion less and less, and then not at all.

In the eighteen months since their visit to the La Collina mansion, the Ramones had produced two more albums, with diminishing returns. And by the beginning of 1979, working with Spector had begun to seem a decidedly more attractive proposition. Seymour Stein negotiated a deal and on May 1, 1979, the Ramones presented themselves at Gold Star.

Under guitarist Johnny's guidance, the Ramones had traditionally spent as little time on recording as possible—regarding the studio as a mere pit stop in the more lucrative, and diverting, round of touring. (The story has it that the group would be given $100,000 to record an album, budget the recording at $60,000 and split the balance between them, reasoning "Why spend more? We're not going to sell more.")

But from the outset, Spector made plain that things would be done his way. To augment the group, he called on the keyboard player Barry Goldberg, drummer Jim Keltner, saxophonist Steve Douglas, and the Kessel brothers playing guitars. It was clear to everybody that the only member of the Ramones he was really interested in was singer Joey. "I think in Phil's mind, the Ramones were basically Joey with a backing group," Roy Carr says. "He looked on Joey as a male Ronnie Spector."

The recording of *End of the Century* would take little more than three weeks—a blink of the eye by Spector's normal standards, "but in Ramones time," Joey would remember later, "it was interminable." The rest of the group had neither the patience nor the proficiency to abide by Spector's traditional routine of wearing his musicians down by having them play the songs over and over again. When he devoted almost an entire session to having Johnny Ramone play the opening chord to

"Rock 'n' Roll High School," Johnny walked out. When Spector ordered him back into the studio, the distracted guitarist snapped back, "What are you going to do? Shoot me?"

When Spector turned his attention to Joey's vocals, coaching the singer long into the night, the others were left largely to their own devices. Marky and Dee Dee immersed themselves in the nightlife of Los Angeles (so enthusiastically in Dee Dee's case that the Kessel brothers would later be obliged to overdub his bass lines), while Johnny fretted in his room at the Tropicana Motel, according to David Kessel, "bored and out of it. It was like: Joey's in the studio with Phil, the other two are out getting wasted and I'm sitting here twiddling my thumbs. Johnny was used to being in control, and he didn't have any control with Phil. No way in the world was Phil going to take orders from Johnny Ramone. Everybody was bitching and uptight and ornery. And of course Phil is Mr. Congeniality, so there was a lot of shouting . . ."

The ultimate symbol of Spector's disregard for the rest of the group came with the recording of "Baby, I Love You"—the third time Spector had recorded the song. He had originally wanted the group to record the Bob B. Soxx song, "Not Too Young to Get Married," but according to David Kessel, Joey "begged" Spector to be allowed to record the Ronettes hit instead. "He said, 'You're going to make me Ronnie Spector? Go for it, please . . .' Phil said, 'Yeah it's my song, I've got the publishing, but do you really want to do this?' But Joey begged him. 'If I'm working with Phil Spector, we're doing a Phil Spector song.' "

Considering the others superfluous to requirements, Spector took Joey into the studio on his own, used his own musicians and, a first for the Ramones, added strings. A disgruntled Johnny would later reflect that the song was "the worst thing we've ever done in our career." But it would give the group their only Top 10 single.

As the sessions dragged on, Spector's worst habits began to reassert themselves, and he began drinking more heavily. Larry Levine, whom Spector had called in to engineer the sessions, had seen it all before. In their long association, Levine had come to think of himself as "pretty much a big brother" figure to Spector, and had developed a fine instinct for knowing when to step in to defuse ugly or awkward situations, and when to leave best alone. But Spector was now more out of control than Levine had ever seen him.

"We would go in sometimes, and Phil had been drinking so much that we would go a whole night without doing a thing, because he wasn't capable of doing anything; he was just out of it. There were a couple of times where I told him that he was not acting correctly, and we got into some heavy arguments. He was abusive to the Ramones, and I told him that; and then he was abusive to me. It was like you couldn't get through to Phil at that point. He was gone, into another place. You couldn't reason with him. And it was all from the drinking. He was never that way not drinking."

With the sessions completed, Spector dismissed the band and got down to mixing the album. With the exception of "Baby, I Love You," which he decorated with a faux-jaunty string arrangement completely at odds with the heartstopping drama and poignancy of the original, Spector had done little to tamper with the Ramones' formula, merely adding texture to the group's amphetamine rush, with echo and reverb and some additional instrumental flourishes. Yet, apparently beset with anxiety, he would labor for almost six months over the mixing. David Kessel was incredulous. "I remember asking him, 'Why's it taking so long? They're just a guitar, bass and drums band—we're not talking about a whole lot here.' And he said, 'I don't care; I've got to get it right. You want me to do it wrong? No. Then let me do it right.' I think he knew the Ramones would be the last album he would do for a long time, and he had a lot riding on it. This was a little different attitude from the art pieces he did with Dion and Leonard Cohen. I think he was conscious of leaving a rock and roll legacy."

For Larry Levine the strain became unbearable. One night he and Spector had a "knock-down, drag-out argument," and the following day Levine suffered a heart attack. Levine refused to attribute the attack to Spector—he had suffered a first heart attack six years earlier but continued to smoke heavily—but Spector was mortified, and fearing he was to blame could not even bring himself to visit Levine in hospital. They would not speak for another ten years.

End of the Century was finally released in January 1980. It had taken seven months to complete, at a cost of some $200,000—more than three times the cost of any previous Ramones album. It would also prove to be the group's most successful record, rising to number 44 in the American album charts and number 14 in Britain. Spector's original contract with the group stipulated that he would produce two albums. But like two boxers who had pummeled each other to a standstill, neither the Ramones nor Spector could face the prospect of going another round.

"Phil was tired, and he needed time to himself," David Kessel says. "When he finished the Ramones album, it was like: Thank you, folks— have a good life."

23

"A Case That No One Can Reach"

At the age of forty-one, Phil Spector entered retirement. There had been periods in the past when he had withdrawn from the studio, and from public life. Longueurs when he had been stricken with self-doubt, recalcitrance. He had always come back. But now he would not enter the studio again for another thirteen years. Better than anybody, Spector knew that the craziness had to end. He was exhausted by his own madness.

He started seeing Janis Zavala again. She had left Screen Gems and was now working in another music publishing job.

On the night of December 8, 1980, John Lennon was shot dead outside his home at the Dakota building in New York by an obsessive fan. Spector and Lennon had had an uneasy relationship in the aftermath of the acrimonious conclusion to the *Rock 'n' Roll* album sessions. According to Yoko Ono they had talked from time to time on the telephone but never actually seen each other again. Spector would later claim that they had discussed the possibility of working together again, on another Lennon album, and as collaborators producing Elvis Presley—an idea that was never put to Presley himself and was scotched when the singer died in 1977.

Spector seemed to have no inner resources to deal with loss. Just as he had been knocked completely off balance by the death of his friend Lenny Bruce fifteen years earlier, so he was now rendered helpless by the shock of Lennon's passing. That same night a handful of friends, including the Kessel brothers, gathered at the mansion, to mourn Lennon, but mostly it seemed to comfort Spector. "He was devastated," Dan Kessel remembers. "I was. Anyone who liked the Beatles or liked John felt the same way. But Phil was particularly close to John; he didn't take it very well at all. He was talking about John, drinking, talking about what a great artist he was and how much he missed him. It was just such a sad moment." When the gathering finally broke up at six in the morning, Spector vanished to his room and locked the door behind him, refusing to emerge for several days.

In January, in an attempt to come to terms with her husband's death, Yoko Ono began recording a solo album, *Season of Glass*. Affection between Spector and Ono had always been somewhat forced; but now, in a gesture as much of conciliation as need, she invited him to co-produce the record. But the sessions were awash with grief, and Spector withdrew before the album was completed. He returned to California with one of Lennon's guitars, which Yoko had given him as a keepsake, and which would occupy a cherished place in the music room thereafter. He had lost any interest in working. "I think, after John died, it was: What the fuck now?" Dan Kessel says. "He'd produced the Beatles, and he'd produced the Ramones, who were like the Beatles of punk rock. So who was he going to produce now? Frank Sinatra? It was very apparent he wasn't all that motivated to create or hustle or anything. It was like the end of an era, and he was going to take a breathing space and just deal with it."

On October 17, 1982, Phil Spector became a proper father for the first time when Janis gave birth to twins, a boy and a girl. Spector was thrilled—and particularly delighted by the fact that they shared a birthday with his hero, Barney Kessel. Horrified at the piped Muzak playing in the ward where the newborn babies were kept, Spector demanded to see the hospital superintendent. "The superintendent came along and Phil was haranguing him," Dan Kessel remembers. "He was saying, 'You've got to change the music.' 'Well, why?' And Phil was saying, 'All I can tell you is you're going to have a serious problem on your hands if you don't change this music to a jazz station. I can't have it that this is the first music my children hear.' And the incredible thing was, they changed it." A boy and a girl . . . To Spector it was obvious—the children should be called Ike and Tina, or perhaps Mickey and Sylvia. At length, they were named Nicole and Phillip Jr.

Janis gave up her job in music publishing and became a full-time mother. It seems that the couple also married around this time, although Spector, who remained intensively secretive about his private life, told almost no one: for years afterward even close friends like Ahmet Ertegun and Nino Tempo would be unsure of his exact marital status.

Family life seemed to transform Spector. He stopped drinking. He was the most contented, the most at peace with himself, that he had ever been. He saw few people, devoting all his time to Janis and the children. The loss of his father had left a deep scar that had never healed, and that Spector seldom talked about with anyone. "I remember once when the Kessels were going down to visit their father, Phil said, 'You're lucky you have one,' " Harvey Kubernik says. "That was a rare thing for him."

His own childhood had hardly provided a model of a happy and harmonious family life. But it now seemed that he was determined to lavish on the twins all the love and affection he had never known himself as a child.

"It was like Phil had had this emotional-paperwork pileup, and he needed to get in touch with himself," Dan Kessel says. "He wanted to be a good father, and he *was* a good father. He became a much more private person. He didn't want to go out, and he didn't want a lot of people coming over to break the vibe. Here was a guy for whom just putting on a funky sweatshirt, going to the supermarket and buying a quart of milk was good for rehabilitation. That's the kind of stuff he needed to do."

When the children were born, he had laid down two conditions to Janis. He would never go to Disneyland, and he would never go to the beach. He was as good as his word, but he delighted in doing other "dad things."

"Phil was a doting father," Dan Kessel says. "He spent most of his time at home with Janis, raising the kids and playing with them; he was very involved in every aspect of their lives, their schooling, everything."

An avid basketball fan, he bought a season ticket to the Lakers, court-side. His seat happened to be directly opposite where Jack Nicholson sat, and Spector enjoyed telling friends that he'd "seen Jack at the game," as if they were the closest of friends.

Spector's newfound peace and equilibrium had come too late to save his adopted family. At 10:00 p.m. on the night of January 23, 1980, ten-year-old Donte walked into a West Hollywood police station and told officers that he had run away from home. When police contacted Spector, he refused to come and collect his son. Donte was taken into temporary care, and in April, Ronnie was awarded custody, with the court ordering Spector to pay child support of $850 a month—"by check or money order," the judge warned Spector, "no pennies, nickels or quarters." Donte joined Ronnie in the small apartment where she was living in New York. But Donte was unhappy in New York, and the arrangement ended after only a few months, when he flew back to California, to spend a few days with an old school friend. At the end of his stay, according to *Be My Baby*, Donte refused to return to New York, telling the friend's mother that Ronnie was an alcoholic and that he was scared to be with her. Instead, he moved in with Bertha. Ronnie would not see her adopted son again for more than ten years. After living for a while with Bertha, Donte moved back into the mansion with Spector, but the relationship was troubled. Donte was going off the rails, and before long he had left home for good.

While Spector had always been devoted to Donte, if incapable of properly playing the part of his father, the twins Gary and Louis had been adopted almost as an afterthought, and for the most part they had been raised by George Brand and a series of nannies and governesses. In 1985, both boys graduated from high school and also left home, Gary to join the air force, Louis to join a Christian community. They would maintain only sporadic contact with Spector.

In 2003, following Spector's arrest, Donte gave an interview to the *Mail on Sunday*, claiming that he had been raised in "an atmosphere of fear" and that Spector had "destroyed" his life. "People looked at me when I was a child and thought I was living a fairy-tale existence," he said. "I lived in a mansion and went to school in a stretch limo. But what people didn't realize was that when I went home I would be locked in my room for hours. My brothers were locked in one room and I was locked in another. I didn't even have a proper toilet—I had a small pot in the corner of the room."

Spector, Donte alleged, "ruled by fear. He always had a gun and if we were bad he'd let his robe fall open so you could see the holster. He would put his hand on it and say, 'Now, just behave' . . . Sometimes I'd want to wet myself with fear." Most shocking were the allegations that after Ronnie had left home, Spector would bring girlfriends back to the mansion and force Donte and his brothers to watch them having sex. "At other times Dad would say, 'There she is, now be a man,' and he would force us to simulate sex with the girl. I was only ten or so at the time. I was terrified."

He went on to describe how, disowned by his adoptive parents, he had slipped into a life on the street, working as a male prostitute in Hollywood to earn money for drugs, eventually becoming HIV-positive. He had last seen Spector, he claimed, two years earlier, when they had gone to a Lakers game. "It was strange—Dad seemed okay to see me, but he didn't give me a hug. I can't remember him ever telling me that he loved me." They had last spoken, he said, in December 2002, two months before Spector's arrest, when Donte had telephoned and asked his father for money. According to Donte, "He just hung up."

In 1983 Gold Star Studios, the crucible of Spector's genius and the scene of his greatest triumphs, was sold when the site where it stood was designated for development as a shopping mall. When the studio burned down the following year, it seemed the final, climactic punctuation mark to the career of the man who, more than anyone, had made Gold Star a legend.

Music had slipped away from Phil Spector's life. There was no financial requirement for him to work. He could rely on a steady stream of income from his catalogue of hits. He would tell the Kessels that the two most important dates of the year were June 15 and December 15—when record companies paid royalties. But he was intensely protective about the use of his material. He had always been contemptuous of his old rival Berry Gordy's willingness to allow Motown songs to be used in films and commercials. Gordy, he mocked, was holding "one long fire sale." And while Spector had occasionally allowed his songs to be used in film soundtracks—Martin Scorsese had used "Be My Baby" for the opening sequence of *Mean Streets*—he was happy to turn down hundreds of thousands of dollars of potential income rather than prostitute his songs, and would make life inordinately difficult for anyone wanting to license them. In 1984 Steven Spielberg approached him about using the Darlene Love song "Christmas (Baby Please Come Home)" for his film *Gremlins*. There was protracted haggling between the two men over the price right up to the last minute, when Spector threatened to pull the song altogether. Spielberg swore he would never again do business with Spector.

His most lucrative licensing opportunity came two years later, when he allowed "Be My Baby" to be used in the film *Dirty Dancing*, which became one of the highest-grossing films of the time. The soundtrack album spent eighteen weeks at number 1 in America, and went on to sell over 11 million copies. For Spector it was a welcome windfall, but the success of the song would later lead to a lawsuit with the Ronettes that would occupy him for much of the next decade. In the same year, Spector allowed three of his songs to be used in the brat-pack movie *The Pick-up Artist:* Darlene Love's "Wait 'til My Bobby Gets Home," the Crystals' "Da Doo Ron Ron," and the Ronettes' "(The Best Part of) Breakin' Up"; for the latter, Spector himself was persuaded into the studio to produce the actress Molly Ringwald singing the lead vocal over the original instrumental track. But the film, and the soundtrack album, failed to repeat the success of *Dirty Dancing* and were quickly forgotten.

While Marty Machat continued to work as Spector's lawyer, it was Janis who was the emissary for most of his contact with the outside world. Most people had no idea that the woman on the other end of the telephone who handled all of Spector's business dealings and correspondence was also the mother of his children. But then most people had no idea Spector had children.

"Janis was excellent for Phil," Dan Kessel says. "She was a real pro, highly intelligent, with sound judgment. She made things run like clockwork."

Spector seemed to have lost all interest in music. It was as if the fear that had haunted him for twenty-five years—that he would never be able to match, let alone surpass, the standards he had set himself in his twenties, and that he was doomed to live forever in the shadow of his own monumental accomplishments—had now hardened into a kind of paralysis.

Occasionally, old friends like Don Randi and Jack Nitzsche would receive a telephone call out of the blue, hinting at a reunion or a recording date, as if Spector were reassuring himself that if ever he were to return to work his old friends would be there for him, just as they had always been. Even Bobby Sheen, who had not worked with Spector for twenty years, would receive the occasional call.

Since separating from Spector in the '6os, Sheen had enjoyed modest success as a solo performer, recording singles for Capitol and Warner Bros., before joining a touring version of the Coasters. While ruing the fact that Spector had allowed his career with Philles to dwindle, Sheen had always felt gratitude and affection for his old producer.

"Everybody else from the Blossoms kind of resented Phil for what he'd done to them, but Bobby would never say anything negative about him," remembers Sheen's widow Frances. "Phil carried on sending him stuff—records, a jacket and T-shirt. He would call up Bobby every now and again and say, 'Hey, we're going back in the studio; it's going to be just like the old days.' But it never happened, of course. He'd call on a Friday, and say, 'I'll give you a call back on Monday.' Bobby would hang up the phone and say, 'Phil says we're going in the studio on Monday.' I'd say, 'That's good!' And Bobby would just laugh and say, 'No, he doesn't mean it. He just calls up and says things like that; he's probably not taking his medicine.'"

On one occasion, Spector insisted that Sheen meet him to discuss a possible recording, suggesting a rendezvous in a parking lot behind a

Hollywood restaurant. Sheen thought it was odd, but duly turned up at the appointed place and hour. They had been talking for only a few minutes when a group of toughs materialized out of the darkness. Spector took fright and fled, leaving a bemused and shaken Sheen to make good his own escape. He never heard from Spector again.

In 1986 an American author James Robert Baker published *Fuel-Injected Dreams*—a classic of contemporary pulp fiction, the book was a blowup caricature of all the myths and legends about the "madness" of Phil Spector. The novel tells the story of Dennis Contrelle, "the original Wagner of vinyl," the "one-man surfing Luftwaffe of car-crash romance," who after a stellar burst in the '60s, creating a series of "epic trash" masterpieces, withdraws to his Malibu mansion, "a drug-damaged Svengali," making a virtual prisoner of his wife Sharlene, the teenage temptress who once sang with his biggest group, the Stingrays.

Guns, drugs, derangement . . . as a Grand Guignol compendium of every myth, rumor and speculation about Spector, as a totem of how deeply his legend had penetrated the collective pop consciousness—and too as a funhouse-mirror, amphetamine-rush evocation of his music—the book was nonpareil. (Trying to write a history of pop in the '60s without Dennis Contrelle, Baker notes, was like "writing the New Testament without mentioning Jesus; a lot of whores and cripples and greedy money-changers wandering around the desert toward no particular end.") But it could hardly have been further from the truth of Phil Spector's current circumstances. At the time of the publication of *Fuel-Injected Dreams*, Spector was doing little more transgressive than playing with his children on the lawn and making occasional excursions to the supermarket and the car wash.

In the summer of 1986, after twenty-one years in the mansion on La Collina Drive, he finally turned his back on Hollywood. The children were coming up to school age; Spector wanted to get away from Hollywood, and Janis wanted to live in a quieter neighborhood, more befitting family life. He purchased a property in Pasadena, half an hour's drive from Hollywood on the Ventura Freeway. It was a symbolic departure from the world of rock and roll. The neighborhood where he settled on Arroyo Boulevard was quiet and elegant, its stately mansions heavy with the aroma of "old money."

Spector told friends he wanted to downscale, but he ended up acquiring an even larger property than the one he had left—a capacious three-storey mansion, built in the Mediterranean style, set in two acres of land. At the rear of the house was a sweeping lawn, with a huge, tiled fish pond decorated with stone figures of Pan and a cascading waterfall and a circular swimming pool with a Jacuzzi.

He had acquired the house from the actor Robert Reed, who played the role of the father in the television series *The Brady Bunch*. But when Spector arrived to take possession of the house, with the Kessels in tow, Reed refused to leave in a dispute over payment. Eventually the police had to be called; Reed was escorted off the premises and Spector was able to move into his new home.

He left his past behind him. George Brand had effectively retired a year earlier, suffering from severe back pain, but had continued to live at La Collina Drive. With the move to Pasadena, Brand now decided to go and live with one of his daughters. (He would develop Alzheimer's and die in 2002.) Spector now had no need for a bodyguard or factotum.

For a brief period, Devra Robitaille came back to work for him. After leaving Spector nine years earlier, Devra had worked for Warner Bros., and then returned to England, working as a studio and touring musician with Mike Oldfield, Mick Taylor and others. Now she was attempting once more to pick up the threads of her life back in America. Once she had played an important part in Spector's life, liaising with musicians, coordinating sessions and budgets. But those days were past. Now her work consisted of girl-Friday chores, "completely low-level stuff," for which she was paid only a few dollars an hour. She worked out of her apartment in Hollywood and seldom visited the Pasadena house. Spector was no longer the intimate he had once been. "He was much more distant, uncommunicative, keeping me at arm's length." She had no idea that he now had a family; it was never mentioned. To Devra, the menial nature of the job began to feel "almost like a perverse joke—as if I was being used." Bored and unhappy, she left after a few months.

Spector had closed himself off from all but a few of his old friends. Even Nino Tempo, who for years had regarded himself as an intimate, now found his old friend remote, unreachable. To Tempo, as much as Spector's growing reclusiveness appeared to be born of a simple desire for sanctuary and privacy, it also seemed a symptom of some deeper yearning to maintain his status as a music business legend.

"I think Phil believed that if he was just a regular, nice guy who was touchable, accessible, not hiding out and not withdrawing, that somehow the level of his importance wouldn't be as great. I think he believed that the only way to be great is to live a life of a legend. Not appearing in public, having three secretaries you have to get past just to talk to him, the unlisted telephone number—it all creates an image.

"He used to say to me that he was the Howard Hughes of the recording industry. But once you set up that lifestyle, you get caught up in it, you become a case that no one can reach. And with Phil it got out of hand, it overwhelmed him and took over his life to a place where he was no longer in control."

From time to time, Tempo would talk to Janis on the telephone. "She said to me one day, 'Whenever Phil and I are talking about the happiest times in his life, he invariably says that he had the most fun when you two were running around together, poor and struggling, doing all the crazy things that young guys do—getting into trouble and laughing about it.' And she would say to Phil, 'Well, if you had so much fun, why don't you call Nino? Why don't you get together and pal around again?' And I would have loved that. But she told me that Phil said, 'I can't. I just can't.' "

Not even the woman who had once been closest to him could penetrate the wall of Spector's self-imposed exile. Since their divorce in 1965 Annette Merar had remarried, given birth to a son and moved back to Los Angeles. She and Spector continued to talk occasionally on the phone, and he would sometimes mark her birthday by sending her a cake. In 1986, Annette took a new job, and Spector agreed to meet her and her new boss for dinner. "And it was the old story—'I'll be there in two hours.' Then somebody calling, 'Stand by, Phil's going to call you back . . .' And I got so pissed off. When he came on the line I yelled at him, maybe for the first time; I really let him have it, told him everything I thought. And then I hung up on him." They would not speak again. For Annette, the incident reawakened all the frustrations, disappointments and lingering anger she had felt over their marriage. "And twenty years on, I can still feel the edge from that. It just brought back exactly what I felt when the marriage ended. I felt absolutely one hundred percent betrayed, lied to, cheated on and never atoned for. Everybody around Phil either made it to the top and had great success in the industry or they were destroyed. And I was one of the casualties, too. And what I always wondered was, Why? Why? Why?

"All I wanted was for Phil to just be regular. I used to wonder, Why does he have to be so eccentric and so bizarre in everything? And then he just got worse and worse. Because he didn't have any awareness of his tendencies, his weaknesses, where he was excessive in the wrong ways. So he ended up just being a victim of himself." Phil, she concluded, was "not a dark soul. I came to see him as a sick soul."

24

"Between Grief and Nothing,
I Will Take Grief"

In 1988 Marty Machat died. It was only some weeks later, while going through his papers, that Spector discovered that for years his lawyer and friend had been siphoning off Spector's money into his own accounts. To handle his affairs, Spector now turned to his old acquaintance, the former manager of the Beatles and the Stones, and the man who had brought him into Apple—Allen Klein. Even before Machat's death, Klein had been courting Spector assiduously, recognizing that the back catalogue of Philles hits constituted a priceless asset that had never been properly exploited. "Phil felt that he'd trusted somebody and got burned, so 'Now who do I trust?'" says David Kessel. Allen Klein might not have been everybody's first choice. But in 1989 Spector signed a deal giving Klein's company ABKCO the right to manage his catalogue.

The music business has a notoriously short memory span. Spector was nearing fifty, and he had not made a record in ten years. His great hits of the '60s belonged to another age. His reputation now rested largely on his eccentricities, the whispered stories of guns, madness and seclusion. Allen Klein realized that his first task was to raise his new client's profile and remind the world that before he was a legendary recluse, Phil Spector was a musical genius.

For Spector himself it had long been a source of deep rancor that the industry had never properly acknowledged the monumental contribution he had made to the history of rock and roll. The failure of "River Deep—Mountain High" had never been forgotten—never mind that it was twenty-five years ago—nor his belief that that failure had nothing to do with the record, and everything to do with the industry holding a grudge against him. No Phil Spector record had ever been nominated for a Grammy, and nobody had ever suggested that he should be considered for a lifetime award for producing or songwriting. But now Spector at last began to receive the industry recognition he had always craved.

In 1988 he flew to Nashville to receive an award for "To Know Him Is to Love Him," which had recently been recorded by Dolly Parton, Linda Ronstadt and Emmylou Harris, as the most played country song of the year. And the following year he was inducted into the Rock and Roll Hall of Fame. The Hall of Fame had been founded in 1986 to honor the artists, producers and entrepreneurs who over the previous thirty years had transformed rock music from a bastard offshoot of popular music into a multibillion-dollar industry. Its principal architects were Jann Wenner, the founder and publisher of *Rolling Stone*, and Spector's old friends Ahmet Ertegun, Jerry Wexler and Seymour Stein. In the Hall's first three years Alan Freed, Sam Phillips, Wexler, Ertegun, Leiber and Stoller, Leonard Chess and Spector's old rival Berry Gordy had all been honored in the "nonperformer" category. Thrilled to be welcomed into this company, Spector invited a group of friends to join him for the ceremony in New York, among them the Kessel brothers and Jack Nitzsche.

Unlike Spector, Nitzsche had embraced the changing fashions in rock music, building a career that had earned him an Olympian respect in the music business. In 1967 he forged a relationship with Neil Young, who was then a member of Buffalo Springfield, working on Young's song "Expecting to Fly." He went on to contribute to numerous Young recordings as a producer and arranger and to record and perform as a sometime member of Young's band Crazy Horse. He had produced Mink DeVille and Graham Parker, and diversified with considerable success into scoring film soundtracks. In 1970 he produced the soundtrack for the Donald Cammell and Nic Roeg film *Performance*, probably the greatest marriage of film and rock music ever. Five years later he was nominated for an Academy Award for Best Film Score for *One Flew over the Cuckoo's Nest;* and in 1982 he provided the score for *An Officer and a Gentleman*, which won an Oscar for Best Original Song for "Up Where We Belong," which Nitzsche composed with his second wife, the singer Buffy Sainte-Marie, and the lyricist Will Jennings.

Over the years, Spector and Nitzsche had maintained a curious sort of friendship. "All the way through Jack's time with Neil Young and Crazy Horse, he never heard a peep from Phil," says Denny Bruce, who for a time acted as Nitzsche's manager. "He'd say, 'I wonder how Phil's doing.' He didn't even know how to reach him. He used to say, 'It's so weird, we were together a lot . . .' He just couldn't figure it out." But the two men continued to maintain an abiding affection for one another. According to another friend, "Jack seemed to have an intuitive understanding of when Phil needed him," and he had a knack of calling or turning up out of the blue when Spector most needed him—he had been one of those who had gathered around in the La Collina mansion on the day after the murder of John Lennon. Once in a while, like Doc Pomus, Bobby Sheen and other old friends from the past, Nitzsche would receive a call from Spector asking 'What are you doing in a month?' and suggesting some project or other was in the offing. Nitzsche would simply shrug and tell friends, 'Like this is going to happen . . .' "

Nitzsche had experienced his own problems over the years, struggling with alcohol and drugs. His old friend Sonny Bono, for one, had always taken a disapproving view of Nitzsche's enthusiastic embrace of the drug culture. "I realized I couldn't talk to Sonny anymore," Nitzsche once recalled, "after he sat me down on a couch and gave me a fatherly lecture about dope—'Jack, are you still taking that . . . stuff? Because I'm just afraid you're going to end up in a mental hospital.' " Bono was a straight arrow by comparison. When his career as an entertainer faltered, he became a restaurateur, moved to Palm Springs and in 1988 was elected as mayor of the city on a Republican ticket. Shortly afterward, Nitzsche was arrested in the town for being drunk and disorderly. At the police station he demanded that a call be put through to his friend the mayor—"We wrote 'Needles and Pins' together!" When Bono declined to get involved and order his old friend's release, Nitzsche railed at his guards. "Who the fuck does he think he is? He and Cher used to sleep on my floor!" He was released after a night in the tank. When Bono later called to apologize, Nitzsche screamed down the phone at him and hung up.

Nitzsche held an ambivalent view of how Spector had changed over the years: Phil, he told friends, would have been happier as a jazz guitarist—"and more humble"; fame "puts you on a pedestal" and it had done Spector no favors. But Nitzsche continued to cherish their friendship. Among his most treasured possessions was a gold watch, engraved with his name, which Spector had given him in the 1960s. Afraid of losing it, Nitzsche never wore the watch, instead keeping it hidden away in a velvet pouch, along with a beaded Indian bracelet made by his wife, Buffy Sainte-Marie. He would tell friends that the watch meant more to him than the Oscar he had won for "Up Where We Belong," which had been consigned to a back room, where it sat on a shelf among the household cleaning products gathering dust.

Nitzsche displayed a blithe indifference to the trappings of show business status, and he was nonplussed when he received a call out of the blue from Spector inviting him to join him at the ceremony to induct Spector into the Rock and Roll Hall of Fame. "Jack said, 'Really?'" Denny Bruce remembers. "He hated award shows and couldn't care less about all that shit; he just assumed it was in L.A. But no—'We will have a limo picking you up; there will be a tuxedo for you . . .'"

Nitzsche dutifully took his place with Spector and a small group of friends, including Gerry Goffin and the Kessel brothers, on the MGM Grand jet for the flight to New York. Checking into the Waldorf Hotel, Nitzsche was bemused to receive a telephone call from Spector's secretary in Los Angeles, asking him to meet Spector in the lobby for dinner. Spector was staying in the room immediately above Nitzsche's own, but had apparently felt it more appropriate to fix the appointment through his office.

Spector was so nervous at the prospect of being honored by his peers that he drank heavily before the ceremony. His old friend Michael Spencer happened to be at the ceremony and was shocked to see him "drunk as a skunk." By the time he appeared onstage to collect his award he was rambling incoherently, making jokes about confusing the induction with President Bush's inauguration.

On the flight back to Los Angeles, Nitzsche turned to Spector with a question. "Jack asked him, 'Look, I hear all these stories and it's been killing me all these years,'" Denny Bruce remembers. "'I hear Leonard Cohen, I hear the Ramones, two or three other people—I have to ask you, Did you really pull a gun on all these guys?' And Phil said, 'You know the problem, Jack? None of these people you mention have the same sense of humor as I do.'"

On the evening of January 17, 1991, at the outbreak of the first Gulf War, Karen Lerner was sitting in her New York apartment, watching the missiles land on Baghdad on CNN when she received a telephone call from her friend Ahmet Ertegun, telling her that he and his wife Mica were having dinner that night with someone that Lerner "might find interesting" and inviting her to join them. Lerner made her way to an Italian restaurant in midtown, where Ahmet introduced her for the first time to Phil Spector.

A former TV executive who was now working as the vice president of the Museum of Television and Radio, Lerner was a vibrant, stylish and highly intelligent woman. Between 1966 and 1974 she had been married to the Broadway lyricist Alan Jay Lerner, who with his partner, the composer Frederick Loewe, was responsible for such hit musicals as *My Fair Lady*, *Camelot* and *Brigadoon*. By her own admission, Karen had "missed the '60s," knew next to nothing about rock and roll, and had barely heard of Phil Spector. But as he held court over dinner, seizing on the fact that she had been married to Lerner and expounding on his knowledge of classic American song, she began to find him "utterly fascinating."

"He was teasing me mercilessly about Alan, who I think Phil thought was old and square, and making jokes about his lyrics. And at the same time I was so intrigued because he seemed to know the tunes and lyrics to all two thousand Irving Berlin songs and Cole Porter too. He said, 'Did you know that Irving Berlin wrote a Cole Porter song, and Cole Porter wrote an Irving Berlin song?' And what it was, was 'Don't Fence Me In'—which you would think was an Irving Berlin type of song, but was actually written by Cole Porter; and then there was 'Cheek to Cheek' that Irving Berlin wrote, but that could have been written by Cole Porter."

Spector, she thought, was "a funny-looking little thing, but he was so smart and charming and funny that he won me over, and I never again thought about what he looked like. Wooing was never really part of our relationship, and there was no physical thing between us, but he was certainly trying to make me adore him."

She was further charmed when they met for dinner the following evening, and Spector took her home. Karen had a small dog named Oliver, whom Spector immediately seemed to fall in love with. The following day, a package arrived for Oliver from the toy shop FAO Schwarz containing a large fluffy toy. "Phil told me later that he'd said to the sales assistant that he wanted to get a present for a little boy. The assistant asked him, 'How old is the little boy?' And Phil said, 'I think he's about three.' He didn't mention it was a dog, and I'm not sure he even remembered. I honestly think at some level he thought he was getting a present for my son. I don't have a son."

A few days later, the Erteguns invited Karen and Spector out to their house at the Hamptons for the weekend. They traveled together in a limousine. Karen had brought a small overnight bag, and she was bemused when Spector appeared with four large suitcases, a portable keyboard and three hatboxes—that he would not let out of his grip, and that Karen assumed contained his wigs. At Ertegun's home, she and Spector were given adjoining rooms. Dressing for dinner, she could hear the sound of Spector's hair dryer through the wall as he labored interminably to tease his hairpiece into place. That evening, a group of Ertegun's friends, including Jann Wenner, sat down to dinner, and Spector entertained the throng at the piano with more selections from the Berlin and Porter songbooks. The next morning, everyone set out along the beach in a stiff breeze for a bracing walk. Spector stayed behind. "I don't think Phil was really a beach person," Karen says.

It was the beginning of a platonic relationship that would last for the next four years. They would meet frequently when Spector was in town, and when he returned to the West Coast, they kept in touch with notes and phone calls. Sometimes Lerner would return home, switch on her answering-machine and find that, in her absence, Spector had been talking to her dog. "I'd hear these messages, 'Oliver, do you want to go out? Do you want to go out?' That's what I always said to him, 'Do you want to go out, Ollie?' And I could picture this poor dog, hearing this voice playing in the apartment, and running up and down the hall, going mad. It was kind of . . . sinister. Who would think of doing something like that? But I actually like sick humor, and that's one reason I was so intrigued by Phil. He had a wild sense of humor, very, very original."

When Spector first played Karen his greatest hits, she was taken aback. "What struck me was the volume and the intensity—this little tiny man making such a big, powerful noise. And the lyrics, which were so lovely in many cases. I'd had no idea. I remember him saying once, 'Your husband wrote music that was on stage and film. But how would you like it if you wrote something and your whole output in life was presented in a 6"×2" box, meaning a car radio. How difficult would it be to write something that would come across in that way?' I think he was saying, 'This is the hurdle I've had to overcome, and I mastered it.' "

Spector would talk for hours about his life and his music, the people he'd known, the people he'd worked with, the friends and the enemies. He would treat her to his impersonations of Ahmet—whom Karen surmised he revered as a father figure—John Lennon and Bob Dylan— "that nasal whine, where you couldn't understand anything. I think Dylan was one of his pet peeves." He proudly told her how he had once thrown Warren Beatty out of a recording session.

Sometimes his conversation would drift back to a subject that had preoccupied him for much of his professional life: being immortalized in film. Over dinner one night he outlined his wish list to Lerner: Tom Wolfe should write the script, and it would be a story in three parts. The first part should be directed by Dennis Hopper; the second part by Stanley Kubrick and the concluding part by Martin Scorsese. Scorsese had used "Be My Baby" in his film *Mean Streets*, and Spector grumbled to Lerner how the director had "ripped me off." But he revered him nonetheless. And, of course, Al Pacino would play the role of Spector.

Spector, Karen thought, liked to give the impression of being powerful and in control, but it was a front that could quickly crumple. On March 14, 1991, his old friend Doc Pomus passed away. As was always the case with Spector, the death of a friend seemed to cut to the heart of his insecurities and left him deeply shaken. A memorial service was held for Pomus at the Riverside Memorial Chapel, where Spector delivered a eulogy. "I remember him writing it," Karen says. "He was afraid he was going to cry; he didn't, but after the service he was a total wreck." Spector did not usually observe Jewish customs, but when Pomus's family invited him to sit Shiva with them, Spector, honored to be asked, agreed, and sat for the customary seven days.

Incredibly, perhaps, for all its historic significance there had never been a compilation of Spector's work on record. Roy Carr had proposed the idea as far back as 1976 but, afraid that it would be seen as an exercise in nostalgia, Spector had decided against it. In 1989 he was approached by another company, Rhino, with a view to licensing his work for a box set, but it was Allen Klein—characteristically alive to the value of the Spector canon—who finally brought the project to fruition.

Spector would play little part in pulling the record together. It was left to Allen Klein to do most of the work. Larry Levine was invited to supervise the remastering of the recordings for release on CD. In recent years Levine had dropped out of the music business and attempted to start a new career, selling condominiums for a builder in Beverly Hills, but his equable nature was ill-suited to the world of real estate. "I ended up getting fired. My boss told me I was too nice a person. He said that one of the people I'd sold a condo to had told him I was more interested in his welfare than my boss's welfare." He had not seen Spector since succumbing to a heart attack during the sessions for the Ramones' album. "I think he felt guilty," Levine says. "But I always felt close to Phil regardless."

The original master tapes that Levine was given to work with were on the point of disintegrating. "They looked like a two-thousand-year-old book," he remembers. Levine and an assistant spent weeks painstakingly transferring the tapes from analog to digital and then remixing them. In an earlier age, Spector would never have left Levine's side, but now he visited the studio only occasionally to critique the engineer's work.

The results were released in a box set of four CDs, *Back to Mono*, which ran the gamut of Spector's career from "To Know Him Is to Love Him" to his 1969 recordings for the Checkmates. One CD was given over in its entirety to the Christmas album. None of Spector's post-1969 productions—for Lennon, Harrison, Dion, Cohen or the Ramones— were included. The final product—in mono, of course—was lavishly presented and beautifully produced. But something was lost in the translation from vinyl to CD, the raw, thrilling impact of the original 45s diluted in their journey to a gleaming collector's artifact. The past could be saluted, but it could never be brought back. Spector dedicated the album to his father, Ben.

When *Back to Mono* was released in October 1991, Allen Klein gave a rare interview to this writer to talk about the project. The record, he insisted, was Spector's vision, "and no one else's, because no one else could do it. I mean, it's not like he's dead. If you wanted to restore the Sistine Chapel and Michelangelo was still around, would you ask some other painter to do it?"

For the past ten years, Klein said, Spector had been doing things "he'd rather not talk about. You know, Phil took a lot of knocks. Lenny Bruce died, Presley died, John Lennon died: these were all people he loved and respected. It points up everyone's mortality, and I think Phil was aware of that." In the meantime, the myths surrounding Spector had been allowed to multiply because "he never stood up and said, 'That's not so.' " Spector, Klein went on, "gets on airplanes and travels by himself. He goes to clubs, listens to music and talks to people"—as if these commonplace pastimes were somehow remarkable. Asked what Spector now wanted from his life, Klein, a man not known for his sentimentality, gave the question a moment's thought. "He's given his music, his heart," Klein said. "He deserves kindness."

On Christmas Day 1991, Spector's son nine-year-old Phillip Jr. passed away after a short struggle with leukemia. It was the day before Spector's fifty-second birthday. Whatever residual belief Spector might have entertained in God was now obliterated. Everybody he had ever loved— his father, Lenny Bruce, John Lennon, and now his son—had been taken from him. There could be no God. As he would put it later, "The most vulgar and obscene four-letter word in this language is 'dead.' It is indecent. It has no redeeming social value."

"The death of Phillip was devastating, and he has never recovered from that," David Kessel says. "Something was lost that will never come back—a piece of his heart, a piece of his soul."

Spector and Janis Zavala had separated shortly before Phillip Jr.'s death. The Pasadena home was now nothing more than a repository of painful memories, and Spector could no longer bear to stay there alone. Early in 1992, in the words of one friend "aimlessly delirious with grief," he left Los Angeles for New York. For a short while he moved into an apartment on Central Park South, where Dennis Hopper remembers visiting one night. Deeply distraught as he talked about the loss of his son, Spector showed Hopper to a room that he said was "Phillip's bedroom" and told Hopper that he was welcome to stay there whenever he wished. Hopper was deeply moved. But the story is a curious one. It appears that little Phillip had never been to New York.

"Between grief and nothing," William Faulkner wrote, "I will take grief." And for Spector the loss of Phillip became the single abiding fact of his existence. He left the apartment, and moved into the presidential suite at the Waldorf-Astoria Hotel, where he was to remain for the best part of a year. In his suite he fabricated a small shrine to Phillip Jr., a photograph of his son with candles. He would bring people to the suite and sob. He was paying tens of thousands of dollars a month for the suite, but he seemed indifferent to the cost.

In his conversations with Karen Lerner, Spector told her about the death of his son, but he would never dwell on it. "You knew it was a terrible thing in his life, as terrible as his father dying," she remembers, "but Phillip was so secretive about it, secretive about everything in his personal life. I don't think he minded being thought of as neurotic, but he didn't want to show he was vulnerable." If he had moved to New York in an attempt to escape the grief of his loss, Karen sensed the city offered no respite or consolation. "It seemed to me that he didn't much like New York and he was scared to be here. He was afraid of flying, afraid of a lot of things. He wanted his security and his bodyguards that he had in Beverly Hills and his Rolls-Royce and all those things, and he didn't have those things here."

Spector's idiosyncratic behavior and his unpredictable hours had begun to put a strain on their friendship. To Karen, it seemed that she was always waiting around for Spector for one reason or another. She held a responsible position and had to be in the office early each morning. His day would invariably be just beginning as hers was coming to an end. When they were alone he would be sweet and considerate, but in public another persona would emerge. "I remember one night we were having dinner in Elaine's. We didn't even get there till eleven. And around midnight, Pia Zadora came over and she was fawning all over Phil. He invited her to join our table. After an hour and a half of this I couldn't stand any more—I thought, I'm not a rock and roll groupie, I'm not interested in anything that's being talked about, and he looks as if he's really enjoying it. So I just left."

Elaine's, which for three decades had tenaciously defended its place as New York's premier celebrity hangout, had become Spector's home away from home, and he struck up an improbable friendship with another of the restaurant's regulars, Jack Maple, New York's deputy commissioner of police. Maple, who died in 2001 at the age of forty-nine, was an ebullient, dandified character who often sported spats, bow ties and a Homburg hat—a sartorial nod to his close physical resemblance to Edward G. Robinson. Maple was a vivid raconteur, and he and Spector loved trading stories. Maple was also a man who could look after himself, and in lieu of Spector's bodyguards sometimes found himself stepping in to handle trouble.

The "kinetic" quality that Larry Levine had noticed when he first met Spector thirty years earlier now manifested itself with increasing frequency. His temper seemingly set on a permanent hair-trigger, Spector would flare up at any slight, real or imagined. Dining in Elaine's one night with Jack Maple, Spector spotted Shannah Goldner, the daughter of his old friend George Goldner. Shannah, who was working as a producer on the television program *A Current Affair*, was dining with the program's reporter Steve Dunleavy. Spector invited Goldner to join his table, but when Dunleavy walked over and sat down, Spector immediately rounded on him; reaching inside his jacket, he told Dunleavy he had a gun and threatened to kill him. Maple quickly stepped in to separate the men, but in the ensuing scuffle Dunleavy landed a punch which caused Spector to bleed profusely. Later that night, Goldner returned home to find a series of bizarre messages on her answering machine, which were subsequently reproduced in the *New York Post*.

"We've got your f——ing number—c——! You're dead f——ing meat. I'll break your f——ing legs and your f——ing fingers! I'll break your f——ing mother's legs! And tell that gray-haired f—— he's dead." Goldner was convinced that it was Spector who had left the messages.

Even Spector's longest-standing friends could be bemused by his volatile temperament and sudden mood swings. Ahmet Ertegun told me of an incident from around this time when he and Spector were doing the round of Manhattan jazz clubs.

"There were two girls with us, we were in two cars, and Phil and I were waiting at the door of this club for the girls to join us. And as we're waiting, two couples came out. The men were over six foot tall, late twenties, very athletic-looking, very chic sports clothes. I think they were Canadians, tourists. One of them looked at Phil, and Phil was wearing this button, 'Back to Mono.' The guy said, 'Excuse me, but what is that?' And Phil says, 'You touch that and you're dead!' Now these are perfectly nice people! I said, 'Excuse me, sir, please don't ask questions; it's better just to leave.' I thought, if we have to fight these guys, here we are, two old schmucks . . . their girlfriends could have beaten us up!

"Phil would do things like that. But it was all bravado—this little shrimp going around saying 'Don't touch me or you're dead' to people who are six foot seven. He'd put on a tough-guy thing, but it's all bullshit. I never felt in any danger from him. The only danger came from being with him, not from him. But that's part of the mystique of the man. Phil is not like other people."

25

"I Honestly Thought
He Was Kidding"

In the autumn of 1992, after a year spent mostly in New York, Spector returned to Los Angeles. For a while, unable to face returning to the Pasadena home, he took up residence in the Bel Air and Beverly Hills Hotels, occasionally returning to the house to collect clothes and mail. At length, he steeled himself to go back.

Although he and Janis were now separated, she continued to work for him, handling his phone calls and business arrangements. And now Paulette Brandt, who had briefly worked for Spector around the time of the John Lennon album, returned as his personal assistant. In the years since she last worked for Spector, Brandt had been involved in the legal case against another of her former employers, and the man who was currently Spector's business manager, Allen Klein. In 1979, Klein served two months in prison for income tax evasion, after illegally selling $216,000 worth of promotional copies of George Harrison's album, *The Concert for Bangla Desh*. Brandt, who had been working for Apple in New York at the time of the offense, was one of those who gave evidence against Klein.

Spector seemed to take a quiet amusement from employing one of the people who had been responsible for sending his partner to prison. He insisted that Paulette use a different name in any correspondence or contact with Klein, instead calling herself "Beverly." Klein, fully aware of the deceit, nonetheless played along with it, sending Christmas gifts to "Beverly" each year, while lamenting to friends, "Does Phil really think I don't know?"

Spector and Paulette had enjoyed a brief affair when she had worked for him in the '70s. But this time it was strictly business. Throughout his life, the one thing Spector had been unable to stand was solitude, and at those times when he had been unable to find companionship, he had hired it. The succession of bodyguards—Emile Farkas, Mac Mashourian, George Brand—had all served as much as companions as hired hands. David Kessel had observed the contradictions in Spector. "Phil likes to be alone in silence; the problem is that when he's alone he starts to think about things he doesn't want to think about, so it's 'Let's go out.' He prefers not to be around people. But then he has to get out and around people because he can't stand being by himself. Everything that was brilliant about Phil, his artistic drive, his genius, was based on an inner torture. It's the agony and ecstasy. That's Phil."

Now in a mansion inhabited only by memories and ghosts, Spector was racked by anxiety and chronic insomnia. "It had always been that Phil would stay up all night, but at least he was fairly consistent with his schedule," Dan Kessel says. "But after Phillip Jr. died, he became a total insomniac. Up at all hours, asleep at all hours; no consistent lifestyle. It went on like that for a couple of years. We'd go visit him and the atmosphere was devastating. It was beyond depressing. After years, Phil still couldn't shake his unbearable grief. He'd lost every ounce of joy in his being."

He became obsessive about his privacy and his solitude. The mansion was divided into two areas which Paulette called "the red" and "the green." The "green area" comprised the family rooms; the "red area" was Spector's private domain, with crimson carpeting and wallpaper, which put Brandt in mind of "a bordello." There was a small office beside the swimming pool, but Spector preferred Brandt to work from her own home, a thirty-minute drive away in Hollywood.

Each day he would fax her a list of duties, "everything from taking care of dog grooming to doctor's appointments. Scheduling and unscheduling. Setting up any meeting would take ten phone calls when it could have been done in one. When I learned how Phil worked, I would call people up and say 'Unless you hear from me differently, this is the deal . . .' "

To protect Spector's privacy, Brandt would schedule the necessary domestic chores for two days of the week, driving over from her home in Hollywood to let in the garbage man, or the gas company to read the meter. Often Spector would not go to bed until 4:00 or 5:00 a.m., and Paulette would schedule the visit for around 8:00 a.m., while he was sleeping, "so he could be comfortable around his own house."

In the period in which they had been lovers, Spector had exercised an obsessively proprietary hold over Paulette. "I learned how to make jewelry, because then I could sit by the telephone and always be there, because if he called and you weren't there, there'd be trouble. Phil loves women, but he doesn't know what to do with them. Because putting them in a cage doesn't work. Even with people who might like cages once in a while."

While the relationship was now platonic, professional, Spector's possessiveness seemed as strong as it ever had been. Sometimes Paulette would see a limousine parked on the street outside her apartment. In the modest, working-class area of Hollywood where she lived, "it looked kind of obvious. He knew everybody who came to my house, and would get very upset if I was dating anybody else. If he knew I was going out, I'd tell him where I was going; he would page me to call my home phone; he wouldn't tell me what it was about, and he'd have a fax there for me, so I'd have to go home to find out what he wanted. He used to call me on Saturday nights to have me come over and light the pilot light on his boiler. It was just to see if I'd do it. I'd think, Okay—he needs to be reassured, so I'd get up and go. It just made me a little sad that he still needed that.

"I don't think Phil liked himself as much as other people liked him. He'd wonder sometimes why people liked to hang out with him, and why they took the way he behaved. But he'd push the limit as far as he could."

Whatever Spector's eccentricities, however unreasonable or demanding he could be, Paulette remained unfailingly loyal. "Most of the crazy stories you hear about Phil are from people who know of somebody else who had the experience. I've never known of anybody who's actually had those experiences. And I think Phil did his utmost to perpetuate those stories. I think he kind of liked it because they're interesting and amusing. Phil keeps his friends for life, and that says something about a person. I care for him and I always will. He's been my rock. When things got pretty bad, people would say, 'Why are you still around?' Well, it's because you remember how special he is. Phil is so truly remarkable that you'd forgive him anything. But I always thought, Phil thinks he's not supposed to be happy, and if he thinks he's not going to be happy, he won't be."

Spector had not been near a recording studio in more than ten years; his only musical activity had been to work on a couple of songs. One of them was called "My Goodbye Song." Spector had begun it long before the death of his son, but that tragedy had brought the song an unintended, and more deeply poignant, meaning.

In Elaine's one night he met a songwriter named Charles Kipps, who had written the hit "Walk Away from Love" for David Ruffin, and worked with Van McCoy, producing Ruffin, Gladys Knight and Aretha Franklin. In his suite at the Waldorf, Spector and Kipps worked on a couple of songs, including "My Goodbye Song," but in the end nothing came of the partnership.

"My Goodbye Song" continued to haunt Spector. In search of a collaborator who could bring the song to fruition he asked Allen Klein to contact the lyricist Hal David, famous for his collaborations with Burt Bacharach. Spector arranged to meet David in the Polo Lounge of the Beverly Hills Hotel, and the pair then spent a day or two at David's Beverly Hills home, working on what David would remember as "a very lovely melody." (Spector complained to Karen Lerner that David's house was always being vacuumed and they could never find a good period of time to work in.) David provided some lyrics, and Spector talked vaguely of trying to place the song with a couple of artists, but David heard nothing more, and the next time they happened to meet, at a Lakers game, it was not even mentioned.

In October 1992 Spector finally roused himself to go back into the studio. He had been told that Linda Ronstadt had expressed an interest in working with him, and decided to record a handful of demos to act as a calling card. Among the material was "My Goodbye Song."

Spector instructed Paulette Brandt to call up a gathering of his old musicians from the Wrecking Crew and to contact Larry Levine. In search of a singer, Spector turned to a vocalist named Mercy Bermudez—who had once sung with a Los Angeles group called the Heaters—whom Spector had met a few years earlier with a view to producing. That collaboration had come to nothing, but Bermudez had left an impression. Furthermore, she sang in the same key as Ronstadt; the perfect vocalist for the sessions.

In need of an arranger, he turned back to his old friend Jack Nitzsche. Nitzsche was not in the best of spirits. His marriage to Buffy Sainte-Marie had recently come to an end, and a disconsolate Nitzsche was drinking too much, taking too many drugs. But he made it a point of principle to answer Spector's call whenever he was needed.

In a meeting at the Beverly Hills Hotel, Spector presented Nitzsche with a tape of two songs, simply labeled "A" and "B," and asked him to provide arrangements. Nitzsche left the meeting utterly confused.

"The tape that Phil gave him was just some dumb melody played on an electric piano," a friend of Nitzsche remembers. "Phil wouldn't even tell him who the sessions were supposed to be for. Jack said, 'This is not how Phil and I used to work.' It used to be they'd play the song, work on it together; he'd know who the performer was going to be, what the song was about. There was never anything on tape, ever. Jack thought Phil was keeping it secret from him. He said, 'I can't work with this.' He was so frustrated."

The recording session, in a small Hollywood studio, had the air of a reunion of battle-scarred veterans; there was Steve Douglas, Jim Horn, Hal Blaine, Jim Keltner, Jay Migliori, Don Randi, even the guitarist Tommy Tedesco, who had recently recovered from a stroke. The keyboard player Al DeLory, who had not played on a Spector session in almost thirty years, flew in from Nashville. Backs were slapped, hugs exchanged, old jokes traded and comic routines rehashed. But when it came to the recording, everything went to hell. Seemingly bemused by Spector's requirements and, according to Don Randi, "not in good shape," Jack Nitzsche had arrived with arrangements that nobody could make sense of. Spector tried to get Nitzsche to correct the charts, but he was unable to do so and finally left the studio in disgrace. The sessions broke up after two hours with nothing committed to tape. "Phil was angry at Jack," Larry Levine remembers. "But he loved having the guys there. In fact, I think that was the only reason he'd organized the session in the first place. You talk about Phil being emotional, there's no doubt . . ."

The emotion did not, however, stretch to forgiveness. Furious with Nitzsche, Spector demanded that his old friend pay the studio costs for the session. Mortified at letting down Spector, Nitzsche readily paid up.

Spector seemed to have few close friends. The Kessels remained as devoted as ever, but the "Three Musketeers" days had passed; with Spector now in a torpor of inactivity the brothers were busily pursuing their own careers. Perhaps Spector's most constant companion was Marvin Mitchelson, the attorney famous for introducing the concept of "palimony" into the American divorce courts.

Mitchelson was a big, booming man with a manner of jovial bon-homie. He had first come to fame in 1978 when representing the singer Michelle Triola Marvin in her claim for support against the actor Lee Marvin, with whom she had lived for six years but never married. Mitchelson lost the case, but his proposal of "palimony" quickly caught on, and he found himself much in demand as a hired gunslinger in the frenetic world of Hollywood celebrity divorces. His clients included Tony Curtis, Bianca Jagger, Zsa Zsa Gabor and Joan Collins. But exposure to the Himalayan sums of money that he would habitually demand on behalf of his clients quickly went to Mitchelson's head. He spent lavishly on Rolls-Royces, Concorde flights and a Hollywood mansion. In 1987 he was accused by a former secretary of using her to ferry cocaine, of which, she alleged, he used "lots and lots." At the same time, he was investigated on two separate allegations of rape by female clients. Mitchelson was not charged, but both women were awarded more than $50,000 by a state crimes-compensation panel. In 1993 Mitchelson was sentenced to thirty months for tax evasion and ordered to pay $2,158,796 in restitution. He wept openly in court when the verdict was passed, telling the judge "This is the second saddest day of my life. My mother's death was the first."

Spector was introduced to Mitchelson at a Hollywood party, and the two men quickly became firm friends. Spector would sometimes take Mitchelson to watch the Lakers, and Mitchelson reciprocated by introducing Spector to the Beverly Hills party circuit. "Marvin got a kick out of Phil," remembers Sy Presten, Mitchelson's friend and press agent, "and Spector loved going to those parties with Marvin and meeting all these celebrities, many of whom Marvin had represented."

On one occasion Spector turned up at his daughter Nicole's school fathers' night in a stretch limousine along with Mitchelson and the Kessel brothers. Whatever mortification Nicole might have felt was assuaged when Spector instructed his driver to give limo rides to all Nicole's classmates. Mitchelson was now barred from practicing law, and his extravagant lifestyle disguised money troubles. It was not unusual at the end of an evening together for Spector to write out a check as a "loan" to keep his friend in fine wine and Brioni suits. Spector's staff knew that when Mitchelson called, it usually meant he needed money. "I don't know whether you could say that Phil was buying the friendship," says Sy Presten. "They enjoyed each other's company. Whether Marvin would have enjoyed it if they ate in a soup kitchen, I don't think so."

Spector's generosity to Mitchelson displayed a side of him that was seldom appreciated by others. The music business revolved around favors, and while Spector would never forgive those whom he believed had turned against him, he always remembered those who had helped him out. He gave financial support to Alan Freed when the disc jockey was down on his luck in the last years of his life. When Ike Turner was imprisoned in 1990 on charges of possessing and transporting cocaine, Spector visited him in jail and helped him out financially on his release. (Spector was on the board of the Rhythm and Blues Foundation, which had been set up to assist veteran performers who found themselves in dire financial straits. The Motown singer Mary Wells was one of the artists the Foundation had helped, paying for her medical bills when Wells was being treated for the cancer that eventually killed her. Spector tried to persuade the Foundation to support Turner, arguing that cocaine addiction was a serious illness, but his request was turned down.) In the late '70s, when Darlene Love was at the lowest point of her life, working as a domestic and unable to make ends meet, she had steeled herself and contacted Spector to ask if he could help her out with her rent. He paid it for a year.

Spector could be recklessly extravagant one minute, nitpickingly parsimonious the next. At home, the big spender who always flew first class and would think nothing of tipping a waiter $200, would clip supermarket coupons from the newspaper and watch household spending like a hawk. When his local liquor store raised the price of his favorite drink by twenty-five cents a bottle, he instructed Paulette to boycott them. "He had a fit . . ." she remembers. "Somebody he didn't know would get a six-hundred-dollar bouquet of flowers. I guess he wanted to impress them. People who knew him and cared about him would get a card. I guess he figured they were already impressed."

Ann Marshall had been a friend of Spector's since the Teddy Bears, and was well accustomed to his eccentricities. On one occasion in the '70s, Marshall visited the La Collina mansion with her friend Michelle Phillips, the singer with the Mamas and Papas. At one point, Michelle announced that she had to leave, to meet another friend who was supposed to be joining them. Spector told her "if you leave this house, you are not coming back in." "I honestly thought he was kidding."

Michelle left, and returned a short while later after collecting her friend. Unable to get an answer at the door, Michelle left her friend at the gate, climbed over the wall and knocked on the French windows. Spector let her in and then locked the door behind her.

"He had a gun in his hand," Michelle remembers, "and then he says, 'Now no one is leaving.' He was as drunk as a sailor. I looked at Ann and she was totally cool. She said, 'Don't worry about it—he does this all the time.' I said, '*He does this all the time?*' I didn't have the feeling that he was going to pull the trigger, and Ann was certainly so calm, but it was a very disquieting feeling him having a gun and for it to be waved around in the room."

At length, two officers from the Bel Air police arrived at the house, alerted by Phillips's friend. "They came into the living room and Phil was standing there with the gun. And they said, 'Mr. Spector, put the gun down.' So he rather reluctantly put the gun down. And they said, 'Is anybody here being held against their will?' And Ann and I put up our hands. They said, 'Would you two come with us, please.' And then they turned to him and they said, 'Mr. Spector, we have warned you about this over and over and over again . . .' "

In the '90s Ann Marshall suffered an aneurysm which almost killed her. Taking leave from her job, she retired to Aspen. "I was on the phone to Phil," she remembers, "and I'm talking about how I'm on disability, and he said, 'How much do you need—a hundred thousand dollars?' I said, 'Phillip, I don't want your money.' But he went on and on. In the end I said, 'The most you can send me is ten thousand dollars.' He was very magnanimous. The next day, Saturday, a FedEx check arrives for ten thousand dollars. On Monday I went to deposit it and he'd stopped the payment. I hadn't asked him for it in the first place. It was all so strange." Marshall never spoke to Spector again.

The more Karen Lerner grew to know Spector, she thought, the less she understood him. He never talked about his life in Los Angeles. She had no idea of his domestic circumstances. He could be entertaining, funny, smart—"mesmerizing"; he could talk knowledgeably and interestingly about music, film, politics, but whenever a conversation became serious or personal, he would change the subject, deflate it with one-liners. He reveled in nonsensical, childlike humor, comic postcards, funny answering machine messages, corny jokes. For a while he carried around in his pocket a little electronic toy that would issue a stream of insults at the touch of a button—fuck you, eat shit, go to hell—which Spector delighted in setting off at the most inappropriate moments. He gave Lerner one of her own.

In March each year, Lerner would fly to Los Angeles for the Academy Awards, and she and Spector would meet. Lerner sensed that for all his outward wit and bravado, it required an effort of will and preparation on Spector's part to go out among people. "Even one person. And whenever we saw each other it was usually with more than one person."

Spector would usually collect her from the Beverly Hills Hotel, asking her to wait outside so that he would not have to go into the lobby. On one occasion, Karen was delayed, keeping Spector waiting for almost an hour. When she finally appeared, she was surprised to see him in the driver's seat of his Rolls-Royce. The valet later told her that rather than parking the car and coming to the hotel to find her, as anyone else would do, he had been driving the car around and around, waiting for her. "I think it took him a lot of courage to muster the ability to go out."

As fond as she was of Spector, it seemed to Karen that everything about their friendship was unnecessarily complicated. When she invited him to be her guest at Irving and Mary Lazar's Academy Award party at Spago, he agreed, but said it was impossible for him to be there for the start of the party at six, because "I'm not even awake then." Nor was he sure he could get there by nine. He eventually turned up at eleven, flanked by two bodyguards. The governor of California, Pete Wilson, arrived at the same time with his bodyguards, and was turned away. But Spector somehow managed to inveigle himself inside. He spent the evening in rapt conversation with Gloria Jones, the widow of James Jones, the author of *From Here to Eternity*, discussing her husband's work. "The bodyguards didn't tell Gloria to stay away," Karen says laconically. "They were just Phil's ego props."

In the end, Karen says, she began to take everything Spector said "with a pinch of salt. I should have cared more, but there was always something to make me not care, to make me annoyed with him. He'd always keep me waiting, or want to know who I was with and why I was with them; and every time I was with him, it was always too late; I'd be exhausted, desperate to go and it would be: 'No, stay . . .' That's the talk of someone who doesn't want to be alone."

One night, he dropped her off at the Beverly Hills Hotel, pleading to come in "just for a minute" and stayed for three hours, the night ending in "a horrendous screaming match, just horrible. It wasn't about anything. It was about some flowers that he'd sent that weren't delivered, and I didn't care, but why didn't I thank him for them . . . and it just went on and on. The most terrible fight."

After Karen got back to New York, the fight was forgotten and the stream of jokey letters and postcards continued to arrive from Los Angeles. One was posted from the Beverly Hills Hotel and addressed to her dog. "Dear Ollie, this is where your mum comes to play when she has you locked up in the kennel. Should we report her to the ASPCA?"

Sometimes Spector would call in the early hours of the morning, and want to talk for hours, about nothing at all. Just to stave off the loneliness, Karen thought. In the end, she could stand it no more and would turn off her phone.

Spector's relations with Janis Zavala had also reached the breaking point. For reasons that are unclear, she stopped working for him. For more than twenty years Janis had been the person closest to Spector, the mother of his two children. It was more than two years since she had moved out of their Pasadena home. But he now instigated a series of small-claims cases against her, for the return of a computer and a television set and VCR, all of which he claimed she had taken from his home. The cases were all dismissed after Janis was able to prove that Spector had in fact given her the items. After that, Spector and Janis would barely talk for the next five years. "You weren't allowed to mention Janis's name," Paulette Brandt remembers. "If you mentioned her name, you could be fired."

In 1993 Jerry Wexler published his autobiography, *Rhythm and the Blues*. In tribute to their friendship, he sent a signed copy to Spector. In the book, Wexler wrote in detail about the death of his daughter Anita from AIDS, contracted from sharing a needle during a period of drug addiction.

On August 9, 1993, Spector replied to Wexler, congratulating him on the book, and saying how distressed he had been to read Wexler's account of his daughter's death. Wexler's inscription had touched him so deeply, he wrote, that he felt the urge to mention the fact of the death of his own son Phillip—a subject he rarely discussed with anyone.

Spector wrote movingly of remembering, when he was about ten years old, his grandmother's grief when one of her sons had died. To try and comfort her, he had reminded her that she had other sons and daughters who were still alive. Didn't that make it any easier? "She looked at me with her loving and tear-filled eyes," he wrote, "and said, 'Phillip, it makes no difference how many children a parent has. . . . A parent can never understand why they have to bury their child.' "

For himself, Spector wrote, it was important to get back into the studio as quickly as possible; it would be therapy, like the tears he shed for his loss. "Tears or the recording studio will never bring him back—but they may bring me back!" Unlike Wexler, he went on, he had no plans to write his own book, although two which he could write and to which he added every day would be simply entitled "Appointments" and "Disappointments." Enclosed with the letter were possible titles and covers, Spector suggested, for two more. One was a postcard of a monkey dressed in a sweatshirt, wearing a *Back to Mono* button, with the title: "Everything I Am Today I Owe to Rock 'n' Roll"; the second a cartoon, with the caption "A Rat Always Knows When He's in with Weasels."

26

"You Don't Tell Mozart
What Operas to Write"

In August 1994, Spector received a telephone call from his friend
Paul Shaffer, telling him to watch that evening's edition of *The Late
Show with David Letterman*. The French-Canadian singer Céline
Dion was performing "River Deep—Mountain High"; Shaffer, the
show's musical director, had labored to create an arrangement as close as
possible to the original version, and wanted Spector's opinion.

Céline Dion had recorded her first English-language album, *Unison*,
in 1990, and scored a breakthrough U.S. hit with the Top 5 single
"Where Does My Heart Beat Now." She had gone on to enjoy a string
of hit singles, and to win both an Academy Award and a Grammy for her
recording of the title track to the soundtrack of an animated version of
Beauty and the Beast. It was a measure of how divorced Spector had
become from the music business that he had never heard of her. But
watching her perform on *Letterman* he was sufficiently impressed to
send a letter to Dion's offices in Montreal, offering his services as a producer. Dion and her husband and manager René Angélil flew to Los
Angeles to meet Spector and agreed to work with him. Spector confided
to Karen Lerner that he "hated" Dion's "screeching" voice, and that he
was doing the project purely "for commercial reasons"; to other friends
he enthused that he was going to "Spectorize" the singer, just as he had
Tina Turner thirty years before.

René Angélil and Dion's record company Sony were not so sure.
Spector had not been in the studio in more than fifteen years. Nobody
knew whether he could be entrusted with an entire album. And fashions
had changed. It had become common practice to employ a number of
different producers, to bring out the varying facets of an artist's identity.
While Spector expected to take command of the entire album, Sony and

Angélil wanted to divide the tracks between Spector and other produc-ers, including David Foster and Jim Steinman. The choice of Steinman was particularly ironic. His reputation rested largely on his productions for Meat Loaf that were basically cartoon blowups of Spector's Wall of Sound. Spector silently seethed at the affront but knuckled down to the project nonetheless.

The prospect of being in the studio appeared to re-energize him. "It was so exciting," Paulette Brandt remembers. "You'd drive up to the house and all of a sudden you'd hear music playing again. And Phil changed. He wasn't drinking so much. Everything was great."

In need of someone to arrange the sessions, Spector might have been expected to once again call on his old friend and most reliable collabora-tor Jack Nitzsche. But Spector had still not forgiven Nitzsche for the farrago of two years earlier. Instead, he turned to the veteran Holly-wood arranger Jimmie Haskell, who as the staff arranger for Liberty Records had salvaged the Teddy Bears album some thirty-five years ear-lier. Haskell had gone on to become one of the most prolific and suc-cessful arrangers in the music business, winning Grammys for his arrangements on Simon and Garfunkel's "Bridge over Troubled Water," Jeannie C. Riley's "Ode to Billie Joe" and Chicago's "If You Leave Me Now."

Haskell was summoned to a meeting at the Beverly Hills Hotel, where he found Spector seated in the lounge with Marvin Mitchelson.

"Phil was drinking vodka, and he asked me, 'What will you have?' " Haskell remembers. "I said, 'If you don't mind, Phil, I'd like some tea and cheesecake.' He said, 'Okay,' and called the waiter over. And the waiter said, 'I'm sorry, Mr. Spector, the kitchen's closed.' So Phil said, 'Please call the captain over.' And the captain came over; and Phil said, 'This is my good friend and he would like some cheesecake and tea. Do you think you could possibly do that for me?' And the captain said, 'We can open the kitchen for you, Mr. Spector, of course.'

"And then Phil said, 'I'd like you to arrange a session for me,' and I said, 'That's great, Phil.' He didn't tell me the name of the artist. He just said 'this girl.' And he said, 'I want you to call the guys.' I said, 'Phil, I usually use a contractor when there are a lot of guys.'

"He said, 'You either call the guys or you don't do the session for me.' So I said, 'Okay, Phil, I'll call the guys.' So he ticked off the people he wanted to use; the first names on the list were the Kessel brothers, Don Randi, Jim Keltner . . . I said, 'Phil, these are all double-scale play-ers.' He said, 'I don't want to pay double scale.' At that time it was prob-ably around $250 for a three-hour session. These guys would have been charging around $500. But he said, 'If they won't work for single scale, I don't want them.' And that's what he got. Don Randi said, 'Well, if that's what Phil wants in his old age, I'll do it.' One of the trumpet players said, 'I won't work for less than double scale, but can I come and watch the session?' "

At the end of the meeting, Spector called for the bill.

"The captain told him how much he owed. Then Phil asked him, 'How many waiters are there here?' The captain said, 'Four.' 'So that makes five, including yourself?' The captain said, 'Yes.' So Phil said, 'Okay, add two hundred dollars for each person to the bill.' I said, 'Phil, how can you give a thousand-dollar tip to the waiters but you won't pay over scale to the musicians?' And he said, 'You don't understand, Jimmie. This room has been closed for remodeling for the last two months; these waiters have been out of work.' "

Outside, Spector invited Haskell to continue the conversation back at his home in Pasadena. "I got in his limousine beside him, and he had a giant bottle of vodka sitting there. He saw me look at it and he said, 'I'm not as drunk as you think I am.' We sat there talking for a while and then he said, 'I'm going to go to the restroom.'

"After he'd gotten out, the driver turned around and said, 'Mr. Haskell, I would advise you to take your own car; otherwise I don't know when you'll ever get home.' I said, 'Thank you.' So I got in my car and followed them.

"On the way we stopped at his mother's house. I got out of my car, and Phil said, 'She's going to hate me for waking her at this hour.' He was up there for about fifteen minutes. This is two o'clock in the morning. He came back and said, 'Yeah, she didn't like the fact I'd woken her up. Sometimes I don't think she likes me.' So I followed him out to Pasadena, and when I got there, there was a young lady to meet us. And she served me cheesecake and tea . . .' "

In June 1995 the Céline Dion sessions finally got under way at Ocean Way Recording studios. Haskell, who had last worked with Spector before he had developed his singular recording techniques, was surprised when Spector ordered the first run-through to be taped. "That was very unusual to me. But on that first playback I heard the Wall of Sound! He knew how to get it instantly! Six guitars all playing the same chord, all playing the same rhythm. But the strumming would vary just slightly, giving it a texture and depth. Also it's very difficult to tune all six guitars perfectly, so you got variation within that—minute variations, but enough to create this symphonic wall of sound. It was extraordinary."

Spector was elated to be back in the studio. It was just like the old Gold Star days—the recording session as performance, as theater—and Spector demanded an audience. The control booth was filled with old friends and new acolytes: the film producer Penny Marshall, the singer Chris Isaak and Spector's old friend and rival Brian Wilson, who, after years of mental troubles, was tentatively making his way back into music. Spector had telephoned Andy Paley, who was writing with Wilson, and asked him to bring Wilson to the sessions.

"There was a big birthday party for Brian at a restaurant on La Cienega," Paley remembers, "and when it was over I told him I was invited to something really special and I wanted to take him along. We drove over to Ocean Way and walked in, and Phil got up and hugged Brian and said, 'Happy birthday. I'm so glad you could come.' Brian was totally overwhelmed."

Spector was back to his old wisecracking, playful self. When Ike Turner turned up, Spector introduced him with the words "This is Ike Turner, and we both wear one of these"—and pulled back his jacket to reveal a pager on his belt. The ubiquitous Rodney Bingenheimer appeared with his friend Brian "Kato" Kaelin. A likeable, goofy, aspiring actor, Kaelin had recently attained a kind of celebrity by testifying in the O. J. Simpson trial, in which Simpson had been acquitted for the murder of his former wife Nicole Brown Simpson and her friend Ronald Goldman. Kaelin, who had been living at Simpson's home, had given crucial evidence about the timing of Simpson's movements on the night of the murder. Spector, who had followed the trial with customary avidity, was delighted with his new acquaintance, and Kaelin quickly became the butt of endless jokes about timing, and "Where's Kato, he's my alibi."

Over the course of a few days, Spector and Dion worked on three tracks, including the old Ronettes song "Is This What I Get for Loving You?" "Céline was so delighted with those tracks," Paulette Brandt says. "She was sitting there, literally kicking her feet up in the air. She said, 'It hits you right between the eyes.'

But the mood quickly began to sour. True to his traditional practice, Spector insisted on keeping Céline waiting for hours while he tinkered with the arrangements, and then working her late into the night—a fact that irked her husband and the representative from Sony. "Phil had a major crush on Céline," one participant in the sessions remembers. "He was working her very hard, and they were wrapping her in cotton wool—'Her throat can't take it—she's got to stop now.' Phil doesn't want to hear that at three in the morning. Céline herself was saying, 'No, no I'm fine.' Phil had gotten her voice in such a great place she wanted to keep doing it." At length, the mounting tensions exploded into a blazing row between Spector and the Sony representative. "The guy from Sony was a typical schmuck executive idiot," remembers David Kessel. "He was pulling all this 'I'm with the label' shit, and Phil told him to go to hell. And then Céline's husband got a little irritated with Phil telling the record executive to shove it up his ass . . ."

René Angélil announced that Spector was off the project, and he and Céline left town, leaving two songs half finished, and only one—"Is This What I Get for Loving You?"—complete. Listening to this, one gets some idea of how magical the collaboration between Spector and Dion could have been. Set against the magnificent tumult of his production—the equal of anything he achieved in his heyday—Dion's voice has never sounded more crystalline nor more emotive. It was the masterpiece Spector had been struggling to make for more than twenty years. Unaware of the rift, Jimmie Haskell continued to fax Spector over the next few weeks, imploring him to complete the tracks. But Spector never replied. "They were wonderful songs," Haskell remembers. "A bit different from what Céline had become known for. If they were released at any time, they would be guaranteed hits."

When the album, *Falling into You*, was released the following year, it contained nothing produced by Spector. But to add insult to injury the album did include a version of "River Deep—Mountain High"—produced by Spector imitator Jim Steinman. Asked to comment on the album by *Entertainment Weekly*, Spector replied by dispatching a vitriolic 800-word letter in which he praised Céline Dion herself but attacked her management and record company for wanting only to record Whitney Houston– and Mariah-rejected soundalike songs. He continued: "You don't tell Shakespeare what plays to write, or how to write them. You don't tell Mozart what operas to write, or how to write them. And you certainly don't tell Phil Spector what songs to write, or how to write them; or what records to produce and how to produce them." Since he had paid for the recordings himself, he added, he intended to release them himself, so that people could compare them to Dion's recordings.

But the Spector recordings would never see the light of day. While it was true that he had paid the studio and musicians' costs, and theoretically owned the backing tracks, he did not own the rights to Céline

Dion's vocals. In an attempt to retrieve the material, Sony agreed with ABKCO to pay Spector all the recording costs and assume clear ownership of the masters. Draft agreements were exchanged between the two parties, but negotiations broke down and the agreements were never signed.

Looking back, Paulette Brandt wondered whether Spector had ever really intended the tracks to be released at all, or whether the whole exercise wasn't just an enormous put-on. "I don't think Phil ever really thought it would happen. I think he did it for kicks, and to show the people he'd invited that he still had it. It was basically a very expensive show for all his friends."

Falling into You became the best-selling album of 1996, topping the charts in eleven countries, and was voted Album of the Year and Best Pop Album at the Thirty-ninth Annual Grammy Awards ceremony. It went on to sell more than 25 million copies worldwide.

The experience of the Céline Dion sessions threw Spector back into a deep trough of depression; once again he began drinking heavily. Henry Diltz ran into him one night at a party at the home of a record producer in Beverly Hills. In the years since Spector had produced Diltz as a member of the Modern Folk Quartet, Diltz had stopped performing music professionally and established a reputation as one of the preeminent photographers in rock music, shooting countless sessions and record covers for such artists as the Doors; Joni Mitchell; Crosby, Stills, Nash and Young and Jackson Browne. He had not seen Spector for years and watched in bewilderment as he reeled around the party, "drunk and very cantankerous. There were musicians there eager to shake his hand and talk to him, and he was just putting them down, withering comments, so they'd withdraw their hands and shrink into the background.

"He had a couple of guys with him. Big guys. And he took great pride in getting them to show their piece. He called one of them over and said, 'Show 'em . . . ,' and the guy got out his .45. A gun that would blow a hole in a house. Harry Dean Stanton and Kato Kaelin were there. And Phil said, 'Come on, Henry, we're going to this club.' This was about three in the morning. And they opened it up for him. And we were sitting in the back room, and Harry Dean Stanton had his guitar, and Phil had him playing 'Goodnight Irene' and we were singing harmonies, over and over. Phil was walking around, playing the producer—'Play it again, Harry . . .'

"At about five in the morning, I said, 'I've got to go. I have to drive my kids to school.' And Phil said, 'No, no—you can't leave, because it'll change things.' He didn't want to change the chemistry, the balance in the room. He didn't want anyone to leave, because he liked it just the way it was."

Those close to Spector noticed a pattern. He would drink to a point of near insensibility, and was prone to furious rages. "Phil could out-scream anybody I knew," says Paulette Brandt. "I've never heard any-body being able to maintain yelling at somebody for ten minutes straight, but he could do that. When you see Phil screaming with bulging red eyes, it's like seeing Satan."

Drink was not a pleasure, but an anesthetic, an escape from the despair over the death of his son that continued to enshroud him. More than once his housekeeper would find a drunken Spector, sitting on Phillip's bed, sobbing.

The incipient mental problems that had incubated for years began to become more obvious. Always a fitful sleeper, he suffered from raging insomnia. The years of buffeting his ears with music at full volume seemed to have had absolutely no effect on his hearing. Spector, it seemed, could isolate the sound of a single raindrop in a storm. "When-ever he went away, he always gave hotels a lot of problems," Paulette says. "He could hear the wind through the dumbwaiter shafts, so he was continually calling maintenance because he couldn't sleep."

Spector had always ritualized his behavior; shaving and showering at the same times each day; always careful to use exactly the same products and fretting if they were unavailable. But now his obsessive-compulsive behavior grew more pronounced. He developed a phobia about germs and became obsessive about hygiene and cleanliness, insisting the house was vacuumed and cleaned until it was spotless, demanding that his cars be ceaselessly cleaned and waxed. He began to wear surgical gloves around the home to protect against dirt, and was seen in restaurants carrying his own plastic cutlery, vacuum-wrapped to guard against any possible contamination.

Furthermore, his drinking had begun to exact a heavy toll on his health. On one occasion Paulette discovered that he was coughing up blood. Without telling him, she called his doctor and Spector was called in for tests. "That was too scary for me. I didn't want to lose him."

Following the death of his son, Spector had started taking a variety of mood-altering and calming drugs, including lithium and Prozac. Prozac made him "a lot more reasonable," according to Paulette Brandt. But, habitually, Spector would stop taking the medication before departing for New York, and the annual round of duties and celebrations for the Rock and Roll Hall of Fame. He had kept up his position on the nominating committee, and would traditionally hold court after the ceremony in a suite at the Waldorf. It was a chance for him to meet old friends, to luxuriate in the respect and admiration of his peers.

"Going to the Rock and Roll Hall of Fame gave Phil a sense of belonging," David Kessel says. "I think for a lot of the time he felt like he was completely drifting in outer space. When you're Phil Spector and you've achieved all those goals, you're on a mountain no one can even imagine, it's exhilarating and confusing and lonely. But he could see Ahmet and Keith Richards and Seymour Stein, and those guys made him feel good and part of something."

The evening would invariably end in a drinking spree, for which his staff back in California would pay the price. "Going to New York was good for Phil," Paulette says. "But it was always a scary time when he came back. You knew that someone would be in the doghouse for no reason."

In October 1995 Bertha died. Her health had been in decline for some years following a traffic accident in which she had broken both legs, leading to circulatory difficulties. Spector was in New York at the time of her death. He asked Karen Lerner if she would fly to Los Angeles with him, because he felt unable to face the flight alone. But Lerner was unable to take the time off work. It was the end of their friendship.

27

"Anybody Have a Calculator?"

At the age of fifty-six, Spector's status as a music legend was assured, and the industry that had once rejected him now clasped him to its bosom. In 1997 he was inducted into the National Academy of Popular Music Songwriter Hall of Fame. His induction coincided with an announcement by BMI that "You've Lost That Lovin' Feelin' " had surpassed John Lennon and Paul McCartney's "Yesterday" to become the most-played song in BMI history, and the first song to exceed 7 million performances.

Later that same year, Spector flew to London to be honored with a Lifetime Achievement Award by the British music magazine Q. Spector had taken on an additional secretary, Norma Kemper, the wife of the drummer David Kemper, who was a regular member of Bob Dylan's touring band. It required an exchange of some forty faxes between Kemper and the editor of Q and the organizer of the awards, Mark Ellen, over such details as timing, dress code, accommodation and the provision of a six-seater stretch Mercedes, before Spector finally agreed to attend. Kemper concluded her side of the correspondence with the words "He's all yours now . . ."

Spector arrived in London with his daughter Nicole and Jay Romaine, a Los Angeles policeman whom he had recently taken on as a factotum and bodyguard, much the same role that George Brand had once filled. The party put up at the Savoy. In his acceptance speech, Spector launched a comedic attack on Britain's current pop sensation: "Am I the only one who believes the Spice Girls are the anti-Christ?" Referring to American right-wingers who had compared the Spice Girls to porno-movie stars, Spector joked "at least in porno films the music's sometimes good."

He dedicated the award to Nicole, seated at his table, "and her brother Phillip, who died age nine, six years ago." Paul McCartney, who was also present, walked out during Spector's speech, apparently in a huff about the award being given to his old enemy.

It seemed that even Spector's long-held dream for a movie about his life was about to be realized. Cameron Crowe had made his name in the '70s as a precociously talented young journalist for *Rolling Stone* magazine, before moving into films, writing and directing *Fast Times at Ridgemont High*.

Now Crowe had been approached with a view to directing a film about Spector by the producer Paula Wagner and the actor Tom Cruise, who was a huge Spector fan. From the moment the project was mooted, Cruise was so excited by the prospect of playing Spector that in preparation for the role he had taken to wearing a pair of Spector-esque shades and rehearsing his posture, pulling in his chin to look more like his subject. In March 1997, two days after the Academy Awards at which he had been nominated for Best Actor for his role in *Jerry Maguire*, Cruise met Spector for the first time at his Pasadena home. Apparently psyching himself up for the meeting, Cruise arrived with "You've Lost That Lovin' Feelin' " blaring from the car stereo. Over the next few months Crowe would spend time with Spector at the Pasadena house and in New York, poring over the details of his life and work and deliberating how best to commit the story to film. Spector, he believed, was one of the great characters and stories of rock and roll, but he simply couldn't resolve where the film would end—at least, not at that point—and at length the project petered out.

In November, Tommy Tedesco, guitarist on so many of Spector's great recordings, died. A memorial service was held at Our Lady of Lourdes Church in Northridge, featuring an "orchestra" of some thirty guitar players performing in tribute. Jimmie Haskell was among the congregation. "At one point I stuck my nose out of the door, and there was Phil, in the back doorway. I said, 'Come on in, Phil.' So we stepped in. And he said, 'Gosh, can you get those guitar players' names; they're good aren't they?' I said, 'Yes, I can, Phil—do you really want to use all of them?' And he said, 'Well, maybe . . .' "

Haskell dutifully took note of all the guitarists onstage, but when he called Spector to give him the names Haskell was unable to get through, and Spector didn't return his calls.

In the years since she had recorded "Da Doo Ron Ron" and "Then He Kissed Me," LaLa Brooks's thoughts had often turned to what she'd been paid for her part in Spector's success, and what she might be owed.

By her own account, LaLa had received just $1,000 for singing on the Crystals' hits. "We got no royalties from Phil; not one dime. Nothing."

After leaving Philles, the Crystals moved to United Artists, and then split in an acrimonious row over the ownership of the group's name. Dee Dee Kenniebrew toured with another set of girls as the Crystals. LaLa married the jazz drummer Idris Muhammad and set about raising a family. "Da Doo Ron Ron" and "Then He Kissed Me" were a precious part of her past—but they were the past. By the 1980s, however, '60s rock and roll was once again becoming big business, with the proliferation of oldies stations and classic hits being repackaged for compilation albums and used on the soundtracks of new films.

"I remember when the babies were small and I was in the kitchen and 'Da Doo Ron Ron' came on the radio, and I thought, 'God, why aren't I being paid for this?' Then I would call California and speak to Phil's secretary and say, 'Listen, can you tell Phil that I called and please can he give me some of my money, just give me something.' And his secretary would say, 'I'll get him to call you back.' One time he did call me back and I said to him, 'Phil, can you just give me what I deserve. I've made you hits.' And he said, 'I'll get back to you,' but he never did. Nothing. I wasn't going down the tubes, you know—my husband made a salary—but I just wanted what I deserved."

Eventually LaLa made an appointment to meet Allen Klein. "He said that Phil would do anything for me because I was the only one that Phil ever cared about . . . bullshit things like that," she remembers.

"Then he gave me a copy of the box set and said, 'Phil said to give you this, he loves you and misses you badly.' I said, 'Do you know what? Phil, in my eyes, could have taken a piece of shit and put it in the middle of the floor and told me to sit in it, that's how insulting that it is.'

"Allen Klein's son was there with him and he was trying to calm me down, but by this time I was so pissed off. I told Allen Klein that he could go to hell. I was crazy as could be. When I was walking out of the door he was still telling me, 'Phil loves you and would do anything for you.' But it didn't come to nothing. I told him that I was a child that Phil had taken advantage of and that he would reap what he had sowed."

LaLa wasn't the only Philles artist whose thoughts had turned to the question of just reward. In 1988, the Ronettes had begun litigation against Spector to retrieve what they alleged were unpaid royalties. They were joined by Darlene Love.

The Ronettes had long been a group in name only. Ronnie had remarried, to a show business manager named Jonathan Greenfield, and continued to pursue a solo career. Nedra had effectively retired from music to raise a family and help her husband Scott in the Christian ministry. Estelle had led a more troubled life, experiencing psychiatric problems. Apparently unable to accept that the Ronettes had long since ceased to exist, she would sometimes talk of going into the studio with Spector and taking dance lessons in readiness for going back onstage.

The architect behind both the Ronettes and Darlene Love suits was Chuck Rubin. In the '60s Rubin had worked for the booking agency GAC, which represented, among its many other acts, the Crystals, the Ronettes and the Righteous Brothers. But Rubin says his attempts to promote the groups were often thwarted by Spector. On one occasion he proposed that the Ronettes and Righteous Brothers should tour together as a package, but Spector vetoed the idea.

"Because of his unusual way of dealing with his artists we couldn't put too much focus on them," Rubin says. "The prevailing view was that Spector was very proprietorial about his artists—overly proprietorial, sometimes irrationally proprietorial. We knew not even to bother him with certain kinds of offers."

Rubin moved into management, handling acts including the Shirelles, B. J. Thomas and the R&B singer Wilbert Harrison. In 1971, Harrison asked Rubin for his help in retrieving unpaid royalties he believed he was owed for his 1959 hit "Kansas City." Every lawyer Rubin approached to help him in the task turned him down. "One of them eventually told me, 'Look, Chuck, nobody's going to try and get Wilbert Harrison his royalties from twenty years ago because they'll ruin their relationship with the industry doing that. And the minute you find an attorney and do it, you will be an outcast and a pariah, too.'"

Undeterred, at length Rubin found a patent and archive attorney, who happened to be a rock and roll fan, who agreed to take on Harrison's case on a contingency basis. Seeing an opportunity, Rubin set up his own company, Artists Rights Enforcement Corporation, and contacted all the artists he had worked with in the '60s. "And I was shocked to find out that none of them were getting royalties. None. They said to me, 'If you can get Wilbert paid, call me.' It took two years to get Wilbert his money. He was the only artist I had. The next day I had one hundred. And they were right. I became a pariah."

Rubin charged his clients 50 percent of whatever he could secure on their behalf, painstakingly following the paper trail of missing money himself—often down an endless tunnel of masters being sold and resold by various companies—and employing lawyers to prosecute the cases.

"By the time we came to represent these artists, half the original companies didn't even exist anymore. A company would go down and sell their entire catalogue in bankruptcy for a couple of thousand dollars. No one knew that these songs were valuable; that there would be this second life—third life." His first case involving a Spector act was over a videocassette called *The Girl Groups* produced by MGM in 1983, and featuring material leased from vintage TV programs such as *American Bandstand* and *Shindig!* Rubin ended up representing a number of the acts featured in the film, including Darlene Love; Fanita Barrett and Gloria Jones as the Blossoms; and Nedra Talley and Estelle Bennett from the Ronettes (but not, at that point, Ronnie).

After securing a share of the spoils from MGM, Rubin turned his attention to scrutinizing the royalties from Spector's recordings. The Ronettes, he discovered, had signed a standard contract in May 1963 giving them a basic 3 percent royalty on the net retail list price, based on 90 percent of all double-sided records manufactured and sold. "Most artists signed a contract like that. And you know how they'd sign it? 'Come in, sit down, sign here and you'll be a star. Don't bring anyone with you, just sign . . .' "

The Ronettes claimed that they had received just one check from Philles for $14,482 in 1963 but had received no royalties after that. Like virtually every other record company of the day, Philles had claimed that "offsets"—the costs for recording, promotion and the like—that were built into the contract had absorbed any profits accruing to the group from the record sales.

In 1988, Rubin launched suits against Spector on behalf of both the Ronettes and Darlene Love. It was the beginning of a protracted saga that would still be running twelve years later.

The first case to come to court, in 1997, involved Darlene Love. Love could remember signing a contract with Spector in 1963 but had long since lost it. (She would subsequently claim she had only received one royalty statement for her recordings, listing deductions for such things as "cartage"—delivery of musical instruments to the studio—with a handwritten note from Spector at the bottom of the statement: "Hopefully there will be something left next time.") However, Fanita Barrett did have a royalty report that included Love's name, and from that Rubin was able to extrapolate what Love's contract would have entailed.

The case was tried in front of a jury. Prior to the trial itself Spector was obliged to give a deposition to Love's lawyer, Ira Greenberg, which was taped. "Spector was sitting there, sparring with Ira, but Ira was ignoring him," Rubin remembers. "Then Ira got to the documents. These were originals that we had gotten from Harold Lipsius; these were old, dirty—the original contract of the Crystals, letters, documents showing the incorporation of Spector and Lester Sill in Philles and so on, because Lester Sill signed the Crystals contract. When Ira handed them to him, Spector raised his hands and he was wearing surgical gloves . . ."

On the first day of the trial itself, Spector was at his grandstanding best. "Phil gets on the stand, and he knocks the jury senseless," Rubin says. "They were rolling in the aisles. It was like a comedy show. The judge was laughing. Even Darlene was laughing. The second day, it was Ira's turn."

Spector had claimed that Love was simply a session singer who had never had a contract, but he could offer no explanation for her name appearing on Fanita Barrett's royalty statement.

"It was clear that he thought he was the only one that was really contributing to the recordings," Ira Greenberg remembers. "He said nice things about Darlene, but he basically said the singers were interchangeable parts, no different from members of the band. I pointed out that he had put out recordings *The Best of Darlene Love, The Best of the Ronettes*—but there was no *The Best of the Sound Engineer* or *The Best of the Drummer.*

"Phil was wearing these little granny glasses, and you could see his eyes starting to roll around in his head," Rubin says. "Then Ira pulls his punch, takes one of the dusty documents, drops it on the floor, then puts it on the stand and says, 'Could you identify that document? Would you pick it up and read it?' Phil said: 'I refuse to touch it. You can't make me touch it.' Now the jury is looking at him like he's a little crazy. So he was eventually forced to touch it. Then Ira picks another document, and so it goes. That was it. When the jury ended deliberations, we heard the magic words 'Anybody have a calculator?' "

Love was awarded $263,000 by the jury, subsequently halved by the judge after he ruled they had miscalculated the royalty rate.

The stakes in the Ronettes' case were immeasurably higher, centered largely around the monies that Spector had received for synchronization rights—that is, licensing the group's tracks to be used in films and television commercials, notably the use of "Be My Baby" in the film *Dirty Dancing,* the low-budget nostalgia film that had been released in

1987 and become an international box office hit. (One of Rubin's first victories was to extract a settlement of $100,000 from American Express for the use of the same song in an advertisement. Rubin was able to argue that while American Express had negotiated the right with Spector to use the master recording, they had violated the advertising code by airing the commercial without the necessary written permission from the group to use their vocal performance.)

In June 1998 the case of *Ronnie Greenfield et al. vs. Philles Records, Inc. et al.* finally came to trial in a civil lawsuit in the cramped chambers of the State Supreme Court in Manhattan.

Alleging that Spector had deprived the group of royalties and synchronization rights for movies, television and advertisements, the Ronettes were seeking damages amounting to $11 million. They were also seeking custody of the masters of all tracks recorded by the group for Spector, and the reimbursement of "all monies received by the Spector corporate defendants and defendant Phil Spector" from 1963 until the present day. The group claimed to have recorded some twenty-eight songs for Spector, for which they had received only $14,482 in royalties. Under this contract, the Ronettes argued, Spector was given the right to record, manufacture and sell phonograph records, but that exploitation of the synchronization rights without their permission or compensation was a breach of contract.

In his defense, Spector claimed that the original contract obligated Philles to compensate the Ronettes solely on income derived from phonograph records, and that Ronnie Spector had given up her rights to royalties by signing a release agreement as part of her divorce proceedings when the marriage was dissolved in 1974.

Spector appeared each day in court dressed in his now-trademark aviator shades, black suit and black shirt, set off by a red AIDS ribbon and a diamond earring in his left ear. A reporter for the *Independent*, David Usborne, took note of his "diminished physical appearance—the broken veins streaking vertically down the gray pallor of his cheeks, the beard stubble and his feeble rasping voice. Disconcertingly, he occasionally sips water from a paper cup and makes a loud whistling sound as he sucks it through his teeth."

The case brought Spector and Ronnie face-to-face for the first time since 1974, providing an opportunity for Ronnie to once again rehearse all of the grisly details of her marriage to Spector. Wearing shades, one reporter noted, "even more nocturnal" than Spector's, she testified that he had frustrated her singing career and held her as a virtual prisoner in their home, confiscating her shoes and surrounding her with guard dogs.

She had signed their 1974 divorce settlement, including a clause forfeiting all future record profits, she claimed, only because "Phil threatened me several times"—adding, "He told me 'I'll kill you' and said 'I'll have a hit man kill you.' "

Taking the stand, Spector denied that he had kept his wife as an involuntary prisoner and rejected the hit-man allegations, adding "I've heard them over the last twenty years." He described their marriage as "a good strong loving relationship," adding that "Veronica had a lot of problems with drinking and mixing medication."

One person in the court at least seemed to fall under Spector's spell. The *Independent* reporter noted that he seemed to have the judge, Paula Omansky, "in his pocket. 'Bless you,' he interrupts one time when she sneezes. Judge Omansky simpers appreciatively."

But Spector's charm offensive on Judge Omansky was to prove unsuccessful. In July 2000 the judge ruled in the Ronettes' favor, awarding the group $3 million. However, Judge Omansky turned down the group's demand that the masters of the recordings should be handed over to them. "Spector's contributions to the Ronettes' success cannot be underestimated," she ruled, "as composer of their songs, as creator of the sound for which the Ronettes' recording hits became famous. Rescinding the 1963 recording contract and taking ownership of the masters away from Spector is not warranted."

Spector appealed against the award for synchronization royalties, and in 2002 a five-judge panel of the New York State Court of Appeals upheld his appeal, ruling that the Ronettes' 1963 contract contained no provisions for synchronization rights. The judgment was remanded back to the lower court to recalculate damages based on the royalty schedules contained in the original contract. The Ronettes would eventually receive around $900,000, for unpaid royalties.

In the early part of 1998, Spector moved again. The Pasadena house contained too many memories. All his life, Spector had wanted to live in a castle—an echo, perhaps, of the crenellated roof of his childhood home in the Bronx. To help him find one he now turned to the person who had always been the most reliable mainstay in his life. Relations with Janis Zavala had been strained for some years, conducted largely through their daughter Nicole. But Janis agreed to help, and after a search of several months she found the castle that Spector was looking for. Its location was the last place one might have expected to find Phil Spector. Alhambra was a working-class neighborhood, a thirty-minute drive down the 101 Freeway from Hollywood, populated largely by Asian and Hispanic families.

The Pyrenees Castle, as Spector's new property was called, had been built in 1925 by a wealthy sheep rancher named Sylvester Dupuy, apparently inspired by the memory of the châteaux in the Basque region where he had lived as a child. An imposing property, with ten bedrooms and turrets at each corner, it was set on a hill in three acres of wooded grounds, hidden behind high walls and an electronic gate. At the foot of the hill was Alhambra's industrial section; behind the property was a railroad track; at night you could hear the sounds of the trains carrying freight to and from the docks at Long Beach. A white elephant, the property had been on the market for almost five years—who, after all, would want a castle in Alhambra? But that was one of the reasons Spector liked it. He liked the fact that it was isolated; that the area was terminally unfashionable; that he was never going to know his neighbors; that he would be left alone.

He quickly settled into a life of seclusion. He lived alone and saw few people. When he ventured out, it was usually in the company of his bodyguard Jay Romaine. A housekeeper came each day to clean and prepare his food, and departed each evening, leaving Spector to face the long hours of night in solitude.

While it was years since they had lived together, Janis, ever loyal, now took the role of his helpmate, looking after Spector's daily requirements and regularly dropping by the castle to ensure that he was okay.

Paulette Brandt continued to work for him in a secretarial capacity, but nowadays she rarely saw him. She was not given a key to the castle. Instead, she would collect and deposit papers at a mailbox at the gate, usually communicating with Spector only by telephone or fax. On one occasion, she was surprised to receive a telephone call at two in the morning, summoning her to Dan Tana's, a restaurant on Santa Monica Boulevard, and one of Spector's favorite haunts. Paulette roused herself from her bed and hurried to the restaurant.

"It was past closing time, but they'd stayed open for Phil, because he'd made it worth their while. The streets were empty, but there was a limousine right outside Dan Tana's. I went inside, and Jay was sitting next to Phil, who was obliterated, he could hardly see. And he said, 'I just wanted you to know you're a very special lady; I love you, and you're in my life.' I thought, That's great, Phil. And then he fell off the seat. And that was it.

"He had Jay follow me home, and I was thinking, Oh no. Because we'd done this a couple of times before; Phil would forget that it was just work. So I parked on the next street. Jay came over and said, 'You okay?' And he followed me back to my house. Phil couldn't make it that far. I was so grateful."

Spector had not been in the studio since the ill-fated Céline Dion sessions, but in 1998 he was approached by his old friend Ahmet Ertegun, asking whether he could help with a new Atlantic signing, Ashley Ballard. Ballard was a teenage prodigy who had emerged from a TV talent contest, sung on the occasion of Bill Clinton's second inauguration in Washington and been spotted by Ertegun performing at the Blues Foundation Lifetime Achievement Awards ceremony, where she had shared the stage with Ray Charles, Ruth Brown and Bobby "Blue" Bland.

Ertegun signed her to Atlantic, and asked Spector to "prep" her for her recording debut. Unsure who to call on for help, Spector turned back to Jack Nitzsche to see whether he would handle arrangements on the new project. But Nitzsche refused. After all the ups and downs he had endured with Spector over the years, Nitzsche felt unable to steel himself for another round. He told Spector he should find a young kid, fresh out of music school who lived and breathed music "and wasn't into young chicks," to do the job.

In March, Spector made his annual pilgrimage to the Rock and Roll Hall of Fame, this time taking his daughter Nicole with him. Michelle Phillips was attending the ceremonies for the induction of the Mamas and the Papas and ran into Spector at the awards dinner. He greeted her warmly, congratulated her on her induction and invited her to a party at his hotel later that evening.

By the time she arrived, Spector was roaring drunk, launching a tirade of "fuck you"s at anyone who crossed his path. Watching Spector embarrass himself, an executive from Atlantic Records quietly eliminated him from their plans for Ashley Ballard. The genial figure who had greeted Michelle so effusively a couple of hours earlier was now looking daggers at her across the room. Unsure what was wrong, she went over to ask Spector if he was all right. Fixing her with a baleful look he said, "You don't deserve being in the Rock and Roll Hall of Fame," and pitched forward unconscious on the rug. The party was over.

Chastened, Spector quit drinking—this time, he vowed, for good.

28

"He Wanted to Prove
He Really Was Human"

In September 1999, *Esquire* magazine published a short interview with Spector in its series "What I've Learned."

His answers were the customary mixture of off-the-cuff one-liners, corny jokes and received wisdom.

> I wonder how Michael Jackson started out as a black man and ended up as a white girl. But in a world where carpenters get resurrected, anything is possible. [Spector seemed to have a particular liking for this joke. He would repeat it ad infinitum, and still be telling it three years later when I met him.]
>
> Since I'm one of those people who are not happy unless they are not happy, it's comforting to know that mental health doesn't always mean being happy. [Otherwise], nobody would qualify.

Only the last aphorism seemed to be spoken from the heart.

Jack Nitzsche's fortunes had continued to decline. In 1998 he suffered a stroke that effectively ended his career. His thoughts turned more and more to his past successes, and the growing feeling that he had not received his just deserts. Seeing what Chuck Rubin had achieved for Darlene Love, Nitzsche contacted Rubin about trying to retrieve unpaid royalties on his behalf, but he balked at paying Rubin's 50 percent commission.

In the summer of 2000, Nitzsche organized a reunion with another artist from his past, LaLa Brooks. According to LaLa, Nitzsche was keen on recording her, and had gone so far as to trace her to Europe, where she was living and working. Nitzsche was staying in New York at the Mayflower Hotel, where LaLa visited him. Over the course of the evening they shared their feelings about Spector. "He said to me, 'LaLa, Phil used to treat you like a piece of shit,' " she remembers. "I thought, Wow, are you going to burst my bubble! He hit me and it felt like a kiss! I was baffled when Jack said that. But he said, 'All those nights in the studio when we'd be there until two in the morning and Phil wouldn't even buy you food.' I said, 'Boy, I used to wonder why I was so hungry, because all I was fed was peanuts.' Jack said, 'Oh, he was so selfish—the motherfucker . . .' because Jack felt he was stolen from, too. Then he said he would always argue with Sonny Bono about which one had the better voice, was it Ronnie Spector or me, and he said he would always say LaLa. He said, 'I always loved your sound'—he gave me all that, but I think he was telling the truth."

As the evening wore on, Nitzsche began to talk about taking LaLa back into the studio. In a flurry of enthusiasm, he reached for the phone and put in a call to his old friend the singer and songwriter Jackie DeShannon in Los Angeles. "I spoke to Jackie, and I told her, 'I want to do one of your songs. We were all going to come together.' " LaLa left the hotel excited about the future.

A few weeks later, on August 25, 2000, Jack Nitzsche died of a cardiac arrest in Hollywood's Queen of Angels Hospital, brought on by a recurring bronchial infection. He was sixty-three.

Some two hundred people attended the memorial service at the Hollywood Forever Cemetery, among them Gerry Goffin, the actor Sean Penn, Jackie DeShannon, Nancy Sinatra and a number of Wrecking Crew musicians, including Don Randi, Earl Palmer and Carol Kaye. It fell to Spector to deliver a tearful eulogy to "My beloved Jack Nitzsche" thanking him for "almost forty years of friendship and loyalty."

Nitzsche, he went on, was a man who left "footprints on your heart," a source of inspiration who had helped Spector to create "beautiful and historical art. And for that I will forever be indebted to you.

"And, if I may, to paraphrase from my own song, to know you is to love you, Jack, and I always have and I always will. And I would be remiss if I did not mention to you that my little boy, Phillip Jr., whom you met a few times down here, is up there waiting for you. So look for him, Jack, you'll know him right away. Just look and listen for the loudest little angel and that's him. I know the two of you will take care of each other."

Eulogies were becoming something of a habit for Spector. On April 15, 2001, Joey Ramone died of lymphoma. Spector wrote an effusive—and in parts identical—tribute that was read at a memorial party for the singer in New York.

"Losing you like this is so very hard to understand, and there are no words that can truly ease the pain," he wrote, concluding, "And I would be remiss if I did not mention to you that my little boy Phillip Jr. is up there waiting for you. So look out for him, Joey. And you'll know him right away. Just look and listen for the loudest little angel and that's him. I know the two of you will take good care of each other . . . Your devoted and loving friend, Phil Spector."

Among the mourners at Nitzsche's funeral service was Lynn Castle, Spector's old girlfriend, who had not seen him in more than thirty years. "Phil was so damn great at the funeral," she remembers. "What he had to say about Jack and the way he felt, it was really great. And afterward he was so happy to see me. It was that same beauty that I'd loved in him all those years ago. I totally saw that, despite his sadness and nightmares and losses. He was very positive. He was absolutely darling. He gave me the sweetest kiss, I was so surprised. He was so damn sweet." They started exchanging notes and postcards. Spector, who knew of Castle's interest in Eastern philosophy, sent one notecard picturing a golden Buddha, holding up his hands. The message inside read simply: "Yes! Love Phillip."

Another mourner was Nancy Sinatra, who had been brought to the service by Don Randi, who sometimes played in her band. Afterward, she and Spector were introduced, and before long they had begun seeing each other regularly.

For Spector, ever in thrall to the Sinatra legend, the relationship carried a particular sweetness. The peerless singing technique, the effortless sense of style, the imperial presence, the palpable aroma of history—Frank was one of his idols, and now he was dating his daughter! According to Paulette Brandt, Nancy was equally enamored of Spector and wanted to marry him.

Spector had turned his back on many of his oldest friends, but now, apparently in better shape than he had been for years, he began to emerge from his self-imposed exile and to rebuild bridges.

In September 2001 Nicole graduated from high school and won a place at a university in New York to study literature. To celebrate, Spector rented a small bowling lane in Montrose, a dormitory town thirty minutes down the freeway from Pasadena, and threw a party. Spector enjoyed it so much that he hosted another the following year. The parties were his way of announcing he was back on the map—"the great Phil Spector show," as Paulette Brandt remembers. "He wouldn't get there until everybody was ready to leave—because they were tired and they had to go to work next day. It would get dark, and the bodyguards would come through and then Phil. All you needed was the theme from *Rocky*. And he'd sit down and everybody would come up and thank him as they left. He'd made his appearance and they'd had a good night. It was always successful, and it wasn't expensive, so he didn't mind the cost."

Old friends such as Larry Levine, Stan Ross, Hal Blaine and Harvey Kubernik were invited back into the fold. Ike Turner was pleased to receive an invitation, although for Turner the evening did not quite go as planned.

"Phil said he'd send a limousine," he recalls. "I said okay. So there's five of us, but the limo never showed; so I called up Phil's secretary, and she said, 'Take a cab and we'll pay for it.' So I called two cabs because three of us would have to ride in one and two in the other, and we rode out to the bowling alley, wherever it was. Why am I going? I'm going because he has asked me to go. So we go inside, I tell the cab driver, 'Thank you and someone'll take care of the fare.' Forty-five minutes later the cab driver is still sitting there, he hasn't been paid. So I told this girl, 'Tell Phil to take care of the cab,' so she says, "Okay, he will.' Twenty-five minutes later he still hasn't paid the cab. So then I go up to Phil and say, 'Hey, man, this cab is out there and I don't have the money to pay him. You told me to come, you should pay the cab.' He said, 'I'll take care of it.' I say to him, 'When?' He said, 'It's Christmas coming, too.' Another ten minutes go by and he still ain't paid the cab. I've got everybody with me and I say, 'Okay, let's go.' And as we're leaving I introduce one of my friends to Phil; I say, 'This is a friend of mine, and he's a friend of Hugh Hefner and they used to do business together,' and Spector said, 'So fucking what, and what else do you do?' So this was embarrassing for me. Not to mention that I didn't have the money to pay for the cab. So we all go out and I tell the cab driver, 'Take us back where you picked us up at.' Man, he was livid. We're ready to pull off when Spector comes out and he says, 'Ike, where are you going?' and I say, 'Man, leave away from all this bullshit, man.' He said, 'If you leave, you're no friend of mine.' So I told him, 'You can't lose something that you never had.' So we finally get home, and I have to borrow the money to pay for the cab. At that point, I called Phil's phone and his service answered. And I left a message. I told him, 'You know I'm never the kind to kiss ass and I never will be.' I told him, 'I don't appreciate the way you talked to my friend,' and that all he's got around him are a lot of people who lick ass. I told him, 'You need to take a long look at yourself; I think you're a lonely man and I feel really sorry for you. I took that car over there, I did it at your request and then I find myself in an embarrassing position.' I left this long, long message on his service. And do you know what? The next day a messenger came with twenty-four roses and a check for two thousand dollars and note saying thank you for coming. A lot of people would have called back and said, 'Screw you—who needs your advice?' But Spector? He sends twenty-four roses. I just called that acceptance, man."

In addition to the bowling parties, Spector also began to host regular Saturday luncheons at the castle, the guest lists made up of a revolving cast of music business friends and cronies: Bob Merlis, who handled press relations for Warner Bros.; Art Fein, who hosted a cable TV show called *Little Art's Poker Party;* Marvin Mitchelson; the oldies DJs Dr. Demento and Huggy Boy. Invitees soon began referring to the luncheons as "the king and his court."

Spector insisted that on arriving, guests should make the laborious climb up the eighty-eight steps to be greeted at the front door. "Huggy Boy has to be nearly eighty," says Denny Bruce, who attended on a couple of occasions. "He damn near needed oxygen when he got to the top."

Drinks and canapés would be served in the living room. "You'd sit around for an hour," Bruce remembers, "and there'd be stories about Doc Pomus and people who take too much credit for things they've done in the music business.

"Then finally, well, okay, lunch is served. And people would jockey for position next to Phil. If you were at the other end of the table you'd end up talking to Dr. Demento. Phil would sit on a slightly higher, velvety chair, just entertaining everyone. He'd do his imitation of voices— when John Lennon turned up backstage at Bangladesh, wanting to get in, and George saying, 'Fuck you, John, you can't just walk in like this. This is my show.'

"I remember Billy Swan [the country artist and producer] asking, 'How did you get the vocal sound on "My Sweet Lord"?' And Phil would be more than happy to share that information. One of the reasons everybody loves Phil is: his storytelling is superb. Once the stories start rolling . . . hilarious. Phil is Everyman on so many levels; he loves sports, he loves the Lakers. And he was getting that camaraderie by having these gatherings. I think he wanted to prove that coming into the new decade he really was human."

His daughter Nicole had played a particularly important role in Spector's renaissance. Over the years, his relationship to family had often been fraught and painful, but as Nicole blossomed into a mature, beautiful and intelligent young woman, so Spector's bond with her deepened. It was as if Nicole was giving him a reason to make peace with himself and the world around him.

Not unexpectedly, Nicole had developed an avid interest in rock and roll, and began to introduce her father to a new generation of bands. She had become friends with the English group Starsailor, and in the winter of 2001, when the group performed in Los Angeles, Spector invited them for lunch at the castle, and that same evening joined Nicole in the audience for the group's show. Watching them perform, Spector grew progressively more exhilarated. He had not completed a record since the Ramones' in 1979. Effectively, he had been out of the record business for longer than he had been in it. But he now apparently made up his mind that he wanted to produce Starsailor. James Stelfox, the bass player, would remember being taken aback by his full-frontal enthusiasm. "He was like: 'Okay, so we're going to do the record in Abbey Road, my guy is going to engineer it, and it'll be great!' We were a little surprised, since it was the first we'd heard about it. But, you know, Phil Spector is Phil Spector." After discussions with the group's label, Capitol, the deal was agreed, and at the end of January 2002, Spector sent out a circular letter to friends informing them that he would be producing Starsailor.

> Their new album, which I remixed, is already number one in England and came out in America last week. I think it will do very well here and that will be the beginning of a long and beautiful relationship. They are four poor boys from England. Sound familiar? I have much bigger plans for their second album, which I will be producing with them in the fall/winter after their present world tour, at Abbey Road in England where I recorded all the Beatles together and solo albums.

He had recently seen the group perform at the Palace Theater in Hollywood, he wrote, "and they were sensational."

The letter was the characteristic mixture of showboating and self-mythologizing. In fact, Spector had had nothing to do with remixing Starsailor's first album, *Love Is Here*, which had not been a number 1 record in Britain; it had stalled at number 2. But his joy at being back in the races was apparently unconfined. He e-mailed his old friend Bill Walsh. "He said, 'Bill, can you imagine at our age! Recording rock and roll again!' He was very excited about it."

In March 2002, as was his habit, Spector traveled to New York for the seventeenth annual induction dinner at the Rock and Roll Hall of Fame, held at the Waldorf-Astoria. The following month, his old friend Helen Noga died, at the age of eighty-eight. She was buried at the Forest Lawn Cemetery; Spector, inevitably, delivered the eulogy.

Now, it seemed, Spector had decided to completely remake his life. While it had been years since they'd lived together, Janis had continued to function as Spector's prop—the person who took care of his daily needs and effectively kept his life on an even keel. But relations between them had become increasingly strained, and in March 2002 Janis decided that she had had enough and stopped working for him. A month later, Spector fired his driver Morgan Martin, who had worked for him for the previous five years. Paulette Brandt was also let go. Paulette was crushed. It had been a long time since she had been "in love" with Spector, but she continued to love him. For years she had been unfalteringly loyal; now, without a word of explanation, he had cut her out of his life. Paulette saw it as just another example of Spector's perversity. "Things had been running quite smoothly for the last couple of years, and I think that's part of what upset him—things were too good. It's like the Lenny Bruce cartoon 'Thank You, Mask Man,' where the people tell him there's no more need for him because the Messiah has returned. And then Mask Man says, 'Well, I'll make trouble because I'm geared for it.' And I think that's a lot of what Phil's problem is. Things were getting boring for him. Everything was going smoothly, no problems. So then he let everybody go, and then this whole thing happened."

With Janis and Paulette now gone, Spector took on a new personal assistant, Michelle Blaine, the daughter of the drummer Hal Blaine. Spector had known Michelle as a child, but the acquaintance had been renewed two years earlier, when Hal Blaine was inducted into the Rock and Roll Hall of Fame. Blaine had injured his foot and was unable to attend the ceremony, and Michelle collected the award on his behalf. Michelle was working in film production, and married with six children. She quickly became what one observer describes as "the go-to person"—the sole intermediary in all of Spector's dealings with the outside world.

At the end of August 2002 Spector flew to London to begin work with Starsailor, taking with him Nicole and his bodyguard and aide-de-camp Jay Romaine. It was—though nobody actually used the word—an audition. Starsailor would not commit themselves to Spector producing an entire album until they were sure he was the right man. But Spector had no doubts about the outcome: he told the Kessels that it was "the Beatles all over again." In search of a talisman, Spector had told Starsailor that he wanted to use the engineer who had worked with him on the Lennon and Harrison albums, Phil McDonald. But McDonald had long since retired from the music business and was now working as a masseur. Instead, Starsailor suggested a young engineer named Danton Supple, who had recently been working with Coldplay.

Spector spent a week with the band working at Metropolis Studios, recording two tracks, "Silence Is Easy" and "White Dove." He was in good spirits, cracking jokes, regaling the band with stories: cranking the playback up to his preferred deafening volume, he blew two speakers that had not needed to be replaced in years.

The results were so impressive that Starsailor had no hesitation in deciding that Spector should take on the rest of the album.

Returning to Los Angeles, Spector now made the decision to fire Jay Romaine. For the past four years, Romaine had served much the same function as George Brand had fulfilled for so many years—not simply a bodyguard, but a companion and watchdog. When Spector ventured out for an evening's carousing, Romaine would usually be with him, keeping a watchful eye. But when Spector moved into the castle, relations between the two men began to sour. And now that he was sober, he had less need of someone to act as his minder. For most of his life Spector had surrounded himself with people—secretaries, bodyguards, lovers, flunkies—who could look after him and keep him out of the worst kind of trouble. But now, with the departure of Jay Romaine, he had let the last of them go.

"It was like the old drunk who insists he's all right to drive," says Denny Bruce. "Like, 'Hey, I'm okay now.' 'Well, are you sure you can drive?' 'Yup, I'm okay now, I'm okay; just give me the fucking keys . . .' "

In October 2002 Spector returned to London to resume recording with Starsailor, this time in the company of Nicole and Michelle Blaine. The sessions had now transferred to Abbey Road Studios, the scene of Spector's earlier triumphs with Lennon and Harrison.

But while the earlier sessions with Starsailor had gone without a hitch, it quickly became apparent that all was not well with Spector.

"It was almost as if he wasn't there at all," one participant remembers. "Sometimes you couldn't get through to him, like he couldn't hear you. It was as if he'd been given something to make him normal for that first week, but then he'd lapsed back into something else. He was kind of really distant; like he was overmedicated. Sometimes he could be the nicest bloke in the world; you'd sit with him telling you stories and laughing our heads off. But other days he was not himself at all."

Musically, too, Spector seemed to have run out of ideas. "Silence Is Easy" had established a distinctive motif with its echoing drum sound and characteristically thunderous mix—pure Spector brilliance, the band thought. But now it seemed that every song Spector touched came out sounding very much the same. "The tracks weren't anything near like what the band wanted. Phil was about overlaying and overlaying and capturing a moment; but they were musicians saying, 'I can hear bum notes.' "

Nor were matters improved by Michelle Blaine, who some around the sessions thought was behaving more like Spector's manager than his assistant, offering her thoughts on how the music should sound and, in the words of one participant, "generally throwing her weight around."

After five laborious and anguished weeks, the band's manager, Andrew Walsh, and Jeff Barrett, the A&R manager for their record label Capitol, asked for a crisis meeting with Spector and his business manager, Allen Klein. Klein flew over to London. When Michelle Blaine walked in expecting to join the meeting, Klein pointedly told her to leave the room. Mortified at having to sack the most famous record producer in the world, Walsh and Barrett announced that the band was unable to work with Spector and the collaboration was over. Spector was stunned. He told Harvey and Barrett, "You've got big balls . . ."

The five weeks' worth of recordings at Abbey Road were scrapped, and the band went on to produce the album themselves, with Danton Supple. "White Dove" and "Silence Is Easy" would both subsequently appear on the record—although Spector's mix of the latter song was replaced with a new mix by the New York–based "mixmaster" Michael Brauer, which featured more guitar, brought the vocal further forward and speeded up the track. The drum sound, however, could only be Spector.

The album, entitled *Silence Is Easy*, went to number 2 in the British charts, and the single of the same name went to number 8.

Disconsolate, Spector returned to Los Angeles. His comeback was over. "He was pissed off, blaming the group, and saying 'They don't know what they could have had,' " one friend remembers. "He was broken-hearted."

29

"It's Very Difficult, Very Difficult to Be Reasonable"

It was barely two weeks after his return to Los Angeles that Spector's white Rolls-Royce arrived to collect me from my hotel on the Sunset Strip and ferried me down the freeway to Alhambra; that I climbed the eighty-eight steps to the door of the castle to be greeted by Michelle Blaine; that I sat in the living room, waiting for Spector, and that he appeared at the top of the wooden staircase to the strains of Handel, dressed in his black silk pajama suit with the initials PS picked out in silver thread, his blue glasses, his shoulder-length wig, his three-inch Cuban heels—looking bizarre, yet curiously magnificent.

"I always wanted to live in a castle . . . ," he said, "and they don't have many left . . ."

He sat, hunched, a small figure on a large white sofa. His face was pale, his skin looked like parchment, and his hands trembled.

For the next four hours he talked almost without pause. He was bombastic, funny, furious and melancholic by turns. His wristwatch made its whirring call, like a cuckoo clock, announcing the hour. *It's two o'clock.*

He had always wanted to win, he said. And from childhood he knew he was smarter than most. "That's how I figured I'd get by. I cheated. People ask me today, 'Do you play computer games?'—the guys at the studio. I don't play if I can't win. I don't play anything if I can't win. And I'm never going to win against a computer, so what the fuck do I want to play for? To lose? So those guys playing, they're morons. When I was a kid everybody used to get ecstatic winning at Monopoly, or Scrabble. I just figured out, Shit, if it's all about winning . . . so I just went out and bought another Monopoly game, took the money and hid it in my pocket, and then go to people's houses and add an extra one hundred or five hundred and I'd win every time. I'd beat Nicole playing Monopoly when she was twelve years old. Beat the shit out of her! I don't care! I ain't going to lose at some fucking board game with dice. Scrabble, I would take the 'X's and the blanks and when somebody turned their head I'd put a blank tile on my rack. I'd always have to win. Because I'm not going to lose, so don't invite me over! Because everybody takes winning so seriously—I beat your ass at Scrabble, Phil. Oh yeah, so try again. If you can't win, don't play. What's the fucking fun in losing? Where's the joy in that? The breakfast of champions is the opposition."

He laughed—once more the small and furious boy, delighted to be putting one over on the world.

"I like the idea of winning. I've made art that wasn't successful; and I didn't enjoy the art as much as when it was successful. What's so great about making a record or a movie and it not being a hit?"

Where, I asked him, did this need to succeed come from?

"I don't know. It's about seeing success around you and wanting to work with the best and bring out the best in those around you. I know a lot of people who like to work with mediocre people and feel they're the most important. I like to work with the best—geniuses. It brings out the best in me.

"It's very hard in the business today to find extremely talented young people. But it was very hard to find extremely talented people thirty years ago too; I was fortunate I fell into the Stones, John Lennon, rest his soul, people with extraordinary talent—Tina Turner. Timing is the key to everything."

He jabbed a finger at me across the table. "Okay. You ask me, 'What's your name?' And then you ask me, 'What do you do for a living, and what's the most important part of what you do for a living?' Go ahead! Just for the conversation."

"Okay. What's your name?"

"Phil Spector."

"And what do you do for a living?"

"I'm a record producer."

"And what's the most important—"

"*Timing*—" and he broke up in laughter.

"So that is the key. For some reason, if you say 'lucky' about people, people say, 'Oh, you're demeaning their talent.' No—there's an element of luck in everything. But I call it timing."

It was timing that took him into Gold Star Records in 1958, with "To Know Him Is to Love Him." Luck that took him to Lew Bedell at Era Records; luck, timing and maybe something else too that had gotten

"To Know Him Is to Love Him" played on *American Bandstand.* "I learned a lot by being in the Teddy Bears," he said. "I learned I didn't want to be a singer. I learned about payola and distributors and manufacturing. I learned about the Mafia. I did *American Bandstand, The Dick Clark Show.* If you broke your record in Philadelphia, it became a national hit. And if Dick Clark played you on national TV, well . . . that's where payola started." He paused and gave a sly smile. "Everybody around Dick Clark went to jail, except for Dick Clark.

"But that's where black music broke," he went on. "The black disc jockeys started taking on their names—Rosco, Big Mama—and for fifty dollars you could get them to play your record and it meant something. They would have a record hop and charge a dollar, and eight thousand kids would show up. No overheads. The groups would come for free and lip-synch, so it was eight thousand dollars' profit. It was an incredible time."

"And that's when you decided you wanted to be a producer," I said.

"I wanted to be in the background—but I wanted to be *important* in the background. I knew about Toscanini. I knew that Mozart was more important than his operas. That Beethoven was more important than whoever was playing his music. I knew that the real folk music of America was George Gershwin, Jerome Kern, Irving Berlin. Those names were bigger than the music. That's what I wanted to be."

I asked how had he educated himself musically?

"Just by listening. By going downtown and buying the sheet music." He paused.

"Black music is our American culture. But our folk music is George Gershwin and Jerome Kern. I was always listening to jazz, rock and roll—sepia music, they called it then; black music. The thing that I liked about rock and roll music, before they called it rock and roll, was that they didn't only sing their own songs. The Fortunes would sing 'Marie' by Irving Berlin. They were open about it. That was what was wonderful in those days. When we were number one with 'To Know Him Is to Love Him,' number two was 'Nel Blu Dipinto di Blu' by Domenico Modugno; number three was Conway Twitty with 'It's Only Make Believe'—a country and western song. So rock and roll really gave everybody a chance."

He reached for his glass, enjoying the roll of the conversation.

Did I know he'd first met Elvis Presley in 1958?

"Sure . . . And in 1960 I worked on his album, coming out of the army. Very few people know that. But Elvis was terrific, wonderful . . .

"I went to New York and tracked down his publishers, Hill and

Range music. I went to them and said, 'I'm a genius and I want to meet Elvis Presley.' They said, 'Sign a contract.' I said, 'I don't want to sign a contract.' I looked up all the writers—Doc Pomus—all the names I saw on records, and I knocked on all their doors and told them who I was and what I did. I had already recorded 'To Know Him Is to Love Him.' I was working at the UN as a translator and as a court reporter. I went to see all these people and just pushed my way in. And these people introduced me to Elvis, and Elvis liked me."

He laughed. "I believed I was the best in the world. I really believed that. Everybody I met from Johnny Mercer to Ahmet Ertegun, I would tell them I was a genius. And then they would agree with me. I'd prove it to them, by conversation, talk. I made demos for Elvis, for songwriters. I made 'Suspicion' for Terry Stafford—I didn't get any credit or any money. I didn't care. I just loved making records. I did a lot of songs for Ahmet and Jerry Wexler that I didn't take credit for, because I loved them. Ahmet was like a father to me. All these people loved me; they saw money in me. And I was willing to work for nothing. I did Elvis's album for nothing. I just wanted a reputation, and the way you earn a reputation is by working and people start buzzing. And to have Elvis talking about you—very important. To have Ahmet Ertegun talking about you—he's brilliant, he's a genius—that's more important than money. I was living in a seventy-five-dollar-a-month apartment. Didn't matter. I was young and vital and they wanted young blood. It was a great fucking time.

"In the '60s I was motivated by a sense of destiny. I didn't know that Lincoln Ford Mercury, McDonald's and Kentucky Fried Chicken were going to be using our songs. But I sure as hell knew our songs were going to be around in forty years. I tried to tell all the musicians about a sense of destiny. Because they made fun of me. Even my good friends today, they made fun of the little kid who was making rock and roll records, and the hold notes—over and over, the same thing, the same thing, the same thing; and not playing for three hours and then at the last minute we play. Six hours and nine hours and twelve hours, the same thing over and over. I *knew* . . .

"These were the greatest musicians in the world. I would want these guys and only these guys. I knew it was demeaning to them, to have these giants playing 'hold' notes, because they were much better than this, but I didn't care. Barney Kessel, Red Norvo. I knew these guys were saying 'Shit' . . . But when they were doing it for one hundred thousand dollars a year for everyone else, trying to get the same sound, they were laughing all the way to the bank.

"I would try to tell all the groups, to impose a sense of destiny on them. We're doing something very important to me. Trust me. I always called it art. And I was the first person that took the words A&R and called it 'producer.' I said, I am the producer. I do everything. I produce this work. I was concerned with art. And it was very hard because these people didn't have that sense of destiny. They didn't know how good they were. They didn't know they were producing art that would change the world. And it did change the world.

"I heard something different, and I saw a different kind of music coming out. I waited eight, ten records before I added strings. I heard a different kind of rock and roll than Fats Domino or Chuck Berry, who were big influences for me. I didn't want to imitate or copy them. I never knew why I was commercial. I couldn't figure that out. I didn't think that what I was doing was commercial. Except I knew I was *writing* hits; I always knew what a hit song was. But I thought that what I was doing was a little too sophisticated compared to Fats Domino.

"I thought we had gone a little too far and each time I felt we were breaking the barrier a little too much. I thought we'd gone too far with 'Zip-a-Dee Doo-Dah.' It was so big and busy that I couldn't even put the drum in. There's no drum on that record; only a bass drum. There was nowhere sound-wise I could fit it in. I tried for six hours and couldn't fit it in. And then I thought, Well, maybe this record won't work. And I always had that dilemma."

What he had always wanted, he said, was the best, and to be best, and only the best. "I was very sure of what I was doing. I convinced myself that Gold Star was good, but it was the hardest studio in the world to work in. It would take me days and days to get the right sound, whereas at Motown . . . I used to be so envious of them, because they could go in and in five minutes get that same drum sound and 'ooh, ooh, baby, baby,' and make number-one record after number-one record. I'd say, 'Shit—how do they do it so fucking easily?' The Supremes, thirteen number-one records or whatever it was and I'm working my ass off, and my groups are leaving me left and right because I'm not putting out records. They loved me, but they couldn't stand it. But it was more important to create the revolution to make the change. You think back on the history of American music and only a few names come up; not quantities of names. So I figured that's okay.

"At Philles I was turning down records every day. I turned down 'Louie, Louie'—all these number-one records. My distributors would call me, asking me to put them on Philles. I said, 'I can't put this shit on Philles, even if it is number one in Seattle or wherever. I mean, I love

"Louie, Louie," but I can't put this shit on my label with "Be My Baby." I have a standard, and I can't lower it for money. I can't do it.' "

He shrugged, as if to say, What could be clearer than that?

"Y'know, the hardest part was convincing people that it could be done. I've tried to teach Nicole, the hardest thing in life is people who don't get it. About anything. I would explain what I was doing to people and they just didn't get it.

"If I wanted three pianos, I couldn't get three pianos in the studio, so I'd get three piano players sitting at one piano, fighting to get their hands on it. Leon Russell, Brian Wilson sometimes . . ."

He laughed at the memory.

"People said, 'Three people sitting at a piano? You can't do that! You can't make the needle go into the red! You can't do this or that.' It's always: You can't, you can't, you can't. So timing put me in a position where I *can* do these things. Because I had these ideas, these thoughts, these sounds in my head. I would read about Mozart and Beethoven and Wagner and it was all about what they had, how they could express themselves and how many people didn't believe in them."

So you wanted immortality? I asked.

He nodded vigorously. "Yes. Very much. I think when Jefferson wrote the Declaration of Independence, he was thinking, People will remember this. When Gershwin wrote, he may have said, 'I don't know about this *American in Paris*,' but I think he said, 'This is something special.' I think Irving Berlin had an ego, that he wanted people to remember this. I think he wanted to be number one. And so did I."

He fell silent, as if, for a moment, awed himself by the story he had told, and the magnitude of its accomplishment, woven as it was from truth and myth so entangled it was impossible to tell one from the other. In the silence, I noticed that the classical music was still playing in the background.

He didn't like to talk about the past, he said. But that couldn't be right, because here, seated on the sofa talking about the past, he flamed into life—names, dates and song titles spilling out, old friends saluted, old enemies traduced.

"Berry Gordy?" He laughed. "I don't see Berry doing very much. Wrote some good songs, 'Money' and all of that. But beyond that I feel there were more talented people in the organization. Like I think Holland, Dozier and Holland, they are genuinely giants in terms of writing and producing. They made some interesting statements. 'Reach Out I'll Be There.' "

When I asked him about the Righteous Brothers and "You've Lost That Lovin' Feelin' " he appeared to enter a reverie.

"You know, they didn't want to do 'Lovin' Feelin'." They wanted to do rock and roll, ooh-boop-a-doop stuff—the kind of stuff they were doing on Moonglow. They didn't want to do a ballad." He shook his head, as if to say, "idiots."

"I worked six months on that fucking record. And a lot of people had come down to the studio and said, 'It's marvelous, it's wonderful.' Herb Alpert came down and said, 'It's incredible,' this and that. I'd spent months overdubbing and re-overdubbing, and finally I had it down right where I thought it was pretty good, but that nobody would get it. Nobody would get the fucking record.

"I played it for a few people and nobody had heard anything like it. I didn't know if we'd changed the musical world or done something completely catastrophic. So I had to go back to New York.

"I played it for Barry Mann and Cynthia Weil in my office on Sixty-second Street. I put it on, the record goes 'You never close your eyes . . .' and Barry says, 'Whoah, whoah, wait. Wrong speed.' I said, 'What?' He says, 'You've got it on thirty-three; that's the wrong speed, Phil.' That's the first comment I hear!

"So I immediately called Dr. Kaplan, my psychiatrist, and I said, 'Doc, I have to see you right away. I just worked six months on this record; it cost me thirty-five thousand dollars and the fucking co-writer thinks it's on the wrong fucking speed.' I called Larry Levine my engineer and said, 'Have you given me the right pressing?' I'm fucking paranoid: I didn't know what to do. I called Donny Kirshner, the co-publisher—he's got Carole King, Barry Mann, Cynthia Weil, Gerry Goffin. I said, 'Donny, I got to play you this record.' He said, 'I hear it's a monster.' I said, 'You've got the best ears in the business, I've got to bring it over to you.' So I bring it over and put it on. He goes, 'Boops—it's great, it's great, it's great; what do you call it?' I said, ' "You've Lost That Lovin' Feelin'." ' He said, 'How many you got pressed up?' I said, 'Half a million.' He said, ' "Bring Back That Lovin' Feelin' ". . .' I said, 'What are you talking about?' He said, ' "Bring Back That Lovin' Feelin' "—that's your title.' I said, 'No, no, no—"You've *Lost* That Lovin' Feelin'." Trust me.' That's the second opinion. So I call Dr. Kaplan again . . .

"Then I call Murray the K, the biggest DJ in New York City. I said, 'Murray, I need you to do me a favor. I have this new Righteous Brothers record. I need it to win the show tonight, because it's a four-minute-and-five-second record; there's never been a record this long before.'

And I'm lying on the label; I put three minutes five seconds—I got in a lot of fucking trouble. So he comes over and he listens to the record. This is the last opinion of the day—five o'clock in the afternoon. And he's listening and listening, and it gets to the middle section—where the bass guitar line is. So Murray the K listens to it, and he says, 'That bass line—that "La Bamba" thing, what's that?' I said, 'That's part of the song.' He said, 'That's fucking sensational.' I said, 'Well, yeah.' He said, 'That's how it should begin . . .' I said, 'It can't begin that way.' He said, 'Make that the beginning.' I said, 'I can't make that the beginning, Murray.' And those are my three experts; the co-writer, the co-publisher and the number-one disc jockey in America, all killed me. I didn't sleep for a week when that record came out. I was so sick, I got spastic colon; I had an ulcer.

"We did 'Lovin' Feelin',' 'Unchained Melody.' And in appreciation they left me; they went for the big bucks to MGM." He paused. "They never had a hit again. I had all the hits. They had nothing."

The Top 40 hits, the power plays, the tantrums, all the hype and bombast that came with being the First Tycoon of Teen—"We did it all! We did it all . . . !"

He threw himself back on the sofa and fell silent.

"We played the part . . . Tom Wolfe wrote about that. It just seemed natural at the time. I just felt I didn't fit in. I was different. So I had to make my own world. And it made life complicated for me, but it made it justifiable. Oh, there's the reason they hate my fucking guts; I look strange, I act strange, I make these strange records, so there's a reason to hate my guts. Because I felt hated. Even when the music became big, I never felt like I fit in. I never hung out with everybody. I never did all the drugs and the parties. I didn't feel comfortable. It felt too commercial to me. I preferred the studio. The outside world was like being the star again. Going out was always the big ordeal. Too hard. It was like being in front of an audience."

Fame, success, the recognition he had always craved—when finally he found it, all of it was "a burden," he said. "It was . . . scary. It was very frightening. It was a power. I felt powerful. But it was frightening because you always think of losing it every minute of the day. You look at poor people all the time. You think of yourself as poor all the time. You're *remembering* yourself as poor all the time. You never quite accept it. Guilt all the time. And if you're not too stable to begin with . . . Now I realize that if money can't buy happiness you're looking in the wrong places; you don't know how to spend your money."

Did he honestly believe that?

"Well, you can certainly get things to help you make yourself happy. People who say they don't give a shit about money, I don't know if they're telling me the truth."

What did money bring him?

"I never thought about it. Money just came with the art. It was a gift. It never was part of the plan."

So he hadn't dreamed of being rich?

"Never. Recognition, and power and control. But never, never that money was part of it. No, that wasn't part of the game plan . . ."

I was reminded of something that Spector had once said about Lenny Bruce; that the great tragedy of Bruce was that he was remembered for all the wrong reasons—as a junkie, rather than a wise, funny and fearless man. Did Spector ever worry that a similar fate might befall him, remembered not for his brilliance but as . . .

"Maniacal?" He gave a thin smile. "Yeah, that's why I say now: Let the art speak for itself. If the art's maniacal, I'm maniacal."

He paused. "Orson Welles spent his whole life chasing money, because he never made any money. And then he ended up being three hundred pounds, doing wine commercials. He never lived up to the genius that he was because he never knew what he wanted to do. He never made that commitment to what to be. He was caught up in being a playboy, a movie star, maybe being a senator. He didn't know what he wanted to be. I made a commitment to what I wanted to be. I let the art speak for itself."

I wondered, had he felt frightened when music changed in the mid-'60s, and the Wall of Sound began to fall out of fashion?

"It never bothered me."

Surely, it must have, I protested.

He shook his head. "It really didn't. I was a manufacturer of records, and a publisher and a writer. I was more intellectually surprised by the Beatle invasion and how to deal with that. But when the Beatles were still number one, two, three, four and five, I was still doing my thing. I was more devastated when the Christmas album didn't sell. That was devastating to me, but I couldn't take it personally because Kennedy was killed.

"But that was a monumental thing to me—all the groups, all the work, all the time, all the money. Columbia had offered me a fortune for them to put it out . . . That was devastating. But when the winds changed, no. You know when I got a little concerned? When folk music came in. Peter, Paul and all that shit. Joan Baez . . . Dylan I could understand, because he was unique. But when all these fucking terrible folk groups from the Troubadour . . . and then when disco came in, whoah . . . That was disconcerting to me. When I don't understand something, I get confused by it."

He had lost his enthusiasm for music in the '70s, he said. After working with the Beatles, what could possibly interest him?

"I did Dion because he was the king of doo-wop and I grew up listening to his music. I wanted him to be the next Bobby Darin, who was my dearest friend and I miss him very much. But I didn't spend as much time with Dion on the album as I should have, because I really wasn't interested. It was winding down for me, getting ready to pack it in."

And Leonard Cohen?

"I wanted to work with Leonard and I like him. I knew it wouldn't sell shit." He shrugged. "I didn't care."

What could interest him after that? Michael Jackson?

"The most depressing, heinous thing. Starting out life as a black man and ending up as a white woman, what's that all about? But the King? He's no king. He's a good singer, a good dancer. Good, but not Fred Astaire, not Elvis Presley . . ."

Rap music?

"Like the *c* got left off at the printers."

Oasis?

"Jerks."

Kurt Cobain?

"When Kurt Cobain died, somebody phoned me from *Time* magazine and said, 'I haven't been this upset since John Lennon died.' I said, 'You don't know the difference between Kurt Cobain and John Lennon?' He said, 'No, what's the difference?' I said, 'That's too bad, because Kurt Cobain did!' "

Spector fell back on the sofa, as if exhausted by his tirade. "It's all been done! It's all been done!"

Lunch was served in the dining room, but Spector excused himself and vanished upstairs. In the hallway a photograph of Spector with Nancy Sinatra stood on a console table, with three slim books on psychiatry, between bookends, like an ironic display. I ate alone, then walked in the garden, looking down through the trees to the rooftops of Alhambra far below. When at length he returned, Spector looked at the food, shook his head, and led the way back into the sitting room.

"I'm not addicted to applause," he said, "because I live a life of reclusiveness." He paused. "My friend Doc Pomus, when people used to say, 'I hear Phil Spector's a recluse,' he would say, 'Not recluse, *reckless*, baby! *Reckless!*' " Spector smiled to himself.

He paused. "I learned there's not much in the world that appeals to me. Like, normal society doesn't really appeal to me. Television—chewing gum for the eyes. It's nonsense. Y'know, the real world—the nine-to-five, the banking—that doesn't appeal to me. I'm not missing out on much by missing out on the real world. You've been on a plane. Is there much to miss out on there? Actually I'm flown in my own plane. I don't see I'm missing out on much by going through security, or standing in line in the market reading the *Enquirer*, or watching *Jerry Springer*. What am I missing? I used to think I was missing a lot by not being normal; that I was an outcast. But not now."

For years, he said, he had not been well. "I was crippled inside. Emotionally. Insane is a hard word, but it's manic-depressive, bipolar. I take medication for schizophrenia, but I wouldn't say I'm schizophrenic. But I have a bipolar personality, which is strange. I have devils inside that fight me. And I'm my own worst enemy."

For a long time—many years—he said, he had been unable to function as "a regular part of society. So I chose not to. Nicole is a twin. Her brother, Phillip, died when he was ten years old. Ten years ago. I don't look for sympathy, but I had a difficult time after that. And Nicole and I went through a lot. It was a difficult time and all my close friends throughout my life—Lenny Bruce, John Lennon—had passed on. All the people I could talk to were gone. So I just sort of struggled along alone and chose not to work, and raise a daughter. And I chose, after the loss of Phillip, to get my life back on track."

For years he did . . . nothing. He was incapable of action, he said. Paralyzed. Projects came and went unfulfilled. Nothing interested him. How, I asked, did he pass the time—the weeks, the months, the years? "I studied languages . . ." The sentence petered into silence. "I don't remember how I spent a lot of that time. I don't think it was a particularly good time."

His mother and father were first cousins, he said. "I don't know genetically whether or not that had something to do with what I am or who I became. And I was petrified by that fact. I was very scared and frightened by it. And as Nicole became older, I thought it would pass on to her. And even if she genetically wasn't unwell, that she would become, by seeing me as an example, unwell herself, and be attracted to men like that—manic-depressive, or psychotic, or cuckoo.

"So getting myself together had a lot to do with having a relationship with my daughter. And I was determined to do it because of my daughter. I wanted her to know what a healthier relationship was like. And I wanted to have a healthier relationship with her than I could have as a neurotic, sick person. I wanted her to look up to me and say, 'This is what a reasonable man is like.' So she could have a reasonable relationship with me, and find a reasonable person, reasonable relationship in her life. I wanted to go places with her, do things with her—things that I couldn't do before. It's very important I could have a reasonable relationship with her. To be friends."

He paused.

"You have to conquer yourself," he said, "and take control of yourself.

"I make fun of a lot of people, like Brian Wilson, because they don't have control over themselves. I think they're largely phonies. They use their illness as an excuse. I have no mercy for that."

But Wilson, I said, idolized him.

"I know. He does interviews; he writes his autobiography about me. I know, I know, I know."

He shrugged. "It's sad, you know, but I don't know if you can feel sorry for untalented people. Maybe he's not that talented. Maybe he's overrated. Maybe. Jimi Hendrix was not overrated. Janis Joplin was not overrated. I feel sorry that they died, because they shouldn't have. They should have been a little smarter. Brian Wilson outlived his brothers, for God's fucking sake. How do you figure that? Carl Wilson—pretty bright guy. Dennis—pretty silly guy; y'know, a muppet. And Brian outlives them? But maybe Brian wasn't that talented to begin with, and we're burdening him with that. We make these people more than they are. I don't feel sorry for Brian Wilson; I never thought he was that talented to begin with. I'm glad he idolizes me; I wish that Jimi Hendrix idolized me. I heard he did. I'd be more impressed if somebody with a brain idolized me."

I told him that when I had met Brian Wilson he had talked of perhaps wanting to be produced by Spector.

He smiled. The idea was clearly preposterous.

"I don't know if I have a feeling for what Brian might want to express today," he said. "I don't know if I have a feeling for what Bob Dylan might want to express today. Or Bruce Springsteen. I went to see Bruce and he's put himself back in that place he was in the '70s, with the E Street Band and Clarence and Stevie Van Zandt. And he's protected himself with three new songs and twenty-five old ones.

"Springsteen said, 'I want to sing like Roy Orbison, write songs like Bob Dylan and make records like Phil Spector.' He said that at the Rock and Roll Hall of Fame, and we appreciate that and God bless him . . ."

What did he think when he first heard *Born to Run*?

"I thought he should have paid me some royalties!" He laughed. "Jerry Wexler called me and said, 'He should pay you royalties, Phil.' But, again, that's a lot more exciting, appetizing, interesting than being idolized by Brian Wilson. Because there's a vibrant force in music who cares and is influenced by you. That means something. Imitation is the greatest form of flattery until it becomes plagiarism. Better they should imitate me than somebody else."

His wristwatch spoke. *"It's four o'clock."*

Who, I asked, had been the greatest love of his life?

He looked away in silence. "Good friends," he said. "It's been Lenny; it's been John . . . It's been my friends and my little boy Phillip was probably the greatest love of my life."

Both John and Lenny, he said, were like brothers. "John—it was the perfect marriage. Just perfect. He loved the way I worked. He loved the way I thought. We just loved each other."

And Lenny?

"Lenny was like an older brother. I recorded him, supported him when he couldn't work—when they wouldn't allow him to work, and I buried him when he died. Losing Lenny and John was like losing my dad. Very, very emotional. Although I was too young to understand the value of losing my dad. Old enough to feel the loss, but not old enough to appreciate the loss until I was much older, and then I realized."

He fell silent.

"But you just learn to put things in perspective . . ." he said at last. "It's like those records; they were the greatest love of my life when I was making them. I lived for those records. I lived and breathed those records. That's why I never had relationships with anybody that could last. They were my life; they were more important than anything. Nothing competed with them." He paused, bewilderment flickering in his face. "That's why I can't figure out why they have so little significance to me today."

I asked about his three adopted children—Donte, Gary and Louis—and his face became a mask.

"I see them occasionally, but I don't have a close relationship with them; I don't pretend to. We're friends. But the only relationship I have with my children is with Nicole, with whom I'm very close. You have to have children when you're ready to have children. It's like anything. If I had made these records when I was forty, I would have been able to handle it a lot better. I didn't know what the fuck I was doing. I knew what I was doing artistically, but I didn't know what I was doing emotionally or physically. I couldn't answer any of the questions; I didn't know what I was doing. So I certainly didn't know anything about having children or relationships."

He made no mention of his first marriage, to Annette Merar. Nor of Janis Zavala, the person who, more than anyone, had loved and cared for Spector over the past thirty years. And when I asked about Ronnie, he could not even bring himself to speak her name.

"Not to get on a dissertation about ex-wives and shit like that. But wives and marriage isn't a word, it's a sentence; and wives last through our marriage, ex-wives last forever, and all that other bullshit. No disrespect, but I haven't spoken to my ex-wife in more than thirty years; I couldn't give a shit whether she lives or dies. I've been vindicated in the courts over and over. But she can still get up forty years later and sing the same fucking song and get applause. Could a typist do that? Could a stenographer? Look at it this way; I also recorded Tina Turner. She's not complaining; she's not suing anybody. Is it my fault that this ex-wife is not Tina Turner? Maybe it has something to do with a lack of a talent there that she can't get justification in the courts. Maybe the courts should say, 'You should be more talented,' but they can't say that. Maybe she's not Diana Ross, Tina Turner. I made her famous, and she resents that. But give it up, for God's sake. I don't want anybody to thank me. I just say, 'Why say, "Fuck you." ' Just leave me alone! 'Oh, but he's a control freak . . .'

"If you come down to what people really hate about Phil Spector, it's that he controls everything . . ."

Did he care, I asked, what people thought of him?

"Very much. What's very important to me is respect, that people respect me, respect what I did, and think that I'm the best at what I do. Other than that, I don't care . . ."

And did he think he had been a good person?

The question stopped him for a moment. "Reasonable," he said at last. "Reasonably good. I mean I haven't done anything . . ." The thought went to silence.

"It's funny—there isn't anybody who has touched me who hasn't had some sort of success with me; *anyone* who has touched me in the business who hasn't made money; anyone at all. Not that it means anything, but it's interesting. Because you hear such negative shit that people say, and yet every one of them has achieved some sort of success with me. So, yeah, yeah . . . good person."

He paused, lost in thought. "My daughter sometimes asks me, 'Dad, are you lonely?' And I say, 'Why do you ask me that?' And she says, 'Because you're alone a lot of the time, and you keep to yourself and you don't tell much about yourself.' And I say, 'Well, there's a difference between being alone and lonely.' I am alone, but I'm not lonely. I've talked to women about relationships, and I've heard what they wanted, and I walked away saying, 'Gee . . . that's what she wants in a relationship?' And I've thought, I don't know what I want in a relationship, but I know one thing; I want a hell of a lot more than that. And maybe I can't find it with anyone. I'm not searching; I'm not looking for a relationship, because maybe it's not there.

"I've got to learn to have a relationship with me and feel comfortable with me, doing what I'm doing and what I'm about. I would feel comfortable, as corny as it sounds, having a good relationship with myself. It's what I've always wanted. For forty fucking years. A decent relationship with myself. A reasonable relationship with myself.

"I'm not going to ever be happy. Happiness isn't on. Because happiness is temporary. Unhappiness is temporary. Ecstasy is temporary. Orgasm is temporary. Everything is temporary. But being reasonable is an approach. And being reasonable with yourself. It's very difficult, very difficult to be reasonable."

Once again he rose from the sofa and left the room. We had been talking for more than three hours, and now it was growing dark outside, the shadows lengthening in the room. Someone, I noticed, had turned off the music.

At length, Spector returned. In the growing twilight, he suddenly looked very old, and very vulnerable.

Had he reached a point in his life, I asked, where he knew he had to change or he would die?

"Well, I don't want to sound like those people . . . like Charlie Sheen, who has gone through drug problems . . ." He gave a grim laugh.

"It was evolving . . . It had something to do with Nicole, but it evolved. I just couldn't stand the way I was anymore. I don't know if it was a question of dying; it was a question of not being able to live that way anymore. I had to find a way to approach life reasonably. And I was not . . . there. And a couple of years ago I just made a pronouncement that I would . . . beat it. That I would beat my brain and do it.

"I was an insomniac. You get addicted to that. And then I said to myself one day: What the fuck's so great about being addicted to insomnia? What's that all about? You sit up all night and you go crazy. You don't sleep. Your mind starts playing tricks on you; you do terrible things to yourself. It's a terrible situation. So a couple of years ago I decided I was going to beat the devil; I was going to get better."

So how did he set about accomplishing that?

"I just waged war with myself."

With medication?

He nodded. "Medication. I started to work with doctors and work with drugs that would work on my mind that would produce results; and I was not getting them. I'm very frightened of drugs; I'm very frightened of fucking with my brain, and I didn't want to interfere with anything that could hurt me creatively or anything like that. So I was filled with fear and trepidation. Actually it was longer—three or four years ago—and over a slow, slow period of time and this and that, and very methodically, and every day getting up saying, 'No, you're not there yet,' and months would go by, years would go by . . ."

Had all his years of therapy been of any help?

"Not enough." He shrugged. "I don't know. There's something I'd either not accepted, or I'm not prepared to accept or live with in my life, that I don't know about perhaps. That I'm facing now. I didn't want it to be because of Nicole. I want it to be because of me. I want to get back in the record business because of me. I don't want to be like these people . . . 'I found the woman of my dreams; I'm going to be so happy, blah, blah, blah.' I made this commitment to me. I want to change for me. I want to try and have a reasonable existence, and if I can't, I can't. So I've been experimenting with medication that I think would help, and not interfere with my creative process and my thinking process, and it's been very slow, very difficult." He paused. "I couldn't have done this conversation six months ago."

Six years ago?

"Absolutely not."

Sixteen years ago?

"Maybe under false pretenses, but probably no. I wouldn't have even thought of it. I was completely . . . I was another person. I'm a completely different person than I was three months ago, six months ago, nine months ago. I'm constantly evolving, constantly changing."

Even now, he said, it was difficult for him to have a meeting like this.

"I can't stand to be talked about. I can't stand to be looked at. I can't stand the attention. I don't defend myself. I don't defend others. I decided many years ago that I wasn't going to make any public statements. I'm a diabetic and as a young child I was told I could never eat chocolate and drink Coca-Cola, so I have great willpower. And it takes a tremendous amount of willpower to abstain from commenting. I commented my heart out in the '60s. I controlled everything. I was a control freak." He laughed.

"I don't like talking about the past. I don't even like meeting people from the past. It's difficult for me. I have a difficult time. Reunions . . . troublesome for me; very troublesome." It was only recently that he had been able to start bringing his old friends back into his life. "A lot of my enemies are dying off, which is a shame, because they define me in so many ways."

So who were his closest friends?

He thought for a moment. "My attorneys," he said, and laughed. Neither of us could have imagined at that moment just how prescient that statement would be.

I asked him to tell me about the Starsailor sessions and he shrugged. He liked their songs, and the singer James Walsh's voice. He found it "intriguing to do a couple of sides with them. No particular reason beyond that . . ."

For years nothing in music had interested him, but now, he said, he could feel the inkling of something in the air, like the '60s all over again. "That's all it is, a feeling. I never thought about anything I did before. I didn't think, Why the Ronettes, why the Righteous Brothers, why John Lennon? I just did it. So I didn't think, Why Starsailor? It just feels okay. And I haven't had that instinct in me for years and years."

He made no mention of the difficulties during the session, the fact that he had expected to record the complete album and had been fired. "I don't know if I can devote the time to a group now that I devoted to John and George. So I go in with Starsailor, I do a couple of sides. I perhaps go in with Coldplay and do a couple of sides . . .

"I feel comfortable in the studio. I feel *reasonable*." He stopped for a moment. "Really, I'm not even sure what I want to do. I just know that what I do is better than what anybody else does."

His wristwatch spoke: "*It's six o'clock.*"

"I don't know what to say anymore," he said. He was tired of talking about himself. "I'm scared of interviews because I don't have the answers to a lot of questions."

None of us do, I said.

"I mean, I don't know the answers to why . . . I keep asking myself, What will he ask that I don't know the answers to? I can't even tell you about some of the things from the past because . . ." He fell silent. Then leaned forward intently. "Listen. People tell me they idolize me, want to be like me, but I tell them, 'Trust me, you don't want my life.' Because it hasn't been a very pleasant life. I've been a very tortured soul. I have not been at peace with myself. I have not been happy."

But then, what is happiness? It's not a good woman, Phil Spector said, or a good man. It's not money. It's not hit records. "Happiness is when you feel pretty fucking good and you've no bad shit on your mind." He closed his eyes. "A memory is a curse. Good health, bad memory, that's about as happy as you're going to fucking get, buddy . . ."

Spector was still not drinking. But shortly before Christmas, he was involved in an accident that was to change things.

He was driving himself to visit a friend at her home in Beverly Hills, according to one source. Near his destination, Spector ran off the road and hit a fire hydrant. The car was undriveable. Shaken, Spector walked the rest of the way to the friend's house, where he poured himself a drink. By the time his driver arrived to collect him, Spector had to be helped to the car.

In January, Starsailor began giving interviews to plug the release of *Silence Is Easy*. Asked about Phil Spector's participation in the record, the bass player James Stelfox was quoted as saying that Spector showed Starsailor "how records used to be made" and they had shown him how recordings were made today. How that must have hurt.

At the same time word began to leak out that Paul McCartney would shortly be releasing a remixed version of *Let It Be*, shorn of all Spector's additions and embellishments, and entitled *Let It Be . . . Naked*. After thirty-five years McCartney had finally gotten his revenge.

On February 1, 2003, my interview with Phil Spector was published in the *Telegraph* magazine. The cover line read "Found! Rock's Lost Genius." Thirty-six hours later, Phil Spector walked into the House of Blues and met Lana Clarkson.

30

"I Think I Killed Somebody . . ."

It's an old axiom that actresses die twice in Hollywood, the first time around their mid-thirties, when they can no longer pretend to play young. At the age of forty, Lana Clarkson, an actress who had appeared in some fifteen movies and countless TV shows, had hit a lean time in her career, and was trying to get back on her feet.

For Lana, 2002 had been a particularly difficult year. The movie and television roles that had made her a minor cult star in her twenties, and sustained her through her early thirties, had all but dried up, and her attempts to forge a new career as a comedienne had been sorely hampered by an accident that had resulted in her breaking both of her wrists. By Christmas 2002, in search of employment that would both pay the rent and, she hoped, turn her career around, she had taken a job as the hostess in the VIP room of the Hollywood nightclub, the House of Blues.

She had been named after the Hollywood movie star Lana Turner, a fact that seemed to set her destiny in stone. As a child growing up in the Napa Valley in Northern California she dreamed of being an entertainer, and when the family moved to Los Angeles in 1978, when Lana was sixteen, she began a career in modeling and acting. At the age of twenty she made her film debut in *Fast Times at Ridgemont High*, playing the role of a geekish schoolteacher's improbably beautiful wife. She had one line of dialogue. "Hi."

Her big break came in 1985, in *Barbarian Queen*, a sword-and-sorcery movie produced by Roger Corman, the king of the Hollywood B-movie. Clarkson played the lead role of Amethea, a warrior in a fur leotard, leading an uprising of slaves. It was a part that the statuesque, six-foot-tall Lana seemed to be made for. Corman would later claim that the film—"loaded," according to one approving review, "with action and gratuitous nudity"—was the inspiration for the highly successful television show *Xena: Warrior Princess.*

For Clarkson, the role was the passport to a succession of similarly low-budget, and low-concept, films: *Amazon Women on the Moon, Death-stalker, Barbarian Queen II: The Empress Strikes Back*—spoofy sword-and-sorcery films and formulaic serial-killer pictures, shot on low budgets in Argentina, Mexico and France. She also featured in modest roles in TV dramas and serials. Nobody could pretend these films were art—in her last major role, in Roger Corman's *Vice Girls* ("three beauteous vice cops go undercover as porno actresses to catch a killer"), Clarkson was obliged to utter the timeless line "You're obedient, Russo. I like that in a sex slave"—but in the peculiar parallel universe of schlock movies they made Clarkson a star, bringing her a large and devoted fan base.

Semi-nudity was an almost obligatory requirement of such films, but Clarkson was never comfortable with it. One story tells of her being furious after discovering that some nude publicity stills had been reproduced in a San Francisco paper, and confronting Roger Corman, demanding to know who was responsible. Denying all knowledge, Corman marched Clarkson to the publicity department, where he proceeded to tear a strip off the hapless publicist. When Clarkson was safely out of the door, Corman is said to have turned to the publicist and told him: "Don't send the nudes to California. East Coast and Europe only."

According to her friend Eric Root, Lana "wanted to be a superstar. And she was gorgeous enough."

The self-proclaimed "hairstylist to the stars," Root ran a salon in Beverly Hills and used Lana as a model when she was first starting out. Root was also the longtime hairdresser and confidant of Lana Turner (he would later write a book, *The Private Diary of My Life with Lana*), and he made a point of introducing the veteran Hollywood star to the young ingenue.

"Lana Turner was very dignified and very sophisticated. Lana Clarkson also was very, very elegant. She never acted slutty; she'd cross her legs and the way she would sit . . . Even Lana Turner said to me, 'What a magnificent lady!' And she said, 'What is she doing, Eric?' I said, 'Well, she's trying to be . . .' And Lana Turner said, 'One day I'm sure a movie will be made of me after I'm gone, but Lana Clarkson would be too tall to play me.' When I told Lana Clarkson that, she laughed and said, 'Couldn't I kneel?' "

Clarkson's dream of fame is the oldest story in Hollywood, of course. She worshiped the twin doomed deities of Elvis and Marilyn, and collected Monroe memorabilia, covering her walls with pictures of the star. "This is not to imply that I wish to live the sort of lonely and narcotics-shrouded existence she did," she wrote on her website. "What I love about her is her essence, her work and her commitment to it. She was an ACTRESS with a capital 'A.' " In another posting she added, "We as humans at our deepest level are pure love . . . [Marilyn] through all of her difficulties gave LOVE!"

That's how Lana befriended A. J. Benza. A gossip columnist and the author of a book called *Fame: Ain't It a Bitch*, Benza first met Clarkson in 1998 at a music club called the Backstage in Beverly Hills. He had recently arrived from New York to host a celebrity cable TV show and had moved into an apartment at Normandie Towers in Hollywood where Monroe had once lived. "Lana loved that," Benza says. "She told me she wanted to wake up looking up at the same ceiling that Marilyn had."

Lana took Benza under her wing; got him backstage passes, introduced him around, told him who was important and "who was an asshole." Hollywood, says Benza, is filled with beautiful blondes. "They're like orange trees. But Lana had class. She wasn't a bimbo; she wasn't stupid. She'd been through ups and downs. She knew about life. And she was a good listener; you'd want her at your table."

Another friend, Bill Craig, who ran the MIDEM music festival in Cannes, would call on Clarkson whenever he came to Los Angeles, to help him work the room at music events. "She was polite, intelligent, very smart," he remembers. "Everybody loved her."

Lana knew everybody. She was said to have dated Jack Nicholson and Warren Beatty; and to have partied at film producer Robert Evans's house; she was good friends with Chris Blackwell, the founder of Island Records, and hung out with musicians like Bonnie Raitt and Don Henley. "A guy-girl" is how Benza describes it. "The kind of girl who could sit down and watch the ball game with you, curse with you and drink with you. She was always up for a good time. Lana was intrigued by people with power, people who'd made it—but in this town, who isn't? You can't be here twenty years, when your career is made up of being a six foot tall, blonde, buxom woman, and not have the men come around you. So it was not unusual for Lana to have known Jack, Warren, Bob Evans—those were all her friends."

Answering fans' queries on her website, Lana was careful not to give too much of herself away: "I prefer to keep my love life private!" she wrote in one posting, then hinted teasingly at revelations to come. "As far as past relationships, there have been some great loves (some of them famous), but you'll have to read about them in my book. That won't be completed for a couple of years yet."

She was the kind of girl whom men showered with gifts, flew to parties in Mexico and on the French Riviera. But while there was never a shortage of admirers, one way or another none of these relationships stuck.

"The last time I spoke to her," Eric Root remembers, "I asked her, 'You got a boyfriend?' She said, 'I've got several.' I said, 'Anybody famous?' She said, 'No, but they're trying to be, like me . . .' "

Lana, according to another friend, "really didn't want a significant other stopping her getting what she dreamed of. She was not short of men giving her offers to whisk her away; oil tycoons, this, that and the other. She had no interest. She didn't want to be somebody's arm-piece."

"The thing about Lana," says A. J. Benza, "when she reached her level of fame she was just having too much fun; and all of a sudden she turned around and maybe she was thirty-five or whatever, and in this town that's not the age where a man pins you down and says, 'Let's get out of here, you're mine.' "

By the mid-'90s, Clarkson's film and television career was on the wane. Too old to play warrior queens, she continued to do television commercials and modeling jobs, and she was still in demand at science-fiction and comic conventions, dutifully signing autographs and talking to fans. ("She could have been the head of protocol for the Queen, she was so good with people," says one friend.) But to anybody who asked, she would say that nowadays she considered herself a comedienne.

She devised a stand-up routine, developing a range of comic characters, along the lines of Lily Tomlin or Tracey Ullman, and started working small comedy clubs—the kind of places that book a performer on the condition that they can guarantee an audience of forty or more friends to boost the bar takings. Lana's shows were always full.

In the autumn of 2001 she enrolled for lessons with a Hollywood voice coach, Patrick Fraley, who taught character and cartoon voices, primarily for animation films or TV commercials. Fraley had no idea that Clarkson had had any sort of movie career. "She never mentioned it. She looked good. She didn't look like she was faded and scary. And she was no more needy than most actors."

Lana took two workshops at $350 each and a couple of private sessions at $100—an investment that to Fraley showed serious intent. He thought she had the talent to make a career in cartoon voices, but Lana was more interested in "fine-tuning" the characters and impressions she had worked up for her one-woman show.

"I teach seven hundred students a year," Fraley says, "and I have a sense of who is motivated and who is ambitious—and she was highly ambitious. And one aspect of that was that she was willing to open up even the smallest or most difficult area of performance to get into."

"Most people who come into this city," says one friend, "they chase the dream, it doesn't happen, they give up. But Lana just kept chasing. It was always, 'We're going to be huge, darling; we're going to be huge.' It was always bigger than life."

"She was definitely someone who always saw the glass as half full rather than half empty," says Courtney Kanner. "Someone who always saw the good in things rather than the bad."

Kanner, an aspiring fashion designer, had met Clarkson in a Brentwood hair salon. Kanner was designing cell phone covers sprinkled with diamanté; Clarkson loved them, and according to Kanner immediately threw herself into helping the young designer's career, handing out business cards and featuring Kanner's designs on her website. Lana, she says, "was everyone's best friend," someone who always saw the best in people, sometimes to an almost naïve degree.

As her forties approached, she started taking more care of herself. She had developed an interest in spirituality and started attending the Self-Realization Fellowship Temple in Santa Monica, founded in the 1940s by the Indian swami Paramahansa Yogananda. Set in two acres of woodland around a large lake, the center is an oasis of tranquillity close to the busy Sunset Boulevard. Clarkson would attend regularly for meditation and yoga classes. It was where her funeral service would be held. She also did voluntary work for a charity called Project Angel Food, delivering food to AIDS patients.

Bill Craig remembers arriving in Los Angeles and taking her to "the nicest sushi bar in Hollywood, expensive, the best. She wouldn't touch a piece of fish—she's eating seaweed, she's eating soup, she's eating rice. No alcohol. She never smoked cigarettes. I said, 'What's going on?' And she said, 'I'm really focusing on my career, I really need to get this together.' She knew she had to change her life and her style in order to be taken seriously."

It was shortly after that, in December 2001, that she suffered a freak accident at a family party. As Lana was dancing with some children, a rug slipped under her feet on the wooden floor, and she fell, breaking both her wrists. Medical bills were high, and she was unable to work. But she put on a brave face. Two months after the accident she attended the Grammy Awards in Los Angeles with Bill Craig and his girlfriend. Lana wore an outfit that had been made for her by Courtney Kanner, one arm in a leopard-skin print sling, with her name picked out in rhinestones on the strap. Stepping into her limousine she made sure that Courtney was beside her for the paparazzi pictures. "The Grammys are a big deal for anyone," says Kanner, "but all she did was talk about me and my designs. She didn't take that moment up for herself ever."

On her website, Clarkson maintained a message board, where she would answer questions about her life and career—fans' stuff ("The torture scene in *Barbarian Queen I* is intense and stimulating, you demonstrate great bravery and unwavering courage. How long did the scene take you to shoot?"). Her replies were always sassy, smart and resolutely upbeat.

"I have been blessed to work in an extremely difficult industry," she wrote in September 2002, "but in my opinion I have not even begun to reach my full potential. I have been pounding my head against a Plexiglas ceiling trying to break through to a completely new level for a while now. God willing, this year it will happen. Keep your eye out for a new quality of work from Ms. Clarkson!"

A month later, she was talking of reading for a new TV show, playing the part of a prison warden. It did not materialize.

"I have been around and working continually," she wrote in November. "I just haven't booked myself a series. Then you would hear about me all the time. Unfortunately, that's how my industry is. You're hot when they decide you are! I am working on several new ventures and God willing, I'll finally make that huge breakthru I've been working toward this next year."

But in the absence of acting roles, she needed something else.

Toward the end of December, she applied for the job as hostess in the Foundation Room at the House of Blues. Built in the studiedly ramshackle style of a Mississippi juke joint, the HOB stands on the Sunset Strip, across from the Chateau Marmont hotel. The Foundation Room, or VIP lounge, is frequented mostly by high rollers from the rock and film worlds. Decorated in the style of a maharajah's palace, with ornately carved wooden panels and plush velvet couches, it offers panoramic views across Los Angeles and what the promotional literature describes as "sacred prayer rooms." Membership costs $1,000 a year; champagne, $250 a bottle. Spector was a member and had often attended events there, such as the celebration for Ray Charles's seventieth birthday in 2000.

It wasn't Clarkson's first choice for a job, but friends say she was determined to make the best of it, a way of tiding things over until her acting career picked up. Bill Craig provided a reference. "She was very proud of getting the job," he remembers, "because it was the VIP room, it was associating with people at the top."

A. J. Benza puts it another way. "Taking that job showed a lot of nerve. In this town, if you have a bit of fame, and the fame starts to trickle away, you can hear the people talking and whispering about you. And at forty years old, for Lana to go back to work as a hostess, in a town where she made herself more or less a star, knowing that she would be seeing the same people who knew that her star had faded . . . To me, that's a real strong character."

Clarkson told friends that she enjoyed the work, and she was optimistic it could lead to better things. "I am going to meet people," she told one friend. "They will remember that I am here and it might get me another job."

She would drive in from her home near the beach in Venice, arriving at the HOB at six each evening, and work until 2:00 a.m. The days she had to herself. On February 1, 2003, she made a personal appearance at the Creation Comic Book Convention in Pasadena, signing autographs for fans and posing for pictures. She spoke to her lawyer, who was reviewing contracts for an infomercial that she had been lined up to appear in. Things were looking up. She spent February 2 shopping for shoes with her mother and e-mailing friends, including a reply to a birthday party invitation. "Can't wait," she wrote. "XOXO Lana." That afternoon, shopping with her mother at Nordstrom in the Grove shopping center, she bumped into a friend, Dianne Bennett, a former columnist for the *Hollywood Reporter* who was now running a dating service, Beautiful Women–Successful Men. Bennett had long been pressing Clarkson to send in her picture, but Clarkson had always replied that she wanted to concentrate on her acting. But now, she told Bennett, "I'm finally ready to get married and have a family."

Bennett replied, "I have the perfect man for you," and told Clarkson about a good-looking, successful forty-year-old entrepreneur who lived in Malibu. Bennett promised that she would get in touch the following week. "Be sure and give me a call," Clarkson said as she waved goodbye.

That evening she reported for work as usual at the HOB. At around 1:30 a.m., just as her night was winding down, Phil Spector walked through the door.

The details of what occurred on the evening of February 2, and the early hours of February 3, would emerge over the next two years, from a combination of police evidence, the coroner's report and testimony to the grand jury that would ultimately decide that Spector should stand trial, accused of the murder of Lana Clarkson.

At a few minutes before 7:00 p.m. on February 2, Adriano De Souza drove into the grounds of the Alhambra castle, parked his car in the courtyard at the back of the house, and pulled Phil Spector's new black Mercedes limousine up to the back door.

Spector's regular driver, Dylan, had been given the evening off. De Souza, a Brazilian, was the "relief driver," a position he had held for the past two months. (In fact, his first job had been collecting me from my hotel on the Sunset Strip in Spector's Rolls. We were delayed outside when the car stalled, necessitating a taxi jump-starting us with a pair of leads. I remember De Souza anxiously calling on his cell phone to explain that we would be late. He told me it was his first day working for Spector, and he was keen to make a good impression.)

At 7:00 p.m. Spector walked out of the back door. He was wearing a black shirt and trousers and a white jacket, and carrying a briefcase, which he threw onto the backseat of the car before climbing in himself. Spector had a dinner date with a woman friend, Romy Davis. Romy had been a prom queen at Fairfax—the sort of girl Spector could only gaze on wistfully from afar as a schoolboy. But in recent years they had become friends. De Souza and Spector set off to collect Davis and they drove to the Grill on the Alley, a Beverly Hills restaurant, where Spector and Davis had dinner. Two hours later, Spector dropped off Davis at her home and instructed De Souza to return to the Grill. He had made another assignation: a waitress, Kathy Sullivan, was waiting for him outside. De Souza drove them first to Trader Vic's bar, and then to Dan Tana's restaurant, one of Spector's regular haunts. By now, Kathy was complaining that she was tired and wanted to go home. But Spector evidently did not want the evening to end and insisted they should go on to the House of Blues, where they arrived at 1:30 a.m. According to the police Spector had been drinking alcohol at each stop along the way, consuming three, possibly four daiquiri cocktails, as well as two Navy Grog cocktails, each containing three shots of different kinds of rum. De Souza said he was "slurring his words."

Spector and Kathy went inside. Lana Clarkson was waiting at her post at the entrance of the Foundation Room to greet new arrivals. There was a moment's confusion; Clarkson did not know or recognize Spector, and initially refused to let him in to the members-only area. Spector began to complain loudly, and another House of Blues employee, Euphrates Lalondriz, came to smooth things over, telling Clarkson who Spector was and that he was to be treated "like Dan Aykroyd—like gold." (Aykroyd has a share in the club.) Clarkson apologized to Spector, introduced herself, and then led him and Kathy to a seating area within the Foundation Room known as the Buddha Room.

Spector ordered a shot of Bacardi 151 rum "straight up" from waitress Sophia Holguin. When Kathy ordered only water, Spector grew angry, telling her to "get a fucking drink." Kathy refused, and while Holguin was fetching the order, Spector told Kathy, "That's it—you're going home."

Spector called for Lana Clarkson and told her to walk Kathy to his car and tell De Souza to take her home, then return to collect Spector. Meanwhile, Holguin returned with the order. Spector told her he didn't want "the fucking water" and called for his tab. He had purchased an $8.50 alcoholic drink and a $5.00 water and left a tip of $450. After settling the bill, Spector tried to order another drink, but Holguin told him the bar was closed.

At around 2:00 a.m., Euphrates Lalondriz overheard Clarkson over his headset asking if she could accept an invitation from Spector to have a drink. Lalondriz heard the club manager tell her that she could not drink, but could sit down with Spector. Holguin saw Clarkson walk into the Buddha Room and talk to Spector for a few minutes. She then saw them walk out of the room together. House of Blues employee records show that Clarkson clocked out at 2:21 a.m.

Two minutes later De Souza, who was waiting outside, saw Spector emerge from the club. He seemed to be having difficulty walking, and was being helped by Clarkson. As De Souza opened the car door for him, Spector invited Clarkson to go home with him. She declined. Spector then offered her a lift to her car, which Clarkson accepted. During the drive, Spector continued to press his invitation, "More than once. Two, three times," according to De Souza. Finally, Clarkson relented.

At the House of Blues employee parking lot, Clarkson got into her car. Spector got out of the Mercedes, stumbled over to a stairwell to relieve himself, and then stumbled back to his car. De Souza could smell the strong odor of alcohol coming from the backseat. De Souza and Spector now followed Clarkson to a side street off La Cienega Boulevard where she parked her car.

As Clarkson got into the Mercedes, she leaned forward to De Souza and told him, "This will be quick. Only one drink." Spector turned to her. "You don't need to talk to the driver."

At around 3:00 a.m., the Mercedes drove through the gates of the castle, and pulled to a halt. Spector and Clarkson got out and set off up the eighty-eight steps toward the house. According to De Souza, Spector had some difficulty walking, and Clarkson was "like, grabbing his arm and shoulder and helping him up the stairs." De Souza continued up the drive, parked at the rear of the house, and settled down to wait. Around fifteen minutes later, Spector came out of the back door. According to De Souza "he looks mad" and disoriented. De Souza asked him whether he wanted to collect his briefcase and a portable DVD player that he had left in the car. "No, no, no," said Spector—but then changed his mind and took the DVD player. De Souza followed him into the house and placed the briefcase inside the hall. There was no sign of Lana Clarkson.

For the next ninety minutes or so De Souza waited in the car. Then, shortly before 5:00 a.m., he heard what he would later describe as a soft popping sound. De Souza, who had served in the Brazilian military, thought he recognized it as a gunshot. He got out of the car, but could see nothing amiss and returned to the Mercedes. It was then that Spector emerged from the back door. De Souza again got out of the car. Spector was still dressed in the clothes he had worn that evening—white jacket, black trousers and shirt; in his right hand was a revolver, which he was holding across his body. De Souza could see blood on the back of Spector's hand. It was at that point, according to De Souza, that Spector said, "I think I killed somebody." Looking past him into the hallway, De Souza could see Lana Clarkson, slumped in a chair with blood on her face.

He asked, "What happened, sir?" Spector shrugged and said, "I don't know." He then turned back toward the house. De Souza tried to call 911 on his cell phone, but was so shaken he was unable to make the call. He climbed back into the car and set off back down the drive. Partway down, he stopped and telephoned Spector's assistant Michelle Blaine, leaving a message on her voice mail: "You have to come here. I think Mr. Spector killed somebody." He then continued down the driveway to the entrance and dialed 911.

Spector would later assert that it was he who had called the police— "I called the police"—but according to police evidence the emergency services logged only one 911 call relating to the incident, De Souza's.

De Souza's call, logged at 5:00 a.m. at the California Highway Patrol, Los Angeles Communications Center, quickly became a black comedy of misunderstandings.

ALHAMBRA POLICE: Okay. And your name, sir?
DE SOUZA: Adriano.
ALHAMBRA: Okay. And your boss's name?
DE SOUZA: It's, uh, Phil Spector.
ALHAMBRA: I'm sorry?
DE SOUZA: Phil Spector.
ALHAMBRA: Seal?
DE SOUZA: Spector.
ALHAMBRA: Seal Inspector?
DE SOUZA: Yeah. Phil Spector.
ALHAMBRA: That's his name?
DE SOUZA: Yes.
ALHAMBRA: S-e-a-l?
DE SOUZA: P-h-i-l.
ALHAMBRA: C-h—
DE SOUZA: Spector.
ALHAMBRA: —i-l. Is he Asian or white or—
DE SOUZA: Sorry?
ALHAMBRA: Is he male white or Asian. Is he an Asian person, a Hispanic person, or a white person?
DE SOUZA: No, it's a white person.
ALHAMBRA: And his name is Chil—C-h-i-l?
DE SOUZA: Yeah, P-h-i-l.
ALHAMBRA: Oh, Phil.

DE SOUZA: Phil, yeah.
ALHAMBRA: Phil Spector? Okay . . .

The first police car arrived at the gate of Spector's house, where Adriano De Souza was waiting, shortly after 5:00 a.m., but it would be a further twenty or so minutes before a group of five officers had made a careful approach up the drive and assembled outside the back door of the house. Spector could be seen on the first floor but made his way down the stairs and appeared at the back door. He was no longer wearing the white jacket and his hands were in his pockets. According to Officer Michael Page, he appeared "mildly agitated." An officer told him to raise his hands above his head. Spector did so, then put his hands back into his pockets again and turned to go into the house saying, "You got to come see this." He was again warned to take his hands out of his pockets, and when he refused, Officer Page deployed a Taser dart at him. "It had no effect," said Page. Spector now backed further into the house, pursued by another officer, Brandon Cardella, who knocked Spector against the stairwell. Page, who had followed Cardella into the house, fired another Taser dart, again with no effect, and then wrestled Spector to the ground. (Page would later testify that he had used a Taser four times in his career, and "I am yet to have one work.") After a brief struggle, Page and Officer Jim Hammond managed to handcuff Spector as he lay facedown on the floor.

Then Page looked up and saw the body of Lana Clarkson slumped in a chair. "She was bloody around the face," Page testified before the grand jury, answering questions from the deputy DA Douglas Sortino. "Exact trauma I couldn't tell at the time."

SORTINO: Was she reacting at all to anything that happened in front of her?
PAGE: Nothing.
SORTINO: What did she appear to be?
PAGE: Dead.

"She had what appeared to be a single-entry gunshot wound to the mouth," the police report would state.

Broken teeth from the victim were scattered about the foyer and an adjacent stairway. Lying on the floor under the victim's left leg was a Colt, 2-inch, blue-steel, .38-caliber, six-shot revolver. This weapon had five live cartridges in the cylinder, and under the hammer, a spent cartridge. A check of the weapon serial number via the automated firearms system was negative. There was blood splatter on the weapon.

It was at this point that a fourth officer, Beatrice Rodriguez, came into the house. As she covered the hallway, Officer Rodriguez would subsequently state, she heard Spector say, "What's wrong with you guys? What are you doing? I didn't mean to shoot her. It was an accident. I have an explanation."

That statement was not captured on tape. But immediately afterward Officer Page activated his microcassette recorder and captured the subsequent exchanges between Spector and the police.

"Just ask me and I'll tell you," Spector said as officers held him down. "I'm not Robert Blake . . . I can tell you what happened."

"Only if you want to . . ." Page said.

Spector continued: "If you're gonna arrest me, just tell me what happened . . . Jesus. You know you're acting stupid. Get the fuck off of me! This is stupid. I'm sorry there's a dead woman here. But I'm sorry but this happened. I can explain it, but if you'd just give me a chance . . . You don't have to handcuff me. I can tell you what happened. What's wrong with you people? Jack Maple worked for me. Jesus Christ, the chief of police worked for me . . . I'm sorry this happened. I don't know how it happened, but it happened and I'm sorry this happened. But, excuse me . . . The gun went off accidentally. She works at the House of Blues. It was a mistake. I don't understand what the fuck, you people, is wrong with you. Jack Maple worked for me. He worked for the chief of police. Oh, God. I'm just gonna go to sleep. Would you like me to go to sleep . . . ?

"If Jack Maple were alive, he wouldn't allow this shit to be done . . . excuse me. When I see the damage that's been done—this is the most devastating thing I've ever seen in my life."

As Spector was being held down, other officers continued with their search of the property. The coroner's report would later note that the weapon found under Clarkson's leg was "apparently taken" from a holster, which the police found, also stained with blood, in a drawer in the hall.

Although Clarkson's blood remained in the engraving and in other recessed areas of the weapon, the gun had been wiped off after the shooting. In a powder room off the hall police found a cloth diaper soaked in both water and Clarkson's blood lying on the floor, and a wet hand towel on the sink top. Smears of Clarkson's blood were also found on the back door handle and on the wooden banister leading upstairs "about seven feet west of the victim's remains."

In an upstairs dressing room, thrown on the floor, police found the white jacket that Spector had been wearing that evening; the left sleeve and front of the jacket were covered in a mist-like spray of Clarkson's blood. A search of the house uncovered thirteen other firearms. Ammunition found in a plastic sack upstairs was the same as the bullets in the gun that had killed Clarkson.

In the living room—where I had sat with Spector some six weeks earlier—police noted that "candles had been lit atop a fireplace mantel. The coffee table between two couches had a brandy glass partially filled with alcohol, and atop the table was a Jose Cuervo tequila bottle and a partially empty Canada Dry soft drink."

Two cocktail glasses, one containing trace amounts of alcohol, were found; one on the table in the living room and one on the sink of the powder room adjacent to the rear hallway.

Toxicology tests by the coroner's office would show Clarkson's blood alcohol level to be .12 percent, and she also had "therapeutic levels" of Vicodin—an opiate-based painkiller—in her system.

Paramedics had been waiting at the front gate for almost an hour, and at 6:09 a.m. they were given clearance and proceeded up the long stone steps to the property. At 6:24 a.m. Lana Clarkson was pronounced dead.

Spector was taken to the Alhambra police station for booking, where he arrived at 6:28 a.m. According to the police, he was belligerent and verbally abusive, calling the jailer "a fat ass." He smelled of alcohol and appeared to be intoxicated. But he twice refused to take an alcohol breath test. (A urine sample eventually obtained from Spector thirteen and a half hours after the shooting, during a sexual-assault examination, showed a .08 percent blood alcohol level.)

Spector asked if he could call his lawyer Robert Shapiro and was told he could do so after he had calmed down and cooperated with the jailers and provided booking information. Spector was placed in the interview room, without handcuffs, and an officer, Derek Gilliam, was told to sit with him, but not to ask questions.

Spector, said Gilliam, began to talk about songwriting and some of the big names he had worked with, including George Harrison. By an odd coincidence, Gilliam is the nephew of Terry Gilliam, the film director and Monty Python veteran. He mentioned that his uncle knew Harrison and had been a member of the Monty Python team. "He called me a liar," Gilliam stated, then said, "I basically have the rights to Monty Python."

Spector then began to talk about the events of that night, telling Gilliam there was a dead girl at his house and demanding to know what Gilliam was going to do about it. He then asked Gilliam what had happened at the house. Gilliam responded, "I don't know. I wasn't there."

Spector repeated the question twice, then told Gilliam that Lana Clarkson worked at the House of Blues and that she was a friend of his.

Spector then began telling Gilliam about music groups that he had worked with "such as Bush, Bono, the Beatles," and said he needed to go in order to catch a plane for New York for an upcoming performance with Bono.

It was at this point that Spector suddenly changed the subject and said, "I don't know where she got the gun from but she started waving it around." Spector claimed that he had told her to put the gun down, but she refused. "He said that the young lady began singing his songs, two of them, one being 'Da Doo Run Run' and the other . . . 'You've Lost That Lovin' Feelin',' " [sic] Gilliam stated.

"He said that she took the gun into her hand and basically put it to her head . . . And basically said, 'It went like this, bang,' and he basically fell back into his chair, throwing his head back. And he sat there for about five seconds in that position. He said that she was singing the song and continued with the process. He was real animated about it."

According to Gilliam, Spector re-enacted the scene two or three times, demonstrating the shooting by forming his right hand in the shape of a gun, placing his index finger against the right side of his head and letting his thumb fall as if the hammer of a handgun. The last time, he threw his head back and for a long time didn't move. Gilliam said he was afraid "that maybe he had gone into some form of an attack." Then with an expression that Gilliam described as "a half-slanted smile," "Spector said, 'You don't pull a gun out on me.'

"And then he giggled, like 'huh.' But he said it very quietly and very calmly. He didn't get excited. This was the calmest I had seen him throughout the time that I sat with him."

Spector was then taken for booking, and placed in a holding cell, where he indicated he was ready to talk to detectives. Detective Esther Pineda made her way to the jail, where Spector was still in an apparently agitated state. For some fifteen minutes the conversation between Spector and Pineda rambled inconclusively around Spector's complaints about not receiving telephone calls, and him asking to see Jay Romaine and Michelle Blaine, who had by now arrived at the police station.

Then Pineda asked whether he wanted to talk to Romy Davis, who had called to say that she would contact Robert Shapiro. At this point Spector exploded.

"This is nonsense. You people have had me here for six fucking hours, maybe nine hours. And you have me locked up like some goddamn fucking turd in some fucking piece of shit. And you treat me . . . and then while this person eats and shits and farts. And you have me jerking around. And when somebody comes over to my house who pretends to be security at the House of Blues and comes over to my house . . . and remember I own the House of Blues. Where this lady pretended to work, okay? And then just blows her fucking head open in my fucking house and then comes and . . . and then . . . and you people come around and . . . arrest me and bang the shit out of my fucking ass and beat the shit out of me and then you pretend and arrest me and then pretend like you're fucking Alhambra.

"And the . . . the mayor of Alhambra wants me to have Bono come and sing at the anniversary of . . . bullshit. This is nonsense. This is absolute fucking nonsense. I don't know what the fucking lady . . . what her problem is, but she wasn't a security at the House of Blues and she's a piece of shit. And I don't know what her fucking problem was, but she certainly had no right to come to my fucking castle, blow her fucking head open and [indecipherable] a murder. What the fuck is wrong with you people?"

Pineda tried to interject with "Tell you what I'm going to do."

"Yeah, I'll tell you what I'm gonna do," said Spector. "I'm gonna be fucking . . . somebody's gonna pay for the fucking . . . I have been locked up for the fucking last twelve hours. And you fucking people come in my house and rummage through my fucking house, and you tie me down like a fucking pig and, you know, while somebody's dying there. And you know, and . . . and . . . and . . . and it scared the shit out of everybody . . . while somebody commits suicide."

31

"A Genius Is Not
There All the Time"

At 7:00 p.m. that same day Phil Spector was released from police custody on bail of $1 million. He was allowed to leave the Alhambra police station through a back entrance, to avoid the waiting press. Temporarily unable to return to the castle, he was booked into the Hotel Bel-Air, again through the back entrance.

A few days later, Spector moved back into the castle. The carpets were cleaned and the chair where Lana Clarkson's body had been found was removed.

Meanwhile, a memorial service was held for Clarkson at the Music Box Theatre in Hollywood, where forty years earlier Spector had tried in vain to resurrect the dying career of Lenny Bruce. The service was attended by more than three hundred people, "and there had to be twenty girls," says one observer, "who stood up and said Lana was their best friend."

The man who arrived at Alhambra police station to arrange Spector's release on bail was his lawyer and friend Robert Shapiro. One of America's best-known defense attorneys, Shapiro enjoyed a formidable reputation for smoothness and charm; he was a man who, according to another Los Angeles lawyer, "couldn't find his way out of the box" in a trial but was widely regarded as a peerless negotiator and fixer. It was Shapiro who put together the "dream team," led by the flamboyant Johnnie Cochran, which in 1995 secured O. J. Simpson's acquittal over the double murder of his wife Nicole Brown Simpson and her friend Ronald Goldman.

With the Los Angeles Sheriff's Department apparently in no hurry to formally charge Spector with murder, Shapiro quickly moved to secure expert witnesses for Spector's defense, including the forensic scientist Dr. Henry Lee and the pathologist Dr. Michael Baden, both of whom had testified in the O. J. Simpson case. Shapiro quietly let it be known to the media that Baden had attended the autopsy on Lana Clarkson, where tests had shown that Clarkson had gunshot residue (GSR) on her hands. The results, Baden had apparently told Shapiro, were "not inconsistent with suicide."

In March, two months after Clarkson's death, Shapiro told the Associated Press that "a thorough and accurate investigation" would prove that Spector was "innocent of any crime." Shapiro, it seemed, had been bounced into his statement by an e-mail, sent by Spector himself to friends, and apparently leaked to a local radio station by lawyer Marvin Mitchelson, stating that police had no intention of pressing charges against him. "I hate to use the words I told you so," Spector's e-mail read. "But I did tell you so. After seven weeks of silence, we can say with certainty this will speak for itself, and boy, does it speak volumes." The death, Spector said, would be ruled as "accidental suicide."

In fact, the sheriff's department had made no such decision. Spector, it appeared, had jumped to the erroneous conclusion that charges would be dropped after police had returned his computer. The allegation was immediately refuted by Captain Frank Merriman of the Los Angeles Sheriff's Department, who stated unequivocally that "we believe a crime occurred," and suggested that the e-mail was being circulated to plant the seeds of doubt in potential jurors.

In July, Spector went one step further, giving an interview to *Esquire* magazine in which he described the case as "Anatomy of a Frame-Up." Written by Scott Raab, and conducted largely on a private plane ("four grand an hour") flying Spector from Los Angeles to New York, the piece was a fulsome celebration of Spector's life and genius in which, bizarrely, Lana Clarkson being shot dead in his home was depicted as merely a minor disturbance. Raab dismissed Clarkson as "a chronically aspiring buxom blond B-movie actress/model/comedienne/hostess—a type always common in Hollywood and not unknown in the castle," grotesquely adding that "Whatever her agenda, and however sunny her memory, the chance that, after twenty years of swimming after stardom in Los Angeles, she didn't know exactly what she was up to—and who she was riding with, and why—when she left the House of Blues that night is exactly the same chance she had of becoming Marilyn Monroe: zero.

"I didn't do *anything* wrong," Spector was quoted as saying. "I didn't do anything. I called the police myself. *I called the police . . .*

"She kissed the gun," he went on. "I have no idea why—I never knew her, never even saw her before that night. I have no idea who she was or what her agenda was. They have the gun—I don't know where or how she got the gun. She asked me for a ride home. Then she wanted to see the castle. She was loud—she was loud and drunk even before we left the House of Blues. She grabbed a bottle of tequila from the bar to take with her. I was *not* drunk. I wasn't drunk *at all. There is no case.* She killed herself."

Remarkably, it seemed that Spector was not asked to provide a full account of exactly what had occurred in the period leading up to Clarkson's death, the circumstances in which she had allegedly taken her own life, or what he had been doing at the time. Or if he was asked, he evidently chose not to answer.

Not only did Spector depict himself as the real victim of events—"it's 'Anatomy of a Frame-Up' "—but, the article suggested, he also felt let down by those around him: Marvin Mitchelson, "for speaking with reporters," Robert Shapiro, "for charging him a huge fee," and Nancy Sinatra, "for failing to stand by him."

"You know what she told me?" Spector was reported as saying. "She says, 'My mother told me, Omigod—Nancy, it could've been you.' "

In fact, Spector's relationship with Sinatra seems to have broken up sometime between Christmas 2002 and the Clarkson killing, apparently to the relief of Sinatra's family, who had never approved of the friendship.

Mitchelson had proved a loyal friend, quickly coming to Spector's defense in the aftermath of the shooting, saying that it was inconceivable that he could have killed anybody. But it seems he had made the mistake of talking too much. A few days after the killing, he was quoted in the *Los Angeles Times*, commenting on the fact that Spector had let his bodyguard (Jay Romaine) go. "I can't help thinking that if he still had a bodyguard, none of this would have happened." He went on to talk about a film project that he was supposed to be developing with Spector: the original plan, Mitchelson said, was for the film to end with Spector returning to Abbey Road in triumph with Starsailor. "That was the last scene, the happy ending, the comeback. But now, I just don't know how it's all going to end."

What he clearly did not expect was that it would spell the end of his friendship with Spector. According to Mitchelson's friend and press agent Sy Presten, Spector, believing that Mitchelson was "capitalizing on the tragedy for personal publicity," cut Mitchelson off.

"When news got out about the killing, Marvin was inundated with phone calls from the press, and so was I," Presten recalls. "And we both agreed that Spector was incapable of doing anything like this. Marvin said, 'I've known him for fifteen years, he would never do this.' He said the nicest things about Spector. But after that Spector wouldn't answer his calls, his e-mails or have anything to do with him. And this was the time when Marvin was racked with cancer, which he died of. And Marvin was very hurt by that. He'd never come out and say it. I'd ask, 'Did you hear from Phil?' and he'd say, 'Well, not exactly . . .' It was a terrible shame." (Mitchelson died on September 18, 2004.)

For Spector, the prospect that he might be charged with murder seemed to have little effect on his activities or his appetite. Through the spring and summer of 2003 he was seen dining out at Elaine's in New York with Paul Shaffer and the actor Richard Belzer, and, back in Los Angeles, at both Dan Tana's and the Grill—the restaurants he had visited on the night that Lana Clarkson died—telling anybody who asked that he would soon be exonerated over any blame.

In the castle, he whiled away the hours sending e-mails to friends. Rather than protestations of innocence or cries of existential despair, these tended to take the form of Spector's beloved corny jokes and squibs.

Among them was a sequence of jokes on the theme of "only in America . . ." "Only in America do drugstores make the sick walk all the way to the back of the store to get their prescriptions while healthy people can buy their cigarettes at the front. Only in America do people order double cheeseburgers, large fries and a Diet Coke. Only in America do banks leave both doors open and then chain the pens to the counters."

In September 2003, seven and a half months after the killing, the L.A. County Coroner finally signed off on the autopsy of Lana Clarkson. The report ruled that her death was homicide. Two months later, on November 20, Spector was charged with murder.

Spector was accused of two separate crimes: murder, defined as the unlawful taking of a human life "with malice aforethought," which carried a sentence of fifteen years to life; and the use of a gun in the commission of a violent felony. The second charge was a so-called sentence enhancement that could add as much as ten years to the sentence. Were Spector to be convicted and the sentences served concurrently, he would be facing the prospect of a minimum of fifteen years in a state penitentiary. Under California law a defendant has a right to a speedy trial. But Spector would display no apparent urgency to avail himself of this right. There would be another three and a half years of procedural red tape, obfuscations and prevarications before the case of *The People vs. Phil Spector* would at last come to its conclusion.

In January 2004—just a few weeks after Spector had been formally charged with murder—he fired Robert Shapiro. The background to the dismissal would be revealed six months later, in July, when Spector filed suit (which he ultimately abandoned) against Shapiro and his firm of Christensen, Miller, Fink, Jacobs, Glaser, Weil and Shapiro, claiming that Shapiro and his colleagues had taken advantage of their friendship with Spector "and used his legal plight as an opportunity to unabashedly line their own pockets."

The action claimed that on February 7, 2003, Spector had signed a letter—which the suit described as "vague, ambiguous and confusing"—engaging Shapiro's professional services, with Spector to pay $1.5 million as a nonrefundable retainer. He had made an immediate down payment of $1 million.

The suit noted that Spector and Shapiro had been friends for several years, and that Shapiro was aware that Spector "was under the care of a mental health professional and was prescribed medications for the purpose of stabilizing [his] mental condition." But it claimed that at the time Spector signed the agreement he had not taken his medication for several days and "was laboring under a tremendous amount of mental stress that comes with being arrested for murder."

Shapiro and his colleagues, the suit went on, had not devoted "significant time or energy" to Spector's case; had only a rudimentary understanding of the facts, evidence or issues involved; had "failed to properly store or examine evidence," and also failed to interview key witnesses.

"As a result of Shapiro's representation," it continued, "the prosecution had a year to prepare, while the defense of the case went nowhere"; indeed it was "likely that the 'services' provided by [Shapiro] had actually led prosecutors to file the formal criminal charges."

A billing statement indicated that Shapiro's work on the case had generated only $95,407 in billable time, and this figure, it was alleged, was "grossly inflated." Spector was now seeking the return of the unused portion of the $1 million down payment he had made on the $1.5 million retainer. (According to the suit, Shapiro had asked for the remaining $500,000.) These allegations were vigorously contested by Shapiro. Responding to the suit, Shapiro's attorneys argued that he had provided "stellar representation" for Spector, including pressuring the police for his immediate release from jail out of sight of the media. Shapiro also maintained that Spector was simply "a friendly acquaintance, I have never considered him a close friend."

Changing lawyers is almost de rigueur in California "celebrity trials." For the defendant, there may be any number of sound strategic reasons, but it also has the happy consequence of slowing things down. Unlike a fine wine, criminal cases tend not to improve with age. Witnesses' memories fade, or doubt and confusion sets in to their stories; public indignation and interest begin to pall—at least in some cases.

Michael Jackson had twice changed lawyers before his trial, on charges of molesting a thirteen-year-old boy, began in 2005. Jackson was acquitted. The actor Robert Blake—as Spector would do—changed lawyers no fewer than three times, in the process delaying proceedings for a full two and a half years, before finally going on trial, again in 2005, charged with murdering his wife. He too was acquitted.

To replace Shapiro, Spector hired another, equally high-profile California attorney, Leslie Abramson. If Shapiro's reputation was as a smooth negotiator, Abramson was more renowned for her ferocious powers of attack and persuasion in court. One client, a contract killer, is said to have remarked that "Leslie was so good, for a while there she even had me believing I didn't do it." But curiously, perhaps, she was probably best known for a case that she lost, defending Erik Menendez, who with his brother Lyle was convicted in 1996 of murdering their wealthy parents in their Beverly Hills home. Both are now serving life sentences without possibility of parole. Abramson had been contemplating retirement when Spector approached her. "No other defendant would get me to give up my freedom," she remarked at the time. "No other defendant was someone I considered an idol, an icon, and the definition of cool." Spector, she added, was "fabulous. I could not picture him hurting anyone." She immediately went on the offensive.

For almost a year, the coroner's report into Clarkson's death had been kept on "security hold" at the coroner's office. But in May 2004, a few days before Spector was due to appear in court for a procedural hearing, Abramson leaked a copy of the report to the Associated Press and the *Los Angeles Times*, at the same time releasing a statement that the coroner's ruling that Clarkson's death was "homicide" was based not on the findings of the autopsy but on certain unspecified "information" that originated with the L.A. County Sheriff's Department. "In other words," Abramson stated, "the Coroner's office, without conducting their own follow-up investigation, relied on secondhand hearsay from witnesses of undetermined credibility to make the crucial decision to rule the death a homicide and to reject the obvious implications of the physical examination of the body—that the single gunshot wound suffered by Ms. Clarkson was self-inflicted."

Contained in the report was what appeared to be crucial evidence on behalf of the defense, which seemed to confirm Shapiro's leak of a few months earlier. According to the report, analysis had revealed "several highly specific particles and many consistent particles of gunshot residue on both the right and left hand" (of Clarkson). "Therefore," the report went on, "the decedent may have discharged a firearm or had his [sic] hands otherwise in an environment of gunshot residue."

The DA's office quickly moved to give its own interpretation of the findings. A spokeswoman, Sandi Gibbons, said that the residue on Clarkson's hands could be explained because a gunshot releases a cloud of residue within a three-foot radius. "She could have had her hands on her lap when the gunshot went off and residue would still have been on her hands." Spector, Gibbons went on, also had GSR, and Clarkson's blood, on him. Furthermore, there was evidence that Spector had wiped the gun and moved it after the shooting. The gun was found under Clarkson's left leg, and she was right-handed.

Clarkson, the coroner's report stated, had died from a gunshot entering "front to back and slightly upwards" and lodging in the skull. The weapon was actually "in the mouth" when it was fired: "The entrance wound of the oral cavity to include the tongue shows gunshot residue consistent with close range of fire."

Describing the death scene, it noted that "directly in front of the decedent, next to the stairs" were "two small white objects that appear to be tooth material." Two more fragments were noted "about halfway up on the stairs."

Lana Clarkson's waist-to-ankle black skirt, it stated, had been found in her handbag along with long black dress gloves.

The report went on to note that traces of hydrocodone—better known as Vicodin, a powerful opiate-based painkiller—had been found in Clarkson's bloodstream, along with traces of alcohol. A county coroner pathologist would later testify at the grand jury that the combination of Vicodin and alcohol would "most likely" have made Clarkson "very sleepy."

The report concluded: "It should be noted that there was no history of suicidal ideations of the decedent and there was no suicide note found at the scene."

Police visiting Lana Clarkson's home in Venice after the killing had found her work records laid out neatly on her desk. She was apparently in the midst of filing her tax returns.

"Based on the history, circumstances, law enforcement police reports and autopsy, as currently known," the coroner's report concluded, "the manner of death is homicide."

Three days after the release of the report, Spector appeared in court for a procedural hearing. The occasion quickly turned into a fireworks display. In the course of the hearing, the deputy DA, Douglas Sortino, asserted that police had collected three incidents over the past ten years in which Spector had allegedly threatened women with a gun. Abramson retorted that the DA was playing to the media, and that the women were all liars "who had crawled out from under rocks" turned over by the sheriff's department, and were simply trying to cash in on a high-profile case.

Outside the courtroom Spector could hardly be restrained, interrupting Abramson on several occasions as she staged an impromptu press conference. When Abramson mentioned the coroner's report, Spector interjected, "He works for the sheriff." Abramson tried to shush him—"Phillip, darling . . ."—but Spector plowed on. "He stated in the *L.A. Times* he would not have ruled it a homicide were it not for the sheriff. He said that in the *L.A. Times*."

When Abramson raised the matter of Spector having been Tasered by police in the hall, and "thrown to the ground at the feet of the poor, deceased Ms. Clarkson—," Spector again interrupted. "Broken nose and two black eyes, and 50,000 volts of electricity shot through me, unarmed, inviting the police into my house . . ." (This conflicted with the statement by Officer Page that the Taser had actually failed on both occasions.)

A few minutes later, Spector erupted again when Abramson was asked how the defense would deal with Adriano De Souza's claim that he had heard Spector say "I think I killed somebody."

De Souza, said Abramson, was "sitting inside a closed car, with the radio on . . ."

"Asleep . . ." interjected Spector.

"Asleep . . . Phillip, please, darling. I do wish you wouldn't say anything," said Abramson, adding to reporters, "You can't stop a starring talent from being a starring talent, you just can't! But it's okay, I don't mind."

SPECTOR: I should stop now?
ABRAMSON: You have to stop me, darling, and I have to stop you.

De Souza's native language, Abramson went on, was Portuguese. "He is not perfect in his English. I will not say he is illiterate, he is not. I will not say he is stupid, he is not . . ."

SPECTOR: But he is illegal!
ABRAMSON: Well, that's a different issue.
SPECTOR: Yeah, he's an illegal alien. And he was threatened with deportation.
ABRAMSON: Exactly. He is undergoing deportation proceedings but the district attorney's office has interceded on his behalf . . .

At the end of the conference Spector exploded again, referring to one of the prosecutors as "the one who proves you have children through anal sex," before again being cut short by Abramson saying, "Phil, I get to be nasty, you don't."

If Spector's outbursts had occasioned a certain *froideur* between him and Abramson, matters could hardly have been improved a few days later when Spector again found himself in trouble in a bizarre incident in which he and his new chauffeur, Tobie Wheeler, attempted to put each other under citizen's arrest, following a fight over what police described as their "business relationship." Both were arrested for investigation of misdemeanor battery.

Rumors now began to surface of discontent in the Spector camp, and were confirmed in August, when, after barely eight months as Spector's counsel, Abramson abruptly resigned, after discovering that Spector had been talking with yet another high-profile defense attorney, Bruce Cutler—best known as the longtime attorney of convicted Mafia boss John Gotti, the so-called Teflon Don. Cutler, whom Spector described as "a genius," had successfully defended Gotti in three trials, before he was finally convicted on racketeering charges in 1992. (He died in prison ten years later.) Explaining her resignation, Abramson said she and her associate Marcia Morrissey had been taken by surprise when Cutler filed a motion to take over the case while Abramson was out of the country.

"We were put in an untenable position," Abramson said. "If we wanted to be ethical and competent, we had to resign." Cutler stated that he had been engaged as Spector's "attorney and confidant" the previous January. "Leslie and Marcia were brought on in February and they quit in July. They just jumped ship, and I had to take control of the ship and bring it in into port."

Cutler is famous for his booming voice, finger-jabbing theatrics and intimidating demeanor. His habitual strategy, he once boasted, is "to pulverize, to eviscerate [his opponent's case]. That's my defense—attack." One reporter noted that, on occasion, talking to Cutler, "you get the sense that he is about to grab your throat with both hands and pop your head off with his thumbs."

His appointment seemed to have had the effect of buying Spector more time. In September he was granted a court delay in scheduling what might, in normal circumstances, have been the next stage in the proceedings—a preliminary hearing. This is where a judge listens to arguments from both the prosecution and defense, and then decides whether there is enough evidence for the case to go to trial.

However, in order to speed proceedings along, it is within the gift of the DA to opt instead for a grand jury—a sitting jury of "community stalwarts" who consider a scaled-down version of the prosecution case behind closed doors and decide whether the evidence connecting the accused to the crime "is not beyond a reasonable doubt." In a preliminary hearing witnesses can be interrogated by a defense attorney—a useful device, since in the trial itself any anomalies and contradictions in their testimony can be pounced on to undermine their credibility. However, no defense attorney is permitted in the grand jury room. Defense attorneys often claim that grand juries favor the prosecution, and "would indict a ham sandwich" if the prosecutor told them to.

In September, Spector's preliminary hearing was waived, and he was indicted by a grand jury, finally paving the way for the murder trial itself to begin. Grand jury testimony is usually made public, but Spector's lawyers immediately appealed to have it sealed. In a bizarre courtroom exchange over the currency of fame, they argued that such was Spector's renown as a "musical icon all over the world" that the testimony would inevitably influence any future jury. In a riposte that must have wounded Spector's ego more than anything, the DA countered that most of Spector's hits had been made in the '60s and '70s and that therefore "most people who came of age after that period have no idea of who he is." Spector's appeal was turned down, and the judge ruled that the testimony should be made public.

Spector immediately called foul. After appearing in court to enter a not-guilty plea, he dramatically addressed reporters outside the courthouse, likening the district attorney, Steve Cooley, to Hitler and accusing Cooley "and his storm-trooping henchmen" of conspiring to deny him California's constitutional right to a preliminary hearing.

"Instead," Spector went on, "he secretly, as fascists would, went to a secret grand jury, to seek, and get an indictment. Why? Is anyone about to flee the jurisdiction? The only one involved in this case, I know, who is seeking to flee the jurisdiction, is the district attorney himself, who longs to get on an airplane to Sacramento to become the attorney general of California."

By not having a preliminary hearing, Spector argued, his expert witnesses, Dr. Henry Lee, Dr. Michael Baden and Dr. Cyril Wecht—"three of the most respected forensic scientists, pathologists and coroners in the world"—had been prevented from testifying. All, Spector said, had examined the coroner's report "and concluded, beyond a reasonable doubt, that the deceased's wounds were consistent with that of a self-inflicted wound"; he claimed that these three eminent coroners would not have ruled it a homicide.

"Why does the district attorney not want that evidence brought forth to a judge and to the public? And why does he not want the judge and the public to know that the deceased was legally intoxicated on the drug Vicodin and alcohol at the time she took her own life? And that her DNA was found on the gun, not mine; and that my fingerprints were not on the gun; and that Dr. Henry Lee found no 'crime scene' in my home on the morning of February 3, 2003, and that the gun the deceased used to kill herself was not owned by me, nor registered to me. Ask yourself why, and you'll see why I am not getting a preliminary hearing."

Spector further urged "fellow artist" Governor Arnold Schwarzenegger to "stop this miscarriage of justice . . . so I, and my attorney, Mr. Bruce Cutler, can put an end to this travesty of justice, once and for all, and I can get on with my life."

In fact, Spector was wrong; under California law, a defendant is not guaranteed a preliminary hearing; only a trial by jury, once indicted. But his outburst had the effect of keeping his declaration of innocence in the public eye, and portraying him, not Lana Clarkson, as the victim of horrendous circumstance.

In January 2005, the grand jury testimony was finally made public. Contained in the five volumes of 1,000 pages was the most complete accounting thus far of the events of the night of Lana Clarkson's death and the prosecution case against Spector. They included police accounts of Spector's behavior and his statements at the time of his arrest, expert forensic evidence, and testimony about Lana Clarkson. Among the thirty-one witnesses who gave evidence were the three women cited earlier by Douglas Sortino, describing incidents in the past in which Spector had allegedly threatened them with firearms.

Deborah Strand told of an incident at a party in Beverly Hills in 1999, when Spector allegedly flicked cigar ash at her dog after it had jumped up at him and then, when Strand asked him to leave, pointed a handgun at her right cheek. More significant would be the testimony from two other women, Dorothy Melvin and Stephanie Jennings.

Melvin, who had worked as Joan Rivers's personal manager, stated that she had dated Spector sporadically from 1989 to 1993, seeing him between five and ten times a year, mostly when Spector was visiting New York. On July 2, 1993, Melvin said, she visited Spector for the first time at his home in Pasadena. They spent the evening playing pool and listening to music, Spector consuming almost a whole bottle of Smirnoff vodka, Melvin drinking nothing. At around midnight she fell asleep on the sofa. At about 5:00 a.m. she awoke, went outside and found Spector pointing a handgun at her new car that was parked in the driveway. When she went to confront him, she alleged, he struck her with the back of the hand that was holding the gun and told her to "get the fuck back in the house." Inside, Spector sat on a staircase in the foyer, pointing the gun at her, repeatedly demanding that she undress and go upstairs to the bedrooms. When Melvin didn't immediately respond, she alleged, Spector hit her again. He then accused her of searching his house, "snooping" and "stealing things," and took her purse and went through it. When, at last, he ordered her out of the house, Melvin said, she ran sobbing to her car and drove to the locked gate. "I heard him running down the drive, and then I heard the pump of a shotgun," she said. When she turned around to look she could see Spector pointing the shotgun at her. Eventually Spector opened the gate and Melvin made good her escape. Outside, she called the police, who came to the house and handcuffed Spector in the kitchen. Melvin was able to retrieve her purse, but declined to press charges, she explained, because she did not want to bring Joan Rivers's name into the newspapers.

The following day, she alleged, Spector left threatening messages on her answering machine, complaining that she had called the police on him. "He had Marvin Mitchelson ready to sue me."

(Joan Rivers recalls another incident at a Christmas party she threw where both Melvin and Spector were present. "He got angry," says

Rivers, "and pulled a gun on Walter Cronkite's daughter. We had a security guard who got him out very quickly. That was the last time I saw him, going down the elevator in his little shoes with lifts. He was escorted out of my building. I have a very nice neighbor on the ground floor, an elderly lady who was dressed in Chanel. On his way out, she said to him 'Merry Christmas.' He said to her 'Fuck you.' Later I said, 'Cindy, you could have been shot. You could have been in a Chanel suit that was black, white *and* red.' ")

Stephanie Jennings, a photographer, testified that she had first met Spector in April 1994 at a music awards show in Philadelphia and then a few months later in New York, when she had spent the night with him in his suite at the Carlyle Hotel. In September 1994 he invited her to come to Pasadena. She stayed the night, but in the morning when she wanted to leave, she alleged, Spector locked the doors and refused to let her go. He then left. Jennings contacted Spector's assistant Paulette Brandt, who advised her to wait Spector out. Jennings said she remained in Spector's bedroom for most of the day, until he finally returned and let her go.

Jennings next met Spector at the induction ceremony for the Rock and Roll Hall of Fame in 1995. Spector, she said, paid for her room at the Carlyle Hotel, but at the party that night he drank heavily, becoming increasingly obnoxious. She eventually went to her room alone. At about 4:00 a.m., Spector's bodyguard appeared at her door and told her Spector wanted her to join him. When she refused, Spector himself came to her room, and when she again refused his request to join him, sat in a chair in front of the door with a gun in his hand, refusing to let her leave. Jennings used the hotel phone to dial 911, Spector apparently thinking she was calling her mother. "He said, 'You can call your mom. She can't do anything,' " Jennings testified. After the call, Spector left the room. When the police arrived, Jennings told them she did not want to press charges and left.

The testimony also provided compelling forensic evidence that would prove highly significant in building the case against Spector.

Looking at the question of the gunshot residue found on Spector and Lana Clarkson, Christine Pinto, a Los Angeles Sheriff's Office (LASO) criminalist, and an expert in GSR, said that it was possible for a person to fire a gun and not have residue on their hands—a crucial point pertaining to the relatively small amount found on Spector, one particle on each hand. Pulling one's hands in and out of one's pockets several times would easily dislodge particles, she said; and about 90 percent would fall off within the first hour just by normal use of the hands. The amount isn't important, she said, only the fact that it's there.

Steven Dowell, a criminalist for the coroner's office, testified that the GSR on Clarkson could have come from her putting up her hands in a defensive gesture, from her wrapping her hands around the cylinder of the gun in an attempt to push it away, or even if her hands had been in her lap. The pattern of GSR makes a cloud of about three feet anywhere from three to fifteen feet in distance, he said, and most of the particles fall downward.

Most critical was the testimony of Lynne Herold, an LASO forensic scientist, since it seemed to establish that Spector was standing in front of Lana Clarkson when the gun was fired. Herrold determined that the gun had been fired from the normal, upright position, rather than turned to the side (as might be expected in suicide), and that the "mist-like spray" of blood found on Spector's white jacket could only have come from the backflow of bullet gases from the mouth, and put Spector "within two or three feet" of the discharging weapon.

Herrold had examined the gun and found evidence that someone had wiped blood off it, but leaving some inside the cylinder and on the remaining bullets. She said it was possible that the cloth, or diaper, as she described it, found in the bathroom had been used to wipe the gun after it had been fired. This diaper was identical to others found with Spector's guns upstairs: such diapers were ordinarily used to clean guns. Herrold thought it was possible that someone had tried to wipe the blood from Lana Clarkson's face, because there were obvious smears on it. Someone had moved Clarkson's head in trying to wipe the blood, she believed, and it was possible that some of this blood had been trans-ferred to the diaper found in the bathroom—in fact, that the diaper had been used to wipe Clarkson's face.

Louis Pena, the pathologist at the L.A. County Coroner's Office who had performed the autopsy on Lana Clarkson, said the amount of Vicodin in Clarkson's system was at "the lower end of the therapeutic level," and stated that the combination of alcohol and Vicodin "can make you sleepy in general." Pena also stated that he had found bruising on Clarkson's body—on the right hand, right forearm, right lower leg and upper right thigh. A bruise on the back of her left hand was "acute." The bruising, Pena thought, had occurred anywhere "from zero to four or five hours" before her death, not a day or so earlier. Asked to explain how the bruising might have occurred, Pena replied, "I will decline."

Spector made no comment on the grand jury testimony. But Bruce

Cutler described it to this reporter as "very deceptive, one-sided and biased. Putting this poison in the public domain is for one purpose and one purpose only: to try and paint Phil in a negative light and to influence a potential jury pool. It's inherently unfair."

Everything the defense's own forensic experts had found, Cutler went on, was consistent with a self-inflicted gunshot wound. "I don't want to get into the drugs and the liquor in the lady's system. I don't want to get into the gunplay. I don't want to get into the fact that Phil's fingerprints are not on that gun, and that gun was not registered to him and that's not his gun. Where is the motive for this crime? There is none."

Spector's "so-called confession," Cutler told me, was "not true." De Souza was "not facile" in the English language, and there had been no confession to the police officer Beatrice Rodriguez.

"It's another lie, Mick. How would you like it if somebody died in your house and you were famous and twelve to fifteen policemen came in and beat the shit out of you and then made up stories about what you did and didn't say?"

Was he saying the police had made it up?

"I'm saying there is no memorialized evidence of this. It's unfounded and untrue." Spector, he said, maintained his innocence. "He didn't kill the woman." And the case would go to trial "unless [the judge] dismisses it for prosecutorial misconduct and some of the shenanigans they've pulled. And we're going to win."

Later that same month, on January 31, 2005, Donna Clarkson, Lana's mother, filed a civil lawsuit against Spector, alleging wrongful death, negligence and battery against her daughter, and seeking "punitive and exemplary damages according to proof." It was necessary to file the suit, the Clarkson family's lawyer Roderick Lindblom explained, before February 3, 2005, based on California's two-year statute of limitations for wrongful-death actions. The suit would not be heard until after the criminal trial.

In the midst of his legal tribulations, Spector had acquired the most improbable of new companions—a girlfriend forty years his junior. According to her website, Rachelle Short—or Chelle as she liked to be known—was a "lead singer/songwriter/trombone player" who had worked with various artists, including Savage Garden and Slim Jim Phantom of the Stray Cats, as well as performing at televised NASCAR and NHRA events. Not mentioned on her website was an uncredited part in a Joel Schumacher film, *Tigerland*, and a spell working as the downtown L.A. sales representative for the ABB label company ("Ordering labels . . . as easy as applying one!"). Photographs of Short showed a pert, pretty blonde—some bore a distinct resemblance to Lana Clarkson. According to a lawsuit later launched by Michelle Blaine, his personal assistant, Short had originally been employed by Spector as Blaine's assistant; however, it seems that Spector and Short quickly formed a relationship. The mood between Blaine and Short grew progressively strained.

In March 2005 Spector threw a party at the Dolce Vita restaurant in Beverly Hills to announce his engagement to Rachelle. Among the forty or so guests were old friends including Nino Tempo, Don Randi and Dan and David Kessel, as well as a healthy sprinkling of new friends—Spector's numerous lawyers and their wives.

Within a few months of the engagement, Michelle Blaine had left Spector's employ. It would be another piece in what was already an increasingly complicated jigsaw.

At the same time, Spector again went on the offensive, giving an interview to BBC TV, as part of a tabloid documentary series entitled *Secret Hollywood*. In the interview, conducted in a Los Angeles hotel, Spector spent almost an hour talking about his music and his career, all clearly designed to boost his pedigree in advance of the case. The BBC, however, chose to broadcast only the three or four minutes during which he spoke of the killing.

Describing his arrest, Spector was at his most self-righteously indignant. "They behaved like cowboys," he said. "I had no weapon. I'm five foot five. They came in with weapons drawn. There wasn't one of them under six foot tall. There was not a medic to be seen . . .

"They Tasered me with 50,000 volts of electricity . . . the police manual says you never do that to a subject unless he is violent or uncontrollable . . .

"A tragedy happened, but it could have happened in anybody's house. It's not for me to explain why. She. Took. Her. Life. It's only for me to explain that I had nothing to do with it. And I didn't.

"This prosecution is bogus. I mean, it has to be because of who I am. It has to be because I live in a castle. It has to be a frame-up, because it's not based on real evidence. I had nothing to do with her death, and three coroners have stated that. Case closed. Move on. You know, forget Phil Spector. Forget the castle. Forget rock and roll. Forget all that."

Even some of Spector's friends were shocked at his attitude toward Clarkson's death, his apparent absence of sympathy for Clarkson or her bereaved family. The death of Lana Clarkson had become first and foremost another example of the ongoing persecution of Phil Spector, further confirmation of his own martyrdom. It was Phil's Lenny Bruce moment.

On May 23, 2005, Spector was back in court again for a hearing on a prosecution motion to admit into the trial evidence from women claiming he had pulled guns on them in the past. Again Spector was having to deal with the allegations made by the prosecution witnesses without the opportunity at that stage of cross-examining them or giving his account of the incidents. This included the testimony from Dorothy Melvin and Stephanie Jennings that had already been part of the grand jury proceedings, as well as additional testimony from two women, Dianne Ogden and Melissa Grosvenor.

Spector walked into the courtroom to a ripple of disbelieving laughter. For previous hearings, Spector had erred on the side of conservatism, invariably appearing in a suit and forsaking the shoulder-length Louis Quinze wig for less ostentatious models. But for this most crucial of appearances, he had chosen to wear a new concoction—a permed, blond Afro, which towered nine inches above his head, and which, with his tinted glasses, lent him the appearance of a surrealist comedy turn. Taking his seat in the court, Spector seemed indifferent to the amusement his appearance had caused.

In the new evidence, Dianne Ogden stated that she had first met Spector in 1982 and dated him sporadically over the years until 1987, when she became one of his paid assistants. The following year, she claimed, she returned to his Pasadena home after a dinner date. Spector had been drinking. At 2:00 a.m. Ogden said she wanted to leave. Spector, she alleged, began to scream profanities at her, locked the door and then pointed a handgun at her face, touching the muzzle to her skin. "Afraid for her life," Ogden agreed to spend the night with Spector. When he woke up next morning, she claimed, he acted as if nothing had happened, and she said nothing about the incident to him.

Two weeks later, she claimed, she organized a dinner party at Spector's house for Allen Klein and a number of other guests. Afterward, as she prepared to leave, Spector became angry and came after her with what she described as an Uzi-type assault rifle, chasing her to her car, before she was able to make good her escape. She never returned to Spector's home again.

Melissa Grosvenor stated that she had met Spector in New York in 1991 at a party and subsequently flown to see him in Los Angeles, booking in to a hotel. After dinner they returned to Spector's home, but when Grosvenor tried to leave, Spector pointed a gun at her head and began to yell and swear at her. Terrified, Grosvenor remained sitting in her chair as Spector hovered over her with the gun. She eventually cried herself to sleep. She was woken next morning by Spector tapping her leg and asking if she wanted to go for breakfast. Grosvenor agreed, believing it was her chance to get out of the house. He later dropped her back at her hotel. She returned to New York and never saw him again.

American law usually prohibits prosecutors from introducing evidence of "prior bad acts" to show that a defendant had a propensity for committing a crime. But such evidence can be allowed to demonstrate a pattern of conduct. In court, Douglas Sortino argued that Spector had used guns to intimidate people "again and again and again," and that the evidence would demonstrate "the absence of accident or mistake" in the killing of Clarkson.

Bruce Cutler countered by disparaging the four women as "gold diggers" and "toadies" who had taken advantage of "one of the greatest music icons in the last fifty years," and described the prosecution as "desperate" and guilty of "character assassination."

But Judge Larry Fidler was apparently unmoved by Cutler's argument. The evidence from Melvin, Jennings, Grosvenor and Ogden, he said, went "to the People's theory of the case" that Spector shot Clarkson in anger when she wanted to leave his mansion. However, Fidler rejected six other incidents, including the two misdemeanor convictions on gun charges from the 1970s; the claim by Deborah Strand that Spector had held the barrel of a gun against her cheek at a party in 1999, and an account of the 1977 incident when Spector had allegedly pulled a gun on Leonard Cohen ("Leonard, I love you . . .") in the studio.

Outside the courtroom, Spector made a brief statement to waiting reporters, veering into the third person: "Mr. Spector never pulled a gun on any of these women." His denial was submerged in the tide of media ribaldry about what quickly became known as "the Wall of Hair." On his talk show that evening, Jay Leno commented that Spector "looks like he already got the electric chair." The erstwhile Tycoon of Teen, the greatest record producer ever in rock and roll, had now become a figure of ridicule.

A month later, at the annual awards presentation at the Songwriters Hall of Fame in New York, Spector's greatest creation, "You've Lost

That Lovin' Feelin'," was awarded the ultimate accolade of the Towering Song Award. Bill Medley received the award. Spector was not in the
audience.

Having failed to exclude the evidence of "prior bad acts" from the
prosecution case, Bruce Cutler now set about attempting to suppress
perhaps the most potentially damaging evidence against Spector—his
alleged admission to police officer Beatrice Rodriguez that "I didn't
mean to shoot her. It was an accident."

Cutler claimed that police had violated Miranda rights by not cau-
tioning Spector, and that he had made his statements when he was
intoxicated, suffering from lack of sleep, and experiencing symptoms of
prescription-drug withdrawal.

Spector was back in court on October 27 to hear the judge's ruling,
accompanied by a retinue of bodyguards and Rachelle, clutching his
arm, according to one witness, "like Phil was gonna fall off his shoes."

The extravagant Afro wig had now been replaced by a more conservative, blond-tinted and permed hairstyle. Furthermore, it appeared
from pictures that in the five months since his last appearance Spector
had undergone plastic surgery, his sagging face now tightened to resem-
ble a mask.

In court, Cutler sought to undermine Rodriguez's statement as "only
the bare recollection of a woman doing her job with all this chaos and
danger and violence around her." What Spector had most likely said,
Cutler went on, was "I didn't shoot her. It was an accident."

Cutler claimed that police had "crashed" through Spector's home
"like storm troopers," attacked him, hog-tied him, Tasered him and
"figuratively punched him around until he said something."

Furthermore, he argued, at the time of his arrest Spector was suffering from withdrawal symptoms from seven prescription drugs, "which
could include hallucinations, forgetfulness, serious fatigue, and/or slurring."

These medications were Neurontin, Topamax, Prozac, Loxitane,
Klonopin, Prevacid and tetracycline. Put simply: Neurontin controls
seizures and manages pain; Topamax prevents migraines; Prozac and
Loxitane are both antidepressants; Klonopin is also used to control
seizures, and to relieve anxiety; Prevacid treats excessive stomach acid,
and tetracycline is an antibiotic.

"I am informed and believe," Cutler went on, "that once the defendant was taken into custody at his home, his requests for this medication
were either refused or ignored by Alhambra police officers."

But Judge Fidler was unimpressed by Cutler's arguments. Spector, he argued, "was treated a lot better than most people." He ruled that all of the statements that Spector made to authorities on the night of the murder were admissible because they were voluntarily offered and he did not need to be read his "Miranda rights" because he was never interrogated.

Fidler also granted a prosecutor's motion to rule inadmissible Spector's statements to officers Gilliam and Pineda on the morning of his arrest, in which he'd claimed that Clarkson had killed herself. These were self-serving hearsay, the prosecution argued, and the judge seemed to agree. "They did nothing to encourage him to talk. They did nothing to get him to talk."

The implication of this ruling was to make it impossible for anyone other than Spector himself to say that Clarkson had taken her own life, and Spector would have to say it from the witness stand—not necessarily a place his lawyers might advise him to be. At the same time, Cutler also tried to suppress the admission of crucial police evidence about the other firearms found at the castle, restricting it simply to the gun that had killed Lana Clarkson. The existence of the other weapons, Cutler argued, was irrelevant and would be used by the prosecution only to show that Spector was "the type of person who surrounds himself with guns."

According to the DA's submission, police had found thirteen firearms in Spector's home, in addition to the murder weapon, although two—an air pistol and a blank gun—were dropped from evidence.

The .38-caliber Colt Cobra revolver that had killed Lana Clarkson was loaded with five live rounds and one discharged round under the hammer. Four of the live rounds, as well as the discharged one, were Smith & Wesson .38 Special +P rounds—a relatively obscure, high-velocity .38 ammunition that had not been manufactured in more than ten years. The sixth round was a more common Speer .38 Special round.

In the master bedroom on the first floor, detectives found five guns. These included two Smith & Wesson .38s, both loaded with the same unusual .38 Special +P rounds found in the murder weapon. Also found were a Browning 9 mm semi-automatic pistol; a Star .25-caliber semi-automatic pistol; and a High Standard 12-gauge pump-action shotgun.

In the same room, detectives also recovered a Ziploc bag containing eight live rounds of the same .38 Special +P ammunition found in the death gun, as well as an ammunition box containing other live rounds, including one live Speer .38 Special round and two live .38 Special +P rounds.

In an upstairs office, detectives found six more handguns: a

.38-caliber Colt Army revolver; two .38-caliber Colt Detective Special revolvers, one loaded; a Smith & Wesson .38-caliber revolver; and a High Standard .22-caliber revolver. Police also found some seventy rounds of live ammunition in a box and a plastic tub, including thirty-three Speer .38 Special rounds and two more .38 Special +P rounds.

Checking into the histories of the firearms, police discovered that two of the guns—the High Standard .22 revolver and the High Standard shotgun—had been purchased by Spector in 1967 and 1972 respectively. Five of the guns—the two Smith & Wesson revolvers found in the office; one of the Colt Detective Special revolvers found in the office; a Smith and Wesson revolver found in the master bedroom and the Browning pistol found in the master bedroom—had been purchased by Spector's old friend Nino Tempo. Tempo told investigators he had bought the guns in the 1970s and subsequently sold them to Spector. These private-party transactions had predated modern firearms-reporting laws and were not recorded.

The remaining five, including the weapon that had killed Lana Clarkson, had incomplete histories. The second Colt Detective Special found in the office had been purchased by a Dr. Brian Alpert from a pawnshop in Kentucky in August 1974, and there were no further records of ownership. The Colt Army revolver had been manufactured in 1920, and no further records existed. One of the Smith & Wesson revolvers found in the master bedroom had been purchased by a Joseph Surgent in April 1975, and no further records existed; and the same was true of the Star .25-caliber pistol, which had last been logged as being shipped to a Texas gun dealer in 1965. The Colt Cobra that had killed Clarkson had been shipped from Colt to a Texas gun dealer in May 1971, and there were no further records of ownership after that.

Douglas Sortino argued that admission of all this evidence was crucial to the prosecution case. Spector had always maintained that the gun was not his and that he had no idea where Clarkson had gotten it from. That's what he had told Officer Derek Gilliam while he was cooling off in the Alhambra police station on the morning of his arrest, and he repeated that assertion in his interview with *Esquire* magazine—"I don't know where or how she got the gun."

Establishing that Spector owned the murder weapon was "absolutely essential" to establishing homicide, Sortino argued. Once that had been proved, the jury, in order to conclude that Clarkson had killed herself, would have to believe that she had come unprepared to kill herself to a home she had never visited before, but for some reason decided to commit suicide, looked around for the means to do so, and just happened to find a loaded revolver nearby.

It was clear from all Spector's statements, Sortino argued, that his defense would try to suggest that Clarkson had brought the Colt with her and then killed herself. To be successful, Spector need only raise reasonable doubt about the ownership of the gun. But the fact that there were eleven other firearms in the house, eight of them revolvers similar to the murder weapon; that three of them were loaded (like the murder weapon), and two with the same Smith & Wesson .38 Special +P ammunition that made up five of the six rounds in the Cobra—all tended to suggest that the murder weapon belonged to Spector. The additional loose rounds of Smith & Wesson .38 Special +P ammunition found upstairs, as well as the loose rounds of Speer .38 Special ammunition (the same ammunition as the sixth round in the Cobra), further reinforced the suggestion that the gun belonged to Spector, as did the fact that two of the guns found upstairs were housed in Hunter-brand holsters—the same company that manufactured the empty holster found in the bureau next to Clarkson, and that fit the murder weapon.

Finally, the fact that only two of the eleven weapons found were actually registered in Spector's name would suggest there was no inconsistency in the murder weapon also not being registered in his name. Indeed, Spector's habit of buying firearms through unrecorded private-party transactions—as he did with Nino Tempo—showed that he was actually more likely to own weapons that, technically, were not registered to him. Fidler, it seemed, did not go all the way to accepting this argument. He ruled that the only weapons that could come into evidence were those containing ammunition that matched the ammo found in the gun that killed Clarkson—i.e., the two Smith & Wesson .38-caliber handguns found in the master bedroom.

Fidler also ruled that the state could use in evidence the pump-action shotgun, since it was the same type of weapon that Dorothy Melvin claimed she had been threatened with in 1993, which gave her story credibility.

In another setback for Spector, the judge also refused to grant the defense motion to rule as inadmissible the testimony of two previous incidents involving Spector and guns—the incident in 1972 when he had threatened a woman in the Daisy club on Rodeo Drive, and was arrested; and the incident in 1975 at the Beverly Hills Hotel when he had threatened a valet parking attendant.

The 1975 incident, Sortino argued, was "just the beginning of a long series of events" in which Spector "would resort to firearms-related violence against men and women if he doesn't get what he wants."

The prosecution had already been barred from using these incidents in their case-in-chief, but having them as "admissible testimony" meant that if Spector tried to argue from the stand that he was a peaceable man who had always hated guns, they could be used to rebut his testimony.

Everything, it seemed, was now ready to go to trial—but with one hitch. Bruce Cutler was scheduled to appear in federal court on another case, defending two former NYPD detectives accused of being Mafia hitmen. Judge Fidler now set two alternative trial dates: the first, within ten days of January 30, 2006; or alternatively, if Cutler was unavailable, within thirty days of April 24.

Through the spring and early summer of 2005, relations between Spector and his personal assistant Michelle Blaine seemed to go from bad to worse. Blaine was seen at the castle less and less. "It was," one friend says, "as if Rachelle was taking over."

In September it became apparent just how bad things had become when Spector launched a lawsuit against Blaine, alleging that she had embezzled money from him. In his declaration to the court, Spector claimed that he had discovered that Blaine was making unauthorized withdrawals from his personal bank accounts, and that she had confessed to erroneously spending hundreds of thousands of dollars of his money, and promised to pay him back the "stolen money." He further alleged that Blaine had gone to his accountant and secured a $425,000 loan from his pension plan without his knowledge and deposited the money into two limited-liability companies she controlled. All told, Spector stated, he believed that Blaine had embezzled "somewhere between $500,000 to $1 million from his various accounts."

In March 2006 Blaine responded by launching a countersuit, alleging sexual harassment and wrongful termination and claiming more than $5 million in damages. Spector, she claimed, had given her $635,000 to buy a house, and the $425,000 was to be used to help finance a movie, *3:15*, "a noble and heartfelt story" about a teacher working with underprivileged children that Spector hoped would "rehabilitate his tarnished image." He also wanted $102,000 of the $425,000 to buy an RV that could be used as "a mobile lounge and office" during the criminal trial.

Her suit also alleged that Spector had "constantly" asked her to have sex with him and had a habit of asking her to work around him when he was naked. On one occasion when the two were traveling to New York, she alleged, he had asked her to find him a prostitute, and on another he had invited her to join him and a prostitute in his hotel room. Blaine said she had declined. Most damagingly, she alleged that Spector had twice proposed marriage, in order to prevent her testifying against him in court. Blaine claimed that she had tried to leave Spector's employ, but he had persuaded her to stay by giving her the money to buy the house and offering an employment package that included a $72,000 salary, a $600 car allowance, a retirement plan and a $500,000 life insurance policy. Matters had finally soured, she claimed, when Rachelle Short convinced Spector that Blaine was stealing from him, and he had fired her after she had refused to promise not to talk to prosecutors about what he may have told her about the death of Lana Clarkson. In answering written questions for the suit, Spector said he did not kill Clarkson but invoked his right under the Fifth Amendment not to disclose whether he had discussed her death with Blaine. He also denied offering to marry Blaine or pay her money to keep her quiet.

In a subsequent interview with a reporter from the *Los Angeles Times*, conducted in her lawyer's office, Blaine described how Spector had become obsessed with the trial, keeping two copies of his "murder book," the compilation of evidence against him, and reading them constantly. His only regular visitors were his housekeepers, his attorneys and his hairdresser, who came as often as three times a week to groom Spector's wigs. Blaine's own duties, she said, had come to focus largely on protecting him from the ensuing media circus and attempting to rehabilitate his image. One idea, she said, was to make a movie or reality television show (working title "Phil Spector's The Producers") that would show his "human side." She also claimed that Spector had tried to dispatch her to music business parties to pass out fliers proclaiming his innocence. She refused to go. In February 2007, however, the case was settled out of court when Blaine agreed to return $900,000 to Spector, at the same time dropping her suit against him.

The money would prove extremely useful. Over the past four years he had employed three of the most expensive criminal defense attorneys in America—Shapiro, Abramson and Cutler—along with their attendant retinues of counsels and advisers. One estimate put Spector's legal bill at around $1 million a year.

His income from recordings had dwindled dramatically in recent years. It had been twenty-five years since he had released a new album—the Ramones' *End of the Century*; fifteen since the release of the *Back to Mono* CD box set. That collection remained in print, along with "greatest hits" packages by the Ronettes, Darlene Love and the Crystals. And in a bid to breathe new life into the catalogue, in December 2006 Allen Klein arranged for the release of yet another "best of Spector" package, along with the Christmas album. Added to that were the ongoing producer royalties from his recordings with John Lennon and George Harrison, and the songwriting royalties from radio plays of his old hits. Of these, the biggest revenue earner by far was "You've Lost That Lovin' Feelin'," which in 1999 had been named by BMI as the most played song on American radio and television in history—8 million performances, or the equivalent of forty-five years of continuous back-to-back airplay.

Perhaps the most telling indication of Spector's financial circumstances came, oddly enough, during the TV broadcast of the Super Bowl in February 2005. Spector had always been highly protective of his music being used in advertisements, and had poured contempt on others—notably Berry Gordy—who allowed theirs to be. It came as something of a surprise, then, to hear probably his most famous song, "Be My Baby," being used to sell the male sexual aid Cialis during one of the Super Bowl's innumerable commercial breaks.

Nor, at this point, it seemed, could Spector rely on any of the money that he was seeking to recoup in his lawsuit against his original lawyer Robert Shapiro. In October 2005, Shapiro's twenty-four-year-old son Brent died from an accidental overdose of Ecstasy. Two months later, Spector dropped his suit against the attorney.

But in January 2006, Judge Fidler ruled that Spector's deposition in the Shapiro suit, which he had given the previous July, should be made available to the prosecution in the Clarkson case. Fidler noted that he had read the material but had found "no smoking gun" in the testimony.

For the deposition, Spector had been cross-examined by Shapiro himself, whose intention was clearly to establish just how important his services had been to Spector at the time of his arrest. Spector's answers provided a fascinating insight into his psychological condition.

Responding to Shapiro's questioning, Spector stated that he had habitually been taking five medications daily, for "sleep and emotional stability" for the previous eight years. A psychiatrist, he said, had diagnosed him with "manic depressiveness," which had manifested in "no sleep, depression, mood changes, mood swings, hard to live with, hard to concentrate, hard . . . just hard."

Medication, Spector said, had helped him "immensely" with his problems. Pushed on whether he had ever drunk while using the medication, Spector replied "occasionally," but never more than three drinks. His favorite tipple was vodka and orange. Shapiro then asked whether Spector had discussed his mental condition with any newspaper reporters since the death of Lana Clarkson.

Spector, apparently referring to my meeting with him, but forgetting that it had taken place before the killing, said he had—with "a gentleman from London." At this point amnesia seemed to envelop Spector.

> Question: Did you ever tell the reporter that you had mental disorders?
> Answer: No, I don't think I used that word, but I . . . it's possible.
> Q: Did you ever tell the reporter that you sometimes felt you were insane?
> A: No, but I might have. It's not . . . I might have . . . He might have concluded that, but I don't recall saying that, no.
> Q: So what would be the basis for him concluding that?
> A: I don't know.
> Q: Did you ever tell the reporter that you were borderline insane?
> A: I don't recall saying that.
> Q: Have you ever said that to anyone?
> A: I might have jestingly said that, yes.
> Q: But not in seriousness?
> A: I don't know what insane is, insanity, so I don't know how I could say it knowingly.
> Q: What does the term mean to you?
> A: Somebody who's not there all the time.
> Q: And would you describe yourself as not being there all the time?
> A: Yeah, because I've been called a genius and I think a genius is not there all the time and has borderline insanity.
> Q: And would you say that would be your . . . The description of yourself on the day of Lana Clarkson's death?
> A: No.

Spector's forgetfulness even extended to the name of his driver, Adriano De Souza, on the night of Clarkson's killing. "Le . . . something is his last name. I never knew what his name was when . . . he came to call. I used to call him 'Tony,' but that wasn't his name."

He had evidently forgotten too that he "owned a lot of weapons" until the police told him after the killing. "They were locked away."

However, his memory apparently sharpened up in recollecting his alcohol consumption on the night of the killing. Contradicting police evidence about the amount of alcohol he had consumed that evening, and testimony from Adriano De Souza and various police officers about his inebriated condition, Spector maintained that he had actually drunk no alcohol at the Grill, despite the fact that it had been brought to the table. Nor, he claimed, had he ordered or drunk anything at Dan Tana's, despite the bartender sending over "something which he wanted me to try." Spector said he had a habit of ordering "a lot of stuff that I don't consume, food and alcohol."

Shapiro then pressed Spector on the gratuities he had left during the evening—a hundred dollars each to the "five or six" waiters at Trader Vic's; a $300 tip at Dan Tana's.

"Would you describe yourself, in the circumstances, at least, of being in a restaurant, as being overly generous?" Shapiro asked.

"Extraordinarily," Spector replied.

"And would you describe yourself as being that way in most things in your life?"

"Yes, especially with you."

Shapiro then moved on to question Spector about going to the House of Blues, meeting Lana Clarkson and what had occurred after that. Invoking the Fifth Amendment, Spector refused to answer.

Deciding that this deposition could be included by the prosecution in the trial was one thing; deciding when that trial should actually take place, quite another.

The first date set by Judge Fidler—January 2006—passed, and in March he agreed to a further postponement, noting that prosecutors and defense attorneys had scheduling conflicts. Bruce Cutler was still involved in his case in New York; prosecution attorneys, in the case of Michael Goodwin, who had been charged with the 1988 shooting of racing driver Mickey Thompson and his wife.

Spector's trial was rescheduled for September, but in June, Fidler ruled that it should be postponed for the third time, until January 2007. That date too would later be moved back to March. At the same time, the wrongful-death lawsuit was also postponed, until after the criminal trial.

In September 2006, Spector married Rachelle Short in a private ceremony at the Alhambra castle. Only a handful of guests attended, among them Spector's bodyguard.

Spector didn't get out much anymore. Secluded behind high walls with his lawyers and his hairdressers, he fretted and agitated about his forthcoming trial. The jukebox in the music room was silent. It was a long time since he had played his old hits. They seemed to belong not just to another era, but to another lifetime. Now that they were married, Rachelle seemed to spend less and less time at the castle. Friends said she was planning to record an album, and maybe Spector would produce—after the acquittal. It would, they said, be the comeback to end them all.

Acknowledgments

This book would not have been possible without the help of Caspar Llewellyn Smith who, as commissioning editor on the *Telegraph* magazine, was complicit in initiating my interview with Phil Spector in December 2002. I am indebted to Caspar, Michele Lavery, editor of the *Telegraph* magazine, and Kathryn Holliday, deputy editor of the *Telegraph* magazine, for all their support, enthusiasm and friendship throughout the project.

Special thanks are due to the redoubtable Harvey Kubernik, authority on Los Angeles music, for spiritual traffic-cop duties; to Denny Bruce, Michael Spencer and to Carlton Smith, who has written his own compelling account of the Lana Clarkson case and who has been extraordinarily generous with his advice and help on this book. I would also like to thank Isabel Albiston, Myra Amorosi, Robert Sam Anson, Eugen Beer, Graham Boynton, Tim Burrows, Tony Calder, Robert Chalmers, Rachel Coat, Bobbi Cowan, Hamish Dewar, Dominick Dunne, Andy Greenacre, Richard Havers, Barney Hoskyns, Simon Jameson, Dan Kessel, David Kessel, Eric Lee, Susan Leibowitz, Roderick Lindblom, David May, Jeremy Marre, Frank and Catherine Mazzola, Cheryl Newman, Ajesh Patalay, Dave Platel, Martin Roberts, Scott Ross, Francesca Ryan, Chris Salewicz, Krishna Sheth, Brian Southall, Peregrine and Catherine St. Germans, Professor Lloyd Utan, Richard Williams and Blake Xolton. I owe particular thanks to Naomi West for all her sterling help.

I am grateful to Gary Fisketjon, my editor at Knopf, for all his unstinting encouragement and enthusiasm, and to Liz Van Hoose at Knopf for all her patience and help. I am particularly indebted to Maria Massey, Hugo de Klee and Patty Romanowski for their painstaking and meticulous copyediting.

I would particularly like to thank my agent Kate Jones at ICM in London, who has been a tower of strength and wise counsel throughout the writing of this book and beyond, and Amanda Urban at ICM in New York for all her support, encouragement and advice. Above all, I owe thanks to my wife, Patricia, for everything.

Notes

1. "Mr. Spector Likes People to Walk Up"

AUTHOR INTERVIEWS
Ahmet Ertegun, Don Kirshner, Larry Levine, Phil Spector.

BOOKS
Smith, op. cit.
Tynan, op. cit.
Wolfe, op. cit.

OTHER MEDIA
Cohn, art. cit.
Brown, "Found: Rock's Lost Genius."
County of Los Angeles, Search Warrants and Affidavits, February 2003.

2. "It Was Phillip Who Was Moving Fastest"

AUTHOR INTERVIEWS
Susan Cooder, Cary Cooper, Kim Fowley, Bruce Johnston, David Kessel, Annette Kleinbard, Annette Merar, Ron Milstein, Burt Prelutsky, Phil Spector, Michael Spencer.

BOOKS
Finnis, op. cit.
Gillett, *The Sound of the City*.
Ribowsky, op. cit.
Smith, op. cit.
Thompson, op. cit.
Williams, op. cit.

OTHER MEDIA
Office of Chief Medical Examiner, NYC.
U.S. National Archives and Records Administration, NYC.
Priore, art. cit.

3. "To Know Him Is to Love Him"

AUTHOR INTERVIEWS
Lynn Castle, Kim Fowley, Jimmie Haskell, Bruce Johnston, Annette Kleinbard, Jerry Leiber, Larry Levine, Annette Merar, Stan Ross, Phil Spector, Michael Spencer, Russ Titelman.

BOOKS
Boyd, op. cit.
Finnis, op. cit.
Picardie and Wade, op. cit.

Ribowsky, op. cit.
Thompson, op. cit.
Williams, ibid.

OTHER MEDIA
www.usc.edu/libraries/archives/la/scandals/chessman.htm: Caryl Chessman website.
www.carolconnors.com
www.goldstarrecordingstudios.com
http://web.inter.nl/users/wilkens/Lho6.html: the Lee Hazlewood Story website.
http://www.lincolnu.edu/~nordstro/jou335/payola.htm: Payola history, Lincoln University of Missouri website.
Era Records contract July 3, 1958.

4. On Broadway

AUTHOR INTERVIEWS
Ahmet Ertegun, Jerry Leiber, Beverly Ross, Michael Spencer, Nino Tempo, Jerry Wexler.

BOOKS
Emerson, op. cit.
Gillett, *Making Tracks.*
Gillett, *The Sound of the City.*
McKeen (ed.), op. cit.
Picardie and Wade, op. cit.
Ribowsky, op. cit.
Wexler, op. cit.
Williams, Richard, op. cit.

OTHER MEDIA
www.felderpomus.com: Doc Pomus website.

5. "A Big Hoot and Howl"

AUTHOR INTERVIEWS
Freddy Beinstock, Miriam Beinstock, Ahmet Ertegun, Don Kirshner, Annette Kleinbard, Jerry Leiber, Annette Merar, Stan Ross, Michael Spencer, Russ Titelman, Jerry Wexler, Toni Wine.

BOOKS
Betrock, op. cit.
Emerson, op. cit.
Gillett, *Making Tracks.*
Picardie and Wade, op. cit.
Ribowsky, op. cit.
Thompson, op. cit.
Wexler, op. cit.

OTHER MEDIA
Trow, art. cit.
http://web.inter.nl/users/wilkens/Lho6.html: the Lee Hazlewood Story website.
www.wtv-zone.com/dpjohnson/parissisters: Paris Sisters website.
"Phil Spector," *The Story of Pop*, BBC Radio.

6. "They All Thought He Was a Genius"

AUTHOR INTERVIEWS
LaLa Brooks, Arnold Goland, Al Hazan, Don Kirshner, Al Kooper, Jerry Leiber, Annette Merar, Beverly Noga, Phil Spector, Michael Spencer.

BOOKS
Betrock, op. cit.
Emerson, op. cit.
Finnis, op. cit.
Kooper, op. cit.
Ribowsky, op. cit.
Williams, op. cit.

OTHER MEDIA
Petridis, art. cit.
Kubernik, "Wild Colonial Boy: Phil Spector."
www.spectropop.com: entry on the Crystals.
www.history-of-rock.com: entry on the Crystals.

7. Building the Wall of Sound

AUTHOR INTERVIEWS
Fanita Barrett, Hal Blaine, LaLa Brooks, Denny Bruce, Al DeLory, Al Hazan, Gloria Jones, Larry Levine, Annette Merar, Don Randi, Stan Ross, Phil Spector, Michael Spencer, Nino Tempo, Russ Titelman.

BOOKS
Betrock, op. cit.
Emerson, op. cit.
Finnis, op. cit.
Love, op. cit.
Ribowsky, op. cit.
Smith, Carlton, op. cit.
Williams, op. cit.

OTHER MEDIA
Lloyd, art. cit.
Puterbaugh, art. cit.
http://lpintop.tripod.com/jeffbarry: Jeff Barry—The Man and His Music.
http://web.inter.nl/users/wilkens/Lho6.html: the Lee Hazlewood Story website.
www.spectropop.com: entry on Jack Nitzsche.

8. "He Wanted to Be Thought Of as Interesting"

AUTHOR INTERVIEWS
LaLa Brooks, Denny Bruce, Annette Kleinbard, Larry Levine, Annette Merar, Don Randi, Bill Walsh.

BOOKS
Bono, op. cit.
Egan, op. cit.
Finnis, op. cit.
McDonough, op. cit.

OTHER MEDIA
Talbot and Zheutlin, art. cit.
Kubernik, "Phil Spector: Jack Nitzsche Remembers the Wall of Sound."
www.spectropop.com: Sylvie Simmons: Interview with Jack Nitzsche.

9. Little Symphonies for the Kids

AUTHOR INTERVIEWS
LaLa Brooks, Ahmet Ertegun, Mitchell Geffen, Dennis Hopper, Bruce Johnston, Annette Merar, Joe Smith, Nino Tempo, Jerry Wexler.

BOOKS
King, op. cit.
Picardie and Wade, op. cit.
Ribowsky, op. cit.
Williams, Richard, op. cit.
Wolfe, op. cit.

OTHER MEDIA
Talbot and Zheutlin, art. cit.

10. Going to the Chapel

AUTHOR INTERVIEWS
LaLa Brooks, Denny Bruce, Larry Levine, Annette Merar, Beverly Noga, Stu Phillips, Don Randi, Stan Ross, Frances Sheen, Michael Spencer, Nedra Talley, Nino Tempo.

BOOKS
Betrock, op. cit.
Emerson, op. cit.
Finnis, op. cit.
Love, op. cit.
Spector, op. cit.

OTHER MEDIA
Wenner, art. cit.

11. "The Wall of Sound, It Kinda Sounds Tired"

AUTHOR INTERVIEWS
Tony Calder, Maureen Cleave, Tony Hall, Tony King, Larry Levine, Annette Merar, Nedra Talley.

BOOKS
Betrock, op. cit.
Bono, op. cit.
Emerson, op. cit.
Finnis, op. cit.
Loog Oldham, *Stoned.*
Loog Oldham, 2*Stoned.*
Norman, *The Stones.*
Ribowsky, op. cit.

OTHER MEDIA
Cleave, art. cit.
Doncaster, art. cit.

12. "The Last Word in Tomorrow's Sound Today"

AUTHOR INTERVIEWS
Denny Bruce, Tony Hall, Larry Levine, Annette Merar, Bill Walsh.

BOOKS
Emerson, op. cit.
Hoskyns, op. cit.
Ribowsky, op. cit.
Smith, Carlton, op. cit.
Williams, op. cit.

OTHER MEDIA
www.mann-weil.com: Barry Mann and Cynthia Weil website.
www.spectropop.com: entry on Jack Nitzsche.

13. "A Giant Stands 5'7""

AUTHOR INTERVIEWS
Denny Bruce, Henry Diltz, Ahmet Ertegun, Emil Farkas, Bruce Johnston, Linda Lawrence, Larry Levine, Annette Merar, Don Randi, Diana Ross, Catherine Sebastian, John Sebastian, Michael Spencer, Jerry Wexler, Brian Wilson.

BOOKS
Abbott, op. cit.
Benjaminson, op. cit.
Finnis, op. cit.
Goldman (and Schiller), *Ladies and Gentlemen—Lenny Bruce!*
Gordy, op. cit.
Hoskyns, op. cit.
Miles, *Frank Zappa.*
Ribowsky, op. cit.
Spector, op. cit.
Thompson, op. cit.
Wilson, *Wouldn't It Be Nice.*
Wolfe, op. cit.

OTHER MEDIA
"A Giant Stands," art. cit.
http://members.aol.com/dcspohr/lenny/original.htm: Lenny Bruce, extract from Lenny Bruce essay "I Remember Lenny" by Grover Sales.
www.freenetpages.co.uk/hp/lennybruce: The Complete Lenny Bruce.

14. River Deep, Mountain Low

AUTHOR INTERVIEWS
Rodney Bingenheimer, Denny Bruce, Larry Levine, Don Randi, Catherine Sebastian, Phil Spector, Ike Turner.

BOOKS
Emerson, op. cit.
Finnis, op. cit.
Ribowsky, op. cit.
Thompson, op. cit.
Williams, Richard, op. cit.

OTHER MEDIA
Kubernik, "Phil Spector: Jack Nitzsche Remembers the Wall of Sound."
Wenner, art. cit.

15. Marriage in Purgatory

AUTHOR INTERVIEWS
Tony Calder, Lynn Castle, Ahmet Ertegun, Peter Fonda, Tony Hall, Dennis Hopper, Phil Spector, Michael Spencer, Stewart Stern, Nedra Talley.

BOOKS
Biskind, op. cit.
Finnis, op. cit.
Goldman, op. cit.
Ribowsky, op. cit.
Spector, op. cit.

OTHER MEDIA
Bart, art. cit.
Wenner, art. cit.

16. "Out There, but in a Beautiful Way"

AUTHOR INTERVIEWS
Larry Levine, Jerry Moss, Toni Wine.

BOOKS
Thompson, op. cit.

OTHER MEDIA
Wenner, art. cit.

17. The Lonely Bird in the Gilded Cage

AUTHOR INTERVIEWS
Nik Cohn, Peter Fonda, Don Kirshner, Nedra Talley.

BOOKS
Abbott, op. cit.
Spector, op. cit.

OTHER MEDIA
Cohn, art. cit.

18. With the Beatles

AUTHOR INTERVIEWS
Peter Brown, Dennis Hopper, Dan Kessel, David Kessel, John Leckie, Annette Merar, Phil Spector, Klaus Voormann.

BOOKS
DiLello, op. cit.
Emerson, op. cit.
Goldman, op. cit.
MacDonald, op. cit.
Miles, *Ginsberg*.

Norman, *The True Story of the Beatles.*
Ribowsky, op. cit.
Spector, op. cit.
Williams, Richard, op. cit.

OTHER MEDIA
Hilburn, "Tearing down the Wall of Silence."
http://homepage.ntlworld.com/carousel/poboo.html: You Are the Plastic Ono Band.
http://rarebeatles.com/ghpsatmp.htm: Letter from Phil Spector to George Harrison re: All Things Must Pass.
www.performingsongwriter.com: Bill DeMain.

19. "These Are Pretty Wild Sessions, They Get Pretty Out There"

AUTHOR INTERVIEWS
Tim Blackmore, Joe Boyd, Paulette Brandt, Emil Farkas, Dan Kessel, Dave Kessel, Tony King, Bob Mercer, May Pang, Stan Ross, Harold Seider, Joe Smith, Nedra Talley.

BOOKS
Goldman, op. cit.
Norman, op. cit.
Spector, op. cit.

OTHER MEDIA
Affidavits and statements, Superior Court of the State of California for the County of Los Angeles, in re the marriage of Veronica Yvette Spector and Phillip Spector.
"Phil Spector," *The Story of Pop,* written by Tim Blackmore and Charlie Gillett, BBC Radio.

20. "Let's Take Five"

AUTHOR INTERVIEWS
Roy Carr, Mitchell Geffen, Zach Glickman, Dan Kessel, David Kessel, Harvey Kubernik, Devra Robitaille, Stan Ross, Nino Tempo.

BOOKS
Love, op. cit.
Williams, op. cit.

OTHER MEDIA
Carr, art. cit.
"Phil Spector in Mystery Mishap," *Rolling Stone.*
Wexler, art. cit.
http://acereco01.uuhost.uk.uu.net/gotrt/feb01/cdchd793.html: Dion—Born to Be with You, by Sean Rowley, Ace Records.

21. "Leonard, I Love You . . ."

AUTHOR INTERVIEWS
David Kessel, Harvey Kubernik, Larry Levine, Devra Robitaille, Joe Smith.

BOOKS
Nadel, op. cit.
Ribowsky, op. cit.

OTHER MEDIA
DeCurtis, art. cit.
Holden, art. cit.
www.serve.com/cpage/LCohen/BBCshow.html: Leonard Cohen on BBC Radio.

22. "Thank You, Folks—Have a Good Life"

AUTHOR INTERVIEWS
Roy Carr, Carol Connors, Dan Kessel, David Kessel, Harvey Kubernik, Nola Leone, Larry Levine, Andy Paley.

BOOKS
Spector, op. cit.
True, op. cit.
Twiggy, op. cit.

OTHER MEDIA
www.ramones.com

23. "A Case That No One Can Reach"

AUTHOR INTERVIEWS
Dan Kessel, Harvey Kubernik, Larry Levine, Annette Merar, Yoko Ono, Devra Robitaille, Charlie Sheen, Frances Sheen, Phil Spector, Nino Tempo.

BOOKS
Baker, op. cit.
Goldman, *The Lives of John Lennon.*
Ribowsky, op. cit.
Spector, op. cit.

OTHER MEDIA
Graham, art. cit.

24. "Between Grief and Nothing, I Will Take Grief"

AUTHOR INTERVIEWS
Denny Bruce, Roy Carr, Steve Dunleavy, Ahmet Ertegun, Dennis Hopper, David Kessel, Karen Lerner, Larry Levine, Michael Spencer.

OTHER MEDIA
Talbot and Zheutlin, art. cit.
Brown, "Behind the Wall of Sound."
http://www.richmondhillhistory.org/JackMaple.html: Jack Maple Remembered.

25. "I Honestly Thought He Was Kidding"

AUTHOR INTERVIEWS
Paulette Brandt, Hal David, Dan Kessel, David Kessel, Charles Kipps, Karen Lerner, Larry Levine, Ann Marshall, Michelle Phillips, Sy Presten, Don Randi.

BOOKS
Smith, Carlton, op. cit.

OTHER MEDIA
Macintyre, art. cit.

26. "You Don't Tell Mozart What Operas to Write"

AUTHOR INTERVIEWS
Rodney Bingenheimer, Paulette Brandt, Henry Diltz, Jimmie Haskell, David Kessel, Karen Lerner, Andy Paley.

OTHER MEDIA
Gordinier, art. cit.

27. "Anybody Have a Calculator?"

AUTHOR INTERVIEWS
Paulette Brandt, LaLa Brooks, Mark Ellen, Ahmet Ertegun, Ira Greenberg, Jimmie Haskell, Alex Peltz, Michelle Phillips, Chuck Rubin.

BOOKS
Smith, Carlton, op. cit.

OTHER MEDIA
Court of Appeals of New York: *Ronnie Greenfield, et al., Respondents, v. Philles Records, Inc. et al. and American Express Corporation*, 2002.
Collins, art. cit.
Usborne, art. cit.
Hoerburger, art. cit.
www.bigmagic.com./blackj: The Blacklisted Journalist: Al Aronowitz.

28. "He Wanted to Prove He Really Was Human"

AUTHOR INTERVIEWS
Paulette Brandt, LaLa Brooks, Denny Bruce, Lynn Castle, Dan Kessel, Ike Turner.

OTHER MEDIA
"What I've learned: Phil Spector": *Esquire*, September 1999.
www.bpfallon.com/joey_spector.html: "A Goodbye Note to Joey Ramone from Phil Spector."

29. "It's Very Difficult, Very Difficult to Be Reasonable"

AUTHOR INTERVIEW
Phil Spector.

30. "I Think I Killed Somebody . . ."

AUTHOR INTERVIEWS
A. J. Benza, Bill Craig, Patrick Fraley, Courtney Kanner, Eric Root. Interviews with Craig and Kanner were conducted by Naomi West.

BOOKS
Smith, Carlton, op. cit.

OTHER MEDIA
County of Los Angeles, Search Warrants and Affidavits, February 2003.
County of Los Angeles, Coroner's Report, Lana Clarkson, February 2003.
Testimony to Los Angeles County Grand Jury proceedings, September 2004.
Pretrial motions (various). *The People of the State of California v. Phillip Spector.*
Brennan, art. cit.

Briggs, art. cit.
Brown, "Spector's Unscripted Ending."
www.livingdollproductions.com: Lana Clarkson website.

31. "A Genius Is Not There All the Time"

AUTHOR INTERVIEWS
Sy Presten, Joan Rivers (interview conducted by Ajesh Patalay).

BOOKS
Smith, Carlton, op. cit.

OTHER MEDIA
County of Los Angeles, Search Warrants and Affidavits, February 2003.
County of Los Angeles, Coroner's Report, Lana Clarkson, February 2003.
Testimony to Los Angeles County Grand Jury proceedings, September 2004.
Pretrial motions (various): *The People of the State of California v. Phillip Spector.*
Transcript of deposition of Phillip Spector: *Spector v. Shapiro*, July 2005.
"Behind the shooting at Phil Spector's home," Fox News.
"Gotti Lawyer to Rep Spector," CBS News.com
"Judge: Prosecutors Can Scan Spector's civil-suit deposition," Lisa Sweetingham, Court TV.
Anson, art. cit.
Boucher, art. cit.
Brown, "Juke box jury."
Deutsch, "Coroner: Spector May Not Have Shot Victim."
Deutsch, "Phil Spector Replaces Lawyer, Hires Leslie Abramson to Replace Him."
Deutsch, "Phil Spector's Former Personal Assistant Claims Sex Harassment."
Garrison, art. cit.
"Lawyer Defends Work for 'Mafia Cops,' " Associated Press.
Raab, art. cit.
Segal, art. cit.
"Spector Drops Suit Against Former Attorney," Associated Press.
www.rachellemarie.com

Interviews

More than one hundred people were interviewed in the course of researching this book. I have respected the wishes of those who asked to remain anonymous. I am extremely grateful to all who agreed to be interviewed for their help, their time and their candor.

Fanita Barrett, Los Angeles, October 2003 (by telephone).

A. J. Benza, Los Angeles, May 2003 (by telephone).

Freddy Bienstock, London, November 2003.

Miriam Bienstock, London, November 2003.

Rodney Bingenheimer, Los Angeles, August 2003.

Tim Blackmore, London, April 2004.

Hal Blaine, Los Angeles, December 2002 (by telephone).

Joe Boyd, London, February 2006.

Paulette Brandt, Los Angeles, August 2003.

Peter Brown, London, October 2003.

LaLa Brooks, New York, December 2004.

Denny Bruce, Los Angeles, August 2003.

Tony Calder, London, September 2003.

Roy Carr, London, November 2003.

Lynn Castle, Los Angeles, June 2004.

Maureen Cleave, London, September 2003.

Nik Cohn, New York, April 2004.

Carol Connors (formerly Annette Kleinbard), Los Angeles, August 2003.

Susan Cooder, Los Angeles, December 2005 (by telephone).

Professor Cary Cooper, Liverpool, October 2005 (by telephone).

Bobbi Cowan, Los Angeles, June 2004.

Hal David, Los Angeles, October 2004 (by telephone).

Al DeLory, Nashville, October 2003 (by telephone).

Henry Diltz, Los Angeles, August 2003.

Steve Dunleavy, New York, December 2005 (by telephone).

Mark Ellen, London, February 2005.

Ahmet Ertegun (who, sadly, passed away in 2006), New York, May 2003.

Emil Farkas, Los Angeles, October 2005.

Peter Fonda, Montana, August 2003 (by telephone).

Kim Fowley, Redlands, California, August 2003.

Patrick Fraley, Los Angeles, May 2003 (by telephone).

Mitchell Geffen, Los Angeles, October 2005.

Arnold Golan, Los Angeles, September 2004 (by telephone).

Zach Glickman, Los Angeles, October 2005.

Ira Greenberg, New York, April 2004.

Tony Hall, London, October 2003.

Jimmie Haskell, Los Angeles, August 2003.

Al Hazan, Los Angeles, August 2003.

Dennis Hopper, Los Angeles, April 2006 (by telephone).

Gloria Jones, Los Angeles, October 2003 (by telephone).

Bruce Johnston, Santa Barbara, January 2005 (by telephone).

Courtney Kanner, Los Angeles, July 2003 (by telephone).

Dan Kessel, Palm Springs, California, August 2003; Los Angeles, October 2005.

David Kessel, Los Angeles, October 2003 (by telephone).

Tony King, London, October 2003.

Charles Kipps, New York, June 2005 (by telephone).

Don Kirshner, Boca Raton, Florida, December 2003.

Al Kooper, Boston, May 2004 (by telephone).

Harvey Kubernik, Los Angeles, August 2003.

John Leckie, London, April 2004 (by telephone).

Jerry Leiber, Los Angeles, August 2003.

Linda Leitch (née Lawrence), Ireland, November 2003 (by telephone).

Nola Leone, Los Angeles, October 2004 (by telephone).

Karen Lerner, New York, December 2004.

Larry Levine, Los Angeles, August 2003.

Ann Marshall, Los Angeles, August 2003.

Annette Merar, Los Angeles, October 2004.

Bob Mercer, Los Angeles, March 2005 (by telephone).

Ron Milstein, Los Angeles, March 2005 (by telephone).

Jerry Moss, Los Angeles, August 2003.

Beverly Noga, Los Angeles, June 2004.

Yoko Ono, Paris, September 2003.

Andy Paley, Los Angeles, August 2003.

May Pang, London, June 2003.

Alex Peltz, New York, April 2004.

Michelle Phillips, Los Angeles, August 2003.

Stu Phillips, New York, March 2005 (by telephone).

Burt Prelutsky, Los Angeles, August 2003 (by telephone).

Sy Presten, New York, August 2006 (by telephone).

Don Randi, Los Angeles, August 2003.

Joan Rivers, New York, September 2005 (by telephone).

Devra Robitaille, Los Angeles, June 2004.

Eric Root, Los Angeles, May 2003 (by telephone).

Beverly Ross, Nashville, July 2004 (by telephone).

Diana Ross, New York, February 2004.

Stan Ross, Los Angeles, August 2003.

Chuck Rubin, Woodstock, April 2004.

Catherine Sebastian, New York, December 2003.

John Sebastian, Woodstock, December 2003 (by telephone).

Harold Seider, Los Angeles, October 2003.

Frances Sheen, DeSoto, Texas, October 2003 (by telephone).

Charlie Sheen, Los Angeles, October 2003 (by telephone).

Joe Smith, Los Angeles, August 2003.

Phil Spector, Los Angeles, December 2002.

Michael Spencer, New York, February 2005; January 2006.

Stewart Stern, Washington State, April 2006 (by telephone).

Nedra Talley, Virginia, December 2004.

Nino Tempo, Los Angeles, August 2003.

Russ Titelman, New York, January 2006.

Ike Turner, Los Angeles, August 2003.

Klaus Voormann, Bernried, Germany, April 2004 (by telephone).

Bill Walsh, Boston, March 2005 (by telephone).

Jerry Wexler, Tampa, Florida, August 2003.

Brian Wilson, Los Angeles, November 2001.

Toni Wine, Los Angeles, June 2004 (by telephone).

Selected Bibliography

There have been five books written about Phil Spector prior to this one: those by Richard Williams, Rob Finnis, Mark Ribowsky, Dave Thompson and Carlton Smith. I have drawn on all of them in researching this book, and I salute all five authors. Other books consulted include:

Abbott, Kingsley. *Back to the Beach: A Brian Wilson and the Beach Boys Reader* (Helter Skelter: London, 2002).

Baker, James Robert. *Fuel-Injected Dreams* (Bantam Press: New York, 1986).

Benjaminson, Peter. *The Story of Motown* (Grove Press: New York, 1979).

Betrock, Alan. *Girl Groups: The Story of a Sound* (Delilah Books: New York, 1982).

Biskind, Peter. *Easy Riders, Raging Bulls* (Simon & Schuster: New York, 1998).

Bono, Sonny. *And the Beat Goes On* (Pocket Books: New York, 1991).

Boyd, Joe. *White Bicycles: Making Music in the 1960s* (Serpent's Tail: London, 2006).

DiLello, Richard. *The Longest Cocktail Party* (Canongate: Edinburgh, 2005).

Egan, Sean. *The Guys Who Wrote 'Em* (Askill: London, 2004).

Emerson, Ken. *Always Magic in the Air: The Bomp and Brilliance of the Brill Building Era* (Viking: New York, 2005).

Finnis, Rob. *The Phil Spector Story* (Rockon: London, 1975).

Gillett, Charlie. *Making Tracks: The Story of Atlantic Records* (Souvenir Press: London, 1988).

Gillett, Charlie. *The Sound of the City* (Souvenir Press: London, 1996).

Goldman, Albert. *The Lives of John Lennon* (Bantam: London, 1998).

Goldman, Albert, and Lawrence Schiller. *Ladies and Gentlemen—Lenny Bruce!* (Ballantine: New York, 1974).

Gordy, Berry. *To Be Loved: An Autobiography* (Headline: London, 1994).

Hoskyns, Barney. *Waiting for the Sun: The Story of the Los Angeles Music Scene* (Viking: London, 1996).

King, Tom. *The Operator: David Geffen Builds, Buys, and Sells the New Hollywood* (Broadway Books: New York, 2001).

Kooper, Al. *Backstage Passes and Backstabbing Bastards* (Billboard Books: New York, 1998).

Loog Oldham, Andrew. *Stoned* (Secker & Warburg: London, 2000).

———. *2Stoned* (Secker & Warburg: London, 2002).

Love, Darlene, with Rob Hoerburger. *My Name Is Love* (William Morrow: New York, 1998).

MacDonald, Ian. *Revolution in the Head: The Beatles' Records & the Sixties* (Fourth Estate: London, 1994).

McDonough, Jimmy. *Shakey: Neil Young's Biography* (Vintage: London, 2003).

McKeen, William (ed.) *Rock and Roll Is Here to Stay* (Norton: New York, 2000).

Miles, Barry. *Ginsberg* (Viking: London, 1990).

———. *Frank Zappa: A Biography* (Atlantic Books, London: 2004).

Nadel, Ira B. *Various Positions: A Life of Leonard Cohen* (Bloomsbury: London, 1996).

Norman, Philip. *The Stones* (Penguin: London 1993).

———. *The True Story of the Beatles* (Hamish Hamilton: London 1981).

Picardie, Justine, and Dorothy Wade. *Atlantic and the Godfathers of Rock and Roll* (Fourth Estate: London, 1993).

Ribowsky, Mark. *He's a Rebel: Phil Spector, Rock and Roll's Legendary Producer* (Cooper Square Press: New York, 2000).

Rice, Tim, Joe Rice, and Paul Gambaccini (eds.) *Guinness Book of British Hit Singles of the 60s* (Guinness: London, 1979).

The Rolling Stone Interviews (1967–1980) (St. Martin's/Rolling Stone Press: New York, 1981).

Smith, Carlton. *Reckless: Millionaire Record Producer Phil Spector and the Violent Death of Lana Clarkson* (St. Martin's Paperbacks: New York, 2004).

Smith, Joe. *Off the Record: An Oral History of Popular Music* (Warner Books: New York, 1990).

Spector, Ronnie, with Vince Waldron. *Be My Baby* (Pan: London, 1991).

Strongman, Phil and Alan Parker. *John Lennon and the FBI Files* (Sanctuary: London, 2003).

Thompson, Dave. *Wall of Pain: The Biography of Phil Spector* (Sanctuary: London, 2003).

True, Everett. *Hey Ho Let's Go, The Story of the Ramones* (Omnibus: London, 2002).

Twiggy. *In Black and White* (Pocket Books: London, 1998).

Tynan, Kenneth, John Lahr (ed.) *The Diaries of Kenneth Tynan* (Bloomsbury: London, 2001).

Wexler, Jerry, and David Ritz. *Rhythm and the Blues* (Jonathan Cape: London, 1994).

Wilson, Brian, with Todd Gold. *Wouldn't It Be Nice: My Own Story* (Harper Collins: New York, 1991).

Williams, Paul. *Brian Wilson and the Beach Boys: How Deep Is the Ocean* (Omnibus: London, 2003).

Williams, Richard. *Phil Spector: Out of His Head* (Omnibus: London, 2003).

Wolfe, Tom. *The Kandy-Kolored Tangerine-Flake Streamline Baby* (Jonathan Cape: London, 1965).

Newspapers, Periodicals and Broadcasts

"A Giant Stands 5 ft 7 in," *Time*, February 19, 1965.

Anson, Robert Sam. "Legend with a Bullet" *Vanity Fair*, June 2003.

Bart, Peter. "A Groovy Kind of Genius," *New York Times*, July 10, 1966.

"Behind the Shooting at Phil Spector's Home," Fox News, March 17, 2003.

Blackmore, Tim, and Charlie Gillett. "Phil Spector: The Story of Pop," BBC Radio, 1983.

Boucher, Geoff. "Spector Was in Dark Place, Friends Say," *Los Angeles Times*, February 7, 2003.

Brennan, Sandra. "Vice girls" (synopsis), http://www.allmovie.com/cg/avg.dll?p=avg &sql=1:162035.

Briggs, Joe Bob. "Lana Clarkson: Requiem for the Barbarian Queen," *Slate*, http://www.slate.com/id/2078263/.

Brown, Mick. "Behind the Wall of Sound," *Sunday Telegraph*, November 10, 1991.

———. "Found: Rock's Lost Genius," *Telegraph* magazine, February 1, 2003.

———. "Juke Box Jury," *Telegraph* magazine, February 5, 2005.

———. "Unscripted Ending," *Telegraph* magazine, August 26, 2003.

Carr, Roy. "The Phil Spector Story," *New Musical Express*, March 6, 1976.

Cleave, Maureen. "Fifteen Hits in a Row," *Evening Standard*, January 25, 1964.

Cohn, Nik. "Phil Spector," *The Rolling Stone Illustrated History of Rock & Roll*, 1976.

Collins, Glenn. "A '90s Refrain for a '60s Girl Group," *New York Times*, June 26, 1998.

DeCurtis, Anthony. "No Mercy: Leonard Cohen's Tales from the Dark Side," *Rolling Stone*, February 21, 1993.

Deutsch, Linda. "Coroner: Spector May Not Have Shot Victim," Associated Press, May 7, 2004.

———. "Phil Spector Replaces Lawyer, Hires Leslie Abramson to Replace Him," Associated Press, February 3, 2004.

———. "Phil Spector's Former Personal Assistant Claims Sex Harassment," Associated Press, March 29, 2006.

"Devra Robitaille to Warner/Spector Post," *Cash Box*, July 19, 1975.

Doncaster, Patrick. "The Man Who Said No to a Million," *Daily Mirror*, February 7, 1964.

Garrison, Jessica. "Behind Wall of Silence, Spector Busy with Suits," *Los Angeles Times*, May 24, 2006.

Gordinier, Jeff. "Naked Ambition: with the No. 1 hit 'Because You Loved Me' Canadian Songbird Céline Dion Finally Seduces America," *Entertainment Weekly*, March 29, 1996.

"Gotti Lawyer to Rep Spector," CBS News.com, August 25, 2004.

Graham, Caroline. "Dad Always Had a Gun on Him: He Ruled by Fear," *Mail on Sunday*, December 14, 2003.

Hilburn, Robert. "Spector on Spector: 10 Golden Memories," *Los Angeles Times*, November 10, 1991.

———. "Tearing Down the Wall of Silence," *Los Angeles Times*, November 10, 1991.

Hoerburger, Rob. "The Power of Love," *New York Times*, June 20, 1993.

Holden, Stephen. "Leonard Cohen Obscured: a Haunting by Spector," *Rolling Stone*, January 26, 1978.

Kubernik, Harvey. "Phil Spector," *Goldmine*, August 2000.

———. "Wild Colonial Boy: Phil Spector," copyright 2003.

———. "Phil Spector: Jack Nitzsche Remembers the Wall of Sound," *Goldmine*, June 1988.

"Lawyer Defends Work for 'Mafia Cops,' " Associated Press, June 30, 2006.

Lloyd, Robert. " 'Time of the Session': When the Music Was Fast, and the Players Anonymous," *LA Weekly*, April 8, 2004.

Macintyre, Ben. "Down with Blazing Wallet," *The Times*, April 16, 1993.

Nitzsche, Jack. "Sylvie Simmons: Interview with Jack Nitzsche," Spectropop, http://www.spectropop.com/JackNitzsche/sylviesimmonspage1.htm.

Peterson, Helen. "Spector's Ex-Wife Shocked," *Daily News*, December 9, 2003.

Petridis, Alexis. "Life After Tulsa," *Guardian*, May 14, 2003.

"Phil Spector in Mystery Mishap," *Rolling Stone*, April 11, 1974.

Priore, Domenic. "Steve Douglas," *Dumb Angel*, no. 4, 2005.

Puterbaugh, Parke. "Reconstructing Producer Phil Spector's Legendary Style," *Rolling Stone*, August 23, 1990.

Raab, Scott. "Be My, Be My Baby: The Phil Spector Story," *Esquire*, July 2003.

Rose, Derek. "Spector's Sons: Dad Caged Us," *Daily News*, May 26, 2003.

Segal, David. "Crossly Examined," *Washington Post*, June 24, 2006.

Selvin, Joel. "Over the Wall," *Mojo*, May 2003.

"Spector Drops Suit Against Former Attorney," Associated Press, December 17, 2005.

Sweetingham, Lisa. "Judge: Prosecutors Can Scan Spector's Civil-suit Deposition," Court TV, January 27, 2006.

Talbot, David, and Barbara Zheutlin. "Expecting to Fly: Jack Nitzsche," *Crawdaddy*, November 1974.

Trow, George. "Eclectic, Reminiscent, Amused, Fickle, Perverse": 2-part profile of Ahmet Ertegun, *The New Yorker*, 1978.

Usborne, David. "The Control Freak," *Independent*, June 27, 1998.

Wenner, Jann. "The Phil Spector Interview," *Rolling Stone*, November 1, 1969.

Wexler, Mark. "Phil Spector: Freaky Genius of Rock . . . ," *People*, September 22, 1975.

"What I've learned: Phil Spector," *Esquire*, September 1999.

Williams, Richard. "The Producer," *Guardian*, February 5, 2003.

Websites

www.spectropop.com: the definitive website for anyone interested in '60s pop music.

www.history-of-rock.com: a useful, comprehensive overview of the history of pop.

www.rocksbackpages.com: probably the world's most extensive online library of rock journalism.

http://lpintop.tripod.com/jeffbarry: Jeff Barry: The Man and His Music.

www.bigmagic.com/blackj: The Blacklisted Journalist: Al Aronowitz.

www.usc.edu/libraries/archives/la/scandals/chessman.html: Caryl Chessman.

www.carolconnors.com: Carol Connors/Annette Kleinbard.

http://acerec001.uuhost.uk.uu.net/gotrt/feb01/cdchd793.html: Dion: Born to Be with You, by Sean Rowley, Ace Records.

www.felderpomus.com: Doc Pomus.

www.rachellemarie.com: Rachelle Spector.

www.goldstarrecordingstudios.com: Gold Star Studios.

www.bpfallon.com/jocy_spector.html: "A Goodbye Note to Joey Ramone from Phil Spector."

www.livingdollproductions.com: Lana Clarkson.

http://web.inter.nl/users/wilkens/Lh06.html: The Lee Hazlewood Story.

www.serve.com/cpage/LCohen/BBCshow.html: Leonard Cohen on BBC Radio.

www.snopes.com/music/artists/spector.htm: "(Let's Dance) The Screw."

http://rarebeatles.com/ghpsatmp.htm: Letter from Phil Spector to George Harrison re: *All Things Must Pass*.

http://members.aol.com/dcspohr/lenny/original.htm: Lenny Bruce—extract from Lenny Bruce essay "I Remember Lenny" by Grover Sales.

www.freenetpages.co.uk/hp/lennybruce: The Complete Lenny Bruce.

www.mann-weil.com: Barry Mann and Cynthia Weil.

www.richmondhillhistory.org/JackMaple.html: Jack Maple remembered.

www.spectropop.com/JackNitzsche: Jack Nitzsche.

www.wtv-zone.com/dpjohnson/parissisters: Paris Sisters.

http://www.lincolnu.edu/~nordstro/jou335/payola.htm: Payola history, Lincoln University of Missouri.

www.philspector.com

http://home.tbbs.net/~msland/Spector: the Phil Spector record label gallery.

www.righteousbrothersdiscography.com

www.performingsongwriter.com: They Call Me Mr. Big: Notorious Rock Managers, Bill DeMain.

www.ramones.com

http://homepage.ntlworld.com/carousel/poboo.html: You Are the Plastic Ono Band.

The Spector family: Harvey, Benjamin, Bertha and Shirley. A celebratory dinner, circa 1947—Courtesy of Paulette Brandt.

The Teddy Bears, 1958. (*Left to right*) Phil Spector, Annette Kleinbard and Marshall Lieb—Corbis.

With Jack Nitzsche (*left*) and Darlene Love, Gold Star Studios, 1963—Ray Avery/ CTSIMAGES.COM.

With Larry Levine and Annette Spector, Gold Star Studios, 1963—Ray Avery/ CTSIMAGES.COM.

With the Ronettes, Gold Star Studios, 1963—Ray Avery/CTSIMAGES.COM.

With Tina and Ike Turner, Gold Star Studios, 1966—Ray Avery/CTSIMAGES.COM.

Phil Spector and George Brand guarding the La Collina mansion, 1975—Corbis.

The Pyrenees Castle, Alhambra, photographed on the morning of Spector's arrest— AP.

Lana Clarkson—AP.

Rachelle Spector—Neil Zlozower.

Phil Spector appears in court, May 2005—AP.

A NOTE ON THE TYPE

This book was set in Janson, a typeface long thought to have been made by the Dutchman Anton Janson, who was a practicing type-founder in Leipzig during the years 1668–1687. However, it has been conclusively demonstrated that these types are actually the work of Nicholas Kis (1650–1702), a Hungarian, who most proba-bly learned his trade from the master Dutch typefounder Dirk Voskens. The type is an excellent example of the influential and sturdy Dutch types that prevailed in England up to the time William Caslon (1692–1766) developed his own incomparable designs from them.

Composed by North Market Street Graphics,
Lancaster, Pennsylvania
Printed and bound by R. R. Donnelley & Sons,
Harrisonburg, Virginia
Designed by Virginia Tan